Henry Demarest Lloyd
and the Empire of Reform

Henry D. Lloyd, Boston, 1903

Henry Demarest Lloyd
and the Empire of Reform

By Chester McArthur Destler

University of Pennsylvania Press

Philadelphia

❧ *Preface and Acknowledgments*

To HIS GENERATION Henry Demarest Lloyd was the brilliant, selfless knight errant of reform, unstained by fear or cowardice. Conservative educators, industrial protectionists, the Tweed Ring, Grantism, orthodox Protestant clergy, foes of intellectual freedom, railroad and industrial monopolists, antilabor employers, Wall street, private utilities, Bourbonism, and McKinleyism winced under the thrusts of his critical blade. Lloyd crusaded for untrammeled intellectuality, honest politics, against special privilege, for genuine business competition or government ownership where this was unrealizable, for an up-to-date social conscience, for industrial democracy and civil rights for the underprivileged, and for economic and social justice to be achieved by a new, positive democracy. While establishing the facts of abuses and novel problems Lloyd became America's greatest muckraker. Invoking Jacksonian equalitarianism he became its greatest antimonopolist. His attempt to develop a theory adequate to resolve complex problems led him away from Cobdenism. He became the first great publicist of a new liberal, progressive policy. Subsequently, he formulated a social welfare philosophy that exerted equally wide influence. Hence, although he is remembered chiefly for his extraordinary campaign against Rockefeller and the Trusts, he was more significant to his era as a unique contributor to democratic theory and policy, and as the great prophet of social justice.

Following Emerson he was an intellectual activist. Among his collaborators and disciples could be found the leading economic and social reformers of the United States and many similar figures in Europe and the Antipodes. His new liberal journalism established the theory and techniques of emergent Progressivism, the ethical basis of social criticism, the actual facts of existing problems, and the need for limited state intervention. Journalistic disciples employed Lloyd's crusading methods for a generation. His social philosophy and championship of social justice and of all elements degraded by the Status Revolution wrought by industrial change and business-political Bourbonism established the new liberal, progressive political tradition. Thereafter he introduced non-Marxian Fabianism to direct the social protest of the American left.

During his attempts to achieve practical reforms Lloyd developed new reform techniques also. His leadership and philosophy, supplemented by unique hospitality to reformers and the underprivileged, made him the center of a wide circle of liberals and radicals in the transoceanic Empire of Reform. He emerged during the McKinley Era as the Dean of American Reform, a radical whose influence accelerated Theodore Roosevelt's emergence later as the presidential advocate of moderate progressivism that would redress evils while fending off the growing threat from the left. As a social critic Lloyd had no peer. As an inspirer of innovating, remedial statesmanship he ranked with Simon Sterne, Henry George, Albert Shaw, and the New Zealand Progressives. As the prophet of a unique ethical, social welfare philosophy he exerted a wide and pregnant influence.

Lack of a diary and intimate correspondence prevent writing Lloyd's intimate biography. Definitive portrayal of his intellectual development and reform career is facilitated by his voluminous publications and reform correspondence. Analyses of his theories and techniques establish their close interrelationship, their pertinence to the great problems of that transitional era, and his great seminal role as the leading philosopher and advocate of the "New Democracy" of the early twentieth century.

Formal research on this project began in 1937, after voluminous Lloyd manuscript materials were discovered during a study of Illinois Populism under the direction of Professor Avery

Craven of the University of Chicago. The loan of a microfilm camera by the Julius Rosenwald Foundation, grants from the American Philosophical Society and the Rutherford B. Hayes Foundations, a Library of Congress Fellowship in American Civilization accompanied by a fellowship at Berkeley College, Yale University, and Connecticut College research grants when I was a member of its faculty facilitated research.

Access to privately held materials was granted by Mrs. Hazel Albertson, Professor Charles B. Bakewell, Harry Barnard, Mr. and Mrs. William Bross, Mrs. S. P. Capen, the Chancellor's Office, University of Chicago, Conrad Godwin-Goddard, Ethical Culture Society of Chicago, Morris Hadley, George Davis Herron, Clara W. Hill, Hull-House, Mason B. Jones, Professor Philip Jordan, Professor Sherman Kent and Mrs. William Kent, Ernest C. Miller, T. W. Phillips, Jr., John Scheide, Catherine B. Schilling, Margaret Winfield Stewart, Mrs. Caro Lloyd Strobell, *Titusville Morning Herald,* James T. White & Company, Mrs. Nellie W. Williams, and The Women's Christian Temperance Union. Professors Paul Wallace Gates and Alpheus T. Mason, the Henry E. Huntington Library and Art Gallery, Lee Benson, and Raymond C. Ginger loaned manuscript items. Interviews were granted by Walter S. Bemis, Mrs. Zelda Stewart Charters, Dr. Alice Hamilton, Professor Samuel Harper, Mr. and Mrs. Nicholas Kelley, Fola La Follette, Mrs. Henry D. Lloyd, Jr., Mrs. Jessie Lloyd O'Connor, T. W. Phillips, Jr., and Mrs. Nellie W. Williams.

I am especially indebted for assistance during research to Alice E. Smith, State Historical Society of Wisconsin, the staff of the Library of Congress, Librarian James T. Babb and others of Yale University Library, A. C. Brown, Curator, Drake Well Museum, Curtis W. Garrison of the Hayes Memorial, Robert W. Hill, Curator of Manuscripts of New York Public Library, and Agnes A. Inglis, Curator, Joseph A. Labadie Labor Collection, University of Michigan Library. I am grateful for courtesies extended by the Boston Public Library; Chicago Public Library; Columbia University Alumni Office and Library; Connecticut College Library; Cook County, Illinois, Clerk; Cornell

University Library; Cuyahoga County, Ohio, Clerk; Erie County, New York, Clerk, Court of Sessions; Illinois Historical Society; Massachusetts Historical Society; Minnesota Historical Society; Northwestern University Library; Oberlin College Library; Ohio Archaeological and Historical Society; Ohio Historical and Philosophical Society; Ohio State University Library; Passaic Public Library; Rochester Public Library; University of Chicago Library; University of Illinois Library; University of Pennsylvania Library; University of Wisconsin Library; Widener Library; Harvard University; and Winnetka Public Library.

Professor Avery Craven has read and criticized the manuscript. Professor Paul W. Gates suggested the new approaches to some problems of the Gilded Age. Discussions of entrepreneurical history with Professor Arthur H. Cole and of problems of historical evidence with Professor David M. Potter provided valuable perspectives. Professor Allan Nevins' reminder of the obligations of the biographer when treating a controversial subject has been kept steadily in mind. Conversations with Professor Charles L. Stevenson provided understanding of Immanuel Kant and bibliographical guidance to other philosophers who influenced Lloyd's thought.

The Lloyd family accorded access without restriction to all pertinent manuscript and printed materials in its possession.

My wife assisted in the early research and in preparation of the index.

CHESTER MCARTHUR DESTLER

West Hartford, Connecticut
June 15, 1962

Contents

Illustrations

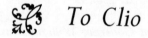 *To Clio*

Henry Demarest Lloyd

and the Empire of Reform

Mr. Lloyd was in many respects, both as regards intellect and as regards character, an absolutely unique figure in the economic history of the country. But when I think of him what I most remember is not the brilliant writer, the active champion, but the man of such wonderful personal charm in his daily conversation.

— Arthur Twining Hadley

Chapter I

Locofoco or Patrician?

YOUTH

A NONCONFORMIST TRADITION is part of many an American family heritage. Possession of it has stimulated opposition to intolerance, misgovernment, special privilege, and social wrong. The Aaron Lloyds, a century ago, were such a family, although they were ignorant of their descent from the regicides Edward Whalley and William Goffe until the children reached middle age. Before this Henry Demarest Lloyd and David Demarest Lloyd became noted foes of corruption, monopoly, injustice, and intolerance. Caro, their oldest sister, became a social rebel.

The children's consciousness of family antipathy to tyranny derived from less sensational grounds. Their mother's family, the Demarests of upper New Jersey and New York City, possessed a legendary history of early struggles for freedom. The founder, David De Marest, was a Picard Huguenot who resided in Holland for forty years before emigrating to Perth Amboy in 1663 to settle in Upper Jersey. David James Demarest, a descendant of Demarest-Dutch intermarriage, had moved to Greenwich Village in 1825. There he became city weigher and then a customs house official. He built and rented houses on Washington Square and was an elder in the Collegiate Reformed Church. His wife, a Christie, was Scottish. Her mother was a Banta of a Waldensian family that had fled to Scotland from Italy. Marie Christie, their daughter, blended Dutch, French, Italian, and Scottish strains. She was educated in the romantic

15

English mode after the custom of the seaboard gentry.[1]

To rough-hewn Aaron Lloyd, whom she married in February 1846, she symbolized the rebel heritage and the Dutch patrician tradition, whose family pride survived beside staunch Calvinism and love of art and letters. He told their children little of his ancestry until they reached maturity, and was ignorant of descent from the regicides until he visited his aged mother when they were grown. His father, John Crilley Lloyd of Belleville, New Jersey, was a foe of patricianism, a War of 1812 veteran, a Jacksonian Locofoco tailor still bearding the "monopolists" and gentry in 1846. He managed his shop with an iron hand, had read law and risen to postmaster, justice of the peace, coroner, and judge of the Essex County Court. He was proud of the Welsh Lloyds's artisan tradition.

Aaron Lloyd was the only child of his father's early marriage with Anna Stancliff, a descendant of Mehitabel Whalley Goffe, on the frontier of Erie County, Pennsylvania. Shortly after his birth Aaron had been taken by his father to New Jersey to be reared as a tailor's apprentice, permanently attached to equal rights and antipathetic to "consolidated government." When he was twenty-one he abandoned his trade and entered Rutgers College, working his way through there and the seminary by selling books and writing for the press. After success in his first pastorate as a Dutch Reformed minister he won Marie Christie Demarest's hand. Fifteen months after their wedding on May 1, 1849, she presented him with their first born, Henry Demarest Lloyd, in the red brick Demarest home at 56 Sixth Avenue, New York.[2]

Aaron Lloyd's career did not prosper after that. Except for those from the best families there were limited opportunities for native-born ministers in his denomination. The best pulpits were reserved for Dutch Dominies. Most churches averaged hardly a hundred communicants. The Board of Domestic Missions supported young ministers in upstate New York and the Middle West in an attempt to carry the Dutch liturgy to the settlers of the "Great Migration." Aaron Lloyd held country pastorates in New York and New Jersey for ten years before trying his fortunes in the West. Influenced by the missionary spirit impelling all Protestant denominations to plant its soil with Christian institutions,[3] he accepted a call to the Pekin, Illinois, Dutch Reformed Church.

For the Lloyd children the journey there was a great adventure. At Pekin steamboats on the Illinois River and the Illinois Railroad stirred imaginations. Pekin was one of ten incorporated Illinois towns, although pigs still roamed its unpaved streets. The wooden mains of the water system served shops and homes. There was talk of organizing a gas, light, and coke company like Chicago's. During harvest wagons hauled wheat and corn to the wharf or railroad station. After the first frost drovers urged their herds toward the pens beside the river. During the spring new settlers outfitted in the stores. On nearby prairies German immigrants perpetuated their native tongue and customs. The frontier had passed, leaving behind an "Old West" whose farm and town life was being assimilated to eastern patterns while still flavored by the optimistic, speculative spirit born of large opportunities and unoccupied lands.[4]

The Lloyds were Democrats. Table talk about politics was a welcome diversion from unbending Calvinism. Family prayers, instruction in the creed of the elect, rigid piety, and stern discipline tempered only by maternal affection were daily fare. High thinking and plain living were the children's lot as in other ministerial families. With this discipline was imparted the virile ethical code, idealism, optimism, and social vision of American Protestantism, which stimulated the sons to aspire to national leadership.[5]

Their training was enriched by the West's democratic idealism. The prairie farmers were imbued with a passion for equal rights and equality of opportunity. They believed in the superiority of an economic system of self-respecting freeholders, handicraft suppliers, and farm produce processors that was preferred by Jacksonian Locofocos and Jeffersonian upland southerners whose tradition Thomas Hart Benton had verbalized and disseminated. Both schools of democratic thought hated monopoly, corporations, and banks. The Locofoco insistence that "Democ-

racy is the cause of Humanity" broadened the humanitarian
impulse that Jeffersonian ideas and the Second Great Awakening, a far-reaching religious revival, had brought to the Northwest.

This ideological heritage provided the frame of reference in
1858 for nonabolitionists alarmed by the pretensions of "the
slave power" in Kansas. It supplied the rationale of hard-
pressed Douglas Democrats in Tazewell County where Pekin
was situated in the doubtful area between "Yankee" north
Illinois and "Egypt" south of Springfield. After his Great Debate with Abraham Lincoln, Stephen A. Douglas carried Tazewell by a narrow margin.[6]

The equal rights creed was invoked there by indignant farmers for other reasons. Money was tight. Produce prices were
low. Boys on errands downtown heard agriculturalists' pungent
complaints against banks, extortionate railroad rates, and
Chicago "trading combinations." Farmers believed that they
were sacrificed to the avarice of lawyers, middlemen, and financiers. Sturdy shoots of agrarian antimonopolism were emerging
from the prairies, and confirmed attachment to the Jacksonian
faith.

Henry D. Lloyd benefited from the education crusade in Illinois. He attended W. Plenkeron's Academy, which enforced
exacting standards. These provoked student protests that the
"restraint" of essay writing would lead to deterioration of the
intellect. Lloyd observed in his notebook that his classmates were
foolish if they thought they could assert their independence by
writing short, poor essays or by arguing that they could not
"talk and think like the seven wise men of Greece." That writing
came easier with practice he knew "from experience." They
should want to write longer and frequent essays and gain thereby the self-confidence and ability needed to seize future opportunities to rise to "Fame and Wealth." With this ambition he
combined a desire to "promote the knowledge and happiness of
mankind," for which he collected "many valuable hints." He
developed a talent for factual, critical presentation that won
commendation.[7]

His father's prospects were dashed by collapse of the railroad boom. Country congregations paid him their contributions slowly. Although he farmed on the side, his sons helping with eleven acres of corn, the hard life obliged him to return to the East after a three-year pastorate. The Dutch liturgy could not compete with the English service and western manners of the Methodists and Baptists. Early in 1860, with his educated wife, three sons, and infant daughter, Aaron Lloyd traveled to New York City and lodged them with his father-in-law. He was a victim of intense sectarian competition.[8]

At 27 West Washington Street the Lloyd children were subjected to an even more rigorous Calvinism. They crowded their grandfather's pew in the Collegiate Church on Sundays. Dutch liturgy there, speaking Dutch in the Demarest home, and the Demarests' collateral Dutch ancestry so impressed Henry D. Lloyd that he became an active member of the Chicago Holland Society in later years. Such an atmosphere, duplicated by the starched piety of his uncle Henry Demarest's home next door, was anachronistic. Intense religious fervor, hostility to the theater, and preoccupation with the responsibilities of the "elect" featured both homes. "Only a stone's throw" from crowded Broadway, Washington Square preserved its "ancient peace," distinguished by architectural survivals from the Knickerbocker past.[9]

Life in the metropolis during the Civil War acted as a catalyst on the Lloyd sons' development, diverting it from the course projected by their Calvinist rearing and prairie years. Family poverty made adjustment from Pekin's semirural simplicities difficult, but their grandfather's dignified, cultured home gave them social position. This shelter was no subsidy. Their mother did the housework and made the children's clothes, which were so short of current fashion as to provoke youthful ridicule.

Aaron Lloyd's domestic standing was not enhanced by a slender income from his "Ye Olde Book Shoppe" on winding Nassau Street in the mercantile quarter. His profits were insufficient during war inflation to defray his family's expenses. His sons went to work in the Mercantile Library in Clinton Hall, a

three-story Ionic structure on Astor Place, to defray the inci-
dentals of their education. The work opened to them a new
world of books, ideas, and junior clerks.

Influenced by life in the great city, Henry D. Lloyd began to
question the Calvinist creed. He broached his doubts to his uncle
Henry, who turned him out of his house. Rebellion followed.
Joined by his brothers he attended Henry Ward Beecher's Plymouth Church. This breach with their father was widened by
wartime politics. Local "rebel sympathizers" led by Mayor Fer-
nando Wood were outspoken. Unionists challenged them in
great, emotional gatherings. Aaron Lloyd was a states rights
Democrat opposed to Lincoln's centralizing war policy. Small
Republicans were horrified when they saw him sitting on the
Demarest stoop reading the "Copperhead" *Daily News.* His
father at Belleville was an outspoken "peace" Democrat.

The Demarests joined the Union Republican Party. Washington Square, led by James Demarest, rallied in defense of law,
order, and the Union during July 1863 when antidraft riots
overran the uptown district. For the Lloyd children there could
be no neutrality on such issues. The Lloyd sons became Union
Republicans like their maternal grandfather, but family affection and Mrs. Lloyd's tact prevented a bitter schism. Despite
their religious and political differences Henry D. Lloyd remained loyal to his father's ethical and democratic principles.

His mother dealt skillfully with her sons' revolt from the
Reformed Church. She read liberal religious books, left the Collegiate Church, and with her daughters attended the Church
of the Strangers where "Commodore" Cornelius Vanderbilt's attendance persuaded her sons to join them. She invited her children's new friends to her house to leaven the society of their
cousins. When Henry D. Lloyd decided to attend Columbia
College she secured a scholarship for him at the Columbia
Grammar (preparatory) School. When he completed the course
his father helped him to secure a four-year scholarship at
Columbia College from Andrew Mills of the Drydock Savings
Bank, which enabled him to enter the class of 1867.[10]

Thus, while shoddyite extravagance, unprecedented vice and

crime, municipal corruption, and spreading materialism corrupted business and politics and Wall Street "bulls" and "bears" trampled down all standards but those of the Spanish Main, Henry and David Demarest Lloyd developed into hard-working, clean-limbed, high-spirited, handsome, and idealistic young men. Their basic happiness was expressed in a gaiety and fine wit that distinguished each for life. Confidence bred of being gentlemen born, some of their intelligence, and much of their literary taste were their mother's contributions to their training. They repaid her with wholesome affection, respect for her judgment, keen appreciation, and by becoming distinguished journalists and men of letters.

LEADER OF THE BARBS

When Henry D. Lloyd entered Columbia College in September 1863 it was a wealthy, self-satisfied Episcopalian liberal arts institution. It attracted sons from Manhattan's "better" families and some boys of undistinguished parentage. Aside from Dr. Francis Lieber, noted publicist and "philosophic historian," the faculty was undistinguished. Although heavily weighted with Greek and mathematics the curriculum included the physical sciences, German, philosophy, English literature, and history. Although this symbolized patrician culture it was not designed to satisfy adolescents alert to the dynamics of American life. Proof of this was seen in Lieber's popularity, which led the new president, Frederick A. P. Barnard, to shunt him soon into the Law School, away from contact with the undergraduates whom his views and classroom talents stimulated.

Of different ferment Columbia possessed a sturdy tradition. Cramped by a rigid curriculum and stiff discipline, the students had long been notriously turbulent. The Class of '67 perpetuated this energetically. Simultaneously the stirring caused by the war penetrated the musty campus on Fourth Avenue at Fiftieth Street, and stimulated student attempts to enrich undergraduate life with new activities and traditions. Interclass sports developed into intercollegiate athletics. The "67 Base Ball Club" had an unbeaten record. Field and water sports diverted student energies from rioting.

Simultaneously the democratic Philolexian and Peithologian literary societies were challenged by the secret fraternities, which grew rapidly, stimulated by the war boom's materialism and snobbishness. Before the close of Reconstruction they would crowd the Peithologian Society to the wall. Meanwhile, the Greeks' attempts to monopolize class offices and honors precipitated a struggle for control within '67 that became the central theme of its history."

Despite his Demarest connection Lloyd was not pledged. Perforce he found himself among the Barbs. Earning his expenses debarred him from sports, and limited excursions into the city with classmates, although work at the Mercantile Library provided opportunities to extend his education into fields untouched by the professors. He was passed over in the freshman elections, which were carried by the fraternity pledges led by Nicholas Fish, son of Hamilton Fish, a college trustee and head of a distinguished New York family.

During Lloyd's sophomore year he was elected to the Philolexian, the largest literary society. Friendly competition on its programs whetted literary ambitions. He signed himself "Lloyde." He aspired to become class poet as he wrote "Halusis" about the Colege. The English professor complimented his style and predicted that with practice he would become "a popular writer."

As "Lloyde" he gradually came forward from the back benches. Unsuccessful as candidate for marshall of the important "Semi-Annual" festivity, he won a place on the committee. The following spring, during preparation for the newly instituted "Burial of the Ancient Geography," he was badly beaten for poet and relegated to pall bearer. He helped to carry "the body" on the night of June 19, 1864, "when the sky was without a star" on a "bier and covered with a pall . . . to its final resting-place beneath the College sod." After oratory and the poet's verses all adjourned to the "Groton" for liquid refreshment at "reasonable prices." There repetition of the last funeral song,

"Benny Havens," provoked gales of laughter at the caricatured professors.[12]

During his first college years Lloyd was influenced by Professor Lieber, who "loved his students and was greatly beloved by them." They liked his vigorous classroom procedures and allusions to poetry and fiction to enrich the study of history. His exacting standards required mastery of geography, knowledge of great men, and notebooks filled with references for future reading. His zeal for liberal causes and reform, ardor for "the noblest sentiments," and witty, cheerful, and stimulating conversations fascinated Lloyd. To those years can be attributed his later notebooks containing excerpts from wide reading, his knowledge and appreciation of history, his zest for public affairs.[13]

The forums provided by his literary society and class were next in importance in Lloyd's development. He wrote a precocious "Editorial" for Philolexian, urging that the College unite its schools on a new site removed from the city and there become a university influencing and dominating the metropolis as Oxford did London. Literary distinction could make such a Columbia "a center of national literary life," he predicted. He became the leading student advocate of reform of the College's antiquated curriculum, discipline, and organization. The professors and students should live in the College as did those of the great English universities, he believed, rather than allow Columbia to remain a "high order of day school" with its stern "systems of coercion" and "invariable course of study." Where within a few years could "Columbians play base ball or cricket" or "find a place for boating, . . . Is physical culture to be altogether neglected?" he asked.

In a composition entitled "Classical Studies," a year later, he sided with "The Moderns" as a practical utilitarian in a renewal of their perennial contest with "The Ancients." He believed it to be wiser to study English grammar directly rather than via the classical languages. Furthermore, "The superiority of the nineteenth century results not from veneration for the ancients and the cultivation of the extinct languages" nor their literature, but rather from science and the attention paid to "politics, law, commerce, mechanical invention, chemistry, and public economy. In this age of utility and progress the educational system has alone remained stationary. Is it natural, is it right?" The languages that should be studied were English, which provided the most authors, and "the tongues of the living world." Memory, taste, attention could be cultivated "by learning things useful" as well as from the "useless" classics. The existing curriculum made French, German, and Italian with their "vast treasures" inaccessible.[14]

In the spring of 1866 Lloyd won a place among the leaders of his class. Anonymous, autobiographical "Sixty-Seven. A Class Poem," appeared in the *Columbiad* with swift iambics, frank hedonism, and wit that disclosed a sophisticated youth who had traveled far in outlook and confident craftsmanship. The poet expressed the gay junior mood as he described the passage from hard first years to the present, while belittling compulsory chapel, ridiculing class recitations, noticing the girls while walking to the campus, and complimenting "patriarchical Fritz" at the favorite saloon.

> Ambitious Fritz! Thy name in future years
> Shall rank Professors with its proud compeers.[15]

Soon after this appeared the class's gay course from the lecture room was blocked one morning by a locked door, a standing student grievance. '67 invoked its slogan, "Onward and untiringly," without delay. The door was broken through and the juniors proceeded on their way. Whereupon President Barnard announced that he was repairing the door at '67's expense and assessed ten cents each upon all present at the incident.

The juniors alleged that other classes had been involved. They sent a committee headed by Lloyd to present the facts to the president. Since Jacksonian days Barnard had defended property as the bulwark of patricianism. Wealthy, traveled, a noted educator, *persona grata* to industrialists, he had long urged miltary training in the schools. He took advantage of the broken door to vindicate the rights of property and attempted to introduce West Point discipline into the college. He rejected the excuses of Lloyd's committee and suggested that '67 be tried by a court martial. The class accepted trial before a student court on the issue "whether the *class* is to pay." Although Barnard allowed '67 to select the judges he insisted that "wanton" injury to college property be "atoned for" and offered the juniors the alternative of being tried as individuals if they testified against their fellows. He provoked unflinching resistance, as Josiah Quincy had done after a student riot at Harvard. '67 voted again to be tried as a class.

The selection of the judges and counsel precipitated a bitter intraclass struggle. The Greeks insisted that "gentlemen" be the judges and that Fish be added to the counsel that had been appointed from among the Barbs. After Fish and Lloyd were added to the class counsel the Barbs still controlled the defense. This was their first victory in the class's history. Then, when the "Favorite Member" was elected to receive the Goodwood Cup at Commencement and Fish was chosen by a narrow majority, every officer elected for the presentation ceremony was a Barb. Lloyd was placed on the Laureate Committee. In preparation for the class's defense at the court martial he was chosen to argue "A Plea in Bar of Trial" at the outset. His close friend, George G. DeWitt, Jr., would direct the rest of the defense if this move should fail. Fish should assist him. This arrangement so estranged Lloyd and Fish that they did not speak to each other again until months after graduation.

The court martial opened in Dr. Charles Anthon's lecture room on May 2, 1866. Professor William G. Peck presided over a panel of seven senior "jurors." President Barnard as judge advocate presented the charge, "Wanton Damage to the Property of the College." Dramatically, Lloyd replied with his "Special Plea." He impugned the presumption of the charge that '67 enjoyed corporate responsibility since it held no "charter" from the College. He denied that "the whole Class" had "participated" in the incident. If the court found some juniors guilty it could not convict '67 since the College's statutes asserted that only individuals involved in such episodes were "responsible." If the court rejected the "Plea" and ruled that '67 possessed corporate status it could not find innocent those members who had not participated. The dilemma could be resolved only by terminating the trial, Lloyd argued.

On Barnard's insistence "the question of principle" was argued fully. In a stormy colloquy Lloyd cited Benet's *Law of Court Martial* and matched technicalities with the president, who was obliged to concede point after point. Barnard then demanded that the issue be narrowed to *"whether a portion of a Collegiate body could be held responsible for damage done by members. . . .* This is not a college if there is no protection for property," he declared. The court should decide the issue and then draft statutes safeguarding College property for him to present to the Trustees, he added.

After ten minutes' deliberation the court admitted Lloyd's "Special Plea." Crestfallen, Barnard entered a *nolle prosequi.* His young adversary enjoyed a personal triumph. The court adjourned. The juniors carried Lloyd away rejoicing. For years afterward he was known among the alumni as "the man who threw Prex." While leading the Barbs to victory over the Greeks within '67 during the episode he had opposed Barnard's patricianism and won. Distinction denied a scion of the Demarests he had won in fair battle as a self-supporting scholarship student.[16]

Thereafter he was '67's acknowledged leader. At the last meeting of its junior year he delivered an especial Valedictory. This reviewed wittily '67's venture into curriculum reform, its "searching criticism" of the professorial debate on the classics vs. science; its "watch" over, its censure, and its discriminating praise of the professors. "We have not lifted our voices in vain," he said, since "rumours of new changes are not wanting." Reward in student honors came the following year. The Barbs swept the autumn class election and installed Lloyd as secretary for the next four years. He proclaimed then in light verse the pride and unity of '67. After renewed friction with Barnard his party secured appointment of a "Committee on Presidential apologies"! In the spring Lloyd was elected to the coveted office of class poet unanimously as the Barbs captured all Class Day honors.

Lloyd read his Class Day poem after the ivy was planted and the class pipe smoked. When '67 saluted the classrooms he read a proud "Song" celebrating the successful pursuit of the bachelor's degree with lines carrying a dual implication :

And some have lightly borne the toil,
And some have served complaining
Against monopoly of spoil
And arduous campaigning.
And some have stormed the leaguered town,
And won their honors well,
O'erlept the ramparts of renown,
And sacked the citadel.[17]

Lloyd spoke second at Commencement in the Second Class of Honor in the Academy of Music after the program was enlivened by Theodore Thomas' Grand Orchestra. His subject was "Soda and Society." He discussed the civilizing influence of modern science and developed Justus von Liebig's thesis that soda made by the Le Blanc process was "the index of civilization." No other discovery, Lloyd declared extravagantly, had so aided the development of scientific truth. Five years before Henry Stanley would return from the Dark Continent he claimed that the discovery of abundant soda and fats there had started it "on the glorious career that awaits her as the future home of a civilized colored man." By curtailing tribal wars and extinguishing the slave trade the "quiet but resistless weapons of Commerce" were winning where the armed might of the great powers had failed. Thus Lloyd voiced his era's liberal faith, growing zest for science, and confidence in the pacific purposes of the "Manchester School" of English economists.[18]

After graduation he learned that a college diploma unlocked few opportunities in the world of trade in that generation of self-made men. A New Year's note from Nicholas Fish, who was studying at Harvard Law School, proposed that they forget the past and meet in the future "as friends." Lloyd agreed, initiated an exchange of portraits, and announced his determination to study law. Fish informed him that while Columbia Law School prepared for practice based upon the New York Code, Harvard Law School emphasized the "great elementary principles of the Common Law."[19]

Lloyd entered Columbia Law School, the largest and best of its type in the United States, whose two-year course qualified its graduates for admission to the New York bar without examination. While paying his expenses by working at the Mercantile Library he studied with the famous Theodore W. Dwight and Professor Lieber, whose lectures on the history of jurisprudence described the larger function of law in civil society. Lloyd passed the New York bar examination in the spring of 1869 and withdrew from the Law School.

Thereafter his relation to Columbia was that of an interested, loyal alumnus. As the class of '67 secretary he retained the friendship of Fish, Seth Low, George DeWitt, and Julius Sachs, each of whom became influential and successful New Yorkers. At '67's twentieth reunion during the Columbia College Centennial of 1887 he organized the Northwestern Alumni.[20]

Meanwhile, it became evident that although his undergraduate years had confirmed inherited family antipathies to oppression, special privilege, and monopoly, Columbia College had inducted him into the community of educated, professional gentlemen who played a not inconsiderable role in combating the disintegration of business and public ethics and cultural standards during "The Gilded Age."

Chapter II

A Mercantile Gateway to Reform

"No Monopoly"

MOTIVATING LLOYD'S legal studies was his desire to "right some wrongs." The triumph of abolitionism had conferred unprecedented prestige upon reform, whose furtherance in other fields was now a fashionable road to fame. An opening on the American Free-Trade League's staff offered an opportunity to gratify Lloyd's desire to form connections within the mercantile community. President Barnard recommended him warmly as "a gentleman" to David Dudley Field, the League's president, who employed Lloyd as a colporteur in the spring of 1869.[1]

Simultaneously, he began the course of feminine criticism that Disraeli said was essential to young gentlemen. With lovely Louise Haight he "walked, and danced and talked, sang, flirted, discussed Darwinism and theology, and matrimony." She was responsive to his temperament, emancipated like him from "current theologies," and shared his philosophy of life and "doubts of the future." Sensitive as he was to the new currents coursing Manhatten, she provided a charming friendship such as only a modest, intelligent young woman could give. So natural and satisfying was this that it did not occur to him that he loved her or she him until he learned of her sudden death a year later.[2]

He enjoyed working for the Free-Trade League. Its leadership, ideology, and purposes combined mercantile objectives with reform. Disinterested reform was a special social province in which New York rivaled Boston. May was the anniversary month of the great associations, when their leaders celebrated past triumphs, reported current progress, and planned new campaigns.[3]

The Free-Trade League had been founded in 1864 by Simon Sterne, a young anti-Tammany, states rights lawyer and Democrat, and the sons of Alfred Pell, agent of the Liverpool and London and Globe Insurance Company. The League's first object was to redress the injury inflicted by the war tariff upon New York's importing and shipping interests. When William Cullen Bryant, editor of the *New York Evening Post,* became president of the League in 1865, Sterne had continued as its secretary.[4] They had revived the antebellum alliance between the coastal maritime-commercial interests and the West to defeat a protectionist bill pressed by Pennsylvania Radical Republican Congressmen. Aided by the *Chicago Tribune,* Senator Lyman Trumbull of Illinois, and Congressman John A. Kassan of Iowa, they had blocked all attempts to increase the tariff except the Wool and Woollens Act of 1867, when the woolgrowers backed the carpet manufacturers.[5]

Bryant's presidency (1865-69) had brought to the League his prestige, the support of the *Evening Post,* which John Stuart Mill said was America's greatest newspaper, and the adherence of noted economists, intellectuals, reformers, and liberals. The *Evening Post* was renowned for courageous championship of democracy and liberal principles, and for steadfast support of Abraham Lincoln during 1861-65 when the *New York Tribune* had yawed on public issues like an ill-handled clipper ship during a hurricane. The *Post*'s lead in politics, philanthropy, and economic policy influenced Manhattan merchants while its opposition to monopoly and special privilege retained a wage-earner clientele.[6]

The Bryant-Sterne administration attracted to the League men of affairs eager to revive the fisheries, shipbuilding, merchant marine, and importing by reducing the war tariff. So injurious was its impact upon New York's trade that the Merchant's Exchange was sold in 1869 for half the cost of construction to the federal government. It became the new Customs House. Leadership in Wall Street had passed to speculator-promoters dealing in railroad securities. David Dudley Field was obliged to reserve part of his law practice for Daniel Drew and Cornelius Vanderbilt. Hence merchants dependent upon foreign trade looked to the League as a means of restoring commerce to its former position, and rallied to extricate private enterprise from government-conferred special privilege.

In 1869 the League elected David Dudley Field president and Mahlon Day Sands, wealthy retired drug importer, the permanent secretary. Charles H. Marshall, manager of Goodhue and Company (the Black Ball Line of packets) became treasurer. Robert S. Minturn of the London Line and Jackson S. Schulz, wealthy hide importer, went on the executive board. A fund drive netted $30,000 to finance far-reaching propaganda and a Washington lobby.[7]

Greeley's *Tribune* cried promptly that the free-traders were "British importers" financed by "British gold" so as to subordinate America to alien interests. In Philadelphia Henry C. Carey's books, pamphlets, and newspaper articles repudiated the Manchester School. Free trade and the international gold standard, he declared, would perpetuate British economic hegemony. Instead of Ricardo's economics of scarcity he proposed a diversified national economy so encouraged by a protective tariff and a national paper currency that its exploitation of unlimited resources and technological advances would elevate wages above the subsistence level. Fabrication of its own raw materials would develop such "harmony of interests," Carey said, that the United States would capture world industrial leadership and lead civilization to "universal peace." Disseminated by the Philadelphia *North American* and Philadelphia *Press* and by the *New York Tribune*, Carey's economic nationalism rallied manufacturers, coal mine operators, and seaboard investors in minerals and timber in a vigorous campaign for continued tariff protection.[8]

To counteract the Free-Trade League's propaganda Greeley published serially in the *Tribune* his "Essays Designed to Elucidate the Science of Political Economy." His unique pauper labor argument asserted that free trade obliged laborers in competing

countries to underbid each other. Although wages were lowest
in agricultural countries, diversified industry "secured by Protection" could elevate them, provide ample markets for farm
products, and attract skilled immigrants. Replete with American economic facts, cutting in reference to free trade abstrac-
tions, outspoken in attachment to American interests, these
"Essays" were read widely. Manufacturers distributed them
among their employees.[9] So stimulated, the protectionists in
Congress in 1869 enacted a copper bill over President Johnson's
veto and the iron and steel interests demanded higher schedules.
During 1865-68 the United States Revenue Commission, packed
with Carey's disciples led by David Ames Wells of Norwich,
Connecticut, had persuaded Congress to abolish most industrial
excises while retaining the war duties, thus enhancing their
protective benefits.[10]

Overhauling of the free trade argument was necessary to
counteract the protectionist offensive, since quotations from
British authorities, abstract appeals, and neglect of American
conditions in the *Free-Trade Tracts* were ineffective. A Cincinnati sympathizer demanded that the monthly *League* direct its
appeals also to the western and southern "working masses" and
German settlers who resented the high cost of living. A western
antimonopoly revolt against a railroad-steamboat combination,
New Jersey antipathy to the Camden and Amboy Railroad's
monopoly, and the National Anti-Monopoly Cheap Freight
Railway League's propaganda and success in instituting anti-
monopoly conventions from New York to Texas indicated an
issue that would appeal to farmers and laborers loyal to Jacksonian stereotypes. "No Monopoly" had been the victorious
slogan of the British Anti-Corn Law League, whose employment
of colporteurs to distribute literature had been copied by the
American Tract Society before 1861.[11] During a second visit to
London where he was wined and dined at the Cobden Club
Sterne became convinced of the practicability of an appeal to
American antimonopolist sentiment.

Sands renamed the League's monthly *The Free-Trader*. It
attacked protected industries as monopolies, attributed strikes

to the tariff, and declared that the Congressional railroad land grant policy dissipated the public domain, the last refuge of the oppressed laborer. It attacked public jobbery and political corruption. Then the third report of the United States Revenue Commission, written by Wells, who had experienced a secret conversion to free trade after studying the tariff's effects, demonstrated statistically that high manufactured-goods prices resulted from permitting industrialists to write their own tariff schedules. In New York the *World, Nation,* and *Post* published the entire document, which the League distributed as a pamphlet.

The *Evening Post* launched an antimonopolist campaign against all protected industry and its agents, including Senator Roscoe Conkling. It lampooned the frightened *Tribune* as the monopolists' tool and announced that public questions would be discussed "from the standpoint of principle" for the "whole country."[12]

The League abandoned abstract free trade and adopted Wells's realistic approach to tariff reform. "A revenue tariff and no monopolies—*These are our watchwords,*" it proclaimed. In March 1870 it declared it would convert the Union Republicans to the "peculiar Free Trade doctrines of William Leggett," leader of the Locofocos. Meanwhile, a broad campaign for equal rights attempted to terminate the special legislation, corruption, and lobby rule that Walt Whitman would castigate in *Democratic Vistas.* Eight new tracts in German and twenty in English made a varied, at times humorous appeal. In one of these Francis Lieber exposed twenty fallacies peculiar to American protectionists. Horace White, editor of the *Chicago Tribune,* translated Frederic Bastiat's *Sophismes Economique* so skillfully that Professor Andrew White of the University of Michigan used it to convert young protectionists to free trade.[13]

Mahlon Sands trained and directed a corps of lecturers and colporteurs in 1869. The latter distributed pamphlets, recruited voluntary workers, and organized meetings. As "preachers of Free-Trade" they moved "among the Trades Unions" and into the "great West" spreading the message of tariff reform "in every center of thought." Professor Arthur L. Perry of Williams

College led the lecturers who spoke in New England, the Middle States, and the West. Great meetings were held in New York, Brooklyn, Philadelphia, Boston, and Indianapolis.

Edward Atkinson, a cotton mill manager, organized an allied New England Revenue Reform League. Mass meetings addressed by Bryant, Perry, Atkinson, Lieber, and Henry Ward Beecher bid for labor's support. The *Evening Post* cried, "Down with Monopoly! The Rights of Labor!"[14]

Henry D. Lloyd was the youngest colporteur that summer. He was assigned to upstate New York and northern Ohio, former strongholds of Martin Van Buren's following that had followed Bryant into the Republican party. Lloyd's task was to rally that area to antimonopoly and tariff reform. In Ohio he was aided by drought and western competition with the wheat- and wool-raising districts. Wool-growers were concluding, after flocks fell a third in value in three years while increasing by 1,333,000 head, that they had been duped by the industrialists into supporting the Wool and Woollens Act. The Cincinnati *Volksblatt* demanded tariff reform to save the Republican party from disintegration. After General Roelliff Brinkerhoff of Mansfield persuaded his county convention to demand a revenue tariff, which the *Cincinnati Commercial* endorsed, Sands hired him as the midwestern agent of the League.[15]

Lloyd was highly successful. His intelligent zeal, confidence, handsome face with steady eyes, slightly bushy eyebrows, high-bridged nose, straight firm mouth, and determined chin combined with medium height, slender figure, and neat attire to make a favorable impression. A young lawyer and minister's son was sure of a warm reception. After sharing the League's triumph at Rochester he alone won the entire press and organized the second upstate branch league at Buffalo. The Rochester *Union* and *Daily Advertiser* both described his successes in Ohio. There he laid the basis for a state league, enlisting such Cincinnatians in it as George Hoadly, John Shillito, Stanley Matthews, and Joseph Longworth. During three months Lloyd visited four states, canvassed thirty-eight towns and cities, called on more than a thousand people, recruited 372 co-operators, distributed 50,444 documents, visited Brinkerhoff and as avant-courier scheduled his lectures, and interviewed sixty-eight newspaper editors. In Ohio he won or confirmed the free-trade allegiance of twenty-one newspapers in eleven cities. His record surpassed that of all other League agents.[16]

He also perfected a hard-hitting propaganda that transformed industrial and commercial statistics into a two-edged blade. Before he left on his field trip the *Evening Post* published a letter to the editor signed "NO MONOPOLY." It exploded dramatically the *Tribune's* claim that in no other nation could 100 days' labor buy as much iron as in America by showing that a week's wages of five poorer-paid English ironworkers could purchase two tons more of iron than could the earnings of five similar American workers in their protected market. "We are *an iron bound* country in many respects," the piece concluded ironically.

The *Post's* covering editorial, "Where are the 'Pauper Laborers'?" hailed the next "NO MONOPOLY" letter, which disclosed a 30 per cent differential favoring English woolen workers in ability to buy blankets. The third "NO MONOPOLY" letter reviewed Greeley's first "Essay on Political Economy," which attributed pauperism to slavery and free trade. Terming this "a direct insult to our laboring class," the letter cited Wells's letter to Congressman William D. Kelley that alluded to a large ten years' increase in Philadelphia's poor relief budget. Why, if protection produced full employment, "are so many idle now, in our manufacturing cities?" The anonymous correspondent fulfilled Bryant's prediction that he would "give the monopolists trouble." In a month he riddled the pauper labor argument by comparisons of the real wages of American and British fabricators of tableware, cotton hose, Scotch caps, salt, felt carpet, and thread. "NO MONOPOLY" exposed Greeley's falsification of American ship-building costs, his callousness toward the unemployed, the injurious effect of the war tariff upon shipping and western meat-packing, and the exorbitant profits of protected industries.

The *Post* declared that this series confirmed Wells's assertion that the tariff was making the rich richer and the poor poorer. In July Bryant attributed the rapid increase in revenue reform sentiment to the wide circulation of the "NO MONOPOLY" series by "country newspapers in all parts of the Union." In August the *Post* and the *World* reprinted its statistics.

The anonymous author developed a gift for dramatic journalistic controversy. Try as it might the *Tribune* could not divert him from the pauper labor issue or its own garbled statistics. "NO MONOPOLY" turned Greeley's "Essays" into ammunition for tariff reformers. His refusal to abandon a single protected industry enabled "NO MONOPOLY" to saddle the *Tribune* with responsibility for the unpopular Onondaga Salt Company. Greeley's name-calling did not silence his antagonist. "NO MONOPOLY" alluded cuttingly to "the monopolists' attorney," to "Mr. Scudder" who had lured Martin Chuzzlewit to "Eden."

"NO MONOPOLY" did not demur when the *Tribune* called its author "the importers' attorney" and "hired man." The series gradually revealed that he was a New York citizen, an employee of the Free-Trade League, poor, and no "kidgloved promoter" of "free trade" as "a diversion" from "a *fashionable* life." The imperturbable spirit with which the series conducted a long duel with the chief of Printing House Square was that of a former undergraduate who had tilted against the Greeks at Columbia College and unhorsed its President. No other League worker exhibited such penetrating, witty, statistical analysis." His series synchronized with Charles Francis Adams, Jr.'s sensational "Chapter of Erie" and other essays on scandalous conditions.

Such talent was welcomed by Mahlon Sands. He promoted Lloyd to assistant secretary in time for preparation of a merciless supplement to the September *Free-Trader,* "The Tariff of the United States."

Executive Assistant and Amateur Reformer

When Lloyd joined the League's staff he believed that he was joining the company of American reformers. Many of them were intensely religious. Each knew that he was "called" to serve his fellows in the fight against evil. They would free others from misplaced faith, vice, or rotten institutions that shackled mind or body, or degraded the soul. Ranging from generous, enigmatic Ralph Waldo Emerson to eccentric Percy Taylor, they labored at the work of "melioration" as a means of advancing civilization. It was ironical that a sincere neophyte should serve his novitiate as the paid agent of a league whose liberal principles were coupled with materialistic motives. Undoubtedly its supporters were charmed to discover that their interests and principles coincided, as a Radical Unionist textile manufacturer friend of Senator Charles Sumner had been a few years earlier.[18] Despite Lloyd's youthful aspiration to achieve "Fame and Wealth" his idealistic impulse was dominant.

Since knowledge of shorthand was essential to his new post he learned Pitman. He preserved press clippings to keep abreast of the western antimonopoly movement, the anthracite coal monopoly, labor and cooperative movements, and the protectionists' campaign.

He began systematic reading, focusing upon the great reformers and free-traders. In a leather "H. D. L. Private" notebook he transcribed selected passages and wrote comments. He began with Wendell Phillips' "Lincoln's Election" that eulogized John Brown, and declared that "Civilization dwarfs political machinery," which excerpts from Richard Cobden's *Political Writings* confirmed. Lloyd regarded Cobden as the prophet of Liberal doctrine, whose conception of history necessitated reexamination of America's past for illustrations of economic doctrine and of stages of progress represented by America, Great Britain, and Russia. Although he rejected Cobden's warning that America might challenge Britain's manufacturing and commercial supremacy. he learned from him of war's deflationary effect upon real wages. Agreeing that government intervention contributed little to the spread of liberty, he concluded that the "jingle of the Almighty dollar will waken the 'minions of depotism' to a more lasting freedom than the frantic cries

of Red Republicans." In his first New York lecture he expounded Cobden's dogma, "free trade is the international law
of the Almighty." He described himself in 1871 as "radically
economic."[19] In the interim he read books on America's history
and protective policy. After Louise Haight's death he read
James Kent's *Commentaries on American Law,* Blackstone, and
the *New York Revised Statutes* as if to bury his grief in work
and prepare for future practice.

Notebook entries described desired reforms such as application of the merit system to the diplomatic service ! Lloyd
desired simplication of Thomas Hare's system of proportional
representation, which Sterne had imported from England.
While reflecting upon Alexis de Tocqueville's *Democratie en
Amérique* he saw no parallel between the decay of *l'ancien
régime* and "the tendency today." Rejecting Emerson's dictum,
"the march of civilization is a train of felonies," he remarked,
"It is essentially more like a series of pendulations with the
point slowly moving forward." After two years his reading
tapered off with Bastiat's *Oeuvres* and Edmund Burke.[20]

Lloyd's duties as assistant secretary included taking Sands's
dictation, answering inquiries, dickering with agencies supplying blue posters, writing articles on revenue questions for
"a large number of journals," greeting sympathizers, placing
advertisements, and editing the *Free-Trader.* Because of this
heavy load his "NO·MONOPOLY" articles appeared infre-
quently in the *Evening Post.*

He took his turn on the lecture platform in the spring of 1870.
At the Brick Church on Manhattan he declared that Adam
Smith's "declaration of independence . . . had done more to
elevate mankind than the one made by Jefferson and Franklin."
He toured New England with Professor Arthur L. Perry of
Williams College, a paid lecturer of the League, addressing
employers and workers. Then, at the League's new Nassau
Street office opposite the Sub-Treasury Building, he conferred
with Richard Rogers Bowker, editor of the *Evening Mail,*
about the Brooklyn branch league's program.

In October Lloyd was humiliated when the *Tribune* pub-

lished the League's confidential financial report and list of contributors, most of whom were importers and financial houses
with foreign connections. Whitelaw Reid rejected his demand
that he name the League's betrayer. Occurring when the
Evening Post was opposing Greeley's congressional candidacy
in the Sixth District, the incident brought the feud between
the free-traders and the *Tribune* to white heat.[21]

Editing the *Free-Trader* gave Lloyd excellent training. It
resembled the *Nation* with editorials, book reviews, and feature
articles as it campaigned in behalf of all interests injured by
the tariff. It plotted the course of the tariff reform movement,
informed supporters of developments, championed workers' interests, and justified strikes despite adherence to Cobdenism. It
encouraged Wendell Phillips' New England Labor Reform
League and urged miners to support free trade as they fought
the anthracite coal monopoly. It courted the National Labor
Union.[22] Free copies went regularly to colleges and public libraries. Such was Cobdenism's prestige among the educated that
President Mark Hopkins of Williams College protested to
Bryant against the League's policy of "expediency."[23] Most railroad men were cool to Sands's overtures, since they were attempting to develop traffic by fostering industries located along
their rights of way.

The League's social functions, which Lloyd managed, furthered his training as a liberal gentleman. He was admitted to
the home of the Parke Godwins, where John Hay and Whitelaw Reid of the *Tribune* courted Minna, Bryant's grand-
daughter, in witty, semiserious fashion. Undoubtedly Lloyd
called at Bryant's handsome stone house in Roslyn, Long Island,
since the poet-editor introduced him in 1872 to Chicago society.
At the League's formal dinners he met businessmen, journalists,
and public men from many states.

A postelection League dinner in November 1870 at Delmonico's celebrated tariff reform victories in the congressional
campaign, during which the *Free-Trader* and *Evening Post* had
attempted to make that issue a party test. The dinner was preceded by a secret conference to plan strategy to disrupt President

Grant's alliance with the protectionists, prominent promoter-speculators, and spoilsmen. In June Grant had declined to re-appoint Wells to the Revenue Commission despite League pressure. At that time the press had published the scandalous story of "Black Friday," with whose perpetrators, Jay Gould and Jim Fisk, Jr., the President had been intimate. Senate spoilsmen had prevented Attorney General Rockwood Hoar's elevation to the Supreme Court because he sought pure men for the federal bench. Grant had forced Jacob D. Cox, reformist Secretary of the Interior, from office. Grant's personal friend, the corrupt "shoddyite" Thomas Murphy, administered the New York Customs House to the injury of the merchants, and made the protectionist Roscoe Conkling the state Republican "boss."[24]

Because of the Erie Ring's alliance with "Boss" Tweed democracy had ceased to exist in New York. Legislative orgies occurred from Albany to Topeka, Kansas. Eighteen months earlier Henry Adams had predicted that elimination of existing political dishonesty would be "harder than the anti-slavery fight."[25] So it proved to be.

Bryant presided at the conclave, which Carl Schurz and other public men declined to attend. Sands had hoped that it could arrange a bipartisan tariff reform organization of the new House of Representatives as preliminary *"to a new political movement in favor of Revenue and Civil Service Reform."*[26] The meeting consisted of friendly newspaper editors, Edwin L. Godkin of the *Nation,* Henry Adams of the *North American Review,* seven League officers including Lloyd, and a few Republican politicians. Among these was Colonel Wm. M. Grosvenor, editor of the *St. Louis Democrat,* Schurz's warm friend. As chairman of the Missouri Liberal Republican State Committee he was privy to the League's secret political strategy. Lloyd knew that this victor over the Grant faction in Missouri was secretly paid by the League. Grosvenor was author of the free trade manual, *Does Protection Protect?* The conclave established a permanent organization to advance tariff and civil service reform. If Congress rejected these reforms a larger gathering would be con-

voked to plan a national convention, following the example of
the antislavery parties. However, this strategy would be dropped
if Grant abandoned protection and the spoils system. After
the January *Free-Trader* published the plan Speaker James G.
Blaine promised the free-traders control of the next congressional Ways and Means Committee of which James A. Garfield
would be chairman.[27]

Minturn, first president of the Union League Club, presided
at the tariff reform Delmonico dinner of 160 League members
and guests. Sands described there the League's 4,000 co-operators, 2,000 friendly newspapers, active lecturers, associated
leagues, and staff of fourteen. The League had defeated the
Schenck Bill and its author's bid for re-election, he claimed, and
elected a tariff reform majority of forty-three to the new
Congress. While the presence of Grosvenor and S. S. ("Sunset")
Cox, victor over Greeley in the New York Sixth District, at the
speakers' table symbolized the League's opposition to Grant,
David A. Wells gave the main address in response to the toast,
"The War Against Monopoly." He identified himself with the
tariff reform movement as he attacked the highly protected
Onondaga salt monopoly.[28]

Grant was unperturbed by tariff reform election victories and
the threat of a party split. Vice-President Schuyler Colfax had
shown him Greeley's autumn prediction that the Liberal Republicans would win in Missouri, bolt in Illinois, and extinguish
the Republican party unless it declared itself for "Protection"
and eliminated "the traitors." Grant's annual message supported
the proposed "free breakfast bill" abolishing duties on tea,
coffee, and sugar, which would prevent reduction of the protective duties. A Delmonico dinner of 350 protectionists endorsed
this enthusiastically. When the "lame duck" House of Representatives passed the bill despite tariff reform resistance, Blaine
forgot his promise to the League. He named a Massachusetts
protectionist, Henry L. Dawes, chairman of the next Ways
and Means Committee.[29]

The Free-Trade League proceeded with the strategy adopted
in November. Lloyd informed his precocious brother David,

youthful graduate from New York University and now private
secretary to Chief Justice Salmon P. Chase, that "the times are
ripening" and Grosvenor "is in Washington on secret service for
the League." Would David ascertain from Chase his opinion of
the probable "result of the palpable division of the Republicans?" Would power pass "from them to the Democrats or will
it be successfully seized by some third party?" In April 1871
J. D. Cox and the Cincinnati tariff reformers launched a Liberal
Republican movement in Ohio. The *Free-Trader* announced
that only a new party led by men such as he could cure the
"body politic."[30]

As the League fomented revolt within the Republican party
Lloyd's propaganda contribution included preparation of an experimental *People's Pictorial Taxpayer* containing cartoons and
anecdotes at Greeley's expense. Lloyd also replied uncandidly,
but with strong support from the *World*, to the *New York Daily
Bulletin's* protest against the League's "political combinations."[31]

He challenged Greeley's lecture on free trade at the New
York Liberal Club from the floor, remarking incautiously that
"the laws of supply and demand furnished a much safer standard for prices than the determination of a few hundred
'idiots' in Washington." The Club invited him to reply to
Greeley formally. In preparation he asked John Stiles of the
Pension Office for data on Greeley's claim that a favorable
wage differential caused by the tariff had promoted Canadian
immigration to the United States. As he drew upon his "NO
MONOPOLY" series to rebut Greeley on March 24, the *Tribune* published his letter to Stiles together with the latter's
repudiation of "Free-Trade." Lloyd replied so effectively to
Stiles in the *World* that he was complimented by the *Evening
Post* and *Washington Patriot*, which disclosed that the Free-
Trade League had rejected Stiles's application for a position.[32]
This exchange and Lloyd's lecture led to his election as second
vice-president of the Liberal Club when Greeley became president, an unusual honor for a young man.

During two successive winters Lloyd persuaded Professors
Lieber and Perry to discuss free trade and protection before

his class at the Evening High School. This cemented his friendship with Lieber, who advocated "Unchecked Exchange" and sent him pamphlets when he added a course on political science. A student of Lloyd's economics class admitted later that under his tutelage he would have burned the Customs House cheerfully. At graduations an astonishing number of student addresses dealt with economics and politics.[33]

Lloyd declared ardently in the *Phrenological Journal,* January 1872, that political economy was "a valiant ally of the social reformer" because it attacked "violations of economic law which cause social disorders." "Liberty" alone would remedy "monopolies, subsidies, special legislation, land-grants." He alluded caustically to "Boss" Tweed and "Commodore" Vanderbilt as he disclosed his complete acceptance of the Bryant-Sterne school of reform.[34]

The Mercantile Library was the first object of Lloyd's independent reforming zeal. He knew at first hand how its dingy reading-room contrasted with the matchless efficiency of the circulation department. Members resented that Library's Sunday closing, when lack of wholesome recreation was keenly felt. As reform sentiment in the Library Association threatened to overwhelm them the directors secured constitutional amendments strengthening their position. When the president would not reply to Lloyd's criticism of the annual budget at a reform party meeting the press supported the demand for Sunday opening, lower dues, and honest elections. The Lloyd brothers worked late and spent liberally to prepare for the annual election, encouraged by their mother to "acquire some practice" for the "fight . . . with evil and wickedness" in "this crooked world."

Exclusion of some reformers from the annual meeting precipitated an explosion. Surrounded by an indignant, compact minority, but howled down by the majority, Lloyd attempted vainly to strike from the minutes of the previous annual session reference to the irregularly adopted amendments. Refusal to allow him to present an amendment of his own precipitated a minor riot. Despite press support and public sympathy his

party's ticket was defeated in what the *Tribune* termed a
"farcical election" in May 1871. The meeting, the *World*
said, was "most disgracefully conducted." When other papers
criticized Henry D. and John C. Lloyd and other reform leaders
they published rejoinders. The "regulars" replied in a "Manifesto" criticizing the allegedly "riotous and disorderly conduct"
of the elder Lloyd.

The Lloyd brothers and Peter Voorhis of the Equitable Life
Insurance Company circulated petitions that persuaded Henry
Ward Beecher to speak under the reformers' auspices on the
"Sunday Question" at Cooper Union. He emphatically advocated opening all public libraries on Sundays. The meeting then
adopted Henry D. Lloyd's resolutions requesting the Mercantile Library Association directors' consent. Great applause
greeted Abraham S. Hewitt's announcement of Cooper Union's
acquiescence. The Mercantile Library then followed suit. Reconciliation between its rival factions followed. In May 1872 a
"union" ticket for directors including ·Henry D. Lloyd and
Voorhis was elected to the accompaniment of "a band of
twelve string and brass instruments" and a "glee club." As
"the life and soul of the Reform party" Henry D. Lloyd made
"a long speech." The new directors then adjourned with their
friends to the Directors' Room where they "drank champagne
and ate lobster salad."[35]

Seventeen months earlier Henry D. Lloyd had joined the
anti-Tweed movement, to which he made a valuable contribution. Like others he was disgusted with the Ring's organization
of the city's ignorant mass of voters into "a tremendous engine
for political burglary" and its control of the state government.
Ring control of political advertising had obliged Isaac Henderson, publisher of the *Evening Post,* to dismiss Charles Nordhoff
after he had killed with a searing editorial the *Sun's* proposal
to erect a statue of Tweed. It took courage, therefore, for Henry
D. Lloyd to protest in the *Tribune* in January 1871 against the
Ring's ouster of H. W. Twombly from the General Assembly so
as to perpetuate its control there. Lloyd offered $5 to finance
Twombly's contest, declaring "our vaunted representative

government is a lie" if he were not seated. "We must come to bay at some time—now say I." In June he predicted to the New York Political Science Association that if a "few more" young college men of probity entered politics "they could soon do away with the corruption and ignorance which now disgrace the nation."[36] A fortnight later the *New York Times* published the fraudulent City Comptroller's accounts.

At the great Cooper Institute Citizens' Meeting in September that named the anti-Tweed Committee of Seventy with Sterne as secretary, Bryant declared that the young men gave "the spirit, the energy, and the hopefulness" to the movement to overthrow the Ring. The Young Men's Municipal Reform Association was formed to get out the vote and police the polls. Public-spirited citizens rallied in self-constituted bands to ensure honest voting and a fair count. Lloyd drafted the pledge of the Seventh Assembly District's "ballot guard" in which his father and grandfather Demarest enrolled. He urged that the Committee of Seventy assume control of the spontaneous citizens' movement's "crude and inexperienced," unco-ordinated "associations." "The imperative demand of the movement is the insistent and efficient concentration of these disunited elements into a compact and practical organization," he said,[37] before Samuel J. Tilden rallied the reform Democrats and gave the anti-Tweed campaign moral and astute political leadership.

Lloyd then wrote a manual on the election laws to inform the citizenry. At first the *Times* had ridiculed the young men's movement. Now it published Lloyd's manual on October 21, entitled "Every Man His Own Voter." Editorial praise bestowed the accolade upon the author, remarking, "The Young Men's Association has . . . deserved public gratitude for bringing his abilities into the sphere of active politics." The Association adopted the manual and distributed it among campaign workers and voters. It was an effective, practical contribution to the defeat of the "Ring" in November.

Afterward, Lloyd felt able to debate first principles with reformers of any persuasion. Wearing his new spurs he listened to a paper on "Equality and Limitation" at the "Cosmopolitan

Conference." During the discussion, after a "Citizen Roosevelt"
had "thought that goodness was always the result of evil, it
took two evils to make one good, but no one had a right to do
wrong," he urged that wage-earners revise the laws establishing
monopolies, abolish restraints on individuals, and give Illinois
women the suffrage. Lloyd had broadened swiftly from the
sincere junior executive of a thinly disguised pressure groups
organization to a reformer in his own right. He combined
zealous Cobdenism with utilitarian impatience with obsolescent
institutions and restraints upon individual development, and
exhibited an unusually sensitive perception of the implications
of moral evils. He had been among the few to demand purging
corruption from representative government and the excision
of the cancerous spoils system from the governmental structure.
Now, before the Tweed Ring was ousted from Albany, Lloyd
made an irrevocable commitment to moral reform.

Chapter III

A Liberal Republican

THE ANTI-TWEED MOVEMENT encouraged reformers elsewhere to devise "ways and means" of keeping "from being sold out by their appointed guardians."Outraged moral sentiment made political reform the order of the day. Widespread organization of reform clubs was stimulated by the conviction of a Tennessee congressman for taking money for prosecuting fraudulent claims against the national government and by the impeachment of Florida's governor for looting the state treasury.[1] The civil service reformers won so influential a following that Grant began belatedly to enforce the recommendations of George William Curtis' advisory commission. Congressman George W. Julian broke with his Radical colleagues in Congress in searing denunciations of the railroad land grant schemes and frauds that were frustrating the homestead policy. These so aroused western farmers and eastern laborers that Congress refused additional railroad land grants.[2]

During the autumn and winter of 1871-72 secret meetings were held between the Free-Trade League's leaders, officers of the New England Revenue Reform League, western tariff reformers, and Missouri Liberal Republicans. Atkinson led in organizing a Tax-Payers' Union with the aid of Colonel Grosvenor, Schurz, J. D. Cox, Horace White, Wells, and Sands. Its purpose was propaganda and lobbying for practical tariff reform, with headquarters at St. Louis. Grosvenor was executive director, having left the *Democrat* when its proprietors went

47

over to Grant. The Tax-Payers' Union was controlled in the West, but was financed secretly by New York and Boston tariff reformers. Sands entrusted Grosvenor with the Free-Trade League's secret mailing list of 100,000 sympathizers! Early in 1872 the Colonel established an information bureau and lobby in Washington to guide the inexperienced tariff reform majority of the new House of Representatives to comprehensive tariff reduction.[3]

With this work he combined the chairmanship of the Missouri Liberal Republican Committee, which in December invited all anti-Grant men and "friends of practical reform" to unite in a new political party. Its formation had been the object of Free-Trade League strategy since November 1870. In cooperation with Schurz, Grosvenor united the political reform clubs of the West and Southwest with the Missouri movement.[4] The Union delegated the editing of a propaganda organ to Lloyd.

This was the monthly *People's Pictorial Tax-Payer*. Imitating Thomas Nast's success in lampooning Tweed, Lloyd exploited political cartoons skillfully. He fostered reform sentiment, supported the Tax-payer's lobby, discussed revenue reform, and backed the independent political movement. Prior to his January number the *New York Evening Post* announced that the new strategy was to oblige the Republican majority in Congress to enact tariff and civil service reform and to abandon Grant. If this tactic failed a reform party would be organized, supported by Democrats who accepted Clement L. Vallandigham's "New Departure."[5]

Editing the *Tax-Payer* drew Lloyd into national politics and the attempt to overthrow "Grantism," to which the free-traders had given the initial impetus. They supplied the nucleus of mass support, most of the financial backing, and much of the moral enthusiasm and philosophy of the movement. Alone of the Free-Trade League officials Lloyd was a Republican and leader of the anti-Tweed and young men's movements.[6] In the ensuing drama he played a dual role of League executive and independent reformer to the bitter end. The experience was highly educational. It tested his moral fiber, but resulted in heartbreaking defeat. The tariff reformers gave Schurz control of the Liberal movement in the spring, expecting him to hold it to its projected course. Instead, he took the craft off course and allowed political pirates to board it. They captured the ship before it reached the open sea. As a clearheaded defender of the craft against the boarding party and subsequently as a leader of the forlorn attempt to recapture it Lloyd established his reputation as an unflinching champion of reform.

In the *Pictorial Tax-Payer* he contributed importantly to the Liberal Republican bolt. The first number was "brilliant." Grosvenor praised it highly as did the *Chicago Tribune* staff. The Western News Company ordered 5,000 copies and predicted a large sale. Atkinson declared it "wonderfully good." A full-page cartoon ridiculing the farcical Senatorial investigation of the New York Customs House made Horace White laugh harder than he had since the Chicago fire. A leader attributed George Leet's monopoly of the "general order" business to the White House. Lloyd predicted editorially that Boston would join "a united West" in overthrowing the protective tariff.

"Independent in everything, neutral in nothing," the *Tax-payer* flew the pennon of "Equal Rights." It attacked the spoils system, tariff-fostered monopolies, and protectionism's injury to sailors, farmers, and laborers. It demanded "instant" civil service reform, abolition of lobbying (!) and special legislation, a sound currency, proportional representation, and "Free Trade." It rejoiced at the convictions of Philadelphia's defaulting city treasurer and Charles Tyson Yerkes. The "eyes of the master are everywhere and wherever he looks he seeks plenty of work to be done," Lloyd remarked.

To nullify Greeley's identification of tariff reform with British interests he secured advertisements from the Illinois Central and Chicago & Alton railroads, the mercantile firm of Field, Leiter & Company of Chicago, Chicago Life Insurance Company, Edward Harris of Woonsocket, leader of the low tariff woolen manufacturers, Holt & Company, and Duncan, Sherman & Company, Bankers, of New York. These offset those from "importers and British Ins. Cos." that "disfigure Our Columns," he informed Atkinson. Such support promised to make the *Tax-Payer* profitable, as Grosvenor predicted it would become.

Zestful, sincere, its vigorous message made an undeniable appeal. The humorous serials, "Horace Greeley, Henry C. Carey, and John Sherman" and "Mother Carey's Chickens," effective cartoons, and statistical proof that "the monopolists" netted fifty million in profits from duties on building materials that yielded only $4,000,000 revenue powerfully supported Grosvenor's lobby. Lloyd disclosed that greater savings to consumers would accrue from hides and leather on the free list than from duty-free tea and coffee. A comic strip revealed that manufacturers alone benefited from duties on wool, woolens, machinery.[7]

Simultaneously, Sands and Lloyd mobilized delegations of Yankee shoemakers and woolen manufacturers to oppose the Pennsylvania protectionists before the Ways and Means Committee.[8]

However, divided counsels in the Tax-Payers' Union nullified Grosvenor's and Lloyd's instruction of the inexperienced Congressional tariff reformers. Over Grosvenor's protests Wells, White, Sands, and Atkinson agreed to duty-free coffee and tea, coal, salt, and lumber. The protectionists promptly rushed the "free breakfast" bill through Congress. Then, when Atkinson sought reductions on the specified raw materials consumed in New England the western tariff reformers questioned their eastern allies' good faith. These divided counsels repelled Garfield and delayed action on a general tariff bill until after the Liberal Republican Convention at Cincinnati.[9]

The Missouri call to that convention went to Republican reformers of all types. It was intended to mobilize a decisive demonstration of Liberal strength in advance of the Union Republican National Convention at Philadelphia. Schurz was the official leader of the Cincinnati movement, to which Senators Trumbull, T. W. Tipton, and J. C. Robinson adhered. Charles Sumner, deposed chairman of the Senate Foreign Relations Committee, flirted with the Liberals. Such moderates as Garfield were privately sympathetic. Soon demands for a Liberal presidential ticket became irresistible. Charles Francis Adams, former Minister to Great Britain, and Trumbull were especially favored.

Everything depended upon a great, unified Liberal demonstration at Cincinnati, to achieve which the April *Tax-Payer* gave powerful support. It urged that tariff reformers support a tacit alliance between the Liberals and the "passive" Democrats. "Cynicus at the Theatre" contrasted Grant's reform professions with the scandals of his administration. The Cincinnati movement, Lloyd declared, provided an opportunity to strike "at the very root of the whole monopoly system" by means "of thorough reform" which only a reorganization of parties could achieve. If a "resolute" tariff reformer were nominated upon a fearless platform the *Tax-Payer* predicted his election and a "reform Congress." However, if tariff reformers allowed the convention to be controlled by their adversaries or refused to devote time and money to the movement, "no set of politicians" would foster their interests and "grasping monopolists" would continue "oppressive exactions."

A cartoon depicted Schurz on the dock beside the "Cincinnati Convention Direct to the White House" steamboat, bareheaded with wind-blown beard, showing Greeley, burdened with "Pig-Iron," a placard on the smokestack reading "White House via Amnesty for all Civil Service Reform Tariff Reform."[10]

Schurz's admission of Greeley doomed the Liberal Movement. Yet, "The White Hat's" adherence seemed to him and some others to be an important re-enforcement. Greeley opposed Radical Reconstruction, urged amnesty for the southern states and freedmen's enfranchisement, denounced Grant's 'partisan interference with the civil service" and thought him "too small a man for the Presidency." Greeley brought into the Cincinnati movement, however, the Trojan horse of protectionism, crowded with the hungry followers of Senator Reuben E. Fenton, a spoilsman rival of Senator Conkling. Now in disfavor at the White House, the Fentonites announced their conversion to civil service reform. Once admitted to the Liberal movement

as Greeley's adherents they sought to control it by pushing him
for the presidential nomination.

Eastern tariff reformers were divided on the wisdom of admitting Greeley to the movement. The great New York merchant A. T. Stewart feared to oppose Grant because of the vul-
nerability of his mercantile establishment to custom house persecution. Wells would sacrifice tariff reform to secure a harmon-
ious Cincinnati convention. He was convinced that this reform
would be ensured anyway by nominating either Adams or
Trumbull. Samuel Bowles of the *Springfield Republican* preferred Greeley and would also compromise the tariff issue to
achieve harmony at Cincinnati. Greeley took advantage of this
situation to demand that the issue be relegated to the Congressional districts.

Schurz stipulated, however, that the Greeley element sign the
Missouri call with its pledge of tariff reform. After his bid for
the Philadelphia nomination was rejected by Union Republican
leaders the chance to join the Cincinnati movement was a
heaven-sent opportunity for Greeley. His anti-Grant attitude
and demands for amnesty and civil service reform would carry
more weight at Cincinnati. Signing the call aroused no qualms
in him or the Fentonites. They believed that with the *Tribune*
as their trump card they could force abandonment of its revenue
plank.

Grosvenor was greatly alarmed. He declared that the New
York free-traders who had inspired and organized the movement were now betraying it by admitting the protectionists. He
urged that Atkinson and Wells bring strong delegations of
"Yankee" tariff reformers and unite with the western free-
traders to prevent Fenton-financed spoilsmen from controlling
the convention. Parke Godwin aroused Bryant and Godkin,
protested against admitting Greeley, and asked Cox to alert
the Cincinnati free-traders. Cox warned Grosvenor that he
would not enter a Cave of Adullam with the Fenton-Greeley
men. Ohio and Illinois free-traders informed Grosvenor, Wells,
Atkinson, and Trumbull that if Greeley gained control they
would withdraw."

Cox asked Schurz pointedly how he would prevent this and reminded him of the differences on the tariff and currency that divided Greeley's following from the revenue reformers. To ignore these questions at Cincinnati and affiliate "with our most natural and most important political opponent" would wreck the movement, he predicted. He invited tariff reformers from all sections to meet at Cincinnati before the convention to save it "from disaster."[12]

In New York Lloyd had to lead the losing fight against Greeley because Sands could not yet qualify as a Liberal Republican. Alone of the city's leading free-traders Lloyd signed the address to Grosvenor whereby the Liberals adhered supposedly to the Missouri call. Drafted by William Dorsheimer, a Fentonite, the address was ambiguous on the tariff. Fentonites were the most numerous and prominent signers. The *Times* dubbed them "Greeley's Ragged Regiment." Lloyd it termed "a very young man, who was active in some of the Mercantile Library rows last year."

As one of the 200 vice-presidents at the April 12 Cooper Institute meeting that launched the Liberal Republican movement in the East Lloyd was indignant at the omission of the tariff issue from the "Declaration of Principles" and at Greeley's prominence as first vice-president. Schurz and Trumbull attacked party despotism and political corruption, excessive centralization, and Grant's maladministration. It was a tremendous demonstration against "Grantism." Greeley pledged support and a mass delegation of his followers at Cincinnati. Encouraged by the enthusiasm, overflow attendance, and adherence of David Dudley Field, Cyrus W. Field, Godkin, Wells, Hewitt, and the Fentonites, Schurz was convinced that Greeley brought indispensable re-enforcement to the Cincinnati movement. The *Evening Post* complained, however, that tariff reform was ignored in the speeches and asserted that the resolutions did not represent the sentiment of the city.[13]

As secretary of the committee to arrange the New York Liberal Republican delegation's journey to Cincinnati, Lloyd entertained no illusions. He worked "day and night" with

Richard R. Bowker to persuade "Free-Trade Republicans" that "their *duty*" was to attend the convention. Francis Lieber declined, observing that the movement had "been *infilé*." Too many Republican free-traders remained loyal to Grant for that element to regain control of the New York Liberal Republican delegation. George William Curtis taunted Godwin because of the shadow that Greeley's adherence cast upon the Liberal cause. On the eve of the Cincinnati convention Curtis asked sarcastically of Wells to be excused from attending while he "reflected among the graves at Arlington . . . that Cincinnati is hardly the way to peace or reform." To the moderates Grant's dismissal of 192 corrupt officials, his promise to Joseph Medill that he would give the merit system a fair trial, and his abolition of the 'general order business" indicated that reform would come more certainly via Philadelphia. The New York financial district evinced its preference for Grant in a mass meeting led by Henry Clews, banker and speculator.[14]

FIASCO

Lloyd was among the first to arrive in Cincinnati. After arranging housing for the New York delegation he joined the revenue reformers and friendly journalists at Cox's preliminary conclave. The convivial Horace White, Samuel Bowles, Henry Watterson of the Louisville *Courier-Journal,* and Murat Halstead of the *Cincinnati Commercial* formed a "Quadrilateral" that expected to control high convention strategy. Inexplicably, Godwin did not go to Cincinnati as a delegate. The *Evening Post* was content to warn the gathering delegates at long range not to compromise with "political speculators." As for tactics within the New York delegation where the Fentonites formed the majority, Bryant urged Lloyd to resist firmly all attempts to introduce either spoilsmen's tactics or protectionism into the Convention.[15]

Had Bryant attended and persuaded his New York lieutenants to do likewise the result might have been different. In that convention of their own devising the tariff reformers should have

secured a presidential ticket and a declaration of principles
attuned to the moral sentiment that was fighting corruption,
monopolies, special privilege, and the spoilsmen.[16]

August Belmont, the New York banker, had warned Schurz
on April 1 that only "the most unequivocal attitude" could ensure success. Manton Marble, editor of the *New York World,*
telegraphed David A. Wells, "For God's sake don't budge one
inch from Adams and Free Trade. Greetings to the Saints,"[17]
in opposition to advice from John Van Buren, secretary of the
Tweed-dominated Governor J. T. Hoffman at Albany. Yet,
when Whitelaw Reid, Greeley's representative, asked the
"Quadrilateral" at Cincinnatt to admit him its members con
sented.

As chairman of the preliminary conclave Cox was unable to
guide its deliberations or unite the participants sufficiently to
defeat the Fentonites. Interminable debate reopened the division between East and West among the revenue reformers. Of
this, secretly advised by Fenton and Pennsylvania protectionists,
Reid took full advantage. He hinted that if tariff reform were
not shelved Greeley would withdraw. The "Quadrilateral"
accordingly advised the conclave to compromise the tariff issue.
Forgetting his political indebtedness to the Free-Trade League,
Schurz declared that Greeley's support was essential to success.
Neither he nor the "Quadrilateral" realized that Greeley had
nowhere else to go politically. They forgot that tariff reform embodied the moral and antistatist principles of the Liberal movement. Instead, they made a self-stultifying harmony their major
objective. As permanent chairman designate of the convention
Schurz decided to allow the delegates to make their own decisions after inspiring them to high moral idealism with his
address, "This Is Moving Day."[18]

Lloyd occupied a back seat at the conclave. Grosvenor, Atkinson, and the Ohio men adhered to the Missouri call. The New
York free-traders divided. Field sided with Wells, who ignored
Marble's advice, and urged negotiation of a formula on the
tariff with Reid. Despite Cox's protest, but backed by Schurz
and the "Quadrilateral," they persuaded the conclave to agree

to this. During the negotiations Reid and Dorsheimer enjoyed the status of equals. Cox withdrew from the conclave. Reid and Greeley rejected successive draft compromises. Immediately before the Convention convened Greeley rejected Bowles' last-minute attempt to pledge his faction to the New York Liberal address that it had signed.[19]

Had the tariff reformers stood firmly on their principles during that conclave the convention might have realized their expectations. Instead, at General Henry Lawrence Burnet's dinner they joined their opponents in pledging advance support to the nominees. Fenton left the city, having set the stage for Greeley's victory.[20]

The labor reformers were a forgotten element in the situation. Some had arrived early in company with Lloyd. They favored tariff reform and appreciated the Free-Trade League's interest in them. However, their demands for a national fiat currency derived from Edward Kellogg's proposed system of district government loan offices clashed with Cobdenite antistatism. Between them and Carey-Greeley protectionism with its preference for a managed paper currency there was a certain affinity. If tariff reform were eliminated from the platform and Schurz should reject the labor reformers' overtures, as he did, they might desert Judge David Davis, their candidate, for Greeley.[21]

The tariff reformers were decisively beaten by "machine" tactics in the New York mass delegation. During this episode Lloyd passed the acid test of his courage, insight, and fighting ability. David Dudley Field was excluded with other free-traders arbitrarily from the caucus by Fentonites determined to control the delegation. Division of it, with a substantial vote for Adams, would have wrecked Greeley's chances. Although Lloyd won the right for each congressional district to select its delegates at the convention, the caucus voted that these had to be approved by a Fentonite committee. Despite Sands's vehement protest and Lloyd's spirited quoting of the Missouri call's denunciation of machine methods, the Fentonites imposed the unit rule upon the official delegation by a vote of ninety-nine to twenty-two. General John Cochrane's committee then re-

ported an approved list of Empire State delegates; among the
sixty-eight only three were free-traders. Sands was excluded.
Although Lloyd was listed he had declared that a unit rule
would oblige him to refuse to represent his district. Theodore
Tilton defended his refusal to promise to support Greeley
under that rule. When Ethan Allen declared that each official
delegate must obey it Lloyd withdrew from the delegation as
did the other free-trader from his district. They were replaced
with Greeley men.[22]

The infuriated New York free-traders led by Lloyd, Sands,
and Field circulated a protest against seating the packed New
York delegation. Indignant Judge Henry R. Seldon, former
lieutenant governor of New York, presented this to the convention. When argued in the Credentials Committee the contest
attracted a great crowd of demonstrating sympathizers. There,
as the contestants' spokesman, Sands was discredited by his
recent status as a Democrat and his refusal to abide by the unit
rule. The Credentials Committee reported on the New York
contest adversely, to the astonishment of many delegates. When
confirmed by a majority vote, this action demoralized the tariff
reformers who had just begun their fight for a revenue tariff
plank before the Resolutions Committee.[23]

Schurz had packed this committee with protectionists. After
an all-night fight with the embittered tariff reformers, the committee adopted Greeley's proposal that the issue be relegated to
the congressional districts. Although some free-traders threatened to bolt, Wells, Atkinson, and Grosvenor agreed to "stand
upon" this stultification of their principles.[24] Thus, after their
exclusion from the convention the New York free-traders witnessed the virtual rejection of the issue most vital to them.

Lloyd was crushed, plunged into cynical despair. Tempted
to throw his ideals overboard and drown himself in dissipation,
he was saved from disaster by his brother David, acting as
Chase's observer, and Henry Francis Keenan, a friendly *New
York Tribune* reporter. The Irish wit and understanding of
this experienced political journalist pulled him off the rocks in
time to witness the climactic fiasco of the Liberal cause.[25]

This resulted from the division of the tariff and civil service reformers on the candidacies of Adams and Trumbull. Their backers hoped to nullify the nonsensical tariff plank by nominating a tariff reformer. Their rivalry prevented the nomination of either man. After initial balloting those groups were caught unprepared by a deal between Frank Blair of Missouri and Whitelaw Reid. They persuaded the Missouri and Kansas followers of Governor B. Gratz Brown to switch to Greeley in return for promising Brown the vice-presidential nomination. Schurz, when appealed to, refused to intervene. The tariff and civil service reformers were unable to unite on a candidate before a stampede for Greeley was started on the sixth ballot by the diversion of Davis delegates to him, accompanied by stentorian shouting from machine politicians that only Greeley could "beat Grant." This swept confused delegates into his camp and nominated him.

Thus, "the embodiment of centralization and monopoly" became the Liberal Republican presidential nominee. Brown, a low tariff Liberal, was named his running mate. Rumor said the deal had been arranged by Grosvenor.[26]

Isaac H. Bromley of the *Hartford Post* remarked later that if the free-traders had replied instantly that on no condition would they support that ticket they could have obliged both nominees to withdraw to make way for genuine reform candidates. Instead, Cox and Atkinson withdrew from the convention to engage that night in interminable discussions with Wells, White, Godkin, and leading Ohio free-traders. They agreed that the manner in which the "original Reformers" had been overwhelmed released them from obligation to support the convention's actions. Since the New York free-traders had left precipitately the meeting was unable to act. Cox informed Garfield, "We have fallen among thieves." The *Chicago Tribune's* decision to support Greeley for business reasons muzzled White and excluded him from the subsequent free-traders' attempts to extricate themselves from their humiliating position.[27]

The regular Republicans in Congress and the East greeted

the ticket with raucous glee. Its announcement in Chicago "fell
dead on the city." Republican moderates in New England re-
affirmed their loyalty to Grant.[28] Sincere reformers were confronted by the mortifying choice between stultifying themselves
by supporting Greeley or by supporting Grant to defeat the
former.

Lloyd alone of the New Yorkers returned home with enhanced prestige. The *Evening Post* termed him "a gallant and
upright devotee of principle" who should be thanked "by all
genuine reformers for his persistency and daring and determination," and attributed Greeley's nomination to "wirepullers, chi-
canery, intrigue, bargaining, and compromise." Then Lloyd
and Sands learned that Grosvenor was in New York conferring
with Fenton. This apparently confirmed the rumor that he had
betrayed tariff reform at the convention. Few League officials
recalled that he had warned them vainly against the Fenton-
Greeley "Trojan Horse," or that he had fought stoutly in the
preconvention conferences against compromise. What they remembered was the Greeley-Brown deal.[29]

Determined to retrieve the League's confidential mailing list,
Lloyd secured authority to take charge of the Tax-Payers'
Union Washington headquarters. After receipt of his telegraphed order David Demarest Lloyd ransacked Grosvenor's
apartment, carried off the Union's records, Grosvenor's political
papers, and the Missouri Liberal Republican Committee's
books.[30] After returning to his ransacked quarters the Colonel
conferred with Schurz, secured a letter from him vindicating
his course at Cincinnati, and entrained for New York shadowed
by David and John C. Lloyd.

Sands, Henry D. Lloyd, and several directors informed Grosvenor at Free-Trade headquarters that they believed he had
" 'sold out' the cause of Free Trade." Grosvenor presented
Schurz's letter but refused to oppose Greeley. The League declined to return to him its confidential mailing list but handed
him his personal papers, while asserting its ownership of the
Tax-Payers' Union from which Grosvenor was dismissed forth-
with. Although Atkinson assured the Colonel of his confidence

and censured the League for acting "on suspicion" the Boston tariff reformers withdrew support from Grosvenor's lobby.[31] In Congress Greeley's nomination modified tariff revision into a ten per cent horizontal reduction that left the protective principle intact.

The *Evening Post* proposed a meeting of liberal notables. Bryant was encouraged by Schurz's silence after the Cincinnati convention, the refusal of the German press to support Greeley, and the attempts of Cox and the Reunion and Reform associations to nominate a ticket "on the Missouri Platform." Bryant's strategy was to force Greeley to retire from the race by drawing the Liberals from him to acceptable nominees who would be palatable to the Democrats.

Greeley was antagonized, however, by a scathing letter from Schurz and the obvious purpose of Bryant's maneuver. He refused indignantly to withdraw and excoriated the free-traders. When Schurz disclosed to Reid sympathy with the plan to call a second Liberal convention, that astute guardian of Greeley's interests brought decisive pressure to bear upon him via Bowles and Grosvenor. This doomed the free-traders' attempt to rescue the cause of economic and political reform from the "pitiable condition" in which it had been left by the Cincinnati fiasco.[32]

Bowles appraised the free-traders' strategy realistically to Wells, when he predicted Grant's re-election. Although sympathetic with the attempt to supplant Greeley with Adams as "satisfactory to me," he did not believe it feasible. "I do not like the issue of Greeley or Grant. I wish it could be Adams and Colfax instead. But I suspect the eyes of that animal are 'sot,' and you have got to look at him just as he is."[33] The Free-Trade League might have accomplished more had its officials not been obsessed with Schurz's indispensability. Cox wanted them to organize a small party modeled on the Free-Soilers to hold aloft the banner of tariff and civil service reform.

Lloyd figured prominently in this desperate attempt to extricate the cause of economic, political, and moral reform from its dilemma. While Stewart and other League supporters declared themselves for Grant, Bryant exerted his utmost influence to reunite the divided reformers. He headed the sponsors, including Lloyd, of a May 30 Steinway Hall meeting to repudiate the Cincinnati ticket because of that convention's "betrayal of reform." Divisions among the tariff reformers deprived this later gathering of major influence. Bowles and Schurz declined to attend. Horace White reproached the sponsors for their bitterness at Greeley's unfair tactics. Tilden, leader of the reform Democrats, preferred Greeley.

Bryant presided at Steinway Hall over an ardent, youthful following recruited almost entirely from the city that shouted down a Greeley claque and applauded Adams roundly. Lloyd was a vice-president. He spoke after Bryant, Wells, Atkinson, Sterne, and Perry, and declared that free-traders must fight "Protectionist Greeley" to the end, ridiculed his pledge not to veto any tariff bill, and attributed his nomination to free-trader weakness in "surrendering the platform" to the Fentonites at Cincinnati. The meeting placed Lloyd on a Committee of Ten to co-operate with other organizations in naming a more satisfactory ticket.[34]

This plunged him into an intricate political intrigue. However, Reid worked with finesse to restrict the free-trader bolt, while noting the moribund condition of the Free-Trade League in the *Tribune*. Encouraged by Marble and Wilbur F. Storey of the *Chicago Times,* the Ten attempted to induce disgruntled Democrats such as ex-Governor Theodore F. Randolph of New Jersey and Oswald Ottendorer of the *New Yorker Staats-Zeitung* to prevent Greeley's endorsement by the Democratic National Convention. Godwin, Wells, and Carl Daenzer of the St. Louis *Anzeiger des Westerns* worked closely with the Ten.[35]

As its secretary, Lloyd went to Washington to secure Schurz's signature to Randolph's draft call for a new convention. When he went to breakfast with his brother and Chief Justice Chase at Mrs. Kate Sprague's he met Reid, whose presence was motivated ostensibly by a desire to recruit David D. Lloyd for the *New York Tribune*. As Reid drove away with him after this repast Henry D. Lloyd argued that his brother should remain with Chase "at least two years" before entering journalism.

Within two months David joined Reid, who must have authorized Keenan's hint of a minor diplomatic post for the eldest
Lloyd son if he would support Greeley. The *Tribune*'s new
chief appreciated the worth of an opponent who had declined
to betray to Keenan the political secrets of the League.[36]

Schurz revised the draft call so as to invite to the second conference all opponents of Grant who wished to unite in the campaign. Lloyd detected the implications of Schurz's explanation
that he desired to "leave his bridges open." He intended to
finesse the discouraged tariff reformers into supporting Greeley
and Brown, and stipulated that prominent Greeley men be
among the sponsors. All this the Ten accepted, but Bowles,
Dorsheimer, and Horace White would not sign the call. Bryant,
Schurz, Cox, Wells, Brinkerhoff, and Ottendorfer sponsored the
new conference.[37]

Lloyd attempted to ensure that the majority at the gathering
"would be anti-Greeley unalterably." Godkin, Cox, Bryant,
and Randolph supported his attempt to beguile Schurz into
breaking with Greeley. Randolph wanted an alternative Liberal
ticket to present to the Baltimore convention. Lloyd was deep
in his plans, flattered by confidential association with him and
Schurz. He teased Keenan, absent in the West as the *Tribune*'s
political representative, with hints of such activities and of flir-
tation with a New Jersey maiden whom both admired. He was
in charge of the Free-Trade League Office, and at a press conference denied that the new conference derivd from it or would
represent its views. He predicted Greeley's defeat because of
opposition to him of the free-traders, Democrats, Germans, and
southern Negroes.[38] In reply the *Tribune* called him the "infant
Secretary of the Free Trade League" linked with Bryant and
belittled their influence. The metropolitan press took up that
refrain as Henry and David Lloyd tried to preserve the conference's secrecy.

It was held at the Fifth Avenue Hotel on June 20. There
Henry D. Lloyd, smilingly uncommunicative, blocked Gros-
venor's attempt to hide a *Tribune* reporter in the meeting place.
David Lloyd guarded the door. Frustrated reporters took re-

venge in their stories of the episode. "Gath" of the *Herald* dubbed the gathering the "Vario-Lloyd Conference." He described Henry D. Lloyd as "fair-skinned, brown-haired, cool and good-looking, with more than ordinary *aplomb,*" but, while "tall, mannerly, and good-tempered," only "a fine sophomoric political economist" with "good clerical and promising executive ability." Reid declared accurately that Lloyd was acting for Bryant and Godwin, Greeley's "unappeasable enemies," while claiming that he had packed the conference "in the free-trade interest."[39]

He was secretary of the conference, where the anti-Greeley element was stronger than had been supposed. Led by Bryant, Godkin, Godwin, Sands, Atkinson, Judge J. B. Stallo of Cincinnati, and Daenzer, the majority demanded a presidential ticket of Adams and William S. Groesbeck of Ohio. Henry Watterson opposed this action. Brinkerhoff and Grosvenor supported the Cincinnati ticket, the latter declaring falsely that all but two working trans-Allegheny free-traders did likewise. Schurz declared that a third ticket would only divide the reformers and re-elect Grant. He told Bryant and his friends bluntly that if they had exhibited at Cincinnati the energy and eloquence now displayed "they would not have cause to meet here."

Cox like Bryant wanted a new ticket. When this did not receive support of a majority of the states represented he discouraged "any attempt to go further." On Schurz's motion the conference adjourned.

At Judge Stallo's suggestion the German-Americans and the "saving remnant" of anti-Grant, anti-Greeley free-traders from New York, southern Ohio, and Massachusetts whom Lloyd led reconvened the next morning. Lloyd spoke vigorously for an outright reform platform and ticket in a manner that the *Chicago Tribune* declared was "too transcendental for this world." Despite opposition from Cox and Wells he carried this rump conference for free-trade, civil service reform, states rights, and sound money. It recommended to all "patriotic, independent liberal voters" the relatively unknown Groesbeck

and Frederick Law Olmstead, the New York landscape architect. This was Lloyd's final attempt to draw the Germans and
Reunion and Reform associations away from Greeley. The
Nation praised the platform. Bryant termed this last stand
against huckstering politics "essentially admirable." Reid, on
the other hand, dubbed the rump conference "The Little End
of Nothing." John Hay, his editorial assistant, turned his wit
in mocking sympathy on the *Post* and "Mr. Lloyd," who preserved his editorials with comments from the Grant press and
Bryant's praise. He had learned from this "most distinguished"
older Liberal to adhere to principle when all seemed lost in the
stampede for selfish advantage, and had acquired much of the
poet-editor's gentility and tenacious loyalty to "Equal Rights."
For the present he had to endure the *Tribune*'s satire and the
Golden Age's twisted story of his relations with Bryant and
Godwin.[40]

A year later, after Greeley's defeat and more scandals in
Grant's administration, the *Atlantic Monthly* declared that despite its disastrous end the Cincinnati movement had disclosed
the existence of a "small class of sincere reformers" capable of
attacking the party in power boldly and of ruining "soidisant
followers" who joined the reform movement for selfish purposes.[41] In this element Lloyd had won a distinguished place. It
remained to be seen if his commitment to moral reform would
endure during the disgraceful years of Grant's second administration.

Chapter IV

The 'Chicago Tribune' and Jessie Bross

JOURNALISM

LLOYD DECLARED FACETIOUSLY after the Fifth Avenue Hotel conferences, "My present condition is one like Murat Halstead's. 'I ain't got no principles and I don't care a damn.' This Free Trade business has drained my vitality." Reaction from overwork precipitated indigestion, an indication of a nervous temperament. Not even an excursion on Dundee Lake with David and four girls eased the shock of disappointment. He was eager for little more than the sunshine at Long Beach.

Friendship with Keenan helped him to chart a new course. "Trajan," as Keenan's friends called him, had befriended David Lloyd during his shorthand reporting for the *Tribune* while studying at New York University. Although Henry D. Lloyd had renounced feminine society after Louise Haight's death, "Trajan's" humor and affection revived his sociability. Being on opposite sides of the tariff issue led to mutual twitting but did not impede the development of a gay, spirited friendship. "Henry le premier," Keenan was to Lloyd, who signed himself "le deuxième."[1]

Keenan drew him into a charming circle at General Thomas D. Hoxsey's "Castle" at Haledon near Passaic, New Jersey. There, with the Hoxsey daughters they rowed, read "Goethe's Life" aloud, talked, walked, sang duets and quartettes, visited neighbors, and conversed. Lloyd visited the Castle after Keenan went West as Reid's emissary. To "Trajan" he wrote that he learned there that thirst for knowledge and attachment to prin-

ciple were not incompatible with the "purest pleasure" of
social intercourse. The General was a vigorous abolitionist, antimonopolist, and teetotaler, and just the man to restore Lloyd's
faith in reform. Lloyd escorted Belle Hoxsey to Theodore
Thomas' concerts.[2] In reply Keenan demanded news of Haledon
and intimate confidences. His accounts of "Fanny" Huntington
and other Chicago belles drew Lloyd into a frank interchange.
"Trajan" soothed "le deuxième's" fury at the jibes of the
Golden Age. When Reid treated "le premier" arbitrarily both
Henries damned him. Lloyd wrote of his early love of Louise
Haight. He confided a longing for the friendship and "restraining and yet vivifying influence" of such a young woman as
Frances Huntington. Keenan's reply to his request that he tell
what he knew of Belle Hoxsey prevented any sentimental con-
nection at Haledon.[3]

To "le premier" Lloyd appraised the recent free-trader bolt
in retrospect as an attempt "to unite fire and gunpowder without an explosion." He had felt while conferring with Schurz and
Randolph that the attempt to rescue the Liberal movement
from the Greeley blight would fail. The "slaughter" at Cincinnati and the later conferences be attributed to the League's
reliance upon "a great and dangerous man like Schurz," whose
insistence upon admitting the Greeley faction to them as
"Free-Traders" had wrecked tariff reform. "Schurz and the
others . . . came, they saw, and *we* were conquered," he admitted ruefully, having learned to eschew false pride and
"thimble-rigging in politics." In the future, he said, he would
"make a straight persistent fight—with homogeneous elements
and in utter disregard of political compromises. I will make
success come to me—I will not run after it," he added confidently.

Yet, since free trade meant "Equal rights and self government" it must "guide the successful party of the future." In this
he would take a hand. It would not place "success today with
discord beyond success tomorrow in harmony." Keenan and
Tilton must both join it. Meanwhile, if given a vacation he
would recuperate in England and then go to Chicago "on

business of the campaign." Keenan urged him to leave the
League and enter the practical world.

Lloyd decided to enter journalism despite his mother's advice
not to leave the free trade agitation. Editing the *Tax-Payer*
and *Free-Trader* and contributing to the *Post* had given him
experience. He had met the co-operating editors at League
conferences, including Henry Adams of the *North American
Review*. Greeley symbolized the power of the press to Lloyd,
who concluded that "a purely eleemosynary institution like"
the League would never be followed far "by so practical and
selfish a people as we." His influence for reform would be much
greater as a respected, "independent" journalist who "sought
individual success . . . in alliance with a righteous cause." For
"ultimate results" he preferred a four-year journalistic apprenticeship rather than "an agitation I could not control."[4]

While he sought a position on the *Evening Post* Keenan informed Horace White of Lloyd's desire to work for a cour-
ageously liberal paper. His brother David warned him against
the *Post* because of Henderson's "despotic traits and uncon-
sciousness." After the *Post* declared for Grant, Henry D. Lloyd
rejected an invitation to write for it "from the outside," pending
a regular appointment. Then White informed him during a
brief conference in New York that he would give him the first
opening on his staff because of his work on the *Tax-Payer* and
his courageous stand for Liberal reform.[5] Reluctant to leave the
League "*Now* we are whipped," preferring to remain with it
"till we have done something," Lloyd was eager to begin journalistic preparation for the future "fight that must ensue on
questions of equal rights." He was interested in "even a tolerable
position" if White offered it.[6]

He desired editorial power free from political obligation that
would lift him "above and upon the insensate masses who flood
the stage of life in their passage to oblivion," he wrote Keenan.
He preferred to be a "Bowles or White or Greeley or Bennett"
rather than "the most successful lawyer or richest merchant
or most brilliant author in America. I had rather raise myself
to their height than be raised by others to the Presidency."

While wishing to be fully rounded and cultivated, "all that is musical, humanitarian, muscular, imaginative, brainy, poetic, powerful with men and material" developed "to the highest point," he disliked the physical sciences. He found "mere literary culture" irksome, impractical. "All forms of money making I despise as pursuits in themselves for themselves, the law is too technical and traditional. I am too unconventionally and un-affectedly pious to be a minister." He could not "brook the idea" of "endangering my independence" by truckling to others' "will" as an office-seeker.

Such was his decision at a time when independent journalism was the greatest force opposing the disintegration of business and public ethics in the United States.[7] Its exposures, its fight for socially responsible governments and business leadership, its belief in rationally achieved progress, its zeal for equal rights, and its humanitarianism transcended the service of urban, regional, political, and special interest elements. Such techniques, purposes, and values characterized Lloyd's career thenceforth. His attempt to combine burning ambition with the reform impulse, while he linked his private contempt for the "insensate masses" quixotically with ardor for "Equal Rights," indicated a not untypical liberal-patrician intellectual confusion. Like Bryant he aspired to be the gentleman liberal editorial leader of the democracy. This resembled the Adams brothers' attempt to terminate political corruption and business "Caesarism" by exposing their character and restoring leadership to Harvard gentlemen.

In August Lloyd traveled West in behalf of the tariff reform movement, an oblique thrust at Greeley's campaign. He shared quarters with Keenan in Chicago for four weeks. Again they were "part and parcel of the same hope—dreamers of the same dream." They explored the half-destroyed city and saw permanent structures rising on half the frontage of the "burnt district." Keenan introduced Lloyd to "Fanny" Huntington and other South Division belles.

The two Henries called together upon Horace White at the *Tribune*'s temporary office on South Canal Street. Keenan took

Lloyd to call upon warmhearted Jessie Bross, the only surviving child of William Bross, the publisher. He was a kindly, shrewd judge of men who had directed the paper's plant without a strike. Although he was a founder of the Republican party, Lincoln's friend, and a former lieutenant governor, he had broken with Grant. Since 1865, with Alfred Cowles, treasurer of the Chicago Tribune company, he had backed White in a free trade, liberal policy against Joseph Medill, the fourth owner, the paper's noted Civil War editor, and now "Fire Mayor." Medill was inactive on the *Tribune* while reconstructing Chicago and remaining loyal to Grant.[8] Bross was a former "Free Democrat." He opposed monopoly, whether tariff fostered or emergent among the railroads.

The Brosses were prominent among the old residents who set the tone of South Division society. Before "The Fire" they had resided in Terrace Row, Michigan Avenue, whose white limestone had contrasted so sharply with the city's wooden homes that it had provoked an envious characterization, "The *Marble* Terrace." In 1872 they lived in rented rooms while their new house was being built on fashionable Calumet. "The Governor" was relaxing after strenuous efforts to secure private capital and congressional aid for Chicago. As a close friend he visited Samuel Bowles during directors' meetings of the Massachusetts Mutual Life Insurance Company. He had staked his fortunes on the future of Chicago, and on the expanding West that he explored repeatedly for the *Tribune*.[9]

Despite opposing views on Greeley's candidacy, Lloyd passed Bross's inspection. Horace White then informed him that he would be pleased to have him join the editorial staff after a brief period of training.

Jessie Bross at twenty-seven was the unspoiled object of her father's devotion, his companion during a recent six months' tour of Europe followed by a journey into the Rocky Mountains. Well read, well educated, assisting her father's attempt to make Chicago the scientific center of the West, she enjoyed intellectual interests of her own. Emerson was her philosopher, George Eliot her favorite novelist. In 1871 she had become a vice-president of the Chicago Philosophical Society with Frances E. Willard, president of the Ladies College in Evanston, and Mrs. Kate Newell Doggett, a "South Side" friend. Because of her mother's ill health Jessie was her father's social coadjutor. She was an unconventional gentlewoman, the heiress of William Bross's swelling fortune in real estate and *Tribune,* industrial, insurance, mining and bank stocks.

Lloyd was already an admirer of Jessie Bross. Tradition has it that she was a lovely young woman with curly reddish golden hair like her father's, and brilliant blue eyes, pink and white skin. She led the young South Division social set with intelligence, charm, and friendliness. Stouthearted like her father, she had refused to entrain for the East on the morning after the "Great Fire" leveled their home. In New York she would have been welcomed by Mrs. Henry T. Field, her former French tutor. Instead, she assisted the Relief and Aid Society while Governor Bross went East to raise capital for rebuilding the business district. The utter destitution of formerly wealthy friends and her experience in distributing food and clothing contributed by cities as remote as London aroused in her compassion for the unfortunate. As a midwestern patrician she combined Jacksonian ideals with warm humanitarianism.[10]

She was attracted by Lloyd's self-confidence, culture, sociability, charm, and handsome, well-groomed person. She knew of his unflinching championship of principles that she and her father cherished. His steady eyes, firm mouth and chin, slightly beaked nose surmounted by a high forehead, and brown hair in pompadour bespoke the patrician Demarests. Of medium height, obviously eager to succeed in journalism, he provoked a response that admitted him to the circle of her admirers. There Keenan had preceded him. Before Lloyd left for New York to resign from the Free-Trade League his portrait by fashionable Rocher was added to others that attested to Jessie Bross's popularity.

Elated by White's offer, he returned home in a "hotel car" in company with a feminine journalist who had declined a position on the *Chicago Tribune* that stipulated that she work in "her rooms." On arrival home he learned that David was working fourteen hours a day as Hay's editorial associate on the *New York Tribune*. David was astonished at White's offer of the night city editorship to his brother. They celebrated with "a swell breakfast at Eleven o'clock" at Delmonico's, after which Henry spent an hour "at the Russian Baths." When journalistic friends told him he could hope for nothing better than the *Chicago Tribune* opening he accepted it and resigned from the Free-Trade League. He boarded Greeley's campaign train and reported to White the Liberal Republican nominee's ineffectual attempt to stem the tide of defeat in the Middle West.[11]

Meanwhile, he had asked Keenan to supply "a daily bulletin" on "how Miss Bross progresses," warning him, "Triangular must be the duel between Miss Bross, yourself and me after this . . . I claim to enter the fray and I will not be second neither."[12] Shocked, "Trajan" plunged into dissipation mixed with obtrusive attentions to Jessie Bross. When he ignored her reproaches she appealed to Lloyd to speak to him. He had hesitated previously to reproach "Henri le premier" for his irregular mode of existence. Now he wrote to him on September 9 in blunt, kindly words, which Jessie read to him, of his "grievous social faults," and warned him that further violation of the gentleman's code would disbar him from Chicago society. Thoroughly embarrassed, his relations with Whitelaw Reid strained, Keenan left Chicago and resigned from the *New York Tribune* to accept the editorship of the Democratic *Indianapolis Sentinel* before Lloyd returned as he and "Gath" advised. "Henri le deuxième" wished him Godspeed and begged forgiveness "for all the pain I ever gave you."[13]

Lloyd worked hard during his *Tribune* apprenticeship, writing paragraphs and making up the paper before it was put to bed at 4 A.M. He stood in daily fear of taciturn White's displeasure, which might blast his hope of establishing himself better in Miss Bross's esteem. Then White relieved him of the "make-up" and informed him he had done "very well so far." Lloyd was seemingly secure as night city editor. Miss Bross approved of a quiet apartment that he rented on South Wabash

Avenue below the "burnt district" before she went to "impossible Baraboo" for a holiday.[14]

Then the Liberal Republicans lost the October states, a foretaste of disaster. This event embarrassed the *Chicago Tribune*'s managers, who were alarmed by the rise of the Republican *Inter Ocean*.

After Lloyd attacked the protectionists in an editorial on October 15, White relieved him of the night city editorship and assigned him to the literary editor's chair while commending his "zeal and application." The editor blamed himself for having assigned him to "so difficult a place" when he required "further practice in the lower walks of the profession." His "matter should be revised before it goes into the printer's hands."[15] An experienced journalist would have resigned at once. Lloyd was tempted to seek a position on the *Chicago Times*, whose "independence" appealed to him. Such a move would have alienated the Brosses. He was encouraged by Jessie Bross's observation, "H W. can't live forever," and assurances from his brother David and Keenan that he had done well. He accepted the literary chair, told White that he would continue to do his best, and informed Keenan that he was determined to "show H. W. how to write, and run a newspaper."[16]

This decision appealed to Jessie Bross. To encourage him she left her portrait and George Eliot's *Adam Bede* at his apartment when she left for a three months' visit in Boston, having accepted Keenan's escort as far as Fort Wayne. Lloyd returned after long hours in the new Tribune Building at Madison and Dearborn streets late at night to find her portrait.

He picked up *Adam Bede*. Leafing through it he came upon a marked passage, where Adam combined praise of beautiful, high-minded Dinah Morris with encouragement of his brother's suit for her hand : "Nay, lad . . . thee mustna lose heart. She's made out of stuff with a finer grain than most o' the women . . . But if she's better than they are in other things, I canna think she'll fall short of 'em in loving." Seth Bede's love for her suggested a parallel for his own devotion to popular Jessie Bross. Rereading the inspiring passage that *"she herself had*

marked" convinced him she intended it as a "happy omen."
This made him "almost hilarious." He wrote Keenan that he
"never knew" he had "loved our dear girl till now that she has
gone." He could not "find drudgery in a path which is lit by
the hope which is now my life. . . . All my paths—of pleasure,
work, memory and hope, lead, please God, to Jessie.""[17] He began
to develop the best literary department of any midwestern
paper.

A LITERARY COURTSHIP

After Greeley's crushing defeat in November White rededi-
cated the *Chicago Tribune* anew to liberalism and independent
journalism. He possessed brilliant editorial assistants, James M.
Sheahan and James B. Runnion, who had lifted its political
writing to the highest level. The financial editor was so competent that the *Inter Ocean* soon lured him away in a vain
attempt to capture the *Tribune*'s real estate advertising. It was
Lloyd's responsibility to bring the literary department up to
their standard. Lest he fail White engaged Professor William
Mathews of the University of Chicago to contribute literary
articles for the Sunday editorial page. This was a challenge to
the young New Yorker from the handsomest, largest newspaper
west of the Alleghanies, whose income exceeded $200,000 on a
capitalization of that amount.[18]

Lloyd's predecessor had filled his space with borrowed poetry,
serials of popular novels, and inadequate reviews of periodicals.
The *Inter Ocean* was uninterested in literature. The irregular
attention of the *Times* to literature was devoid of merit. The
Tribune's only serious competition in that field was that of the
New York Tribune and *Harper's Weekly*.[19] Lloyd's resources
to meet White's test were not inconsiderable. A college education, legal training, systematic reading, previous teaching of
political economy and political science, contributing to the
Evening Post, editing the *Free-Trader,* and life in New York
had developed his literary taste and sharpened his critical
powers. He wrote concise, eloquent prose.

His task was to evaluate contemporary literary, scientific, and scholarly writing for a clientele comprising liberals, Unitarians, Universalists, adherents of the Congregational and Presbyterian intellectual traditions, and others who were seeking to civilize the "wide-open," materialistic city. He met the challenge squarely. Since Mathews pre-empted literary appreciation, he provided a literary page distinguished by solid criticism and appraisals of trans-atlantic intellectual trends. He reviewed important current books and periodicals of the United States and Europe. He reported literary and scientific news. He commented editorially upon intellectual and literary developments. Inevitably this work broadened and enriched the utilitarian and scientific aspects of his thought, while strengthening its religious liberalism and reformist phases with their emphasis upon human progress.

His first page appeared on the Sunday after Greeley's defeat. It was accompanied by an inspiriting poem, "Sursum Corda!" whose heroic couplets rallied the crushed, divided Liberals to steadfast faith in the "right" and its ultimate victory. His review of Samuel Johnson's *Oriental Religions and Their Relation to Universal Religion* expressed a liberalism certain to shock the orthodox. This praised the scientific spirit that gave "physicists and metaphysicians a freedom of reach and freedom of result impossible in the dull, traditional circle of authority and unthinking faith." Commending Johnson's study to all who love scholarly research irrespective of bearing upon "dominant religious thought," he cited Herbert Spencer's dictum: "The profoundest of all infidelities is the fear lest the truth be bad."[20] That Lloyd believed always.

A week later his critical paragraphs took Bret Harte to task for eccentric discourtesies and described the *London News'* appreciation of the American reception of James Froude's lecture tour. The page reviewed the November British quarterlies with critical acumen and graceful familiarity. The third Sunday page, with a comprehensive analysis of American monthlies and a provocative editorial review of Charles Darwin's *Expression of Emotions in Man and Animals,* dispelled remaining doubts of Lloyd's capacity. The following week, while commenting upon John A. Coleman's "The Fight of a Man with a Railroad" in the *Atlantic,* he condemned railroad managers' disregard of the "commercial code of civility" and their "brutality and oppression." He castigated religious persecution and intolerance while commenting upon "The Spirit of Protestantism" in the *Catholic World,*[21] and ventured into literary criticism by reviewing John Forster's *Charles Dickens.*

Then, on January 19, 1873, he made George Eliot's *Middlemarch* the subject of such an extensive analysis of the Victorian novel that he established himself firmly in the literary chair. Of unprecedented length, it compared well with contemporary and subsequent evaluations. He termed the author correctly the greatest living writer of English fiction. While comparing her character portrayal and "psychological observation" to Shakespeare's he distinguished her realism from the latter's "boundless fancy and exuberant imagination." Not all agreed that she ranked intellectually with Spencer, Buckle, Tyndall, Huxley, and Darwin. He described skillfully the character of this study of Engish rural life and observed perceptively that its "anatomical insight into social and individual nature" helped to raise "social problems" to rank with political economy.

George Henry Lewes wrote him of her appreciation of his "very sympathetic and extremely well written review." This warm note, with its disclosure of the discipline with which George Eliot "steeled herself from the praise of critical charmers," enhanced Lloyd's reputation in Mrs. Doggett's South Side salon, where serious students of modern languages and literature gathered at Michigan Avenue and Harmon Court.[22]

Mutual friends there may have discerned a connection between the review and his interest in Jessie Bross, but only she could have known how daringly and deftly he declared his love for her before the *Tribune*'s public. To the tribute to Dinnah Morris that she had marked in *Adam Bede* he replied with a condensation of Lydgate's description of Dorothea :

This young creature has a heart large enough for the Virgin Mary. She evidently thinks nothing of her own

future, and would pledge away half her income at once,
as if she wanted nothing for herself but a chair to sit in
from which she can look down with those clear eyes at the
poor mortals who pray to her. She seems to have what I
never saw in any woman before—a fountain of friendship
toward man. A man can make a friend of her. *Her love
might help a man more than her money.*

Previous to this Lloyd had been introduced to Chicago society
by William Cullen Bryant in a note to the Nathaniel K. Fairbanks, wealthy social leaders of the South Division. This
strengthened Lloyd's position on the *Tribune.* It furthered his
suit for Jessie Bross's hand.[23]

On the first of January he had joined the merry men who
called upon the ladies whose flowing bowls raised ever higher
the spirit of New Year cheer. Regaled with punch, warmed
by the banter and greetings of friendly belles and matrons, he
attended Major Henry A. Huntington's reception where "Miss
Lizzie Kirkland received." Afterward, he paid his respects to
"the Badgers, the Hamiltons . . . George C. Walkers, Fairbanks,
Doggetts, Lunts, and all." Friends of the absent Keenan were
delighted with the "good accounts" that he gave of him.[24]
Lloyd reported to him Mrs. Bross's and Major Huntington's
praise of the "spicy" *Sentinel,* predicting that he would soon be
"the Sam. Bowles, No, the Keenan of the West."[24] This would
have quashed his fear of a cooled relationship had not Lloyd
written unreservedly also of his love for their mutual friend.
Badly hurt, Keenan ceased correspondence with all his Chicago
friends.

While Keenan sulked Lloyd analyzed Victorian science and
biblical scholarship, philosophy, and social science on his literary page. Although he faced candidly the contradiction between
America's equal rights, humanitarian, and "moral law" tradition and the deterministic naturalism of Darwinian thought,
he was captivated by the vogue for science with its apparent
vindication of the idea of progress and promise of a more abundant life. His opposition to orthodoxy's attempt to censor clerical

and professorial utterances so as to protect religion from Darwinism drew him into the era's heated controversies.

He was certain of White's backing. Bross combined staunch Presbyterianism with patronage of the Chicago Academy of Science. Yet, while he attended the American Association for the Advancement of Science he found it difficult to accept the new valley formation theories and was impatient with agnosticism and religious heterodoxy.[25]

Lloyd featured *Popular Science Monthly,* ranking it first among American magazines because of "its sympathy with the foremost scientific thought." This should be accorded "an equal, if not a superior rank" to that of "mere litterateurs and classicists" who would fail "to stay the modern tide" by reverting to "a culture which, however beautiful and lasting . . . cannot fill all the scope of our activities." Darwin, Thomas Huxley, and Herbert Spencer were ushering in a new era of "untrammeled thought, active inquiry, fearless reform." Its "practical results" would "enrich our daily lives," make humanity "better," and "rehabilitate even our poetry and romance with new imagery, analogies, and suggestions." Science would attract the "fresh allegiance of young men of ambition" and "imprint its stamp on all the activities of our society."[26]

Yet, Lloyd did not accept the Social Darwinism that John Fiske and Edward L. Youmans disseminated. Cobden and Mill inspired his opposition to "over legislation." His published sympathy with Joseph Arch's attempts to elevate the English agricultural laborers was humanitarianism such as Herbert Spencer repudiated. Lloyd rejected Social Darwinism's mechanistic and amoral aspects, whose application to business seemed to justify ruthless methods. Inconsistently, many converts to this new social philosophy sought governmental favors, while citing Spencer's doctrines against the labor movement because it encroached upon their "liberty." Natural selection became a pseudoscientific élitist concept appealing to ambitious men.

Lloyd remained loyal to the Jacksonian insistence upon the moral responsibility, dignity, and essential equality of free individuals. He continued to oppose special privilege and monopoly. He refused to relegate the wage-earner to the limbo of the "unfit." He exposed Herbert Spencer's illogic by asking how could a theory that regarded employers and workers as "irresponsible cogs in the social mechanism" stigmatize industrial contestants for "ignoble materialism" by implying that their conduct sprang from individual volition.

While reviewing J. F. Collingwood's translation of Louis Buechner's *Kraft und Staff*, he observed that the book claimed that the sole creative force was an "immanent necessary instinct of Nature" while conceding the existence of a soul. Such illogic could not destroy Protestant belief in "Design in Nature" or expel God from the universe, he remarked, while Buechner's rejection of scientists' responsibility for the "moral tendency" of their discoveries made his book more dangerous than earlier French materialism. All this, he added, was dwarfed by Lorenzo's graceful speech under the full moon to Jessica, who had fled her father's house to live with him.[27]

He was now engrossed in his courtship. Tortured by "a wild sea of hopes and fears," he awaited Jessie Bross's return. His grandfather Demarest's death took him to New York, where he informed his mother of his love for Jessie Bross, who inspired him to live "in a broad, generous way so that I seek . . . not only the gratification of my own blissful longings but find delight in giving others, all others, the affection I have."

With Jessie's consent he called upon her in Boston and declared his love. Thrilled when she confessed to reciprocal affection, he was dismayed when she said that her slightly greater age was a possible obstacle to marriage. She would wait until certain that it was "God's leading and his will" that they should wed, but intimated that "years were not absolutisms."[28] He returned to the *Tribune* to defend journalism from the accusation of being afflicted with money madness. She returned home soon afterward.

Once informed by "le deuxième" that Lloyd had won her heart, Keenan renewed their friendship. Then he jeopardized Lloyd's position and distressed the Brosses by publishing in the *Sentinel* a confidential story that Lloyd had written him of

President Grant's final alienation of his remaining *Chicago Tribune* friends. After the *Indianapolis Journal* demanded that Keenan divulge his source,[29] only urgent telegrams from Lloyd, Jessie Bross, and her mother restrained him from publishing the letter with its story of Grant's drunkenness and misconduct.

That summer the *Tribune*'s literary department emphasized sentimental literary themes. Reviewing George Grote's memoir enabled Lloyd to observe how a great historian had been aroused to "his best literary and poetical work" by his devoted wife. He observed that Robert Dale Owen's "Educating a Wife" featured a "Jessie" for whom her spouse entertained "a great and chivalrous passion."[30]

The literary department improved steadily. Concise, critical reviews with a light touch and tendency toward epigram displayed a confident power. No other Chicago paper served so rich and varied a literary fare. Lloyd thanked J. W. Dawson for meeting the evolutionists on their own ground instead of attacking them from "some theological ambush." After introducing a "Boston Letter" in November he published "Literary Notes" on European and American literary news. His review of Hippolyte A. Taine's *Tour Through the Pyrenees* exhibited familiarity with that 'creative critic" and Gustav Doré, the noted illustrator.[31]

Toward Chicago artists and authors Lloyd displayed kindly interest mingled with discriminating analysis. He emphasized George F. Root's importance in American church and Civil War music. While he treated Mrs. Doggett's translation of Charles Blanc's *Grammaire des Arts du Dessein* strictly as a lay manual of appreciation he stressed the importance of enlightening American democracy in those fields and complimented the "superb style" of "one of Chicago's most cultivated and accomplished ladies."[32]

Assured of his devotion, Jessie Bross had given him her consent in the early autumn. Her father had anticipated this culmination of her attachment to the ardent literary champion of liberalism and science, and had called upon David D. Lloyd at the *Tribune* and investigated the Aaron Lloyds. Then, before an excursion into the Dakotas he allowed Henry D. Lloyd to ask for her hand. With "entire confidence in his integrity," believing them to be "well adapted to and worthy of each other's love," the Brosses gave their consent.[33]

A week later the failure of Jay Cooke & Company precipitated a great financial panic. Chicago's feverish building boom collapsed without having fully repaired "The Fire's" devastation.

Bross survived the catastrophe but his funds were "frozen." Jessie's wedding occurred in their home at 57 Calumet. With his own money lent to his brother David, Henry D. Lloyd borrowed to set up his establishment on Eldridge Court. Keenan delayed congratulations until reproached by "H. D. L.," who offered his rooms and influence to help him find money to finance the instalments of his investments in the *Sentinel*.

As winter closed in, Chicago filled with jobless railroad construction workers. Joining thousands of unassisted local unemployed they demonstrated at Twelfth Street Turner Hall on December 21, denouncing the "aristocracy of wealth." They demanded assistance and listened to a small band of Marxian Socialists whose activities alarmed the wealthy and revived memories of the Paris Commune.[34]

Against this background of Chicago's financially embarrassed élite and the distressed unemployed, Henry D. Lloyd and Jessie Bross were wed before a " 'house full' of very excellent people," as her father wrote in his diary that Christmas night of 1873. When viewing this event in retrospect Charles Wendt, a Unitarian minister, thought only of the bride and groom, she who had been his "faithful helper in the 'terrible times' that had followed the 'Great Fire,' " he an editor attempting "to rear an ideal Chicago, as well as a material one."[35] Henry D. Lloyd was assimilated into the city's upper social stratum that night.

Chapter V

For Liberalism, Business Ethics, and Bimetallism

CIVIC LEADERSHIP

THE NEXT MORNING William Bross walked to 6 Eldridge Court to lunch with the newlyweds. "Their first guest," he recorded proudly in his diary. There could have been none earlier! Henry's father and mother and some Chicago friends called in the afternoon. Jessie entertained so successfully that Bross left for the *Tribune* office much gratified. The Rev. R. W. Patterson of the fashionable Second Presbyterian Church on South Michigan Avenue, to which the Brosses belonged, invited Aaron Lloyd to preach. Bross took David D. Lloyd on a tour of the city. Mrs. Aaron Lloyd and her second daughter, Madelein, remained to celebrate Twelfth Night with the Brosses at the Henry D. Lloyds, and were escorted to the opera by "The Governor."[1] Mrs. Doggett gave a luncheon in honor of the newlyweds.

Jessie Bross Lloyd entertained friends and visitors, widening her husband's circle of acquaintances. Among them was Robert Collyer, Unitarian antislavery pastor of Unity Church, whose friendship furthered Henry D. Lloyd's participation in Chicago civic life.[2] Membership in the Beethoven Society, attending the Dogget salon, studying German and Italian together, and reading French literature in the vernacular enhanced the Lloyds' cultural *rapport*.

Jessie would be no Victorian mouse preoccupied with her

household, growing family, and the nonintellectual fare of polite society. She prevented distractions that interfered with her husband's journalism and literary work. She shared his intellectual interests and "causes," which was almost unique among the married women of her day. In June 1875 Henry took her East and introduced her proudly to John Hay, Whitelaw Reid, Isaac H. Bromley, and Noah Brooks. They lionized her. Afterward, she confessed to Keenan that she longed to live on Manhattan Island, because in Chicago "free unconventional women" and "feminine freedom of speech" were lacking. Heartbroken at having lost her, "Trajan" eventually resigned the editorship of the Indianapolis *Sentinel* and fled to Europe, to reside there many years. Before she returned to Chicago Jessie invited Henry's fifteen-year-old sister Caro to live with them to lighten the burden on her mother-in-law.[3]

The Lloyds' marriage was a love match. Its years of comradeship intensified their mutual respect and sensitive consideration. Even William Bross's excessive solicitude and growing rigidity of mind drew them closer. No later action of Henry D. Lloyd can be attributed to frustrations derived from his wedded life. Conscious ones he would experience in journalism, reform, and politics, but these he and his wife would confront together.

Marriage brought him also financial security and sons. On the *Tribune* the Bross connexion gave him immediately the prestige of membership in a stock-owning family. As long as White, Bross, and Cowles retained control he could pursue his career there as far as his ability and industry could take him. For all this he paid a price different from that exacted from John Hay, who soon married the heiress of wealthy Amasa Stone of Cleveland and was there transmuted into the literary and oratorical apologist of "The Gilded Age."[4]

Bross had buried sons among seven children in Rose Hill Cemetery. For a long time he had focused his love and hopes upon Jessie. Now he initiated his son-in-law into the mysteries of Chicago real estate, finance, and business, in which the Bross fortune was invested. Together they inspected "The Governor's" "thirty acres" on Western Avenue and his lots in Lake Forest. Bross was Chicago's greatest commercial journalist and president of the Manufacturers' National Bank. Especially important to Lloyd was his friendship with William F. Coolbaugh, who had come to Chicago as agent of the State Bank of Iowa and political heir of Stephen A. Douglas. Genial, so broad-minded that he rated as a skeptic, well informed, he symbolized the self-made man. His wide reading and fine gallery evinced culture and refinement. As president of the Union National Bank, first president of the Clearing House Association, and president of the National Bankers Association of the West and Southwest, he was the region's leading Banker.[5]

Lloyd and Coolbaugh became warm friends, drawn together by a kindred liberalism, interest in economics, and a desire to build a finer city. Coolbaugh's interest was an indubitable factor in Lloyd's training. Under his and Bross's tutelage he learned patience and caution, to beware of the wolves on the Board of Trade, the value of shrewd calculation before commitment to a venture. The older men valued Lloyd's journalistic crusading in behalf of their principles.[6]

Could the latter's liberalism withstand the erosion of comfort, security, the prospect of inherited wealth, the inevitable journalistic compromises? Could he cope with Bross's aging, and his unanticipated, adverse reactions to his cherished projects? Bross dined frequently at the Lloyds' and became increasingly dependent upon his daughter. Sixty years old at the time of their marriage, he lived until 1890.

Thoroughly happy, Lloyd took his wife "deadhead" to the opera, theater, and Theodore Thomas' concerts, paying his way with program reviews. Reading together books that he reviewed for the literary page gave him the benefit of her taste and judgment.

She encouraged him to participate in attempts to repair the cultural damage inflicted by the fire and panic upon Chicago. She entertained Robert Collyer and Mrs. Wirt Dexter, wife of the president of the Relief and Aid Society. On that occasion, apparently, there was broached the idea of a men's literary club to replace organizations destroyed by the fire. Six weeks later, a group met with Collyer at the Sherman House to organize it. Intensive recruiting gathered an impressive list of authors, editors, statesmen, clergy, lawyers, and judges who, on May 4, 1875, voted to establish a club home and participate in solid Monday night programs. These were followed by midnight collations, and relieved by infrequent "Ladies' Nights." With quarters in the American Express Company Building the Chicago Library Club led the revival of the literary community. Lloyd was active in it, although the surviving list of his program contributions begins with 1880.[7]

Collyer and Charles Wendte joined Lloyd in organizing Sunday afternoon lectures in 1874, stimulated by Joseph Medill's plea for a free popular series despite the post-panic sabbatarianism. The lectures presented nontheological subjects and were financed by a small charge, thus deviating from London's popular series. Lloyd persuaded prominent liberals to sponsor the Chicago Sunday-Afternoon Lecture Society. Younger liberals and journalists did the work, led by himself and Alfred B. Mason, secretary. In the third year Lloyd became president.[8]

The spring of 1874 series, delivered by local volunteers, placed "knowledge at the very doors of the working-class" after Cooper Union's example. Dr. N. W. Abbott's "Science and True Religion Not Antagonistic" challenged the orthodox. Mrs. Doggett's "Raphael" gave the venture cultural standing. The second season's series was presented in the Grand Opera House and McCormick's Hall. Seven hundred heard "The Moon" by Professor Elias Colbert, resuscitator of the Chicago Astronomical Society. Wage-earners attended *en masse* to hear Charles Bradlaugh, British free-thinker under indictment for publishing a pioneer birth control tract. Afterward, the Lloyds entertained him. Attendance at the series, warmly encouraged by the *Tribune,* totaled 19,200. Receipts defrayed expenses.[9] The third season attracted 41,000 to McCormick's Hall to hear such nationally known lecturers as Emerson, Julia Ward Howe, Moncure D. Conway, Frederick Douglass, William Graham Sumner, Edward Everett Hale, Bayard Taylor, and Joaquin Miller, poet of the Sierras. "Long John" Wentworth concluded the series with "Chicago's Men and Manners," backed on the stage by a galaxy of old residents and ex-mayors.[10] Thereafter, competing church lecture series, hard times, and social cleavage between wage-earners and more comfortable residents made a continuance of the secular programs impossible. Lloyd husbanded a slender reserve against a more auspicious future that never came. Mason soon left for business ventures in Mexico.[11]

Lloyd helped, meanwhile, to revive the Illinois Free-Trade League, aided by S. T. K. Prime of Dwight, former agent of the American Free-Trade League who stimulated the powerful Farmers' and Peoples' Anti-Monopoly Party in 1873 and then assisted the International Free Trade Alliance. Lloyd secured funds from New York and Boston and with Huntington, Mason, Edward Osgood Brown of the Chicago Literary Club, and Franklin MacVeagh, a wholesale grocer, reorganized the local Free-Trade Club. He brought William Graham Sumner, Wells, and Charles Francis Adams, Jr. to lecture in Chicago in 1877. The Illinois agitation made tariff reform again a vital issue, and induced Congressman William B. Morrison to begin his campaign for tariff reduction.[12]

Such activity won Lloyd a firm place among the forward-looking young lawyers, journalists, and businessmen of Chicago. The Alfred Masons and the Lloyds were especially intimate, as the latter built their house at 202 Michigan Avenue, the Bross homestead lot that was given to Jessie when her first son was born. Huntington was another warm friend. So was the prospering MacVeagh, who won a reputation for discriminating support of good causes. Years later Prime recalled, as a famous crop reporter, the "delightful friendship and those encouraging talks" at the Lloyds![13]

Bross was delighted with William Bross Lloyd's arrival at his daughter's home. He took them to Grand Haven during the August heat. In 1875 he escorted them to the White Mountains until Henry D. Lloyd could join them for a summer holiday after attending the wedding of his brother David, the exposer of the "Erie Canal Ring," to Alice Walbridge, niece of Salmon

P. Chase.[14] Bross and Lloyd attended together the Chicago concerts of the "Hampton Singers," whom "The Governor" termed
"an honor to their race."[15]

The Lloyds remained devoted to Henry Keenan. "Le
deuxième" vainly urged Horace White to engage him for a
European letter and later asked him to make him financial
editor of the *Chicago Tribune*. "Trajan" remained abroad as a
correspondent for the New York press.[16]

ANTICLERICALISM

1874 brought Horace White's editorship to a climax and
then abrupt deposition after the paper incurred the hostility of
the powerful, orthodox Protestant clergy. Since the *Tribune's*
political liberalism had alienated many Republican businessmen
this placed it in opposition to the two forces that have made
Chicago a bulwark of conservatism during much of its history.
In provoking the conflict with religious orthodoxy Lloyd played
an important role.[17]

He sowed the seeds of this by candid discussion of evolution,
Social Darwinism, and European skepticism and materialism.
While avoiding agnosticism and atheism, he sided with religious
liberalism. He reviewed books on "the higher criticism," which
the seminaries attacked, in brave disregard of possible consequences. This antagonized the orthodox but won him the esteem
of Collyer, Wendt, and David Swing. Lloyd published Colbert's
"Sparks of Science" on Saturdays. Bross identified the paper
further with science by his activity in the American Association
for the Advancement of Science.[18]

Open conflict between the *Tribune* and the conservative
clergy was precipitated by the former's ridicule of the "Women's
Crusade," which attempted to close saloons by kneeling prayer
meetings on barroom floors, and by a demand that the University of Chicago be secularized.[19]

Swing's "heresy" made the breach complete. He had become
nationally known after the fire by preaching to overflowing
crowds at McVicker's Theater. A lovable character, the high
literary quality and eclectic liberalism of his sermons and the

vibrant lyricism of his verse sustained his popularity with all forward-looking people. Whittier hailed him as the poetic star of the West. In reply to Darwinism, he presented Christianity from the pulpit as natural, humane, reasonable. In *The Alliance* he carried the fight for religious liberalism among the religious periodicals.[20] Dr. Francis L. Patton, editor of *The Interior* and professor in the Presbyterian Theological Seminary, was his chief opponent. Patton maneuvered Swing into publishing what he called heresy and brought him to trial before the Chicago Presbytery.

The *Tribune* demanded that the trial panel of local clergy defend him from persecution by a pugnacious newcomer. Despite Swing's deviations from the Westminster creed the Presbytery dismissed the case. Patton then appealed to the North Illinois Synod. Thereupon, Swing resigned from the Presbytery to become pastor of the nonsectarian Central Church at McVicker's, underwritten by fifty wealthy Chicagoans, including William Bross.[21]

During the summer of 1874 Henry Ward Beecher was tried before Plymouth Church. The *Tribune* scooped the American press by publishing the Beecher—Mrs. Theodore Tilton love letters, extracts from her diary, and her "confession" together with "exclusive" interviews with her husband. This demonstrated Beecher's guilt to the openminded, if not to Plymouth Church. He had been the uncrowned "Pope" of American Protestantism. His "fall" was extremely embarrassing to its clergy, who resented the *Tribune*'s publication of the inside history of the scandal. During the episode Lloyd confessed to Keenan that his love of Beecher and his sympathy with Tilton drew his heart and head in opposite directions. Tilton had been "awfully wronged, almost no one gave him fair play," he said. He visited him in New York and learned of his lonely fight for justice.[22]

The *Tribune*'s attitude toward the Swing and Beecher trials precipitated open war with the religious press. Lloyd's editorials backed Swing against the Presbyteryian Synod, publicized his activities, and belabored ecclesiasticism. He risked William

Bross's displeasure by attacking orthodox theology. He attributed the Boston Radical Club's death to unwillingness to grapple with Darwinism, the "Knowable," and the moral problems of daily life. He reviewed, with covering editorials, the books of great European skeptics from Celsus to David Friedrich Strauss, Tyndall, and Huxley. He asked for an honest, rational analysis of skepticism by all.[23]

"The Coming Christian," he predicted editorially, would make common-sense morality and integrity and "the religion of unselfish obligation" the basis for virtuous private life and social reform rather than the "incomprehensible polemics of Christian metaphysicians." He would insist upon marital fidelity from "the minister of an undefiled religion," a sarcastic fling at Beecher. Temperate in imbibing hard liquor and articles of faith, this future Christian would welcome scientific discoveries but be indifferent to such theological issues as the earth's antiquity, the divine method of creation, and the skeptics' materialism, determinism, and atheism.[24] Terse, lucid, well focused, challenging, these editorials were very effective. Equally disagreeable to the orthodox was his appreciative review, November 22, 1874, of Edward von Zeller's *David Friedrich Strauss,* which exposed the neo-Christianity of the cultivated.

The *Tribune*'s war with the clergy and political considerations led Alfred Cowles to terminate his alliance with White and Bross. He joined forces with Joseph Medill, who returned from Europe as the Republican party was defeated in the autumn election by a resurgent Democratic and midwestern antimonopolism. Since the Democrats were reaping the fruits of the Liberal Republican revolt the Medill-Cowles combination, with bare majority control, took the paper back into the Republican fold.

Medill resumed editorial control on November 9. He announced that the *Tribune* would be an independent Republican paper. He terminated its war with the clergy, retreating with a final blistering shot at Patton for hunting Swing down before the Illinois Synod, and became a guarantor of Swing's Central Church.[25]

This revolution in the *Tribune*'s management occurred after the Lloyd's vacation at Prout's Neck, Maine. Learning upon his return of Medill's arrival and the rumor that he had acquired control, Henry D. Lloyd termed this "stuff" to Keenan before the former editor's sudden return to power ousted Bross from the presidency of the company. Medill made his younger brother Samuel the managing editor, and Frederick H. Hall, a loyal friend, city editor. He relieved Lloyd of the literary chair, terminating his crusades for religious liberalism and modern science, but announced that the *Tribune* would continue to advocate "material, moral, and intellectual progress," tariff reform, and specie payments. The Literary Department's rich offering, which included Saturday and Sunday book reviewing, analysis of scientific and literary developments, support of Charles Kingsley's crusade for social justice in Britain and of the feminist movement, "Sparks of Science," literary chitchat, bibliographical guidance, and reprinted stories, was severely curtailed. Prior to Medill's return to control no western newspaper had offered a comparable literary fare. Lloyd's unique literary editorship had won him the esteem of W. Stanley Jevons of Manchester, England, of whose *Principles of Science* he approved.[26]

FRUSTRATION

Medill also hated "the high tariff robbers and professional tax eaters" during the spring of Liberal Republicanism. He promoted Lloyd to the financial chair. By this action he may have intended to conciliate Bross. However, before making the change he tested Lloyd, on the evening after he assumed the editorship, by having him report Professor Bonamy Price's lecture. After mingling with the businessmen who cheered the Oxford don's sallies against reckless American bankers and railroad promoters, Lloyd scooped the *Tribune*'s rivals with a front-page, stenographic report of the lecture and editorial.[27]

Despite his promotion Lloyd concluded that his prospects were jeopardized by Medill's control. The *Tribune*'s advocacy of tariff reform and Colbert's assistance in compiling his annual review of Chicago's business each First of January reconciled him somewhat to the new management. Huntington, new literary editor, was his warm friend who, "After one uncommonly productive night," put him to bed in his front bedroom as the sun rose over the Lake.[28] Why Lloyd remained with the *Tribune* is explained, however, by his inability to establish himself at the head of his own newspaper in the city.

Within a month after Medill assumed control Lloyd attempted to purchase the *Chicago Post and Mail*. During the negotiation he exhibited the shrewdness and caution he had learned from Coolbaugh, from whom he elicited the opinion that it was a good property. The owner of the *Staats Zeitung* believed that it could be made to pay well. Coolbaugh urged Lloyd to acquire his own paper and promised financial support. The younger man believed that affiliation with Samuel J. Tilden and his financial backing were essential to success. He was eager to aid the new attempt to overthrow "Grantism," cleanse Washington, and advance reform while furthering his journalistic fortunes. Although Lloyd promised to make the paper the western Tilden organ if adequately backed, his overtures to Colonel W. I. Felton, Tilden's representative, were abortive.[29] Lacking such support he did not request a loan from Coolbaugh or inform William Bross; who possibly learned of the negotiation. At his daughter's suggestion he gave Henry D. Lloyd a hundred shares of *Tribune* stock.

Although he was grateful for this gift of a 5 per cent interest in the Tribune Company, Lloyd did not take the hint. Soon he was involved in the *Chicago Daily News*, a struggling penny evening paper recently established by Melville Stone, former Washington correspondent of the *Post and Mail*, and Percy H. Meggy, English remittance man. Stone asked Lloyd for financial assistance after Meggy's funds were exhausted and he had left for Australia while majority owner. James E. Scripps of the Detroit *Daily News* advised Lloyd that a penny paper properly edited and supported should net $25,000 annually. Lloyd arranged with Stone to so build up the *Chicago Daily News* that Bross would accord financial backing if needed. Lloyd paid the operating deficit, taking an option giving temporary control and the right to purchase 55 per cent of the stock in a projected publishing company. Retaining his position on the *Tribune,* he brought his brother John from New York to serve as business manager and his representative. Before and after *Tribune* working hours, he, Stone, and John directed the *News.*

Henry D. Lloyd intended to make the *News* a crusading liberal paper, opposed to "Class legislation," business politicians, and every attempt "to rob the people." Publishing "all the news," serving no privileged group or "money power," it would be "absolutely fearless and independent, guided only by what is right and true." Typographically it would be "elegant." Conciseness, lucidity, and "clever expression" would feature news presentation and comment. Circulation increased from 3,000 to 11,000 and advertising in proportion, but deficits continued. Still larger circulation and heavier advertising were necessary for a profit. Encouraged, Lloyd put up more money.

He informed Bross of the venture and asked for a loan to enable him to take up the option and assume permanent control. During acrimonious family conferences "The Governor" and his wife opposed him. The *Tribune* was fighting the *News.* Bross believed that the fledgling threatened its profitable position. Since Lloyd would have to leave the *Tribune* to edit the *News,* his resignation would terminate the Bross and Lloyd active connection with the former. With family pride and purse involved Bross resisted every blandishment. After a final argument he denounced Stone as an adventurer and stalked away from the Lloyds' stoop.

Henry D. Lloyd was encouraged by the *News'* growth to continue, sustaining it from his limited resources. Then he incurred the displeasure of his Cromwellian father-in-law and of Medill by advertising the want ad service of the *News* in the *Tribune.* "The Governor" informed Lloyd angrily that he was disloyal to his paper and to the Brosses, whose fortune he should conserve rather than persist in building up a rival property that would injure theirs. Simultaneously, Lloyd learned from the *Tribune* pressroom's foreman that the *News* was subject to mortgages prior to the chattel mortgage that Stone had given him as security for his advances. Disgusted at such sharp practice, Lloyd declared he would invest no more money in the *News*. Stone then offered to transfer control to him, which he said falsely that Meggy had given him, in return for $100 to complete the week's payroll and a signed contract to continue the paper for six months, provided that if the *News* went on a paying basis during that interval Stone would receive a quarter interest. John C. Lloyd pleaded with his brother to take up this proposition. Henry D. Lloyd took it to Bross, who advised him to withdraw from the venture.

Henry D. Lloyd rejected Stone's offer and terminated his participation in the *News*. John returned to Manhattan after advancing sufficient money to keep it afloat another week.[30] During that time Stone scored a "beat" with the news of Rutheford B. Hayes's presidential nomination. This scoop increased circulation to 15,000 and enabled him to persuade Victor F. Lawson to buy a half-interest. This arrangement established the paper permanently,[31] and laid the foundation of fortunes that would have accrued to Henry D. Lloyd and Stone had it not been for Bross's opposition. Until late in life Lloyd cherished the ambition to head his own paper. In 1881 he negotiated vainly for purchase of the Chicago *Daily Telegraph,* again planning a liberal daily with the newest technical methods. After leaving the *Tribune* he attempted to purchase the *Chicago Evening Journal*. In 1889, 1891, and 1894 he attempted to acquire the *Chicago Times*.[32]

Such was the ambition that Bross and the duplicity of Stone thwarted. Lloyd suffered from "severe neuralgia of the head" after the *Daily News* episode. A photograph in 1878 revealed that some of the fire had faded in eyes once brilliant with faith in his ability to achieve the highest pinnacles of independent journalism. Both Medill and Bross recognized the quality of his talents. Had he become the successful editor of his own newspaper a steady accretion in confidence, judgment, and journalistic leadership would normally have resulted. If he had completed his success with the *News* Chicago would have had a liberal evening newspaper instead of the ally of Charles T. Yorkes, utility promoter. Stone led the witch hunt against organized labor and reform during 1886-92.

FINANCIAL EDITOR

Lloyd was restricted for a decade to important secondary editorial positions on the *Tribune*. Success in those won him unique fame and influence as he developed a field of crusading journalism peculiarly his own. Medill was an easy "chief" who left Chicago for months at a time to reside in Washington or go abroad, allowing the subordinate editors to run the paper subject to his remote control. As financial editor for five to six years Lloyd enjoyed an autonomy and opportunity for journalistic education in American business realities that was surpassed only by Washington Ford of *Bradstreet's* and a few New York City editors. Of Lloyd's former Liberal Republican associates Edwin L. Godkin carried Mill's economic and political liberalism no farther than "mugwumpism." Wells and Atkinson were partially blinded by Manchester School dogma or business ties to fundamental trends.

Lloyd's financial editorship came after the collapse of the postwar speculative bubble during an era of depression, disillusionment, and business stock-taking. Knowledge of Jay Gould's and Jim Fisk's methods, a penchant for reform, a Calvinist ethical code, earlier participation in the free trade, anti-Tweed, and Liberal Republican movements, and Jacksonian principles prevented a surrender like Henry Adams' to a patrician determinism or cynical acceptance of business amorality such as John Hay would exhibit. Instead, Lloyd analyzed the economy, as it burst geographic boundaries, realistically in the light of public interests, the need for effective business ethics, and the threat of promoter-speculator "Caesarism" after the example of the Adams brothers during 1869-72.

After a year in his new chair Lloyd gave no hint of dissatisfaction when he wrote to R. R. Bowker to express warm sympathy with the scratching of undesirable Republican nominees from the ballot during the New York election, as his "band of scratchers" demanded. "I have often thought myself about the desirability of an organization of independents—but have always found a stumbling block in the reflection that independents could never organize. As for myself I have never yet voted a straight ticket, and seldom expect to," Lloyd said.[33]

Chicago was then welding financial and commercial ties with the Great Plains and Rocky Mountain areas. Dependent upon no single route to the Atlantic coast and Europe, it rose like the phoenix to leadership among its western rivals. Chicago businessmen owed litle or nothing before 1880 to the speculator-promoters of New York and San Francisco. Instead, they fought the first and scorned the piratical monopolizers of the Comstock Lode, although some local figures such as Philip D. Armour did not lack ruthlessness or neglect speculative opportunities. Such survivors of the antebellum business generation as Coolbaugh faced competition from less cautious, more unscrupulous men. On the western railroads and eastern trunk-lines hard times incited rate makers to widen the practice of buying traffic from favored firms with exclusive rebates.[34]

Lloyd faced dangerous pitfalls in assuming the financial editorship of the *Chicago Tribune*. The calculations of dealers and speculators depended partially upon his analyses of market trends in produce, provisions, and securities. If he dropped a hint he would be cut in on the profits of speculative rings, who would expect him to modify his predictions accordingly. Such were the means by which not a few financial editors in Chicago and New York accumulated wealth privately. Lloyd had to be devoid of the least taint of suspicion of such liaisons if he would crusade for higher business ethics and enjoy the confidence of LaSalle Street and the Board of Trade. He had also to prove his technical competence as a market analyst to win the respect of warehousemen, brokers, livestock and produce shippers, and financiers. For this the assistance of market reporters was indispensable. So was Bross's and Coolbaugh's counsel at the outset.

Lloyd's first "Money and Commerce" page disclosed his comprehension of the essentials of economic power. After asserting that the solvency of Chicago's banks after 1873 had given its meat-packing industry a decisive lead over St. Louis, he observed that their superior credit in the East now facilitated the purchase of sufficient livestock to enable the packers to retain it. He compressed his department's statistical reporting and gave better market coverage, including new tables on the visible supply of grain. He published New York Stock Market transactions daily, an innovation, and reported on real estate with the loan market on Sundays. Railroad rate wars, pork-packing statistics, and foreign financial news received due attention. This was high-caliber commercial journalism.

Lloyd mastered the technical aspects of finance so well that he was invited to write the article on the clearinghouse system for Lalor's *Cyclopedia of Political Science*. He editorialized on business conditions on the financial page, and on railroads, agriculture, and finance graphically on the editorial page.

Soon he began to campaign against unethical business methods by reporting Board of Trade discussions of the upgrading of new corn. He warned against speculation in produce, provisions, and stocks, stressing its injurious effects upon morals. For years he reported wearily the manipulations of security values by speculative cliques in New York and San Francisco. He supported the attempts of legitimate traders on the Board of Trade to reform its rules against unethical transactions. The Board had been incorporated in 1859 as a cooperative, self-disciplinary body dedicated to "justice and honesty in trade." After 1865 unscrupulous dealers had introduced there the sharp practices of the Erie Ring, which demoralized the Board as they manufactured corners and fraudulently upgraded produce and livestock in alliance with state and private inspectors in elevators, warehouses, stockyards firms, and on the railroads.[35]

This corrupt, speculative, "free and easy" system undermined legitimate trade based upon market requirements, actual supply, and quality. It ramified on the prairies in all directions, binding village and town buyers and elevators to the demoralized Chicago market by telegraph wires and steel rails. It antagonized farmers who suffered from manipulated and artificially depressed produce and livestock prices. In 1874 under agrarian pressure the legislature had prohibited corners on the Board, but defiant speculators had promptly fashioned more during the next six months than in any previous twelve.

Prodded by farmers and the *Tribune* legitimate merchants rallied on the Board to prevent utter demoralization of trading. After the courts backed them in *Fisher* v. *Sturgis* a determined attempt was made to prevent future corners, improve trading practices, and discipline recalcitrant members. After the reformers secured an anticorner rule prohibiting gouging of trapped "shorts," "bulls" attempted corners with indifferent success until 1880, when this rule was repealed with the help of the "bears." Meanwhile, Lloyd induced the Board to require the deposit of cash margins to limit speculation's effect on prices. He supported successful litigation to abolish "puts" and "calls" (outright gambling contracts). He campaigned against the bucket shops that defrauded humble customers, but not until the early eighties did the Board drive them from its floor and "scotch" the "shops" in the Chicago area.[36]

During this long campaign Lloyd was backed by the *Evening Journal* and the literary *Current*. The *Western Rural,* Chicago *Express,* and other farm journals disseminated his exposures of market evils and taught their readers that speculation in farm produce was a major form of urban exploitation of the farmers. Thus, while inspiring the Board of Trade's reform party Lloyd contributed to the realistic sense of grievances that motivated the "agrarian crusade."[37]

He attacked unethical methods in other business fields, stressing the betrayal of fiduciary obligations that was transforming corporation management in many instances into covert buccaneering. He cited the looting of the Comstock Lode mining companies and collusion between San Francisco banks and the Director of the Mint. He summarized *The New York Times* exposure of the great New York life insurance companies' mismanagement. On January 4, 1878, the *Chicago Tribune* republished the *New York Sun*'s four-page compilation of corporation embezzlements and official defalcations. Editorially, Lloyd termed this "The National Black List," an "appalling exhibition of social dishonor and moral corruption" permeating "all ranks of men holding public and private trusts." He emphasized its pertinence for "students of morals" and attributed this situation to the Civil War and concomitant speculative manias.

He exaggerated in February 1878 when he wrote to Keenan that he was losing the ideals of his "green days" by writing daily "financial slush." He retailed society gossip and news of the Literary Club and journalistic community, disclosing a basic happiness derived partially at least from his crusading editorship. A satisfactory adjustment to the Medill régime was implicit in his imperturbable report of the marriage of Nellie Medill, daughter of "The Chief," to Robert A. Patterson of the staff. Yet, this event shut the door to Lloyd's ascension to the chief editorship. The Medill-Patterson-McCormick dynasty would control the *Chicago Tribune* until the mid-twentieth century. Instead of voicing frustrated hopes Lloyd wrote sadly of his great personal loss from Coolbaugh's suicide, "my very fast friend" and "one of the very few human beings for whom I have a tear to shed."[38]

Lloyd's especial responsibility was to foster the Chicago area's economic interests. He voiced the city's ebullient faith in the future. He urged that Canada complete the fourteen-foot channel of the Welland Canal and open up direct exporting of western products to Europe. He defended investment in western railroads and mortgages against the strictures of *The New York Times* on their soundness. In behalf of Chicago's wholesalers, investors, and the rural area he campaigned for custom house reform and tariff reduction, citing the steel rail duty's effect in increased construction costs and rates and merchandise prices and in depressed crop values.[39]

He was less skillful in analyzing real estate trends. As a novice he predicted in December 1874 that local values would see their lowest point within three months. Actually, they declined until after the railway strike of 1877, when buyers were as great a curiosity as the wonders of Barnum's circus. He voiced steadfast faith in Chicago real estate as an investment where values could not "be stolen or Mobilized by Directors," but not until late 1879 could he report the long-awaited real estate boom. Then he bought two and a half blocks at 63rd Street and Cottage Grove Avenue in the South Division and a more extensive property elsewhere in Chicago after consulting William Bross. This speculation identified Lloyd firmly with Chicago.[40]

At this time he was scooped by the *Chicago Times*'s exclusive story of George M. Pullman's removal of his factory to the Chicago area. Lloyd had greater flair for market, mercantile, railroad, financial, and corporation analysis. His annual reviews expressed Chicago's spirit of "manifest destiny" and rejoiced at its recovery from the fire. As the depression lifted he predicted that Chicago would resume its "march towards the proud position of the world's commercial metropolis."[41]

BIMETALLISM

Although there was in this no departure from economic liberalism, Lloyd's reading of the works of Emerson, John Ruskin, and European economists diminished his allegiance to Cobdenism. Furthermore, two *Tribune* campaigns in behalf of western interests made him question the pertinence of orthodox economics to American problems. The first campaign was for bimetallism. This began abruptly on June 8, 1877, during the worst of the depression and continued for two and a half years. The second was a vigorous campaign against railroad abuses. It began a few months later and continued into the next decade. In both Lloyd bore the heat of the battle, although policy was undoubtedly determined in conclave with Medill.

Lloyd conducted these with complete disinterestedness, as he did those for financial and business reform. Nearly twenty years later Robert Patterson would inform him that he had been "almost the solitary exception" to the rule that financial editors were generally accused of "crookedness," and contrasted him with Frank A. Vanderlip, who had left the *Tribune*'s financial chair after losing the "confidence of LaSalle street" because of "grave rumors of improper interests in the market."[42]

During his campaign for bimetallism in behalf of vital

property interests in Chicago and the West, only Jacob D. Cox of the old Liberal Republican leadership agreed upon the necessity of free silver. Both lived west of the Alleghenies. Previously, the *Tribune* had supported the resumption policy of 1875. Now it reversed itself to combat radical greenbackism, which threatened to achieve tidal force by promising economic justice to the masses by fiat currency inflation and decreasing interests rates on mortgages.[43]

Congressman Cox expressed to David A. Wells the conservative purposes of the western men who would enact the Bland Allison Act over President Hayes's veto. Cox voted for that Act and bimetallism, he wrote, as the only way to gain "solid ground from which we can resist the . . . 'fiat' money men" and "all forms of communism."[44]

Medill and Bross were in the forefront of the free silver agitation. The former presided at a great Chicago Silver Meeting of business and professional men in December 1877 and then addressed the Illinois Silver Convention at Springfield.

The *Tribune* fought greenbackism as "Brick" *Pomeroy's Illustrated Democrat* boasted of 100,000 circulation and demanded sufficient inflation to wipe out the national debt. Lloyd argued that only remonetization of silver could convince Greenbackers of their error and make resumption feasible despite gold's scarcity. He demanded repeal of the Resumption Act, to be followed by retirement of the greenbacks and repeal of the war taxes. He cited the bimetallism of the London *Economist, Pall Mall Gazette,* London *Standard,* and Berlin *National Zeitung,* as he warred with the *Nation, New York Evening Post, Journal of Commerce, Hartford Courant, Chicago Times,* and *The New York Times.* Doctrinal encouragement he derived from Professor Francis A. Walker's *Money* and *The Future of Gold* by Professor Edmund Suess of Vienna. Ernest Seyd, a German monetary expert, supplied additional ammunition and posted Lloyd on the Austrian press. Lloyd informed *Tribune* readers of "The Struggle for Gold" between European central banks. He argued that silver's depreciation was solely in terms of gold, a product of the latter's scarcity. *The Economist* and

Pall Mall Gazette agreed. He revived Murat Halstead's claim
that demonetization in 1873 had been fraudulent. He castigated
Wall Street "Shylocks," helping to instill such stereotypes widely
in agrarian minds.[45]

Righteousness, he declared in reply to Godkin, was on the side
of those who would undo "The Crime of '73." Bimetallism
would break the "corner" in gold of European central banks
and great financiers, defeat their "plot," and raise the value of
all commodities. This argument appealed peculiarly to apprehensive urban and rural midwestern debtors because Lloyd
argued that free coinage would produce an honest reflation
in values. To William Graham Sumner's declaration that pay-
ment of the national debt in silver would dishonor the national
faith he replied that it was payable in "standard coin," that
Sumner sought an unethical bounty for "money-lenders."[46]
These arguments were repeated by the Louisville *Courier-
Journal,* Philadelphia *North American,* and *Kansas City Times.*

Three years after Congress enacted the Bland-Allison law the
Des Moines Register declared that the *Tribune's* "splendid fight
on the money question" had been "one of the ablest, strongest,
most powerful, and most effective contests ever engaged in in
Western journalism, and never surpassed by any journal in
America." Its influence in the West, it added, "was well nigh
boundless."[47] When resumption occurred, January 1, 1879, Lloyd
rejoiced at the triumph of "the conservative classes" and public
faith over "the Fiatists" and the "Goldites."[47] It had become
evident in the Tribune Building that Medill possessed in his
financial editor a journalistic swordsman of high caliber.

Not until four years later was it clear that unilateral American
remonetization of silver without free coinage had not restored
it to parity with gold. Instead, new silver discoveries in Colorado
flooded the metals market, while the refusal of France and the
German Empire to return to bimetallism left the United States
with a slender gold reserve burdened by monthly silver pur-
chases made by congressional order. The *Chicago Tribune* re-
treated then as gracefully as it could from a position that
events had made untenable. However, when it championed the

gold standard during the second "Battle of the Standards" in 1896, Governor John Peter Altgeld exhumed Lloyd's silver editorials of 1877-79 as ammunition for his campaign against Mark Hanna and William McKinley.[48] Thus, in the silver propaganda of 1894-96 that refurbished and rang the changes upon his shibboleths of 1877-78, Lloyd's short-lived bimetallism was revived to haunt him at a time when its adherents opposed the broader, far more radical program that he was then offering to the public for adoption.

Chapter VI

 For National Railroad Regulation

CONSTRUCTIVE CRITICISM

LLOYD'S JOURNALISTIC CRUSADING almost invariably placed him at odds with the powerful interests responsible for the abuses that he exposed and sought to remedy. This had first become evident when his literary editorship antagonized the orthodox Protestant clergy. His campaign for Board of Trade reform placed him in opposition to Philip D. Armour, "idol of the market place" of the powerful speculator segment of midwestern business. The *Tribune*'s free silver campaign pitted him against "Wall Street" and orthodox economists who favored Britain's single gold standard.

All this was preliminary to a spectacular campaign for railroad reform and national railroad regulation. During this Lloyd attacked magnates who comprised the most powerful entrepreneurial group in the United States in the late seventies. If William H. Vanderbilt, Thomas A. Scott, Jay Gould, and Collis P. Huntington were not "the gods" of the continuing "Gilded Age" for millions of citizens whose limited perceptions were confined to a simple materialism and admiration for success and power, those figures were the "idols" of the steel roads that bound the nation in a continental economic unit. Lloyd viewed the issues that they raised as social in the broadest sense. His broadly oriented intellectualism enabled him to perceive the incompatibility of orthodox economic dogma with the business behavior of magnates whose entrepreneurship combined astute but speculative operations development with speculation in their

corporations' securities and flagrant favoritism to certain shippers. To expose their maladministration and misdeeds, and their
consequences, required skill and courage. To demand practicable railroad reform and to mobilize decisive support for it was
the work of a publicist.

While the *Tribune*'s free silver campaign obliged Lloyd to
differ from the gold standard economists, his fight for railroad
reform led him to abandon laissez faire completely. He soon
regarded the railroad problem as more important than the tariff
or monetary policy in its implications for free enterprise and
democratic government. Ethical and power considerations combined with Chicago's and regional interests in determining his
policy. The violent antirailroad riots of 1877 taught him and
Medill that railroad management's arrogant disregard of shippers' and laborers' interests fostered a dangerous radicalism.
The *Chicago Tribune*'s ensuing campaign for railroad reform
and regulation was motivated in part, consequently, by the conservative considerations that impelled its free silver crusade.

Prior to Lloyd's financial editorship the *Tribune* had supported new western railroad construction and campaigned for
railroad competition, low rates, and fair treatment of shippers
while opposing combinations. Lloyd had long been familiar with
the railroad problem. As an antimonopolist he was opposed to
railroad combinations on principle. Charles Francis Adams,
Jr.'s findings as a Massachusetts railroad commissioner, he discovered, were largely inapplicable west of the Hudson River.[1]

Adams was America's most influential railroad publicist
during the mid-seventies. All later students of railways became
indebted to his *Railroads: Their Origin and Problems* (1878).
Moderates supported his proposed national fact-finding railroad
commission. In 1879, however, he became president of the
Board of Arbiters of the eastern trunkline association. Although
he left the field of railroad reform open, no economist entered
it until 1885 when Arthur T. Hadley of Yale College published
his *Railroad Transportation,* which favored legalized pools subject to fact-finding commissions, and Richard T. Ely of the
Johns Hopkins University wrote some articles on railroad prob-

lems for *Harper's*. However, between 1877 and 1886 two former
officers of the Free-Trade League contributed importantly to
an understanding of "the railway problem." Simon Sterne's six
months' inquiry into Empire State railroads for the Hepburn
Committee in 1879 ventilated abuses and led to the establishment of a state railroad commission.[2] Lloyd led in the press campaign for national regulation which, combined with the activity
of influential elements, led to its institution after nine years.

The railway problem had attracted the attention of journalists and antimonopolist reformers since 1864 and had produced "Granger" state railroad regulation during 1869-74.
While new construction continued to enjoy popular support as
settlers moved into the public domain and the cutover pine
lands, of greater moment to business and agriculture when
Lloyd first occupied his new chair were the rate and service
policies of the eastern trunklines. Their tracks terminated at
Chicago and St. Louis, connecting there in the yards with
regional and transcontinental systems. As the eastern trunklines
organized and dissolved traffic pools and revised rate schedules
arbitrarily on "through" traffic to and from salt water, the
Chicago railroads that ran to the south, west, and northwest
felt impelled to follow suit while maintaining arrangements for
pro rata division of rates on intersystem shipments.

Chicago's prosperity and pre-eminence and the welfare of its
expanding metropolitan area depended upon the carriers'
management, which a comparatively small local investment in
them could not control. Chicago's wholesale merchants' ability
to compete with those of rival cities, the continuance of the
packers' hard-won leadership in their industry, and the city's
attractiveness to new industries and investment capital were
directly related to the railroad rate structure. Local and regional
wage levels and real estate values depended upon it indirectly.
As Chicago became the world's leading railroad center all
phases of that vitally important transportation system that
affected the welfare and growth of the Middle West possessed
news value.

Initially, as financial editor he continued the paper's earlier railroad policy. He rejoiced at the collapse of the Saratoga combination of eastern trunklines. He approved the four-track reconstruction of the New York Central Railroad. He supported a projected Boston built eastern trunk railroad, asserting that diversity of interests between the north Atlantic cities made a permanent trunkline combination unlikely. In 1877 he demanded that the rival Southern Pacific and Texas and Pacific transcontinental lines be built without government subsidies.[3]

During the railroad strike of 1877 he kept cool and sought a constructive solution, despite a division of opinion among the *Tribune*'s editorial staff. Although he believed that the Baltimore and Ohio's deficit had justified the wage reduction that precipitated the conflict, he alluded scathingly to "Credit Mobilier" methods and the "fictitious" capital that had been wiped out by the bankruptcies of sixty-three other lines. He attributed the spreading violence to specific management deficiencies. He demanded an end to the almost universal "cutthroat and starvation" policies that had precipitated the strike. Quell mob rule; reform railroad policies; restore rates to "a live and let live basis"; and cancel the last two wage reductions were his remedies.

When mob violence reached Chicago Medill shelved this policy. His headlines screamed "RED WAR," "PITCHED BATTLES." *Tribune* editorials declared that "Communism" underlay the strike. He demanded mobilization of all able Chicagoans for defense. Increase the standing army, enforce vagrancy laws against "Communist gentry," and suppress "The Dangerous Classes" was Medill's program during the rioting. After order was restored, prosecutors, judges, and legislators bulwarked society by reviving the common-law doctrine of conspiracy, erecting armories, and strengthening the militia. As this began Lloyd declared on the financial page that damage inflicted by the strike was "exaggerated like everything else about" it. Although he regarded it as "a foretaste of what may happen when better organization attends the revolt of labor," he asserted that the upheaval had not been the result of Communist infiltration. The strike demonstrated that a general redress of grievances instead of repression was in order. He proposed termination of the orgy of special legislation and reform of land policy, corporation management, the "unrighteous and inequitable administration of justice, the currency, the tariff, and the use of public offices for private ends."

In an editorial he demanded national arbitration of railroad disputes and demonstrated that railroad workers' real wages had declined from an index figure of 196 in 1868 to 106 in 1877 prior to the reduction precipitating the strike. That would "furnish a basis for argument after people's heads get cooler," he observed, as he approved Vanderbilt's promise to establish an employees' pension system for the New York Central system.[4]

Continuance of prestrike railroad policies by managers who learned nothing from the episode except the efficacy of contempt proceedings against strikers on lines in federal receivership[5] soon vindicated Lloyd's lonely demand for comprehensive reform. Medill gave him reportorial assistance for development of a distinctive railroad policy. He rapidly acquired an unmatched knowledge of railroad abuses, against which he began a long campaign. He warned the Pennsylvania Railroad to desist from reckless expansion. He seconded the London *Times*'s demand for franker B & O financial statements. He concluded privately that railroad reform could be achieved only by governmental action.

Then he opened fire upon railroad pooling. He began, November 3, 1877, with reporting that the Omaha Pool had been coupled to the revived eastern trunkline pool on the initiative of Albert Fink, executive officer of both. Effected before the close of lake navigation, it facilitated a general freight rate increase that squeezed all possible profit from farm produce shipments to pay dividends on "watered stock," a prime motive for "constant extortion and oppression practiced by the railroad companies," he reported, while predicting that the new interregional pool would precipitate an unprecedented movement for railroad regulations and reform.[6]

He attacked the Gould ring's and the Huntington ring's attempts to persuade Congress to scale the Union and Central

Pacific railroad companies' indebtedness to Washington as "rank villainy." Congress should prohibit dividends on their "watered stock" until this claim was settled, he said.[7] The antagonized railroad magnates retaliated immediately. On railroads entering Chicago the *Tribune*'s patrons found it impossible to purchase their favorite newspaper, but were offered the *Chicago Times* or *Inter Ocean* instead. Medill promptly exposed this "conspiracy," gathered evidence with a view to litigation, and defeated the boycott.

Lloyd supplemented realistic criticism with comprehensive reporting. After declaring that B & O adherence to the eastern trunkline pool was a blunder he opened a railroads department. This supplied daily news of rate wars, new construction, freight agents' meetings, trunkline pool actions, and the activity of the notorious livestock "eveners' pool." He punctured traffic managers' blurbs and exposed abuses and buccaneering. This unmatched service educated the West on the injuries to regional interests inflicted by pools controlled on the Atlantic seaboard. Not even Fink withheld information when Lloyd requested it.[8]

He concentrated editorially upon significant trends in railroading, mixing censure with praise. In January 1878 he urged that Congress extend the time limit of the Northern Pacific's land grant. Stressing the effect on the national economy of railroad abuses, he discussed those most vital to farmers, businessmen, and democratic government. As the decade closed he explained proudly why Chicagoans refused to fawn upon Gould and other barons of railroad rate and stock market manipulations.[9]

For National Regulation

Lloyd's attempts to prevent free enterprise and representative government from being supplanted by a corrupting, arbitrary railroad power elevated his campaign from muckraking to that of publicist. He received his cue for this in September 1879 when William H. Vanderbilt demanded that Congress authorize a national railroad pool, a proposal that Adams and Fink pressed repeatedly during 1879-82. There was no guarantee that such a pool would exercise its power in the public interest, Lloyd replied, since lack of honor among railroad men had been the public's only protection from extortionate rates. The great need was national prohibition of railroad combinations, pooling, and discriminations sueh as the high rates preventing direct rail shipments between Chicago and California. The Reagan Bill would do "for a beginning," and legislators opposing it should be held to "a strict accountability." Thus, Lloyd demanded that Washington abandon laissez faire and apply to the railroad problem William Jevons' empirical-utilitarian method that was influencing Britain's policy.

When Vanderbilt attempted to counteract the Hepburn Committee's revelations and their effect on the New York Central's position by secretly engaging J. Pierpont Morgan to sell a large block of his Central stock to small investors and arrange a community of interest by interchange of stock with the Pennsylvania Railroad and the Erie Railroad, Lloyd detected the stock market preparations for this consolidation of eastern railroad power. He exposed false rumors and deduced brilliantly that Gould was acquiring a minority interest in the Central in return for diverting traffic to it from his southwestern railroads via the Wabash. This he termed a great triumph for Gould, "a colossal thief."[10]

Lloyd then declared journalistic war dramatically upon the gigantic combination, which promptly increased eastbound through freights from Chicago from $3 to $8 a ton. This "Railroad Plunder" added $300,000,000 to the value of the allied railroads' "watered" stock in a hundred days, he claimed, an unearned increment taken "forcibly from the value of the farms" and earnings of "agriculturalists" by the "huge monopoly" that deprived western wheat farmers of most of the recent advance in grain prices. Since Chicago's trade suffered from Gould's diversion of southwestern and transcontinental traffic via Peoria to the New York Central, Lloyd demanded that the Boston- and Chicago-controlled Northwestern, Rock Island, Alton, and Burlington roads join with the Santa Fe to reject Fink's invitation to present plans for a division of westbound freight.[11] By striking appeals to western interests, antimonopolist stereotypes, and "genteel" ethics, personalization of the giant combination, and skillful reporting he attempted to arouse threatened rural and urban interests to effective counteraction in a brilliant campaign in which his partially frustrated ambition found fulfillment.

The "Vanderbilt-Gould Combination" threatened "a railroad mastery of the trade of the country" by a prospective "consolidation of the entire railroad interest," he warned, since Gould was allied with the Huntington coterie of the Central and Southern Pacific railroads. Like "Robbers of the Rhine" Gould and Vanderbilt could "confiscate any proportion of the public's goods that they may desire." Although the Chicago and Santa Fe roads, farmers, and merchants could not resist the great combination's raids, he reminded readers that many of its chartered members enjoyed land grants, the loan of government credit, local government subsidies, and rights of way secured by eminent domain.[12]

The new combination was the Vanderbilt-Gould-Scott reply to the United States Supreme Court's decision in the Granger cases, Lloyd declared, and predicted that the combination's pooled corruption funds would be felt in "every corner of the land." This would force a contest between it and the "people through Congress." The press must define the "issue" and the public should "watch" its representatives.[13] This was a realistic warning in view of railroad methods of controlling Congress and the state legislatures. Politics had become a "business" in service of the railroad power everywhere.[14]

Lloyd's campaign was stimulated by Vanderbilt's scheme, the Hepburn Committee revelations, and the parallel disclosures of the noted Commonwealth Suits in Pennsylvania, and anticipated the National Anti-Monopoly League that would be founded in 1881.[15] Lorane W. Reynolds of Boone, Iowa, wrote Medill in December 1879 of the "almost universal commendation" accorded the *Tribune*'s campaign. Railroad corporations, he observed "own Judges, corrupt juries, buy Legislatures, confiscate property, and in short, rule the land." Although not a

Granger he declared his opposition to the railroads' "over-weening" power.

After publishing this on January 2, 1880, Medill shifted Lloyd from the financial chair to chief editorial writer and head of the special editorial departments. Colbert became "commercial editor." From 1880 to June 1884, however, Lloyd wrote the editorials on business, finance, railroads, labor, and many other subjects. While honored by the responsibility he long resented Medill's withholding of a commensurate salary increase.[16] A fruitless negotiation for purchase of the *Daily Telegraph* indicated his dissatisfaction.

Periodically, thereafter, he gave concentrated attention to the railroad problem, as during the congressional session of 1879-80, when he published a daily leader that aroused public support for national railroad regulation. He backed the congressional railroad reformers against the powerful railroad bloc, whose members he put on record while he smoked out the well-financed railroad lobby.[17]

Specifically, he began by demanding that Congress fix a maximum rate for transportation, a method attempted previously by Britain and Illinois with indifferent success. Public, reasonable rates, devoid of discriminations between shippers and localities, were sought by railroad reformers everywhere, although Lloyd's proposal that rates be changed only at stated intervals was new. His demand for prohibition of higher rates on short hauls than on long hauls was probably derived from the independent oil producers of Pennsylvania and struck at a favorite railroad mode of developing "through" traffic at the expense of noncompetitive "local" shipments. He again anticipated Robert LaFollette with a novel demand that Congress discard the claims of watered stock in determining fair rates when railroad indebtedness equaled or exceeded the value of the property. Lloyd's program for statutory railroad regulation exceeded the scope of the Reagan Bill, which he supported with qualifications.[18]

He denied that the *Tribune* opposed the consolidation of short lines to provide more efficient service. Railroad reformers demanded, he replied to railroad spokesmen, that "men who enjoy great and valuable public franchises shall not use their monopolies for the oppression of those who furnish their business." He reminded Congress that the National Grange and the National Board of Trade demanded a national railroad commission to enforce uniformity and publicity of railroad accounts, publicity of freight classifications, uniformity of rates, an end to discriminations and extortion. He asserted that urban consumers and merchants supported this demand for a national railroad code which Senator William W. Eaton's bill for a national commission provided.[19]

This was a comprehensive program, derived partially from important aggrieved interest groups and designed to remedy the long continued abuses of irresponsible, arbitrary railroad management. It anticipated the twentieth-century regulatory policy developed by the two Roosevelts, Taft, and Wilson, although it did not envisage government control of railroad financing. Lloyd's elaboration of this policy before March 1880 illustrates how early was the seminal period of American Progressivism's moderate but realistic program.

To justify his railroad policy Lloyd cited Britain's strong national railway commission that possessed authority over rates, pooling, and service. Congress should add such a commission to the Reagan Bill. Only in this way, he declared, could effective national regulation be instituted and the dictatorial Vanderbilt-Gould-Huntington attempt to unify the railroads into "one great monopoly" be defeated.[20]

Charles Francis Adams opposed the Reagan Bill and Lloyd's broader program. Instead, he urged federal authorization of a self-policing, voluntary, railroad "Confederation" to fix rates—Vanderbilt's national pool—which would leave unrestricted the "evolutionary competitive struggle" in which combinations resulted from natural selection. A national commission should be limited to gathering statistics and arbitrating intersystem differences.[21]

Adams spoke as a "railroad attorney," Lloyd replied, and his plan left the public unprotected from such a triple increase in rates as Fink had imposed in October '79. If a national railroad pool developed Congress should follow France in subjecting it to national control. What lack of this involved was illustrated by the Hepburn Committee's discovery that the New York Central had had in force in 1878 six thousand secret, special contracts conferring cut rates on privileged shippers, and that the Erie practiced similar discriminations. Lloyd exposed the parasitic terminal, elevator, sleeping car, and fast freight companies on those trunk lines, the secrets of railway executive intersystem meetings, their favoritism to the Standard Oil. Nationwide "extortion and discrimination" originated, he said, with the New York "railroad combinations" and only national regulation could provide "a complete remedy" for the "railway problem."[22] Lloyd complimented Sterne privately for his masterly conduct of the Hepburn Committee investigation, the circulation of whose report fostered the demand for railroad reform.[23]

Although Congress rejected the railroad reform program that presidential year, Lloyd kept up the fight, exposing railroad abuses to stiffen reform sentiment, censuring the Congressional Committee on Commerce's preference for a weak commission, and reminding voters that the remedy lay in their hands in November. He censured President Hayes and Congress for not preventing renewal of the pool between the Union-Central Pacific roads and the Pacific Mail Steamship Company that eliminated transcontinental competition. He attacked the eastern trunkline pool's attempt to gain control of the Great Lakes steamship companies. He printed eyewitness accounts of the use of free passes by a Chicago judge and a member of the Illinois Board of Tax Equalization.[24] As a journalistic warrior for railroad reform Lloyd was unequaled. Success would have been immediately beneficial to Chicago, the Middle West, and competitive business.

During subsequent congressional sessions and whenever opportunity offered Lloyd renewed the fight. His great article on the Standard Oil in the *Atlantic* in March 1881 stressed that industrial monopoly's dependence upon railroad favoritism, demanded a national railroad commission, and cited the Charles River Bridge and Granger cases as establishing its constitutionality. So shattering was the article's impact that John Murray Forbes, chairman of the Board of Directors, Chicago, Burlington & Quincy Railroad, hired a writer to defend all corporations. For Illinois Lloyd demanded strengthening and reconstitution of its negligent Railroad and Warehouse Commission. He published the exposures of railroad abuses by the New York merchant Francis Beatty Thurber, moving spirit of the Anti-Monopoly League.

Lloyd also stressed the ironic contrast between American constitutional government and the concentration of political power in the hands of railroad and telegraph magnates. In "Feudalism in America," he asked editorially, "We are a free people, are we? This is a government of laws, is it? Oh, yes; but one man makes the laws—in the State of New York!"[25] In "King's Horses and King's Men" he finished off Vanderbilt with a sarcastic contrast between the luxury of the Vanderbilt stud and its owner's indifference to the hundreds killed in a New York tunnel wreck of his trains.

To Fink's private plea that publicity was the only means of preventing rate discriminations he replied that only government regulation could stop "oppressive pools," competitive building, and rate cutting, and this "will be the most difficult work ever undertaken by this people." Congressional legalization of pooling that Fink demanded had to be accompanied by statutory protection from discriminations such as the Standard Oil, California, and "the shippers of dressed beef" enjoyed. "Railroad government" must be subjected to "political government." The current application of "Wall Street Morality" to new railroad construction was "the strongest possible argument for the immediate, persistent agitation of the question of National regulation." Able, powerful railroad men must operate within "the strict lines of social duty." Lloyd's railroad reform journalism put carrier executives so on the defensive that they promptly developed public relations policies of counter propaganda and press control.[26]

Simultaneously, Lloyd welcomed constructive developments such as Fink's introduction of the British freight car clearing-house system on the eastern trunklines and the Chicago & Alton's reduction of passenger rates to the Illinois legal maximum. He praised the well-managed Illinois Central and B & O. He urged that the eastern trunklines double-track to the Mississippi River to reduce costs and increase carrying capacity. He suggested that the Pacific railroads institute low seasonal tourist rates, low land prices to settlers, and reduce freight rates as means to profitable operations. He reported significant European railroad developments. He warned against government ownership because of Italy's experience. He did not deduce as he should have from a parliamentary commission report in 1882, which he read, that stock watering had little influence upon rate making. British railroads charged "what the traffic will bear," with special commodity rates when circumstances warranted, instead of basing rates on mileage or cost as the Illinois Commission favored. The former practice, aside from discriminations between shippers and places that was so peculiarly American, was not unlike that evolving on American railroads.[27]

APPRAISING VILLARD AND HUNTINGTON

Because of the *Chicago Tribune*'s policy of supporting railroad construction that broadened the city's trading hinterland Lloyd made an important exception to his indictment of railroad management in the case of Henry Villard, who had gained control of the Northern Pacific by the spectacular "blind pool" of 1881. Lloyd was influenced also undoubtedly by friendship for a fellow journalist, by admiration of Villard's iron nerve in pushing the NP to completion despite Gould-Huntington attacks on the stock exchange, and by ignorance of Villard's disguised resort to the profitable construction company method of self-enrichment. Presumably on Medill's orders he traveled with Villard in 1881 and in 1883 to the NP railhead to report its achievements and the potentialities of the newly opened northwest.

His reports were made in two series of vivid articles. Seven in July 1881 described investment opportunities in the Dakotas and Montana in lands, cattle ranching, and mining. Contrary to his earlier position, Lloyd supported Villard's attempt to sell the huge NP land grant quickly to capitalists in large blocks to finance construction. Lloyd urged that homesteaders locate outside the grant, without noting that this would place them from forty to eighty miles from the railroad! He described the plan to complete the main line and build branches. He approved making Superior the NP's eastern terminus, thereby "Undoing Duluth" in return for "concessions of a third" of the former to Villard and associates. Deceived by unseasonably heavy rainfall Lloyd declared that it was impossible to get "west of the rain-belt" on the NP. He exaggerated the potentialities of the "Good Bad Lands." During this first junket he met Captain Henry R. Gorringe of the Navy, famous for having brought "Cleopatra's Needle" to Central Park, New York. Lloyd was flattered by Villard's praise of his "Yellowstone and Beyond" dispatch, which depicted Montana as an empire of rich valleys "backed by mountains that would support tens of thousands of cattle on the outside and turn out tens of thousands of tons of gold and silver ore from the inside."[28] The promotional tone of these articles contrasted sharply with his earlier critical, crusading editorials.

In September 1883 Lloyd joined the junket of 400 dignitaries, authors, and journalists who, as guests of the NP on special trains, met at Helena, Montana, to witness the well-publicized "Gold Spike" celebration of the completion of the main line. Lloyd traveled with British cabinet members, M.P.'s, British Minister to the United States Lord Sackville-West, James Bryce, and other British notables who informed him unanimously of the undesirability of Irish Home Rule. In the same group of trains were former President Grant, seven state governors, senators, congressmen, and federal cabinet members and judges. Some months later Lloyd depicted the discourtesies and crudities exhibited to their host and fellow travelers by the British nobles in a *Tribune* editorial, "Eastern Manners and Western Criticism." Henry George called the journalists on that junket Villard's "literary-brushers-off of flies." Probably Villard paid many of their editors for their praises.

Until after the "Gold Spike" ceremony near Gold Creek, Montana, Lloyd sent complimentary dispatches to the *Tribune*. These culminated with an account of that romantic episode. Among 3,000 guests, mountaineers, and Indians he listened to William M. Evarts beat time with the Fifth United States Infantry band, and saw the gold spike driven as the sun set behind the Big Hole Mountains. Lloyd's articles praised the NP's construction without loan of government credit, its ownership of terminal facilities and town sites, lack of exclusive contracts with grain elevators, and, inexplicably, lack of a construction company like the Missouri Pacific's, which had netted a 700 per cent profit in a few months. The Oregon and Transcontinental Company was Villard's construction company.

As the most noted of the journalists present Lloyd addressed Villard in their behalf before the party broke up, thanking him for his hospitality and praising his achievement in advancing "civilization" and his fidelity to his fiduciary obligations.[29]

Lloyd continued westward on an independent investigating tour. From Helena he observed that Villard must prove that he could earn profits operating the NP after such lavish construction expenditures. This was an oblique thrust at its overcapitalization. In "Lively Hops" from Tacoma he warned against excessive speculation in the lands of rich Puyallup Valley, Washington. At Portland, Oregon, he asked the NP Land Commissioner pointedly as "an antimonopolist" how Montana could benefit from a proposed NP pool of traffic with the UP.[30] When, a fortnight later, Villard joined Huntington's California railroad pool, Lloyd returned to the Pacific Coast from Salt Lake City, where he had written up the "monopolistic" features of Mormonism. He spent ten days at San Francisco investigating the Huntington railroad empire and sent six dispatches to the *Tribune* describing it.

"California Cornered," the most notable of these, depicted on October 8 and 13 the Southern Pacific Railroad Company's monopoly in California. Citing statements from the management, its business friends, and its critics, this ranged from analysis to description, narrative, and epigrammatic summaries in a masterpiece that would have been a credit to *McClure's* twenty years later. Stuart Daggatt's scholarly study of the Southern Pacific has since corroborated its accuracy.[31] In his study Lloyd described how the SP had developed familiar railroad abuses to the nth power under complete monopoly. It forced shippers to sign "special contracts" to ship exclusively on the Huntington lines in return for rate reductions and to open their books to the railroad's inspection. With passenger and freight rates double those on eastern railroads the SP netted greater profit per mile than did any eastern railroad despite a lower traffic density.

California exhibited the terminus of "the social drift" initiated by railroad pooling, Lloyd concluded. The Southern Pacific Railroad Company controlled all railroad transportation there. The huge fortunes of California's "Big Three," he said, were fruits of their monopoly, garnered by "oppressing the people." No governor, senator, congressman, or two of three state railroad commissioners could be elected without their approval. However, a critical public opinion was obliging these "railroad kings" to modify Leland Stanford's earlier repudiation of any obligation to consider the public interest.[32] This report to the *Tribune's* public broadened the horizon of midwestern antimonopolism.

In December, Mrs. David B. Colton's damage suit against the "Big Three" corroborated Lloyd's analyses spectacularly. During it she produced 300 letters from Huntington to her husband, his former lieutenant. Lloyd arranged their selective republication in the *Chicago Tribune,* thereby scooping the midwestern press. These and his editorial analyses of the letters precipitated a sensation.[33]

More effectively than any "damned interviewers" whom Huntington hated, these letters disclosed his manipulation of western state and territorial governments, purchase of United States senators, control of Congress in his fight against the Texas & Pacific, corrupt securing of federal land grants, and purchase of press support on both sides of the Rockies. "Chesterfield Publicus Huntington," Lloyd dubbed him sarcastically, observing that the letters proved that his fortune was based on "fraud of the grossest kind." The public had paid a hundred million for the laugh it could now enjoy at the expense of Huntington and the senators and bankers whom he called "our men."[34]

FOR RAILROAD LAND GRANT REVOCATION

Such extraordinary disclosures intensified greatly the demand for national railroad regulation and railroad land grant revocations. In the *North American Review* and the *International Review* in March 1883, George W. Julian had demanded an end to the influence of the "Land Grant Railways" in Congress and the Land Office. Lloyd gave immediate, vigorous support. After elaborate, independent research he presented in "Our Land" in the *Tribune,* March 17, a forgotten classic of the literature of exposure. With American preference for a small farming democracy as his frame of reference he described graphically the defeat of the homestead policy, the rise of great private and corporate holdings, the fact of "land monopoly," the corruption that had fostered these developments, and the abuses of the railroad land grants. The latter he depicted on a large map that has been reproduced since. Unfortunately, Lloyd's map included in the land grant belts the alternating government sections and also the broad "indemnity limits," thus exaggerating the actual railroad grants.[35]

This exposure, the map, and Lloyd's editorial demands that Washington revoke all lapsed railroad land grants and reform the General Land Office were undoubted factors in arousing a sudden popular insistence upon congressional action. Forty million acres of government land were still withheld from settlers by Land Office rulings despite certain railroads' inability to qualify for their grants. The popular demand for revocation was intensified by the revelations in the Huntington letters. A flood of bills to revoke the lapsed grants was proposed in Congress. To expedite action Lloyd and the *Tribune* formed an alliance with Senator C. H. Van Wyck, author of Nebraska's

Railroad Act of 1881, who was active in the campaigns for revocation, land policy reform, and national railroad regulation. In May 1884 Lloyd and Van Wyck vainly attempted to get the Senate Public Lands Committee to report the railroad land grant revocation bills.[36]

Neither then nor in the next session of Congress were they able to secure a reform of land policy or national railroad regulation. Senators facing re-election were more sensitive to the railroad viewpoint than to popular demands. Senator Cullom ignored the *Tribune*'s demand that he strengthen the proposed national railway commission. Neither his bill nor the Reagan Bill was seriously considered in 1884. So evident was this that Lloyd boiled over.

On January 10 he attacked the penetration of the American "House of Lords" by the railroads and industrial monopolies. The Standard Oil controlled two senators, he said, the Northern Pacific one, the UP "several," the Pennsylvania Railroad two, the Central Pacific two, the Georgia railroads one, the C & O one, the "lumber monopolists" of Michigan and Wisconsin two or three, the Wilmington Match Company one. At least half of the senators were controlled by "some corporation interested in getting or preventing legislation, or some syndicate that has invaluable contracts or patents to defend or push." He cited Van Wyck's declaration that the Senate had been controlled by "the money power of great corporations" for twenty years. He castigated the Senate's manipulation by "the cattle-eveners and stock-yards millionaires" because of the pleuro-pneumonia bill which was emasculated despite protests from the Cattle Commission, ranchers, and the public.[37]

His robust journalism, aided by other papers, Julian, and Van Wyck so mobilized public opinion that both political parties in 1884 demanded forfeiture of the lapsed railroad land grants. Reformers dubbed the Republican presidential nominee, James G. Blaine, "The Tattooed Man" because of his association with Reconstruction railroad land grant scandals. In the Middle West railroad and land policy reform sentiment was so strong that customary Republican majorities were greatly reduced and urban "mugwumpism" developed, to which Lloyd adhered. This had an undoubted influence upon the subsequent reform of land policy and the Land Office and the first experiment with national railroad regulation.[38]

Immediately after the election Lloyd revived his campaign. He celebrated the defeat, in the courts, of the Hocking Valley and Lake Shore railroads, charged with flagrant discriminations against independent coal dealers and oil refiners. At long last, he rejoiced, "the railroads can be made to obey the laws." Investors were learning that railroad managers lacked the acumen to institute the low rates needed to stimulate the increased traffic necessary for dividends on railroad stocks. He reported protests against rate discriminations from Chicago's Board of Trade, industrialists, and lumber dealers, the Toledo and Kansas City produce markets, and the pig iron and American Iron and Steel associations. What was needed was a strong national commission, he reiterated. When the lame-duck Senate rejected the Reagan Bill he urged reconstitution of its membership so as to terminate railroad nullification of the public will. Twenty-one state regulatory commissions foreshadowed the ultimate solution of the railroad problem, he predicted.[39]

Simultaneously, he exposed frauds of cattle-raising syndicates on Oklahoma Indian lands and demanded that the Secretary of the Interior void illegal leases of railroad lands to similar groups. He castigated President Chester A. Arthur for employing federal troops to drive a few hundred small farmer squatters from Oklahoma. He wrote with bitter realism to Senator Van Wyck of his disappointment at the results of the current senatorial elections :

> With Evarts :—Jay Gould's counsel for years;—Stanford; Spooner of Wisconsin, the attorney of the Minneapolis and Omaha railroad; Teller of Colorado and the old railroad senators being elected all round the circle, the prospects of getting anything for the people from the Senate for the next half dozen years seems to me to be getting slim. All that remains for the railroads is to get

control of the Supreme Court, and the lines of defense for the corporations are all thrown up."

A shrewd prophecy! All that public opinion, which he had done so much to inform and arouse, could secure from Congress two years later was the weak Interstate Commerce Commission. Within twelve years, as he foresaw, the Supreme Court would emasculate the Commission's limited authority. Yet, as Dean John D. Clark has remarked, he was "fairly entitled to much of the credit" for "the growing sentiment for federal regulation."" By synthesizing diverse reform proposals into a comprehensive national program, relating this to regional and special interests, and constantly exposing existing abuses and problem situations he contributed largely to the development of a realistic public opinion that insisted upon this departure from laissez faire. His contribution to the initiation of national railroad regulation ranked, therefore, with that of Simon Sterne, who helped to draft the Interstate Commerce Act, and exceeded that of Thurber and the Anti-Monopoly League. In so doing Lloyd developed into a fighting publicist of the first rank and developed extraordinary influence.

Chapter VII

Originator of the "Progressive Mind," 1879-1885

A New Liberal Theory

LLOYD'S CAMPAIGN for railroad regulation took him far afield from Cobdenism, which in 1870 he had preached as the "international law of the Almighty." Although his invocation of Jacksonian and Cobdenite antimonopolism was an effective tactic that counteracted Darwinian determinism, he was not the "homespun realist" that Vernon Louis Parrington said he was.[1] Lloyd knew the theories of the schools.

Since the crusade for business reform demanded broad government intervention he was unable, as did practical men or aggrieved interest groups, to advocate single interventions as necessary exceptions to laissez faire. As an intellectual he was compelled to develop an adequate theoretical basis for positive political action. As a repudiator of Social Darwinism he was unable to invoke Reform Darwinism that was popular in civic-minded patrician circles. Granger precedents and British experimental-utilitarianism provided a justification in railroad reform for government intervention that could be harmonised with individualism.[2] This did not provide a comprehensive rationale for government action against a broadening range of business problems. Although he accepted much of Mill's positivism, his inherited Locofoco antipathies, acceptance of the Emersonian critical tradition, and recognition of Cobdenism's inadequacies impelled him as financial editor to invent or borrow constructive principles that would serve this end. After he devised his basic conceptions independently, he found

122

justification for them and corollary concepts in the schools of nineteenth-century historical, philosophical, economic, and social thought.

As he and his wife ran the gamut of Emerson's *Works* they studied Thomas Carlyle and John Ruskin and were influenced by their romantic protests against machine-age injustices. Emerson's antimonopolism and insistence upon the intellectual's civic responsibility strengthened existing commitments in Henry D. Lloyd's thought. He readily endorsed Carlyle's blunt insistence that the Abbot Samsons of business honor their social obligations. He understood better after studying the viewpoints of those figures the role of the "hero" in civilization and was influenced, perhaps subconsciously, by it thereafter. Ruskin's aesthetic protest against a sordid, grasping industrialism conditioned Lloyd for affirmative reaction to his denunciations of orthodox economics and his plea for application of the Golden Rule to business. These men influenced him indelibly but unsystematically, chiefly because he had previously discovered the inadequacies of the Ricardian-Mill political economy. He found August Comte of limited value but congenial because of his stress upon progress and the constructive roles of intellectuals and enlightened women in furthering it.

The actual imperatives driving Lloyd's thought forward were derived, however, from the amoralities and pathology of "The Great Barbecue" of The Gilded Age. So Parrington dubbed the unrestrained buccaneering of speculator-promoters who seized control of so large a segment of the economy during Grant's administration and exploited their advantage for a quarter-century afterward. Speculative rigging of the markets, "inside" looting of railroads and other corporations, spreading land monopoly, railroad discriminations, special legislation, rising industrial monopoly, flagrant political corruption, and their deleterious effects upon business and public morals and the distribution of wealth became endemic in a nation committed to the equalitarian tradition. This produced a perilous dichotomy in national life that thinking citizens, such as Lloyd, found increasingly troublesome. Actual circumstance diverged too far from Adam Smith's "law of economic harmonies" and libertarianism, and the assumption of ensuing justice, for the contradictions between theory and American practice to be tolerable. It was his early perception of this, derived from an unusual sensitivity to illogic and moral wrong, that also emancipated Lloyd from blind allegiance to orthodox economics and confirmed his attachment to the four thinkers whom he was studying. However, it was a major crisis that first impelled him to rebel from accepted dogma and to develop for himself a more adequate theory.

The railway strike of 1877 first led him to question laissez faire privately and conceive of a regulatory statism that would checkmate the "tyranny of corporations," submission to which he believed would disintegrate society. The "State," he concluded, was obligated like individuals to "resist wrong and do right." The masses provided the proper basis for remedial action, since they "must love the right" and "hate" injustice, defalcation, tyranny. Worshipping the "golden calf" was an "awful blunder." "When monopolies succeed the people fail. When a rich criminal escapes justice the people are punished." From this position he did not deviate as he grappled editorially with the problems presented by the Second Industrial Revolution.[3]

As he began to campaign for national railroad regulation in 1879 he read James A. Foude's *Caesar* and Adams's *Railroads.* These catalyzed emerging trends in his thought. Classical antiquity had experienced the threat to republican democracy of concentrated wealth. In the plundering of the Roman peasantry by fifty great aristocratic families during the civil wars he discovered an ominous parallel to "the stealing of the land-grants" by "the American rich, the corporations." The growth of tenant farming in Illinois suggested to Lloyd that if "an unchecked accumulation of wealth is allowed the United States will have a land question to end in a war against property." "Present laws and present tendencies will" terminate "free government" in America. While noting that uncorrected abuses and monopolies demanded government controls as "the great weapon, for the masses," he formulated in a notebook a remarkable, seminal statement of the necessary theoretical basis for positive action :

Now that we've got the nation let us use the nation. . . . The only way to checkmate tendencies of individual sel-fishness and power, the aggressions of corporations is by a public opinion acting through the provided organ of a public government. *A new Democracy.*

The new theory of state, the new party, the new dem-ocracy can be only by appealing to the businessmen of the country? or to the masses? The appeal must be made to the *community of interests.*

In addition to this well--defined conception of the necessary interest group basis of expanded, corrective governmental activity, Lloyd believed that *"A new political philosophy"* is needed to underwrite *"new departures"* since "the constitutional era for which Jefferson wrote is near its end." This theory would "acknowledge *the right of the majority to modi-fy the tenure and definition of property,* to confiscate it if need be" as during the French Revolution. It would prevent "primogeniture" by levying *"an income tax . . . vest the state with control of the railroads,"* impose *"heavy succession taxes,"* and "punish breaches of trust in the management of corporations." This would cure 'Vanderbiltism." "Justice" must be the "essence" of such a government in America, which witnessed "warnings of the final struggle between rich and poor." The "cry" of laissez faire raised by "French merchants" was "now used by monopolists." He jotted sarcastically in a notebook : "The rich man and Darwinist—Fittest survive. The Political Economy Professor whom he endows adopts his philosophy."

This prescient theory and polity crystallized in Lloyd's mind as he studied gross business abuses, monopoly trends, labor upheavals, and the fading promise of Jacksonian principles. While his proto-Progressivism justified national regulation of the railroads and resort to government action to correct abuses in other fields it developed in his thought a radical trend of far-reaching implications. Study of history suggested to him a need for authority in America to restore democracy's property basis by correcting the concentration of wealth. His suggestion that social taxation would accomplish this, although radical for his day, was undoubtedly original. Its effectiveness in the twentieth century indicates the practicality of Lloyd's remedy. Far more extreme, and borrowed from French revolutionary precedent, was his private belief that the power to confiscate might be needed as an additional corrective.

He wished that the novel regulatory and taxing powers that he deemed necessary be conferred upon the national government, a departure from Jacksonian states rights that foreshadowed Theodore Roosevelt's attempts to achieve Jacksonian objectives by Hamiltonian methods.

The originality of this startling development in Lloyd's thought is indubitable. The development and attempts to implement this new theory became increasingly important in his career during the next decade, first as a moderate remedy for developing abuses and then as a radical cure for social injustice. This notebook entry foreshadowed Rooseveltian "Progressivism" also in its ethical appeal. "There is a moral force in man," Lloyd continued, "of which the Darwinism of grasses and bugs takes no account. The collective conscience" must be so awakened, educated, and focused as to induce the state to control "the Caesars of Industry." The real struggle was between the "masses and the railroad kings,—the poor and the rich," for America's destiny. The "grandest political mission to which any man or body of men can be committed is to organize this struggle," since the "passion of the American rich man is to enslave labor by monopolies."[4]

Lloyd dedicated himself thenceforth to this task in his journalism and independent writing. He became the first influential publicist to advocate a realistic, positive reorientation of democratic theory and policy so as to reconstruct the property basis of a pluralistic democracy and in this manner ensure its survival. This differentiated him fundamentally from Henry George whose *Progress and Poverty* appeared that same year (1879) in a limited San Francisco edition. Both shared the Jacksonian heritage, invoked its morality, and hated monopoly as undemocratic and antiequalitarian. But Henry George grasped at the central problem facing free economy only to miss and focus instead upon land monopoly, a subsidiary issue that was most acute behind the advancing frontier, and prescribe a pseudo-Ricardian natural rights fiscal method of land nationalization —the so-called single tax—as the panacea for all economic injustice and social malaise. As George swept up a large, ephemeral following in the British Isles and among the Knights of Labor in the United States, Lloyd classified George with "quacks" and "communistic spirits." Several years later he called his theories "lunar" to William Clarke, the London Fabian and journalist.[5] Lloyd rejected the Georgite semiutopian gospel and began to apply to practical situations his theory of a positive regulatory, corrective statism. In this and its intent to redistribute unduly concentrated wealth it anticipated some of the subsequent British "New Liberalism."

In so doing he developed in action the classic method of American Progressivism. Necessarily, as a journalist, he relied upon a combination of exposures of evils with graphic appeals to pertinent moral values, and insistence upon application of American democratic principles applied to specific problems.

His candid, detailed exposures of pathologic trends fostered realism. His moral appeals stimulated a reviving idealism resting upon the reassertion of Jacksonian principles combined with a reinvigorated romanticism, the critical edge of which was sharpened on the grindstone of humanitarianism revived by the vogue for Charles Dickens' novels among the churchgoing middle classes. Lloyd broadened the basis for the reviving democratic impulse that he cultivated by discussing current European thought and policies. Invariably he resorted to this complex technique by focusing it upon specific situations, invoking American tradition and European example to justify extensions of governmental power. As he did so he presented his new liberal theory formally in the leading American periodicals, anticipating by three decades Walter Lippman's attempt to formalize Progressive thought.

Lloyd drew, of course, upon other sources of inspiration as he perfected his theory. He reread Adam Smith's *Wealth of Nations*. He studied Walter Bagehot's treatises on money and banking, Leslie Stephen's *History of English Thought in the Eighteenth Century*, and Sir Henry Maine's *Ancient Law*. In 1881 reading the tracts of Thomas Edward Cliffe Leslie, pioneer British historical economist, provided a doctrinal justification for Lloyd's new theory and polity. So did Emile Louis Victor de Laveleye's *De La Propriété et de ses Formes Primitives*. Lloyd's notebook of 1879 does not mention de Laveleye's appraisal of the historical school that *Bankers Magazine* featured. In 1881, however, he studied Wilhelm Georg Fredrick Roscher's works, origin of the German school of historical economics, which he contrasted with Bastiat, Mill, and Cairnes.[6]

Having abandoned Cobdenism Lloyd now rejected political economy as "the universal science" because of its ignorance of the economic significance of patriotism, the family, community, and state. Hence it was "as complete a failure as the mental philosophy taught usually by the same professions and based upon the same extravagant lack of fact." What was needed, he concluded, was "a natural (empirical?) history" of fiscal policy, banking, corporations, colonies, from which sound generalizations could be drawn.[7]

In this manner Lloyd became the pioneer Gilded Age rebel against doctrinaire formalism in American economic theory. His empiricism and Lieber's influence had led him to apply the historical method in economic analysis *before* he read Leslie, de Laveleye, and Roscher. Their historicism now confirmed his own. De Laveleye's and Maine's demonstration of the relativity of property rights was consistent with the Emersonian relativism that he accepted, and was pertinent to his conclusion that they should be modified by government action when necessary for the public welfare. This position Richard T. Ely and Simeon Patten would soon introduce into American economic theory. In 1883 Lloyd asserted privately, "Property law like Political Economy must be rewritten in terms of man."

He had perceived earlier also the ethical incompatibility of Social Darwinism with Protestantism and Jeffersonianism. Either the public would be converted to the "new gospel of Darwinism," he observed, "or there must be new ways of enforcing the ten commandments" against growing evils. After 1881, five years before Washington Gladden's *Applied Christianity*[8] he advocated extension of the Golden Rule and Christian ethics into business. In denying economic determinism impliedly his faith in American democracy's ability to subject the combination movement in business to the public welfare departed significantly from historical economic theory while repudiating the basic Marxian tenet.

How clearly Lloyd harmonized his expanded theory with traditional antimonopolism he expressed in a 1883 notebook:

> Monopoly represents industrial tendency to pools, combinations. Anti-monopoly stands for collective restraints of public morality and public policy . . .
>
> If combination is irresistible, control is irresistible . . .
>
> Combinations of Middle Ages were mere town affairs —our ascending spiral has developed them into continental combinations. If combinations are permanent tendency we may rest assured we have here key to much if most of our politics, law, morals, etiquette.
>
> Grant that it is the business of those who have industrial spirit to combine. It is the business of those who have public spirit to control combinations, and make them square with the public good. This they will assuredly not do themselves.[9]

The civic spirit of an aroused, informed democracy was clearly ascendant in this statement, despite its concession to the influence of the economic factor.

PUBLICIST

As early as 1880 Lloyd began to present his new theory to the public. He developed and applied it pragmatically during the next five years in application to problems of railroad transportation, business organization and policy, land policy, labor, and British-Irish relations. To his readers it soon became evident that he was proposing a new type of liberalism characterized by a limited statism that reserved wide areas for individual enterprise. Elaborated while he invoked antimonopolist shibboleths, this theory posited the ideal of justice in intergroup relations as the goal of public economic policy and private enterprise.

His editorials made the *Chicago Tribune* the pioneer vehicle of new liberal thought and policy, and America's leading antimonopolist newspaper. Then he presented his theory formally to the general reading public in four notable essays in the *Atlantic Monthly* and *North American Review* during 1881-84 as he continued his new liberal journalistic campaign.

Late in 1878 Lloyd began editorial criticism of the Standard Oil monopoly. His interest focused first upon the revelations of the spectacular Commonwealth Suits in Pennsylvania, where the Petroleum Producers Unions were cooperating with the state in an attempt to overthrow the Standard Oil-trunk-line railroad traffic pool. From Roger Sherman, leading counsel of the Commonwealth and the producers' General Council, he secured printed testimony and other data. This inaugurated an exchange of data that lasted for nineteen years.[10] Then the Hepburn Committee's findings and report of 1879 provided Lloyd with other data for editorial analysis of the Standard Oil and its peculiar relationship to the railways.

As he digested the data from these sources he wrote an essay, "The Cure of Vanderbiltism," for the Chicago Literary Club program, for which Elisha G. Patterson of the Producers' Council and Franklin B. Gowen, president of the Philadelphia and Reading Railroad, also provided material. After presentation to the Club, upon urging by Major Huntington, Lloyd sent the essay to William Dean Howells, editor of the *Atlantic,* who published it as the leading article in March 1881 entitled, "The Story of a Great Monopoly."[11]

Before its appearance Lloyd discussed the famous case of the

Standard Oil Company v. *Scofield, Shurmer & Teagle* editorially in "A Corner on Light," asserting that the former's alliance with the railroads was the basis of its monopoly. Congress should investigate it along with the railroads, he declared, and admirers of Rockefeller's "success" should be nauseated.[12]

His *Atlantic* article appeared dramatically just as Rockefeller was consolidating his position with interregional pipelines and was preparing to merge his many companies into the famous "Trust." Lloyd made a profound impression on the reading public by presenting Standard Oil as a case study of the industrial effects of railroad favoritism as a grave threat to the continuance of free enterprise and democracy. He described realistically the illegal railroad discriminations which, with its gathering pipeline monopoly, had contributed so decisively to the creation of Standard Oil's monopoly. His well-buttressed assertion, "the means by which" this was achieved "was by conspiracy with the railroads" was an oversimplification, although the pipeline control that he mentioned was intimately related to this. His statement that the business talents of the Standard Oil managers would have ensured their "success" in legitimate competition, although not monopoly, Ida Tarbell would reiterate twenty years later. The essay concluded with a powerful plea for effective national railroad regulation, after presenting the pioneer account of how the petroleum monopoly developed.

Lloyd erred in describing Rockefeller's earlier career and in inferring that railroad men owned an interest in the Acme Oil Company, a Standard subsidiary. However, Arthur M. Johnson's *American Petroleum Pipelines* develops Lloyd's thesis that joint managerial investment in the oil business explained the Standard-railroad alliance. Lloyd and Allan Nevins follow opposing lines of evidence in analyzing the "immediate shipment" crisis of 1879, whereas *both* Standard Oil exploitation of transportation control *and* a production glut that enabled it to do so with maximum effect explain that episode. Lloyd's devastating portrayal of the price spread between crude oil and kerosene on the domestic market did not rely

upon the New York prices of low-grade export oil as Nevins'
Rockefeller does. Lloyd's account of pro-Standard Oil railroad discriminations Nevins documented with new data but
demonstrated that Rockefeller did not initiate the secret rebate
practice. Hans B. Thorelli's recent review of the origin and
methods of Standard Oil largely confirms Lloyd's analysis.
New data on Standard Oil's origin substantiate Lloyd's general position, but Harold F. Williamson's and Arnold R.
Daum's findings disclose that that monopoly derived more
from nontransportation factors that he inferred.[13]

Because of the article's wide influence this is especially significant. For the *Atlantic* it was the hit of 1881. Six reprintings were required to satisfy the demand. Lloyd's term, "the
octopus," stuck to Standard thereafter, like the barnacles on
the hulls of tankers. Thousands repeated after him, "The
Standard has done everything with the Pennsylvania legislature, except to refine it." Even the *Nation* endorsed the article
despite Godkin's feud with the Anti-Monopoly League. The
independent oil men were delighted. Sherman said that Titusville considered the article "by far the strongest connected
presentation of the subject." *The Oil, Paint and Drug Reporter* republished the entire article. So did the *Chicago Tribune,*
Medill's resounding compliment to Lloyd. The Anti-Monopoly
League quoted the article extensively in a broadside attacking
Standard and the "Sugar Trust." An Iowa antimonopoly
movement stimulated by it elected Governor William Larra-
bee. The *London Railway Times* commendatory editorial was
distributed among British holders of American railroad securities.[14] Formal railroad public relations began with the carriers'
attempts to counteract the article's influence.

During the "next twenty-five years" the article "became the
starting point for every public investigation and the climax for
every orator endeavoring to describe the sins of the trusts,"
Dean Clark has observed. In the public mind it strengthened
railroad regulation sentiment. It aroused the press and periodicals to attack Standard Oil and the 'Trusts" as the Rockefeller coterie and its imitators resorted to that type of organiza-

tion.[15] Since the essay was unchallenged by the Standard Oil it was regarded as unanswerable, as Lloyd would boast in 1892.

His attack on monopoly in 1881 was not limited to Standard Oil. Before the essay's appearance he editorially analyzed Jay Gould's conquest of the Western Union, ascribing this vividly to exclusive railroad contracts, stock market manipulation, mergers of the Gould lines with the Western Union, and the incentive for monopoly rates inherent in gross stock watering. He endorsed the National Board of Trade's demand for a nationalized postal telegraph following Great Britain's example, a proposal that would be advocated widely and in vain during two decades by Congressional committees, commercial, farmers', and laborers' organizations, and Postmaster General John Wanamaker.[16]

In a noted editorial, "American Pashas," December 30, 1881, Lloyd paid his respects to Gould, Vanderbilt, and Rockefeller and arbitrary political "bosses." "All our business interests are drifting to monopoly," he said, "and each monopoly has its Pasha. . . . Some powerful man or group of men, by wealth, or favor of transportation companies, or the help of corrupt officials, is monopolizing almost every important industry." Their "force and fraud" were redistributing "the wealth of the masses into the pockets of monopolists. . . . There are too many Mehemet Alis in this country," whose leadership in the concentration of wealth was especially furthered by maladministration of "what is called 'Justice'."

This was preliminary to Lloyd's second article on business trends. The product of the Chicago Literary Club's request for a repeat performance, it appeared in the *Atlantic* for July 1882 as "The Political Economy of $73,000,000." This proclaimed the bankruptcy of orthodox economics in a vivid analysis that presented Gould as the chief illustration. It preceded the manifesto of the Ely group of "new economists" by two years. Before any other publicist or important economist in the United States Lloyd pled for the development of a welfare economics based upon realistic analyses of the economic facts and worth of the individual. He developed this thesis during a brilliant survey of recent economic thought in Britain and Germany, reviewing exceptions to the classical school taken by Comte, Ruskin, Emerson, Carlyle, and Maine and lampooning William Graham Sumner's defense of it. Lloyd's welfare theory was no paraphrase of the position of the historical school. It was a synthesis of Jevons' utilitarian empiricism with the humanism of the great romantic critics of modern industrialism. This justified government regulation of the economy in behalf of the general welfare in a manner that made a wide appeal, including experimental state and municipal welfare legislation.

Lloyd invoked Ruskinite humanism to validate the axiom that human welfare should be the chief concern of economic doctrine and practice. This thesis his friend John A. Hobson would develop a decade later. Then, after quoting Emerson's "we want justice, with heart of steel to fight down the proud," he castigated the feline, piratical Gould so searingly that J. S. Aldrich, Howells' successor, took legal advice before publishing. "It is a brave paper," he informed Lloyd, whose article declared that Gould's administration of his corporations was "an orgy of fiduciary harlotry," in which as on the stock exchanges he profited by trapping honest investors and speculators and manipulating "other people's money." Seldom has a powerful American businessman received such a sarcastic, public raking for betrayal of fiduciary trusts. Lloyd called Gould the "Giteau" of economics, a robber within corrupted legalities who illustrated what could be accomplished by scientific devotion to "competition, desire for wealth, and self-interest." Gould's flamboyantly displayed fortune raised an inescapable issue. Theft must not be property, Lloyd declared in a graphic reversal of Proudhon's dictum. The republic must protect private property from such a plunderer if it would preserve itself."

In style and content the article was classic despite its senssational character. The *Independent* called it "tremendously effective." Captain Gorringe wrote Lloyd that every phrase was a mot!" declaring that he was his "ideal writer" who would found a new school. Thurber of the Anti-Monopoly

League called him a "public benefactor" and sought a conference to advance the antimonopolist campaign. Lloyd informed him that if "the men of property and culture of this country" allow the "work of reform" to drop "from their hands into those of more ignorant people it will not be gently done." E. V. Smalley of *Century* and the *New York Tribune* praised the article's style and effectiveness. The *Springfield Republican* endorsed Lloyd's indictment of orthodox economics and declared just his condemnation of Gould, since "monopolists" were providing "justification of communism in America." Lloyd, it added, was a public servant seeking "to meet the great mischief of the money power" before the violent proletarian movement could overtake it. In Paris, Lloyd's friend Henry F. Keenan began his anonymous *The Money Makers,* which exposed Gould's prostitution of the New York press and market manipulations.[18]

However, influential journals rejected Lloyd's welfare theory and his thesis that the combination movement was the dominant business trend. *The New York Times* asked if he contemplated "some sort of principle that might work better than that of free competition?" The *Nation* declared that Gould was the product of corrupt courts and legislatures; laissez faire had never "covered the right to bribe judges or 'gobble' railroads." Even Ruskin would repudiate "this volunteer," Godkin said. Lloyd denied in reply that he had called political economy "bosh" and identified his position with the historical school's criticism of Mill's theory of competition. Why did Godkin take refuge in the "bad man" theory? Laissez faire was responsible for America's toleration of robbing and murder "by wholesale" in "corners" and combinations, "and by legal methods of oppressing the people, betraying trusts, and deceiving the community." Godkin conceded the validity of this, although he did not agree that the "class" perpetrating such evils "must be controlled." Inspired by Lloyd's article Schurz denounced "The Robber Barons" of business in his Phi Beta Rappa oration at Harvard University. In Chicago John McGovern kept Lloyd's portrait of Gould fresh in the public mind by biting editorials in *The Current*. In the *North American Review* for April 1883 the Rev. Ernest Crosby's "Dangerous Classes" demanded drastic curtailment of the power of industrial and railroad "tyrants" and legislative protection of the poor.[19]

On February 12 Lloyd had hailed the "renaissance in political economy" in the *Chicago Tribune*. Citing the ovation accorded Arnold Townbee's London lectures on the land question, he announced his own adherence to the "new school," which combined "the results of economic study with the principles of Christian socialism" while repudiating the dogmas of "unlimited competition and freedom of contract." Then, in November he declared editorially that the social unrest was reviving the "old question of the rights of the many" in new forms. How the masses could co-operate to alleviate industrial wrongs and achieve "industrial liberty" "only quacks like Henry George pretend that they can see. But how to do it is the question to which those who were born to hate wrong are turning above every other. . . . Great changes are impending." The feudalization of "democratic and republican America . . . into industrial Barons by the hundred and serfs by the million" would "not continue forever." When the formulae for this new "reformation" were perfected into "A New Magna Carta" Mills's "competitive political economy" would be "obsolete."

Nine months later Lloyd rejected Matthew Arnold's élitism. The history of social progress, he replied, "is the history of the widening area within which those who had voices could make themselves heard." The problem was how to employ democratic power to cope with the emerging business oligarchy. Since the majority must love justice while hating tyranny "the great reforms before this country are those that will dispossess little groups that have slipped into holdings of social, political, and industrial power," which they administer contrary to democracy's "ideals and interests." Those demanding "these reforms are few," but the mass speak through them.[20] This was brilliant tilting. Like his opposition to the pursuit of unlimited gain that Mill posited as fundamental to competition,

Lloyd's opposition, embodied in the democratic principle, to the caste tendencies of power entrepreneurs and the *nouveaux riches* ran counter to the dominant currents of the era.

In "Making Bread Dear" in the August 1883 *North American Review* he carried his campaign against speculative rigging of the markets to the general public. Encouraged beforehand by the antipathy of Partridge and Smith, New York commission merchants, to "the abominable gambling in wheat and other necessities of life," he contrasted legitimate market functions with the speculation on produce, petroleum, and stock exchanges. With devastating epigrams he dramatized the speculative "manufacture of prices." Strong men built "corners instead of castles" on the exchanges to collect "tribute at the end of a telegraph wire instead of a chain stretched across the Rhine." "The criminal rich" adulterated grain and provisions and manipulated the exchanges so as to seize other people's property by exacting artificially high prices and extorting excessive damages from trapped "shorts." Elsewhere they betrayed fiduciary obligations, looted corporations, and abused franchises. Speculative manipulation, such as Philip Armour's, depressed produce and provisions prices during harvest and raised them artificially afterwards to the injury of farmers and consumers and legitimate merchants. Since the Illinois Supreme Court had exempted the Chicago Board of Trade from state regulation, national regulation of exchanges was needed to enforce there an acceptable ethics and restore legitimate market functions.[21]

"Making Bread Dear" was widely acclaimed, and its oblique thrust at orthodox economics much appreciated. The *Pall Mall Gazette* termed the essay "remarkable." William Clarke's "The Power of Monopolies," Cambridge (England) *Independent Press,* hailed this "blow" and agreed that legislatures everywhere must curtail monopoly in the public interest. American press comments were generally favorable, the *Springfield Republican* and St. Louis *Globe Democrat* presenting long summaries. Although the former and the *Boston Daily Advertiser* minimized the effect of "corners" on living costs, the *Boston*

Globe, Albany Times, New York Journal, Rochester Post-Express and *New England Farmer,* endorsed Lloyd's demand for national regulation of exchanges that anticipated the Securities and Exchange Act by fifty years.[22] Reverberations from the article were perceptible for years in agrarian circles.

Shortly after this essay appeared the Chicago Board of Trade revised the anticorner rule. Then the Illinois Supreme Court reversed the decision that had placed the Board beyond statutory control. C. L. Hutchinson, president of the Board, a noted speculator and later founder of the Chicago Art Institute, attempted a reply before the Chicago Literary Club. In rebuttal there Lloyd quoted him against himself on the evils of corners and cited the Board's rules against them asking, "Are only the priests of the Board of Trade to be allowed to think and speak of its sacred mysteries?" In October Van Buren Denslow replied ineffectively to Lloyd in the *North American Review.*[23]

In June 1884 before the Republican National Convention nominated Gould's friend, James G. Blaine, for the presidency, Lloyd published "The Lords of Industry" in the last-mentioned journal. This essay dealt exclusively with monopoly capitalism, which American and British economists neglected, and was based upon extensive research in court proceedings, legislative investigations, and trade journals. Comparisons with mercantilism and the free trade era pointed up a searching analysis of the combination movement. Fifty-eight industrial monopolistic combinations were identified. Their effects upon consumer welfare were vividly portrayed, as were the ruthlessness with which combinations whipped recalcitrant firms into line, their self-policing, and their secrecy. This documented Lloyd's conclusion that Americans were witnessing an epoch-making revolution. Nothing went "backward" in the United States except "reform," he declared. "Monopoly and anti-monopoly" were the great tendencies of the age. Public control of the combination movement was "imperative." To preserve their freedom men must apply the ethical principles that Emerson and Ruskin asserted were essential to sound values. Only a moral renaissance could enable Americans to recover business freedom or oblige monopolists to adjust their prices to production costs and serve the public interest. State laws and railroad commissions were "but toddling steps in a path in which we need to walk like men."[24]

The moving, elevated tone of this article gave maximum effectiveness to Lloyd's unique style. Jeweled epigrams, irony, coined maxims, sarcasms, vividly presented examples and variation between factual presentation, reference to pertinent doctrine, analysis of trends, and episodic presentation of the case for a welfare economics and regulatory policy elevated the treatment to an unprecedented height in American essay writing. His unique prose method won Lloyd a unique position in American letters, while his realistic and penetrating analysis of business methods and trends made him the pioneer economist and publicist of the new liberalism that he advocated.

The *Pall Mall Gazette* reported that the essay attracted much attention among British economists and statesmen. It completed the destruction of William Clarke's faith in the old liberalism, to which "Our Land" and Lloyd's earlier essays had contributed, and helped to propel that able London journalist into the Fabian Society.

In the United States *Bradstreet's,* organ of the renowned credit-rating company, published a five-column review of the essay. The *Age of Steel* declared that only "government interference and superintendence" could remedy railroad pooling and that Lloyd's analysis of industrial pools should be read everywhere. The *New York World* featured it as disclosing a trend back to "guild slavery." The *Current* cited the *Northwestern Lumberman* in support of Lloyd's identification of a lumber pool. John Swinton, the *New York Sun*'s former chief editorial writer, hailed Lloyd's "heart" when attacking "The New Feudalism" at Christmastime in his *Paper*.[25]

Because of the complexity of the problems that Lloyd's article series and accompanying editorials analyzed, their frontal attack upon the old liberalism and orthodox economics and their cumulative presentation of his welfare economics and new liberal polity exerted a seminal influence upon American reform thought. While they paved the way for the American Economic Association's manifesto of 1885, they provided the rationale of the moderate reform legislation that was enacted in the mid and late eighties. They also laid the ideological foundations of the "Progressive Era."

Lloyd's "other people's money" and "our criminal rich" were widely quoted, the latter by Theodore Roosevelt. Lloyd's analysis of the monopoly trend, welfare theory, and regulatory polity won the admiration of Clarke and the Fabian Society. In the United States he led the intellectual revolt from the doctrinaire formalism in economic theory that obstructed the experimental approach to economicopolitical problems on municipal and state levels that produced 5,000 general welfare laws before 1890. In these ways Lloyd helped to prepare the way for their pragmatic solution as the electorate turned against "Stalwart" Republicanism and timidly ventured into the waters of reform.

CRUSADER

Lloyd's editorials developed a transoceanic view as he applied his new liberalism to practical situations. To the joy of Irish-Americans he declared that peasant proprietorship was the solution for Ireland's land problem, to be achieved by sequestration of Irish estates and their sale to peasants after compensating the landlords. He encouraged the Irish Land League to agitate for land reform and urged resistance to coercion, which won him the lasting friendship of one-armed Michael Davitt, who contributed to the *Chicago Tribune*.[26] This campaign had implications for American land policy that Lloyd developed in "Our Land."

He analyzed other aspects of British life and policy. In "The New England" in December 1882 he predicted editorially that the newly enfranchised British workers would not foster Anglo-American emnity "to increase the outdoor relief" of the British aristocracy. When Disraeli revived imperialism he republished William Clarke's criticism of imperial federation. They agreed that responsible government in the British colonies made that scheme impracticable. Some Englishmen, Clarke said, would avoid this in order to "extend the empire of justice at home!" Lloyd predicted also that Britain's Indian policy, by supplying Hindus with railroads, armaments, education, and newspapers, was leading to the overthrow of the British raj.[27]

He devoted much more time to exposure and analysis of domestic problems, and editorial campaigns for their remedy. He combined antimonopolism and hostility to special privilege with patrician antipathy to "stock-jobbing," despite his seat on the Chicago Stock Exchange, and pride in Chicago's preference for "honorable" trade. New York, he wrote scornfully, was the home of stock market manipulations and promotion of "great monopolies"; its press served the "robbers" and "wreckers" of "Wall Street" while opposing the West's attempt to free itself from "the slavery of railroad monopoly."[28]

Beginning in 1879 Lloyd waged a six-year campaign for pure food legislation. He demanded a city ordinance against selling condemned meat, and supported the pleuro-pneumonia bill that Congress emasculated at the packers' behest despite support from exporters, cattle ranchers, and the National Board of Trade. He endorsed a congressional bill to prevent sale of adulterated foods in the District of Columbia and the territories, although Chicago packers were the chief offenders. After a British investigation of the fraudulent butter "mixers" and the waterers of lard he called such businessmen "public enemies."[29]

He lampooned Congress for withholding adequate funds from the National Board of Health's program of preventive medicine and immigrant inspection. "Of course not. There is no plunder in it." If Dr. John R. Rauch would, instead of suppressing disease, cultivate it in partnership with the quinine monopolists, he would have no difficulty 'in getting help from Congress to keep out" foreign smallpox, yellow fever, and cholera, Lloyd observed sarcastically.[30] On the other hand, he complimented Congress for enacting the Pendleton Act and endorsed the Postmaster General's recommendation for a postal savings bank.[31]

He advocated forest conservation. He demanded immediate state action while supporting the *Nation*'s notable campaign for forestry reserves and reporting the findings of current literature of the conservation campaign.[32] Locally, he fought in vain for the development of the Chicago traction system in the public interest and against granting "corrupt" franchises to railroads and utilities. He campaigned for law reform, to further which he described English agitation for improvement of court procedure, reform of the criminal code, and modernization of the law. He demanded statutes to cope with speculator-promoter depredations, and "lawyer-reform" via higher professional ethics that would debar railroad attorneys in legislatures from voting for bills furthering their clients' interests and prevent evasion of laws prohibiting railroad and utility mergers.[33]

Lloyd's widest, inherently the most dramatic, and most ardent editorial campaign was against monopoly of all types. He identified, analyzed, and depicted their effects upon the public as they emerged into view in a continuing fusillade that has had few parallels in American journalism for range, persistency, and cumulative effect upon public attitudes and policy, if not upon the combination trend. He fathered the slogan of the Progressive Era, "the tariff is the mother of the trusts," as he demonstrated that it spawned monopolies. In January 1880 he reported that the 120 per cent steel rail duty had enabled the Bessemer steel rail pool to raise prices 100 per cent in seven months. He attacked the paper pulpwood monopoly when the congressional owners of the patent prevented reduction of the 20 per cent duty. He exposed 'The Match Monopoly in Congress," with its prohibitive duty and 50 per cent differential and sixty-day credit to large companies on excise payments. "Scratch a monopoly and you will find the Government underneath," he quipped.[34] He supported the tariff reformers who attempted to reduce schedules as the Tariff Commission of 1882 recommended. He ridiculed the pauper labor argument. He exposed the exhorbitant profits of the Pennsylvania Steel Company, the woolen ring's machinations, the barbed wire combination's bleeding of western farmers, the Pennsylvania protectionist lobby. Monopolists generally opposed tariff reduction, he declared, after agitation had produced but limited realization of the Commission's program.[35]

Wit, vivid style, piercing epigrams, and a varied approach enabled Lloyd to continue his antimonopoly campaign for years and maintain reader interest. He reported the Anti-Monopoly League's activities, read *Justice,* its organ, and supplied Thurber with data. He dubbed the Boston owners of the Lake Superior & Hecla raw copper monopoly "Anti-American Millionaires." The similar tariff-favored starch combination he called "The Stiff Monopoly." His "Why Coal Is Dear" and "The Pennsylvania Cold Wave" exposed the Pennsylvania anthracite coal combination. Circulated almost daily in the Chicago area among the *Tribune*'s constituency, these editorials intensified antimonopolist and tariff reform sentiment that he had fostered as a free-trader before 1872.[36] In so doing he demonstrated his effectiveness as a journalist of unique courage, brilliance, and power, while exhibiting keen interest in scientific and literary developments of importance.

Chapter VIII

 A Second Wendell Phillips?

SHOWDOWN WITH MEDILL

LLOYD'S REPUTATION as America's leading antimonopolist journalist and exponent of the new liberalism gave him especial
prestige on the *Chicago Tribune* editorial staff. There he represented the active Bross-Lloyd minority interest in the publishing company. Ranking in importance with the city and
night city editors, he enjoyed large liberty during his crusades
for a socially responsible business leadership, democratic land
policy, and government policy designed to resuscitate decadent
democracy by positive measures. Although Lloyd's private
statement of his politicoeconomic theory was more advanced
than his published position, his editorials and magazine articles
with Medill's backing made the *Tribune* the leader in a press
campaign for moderate, effective reform on all levels of business and government while Chester A. Arthur was President.

Social prominence bulwarked Lloyd's position in the *Tribune*
building also. Well-to-do, he belonged to the Calumet Club,
Chicago Club, and Press Club. His literary fame made him
a leading figure in the Literary Club, where municipal reform
enjoyed a mild vogue. In the city his disinterested civic activity won him "respect and good will."

While entertaining talented men and women Mrs. Lloyd
fostered literary, linguistic, and aesthetic activities in Chicago
long before the arrival of women's college graduates led to the
adoption of her standards in place of the prevailing emphasis
upon family and wealth among married women. In the midst

of child-bearing she was plainer now as the characteristic Bross long straight nose, deep set eyes, and bushy eyebrows became more prominent. Clara Louise Kellogg, opera soprano, Mary Mapes Dodge, editor of *St. Nicholas*, Helen Hunt Jackson, author of *Ramona*, and a great admirer of Henry D. Lloyd's articles, John Root the architect, Frances Root, and Bayard Taylor were her close friends. She was active in the movement to reform national Indian policy, and was disgusted at President-elect Garfield's ignorance of the subject and hostility to the proposal as an imagined attack upon him, when she called. Her report of this led Martha LeB. Goddard of the *Boston Daily Advertiser* circle to denounce him for debasing "a great moral question to a matter of personal vanity." To Mrs. Goddard Mrs. Lloyd was "a noble woman." The Lloyds' unique position in society explains why they were listed separately from the Brosses in the printed program of "Long John" Wentworth's elaborate entertainment of the Calumet Club, December 27, 1882. However, the Lloyds and Brosses attended together the parties of Judge Lambert Tree, the Townsend Roots, and the William Blairs.

Lloyd worked so hard that he endangered his health, although he and his family vacationed annually on the east coast or in the White Mountains. Removal to the village of Winnetka twenty miles north of Chicago on Lake Michigan in 1878, with frequent walks there in Hubbard Woods and hunting in the oak openings with William Bross, freed him from fear that he had inherited the family headache. Previously, recurring headaches had obliged him to go to a New York osteopath for relief. At that time he visited the Perry Richardsons, who admired his charm and sociability, and was "put up at 'The Players Club'." After recovery he plunged into the preparation of his great articles in leisure hours at his Winnetka home. Overwork again—despite friends' warnings—high fever in 1882, and sewer gas poisoning in 1883 were followed by sciatica during the winter of 1884 and serious insomnia early in 1885. However, no breakdown occurred before he left his *Tribune* desk in late February on leave for a trip abroad, as Bross's diary indicates. It was evident to Lloyd's associates, however, that he had risked burning himself out after the example of Runnion and Sheehan, White's brilliant lieutenants, in campaigning for the new liberalism.[2]

The year 1884 had been a time of decision for him as it was for other liberals of insight and moral stamina. It subjected him to shock, emotional strain, and conflict with Medill. "The Chief" stultified himself by supporting Blaine's preconvention campaign before publication of "The Lords of Industry" on the eve of the Republican National Convention announced Lloyds's opposition to "The Plumed Knight's" business backers, among them the hated Gould. Lloyd's rejection of Blaine was commended by William Clarke in London and known to the Goddards in Boston. During the presidential campaign Medill restricted Lloyd's editorials to financial subjects. However, in these Lloyd continued his campaign for railroad regulation, an oblique thrust at Blaine, and exploded the G.O.P. claim that fear of his defeat was precipitating a depression. In "Making Coal Dear" Lloyd demonstrated laissez faire's inability to protect consumers or guide executives to conservation of their markets. He warned that railroad rate discriminations, if continued, would enable private individuals to become "masters of all the great business" and "change the entire aspect of our society, politics and trade. . . . Men cannot remain free citizens who are business slaves." Cleveland was the beneficiary of this, but Lloyd refused to vote for him as a protest against his tarnished private life. That made continuance under "The Chief" possible, although their relations were strained by Lloyd's indirect thrusts at the *Tribune*'s ineffective support of ·Blaine.[3]

After the election Lloyd deftly but dramatically manouvered Medill into the position of a defeated opportunist in a manner that expressed a liberal gentleman's contempt. In "Gilded Grief" Lloyd anticipated Thorstein Veblen by discussing the conspicuous waste of "the plutocratic class" while denouncing its departures from "good sense, good taste, and real hospitality." "The Gas Monopoly in New York" excoriated the eight pooled companies there for "extortions" and predicted government regulation of utilities. "Other People's Money" assailed frauds upon depositors and stockholders perpetrated by Wall Street bankers and executives. "Wall Street Must Divide," Lloyd declared, since eastern controlled railroads had lost the election. He voiced the West's bitterness at their refusal to adjust rate schedules to the decline in produce and merchandise prices when he declared those carriers to be "a separate, independent, and superior interest" like the British aristocracy. He opposed the Union Pacific's attempt to wangle congressional reduction of its debt to Washington, and condemned its annual report so savagely in mid-January that a director called him "a Communist" to Medill in the *Tribune's* editorial office, an obvious attempt to retaliate also for Lloyd's continued exposures and castigation of the greatest disciple of Daniel Drew.[4]

Unknown to Gould's emissary and no doubt to Medill, Lloyd had extended his new liberalism farther to the left. Privately he concluded that the controlling principle governing public policy toward the economy should be : "Is present use consistent with the best interests of society?" This was an empirical-utilitarian axiom that the Fabian Society would accept. Its application to the United States, as the beaten Republicans rallied, would have wrought far-reaching changes in its property system, business system, and structure of "Bourbon" power. Business combinations and monopoly were compelling men to be "collectivists," Lloyd added. The problem was to enforce "the morals of the crowd, the mass," vis-à-vis promoter-speculator and power enterpriser amorality. "Morals and values rise or fall together," he quoted from Emerson.[5] Under that inspiration Lloyd scaled the heights of journalistic heroism.

To have defended Lloyd against Gould would have disrupted Medill's new alliance with "Big Business." Furthermore, important local business interests, the Pullman Palace Car Company, leading merchants, and La Salle Street financiers, were developing close ties with Wall Street and the trunklines upon whose favoritism the packers and cattle eveners were dependent. Charles T. Yerkes bespoke the power in Chicago of the Widener-Elkins syndicate of Philadelphia. Belief in Social Darwinism was spreading as the rationale of extraconstitutional "Bourbon" political and economic power.

Medill told Lloyd what Gould's agent said. Instead of taking the hint Lloyd denounced editorially, in "Wall Street Nihilism," the Gould group's "boundless impudence" in its attempt to stigmatize as "Communists" those who exposed its "scandalous railroad robberies," corrupt political activity, perversion of executive authority, and wrecking of "confidence of man in man." Thus, Lloyd nailed to his editorial mast the colors that he had received from William Cullen Bryant. As a patrician new liberal who attacked the "Insolence of Plutocracy" some years before William Dean Howells would do so in fiction and whose exposures of unethical business and governmental methods long preceded Edward A. Ross's *Sin and Society,* he was too aware of the issues, too courageous morally, ·to stultify himself.[6]

The next day he expanded his new liberalism to include championship of legitimate labor activity and a plea for social justice. Hitherto, like Medill, he had been apprehensive of "Communism" and tended to identify trades unions and the Socialistic Labor Party with it. In 1880 he had attacked "The Folly of Trades-Unionism," branding strikes as futile but permissible as did Carroll D. Wright, and denounced the coercion of strikes and lockouts as "civil war, indefensible in any theory of . . . individual rights." He called the co-operative movement a failure, and condemned "vague discussions of the theoretical reconstitution of society," although he favored slum clearance. He had even hailed George Pullman's factory on Lake Calumet as a remedy for the labor problem despite the obvious "autocracy of its one-man rule" in an essay written for *Harper's,* which he refused to publish when the editor allowed Pullman to revise it. In 1882, however, Lloyd had approved of Terence V. Powderly's demand for a national labor code legalizing trades unions and a National Bureau of Labor only because this was a resort to the democratic process.[7]

In September 1884 a tall, stammering laborer from a Decatur coffin factory called at his *Tribune* office, seeking, he said,
the literary sources of "Making Bread Dear" and the foe of
"the gigantic evils that are sapping the life blood of our
country." "Bert" Stewart preferred "Lords of Industry" to
Sumner's "What the Social Classes Owe to Each Other." He
shunned Spencer, and clung fast to Jacksonian antimonopolism
as he wrote uncompensated articles for Knights of Labor journals in the Middle West. He supplied Lloyd with "inside"
data on the National Burial Case Association which he used
editorially in "A Corner on Coffins." When *The Casket* attacked that exposure of the semiserfdom imposed upon the
Association's employees Stewart informed him of that pool's
price maintenance policy and scheduled plant shutdowns. This
Lloyd also published. Unemployed, virtually penniless, his
children crying for bread, Stewart asked if the *Tribune* would
pay for contributed articles on the labor movement. Although
Medill rejected this application Lloyd encouraged "Bert" "not
to give up the ship." A year later Governor Richard J. Oglesby,
Lloyd's friend, appointed him to the Illinois Bureau of Labor
Statistics.[8]

After Stewart's visit Lloyd secured data from William Clarke
on William Morris and British socialism. He asked Professor
Henry C. Adams of Ann Arbor, whom Cornell had dismissed
because of a prolabor speech offending the Gould group, for
help in studying the French Revolution. Andrew D. White,
Adams' colleague, supplied an illuminating analysis of the inadequate histories of that great upheaval. Lloyd purchased
George Howell's *Handy-Book of the Labour Laws* from London and began to re-examine the labor movement. Together
with a determination to adhere to his new liberalism, this led
Lloyd to ignore Gould's protest and Medill's hint, despite "a
great temptation" to acquiesce in the latter's new policy. He
wrote to his mother, "I have gone to the edge of an abyss, but,
I have not gone over. The battle has left me weak and sore. To
whom should a man confess if not to his mother. Pray for me,
and that the strength wasted on unnecessary temptation may

somehow be given me again for my work." He was, he admitted, "not well."[9] After that he launched an extraordinary counterattack on the Gould group.

He brought this to a climax in a mid-February editorial, "The Mouse-Trap Men's Lobby," by ascribing Gould's congressional lobby and purchasing of a dozen United States senators to a desire to prevent changes in the *status quo*. To this he attributed the Senate's lack of enthusiasm for a national railroad commission. He called the UP's administration, "the sum of all villainies." He portrayed "The Nihilist Revival" as an anti-Communist "struggle against autocracy" in Russia. He defended the right of wage-earners to organize against the Hocking Valley Railroad. "To forbid the trades-union is to feed conspiracy," he said. "Shrewd capitalists should be the first to see this." Finally, he hailed Van Wyck's restoration of the Texas and Pacific land grant forfeiture bill to the Senate calendar as a victory for the public over Gould.[10]

Thus, on two great issues, the new liberalism versus the promoter-speculator oligarchy and the extension of the former to champion legitimate labor activity, Lloyd forced the issue with Medill.

Two days later the Lloyds announced to Bross that they were going to Europe. After two more they entrained for New York on February 28. The Medill-Cowles majority in the Tribune Company settled the issue for the paper in favor of the new conservatism of giant business, high finance, and speculative promotion. Medill gave his gifted gunnery officer a leave of absence, to rest, tour Europe, reflect, and then to return if he wished on the implied condition that "The Chief" would thenceforth designate the targets. Among them the Gould group would not be one. The Lloyds' letters of introduction followed them to Europe. They entrusted their three children to their servants and the Brosses. On the eve of sailing they telegraphed "The Governor" that they were well.[11]

RESIGNATION AND COLLAPSE

They reveled for six weeks in Italian Renaissance art. Then, in May at Venice, Mrs. Lloyd became seriously ill with typhoid. For a month her life hung in the balance while Henry D. Lloyd cared for her, keeping the news from the Brosses until she passed the crisis. After seven weeks together in France and England, when she had recovered, Mrs. Lloyd went home alone, insisting that he remain to complete his "leave." She intended, possibly, to prepare her father for the decision that the *Chicago Tribune*'s diminished hostility to monopolies, railroads, and speculative "dry land pirates" told Lloyd he would have to make.[12]

His first letters to her from London were aglow with excitement produced by new horizons and plans to investigate Irish landlordism. An extraordinary ferment was turning Britain away from individualism to the road leading to the modern welfare state. London had been stirred deeply by George's crusade, the Land Nationalization League, Irish land reform agitations, and huge Hyde Park demonstrations against Gladstone's attempt to quell Ireland's violent rejection of the Land Act. Intelligent and wealthy Britons were developing "a new consciousness" of social sin because of industry's failure to provide "a decent livelihood" for the majority.

Clarke had acquainted Lloyd with the utopian New Life Fellowship and the Fabian Society. Lloyd knew the literary sources of the rising British protest against social injustice. Need for a "new liberal" advance was also being agitated by the trades unions and Christian Socialists. A revolutionary Marxian socialist agitation was led by Henry Hyndman, William Morris, George Bernard Shaw, John Burns, and Keir Hardie. Clarke, like Charles Booth and Beatrice Potter, had abandoned traditional liberalism.[13]

David D. Lloyd came over from Paris, where he was writing the third of his famous comedies, to join his oldest brother in a tour of the British Isles. At the House of Commons Henry Norman, Major Huntington's friend, introduced them to James Bryce and Charles Stuart Parnell. Bryce recognized Henry D. Lloyd instantly, accorded the brothers an interview, and discussed the Socialist agitation with them at breakfast. Parnell had them in to tea to discuss "Irish-American politics." A conference with Professor Thorold Rogers of Oxford University confirmed Henry D. Lloyd's admiration of his economic histories. In the Commons the brothers witnessed Salisbury's attempt to buy peace in Ireland and the support of the Parnellites with the Ashbourne Act, whose peasant land purchase provision Henry D. Lloyd had long advocated. He began a lifelong patronage of B. F. Stevens, London bookseller, who supplied him with the latest books, periodicals, and government reports on all aspects of British, continental and antipodean liberal, labor, and social movements.

Bryce's letters of introduction opened "the best doors in Cambridge, Edinboro, and Aberdeen" to the brothers. T. P. O'Connor, an Irish M.P., prepared the way for their projected tour of Erin's rack-rented counties. As experienced journalistic investigators they were determined to get the facts and make their own appraisals of the changing United Kingdom.[14]

Before starting they attended a gigantic Socialist League meeting. There they met Morris, "a Norse God style of fellow, big, broad, hairy, loud and kind," and Stepniak, the Russian nihilist. The Marxian poet, intoxicated by his own oratory, failed to react to Henry D. Lloyd's graceful compliment, "We have had for many years in our house a most delightful arm chair of your make, which my wife has named the 'Earthly Paradise'." This "mot" Bryce enjoyed hugely when it was repeated to him the next morning. Henry D. Lloyd discerned the insurrectionary mood of that crowd, and reported to his wife its cheers for the "Revolution" and his disgust at "the broadest ideas of Free Love" that Morris voiced, *"so false to nature itself."* So Lloyd remarked to Clarke also, feelingly.

Provoked, he wrote to his wife tenderly of his lofty conceptions of human mating. Purity, fidelity, love and mutual respect, plus high intellectuality and culture, characterized their life together. Lloyd was cast in a mold different from the gifted but bohemian George Bernard Shaw, who was an extreme free thinker on sexual relations and no celibate.[15] Lloyd's letters to her excerpted Sir John Seeley's *Ecce Homo:*

" 'No heart is pure that is not passionate; no virtue is safe that
is not enthusiastic'." Such was the motto of his ardent nature.

While touring the Hebrides and Scotland Lloyd was fascinated by George Eliot's autobiography and its allusions to
Hegel, Kant, Mommsen, and Spencer. He informed his wife
that he had learned from Eliot how "one can do one's life
work despite gravest physical limitations." He described graphically his stimulating voyage "across Scotland" by steamboat
on the Caledonian Canal to Inverness, arriving in Ballater in
time to see the "great rotund, heavily bearded, very pleasant
looking Bon Vivant" Prince of Wales walk up the red carpet
to entrain for Norway while "the ladies waved their handker-
chiefs—and thrilled."[16]

Fatigued but buoyed by his brother's gay companionship,
Henry D. Lloyd made his great decision in the English Lake
Country before bad weather obliged them to depart for London. He wrote to his wife from Ambleside that he would probably not return to the *Chicago Tribune,* a decision that Bross
had foreseen and with which he concurred as Henry D. Lloyd's
mother informed him. What he intended to do he would not
decide until he could talk it over with his wife and Bross. It
would not be work on another newspaper, since he could no
longer afford to burn his candle at both ends in his "enthusiasm," at the risk of ruining himself by "literary excesses," he
wrote tactfully. Financially it wasn't necessary because of
Bross's generosity to him. "Perhaps the time has come for me
to devote myself to a larger constituency, a constituency I already have."[17] If "perhaps" became certainty his new career
would involve renewed combat with the American "Robber
Barons" of business consequently altering Lloyd's role from
that of critic and Progressive publicist to independent reformer. He would explore the plight of the wage-earners who were
demanding a redistribution of the social product. "But with a
new era we must have a new prophet, a new gospel," he concluded.

Had he, instead of embarking upon his continental tour
and experiencing the strain of his wife's typhoid, taken instead

a quiet rest with gradually increasing exercise until his mental resilience and normal sleep were restored he would have regained, probably, his full strength. That this would have altered his decision is improbable. After making it he was exhausted by a five-mile ride in the Lake Country, a walk back through a downpour, and travel to London—during the whole time of which he was experiencing an emotional reaction. Depressed at the prospect of abandoning his life's ambition, he had a nervous breakdown in London in the first week of September.

For six weeks he rested, taking drugs to sleep, his career in shreds at a time when his brother was at the height of his fame as a journalist and playwright. Henry Lloyd lacked strength for the Irish tour or the return to Paris to visit with Major Huntington before sailing. As he wrote him later, "I was . . . more ill than I knew." Thereafter, "the reconquest of fair command of nerves, sleep, working power" was "very slow."[18] David D. Lloyd, who would burn himself out and die before reaching forty, put him on a liner and cabled his wife to meet him. The ocean trip so restored his strength that Bross was agreeably surprised at his appearance when he reached Winnetka. Encouraged, Lloyd attempted vainly to purchase the *Chicago Journal* and experienced a relapse.

His false recovery must be attributed to the urbane shipboard company of Edwin D. Mead of Boston. They became warm friends. A gay, skeptical, liberal intellectual and leading spirit of the Goddard circle, Mead was a cousin-in-law of William Dean Howells, poet, editor of the *New England Magazine,* and active in the Old South Church's citizenship program. On shipboard Lloyd expressed to Mead a need for intellectual guidance. A fortnight after returning home he reminded Mead of a promise to help, adding "I have thrown away bromides." Mead replied with the warm hope that Lloyd at last would be able "to sleep and sleep and sleep," enclosing a critical bibliography of German idealist philosophy from Fichte to Hegel. Mead suggested that he read philosophical classics, British treatises on Kant and Hegel, the *Journal of*

Speculative Philosophy, study Kant's *Critique of Pure Reason* with Wm. M. Salter, and then read Fichte's *Popular Works.*[19]

To Salter, lecturer of the Ethical Culture Society of Chicago, Lloyd expressed interest in the announcement of the new American Economic Association that Ely had drafted. Henry C. Adams urged Lloyd to join. He admitted that he liked the Association's "ideas very much" and might join when "once more in fighting trim," despite his antipathy to the term "Economic," which he associated with the "irreligious, and I think unscientific, doctrines" of the "cruel" orthodox school. Would Salter come "to Winnetka for a sun bath" some bright autumn day? The younger man, who was about to wed William James's sister-in-law, wrote a glowing tribute on this note and forwarded it to Mead :

> This is from one of the noblest men in Chicago—one of the Editors of the Tribune, but out of health. I send that you may see I am not alone in my feeling about ordinary orthodox political economy, with its brute law of supply and demand, governing everything—even the treatment of human beings.[20]

COMMITMENT TO THE OPPRESSED

Guided by Salter in philosophy and reading his books on industrial relations, Lloyd worked ideas so garnered into his expanded new liberalism. He turned away from journalism and espoused labor's struggle for economic justice and civil rights in the *Age of Steel*'s symposium on the labor problem in January 1886. Hadley of Yale and the Rev. Edward Everett Hale favored industrial co-operatives in that as the best solution of the labor problem. Lloyd expressed frank sympathy with the laborers' discontent in his contribution and endorsed trades unions' and producers' co-operatives. The workers, he said, "have the sympathy of the thinkers of the world and of all lovers of mankind. Hence the issue is not doubtful." In our "enlightened age this growth upward should be accomplished

without social discord." Even if "revolution does come it will
be like the French Revolution simply a violent episode in the
emancipation of man."[21] These ringing words struck the keynote of Lloyd's independent reform career. John Swinton republished them. The pro-labor sympathies of the Ethical Culture movement encouraged Lloyd in this course.

Upon returning from abroad eight months later he found
Chicago swept by excitement, fear, and indignation after the
recent Haymarket Riot. Replying to a query, he informed
Swinton : "The Chicago dyamitards have secured able counsel
who will employ all the resources of the law in their behalf."[22]
Lloyd excerpted a sentence from the Illinois Bureau of Labor
Statistics' defense of labor organizations without noticing that
it was written by "Bert" Stewart, who was also coeditor of the
Chicago *Knights of Labor*. There he exposed the open alliance against legitimate labor unions of the police, sheriff, and
prosecuting attorney, and reported the murders of peaceful,
unarmed workers that summer and autumn. He disclaimed
any belief "in anarchy or force." He would "take out the
rotten planks in the ship of state and replace them with new
ones rather than sink the ship itself."[23]

In December Lloyd again referred to the Haymarket anarchists while commenting on Henry C. Adams' argument that
too limited an individualization of property was responsible for
existing "wrongs!" and that the chief problem was how "to
enforce the responsibility that goes with industrial power."
Lloyd differed and rejected Adams' assertion that society could
safely tolerate industrial strife. America, he declared, was
faced with the alternatives of "Reform or Revolution." Redress of "wrongs" must be secured by "state" action or it would
come "through anarchy," he said in a blunt application of
his new liberalism to the crisis. Industrial strife was comparable
to medieval feudal *"private war"* as was illustrated by "Pinkerton men pointing Winchester rifles out of Chicago Packing-
House windows at the rifleless mob outside."

Precedents existed in the state's resumption of control of the
coinage, law enforcement, taxation, and the roads during the

Middle Ages for present-day government intervention in labor-management relations in behalf of the general welfare, Lloyd maintained. "Shall the Rhine belong to the Barons or the people?" If to the latter, the state must resume "for the common good, the powers now misused by a few," although to accomplish this 'the very *roots*" of existing beliefs on politics and industrial relations would have to be "torn up." The "great question of the future" was whether the principles to guide such action would emerge "from a friendly debate" or harsher encounters. Contemporary economics or political science afforded scant guidance, he said.[24]

Then he attempted to aid labor's fight for civil liberty and the right to organize as frightened employers' associations began to smash the unions and terminate the eight-hour day in plants where the Knights and trades unions had won it. Lockouts, blacklisting, ironclad contracts, and armed Pinkerton detectives were employed after Armour & Company's example. A conviction that "radicals" and 'anarchists" must be crushed at all costs produced an employer-contributed fund to "reward" the police, who repressed labor activities indiscriminately instead of restraining only the shattered "Black International." Such was the bitter fruit of the Haymarket.

Labor leaders turned desperately to politics in the hope of electing friendly governments in Chicago, Milwaukee, and New York City to combat repression. In Cook County, Illinois, a United Labor party ticket was nominated. Among its candidates for the superior court bench was a Democratic party nominee John Peter Altgeld, a German-American advocate of penal reform.[25]

Alone of the journalists and his social circle Lloyd perceived the relation between the antisocial business management that he had long opposed and the antiunion drive. He warned Thomas B. Barry, who was attempting to settle the strike of the nonaffiliated pork-packers' union for retention of the eight-hour day, that the Packers' Association intended to crush it and the Knights of Labor that he represented. Armour would surely win, Lloyd predicted, unless his employees were backed

by "the whole Order." Many elements "and all workingmen
and patriots" would support the Knights' attempt to diminish
Armour's "power for evil." Barry accepted a truce until after
the November election, which was followed by the catastrophic
defeat of the pork-packers' union.[26] On the title page of Richard T. Ely's *Labor Movement in America* Lloyd wrote
Charles Kingsley's "The workingman who tries to 'get on,' to
desert his class, enters into a lie, and leaves God's path for his
own."

He rediscovered Ethelbert Stewart, who confessed to him
that from his letter of encouragement had "come the courage
I needed. I have more of it now. But I want to . . . talk with
you." Learning that his coeditor on the *Knights of Labor* regarded him as a "radical," Lloyd replied hotly, "It is about
time that somebody got radical on the side that has been so
radically plundered." He would keep Stewart's letter as long
as he lived. Could he spend the evening at the Lloyd home?

"Bert" accepted, voicing bitterness at Gould and other
"champions of . . . industrial robbery." Conceding that the
solution of the labor problem would come much better "from
above" than be forced "from below," he observed, "robbers
never disband of themselves." After seeing his babies cry for
bread, his wife sick and hungry in a cold house, having been
long unemployed and *"kicked in the breast"* and out of a shop
for asking for work, he was not vindictive,

> but the ashes of memory smolder and burn. You tell me
> I must be wise. . . . While recognizing no vested rights,
> no special grants; I pray Heaven keep me from ever
> touching with tongue or pen the natural rights, the real
> rights of any human soul.

After he had read Lloyd's essay series, unlike Diogenes he had
"put out his lamp."[27]

Thus Lloyd discovered a determined disciple. Stewart was
holding the harassed, embittered midwestern labor movement
faithful to the equal rights, antimonopolist faith despite at-

tempts of surviving anarchists and agents of the Pacific Coast
International Workingmen's Association to chart a revolutionary course. Like Powderly he viewed the Knights as an anti-
monopoly movement, whose objectives included co-operatives
and social legislation. He exposed the monopoly price of coal,
child labor exploitation, and speculative manipulation of food
prices, quoting "Making Bread Dear." He demanded a postal
telegraph. At his request Lloyd contributed "The Political
Economy of Child Labor" to the *Knights of Labor* spring supplement, after cheering Stewart's efforts and the United Labor
party's mayoral campaign and ridiculing businessmen's threats
to withdraw their capital from Chicago if it won.[28] Lloyd toured
the Chicago slums with "Bert." They found there a little boy
"who preferred beef-steak to candy," and saw scenes so depressing that Lloyd wept. Aroused sympathy transformed him into a
vigorous champion of the wage-earners. Thenceforth he employed his pen, purse, and voice in their behalf. He sent a
check to *John Swinton's Paper,* calling the editor "the greatest
patriot" in New York for appealing for clemency for the condemned anarchist leaders.[29]

Lloyd's "Child Labor" article invoked Christian, humanitarian, and democratic concepts and the idea of civilization in
disseminating concepts of social justice, brotherly love, and
welfare economics among wage-earners. It termed orthodox
economics a "pseudo science with its fiction of free contract and
gospel of competition teaching the extermination of the weak
by the strong." Helpless children, Lloyd declared, were the most
cruelly exploited workers. "Civilization in the family" must be
extended to business. "The law of love" as "part of the true
political economy" must abolish business "infanticide."[30] Then,
in a letter to the *Chicago Tribune* he attacked clerical defense
of upper-class luxury. Ministers should apply "the golden rule"
to that phenomenon, he urged, and businessmen should produce
necessities instead of luxuries, thereby ameliorating poverty.[31]

After this the Dubuque *Industrial Leader* urged that Illinois workers nominate him for governor on the Union Labor
ticket and spike the guns of the *Chicago Tribune,* their "worst

enemy." No cry of "socialist, red, etc., could be raised against such a man, and while labor could implicitly trust, capital dare not fight him." As a friend "in the enemy's camp" Lloyd could be elected, it predicted, by an overwhelming majority.[32]

Lloyd was not alone in appreciating the implications of the industrial crisis. Judge Altgeld and C. C. Bonney of the National Law and Order League advocated compulsory arbitration. Professor Hadley remarked to his Yale College class on industrial legislation, "natural selection has its bad as well as its good side." The trustees of the Peabody Foundation, led by former President Rutherford B. Hayes, condemned the blind folly of wealthy men who talked of force as the only solution for the labor problem, and discovered that Social Darwinism encouraged the most reckless business methods and tolerated such abuses as child labor.[33]

For Executive Clemency

Lloyd participated in the clemency movement in behalf of the condemned Haymarket anarchists because they were "connected with the agitation of the great social question of our day," as he informed his father afterward. He believed as did many attorneys that they had been unjustly condemned; he knew the Chicago business community's determination to make an example of the "Black International's" leaders. After attending their trial in Judge Joseph E. Gary's court, Bross wrote in his diary, "A hard looking lot. Cut Throats—nothing less." Medill and Melville Stone agreed. Every journalistic device was employed to arouse the public against them. A storm of public applause greeted the general verdict of guilty and the death sentences imposed upon seven of the eight men. Lloyd wrote Professor Adams that no governor would dare to pardon them. *The Current* asserted that no court would dare to reverse the verdict.[34]

Lloyd discounted the press hue and cry as an experienced journalist. He concluded that the state's evidence in the trial did not sustain its theory that the Haymarket Riot had resulted from a treasonable conspiracy. Although Adams differed, his-

torians have accepted Lloyd's view. He feared that continued
police violation of the civil rights of suspects would lead to
searches and arrests without warrants and "continental methods of government by police." When the Illinois Supreme
Court rejected the anarchists' appeal in mid-September 1887
he declared privately that it deduced "conspiracy and murder
from membership" in the "Black International" and from a
"violent insanity of public speeches," and could not infer prej-
udice when Gary's bailiff admitted he had packed the jury
panel.[35]

Before the United States Supreme Court refused to hear the
anarchists' appeal George A. Schilling and other influential
Knights in Chicago initiated a movement for executive clemency from Governor Oglesby, seeking, perhaps illogically,
to counteract the employers associations' assertions that organized labor and anarchism were synonymous. Many Knights,
despite hatred of anarchism, were driven by police persecution
and the growing hostility to labor to support this self-styled
"Amnesty" movement. The antilabor reaction that Haymarket
had precipitated in America and Europe, the violations in
Chicago of laborers' civil rights, and Judge Gary's misconduct
of the trial aroused the indignation of liberals, radicals, and
labor leaders. They concluded that the anarchist leaders had
been condemned on dubious evidence for a murder that they
had not committed by a court where their propaganda rather
than their acts was on trial.

In Chicago Presiding Judge Samuel P. McConnell, Judge
Murray F. Tuley, the city's most eminent jurist, and Vice-
President Lyman J. Gage of the First National Bank urged
the Governor to commute the anarchists' sentences. Oglesby
promised Gage privately to commute the sentences of Albert
Parsons, August Spies, Samuel Fielden, and Michael Schwab
if Chicago businessmen requested it. Gage called fifty leading
patrons of his bank together, informed them, and asked that
they request this action so as to avoid making the anarchists
"martyrs." Marshall Field defeated the attempt when many
present who agreed with Gage did not dare to challenge his

indignant protest. However, the influential Potter Palmer and Marvin Hughitt, president of the Chicago and Northwestern Railroad, signed the general clemency petition as did 41,000 other Chicagoans.[36]

Howells risked the ruin of his literary career when he published a letter to Governor Oglesby asking commutation in the *New York Tribune*. Robert G. Ingersoll, noted lawyer, orator, and free thinker, secretly urged the Governor to do this. Henry George, mayoral candidate in New York of the United Labor Party, wrote Oglesby on November 5 that there existed "among great bodies of men a deep and bitter consciousness of social injustice" and that despite total lack of sympathy with anarchism, many were convinced that the Haymarket anarchists "did not get a fair trial."[37] This attitude produced huge clemency mass meetings, long clemency petitions, and the clemency demands of the liberal and labor press in many cities, led by London. Leading Chicago lawyers joined former Senator Lyman Trumbull in condemning the anarchists' trial.

Lloyd and Salter attempted to heal the dangerous social schism by securing clemency with the aid of a retraction by the condemned men, whom they interviewed in Cook County Jail, of their revolutionary creed and violent methods and by their admission of previous errors without implying guilt for the Haymarket bomb. Unless they did this, the pair urged, clemency would be impossible, the hangings would ensue, and organized labor would suffer and be embittered for years.

Before the Ethical Culture Society, with the Lloyds and Stewarts present, Salter pleaded earnestly for commutation as a means to social reconciliation. Despite the bitter opposition of the *Chicago Daily News*, Salter appealed for instruction of immigrant workers in democracy and demonstration that the government was not antilabor or the corrupt instrument of reactionary business. He urged that Americans establish social settlements modeled on Toynbee Hall and circulate Mead's Old South Church lectures on American history and politics.[38]

Lloyd and Salter persuaded Fielden and Schwab to petition

for commutation. Adolph Fisher, Albert Parsons, Friedrich Engel, Louis Ling, and Spies rejected mercy and demanded release as innocent men. All admired Lloyd and appreciated his efforts.

Word that the Lloyds with Salter would attend the Governor's clemency hearing reached Medill, whose *Tribune* demanded that the seven doomed anarchists be hung. Knowing that Bross supported this strongly, perhaps because he did not wish to be balked in this demand for "vengeance," Medill warned Mrs. Lloyd that she and her husband would risk disinheritance if they did this. "Do you suppose that any such consideration will stop Henry Lloyd from doing what he believes is right?" she replied.[39]

Before Governor Oglesby's public clearing began on November 9, Henry D. Lloyd, Salter, and Judge McConnell met him and were promised a private audience afterward. They sat to the left of the Governor's desk when Captain Wm. P. Black, the anarchists' counsel, pleaded for clemency and presented the huge Chicago petition. This was supported by General M. M. Trumbull of Chicago, Samuel Gompers, President of the American Federation of Labor, State Senator Alson J. Streeter, Representative Charles G. Dixon, and labor representatives from a dozen eastern and western cities. The clemency petition of 16,000 London workers was also presented.[40]

Oglesby then granted an audience to Lloyd's party. Salter presented a clemency petition that Lloyd had drafted, bearing signatures of more than a hundred prominent men of Chicago and a dozen states. Salter handed Oglesby also Schwab's confession of the error of his former revolutionary agitation. Lloyd then made "a very powerful" plea.

Accepting the trial court decision as "the law," he urged that public considerations made general clemency imperative. In a sociohistorical argument he attributed the anarchists' words and deeds "to the great labor struggle of our day," and impugned the fairness of their sentence by analysis of the court record, adducing new evidence and appealing to equity and history. Although punishment was justified "justice demands" that it be less than death, he said, while rejecting Prosecutor Julius S. Grinnell's thesis that the bomb had resulted from concentric circles of a general anarchist conspiracy. Lloyd then stated inconsistently that the seven anarchists sentenced to death were "legally guilty of murder for what happened at Haymarket, though none of them did it, but two of them planned it." He insisted that the Governor investigate an affidavit from Otis S. Favor, Chicago merchant, that Black had presented and which charged that Gary's bailiff had admittedly packed the jury panel. Francis Lieber had declared that there must be "no constructive treason." Illinois could not afford precedents of arresting and searching without warrants, and executing men for being "leaders!" The cry of danger, he warned, had been "the favorite device of tyrants" as Aristotle said. With the anarchist leaders "caged" the country would be "perfectly safe." Finally, Lloyd insinuated that the citizens' right to resist unlawful acts had justified resistance to the police invasion of the peaceable Haymarket meeting, May 4, 1886, in defiance of the Mayor's orders."

Lloyd's appearance was dramatic proof of his opposition to alarmed conservatism's antiunionism and of his insistence that the social chasm be bridged. The Governor listened carefully to his long, moderate plea. He accorded equal courtesy to Salter's and Judge McConnell's remarks. He asked them many questions, was impressed by Schwab's contrition, but not by the Favor affidavit. The trio's refusal to talk to the press after the hearing aroused much speculation. The Chicago Trade Assembly delegation presented a petition and left.

Then Joseph Buchanan of Denver, who was attempting to unite the anarchists with the revolutionary Marxists, handed Oglesby a letter from Spies asking to be hung alone for advocating revolution and a letter from Parsons asking that his family be hung with him. Unstrung, Oglesby terminated the private audiences.

He commuted the sentences of Schwab and Fielden to life imprisonment, and left five anarchist leaders to the hangman. He handed the commutation papers to Schilling and State

Senator Richard Burke, who accorded Lloyd the privilege of delivering them to the beneficiaries in recognition of what he had accomplished at Springfield. Twenty-two years later he said to a stenographer, "I shall always think more of this good right arm for the service it rendered to those men."[42]

After delivering the commutation papers Lloyd explained to his father that he had entered the clemency movement because the facts justified commutation, and because of the opportunity to identify himself with the underprivileged. "If it were possible to do everything I would attempt to rescue the victims of all injustice." Their agitators "make mistakes, commit crimes . . . but for all that theirs is the right side. I will try to avoid the mistakes and the crimes but I will stay by the cause." He had hardly eaten or rested for three days.[43]

Just as the discovery of some bombs in Ling's cell immediately before the clemency hearing had prejudiced that adversely, his last-minute suicide revived popular hysteria and precipitated more police outrages. Mrs. Parsons, her children, and Mrs. Lizzie Holmes, the labor organizer, were arrested, jailed, and held until after the hanging. Bross typified the relief of the business community when he wrote in his diary : "The anarchists—four of them—were hanged at 11.54 A.M. The Law, thank the Lord, is vendicated [*sic*]. May the peace of the Lord prevail." The fear of an "impending storm" entertained by the wealthy was dispelled."[44]

That event left Lloyd and Howells depressed, convinced that the dead had been wrongly hanged. Howells wished to be identified with the struggling mass, and began to explore the social problem in his writing. At the Lloyds' Winnetka home during the evening after the hanging the entire family sang Henry D. Lloyd's two-stanza verse, "Voice of the Gallows," featuring Parsons' last words, "Let the People's Voice be heard," to the tune of "Annie Laurie." Then Lloyd wept bitterly, confirming thereby his dedication to the cause of social justice.[45]

He then experienced the fate of the patrician peacemaker. Many friends cut him repeatedly in his clubs and on the streets, a tactic to be employed subsequently against others who departed from rigid conservatism. So exceptional was an invitation from James A. Hunt of Winnetka to attend a meeting of the Chicago Literary Club together that he preserved his note, endorsed, "J. A. Hunt after Nov. 11, '87."[46] Bross informed him bluntly that he had disgraced the family by his clemency plea at Springfield, an ominous portent.

Lloyd and Salter sustained each other. Lloyd circulated his "plea" among journalists, lawyers, judges, and businessmen. David Swing promised to preach interclass understanding and sympathy. Charles H. Ham, Chicago's advocate of manual training in the schools and a fellow antimonopolist, complimented Lloyd on having stated the amnesty movement's "philosophy" and attributed its limited victory to Oglesby's political character and antilabor bias. The wife of the French Consul-General in Chicago thanked Lloyd for his work in the anarchists' behalf.

From London the Fabian Clarke congratulated him : "You will never regret having said a word for justice & mercy while the whole press of America was howling for these men's blood." Mead wrote to Lloyd and Salter that they had been *"Christians* enough through this whole trying ordeal," and informed Lloyd of the Tolstoian views motivating Howells' request for clemency that had led to his abuse by the "cheap Jacks of the newspapers."[47]

Meanwhile, Stewart had exposed Buchanan's attempts to merge the anarchists and revolutionary Marxists and exploit the "martyrdom" of the executed anarchists whose funeral he stage-managed. In "Ballot more Powerful than Bullet" in the *Knights of Labor* he asserted that "honest workingmen" had no sympathy with secret negotiations or any resort to force, and declared that only the vote could emancipate "wage-slaves." Until they employed the ballot as "an honest weapon" laborers would have to submit to "police brutality" and "every other injustice and outrage." The advocates of force were their "very worst enemies." Thus, he held the English-speaking workers and most immigrants to the democratic faith when despair born of defeat of the eight-hour movement and repression of the unions might have led many to join the revolutionaries. Buchanan ceased his conspiratorial activity.[48]

PATRICIAN AND PLEBIAN

Lloyd and Stewart drew together into a warm friendship between gentleman and workingman. "Bert" supplied the Winnetkan with data on litigation between the railroads and the Knights' co-operative mines. He loaned Lloyd books on the labor question, including Gladden's *Applied Christianity* (1887), the classic of the emerging Social Gospel movement. Lloyd declared to "Bert," "The Commonwealth—a *truly* Christian State —must be the religious institution of the future," a neo-Calvinist objective that henceforth permeated his social thought. He took the Stewarts to the Ethical Culture Society repeatedly, and entertained them and their children.[49]

He concluded correctly that the executed anarchists had been "killed because property, authority, and public believed that they came to bring not reform but revolution, not peace but a sword," because "vested right" invoked self-preservation. Their deaths had been "in vain" unless from them came "a resurrection and a new life." The intimation in this that the executed anarchists were martyrs exhibited a bias derived from his new championship of the underprivileged and the partial defeat of his clemency effort. This view was shared by many. It stimulated trades unionism and ultimately a later amnesty movement in behalf of the three imprisoned anarchist leaders. In the same manuscript statement Lloyd elaborated upon "social love" for the first time as a force that would abolish business abuses, luxury, political corruption, and institute social justice. Human history is "a history of emancipation," he believed.[50] Gladden's influence had broadened the theoretical basis and practical scope of his new liberalism.

Although many historians agree that the executed anarchists were martyrs, it should be observed that had they been prosecuted for their five-year public conspiracy, and had a patient investigation been made of the origin of the Haymarket bomb before securing grand jury indictments, the perpetrators of both crimes could have been punished for their actual deeds. A dangerous precedent of punishing men for one crime when they are guilty of another would have been avoided, and safeguards against mass hysteria would have been. strengthened. Instead, the post-Haymarket witch hunt and newspaper trial weakened these and strengthened conservative stereotypes at the expense of civil liberties and sound judicial practice, and identified the labor movement in the minds of many citizens with alien, anarchist, and revolutionary doctrines in a manner that retarded the development of the labor movement.

This became clear to perceptive Chicagoans after the Chicago Bar Association dinner on Christmas Day in honor of Judge Gary, the lion of conservatism in Cook County. In introducing him Wirt Dexter declared that the legal profession was the "conservative bulwark" of the state, and in the person of Gary would "hang . . . armed men with destructive theories." The Judge then aroused the diners to frenzied enthusiasm by attacking labor organization, the burden of whose "tyranny," he said, far exceeded those of "monopolies of capital," which, though calling for a remedy, were "so light as to be scarcely felt," and of political corruption that caused only temporary tax increases. As for labor unions' "tyranny," he asked, "What can we do to break it down?"[51]

This gave Lloyd an opportunity. After Medill declined to print it he replied to Gary in a letter to the *Chicago Herald* that appeared on January 3, 1888. It was entitled "Labor and Monopoly." Far more dramatically than his appearance before Governor Oglesby, this communication aligned Lloyd with trades unionism and the opponents of political and business "Bourbonism" in Chicago. "Neither public opinion nor the facts," Lloyd said, sustained Gary. Monopoly prices of kerosene, anthracite coal, gas rates, New York land rents, telegraph rates, railroad rates refuted the Judge's claim that no monopoly deprived people of the "necessities of life." Some of these, Lloyd remarked scornfully, were that no American could "be robbed without redress," be deprived of property by "taxthieveries" of corrupt officials, or be denied the right to judge individually of the burden of monopoly. What "the Judge . . . hardly feels . . . are known to the poor and the middle class as bitter privations," which the correlation of the death rate of the poor with Pennsylvania coal prices documented.

Lloyd then cited Andrew Carnegie's assertion that trades unions improved workers' living standards and labor-management relations. The greatest hope of the day, he said, was for law enforcement and "equal" constitutional government as the result of wage-earners' discussions of "wrongs and remedies." Labor would lead and "the farmers will follow." As for the "arrogant assumptions of labor organizations," Gary should study Great Britain's repeal of the common law of conspiracy and learn that the trades unions' great objective was "to counteract the social, political, and industrial ills of factory life," prevent competitive wage reductions, find work for the unemployed, and restore laborers' contractual rights. The attempt by the Judge, Bar Association, and "money power" to break down the unions would certainly fail. Since any "Trust" coming before the Judge would receive "light punishment," the posterity that "judges the judgements of the courts" would see in his speech a flood of light "pouring backwards," illuminating his conduct of the anarchists' trial.[52] So it did. Gary had thrown down the gauntlet on the issue of biased, anti-labor, promonopoly justice. Before all Chicago Lloyd picked it up, threw it in his face, and made his own disinheritance certain.

At the price of that and social ostracism he purchased the undying love and loyalty of Chicago's wage-earners, and of many of its forward-looking businessmen, lawyers, journalists, and clergy. The Trades and Labor Assembly circulated 50,000 copies of his *Herald* article. Farmer and labor leaders experimented that year in the new Union Labor party with the political alliance that he advised. In New York, Boston, and London the *Herald* piece, which he circulated, enhanced the admiration of liberals, radicals, and intellectuals for Lloyd's new leadership.

To Salter and Stewart he now added Clarence S. Darrow

as a lieutenant. That young attorney, educated to liberalism by a free-thinking father and by studying "Making Bread Dear," Altgeld's *Our Penal Machinery and Its Victims,* and George's classic, arrived in Chicago in time to read "Labor and Monopoly." He wrote Lloyd immediately to thank him, declaring, "it will do much good. Organized labor is fortunate in having such a champion." Although Lloyd's friends, James Hunt in Winnetka and Sarah C. Moseley of Newport, took exceptions to his reply to Gary and accepted the Judge's view of labor unions and monopolies, intelligent, liberal businessmen appreciated Lloyd's gallant intervention into the dangerous post-Haymarket situation.

Sixteen years later W. W. Catlin, a Chicago banker, remembered how he had deliberately incurred "the bitter opposition of nearly all those powers in life which even the most influential desire to placate," when, disinterestedly, he "took up the fight in behalf of despised and hated men, who were denied simple justice." Naturally sensitive, he had risked the respect and good will of Chicago in that "losing fight." But, Catlin said, it "will always remain, a glorious victory for the cause of human welfare throughout the world."[53] In January 1888, however, it was evident that Lloyd's career had completed a great transition from publicist extraordinary of the *Chicago Tribune*'s greatest years of national influence to independent knight errant of social justice. In this role, despite ill health, social pressure, and ostracism, he would win equal distinction. His preparation for it must now be examined.

Chapter IX

A Welfare Philosophy: "The New Conscience"

STUDIES

LLOYD'S RECOVERY of health was not without discouraging relapses. Until the early summer of 1886, as he wrote later to Major Huntington, "More than once but for my wife I would have fallen back into utter hopelessness."[1] Basic soundness of body and mind, and the therapeutic effects of his wife's understanding, cheery encouragement, and wise care facilitated his recovery. Together he and his wife conquered his insomnia and restored his working efficiency. He worked regularly at his desk each morning. After luncheon she read aloud to him until he relaxed and slept for an hour. After more desk work he took a brisk walk. There followed a sociable dinner and evening with "the boys" or numerous guests, or dining out, or atendance at meetings. He realized that his breakdown and ensuing "brain fag"[2] had been caused by excessive work on the *Tribune* and independent writing. His new regimen prevented its recurrence. He adhered to it for the remainder of his life.

William Bross attempted to help his recovery. In late February 1886 he persuaded Lloyd to travel with him to Colorado and then to Mexico. Lloyd's insomnia revived while they were touring Mexico City. Pleading that the altitude did not agree with him, he left for Winnetka on March 11th while Bross remained another week. Yet, when the Lloyds met him on his return to Chicago he described his son-in-law as "very well."[3] In May Lloyd travelled to Europe with a friend but after six weeks there returned unexpectedly.

171

Meanwhile, convinced that correct principles must guide constructive action, he studied philosophy, history, economics, politics, and social reform in preparation for the role of social reformer to which he dedicated himself. So thorough was this that he emerged from retirement early in 1888 as the exponent of a new social philosophy, and soon became the publicist and leader of a crusade for social justice that continued into the twentieth century. This satisfied traditional family impulses while bringing to logical fruition his penchant for applied ethics and democratic welfare theory. After presenting his new philosophy to the public he was persuaded by continued study, the logic of his thought, travel abroad, and campaigns against continuing "Bourbon" abuses to assume gradually a more radical position. This brought him to Fabianism during 1893-94.

For the role of gentleman reformer he found inspiration in English and American examples. Sir Charles Dilke was campaigning in Britain for a "New Liberalism" akin to his own, which would foster wage-earner welfare via social legislation, voluntary slum clearance, and acceptance of collective bargaining. Wealthy John Ruskin was demanding a social democracy characterized by brotherhood, social love, co-operation, mutual service between rich and poor, love of beauty and high ethics. He attempted to create an "Ideal Commonwealth" based upon these concepts and a revived medieval freeman's co-operative craftsmanship and agriculture in his utopian St. George's Guild. He demanded that political economy make "the natural order conform to man's moral and material needs." In *Unto This Last* and *Munera Pulveris* he struck chords with which Lloyd's heart never ceased to vibrate.[4]

He had met William Morris, who had turned from poetry and interior decorating to attack the social problem in lectures on socialism that were circulated by Hyndman's Social Democratic Federation and his own Socialist League. Charles Booth was making his monumental inquest into London's East End with the aid of such dedicated upper-class saints as Beatrice Potter. In this as in St. George's Guild and at Toyn-

bee Hall Lloyd had witnessed in operation the awakened social
conscience of upper and middle-class Britain and its universities. He had met the Christian Socialists and read their publications as well.[5]

More suggestive to Lloyd, perhaps, were Emerson and Wendell Phillips, whom he had known when a young man. Each
had abandoned his profession to lead in unpopular social
criticism, in pioneering in applied ethics, and in advocating
needed reforms despite the opposition and antipathy of vested
interests. During his youth Lloyd had imbibed the philosophy
of reform that they had embodied. The obligation to reshape
the world in which he lived by eradicating evils and creating
the good he had long regarded as a controlling imperative.
Similarly, he had cultivated the self-reliance, subjective self-
sufficiency, and intellectuality focused upon practical problems
that Emerson said must characterize "The American Scholar."
Admiration for Emerson's *Works* had encouraged Lloyd to
perfect the epigram as an effective method of truth-telling. In
his new liberal journalism and magazine essays he had employed it brilliantly as a double-edged blade, illustrating before
he too ascended the lecture platform that "Words are also
actions." As he prepared for his independent reform career
he cast himself for the role expressed in the Concord sage's
other dictum, "Always the seer is a sayer." In Winnetka he
enjoyed the face-to-face intercourse with nature and his fellow
townsmen that had distinguished Emerson's life. Then friendship with "Bert" Stewart produced a direct interest in the lowly
and the everyday facts of the working world such as Phillips
had achieved during Reconstruction. Like both prototypes
Lloyd had risen by 1886 to the selfless, sacrificial devotion to
moral virtues that fostered the general weal irrespective of the
cost.

Until 1885 Lloyd had been primarily an empiricist in his
objectives and preoccupation with practical issues, subordinating thought to the requirements of constructive action. Yet, he
had cultivated the idealizing faculty as Emerson had done as
essential to advancing the public good. Lloyd's general welfare

theory had resulted from the interaction of his driving do-goodism with necessity, guided by his own logic, Jevons, and historical economics. For years Lloyd had exhibited an Emersonian impatience with institutions and policies at odds with ethical and human values. His new liberalism attempted to harmonize Emersonian individualism with the practical need for political action to correct inequities. Cultivation of the fullest individual development remained until 1886 with Lloyd as an enduring objective.

His recreational reading together with his wife had left him ignorant of the German sources of Emerson's and Carlyle's thought, and unacquainted with the St. Louis Movement's neo-Hegelianism and the vogue among American philosophers for the lamented Thomas Hill Green, Oxford University's great neo-Kantian. Both developments indicated that other Americans were seeking also to resolve the dilemma posed by post-Appomattox Darwinism and continuing popular attachment to romantic values and Jacksonian principles.

Lloyd's new studies weakened Emerson's influence upon his formal thought and social objectives, but not upon his self-conceived role as reformer. As he became active initially as a reform essayist and lecturer he exhibited a heightened subjectivism, intense ethicism, and articulation as "seer." Yet the substance, justifications, and methodology of his developing welfare philosophy deviated progressively from transcendentalist individualism. But, while crusading in behalf of the underprivileged he evinced an independence of tradition, insistence upon the priority of American necessities, and the intellectual independence that characterized Emerson's American scholar. Like Emerson, also, Lloyd was not a systematic philosopher. He produced no unified philosophic system, although he advanced to author of books. Beginning as an eclectic Emersonian in his studies he became formulator of a uniquely influential social philosophy which, though unsynthesized, rested upon an Emersonian frame of reference. That Lloyd advocated no utopian communitarianism during 1886-90 such as Edward Bellamy popularized may be attributed partially to Emerson's coolness to Brook Farm and Fruitlands a half-century earlier. Lloyd like Emerson stressed the divinity of the individual man and rebelled from the Christian Church as an outmoded institution. He too sought new revelation while retaining profound respect for spiritual values and the influence of religion upon the social process. This attitude made him susceptible to the influence of the Ethical Culture Society as its Chicago lecturer, Wm. M. Salter, became his guide in the study of philosophy.

Lloyd had accepted earlier Emerson's correlation of the development of governmental forms and law with the progress of thought, and had concluded that all institutions were "outward expressions of inner concepts of the individual or social mind." While he too would build on ideas "for eternity" he placed greater weight upon the role of intuition, after Emerson's use of Coleridge's theory, than at first appears. As a publicist he had already guided men "by showing them facts amidst appearances." Self-relying and self-directed he had won the hostility of "educated society," resisting vulgar prosperity, communicating heroic sentiments and "the conclusions of History." Now he would be "free and brave." His very championship of the lowly whom he would elevate followed the literary tradition of Goldsmith, Wordsworth, and Carlyle who had contributed so significantly to the democratic revolution that had emancipated "The American Scholar." And now, as a fearless hero, Lloyd sought the reformer's "purer frame." By arousing humanity to a new enthusiasm he would persuade it to achieve the impossible once more by making all men lovers in behalf of social justice.[6]

During the spring of 1887 Lloyd read idealist philosophy with Salter, borrowing books on Kant and Hegel from him. He purchased heavily from Stevens and American booksellers books on philosophy, history, religion, education, socialism, and domestic and foreign reform movements and pertinent periodicals that facilitated his intellectual and practical reorientation. While he also kept his technical library on American business and agriculture up to date, many new additions dealt with the labor movement and radical thought, such as those by Morris, Hyndman, Marx, Engels, and Kautsky. He purchased American antislavery publications with emphasis upon Phillips. Salter's bride, an intellectual, accompanied her husband to Winnetka, where she became Mrs. Lloyd's warm friend.[7] Lloyd and Salter discovered a kindred aversion to socially conservative Protestantism, and both rejected the harsh Manchester creed before they intervened together in the clemency movement of 1887.

Salter's *The Problem of Poverty* had attempted to dispel indifference to the poor and rejected Ricardo's wages-fund that doomed workers to a subsistence wage. Salter denied that poverty was necessary or inevitable. With Felix Adler he demanded "a new morality" of employers, "a new conscience" about using the fruits of "unrequited labor."[8] This approach appealed to Lloyd. As rebels from their era's antisocial practices and dominant intellectual currents they struck hands in a reform partnership that bore early fruit.

As early as 1886 a new direction in Lloyd's thought became apparent when he repudiated Mill's "man does as little work as possible" and substituted "the greatest good of all" for the Benthamite formula. His notebook entries stressed reform achieved by "our oppressed classes . . . through law" applied to predatory man, monopoly, concentrated wealth. That "the moral sense of mankind has reached a stage of revolt which demands a wide, sweeping, radical change" was evinced to him by the popularity of the works of Emerson, Carlyle, and Ruskin, business opposition to unfair competition, revolt from political corruption, and the labor protest. Then, with Salter, he traced the sources of Emerson's inspiration and the Ethical Culture movement back to Kant and Comte. He also read Aristotle's *Politics* and Morley's analysis of John Stuart Mill.

Although Kant reasoned a priori rather than empirically Lloyd was inspired by his works and especially by his moral earnestness, as can be inferred fairly from Lloyd's subsequent writing although his correspondence and notebooks do not reveal specifically what he derived from him. Kant's works intensified

his already well-developed sense of moral obligation by clari-
fying his understanding of the categorical imperative. They
strengthened his insistence upon correct ethical principles and
his desire to put them into practice by effective reforms. He
concluded that what was needed was a primary, absolute
ethics plus a secondary relativist ethics to implement it in
changing situations. Previous indebtedness of his neo-Calvinist
ethics of 1872–85 to the categorical imperative, now better
understood, furthered this harmonization of the former's absolutism with the empiricism and historicism of his new liberalism.
Before long he attempted to base his social thought upon this
ethical dualism, anticipating Abraham Edel's *Ethical Judge-
ment*. Ultimately, Lloyd had to face the contradiction in this
position. At an imprecise date, probably in the early nineties,
he would jot on a card, "Truth—There is no truth. It is to
be made. There is no absolute truth, final, and never will be.
There will be whatever truth is created," a pragmatist position
that William James would reach partially in 1909.[9] Derived
in part from Thomas Hill Green's discussion of human rights
and Mazzini, this statement was formulated only after Lloyd
had associated with John Dewey and other philosophers while
lecturing in summer schools.

Kantian free will and its sense of duty confirmed Lloyd's
commitment to social reform to be achieved by education and
appeals to individuals to choose right courses of action. His
study of Kant strengthened his attachment to Emerson but
did not divert his thought completely from English empiricism.
Lloyd's straddling of the absolutist-relativist issue in ethics was
related also to an interest in Comte, whose works he now reread. Comte's insistence that society could be regenerated by
empirical applications of utilitarian ethics to politics, society,
and the economy had supplemented Jevons' influence and
Ruskinite humanism in the development of Lloyd's welfare
economic thought. His interest in Comte was highly selective,
however. While assisting Adler and Salter in the Ethical Culture movement's venture into applied ethics and adaptation
of Comte's religion of humanity, he rejected his authoritarian-

ism, his paternalistic two-class "Système" of rich and poor, and his depreciation of women.

Comte re-enforced Emerson's emphasis upon the dominant role of an élite of dedicated intellectuals in social regeneration. Equally important to Lloyd was Comte's substitution of social altruism working through moral regeneration for individual selfishness as the psychologic dynamic of social change. This validated Ruskinite social love as the activating force in social reform, which Lloyd also accepted. He concluded that "the associated spirit of Humanity" was the creative factor in civilization's advance, but differed with Comte in holding that this was "not God . . . but it is the face of God on earth," led by "lofty" righteous individuals whose high ideals fructified "in the bosom of a common Humanity" and "became efficient agents in human welfare."[10] That Lloyd regarded Comte's religion of humanity with reservations was indicated by his decision not to join the Ethical Culture Society.

Kant and Comte belonged to different philosophic categories. As an eclectic driven by the imperatives of practical problems, Lloyd's limited fusion of idealism with positivism validated his expanded new liberalism and engendered a dynamic optimism. This he confirmed by association with the Ethical liberals and free-thinkers who attended Salter's lectures and patronized the *Radical Review*. That circle admired Lloyd's long new liberal crusade, his championship of labor, and his sincerity, enthusiasm, and vibrant, sympathetic personality.

Salter introduced him to Felix Adler, founder of the movement,[11] who taught that sincere adherents dedicated themselves and their surplus wealth to elevating the wage-earners. This the Lloyds accepted as an irrevocable commitment after the partially successful campaign for clemency for the Haymarket anarchists in November 1887. Lloyd had concluded before this that America was nearing "the end" of its "political liberties" unless it could discover "industrial liberties to set free a new body of fresh, ingenuous, generous, enthusiastic, independent, virtuous minds to seek a further social good."[12] These he determined to discover and cultivate, while aiding the ethical revival that was spreading to socially enlightened Protestant clergy. Simultaneously, released from editorial frustrations on the *Chicago Tribune,* Lloyd formulated the philosophy that guided his reform career thenceforth.

A NEW SOCIAL PHILOSOPHY

As he formulated a broader social philosophy adequate to existing problems Lloyd synthesized principles derived from Kant, Hegel, Comte, T. H. Green, and the ethical movement with those derived earlier from Emerson, Jevons, Carlyle, and Ruskin. He stressed the ideological basis of institutions whose growth fulfilled the promise of the principles they were created to realize, as in the law where rights took precedence over duties. In institutional fulfillment of germinal concepts he detected indications of the course of future social development. He derived from Emerson's naturalist symbolism insight into such social symbols as "social contract," "equality," "fraternity."[13]

His eclecticism produced certain logical and philosophic straddles, inconsistencies, vagueness, and unpursued intuitions. Lloyd derived helpful concepts from philosophers of different categories that assisted and justified his reform career and its purposes, but he did not attempt to synthesize fully these borrowed ideas and those of his own devising into a completely unified system. He did achieve a partial synthesis despite repeated interruption of his studies by practical reform work. Idealist influences now dominated his thought, although he retained and employed the empirical method. This was justified by Kant's experimental bias, Comte's positivism and Green's fusion of experience with the ideal.

Green's influence sharpened the focus of Lloyd's ethics upon practical problems. It validated his repudiation of Social Darwinism, acceptance of the categorical imperative, and assertion of society's responsibility for individual well-being. Green's "Lectures on the English Commonwealth" provided historical perspective for radical democratic reform toward which Lloyd was tending. Green's thesis that moral progress produced by the perfectionist impulse was the indispensable preliminary to constitutional government, was an adaptation from Aristotle that appealed to Lloyd. So did Green's novel assertion that civil rights were a functional social product, entailing upon the beneficiaries the moral obligation to advance "the common well-being." Since the free individual was a social being whose development and civil opportunities depended upon moral progress, interference with individual liberty was justified when laissez faire prevented reforms "promoting conditions favourable to moral life."[4]

Green's political theory had appealed strongly to Oxford students as Britain confronted its wage-earners' insistence that state action was essential to protect their welfare in the machine age. It validated the general welfare and statist aspects of Lloyd's new liberalism, which he had formulated while Green's Oxford disciples were campaigning against London's slums. Green pointed toward an expanding democratic collectivism of an as yet unidentified character, which was glamorized by his example as a devoted liberal reformer and the dynamic perfectionism of his thought.

Lloyd's social philosophy was based upon an empirical and neo-Hegelian use of history, empirical and neo-Kantian ethics, Green's functionalism, positivism's social altruism, Aristotelian perfectionism, *and* the principles of association and co-operation stressed by Comte and Ruskin. It exhibited, as David W. Noble observes, an inevitable metaphysical dualism. This derived from Lloyd's attempt to merge empiricism's preoccupation with concrete experience and idealist philosophy's emphasis upon the supreme importance and influence of thought and the spirit. Lloyd projected this dualism into his ethical theory, the psychology that underpinned his theory of progress, and his theory of progress. Paradoxical though this was it justified and gave direction to a crusade for social justice that was implied by his commitment to the cause of "the opressed."

As early as 1886 Lloyd had observed that the Marxian labor theory of value "has too many exceptions." With Jevons he concluded that value was what could be obtained for a product or service in the market—"search for 'natural' value" in which labor was a factor along with genius, fashion, and "unscrupulousness, . . . search for absolute ethics" as the basis for economic policy, he wrote in his notebook, adding sagely that morbidity and mortality statistics disproved Marx. Instead of his ideas those of "Carlyle, Ruskin and Emerson about relations of men to each other and society" possessed "scientific value and economic precision." Lloyd desired a law to destroy monopolistic combinations in anticipation of the Sherman Act, in opposition to Marx, and would exterminate millionaires as "social saurians." The public interest was paramount to class and monopoly claims, he believed, since neither of them could Darwinism justify.[15]

He related individualist and statist concepts to the ideas of progress and civilization. The individualist aspect of his thought was re-enforced by the influence of Thomas Davidson, friend of William James and William T. Harris. Lloyd found "solid ground" for the statist aspect in Hegel's organic conception of the *"state"* whose "divine power" was "greater than any of its parts." To the "finer" national consciousness with its "sympathetic and ethical standards," a concept derived partially from Emerson, he looked "for all patriotic action, all protection of women, children and the weak," for the "consecrated sacred creed." Patriotism embodied "the life of the whole of the community" and the submission of individual wishes and welfare to the "nation's." In the state there "shines a great principle of Order and Progress."[16]

Individualism, however, contributed "the great leaps forward to discovery, colonization, invention, science, and in leadership." How to curb the state "so that individual liberty shall be saved," and how to restrain individualism lest society disintegrate was a pragmatic problem for "each generation to debate and adjust for itself according to its needs." History recorded an alternation in control between individualism and the state. Among signs of progress was man's ability to focus science, "concerted human effort," and humanitarian agencies upon social ills. Also, the state's repeated resumption of accumulations of antisocial power or wealth that individuals or minority groups used against it disclosed a "law of survival of common-wealth over individual rapacity." Hence, the Industrial Revolution would be followed by equally revolutionary social changes. The internationalization resulting from modern communication, transport, travel, and interchange of technology and ideas indicated a destiny to be achieved "on the broad basis of the ultimate union of all men."[17]

While accepting Green's assertion that fullest individual development was realized in social relations, Lloyd identified an "unerring instinct" impelling men to oppose social encroachments on individual freedom : "the last thing men learn to do is to act with success collectively." Yet, with Green and Ruskin he held that co-operative achievements were superior : "a finer thing than the finest individual is the union in works of love, sympathy, statesmanship, industry, of individuals of all degrees." Yet, although the state and lesser forms of co-operation were central in human progress, individuality should be cultivated lest all be swept into "a diluted cosmopolitanism." Since man's "sixth sense" was his "social sense," the problem was "how to subordinate to the public welfare its modern economy, press, and political parties whose control by the wealthy made them instruments of class dominance." Lloyd learned from Aristotle's *Politics* that the greatest crimes were motivated by ambition, not necessity. He deduced, despite the prevailing corruption, that democracy was a means of selecting "the pre-eminently virtuous in the community" to rule. Recognising that the modern financial system was essentially collectivist and the facts of property "mainly Darwinian," he held that the law followed Christ, Ruskin, and Carlyle who "believe that sympathy and justice are as much economic forces as greed and force" though at "a great distance."

From law and history Lloyd deduced that the "development of the individual and of the common consciousness" occurred simultaneously. "The law of sympathy, the equalizing of human rights, the Golden Rule" tested the utility of institutions. Failing this, like slavery, feudalism, guilds, and "the wages system," they will be superseded by "more successful experiments" in human relations. Recognizing that bad environments produced the bad, he believed that the former could be changed so as to produce the good. "If we wish the morally, socially fittest to survive we must provide the moral, social environment needed." Thus he avoided the double-entendre of natural selection by asserting the validity of what may termed a tellic environmentalism. The production of Vanderbilts and Rockefellers as 'the fittest" by a selfish civilization could be prevented by reform of the latter. For unrestrained individualism Lloyd would substitute a "body of social unities co-operating" as "a higher individual." Thus he fused Hegels theory of social self-consciousness with Lester Frank Ward's theory of telic progress, as expressed in his criticism of Social Darwinism before the American Economic Association.[18] History was partly the "history of association," the expression of human brotherhood, Lloyd added, thereby broadening the Emersonian concept.

Immediately, reformers should oppose capitalistic combinations producing "the multiplication of the poor and the unemployed." Ultimately, they must advance civilization and the better sharing of it, opposing equally capitalist abuses and labor anarchism. Society must develop a co-operative cure for child labor and unemployment caused by monopoly and technological change, or "submit to catastrophe and decay." This fused antimonopolism with association and Ruskinite co-operation. Association was the reformer's chief instrument in promoting progress and civilization; paternalism and pauperism should be avoided. Society's obligation ended when it corrected abuses and provided opportunities for employment. In 1887-88 Lloyd wished to retain a wide area for free economic endeavor.

"What society may do varies with the associative power of the people," he concluded. Society had to break up, reform, or revolutionize its institutions periodically. By re-equalizing "all conditions of struggle" and re-establishing "equilibrium constantly disturbed by fraud, . . . strength, opportunity, and accident" it could prevent violent attempts to change conditions. Therefore, the social sympathy demanding protection of women and children in industry was a "regular" economic force. However, the failure of utopian communitarian experiments demonstrated that "the social problem must be worked out in the bosom of society, not in separation from it." While Lloyd imbibed little of the British socialism that he had witnessed in 1885 and 1886, and was still influenced by Emersonian individualism, the logic of Green's social theory obliged him to re-examine collectivism. In 1889 he concluded that socialism was government restored to control of land and extended to industries which "it can administer better than private enterprise."[19]

The next year he listed "Extensions" needed for reform, i.e., of the Ten Commandments to modern types of stealing, of "Public Peace for Private War—in industry," of co-operation in education and defense, of "brotherly love into the markets," of "Anti-privilege into industrial relations, Of individualism, Of Socialism," "of representative government and no taxation without representation into property and business," "Of property—from some to all," and "Of Patriotism—into love of all men." His developing theory included, therefore, a larger share of collectivism than hitherto.[20]

Progress resulted from the interaction of individualism and social organization, he observed. It was "quite in harmony that the evolution of a higher type of man, and a higher type of association should go on together," interacting. This suggested "how tolerant strong communities can afford to be of those who propose measures either for the enfranchisement of the individual or his associate action." The "centrifugal" principle of "sympathy of the Golden Rule" and the "centripetal principle of the individual's right to "take for himself the rights withheld by privileged classes" would unlock the door of social reform. While inferring from Green's assertion that Locke's and Rousseau's social contracts were myths, that new reform movements could be precipitated by fictionalizing the truth, Lloyd concluded with Comte that the reformer's immediate task was to elevate business, political, and international ethics. Since the quality of association was proportionate to the intelligence and morality of "the controlling individuals," leadership "of the highest spirits" was essential. Adelbert Hamilton documented the need for higher business morality when he told Lloyd that Philip Armour's agents on the Board of Trade periodically cleaned out every one ruthlessly without regard "to anything that is said or done."[21]

Lloyd's philosophy justified inclusion of the weak, wicked, and ignorant in universal suffrage since those elements were "perfectable" and would "do best when made free and responsible." His political theory was unconcerned with mechanics, but his ethical theory sought ever more effective means of implementation. Vitally interested in the relation of poverty and politics and how special privileges enriched men and corporations, he detected behind primary fortunes such as A. T. Stewart's "a derivative circle" created by favoritism such as Rockefeller's. Sarcastically he revised hypocritical business shibboleths to read : "Thrift—with a franchise. Industry—with a Trust. Enterprise—'on advice of counsel'." Observing how Chicago police deprived the populace of personal liberty while pretending to fear "nihilism," he unmasked industrial magnates' hypocritical defense of individual rights while their combinations destroyed those of "whole classes." Intelligent voting should produce police protection of constitutional liberties, he concluded.[22] Agreeing with Henry George that a developing gulf between great wealth and great poverty would wreck civilization as in the past, he rejected his panacea and favored privately the almost equally radical step of guaranteeing each worker a job during good behavior. Industrial relations were not more "sacred" than those of the family which the law regulated, he believed.

Reformers must create "a true civilization" in which highly developed individuals concur spontaneously in beneficent use of social forces as "a great, visible, benevolent, all-present embodiment of the Fatherhood of God and Brotherhood of Man." This would demonstrate "the strength, tenderness, and wisdom of universal love" as exhibited in "the associated spirit of Humanity" and inspired by "lofty individuals" on the "summit of righteousness." Justification for this semi-Positivist élitism Lloyd derived from Emerson and Mill's and Bryce's emphasis upon the civic and social value of the small minority "with convictions." "Life is . . . most sacred," he added, "when spent for the right, least so, when saved selfishly."[23] He held with Green that men would "grow more perfect" in social action. As high ideals, sympathy, and intelligence became "more widespread," the wretched would be "succored," and "the cruelty of the wickedly strong will be more peremptorily repressed." By "being faithful to his brother" man could free the masses from poverty, ignorance, and disease, restore "the happy security of childhood," and possibly discover God.

On the American frontier—he observed five years before Frederick Jackson Turner presented his famous thesis—existed great social equality, "most kindheartedness of man to man, less wolfishness in preying upon fellows, greater ability on the part of the community to think and act together." Contrasted with its "freedom and efficiency" were the antebellum slaveholders and the "Gilded Age's" cynical perversion of "Toil, Thrift and Temperance," into "Toil—with a charter, Thrift—in charging all the traffic will bear, Temperance—with a Trust, and The old flag—with an appropriation."[24]

Lloyd's social philosophy was more pregnant in its ethical and reformist implications than any other contemporary American theory, and richer in its individualism, humanity, tolerance, and stress upon the potentialities of free association and democratic action in business and politics. Its sincerity and impingement upon the Jacksonian and humanitarian traditions, its pragmatic orientation, its optimism and perfectionism, and its moral earnestness and self dedication carried an inevitable appeal to those alarmed by gross abuses. Its realism and gradualism contrasted sharply with Bellamy's utopianism of 1887 and the "Golden Age" promised by Henry George.

Lloyd's logic cut deep into the superficial reform spirit of the late eighties. Ironically he observed that the Chicago Literary Club wished to make politics unmercenary without making the life behind politics so, and that "Protestants vainly and unscientifically want to separate religion and education" and make the latter "materialistic and individual."[25] When at Sebago, Maine, in 1888 he wrote in his notebook that the "new religion, the revolution that is now impending" would practice as well as acknowledge the "humanity, brotherhood and divinity of every man" that Christianity had asserted and make "justice" its first work always. Freeing "brothers, sons of God, men" from "tenement houses, rags, hunger, twelve hours' work, etc.," the new "Christ" would "teach no submission, resistance to tyrants is obedience to God, everywhere; in industry just as much as in politics."

The goal of Lloyd's social philosophy was a welfare democracy evolving as man's associate power increased, resting upon social love as its psychological basis instead of Ricardian and Darwinian individualism. He envisaged an experimental attack upon existing problems, guided by the values and principles that he postulated. Such a theory and method implied a catholic social reform assisting all attempts at amelioration. His pre-1886 new liberalism had been essentially middle class. His new philosophy transcended social barriers with its objectives of social justice, all-embracing brotherhood, and comprehensive reform. Its potential appeal to American and British Protestants, emerging social Catholicism, new liberals, farmers, labor leaders, and social reformers was great. Into Lloyd it instilled a sense of mission and the dynamic obligation to disseminate it as the proper basis of a comprehensive reorganization of machine age society. Hence, he proferred his new philosophy to America first by personal example, as in the clemency movement, and then in his "Child Labor" article and "Labor and Monopoly" reply to Judge Gary. A more formal presentation awaited the appropriate opportunity.

Chicago Reality

The climate of opinion into which he interjected it was not entirely unfavorable. President Grover Cleveland had rejected the high tariff and denounced industrial combinations and "Trusts" as oppressive of the people in a vigorous message to Congress on December 6, 1887. During 1888 the popular demands for reform of the civil service, land policy, tariff, and for forest conservation and antitrust legislation evinced a dynamic realism and moral revulsion from crudities of party "bosses" and promoter-speculators. The burgeoning farmers' alliances were rallying the agrarian "producing masses" for a new crusade against economic injustice.[26] However, the labor movement languished, while renewed prosperity, fear of "radicalism" engendered by Haymarket, and a slight improvement in state governments encouraged fickle citizens to withhold support from reform organizations that opposed corrupt municipal régimes in cities such as New York and Philadelphia.

In Chicago Mayors John A. Roche and Dewitt Cregier gave Marshall Field, Yerkes, the railroads, and business the administration they desired, while the annual corruption fund rewarded police repression of trades unions. As the labor movement split these became non-partisan. Emerging "labor skates" offered to deliver the labor vote to the highest bidders. Socialists organized a labor party of their own.[27]

Yerkes introduced during Roche's administration the business politics for which New York and Philadelphia were notorious. He gave an illuminating lesson also in corporation financial manipulation to the prairie capitalists whom he confidently outwitted. Acquision of the North and West Division traction companies, seizure of the municipal tunnels under the Chicago River, dominance of "The Loop," corrupt procurement of approval of these coups and needed franchises from the Common Council, and reincorporation of his traction companies with swollen capitalization brought him sudden wealth and influence in both major political parties.[28] Aggressive Chicago capitalists and attorneys followed his example.

An era of mergers, a capitalization of future earnings, stock dividends, and stock market manipulations ensued. Rival gas companies joined under the aegis of Philadelphia capital into a hated "Trust." Levy Meyer created the "Whiskey Trust," 85 per cent of its stock "water." Judge W. H. Moore promoted the lucrative New York Biscuit, American Strawboard, and

Diamond Match combinations. Brewery mergers and combinations of grain elevators and independent meat packers followed, while British investors were "scald." The Illinois Steel Company resulted from another merger. Yerkes secured influential local backing when he enabled Field, L. E. Leiter, N. K. Fairbank, and Pullman each to net a quick $800,000 by investment in his West Chicago City Railway Company. During 1888-94 $250 millions new capital resulted from capitalizing the anticipated earning power and "good will" of such combinations and the utilities. As financial capitalism and the combination movement struck Chicago with full force and the middle class was still frightened by Haymarket into uncritical support of the *status quo,* the *Chicago Tribune* proudly listed 200 local millionaires, headed by Field and Armour.[29]

Chicago became the business center of the Middle West as its enterprisers invested in timber, mining, and railroads in the region extending to Canada and the Rocky Mountains. Yet, despite an indubitable regional leadership, Chicago's finance and giant business was held in partial tutelage to eastern and British finance by Yerkes' prominence, British investments, and Morgan sponsorship of the Illinois Steel Company. Such were the powerful interests whose ascendancy, power, and profit position Lloyd's new welfare philosophy challenged.

He watched the crass, ethicless, unbridled materialism and concentrated financial power of these developments with experienced realism. Inexperienced William Kent, fresh from Yale College, was repelled by them. He wrote for himself an unforgettable description of Chicago, itching to divert its energy into constructive channels :

> Like a great, lank, sordid, stoop-shouldered country boy.
> Possibilities immense or nil . . .
> Greedy days of '49 are here outdone. Everyone has struck pay dirt, or could have struck it.
> Backbone is the backbone of Puritanism, but how altered !

All lines of caste are thrown away; nothing but money counts in real social life, and money is quite as good as any other snobby reason for exclusiveness. . . .

There is no line in business relations, neither character nor success nor anything else. There is no line in the clubs. Almost every real estate man is a thief. Shady transactions are entirely overlooked and forgotten. . . .

The seething caldron of the world—the abode of a flame crime riot and damnation. The home of conceit and dissatisfaction, individual liberty running into license and resultant tyranny. . . .

A happy go lucky town where everyone steals for himself and forgets that his neighbor has stolen in his turn.

The poorest place on Earth for *rapid* progress as a result of squeamish honesty. The best in the world for honesty to come with time.

No organized stealing like Tammany, that is too slow, jump in a grab and get out and no one can criticize or prosecute. . . .

Honesty is admired if possible come to think about it but it is ordinarily considered a mild or noxious form of insanity. . . .

Packers steal water and taxes and Ry rebates, but pack good goods of course.

Elevator men mix grain and steal grades of course assessors are bought and of course favor their friends "as they have a perfect right to do."

Such examples are set laborers that they cannot keep a contract or refrain from anarchy.

Railroads own the earth and the water as well.

And it's all a matter of course. It's all a grab bag and if you can bribe the sunday school superintendent you get back more than your stake.[30]

This explains how Lloyd could call Chicago "the Carthage of the modern world" incarnating "all the evil tendencies of a civilization of false ideals," and his castigation of the "falsehood in trade" that deified money. His ideal Chicago, which he would sketch in 1895, would stress community planning as did British cities. Only a sense of duty held him there as Chicago grew increasingly "repulsive" to him.

However, he appreciated the cultural significance of the new John Crerar Library, Newberry Library, and Chicago Art Institute founded by philanthropic businessmen. These institutions and the city's growing literary community made it "one of the most stimulating spots in which a young man could find himself," Thomas Fuller would remark.[31]

Lloyd turned away from this rich upper world to work for the underprivileged in a pioneer attempt to bridge the gulf between the "Gold Coast" and the slum. The latter was "a vast wilderness of shabby houses—a . . . more desolate White-chapel than can hardly have a parallel for sordid dreariness," George Stevens reported to London. Twenty-one immigrant nationalities crowded into front and rear tenements on unswept streets with foul-smelling garbage boxes and alleys piled with manure leading to yards where waste removal was unknown. Dense crowds of the "most wretched and destitute" congregated in rotten tenements on dingy, foul courts that infected children and their impoverished parents. Decayed wooden housing and rising brick tenements extended from near Lake Michigan on Twelfth Street in a great horseshoe across the South and North branches of the River back almost to North Clark Street, an arc distinguished by squalid misery, social deterioration, and persistent growth.

Immigrants and their culturally unassimilated children dominated those slums, where innumerable back tenement families received incomes of less that $5 a week. Factory hands, Bohemian artisans, and Italian railway workers were irregularly employed. Italian wives and children were "home finishers" sewing in ill-lighted, insanitary, back basement rooms for the Bohemian and Russian Jewish "sweaters" of the garment trades, whose thousand sweatshops underbid each other for contracts, recouping by pay reductions.[32] The garments, after cursory cleansing, were retailed by the best State Street stores and distributed to midwestern cities, occasionally spreading smallpox and other diseases.

Employment in Chicago ranged from transportation, building, and manufacturing to clerical work and domestic service. Predominantly alien, divided by ethnic, religious, and national differences, the 250,000 workers and their dependents comprised a majority of the population. The future of democracy in Chicago depended upon the ability of this cosmopolitan mass to achieve assimilation to American civilization and fuller enjoyment of life's comforts and constitutional rights.[33] Such was the *milieu* into which Lloyd introduced his social welfare philosophy and where he first labored in social reform.

THE NEW CONSCIENCE

He and Salter were among the most influential Chicagoans to champion social justice. Only a handful helped Salter's attempts, inspired partly by Lloyd and Stewart, to bridge interclass antipathy. Lloyd wrote Adler a month after the Anarchists' execution of his desire to counteract "the iniquitous precedent" set by their trial and to remedy the evils that "would otherwise lead to anarchy and Communism."[34] "Delicate, sensitive, reticent, a student and a man of letters," he sought practical application for his philosophy.

Fundamentally, the then so-called social problem was intellectual in character. Traditional individualism was at the height of its glamor as the result of spectacular mining bonanzas, the "Cattle Kingdom," great industrial growth, and the rise of huge fortunes. A general complacency prevailed among the wealthy, corporation hierarchies, bankers, small businessmen, well-to-do professional people, and prosperous farmers. Social Darwinism was capturing much of the reading public. This conservative creed rationalized ruthless business methods and taught that competition was appropriately ethicless. Wealth and position were regarded as rewards of the "fittest," which the churches sanctified when receiving the traditional philanthropies, which the *arrivistes* hastened to perform. Unless the fusion of individualism, Darwinism, Cobdenism, and modified Calvinism that constituted the popular "Gospel of Wealth" could be overthrown, the reformer, agrarian, and labor leader would agitate in vain. Since imported "isms" were anathema after Haymarket, the only effective tactics left for protesting elements were either to attack abuses empirically while invoking the Jacksonian and humanitarian formulas, or to justify widening the area of social action by propagating a new, indigenous faith. The latter's potential appeal was suggested by the waning Georgite crusade and especially by the large, ephemeral following among middle class, trades unionists, and farmers that Bellamy's *Looking Backward* was sweeping into the Nationalist movement.

In Chicago Judge Gary was still the hero of conservatives and moderates. The city had given sites for Fort Sheridan and the Great Lakes Naval Station to the federal government at Field's instigation, so as to have federal garrisons available for future labor troubles. Wealthy New Yorkers in 1889 were talking of force as the only remedy for the labor problem. None in that metropolis could "safely make himself heard in behalf of the strikers" on the Burlington Railroad, Howells wrote to Samuel L. Clemens.

Rutherford B. Hayes and Chief Justice M. R. Waite were alarmed at this and at the concentration of wealth. Hayes was ready to extend government authority to control the railroads, destroy monopolies such as the Standard Oil, and curb anti-social economic power.[35]

Adler and probably Davidson, who was lecturing in Chicago when Lloyd's "Labor and Monopoly" appeared, persuaded him to present his social philosophy publicly. Salter tendered the rostrum of the Ethical Culture Society. When Lloyd accepted he joined the ethical leaders of the English-speaking world who were attacking the "moral chaos" of business.

Traveled, interested in serious scholarship, Davidson, Lloyd, Salter, Adler, Mead, and William Clarke were committed to high ideals and social reform. Sensitive to ugliness and social injustice, they were penetrating analysts, stimulating conversationalists, and effective lecturers, a congenial group. As Clarke observed in the (London) *Ethical Record,* they crusaded for "social righteousness," for "a new and better order." Inclusion in this group became for Lloyd an enjoyable, stimulating experience. By correspondence and infrequent meetings in Chicago, New England, and London, the members exchanged views and kept in touch with each other.[36]

When Lloyd addressed "a very large audience" of the Ethical Culture Society and its friends at the Grand Opera House, February 5, 1888, he challenged the expanding system of business power that dominated Chicago and the Middle West. His neo-Emersonian title, "The New Conscience, or the Religion of Labor," prefaced an eloquent statement of his welfare philosophy. It possessed dynamic implications for the ethical movement, philosophy, economic and social theory, the labor movement, and statesmanship as he preached the gospel of social salvation to a sinful generation.

As a literary performance the lecture matched his first essay series.[37] Its tooled, barbed epigrams sank deep into the armor of the "Bourbon" world. Alluding to judicial opposition to abolitionism, Lloyd said, "The courts then, as now, made many things successful which they can never make respectable." His references ranged from Plato, Aristotle, and the Bible, to Carlyle, Emerson, Ruskin, and Mazzini. He invoked Dickens and Garrison while appraising orthodox economics and implied that human freedom and welfare were proper criteria for evaluating business policies.

> The incantations of political economists cannot cure disease. Conscience cares nothing for the fine phrases of professors, . . . employers, for their theories and philosophy of business. It says, "What have you done?" What are the results? Both of your theories and doctrines of facts! It looks . . . at Cain in his palaces and Abel in the slums, at the profits of the "brother" and the wages of the other. . . . What hast thou done? Where is thy brother?

The implication that the truth of abstract doctrine was dem-

onstrated by its practical consequences bespoke Green's influence. Lloyd's radical, ethical instrumentalism combined adherence to social reform, which William James rejected, with
repudiation of snobbery, which he espoused. Lloyd believed
that the universities needed the workers' "culture" in "hard-
ship, and equality, and sacrifice." He arraigned and convicted
the leaders of the era before the bar of a democratic social
ethics whose purpose was the fullest liberty and self-realization
of all. Business excesses, the slums, fourteen-hour working days,
a million unemployed, sweatshops, and the prostitution of workers' daughters demanded "the abolition of the system and the
philosophy that permits them," he cried. He charged accurately
that the great financiers were accomplishing "the revolution"
by capping "the new industry with the high finance," as Morgan's latest biographer has demonstrated.[38] "The Money
Power," Lloyd cried, was organizing "Trusts" in everything,
destroying market competition, and preparing to control "all"
the nation's "other liberties."

The social ferment and labor movement, which "law, church,
culture and wealth" opposed, provided "the greatest cause in
History." With these "The New Conscience" was especially
concerned, he declared. It had motivated Christ and the
Reformation to lead men to a new freedom. It worked for
"ceaseless emancipation, and now demanded that 'civilization'
apply justice, love, and liberty to business and the social system to eliminate abuses and stop treating laborers as 'merchandise'." Its axiom, "Brothers in Industry," discredited Adam
Smith's dogma of individual self-interest and "the false society"
erected upon it.

"The New Conscience" would abolish "the cannibals of
competition, tyrants of monopoly, devourers of men, women
and children." Lloyd claimed, "Monopoly is force, and force
is slavery, and slavery must be abolished." Social love, brotherhood, and God working and growing within the individual and
society would guide the common people in emancipating men
from this new "tyranny," freeing laborers and ensuring their
full development and allaying "hatred" between "the classes

and the masses," ushering in "a new day." All social questions are religious questions, matters "of moral economy." "All political, industrial, and social activities" should be "functions of a new Church—a Church of the deed as well as of the creed, . . . which will make every social wrong a moral wrong, and every moral wrong a legal wrong," recognizing "no vested right in property in man except the right to love and be loved."

Lloyd demanded a moral revolution instituted by "The New Conscience" to reverse "the revolution" wrought by the *arrivistes* of speculation, promotion, and "high finance" and depose "The Monopoly Power" and the "Trusts" so as to create a new democracy. He attempted to make love, whose power Emerson said had never been made the basis of a state, the foundation of a just society in the machine age. Such was his attack upon the pseudo-élitism, power pretensions, and Darwinian creed of ruling "Bourbonism."

"The New Conscience" presented, therefore, a philosophy of social justice founded upon the Christo-democratic faith, Emersonian transcendentalism, Positivist humanism and altruism, the Kantian categorical imperative, empiricism's insistence upon implementing ideals, a profound knowledge of the economic mechanism of the era, and romanticism's evaluation of humanity. Lloyd threw rhetorical javelins drawn from the quiver of his new liberal campaign at "The Money Power," the "tyranny" of the "Trusts," "fraud," and "immorality." Vividly lucid, "The New Conscience" preached a patrician *and* popular crusade to overthrow "The Robber Barons" of "Big Business" and establish a new order based upon the general welfare and social virtue. Of this Lloyd would be the prophetic leader, with only the masses and occasional professional and business disciples in his following, attempting to achieve the impossible by his brilliant insistence that ideas of right, justice, and humanity be applied as correctives for the evils of the age.

Repeated applause informed him of an immediate triumph at the Grand Opera House. The ethical liberals were enthusiastic. An enterpriser present was admittedly convicted of business sin, although that evening Bross wrote dourly in his diary that the lecture had been neither "orthodox" nor religiously "sound." Salter, however, was delighted that Lloyd had developed the ethical movement's position on the labor question so brilliantly. Lloyd had complimented him by borrowing "The New Conscience" as a phrase from *The Problem of Poverty.* Eager to apply Lloyd's brotherhood principle, Salter wrote him that his address was "the best word" spoken "on any platform this year." The excited, converted Buchanan invited Lloyd to repeat it under the *Labor Enquirer's* sponsorship, sought his friendship, joined trades unionism after abandoning revolutionary conspiracy, and became a loyal citizen.[39]

Lloyd published the essay in the September *North American Review.*[40] It reached a wide audience. Henry George endorsed it heartily, declaring "the single tax will satisfy to the uttermost" the "demands of that new conscience which Mr. Lloyd so eloquently speaks." David D. Lloyd reported "echoes" from New York and Washington "of your brilliant article," and urged his brother to write more like it, get them printed in the *Congressional Record,* investigate practical problems, draft remedial legislation, and win thereby an "international reputation." Henry D. Lloyd's Congressman, Republican George E. Adams of the North Shore, agreed with his main position. Dissent came from more conservative quarters, as when the *Chicago Tribune* inferred that Lloyd wanted "sentiment" to "rule in business." The *Pittsburgh Telegraph* approved of "The New Conscience" but demanded "a concrete plan of relief."[41]

In Great Britain the essay attracted "wide attention" as William Clarke informed Lloyd. The Fellowship of the New Life and the Fabian Society were "greatly impressed." The former republished it as a pamphlet, which ran through three editions in four years, contributing significantly to British social thought two years before the *Fabian Essays,* which were also influenced by Lloyd's antimonopolism. British labor was impressed. On "Labour Sunday," May 7, 1893, in Liverpool, the essay was read to a large audience. When Lloyd visited London again, the New Life Fellowship persuaded him to present it to them. Sir William Mather, influential Liberal M.P. and industrialist of Manchester, confessed later that it had troubled him for years.[42]

In Illinois Judge Altgeld wrote Lloyd that he would prefer to be the author "of one such article" to holding any public office. Lloyd's essay, he predicted, would benefit humanity more and bring him greater "fame" than a lifetime in high office. "Accept my congratulations and go on with your work," Altgeld added, "The future will know you—and coming generations of suffering humanity will rise up and bless you." In 1894, George A. Schilling's most effective appeal to Mrs. Lucy E. Parsons to abandon her bitter, revolutionary agitation was to "the new conscience . . . those higher ethical relations of equal rights" that made "progress possible."[43] Altgeld and Schilling, partners in Illinois' first general welfare state administration, accepted Lloyd's social philosophy. So did Jane Addams, who justified social settlements to Chicago as a practical application of "a higher conscience" and regarded labor's cause as basically "an ethical movement" implementing "brotherhood."[44] Thus Lloyd emerged as an original social prophet of great influence.

Chapter X

 The Social Mecca of Reform

LLOYD AGREED WITH Emerson that every great historic change originated "in some seed idea" first denounced as "impractible" and "impious."' He persuaded Salter that ethical principles could be validated only in action when he lectured on "Child Labor and Its Remedy." In April 1888 the Ethical Culture Society instituted an annual series of economic conferences between businessmen and labor leaders. Lyman Gage, Schilling, Thomas J. Morgan, leader of the gradualist Socialists, Hutchinson of the Board of Trade, Buchanan, Franklin MacVeagh, and A. C. Cameron, trades unionist, addressed crowded audiences at Madison Street Theater. "Old Hutch" was surprised at the workingmen's comprehension of the social problem. MacVeagh confessed that competition was "a complete failure," large fortunes "abnormal," and child labor an evil. He advocated a shorter working day. No other employer would appear.[2]

Mead encouraged Lloyd to speak frequently and to read Laurence Gronlund's *Co-operative Commonwealth*. In March Lloyd had met William T. Harris, the leading Hegelian with whom he corresponded. During the summer the Lloyds went to New England, visiting first with the William Lloyd Garrisons of the *Boston Herald* at Wianno on Cape Cod. There Henry D. Lloyd read Clarke's *Essays of Mazzini* and enjoyed an exhilarating rendezvous with Thomas Davidson, who was an intimate of William James, Harris, and the Goddard circle in Boston.

Davidson was the last of the great wandering scholars, an

experienced philosopher whom James attempted vainly to lure
to Harvard. Davidson was "an incomparable linguist," a charming, brilliant conversationalist. He had hobnobbed with the
Boston Radical Club, joined the Cambridge Philosophical Club,
studied Hegel with Harris, and mastered Aristotle. From Ros-
mini, the great, unorthodox Scholastic, he derived a reconstructed individualism. He was fired with the plan to regenerate
society by means of voluntary, cooperative associations in which
a new education would train men and women for world-building. He was planning a new type university when he and Lloyd
talked on the long porch facing the sea. Davidson appealed
to Lloyd because he taught that social reform began with the
individual's education in true values, his cultural development,
and the inspiration to work unceasingly for his fellow men.
Warmed by his scintillating conversation, candor, and learning,
Lloyd was flattered by an invitation to join the faculty of the
new "university."

Soon Davidson purchased a farm in Keene Valley in the
Adirondacks, only to learn that Lloyd had "bought on the sea
shore." At "Glenmore," as the philosopher named his mountain farm, he located his famous Summer School of the Culture
Sciences where James and Harris would teach. Davidson hoped
that his university would be financed by a friendly, wealthy
Chicago speculator, with an initial faculty including Lloyd,
Mead, Harris, Henry George, and a "Mr. Gunton." Lloyd put
Davidson up at the Chicago Club when he lectured in Chicago
on medieval philosophy and joined the Art Institute to hear
him lecture. He was disappointed when Davidson's sponsor
lost his fortune speculating on the Board of Trade.[3] The projected new University of Chicago went glimmering, but the two
men remained friends.

At Boston, in August 1888 after parting with Davidson, Lloyd
discovered in Mrs. Goddard's journals new light on Wendell
Phillips' stormy career. He learned that Charles Eliot Norton
had persuaded James Russell Lowell to omit a sonnet to Phillips
from a volume of verse because of his championship of labor.
Lloyd denounced the "silent conspiracy" to suppress Phillips'

speeches on labor to John Swinton and asked him to publish
"his last and greatest utterances." Since Phillips was otherwise
lacking in originality, it was his discovery of the continuity of
the abolition and labor movements that led Lloyd to declare
him "the greatest social thinker,"[4] thereby justifying by implication a crusade for social justice.

While vacationing at Sebago, Maine, Lloyd read F. W. San-
born's *Emerson,* Oliver Johnson's *William Lloyd Garrison,* and
the *Pall Mall Gazette.* He reflected upon Green's political
theory. With an Emersonian frame of reference, he compared
Mazzini's collectivist thought with Gronlund's interpretation
of Marxism. This led Lloyd to expand his social theory in a
manner that diminished its individualism. As revised it placed
unusual emphasis upon collectivism, despite his friendship for
Davidson.

From Green, validated by Standard Oil example, he derived
the rule that the freedom and power granted "any person,
class, nation, or officer" must be proportionate to "their intelligence and virtue." Because contemporary capitalists abused
their power, he concluded that that should be taken away by
public action or there would be a catastrophe.[5] A *Pall Mall
Gazette* report of Bishop Stubb's religious philanthropy to
labor led him to insist that "the first work of religion" should
always be "justice." Rejecting Renan's cynical *"Gardons nous
de rien fonder,"* he conceived that his own "Authority" was that
of an élitist exponent "of popular inspiration" at odds with
militarism and a business civilization's preoccupation with
money-making. He attributed the hard, sordid, low, transitional
character of the latter to its disregard "of the exhortations and
powers and intuitions of its Emersons and Wordsworths."[6]

Lloyd deduced an interesting theory of reform from the
experiences of Mazzini, the romantic Italian Liberal revolutionary. Reform sects and revolutionary elements could not
combine "in the early stages" of any move for social reconstruction unless forced together by repression. Hence, liberty of
speech and meeting was safest for society. Even a fragmented
movement educated the public on problems and proposed

remedies. It was "a law of social growth" that a reform would be achieved only so far as the common momentum took it, while the results of agitation and revolution were "always extremely conservative in proportion to the presage." Belief in this law explains Lloyd's subsequent championship of freedom of agitation for radical elements and, partially, his extraordinarily broad range of reform interests.

Mazzini stimulated him more than was indicated by his rating of him as the activist, embodying the "predestinator and creator." His example led Lloyd to formulate a new conception of man's role : "Life is a Creation! . . . Man the Creator" in whose activity "through form after form along an ascending spiral, we see Free Will, the Divinity of Man, the creature Creator." Eight years later, after a frustrating experiment with Labor-Populist Fabianism, he would develop that fruitful conception further. Admiration for Mazzini as the "Artist—'priest of the universal life' and prophet of a high social aim" intensified the idealistic, religious, and reformist aspects of Lloyd's thought.[8]

In November 1888 Lloyd concluded that reform was predestined. "The reforming genius . . . discovers the step forward which can be taken in harmony with the development of the past without breaking the continuity of social growth." Progress proceeded "according to an intelligent plan," irresistibly. The reformer's work was to remove the "out-worn, out-grown forms" that obstructed it, by disclosing evils and obstacles to "free growth, the old forms that hamper progress." In reaction to Mazzini's assertion that institutions were relative to the spirit of those operating them in potentiality, he observed that there was "an evolution of instruments as well as principles. Mankind's progress is towards absolute truth, not only in morals but in mechanics . . . of forms, as well as spirit . . . changes of spirit and matter, of principles and institutions, must go on together." Tellic progress fulfilled a predestined end.

Drawing upon history as he philosophized on the long hotel porch, and projecting Mazzini's thought against Emersonian transcendentalism and Hegel's social theory, Lloyd developed an institutional experimentalism. A wise, enfranchised spirit kept its devotion to its ideals paramount to loyalty to the institutions created to attain them. Recalling how "brotherliness, love, . . . liberty and duty" had inspired men to apply them practically at the expense of outmoded institutions he concluded that "numberless moulds must be broken in which we now shape our activities to the realization of our hopes and ideals." Developing this idea further he concluded that the wages system, land monopolies, all types of war, despotisms, and surviving polygamy "must go everywhere." Past progress inspired the individual to new energy in behalf of the general welfare.

This, to be sure, was neo-Emersonian and radical. Oddly, Lloyd regarded the international spirit of social reform as a new phenomenon, expressing Hegelian social self-consciousness and Kantian free will. In practice, Swiss forestry illustrated to Lloyd how conscious self-rectification enabled nations like individuals to reform themselves. As they progressed he believed they would do so with less violence. Mazzinian association appealed to him as a principle despite Emerson's objections to Brook Farm, viz., the role of collective labor in "the constant change of social forms." Mazzini indicated that humanity was about to discard individualism and "devote itself to its task— collectivism," which "is but the highest form of individualism," Lloyd concluded.[9]

"What the collectivity can do is the subject of an experimental development, evolution by experience" as was true of individualism. The larger social fabric would be woven from both. Prophets had stated earlier the right of growth, Golden Rule, individual development, and expansion of the State that were fundamental to human development. To realize these principles, institutions must "constantly change," and new associations would be devised by the social movement, "by sternest encounter, . . . indubitalest survival as fittest" in which human, as distinct from animal, forces would be increasingly in the ascendant.

Lloyd, obviously, was not an unqualified social rebel as some scholars infer. More realistic, more discriminating than many subsequent "Progressives," he expected "the shrewder and sturdier" to adhere to the socially approved good until the superiority of new institutional forms was demonstrated.[10] The pragmatic test would determine that for individualism and collectivism.

Lloyd qualified Emerson's dictum that property flowed into hands fittest to handle it by asserting that wealth and power were subject to an implied general welfare trusteeship. The morally fittest were the strongest and would surely survive, he stated as if he were formulating an Ethical Darwinism. This, too, became an enduring part of his social faith. Moral growth must parallel the increase in scientific knowledge and intelligence. Because of this and the interrelatedness of human experience, there could be "no solitary reforms." He asserted optimistically an indefinite expandability of human capacities. However, recognizing that collectivist rule was invariably despotic, he declared that it should properly be resisted and be accepted "only when it has the power of 'Right and Might' combined." A new people "so wise, strong and good that each cares for all" would have to be produced before there could be "a society in which each is taken care of by all."[11]

All this was part of an unusually complex theory of progress. The collectivist part of it, hedged about with strong reservations, was founded partially upon Mazzini's romantic appreciation of the folk and his insistence that the masses should enjoy fully the right of association and economic justice, and partially upon an understanding of the historical process unprejudiced by the concept of class conflict. Lloyd's revised theory made him sanguine as to the portent of contemporary phenomena, as when he interpreted a wave of strikes as presaging "the decomposition of the wages system" to result from labor's growing strength and humanitarian impatience with misery. His cautious realism prevented him from attempting to blueprint the future. He did forecast, however, that enlightened conscience and thought would insist upon protection of the people "from actual want and suffering" and full opportunity for individual development as "the minimum." Rejecting the orthodox economists' assumptions that men had to be driven to work by hunger and that they could not be trusted to respect others' rights, he insisted that men were naturally honest, loved work, and possessed "physical, moral and social virtues that would make them gloriously successful in maintaining a far more complicated and noble social system than this." Human life could be so perfected in justice, sympathy, transportation, etc., "that social life becomes perfected" and the United States made capable of supporting three billion people.[12]

"The coming revolution" would free "men from industrial privilege" and clear the ground for "the great constructive work of future social perfection of which we get in our most exalted moments brief glimpses." Before it succeeded, he predicted, the resisting industrial privileged class would rally survivors of earlier religious and landed aristocracies to the defense of landlordism, business management, finance, and "the to-be-regulated corporation." After victory, free men for the first time would be able "to build up a true society." The question would then arise, "What will mankind do with this great *means?* For that is all liberty is. . . . The practical adoption of an advanced socialism—I say advanced because we already have a socialism—must wait for this work of industrial Protestantism to be first done." Life would be made infinitely more hellish if it were attempted to found Socialism before men were industrially freed. That would invite certain failure. "No collectivity until it be one without money and without price. Better centuries of transition and purification." British workers who had been free for generations should discover experimentally if Socialism could be genuinely democratic. If not, Lloyd rejected it. Implicitly he rejected Marxism's materialistic determinism, class struggle, and proletarian dictatorship, although he agreed that an ideological and institutional economic revolution was a necessary preliminary to an "advanced Socialism."[13] In Lloyd's expanded social philosophy a democratic collectivism, if and when it came, would result from the fulfillment of liberty, mankind's perfectibility and creativity, and the great ethical tradition of the western world. It was this optimistic, semiromantic,

semirealistic theory of progress that inspired him as he walked
on the reform stage as the philosopher, prophet, and practical
leader of a crusade for social justice.

While in New England that early autumn Lloyd ran for
Congress *in absentia* on the Union Labor ticket at the insistence
of the *Knights of Labor,* which republished "The New Conscience," as did the *Illinois Staats-Zeitung.* Lloyd could have
had the Democratic nomination and given Adams a real contest if he had not declined to speak or contribute to the campaign fund after John Stuart Mill's example. Lloyd lacked
appreciation of the tactical value of compromise, which enabled
the British Socialists within the Liberal Party to elect laborers
to Parliament during that decade. He cherished his nomination
"by workingmen" but was badly beaten with the entire Union
Labor ticket despite the workers' initial enthusiasm."

Afterwards on February 17, 1889, at an economic conference,
he presented Mazzini to Chicago as the "Prophet in Action,"
the "winged and daring spiritual hero of the modern world"
ever conspiring "to overthrow tyranny." Emphasis upon Mazzini's love of humanity, high ethics, and intense religious spirit
helped to fashion the Mazzini myth as a dynamic influence
upon American reform. Lloyd ignored, if he knew of it, that
great Liberal's readiness to denounce innocent men or fellow
conspirators to despotic authorities so as to arouse the Italian
public against reactionary governments which garrotted them.

Lloyd appeared dramatically on the rostrum that day as a
radical, envisaging if not encouraging "THE Revolution."
While delineating Mazzini's Liberalism he described also his
radical solution for the social problem, his demand for abolition
of aristocracy and proletariat, for union of capital and labor in
the same hands, and termination of the privileges of priesthood
and property. Lloyd quoted with enthusiasm Mazzini's prediction that "the sole aristocracy of tomorrow will be the eternal,
divine, beneficent aristocracy of intellect and virtue." In an
eloquent parable of the mountain-top with a golden bird, Lloyd
preached the doctrine that revolution against industrial privilege for industrial democracy would unite all reformers and

complete the Christian, American, and French revolutions. "Political democracy must be backed up by industrial democracy" after the overthrow of industrial popes or czars "or all democracy becomes impossible," Lloyd cried. "The regime of the new liberty will be one in which all will be rich, just as political liberty makes all free." He quoted Mazzini's prophecy that America would intervene in Europe in behalf of liberal self-determination. He ranked him higher than Emerson because he offered a constructive "faith for the future," insisting that "all social arrangements" be adapted to it. In his assertion of the religious basis of all revolutions, Lloyd discovered validation of "The New Conscience" before describing allegorically the cruel competitive struggle of laborers in the contemporary economic arena.

He admitted later that Mazzini was the reformer most akin to his own spirit and intellectual approach to the social problem. During the lecture his stress upon Mazzini's renunciation of the churches for a higher religion of humanity and his disinheritance by an unsympathetic father carried autobiographic connotations to his hearers. Although Lloyd always eschewed conspiracy, his developing radicalism was thereafter strongly influenced by Mazzini's anticlass remedy for social injustice and his prophetic role. During the discussion after the lecture he stressed Mazzini's opposition to Communist materialism. After appreciative press notices in the *Chicago Times, Leader,* and *Arbeiter Zeitung,* he presented the lecture in Evanston and elsewhere.[15]

Simultaneously he published an uncritical review of Thorold Rogers' *The Economic Interpretation of History* in *The* (Chicago) *Dial.*[16] This exaggerated Rogers' importance as a historian and chortled at his attack upon orthodox economics' indifference to "facts." Lloyd approved of Rogers' repudiation of Henry George and urged that American business magnates note his discovery that class legislation caused the post-Tudor impoverishment of English farmers and laborers. Rogers and such "seers and prophets" as Ruskin, Carlyle, Mazzini, and Emerson decried "social injustice," he added.

While the richness and complexity of Lloyd's social thought was evident, his hearers and readers were left in no doubt as to his candid anti-Marxian radicalism. Discerning Chicagoans perceived that he was disseminating a new, radical social gospel that justified trades unions' and farmers alliances' attacks upon economic injustice, business amorality and authoritarianism, and the "Trusts." His institutional experimentalism and denunciations of specific evils, typical power entrepreneurs, the "Money Power," and "Trusts" aroused apprehensions among those who feared an Anarchist revival and approved of the developing business system.

Their reply to Lloyd was voiced by Slason Thompson, editor of *America* and formerly of the *Chicago Tribune*. Thompson criticized him for wasting his influence with appeals to the populace and specifically for criticizing police repression of labor in the Mazzini lecture. Mazzini was an "impractical" criminal conspirator, no fit example for Americans, Thompson said. The applause Lloyd received was "nothing but the spirit of unrest which no Utopian perfection of government could satisfy." Lloyd was "ungenerous and ungrateful" in supporting "the clamor of lawlessness." Would he recall his former position "as one of the few young men in Chicago who . . . bade fair to achieve a national reputation in the field of social and financial letters," whose gentle, honest character had delighted friends and whose "rare mental powers" and reform "enthusiasm" had promised to make him "one of the most useful forces in this —centre of sordid ambition and material progress" and mend his ways?"

Although Lloyd was undoubtedly gratified by this tribute to his character, talents, and former position, he understood the animus behind it. His mother was gratified at Thompson's tribute to his "noble and lofty manhood." She persuaded him not to reply to this "severe criticism" and warned him "to be careful how rapidly you advance." Lloyd should not, she added, "be too hard on the policemen" and "don't alienate the church.""

SUBURBANITE

During 1888-89 the Lloyds transformed their Winnetka home from a suburban outpost of Chicago society into a salon of social reform, dedicating their lives and guest lists to "The New Conscience." They erected on the Rhode Island shore a large summer cottage that became its eastern projection. As an Emersonian lover of nature, Henry D. Lloyd found the Winnetka area a source of unending delight. Walks in Hubbard Woods and occasional hunting so acquainted him with the trees, shrubbery, birds, and small game that his knowledge of local fauna and flora amazed his sons. He wounded himself accidentally on one hunting expedition. Bross called Winnetka "one of the most delightful spots in the West."[19]

Equally attractive were the village's amusements, neighborliness, community activities, and the intellectual and aesthetic interests of the "Yankee" inhabitants. The Georgian church spires and green reproduced a traditional New England scene within an hour's commuting distance from Chicago's opera, music, Exposition gallery, libraries, and literary community. The Lloyds sent their sons to the Withington School, whose director was sister to Anne Withington of Newburyport, later a well-known Boston social settlement resident. The School's accomplished staff dined frequently with the Lloyds, where they joined Caroline Stallbohm, "Will's" former nurse and Henry D. Lloyd's indefatigable secretary, in a round of charades, farces, dances, and musical evenings.[20]

Lloyd became active in the Improvement Society, leading its investigation of the village trustees. During 1886-87 he was village treasurer. He was elected to the Board of Education, revised its by-laws, added a kindergarten to the school system, and despite popular apprehensions introduced manual training for both sexes. He spoke on "Our Duty to the Village" to the Improvement Society. As a member of the Village Council he defended the streets from property-holders' encroachment. When one of them defeated the trustees in a lawsuit, he urged him to return the disputed part of Hazel Street because "as

part of the social compact by which Winnetka was created"
it had been a thoroughfare. Besides, no man of integrity would
rely on a definition of legal rights by the courts, "the sanctu-
aries for wreckers and false trustees." Lloyd practiced what he
preached when he paid the treasurer "estimated taxes on un-
assessed property" in August 1889. The trustees thanked him
unanimously for "the influence" of this "truly honest and
honorable action in these days of greed and gold." Quietly he
aided the Public Library.[21]

Mrs. Lloyd was the beloved mistress of the most cultivated
home in the village. She directed a boys' "Saturday Club,"
which her father took to Chicago to see the new cable engines
and works of the traction companies. She organized an interdenominational sewing school for forty little girls.[22]

After a few years Henry D. Lloyd bought and remodeled an
old inn of moderate size with ample grounds and carefully
trimmed trees on Sheridan Road, south of Hubbard Woods
on a bluff overlooking Lake Michigan. There he wrote his
essays on Gould, speculation in food, and "Lords of Industry."
He and Mrs. Lloyd staged annual all-day Fourth of July picnics
there for guests from the village, Chicago, and elsewhere, mixed
groups of businessmen, lawyers, clergy, journalists, and physicians. Culminating in bonfires and fireworks, these were gay,
informal occasions. Mrs. Lloyd entertained the Chicago
Women's Club there at other picnics, demonstrating her ability
to maintain a suburban residence, bear a third and a fourth
son, shepherd local youth, and maintain her position in Chicago
society simultaneously. The Lloyds were prototypes before 1885
of the families of means and culture who have since settled the
Chicago North Shore. With an express wagon they maintained
communication with the village center, the Northwestern Railroad station, and their friends. They entertained frequently "on
Henry's grounds" with "fish chowder à la the Shackfords and
good things and good cheer generally," the Bross diary records.[23]

Bross visited the Lloyds there frequently. No trip of his to the
Rockies, California, Manitoba, or the East ended until he went
to see how matters were "at Jessie's." When he shot a bag

of snipe she invariably received her "string." On each festive occasion, during every hour of trial, "the Governor" was on hand. In return the Brosses entertained the Lloyds and Miss Withington in Chicago after attending *Twelfth Night* together and on other occasions.

Bross purchased the reddish brown brick "Kef-Lawn," as the Lloyds called their home, after the sewer gas poisoning episode, from Henry D. Lloyd and allowed him to reside there until he could build a new house immediately to the south. Bross planted fruit trees, expecting to reside there beside his daughter's family, with easy access to Lake Forest University, where he was a Trustee, and to his Chicago real estate, banking, insurance, and industrial interests. Meanwhile, he resided at fashionable No. 8 Beaurivage, 194 Michigan Avenue. He purchased and moved a brick house to "Kef-Lawn," joined it to it as a "front addition," redecorated and refurnished the enlarged structure, sank an artesian well, and stocked a large pond on the lawn with trout. The Lloyds vacationed in the East, leaving their sons with him, Miss Stallbohm, and the maids. Henry D. Lloyd expected to build his new house in 1884, but delayed until his breakdown and retirement from the *Chicago Tribune* postponed this indefinitely.[24]

Thin, tall, erect, with white beard, Bross's appearance during 1885-1889 contrasted vividly with the thick, curly brown hair and beard and ruddy plumpness of his middle age. Still eager to elevate Chicago culturally and in business leadership, he did not suffer from comparison with richer, less scrupulous contemporaries. Articulate, learned, wealthy, he was Williams College's finest contribution to Chicago's development.[25] He showered attentions upon his namesake "Will," for whom Mary Mapes Dodge wrote a verse. Bross presented him on his second birthday with a handsome leather-bound *History of Chicago and Other Pamphlets* containing all his important publications, plus a letter enjoining the grandson to model his life after his. Will went with nurse and grandparents regularly to Morris, a Bross family stronghold, to Chicago to attend Barnum's Circus and view the exposition in Grant Park with his grandfather, who gave him a magic lantern with which he regaled his brothers and friends.[26]

Mrs. Lloyd's unquenchable spirit of friendliness, kindness, and gaiety pervaded "Kef-Lawn." Recurring illnesses followed her typhoid, her husband's breakdown, and his intervention in the clemency movement. Yet, she encouraged his literary and reform work, guarded his health and writing, cared for their children, and administered their home. After his recovery she enforced a rule of silence during his working hours and afternoon nap, and encouraged guests to join him in his daily walks. After he left for Europe in 1886 she arranged to add a third floor to the house, with a spacious study possessing north, south, and west windows, fireplace flanked by window seats on the south wall, a desk beneath the skylight beside a revolving bookcase, book shelves, closets, and adjacent roofed and sun porches. When his abrupt return spoiled her surprise for him, she supervised the completion of this transformation[27] of "Kef-Lawn" into "The Wayside," as they renamed it. The new study became the center of Lloyd's writing, studies, and reform correspondence. Without his wife's interest and encouragement, he could hardly have reconstructed his social philosophy during 1886-88 or embarked so early upon his reform career. Together they transformed their home into a unique center of social reform.

So sustained, he attended the Chicago Literary Club instead of licking his wounds in solitude. He began a witty correspondence with Major Huntington, who had left the *Chicago Tribune* to be librarian to Cardinal Howard in Rome. To him Lloyd wrote of how "countless incidents" disclosed an increasing antagonism between America's "classes—employer and employee, of capitalists and people," and that the wife of a wealthy industrialist was so "tired" of the labor question that she wished "all the laborers were drowned." Lloyd said he missed Huntington "tremendously."[28]

THE WATCH HOUSE

William Lloyd Garrison II recommended Osterville, a few miles west of Wianno on Cape Cod's south shore, to the Lloyds in 1888 when they asked about eastern resorts.[29] However, they learned of an unsettled point at the mouth of the Sakonnet River directly opposite Newport, Rhode Island. There a crescent beach faced the ocean to the east and south beneath a hillock offering an admirable location for a cottage. The site was five miles from Little Compton's post office along winding roads flanked by stone fences. Sakonnet Point offered solitude, salt-water recreation, and proximity to Boston, Newport, and Providence. The Lloyds purchased forty acres there and planted trees in the late summer of 1888.

During the spring of 1889 they built their cottage on the south slope of the low granite ridge. As friends of John Root and Daniel Burnham, noted Chicago architects, they selected a simple design whose structural unity, length, breadth, harmony with the site, and adaptation of the Cape Cod cottage style was singularly felicitous. A balustraded captain's walk with a short mast lightened the mass of the large, rectangular house. Its paneled windows bespoke the Colonial Revival that was beginning to win favor with discriminating builders after erection of the Taylor House in Newport.[30] Wide expanses between broad windows on the face of each wing and west wall, where the upper story overhung the ground floor, suggest Richardson's influence. A broad screened porch within the main south wall faced the Atlantic. Shingled in natural wood, the house would turn silver gray as it weathered.

The Lloyds named their cottage "The Watch House." Although it sufficed to house their family, servants, and twenty guests, its unpretentiousness contrasted sharply with the ornate "Queen Anne" cottages of the "Robber Barons" at Newport across the Bay. They enjoyed summers there with the informal, casual hospitality of seasoned residents who avoided Newport's extravaganza. Mrs. Lloyd had been seriously ill during the winter of 1889. After completion of The Watch House Will developed rheumatic fever, for whose cure his father eventually took him to Carlsbad in 1891.[31]

Annually when school "let out," the Lloyd family entrained for Providence, whence they drove to Sakonnet. Once at the

Point, with a sloop in the water and gray mare Peggy on the roads, "the boys" boxed the compass in an unending round of activities. Sunshine, salt breezes, vacation reading, conversing with friends and guests, and visiting along the Shore rehabilitated young and old.

The Lloyds became warm friends of the Edward Everett Hales at Matunck. The popular, literary, pastor of South Congregational Church, Boston, supported Mead's lectures, wrote novels, published source materials on American history, projected settlement houses, advocated world peace, wrote historical articles and short stories, and lectured as far west as Chicago, where the Lloyds first met him. As a romantic realist akin in temper to Henry D. Lloyd, he was a moving spirit at "The Hub" among civic leaders. Residing seventeen miles to the east of The Watch House, Hale communicated with the Lloyds by "flashlight telegraph" and reciprocal visiting. His friendship with the Winnetka reformer stimulated both.[32]

Lloyd continued his morning writing, studying, and correspondence at The Watch House, dictating to his secretary from nine to eleven while clad in a long scarlet bathrobe with hood. Mrs. Lloyd enforced the silent rule until he joined the swimmers after his afternoon nap, or sailed, or drove along the Rhode Island roads behind Peggy in the four-seated "The Democrat" with guests to chat and call upon friends. Peggy became so sophisticated while pulling so many "smart people" from Boston and Chicago, it was said, that she was about to begin painting landscapes. Evenings were enlivened by music and serious conversations with visiting reformers and scholars such as Professor Ely, or Dr. John Graham Brooks and Herbert I. Foster, Harvard economics lecturers seeking light on monopolies.[33]

Mead, the Hales, Howells, Sylvester Baxter of the *Boston Herald,* the Bowles of Springfield, Edward Bemis, John R. Commons, Willis J. Abbot, the Social Gospel evangelist B. Fay Mills and Hugh J. Lusk, New Zealand consul in New York, visited The Watch House frequently. In the long attic Margaret Morley wrote up her research at Wood's Hole and her observations of wild life along the Atlantic Coast. As a campaigner against

Victorian prudery she needed the Lloyds' backing of her books for children that won her a national reputation. Henry Latchford, literary friend of President Daniel Coit Gilman of Johns Hopkins University, remained behind at The Watch House in the autumn of 1894 to alarm Little Compton with postcards mailed to the *Arena*. This won him a local reputation of being "a dangerous man" and Lloyd's agent for "advancing revolutionary and destructive ideas." So he informed him good-naturedly, adding, "You and Mrs. Lloyd have caused people here to think—and that is much."[34]

The Watch House became the summer center of reform thought and planning on many issues confronting America, Great Britain and the Continent. Its changing guest list included reformers of all types, labor leaders, and "social economists of the world." Clarence Darrow humorously invited himself to "Mrs. Lloyd's summer boarding house." Lloyd enjoyed his role as leader and host. As a patriot he depicted the cottage's site with its combination of "red rocks, white foam, and blue sea" as "a perpetual and delightful reminder of the flag" when he joined Chauncey Depew, William C. Whitney, and Mrs. Rebecca Harding Davis in explaining to the *Boston Globe* why New England was the nation's "Favorite Summer Resort."[35]

The Lloyds also entertained their sons' friends of both sexes at The Watch House. These young people romped on the lawn, swarmed on the swimming raft, and shared the yacht. They called their host "Dear Uncle Henry" and were charmed by his interest in them. "Coe" Kelley, son of Mrs. Florence Kelley, was the first regular teenage guest. He carried into later life a vivid impression of the lord of The Watch House, who sent him to Harvard with Will and "Hal," together with enduring attachment to his ideals. Thomas W. Phillips, Jr., son of the wealthy independent oil man of Butler, Pennsylvania, and his sister were other regular visitors. She was on the yacht *Mary Jane* during the squall that swept the Lloyds' chef overboard to drown before he could be rescued.[36]

During meals from six to thirty adult and teenage guests sat around the large table in the huge dining room with its beamed

ceiling, where "grace" was said only when the Aaron Lloyds
were present. An entire reformer's family, such as the Bemises,
would be entertained indefinitely with irresistible graciousness.
The Lloyds' informality and catholic interests delighted their
guests, and drew out the ideas and interests of each, pulling all
together into a stimulating *rapport*.[37]

THE WAYSIDE

During the other nine months of the year The Wayside became the social Mecca of transoceanic reform, with many of
the same guests gathering there at its bountiful table or in the
parlors or tramping together in Hubbard Woods as they discussed the issues of the hour. Thus, instead of dispensing their
social ideas and strategy plus philanthropy from a remote
social pinnacle, the Lloyds gathered around them a unique
circle. This included ethical leaders, socialites, slum-dwellers,
clergy, businessmen, liberal and radical politicians, enlightened
lawyers, labor leaders, Socialists, Single-Taxers, Bellamy's
lieutenants, Hull-House residents, college presidents and professors, newspaper editors, British Fabians and Liberals, and Negro
leaders. The geographic limits of the Lloyd circle, with whose
members Lloyd also kept in touch by correspondence and
travel extended ultimately to central Europe and the Antipodes.

To inform them mutually of developments in their multi-
farious fields of reform, he distributed copies of his and their
publications, clippings from the press and periodicals on current
issues and reform movements and others reporting his activities,
all supplied him at his expense by clipping bureaus. When supplemented by warm personal interest, this developed among
them a community of ideas, an *esprit de corps,* and growing
agreement upon ways and means. Miss Stallbohm operated this
"literary bureau" at The Wayside and The Watch House. It
stimulated a further development of Lloyd's thought and provided him with specific programs congenial to this as he participated in the continuing interchange. His information bureau of
reform enhanced his influence among reformers steadily as it
disseminated his views and news of his activities. It enabled

him to mobilize support swiftly for specific causes, and furthered the continuity and development of non-Marxian reform on three continents.

As early as 1890 it was evident that Lloyd had developed a new personality. Old friends such as the Masons, Franklin MacVeagh, and the distant Huntington still saw in him the patrician liberal, albeit dedicated now to unorthodox causes. Lloyd continued to be the well-dressed clubman, increasingly cosmopolitan, cultivated, a man of elegant tastes. To journalist friends he was still the editorial crusader against the evils of the age, to whom their columns remained generously open. But to these as to Winnetka intimates he had changed from a charming but semi-aloof patrician reformer in a manner that they did not understand fully. The new guests at his table somehow knew him better. A cultivated catholicity of interest in reform movements explained his open-minded sympathy with the proponents of each new cause. His kindly friendship bound the members of the Lloyd circle to him with bands of steel.

Added to this was his relaxed, interested democracy in social intercourse. His keen personal interest in each new friend bridged the gap between patrician and plebian. "Bert" Stewart, "Tommy" Morgan, Debs, Andrew B. Adair of the Typographical Union, and other labor leaders found him congenial and understanding, his warm support devoid of condescension. He appreciated their virtues and the merits of the cause that they led, just as he did the self-sacrificial devotion of the enthusiastic social settlement residents of Chicago, New York, and Boston. They also stressed co-operative self-help in uplift of the underprivileged. Slum-dwellers and sweat-shop workers, embattled agrarians of slender means and their journalistic champions, clerical recruits for the Social Gospel, excited Nationalists of Bellamy's crusade, municipal reformers, the more broadly oriented single taxers, Christian Socialists, Fabians, and tentatious advocates of public utility franchise reform such as Louis D. Brandeis found him eager to learn, generous in time and money to assist. So dedicated was he that Lloyd became the universal reformer of his era.

He achieved this unique position in the Empire of Reform at the price of disinheritance, complete for himself, partial for his wife. Bross died in the spring of 1889 after a partial invalidism, leaving his fortune in trust to their four sons under the management of Azariah T. Galt, whose administration increased it to $6,000,000 by 1910 when "the boys" assumed control. This fortune was subject to annuities of $15,000 for Mrs. Bross and $10,000 for Mrs. Lloyd, plus $1,000 annual expenses for each of the Lloyd sons, the cost of their college and professional education, $5,000 each when they reached twenty-one, $10,000 each when they became twenty-five, $35,000 each when they reached thirty, and $2,000 and $8,000 additional to Will when he came of age and reached twenty-five respectively. Mrs. Lloyd received lifetime use of The Wayside. The Bross 20 per cent interest in the Chicago Tribune Company, control of which with his own holding might have made Henry D. Lloyd a factor in its management, was placed in Galt's hands.[38]

The humiliating implications of this for Henry D. Lloyd, who was obliged to listen to the reading of the will that provided living and educational expenses for his sons, can be imagined. Had he been a fortune hunter, the experience of being unmentioned in the will and unprovided for would have plunged him into cynical dissipation or a final nervous collapse. His previous defiances of "The Governor" had long since indicated that he was not. Not a scintilla of evidence suggests that disinheritance or the disappointment of his wife's expectations as the result of her loyalty to him ruffled their establishment. Their mutual devotion, comradeship, and dedication to reform and the underprivileged was intensified. Lloyd continued to be head of his family, managing its funds, planning with his wife their daily life and future.

Their income was not inconsiderable, although much of it was consumed in the maintenance and hospitality of The Wayside and The Watch House. Mrs. Lloyd's life income, use of the former, and the boys' expenses were equivalent to $16,000 a year. Henry D. Lloyd received approximately $10,000 annually in dividends from his Chicago Tribune Company stock until

1894, then somewhat less until 1897 and again in 1903.[39] This he supplemented with fees from lecturing and writing. His Chicago real estate holdings were worth hundreds of thousands of dollars but yielded no income. Lloyd was a man of means apart from the *Tribune* stock that he had received from Bross, and at any time could have liquidated his real estate speculation for a sum that would have yielded him a good income. Had he and Mrs. Lloyd desired, they could have turned away from social reform at any time to enjoy a life of elegant dilletantism for which their cultural interests, linguistic talents, personal charm, and sociability qualified them.

At The Wayside they eschewed the cult of luxury but unlike Count Tolstoi maintained accepted social standards while entertaining guests from all strata, races, sexes, and reform elements. To this they added unobtrusive philanthropies in behalf of the distressed and various "causes." Thus, they achieved in the Winnetka woods the retirement from the social whirl and devotion to reform and the underprivileged that Howells had longed for but did not realize.

The company around the Lloyds was gathered first from Chicago, beginning with the Stewarts and the ethical leaders. It expanded to include Hull House and Chicago Commons residents; Clarence Darrow, Schilling; Morgan; Eugene V. Debs; the Rev. Jenkin Lloyd Jones, crusading preacher of All Souls Church; Mary Kenney, woman's garment workers' union organizer; and Professor Bemis of the University of Chicago. Judge Altgeld entered the circle early, and President George A. Gates and Professor George D. Herron, of Iowa College, joined after 1895. During the World's Fair Roger Sherman of Titusville, Michael Davitt, some London Fabians and ethical leaders, Booker T. Washington, Eltweed Pomeroy, Henry Legate of Boston, and other eastern reformers and scholars visited at The Wayside. So did James Baird Weaver and Ignatius Donnelly, leading western Populists. Other guests of import were Davidson, James B. Corruthers, Negro poet; Professors Ely and Commons; the Rev. Leighton Williams, representative of the Ogden Estate among the Trustees of the new University of

Chicago; Abbot; Hale; Rev. Wm. D. P. Bliss, the Boston Christian Socialist; Mayor Samuel M. Jones of Toledo; Mayor Tom L. Johnson of Cleveland; and the editors of many lay and religious reform periodicals.

Le Petit Temps of May 8, 1894, described The Wayside's table as a place where a score to thirty persons, "rich and poor, white and black, gentle and simple, college president and seamstress, artist and mechanic, divine and layman" gathered "all on the basis of liberty, fraternity, and equality." Lloyd, it added with gross understatement, was "un philosophe simple et bon," the foe of violence, the leader of the discontented. Actually, his interest in the problems, plans, and views of each guest sharpened his sense of justice and intensified his compassion for the unfortunate as he broadened his grasp on practical problems demanding attention. Mrs. Lloyd regarded his "causes" as "the center of his life," and advanced them by entertainment of their circle and personal participation. With the aid of Jane Addams after 1889, and incidentally to assist Hull House, she regularly brought discouraged slum-dwellers to The Wayside to rest.

How entertainment there affected the intelligent labor leader Thomas J. Morgan expressed retrospectively to her in 1904:

> . . . no one ever linked themselves so closely to my ideal of manhood as Mr. Lloyd. With him I lost all my feeling of class distinction and antagonism, all doubt and bitterness was gone and in its place perfect confidence. All differences of culture and refinement in contrast with the manners and language of the factory lad was merged in the purest simplicity and limitless goodness—like the snow-white table with a live vine lying on it in beautiful curves which I see as vividly as the day years ago when I first sat with you and him in your home—purity and simplicity— . . .[40]

Instead of taking culture to the wage-earners as the Fabians and British universities were doing, the Lloyds stimulated the workers' development by bringing them individually into their cultured reform circle. This imbued them with their high "spirit of brotherhood, of helpfulness, of service, and . . . joy in living and doing." To this Mrs. Lloyd gave "a distinction and charm" that was unequaled "except at Hull House" under Jane Addams. So Nicholas ("Coe") Kelley recalled after he became a New York attorney and expert on labor relations. Both hosts exhibited "a kind of magic compound of informality, decorum, high thinking, interest in all that was going on, including the sports of the young people, and an ever bubbling fun, humor and wit." Great warmth, friendship's equality, and "the helping hand" Mrs. Lloyd extended to all unaffectedly, but with quiet insistence upon decorum and efficient operation of the establishment.[41] As he was describing this, portraits of the Lloyds and their sons hung on the living room walls of his Manhattan home.

Mrs. Lloyd combined Julia Ward Howe's antebellum social co-operation with her reformer husband with cheerful pursuit of the life that his "genius" and social philosophy dictated. As "a sweeter and more sane exponent" of this than the Countess Tolstoi was of her husband's she was presented to the American public as a unique woman by Marian DePew's "Living Out a Theory," which was syndicated in the press in 1897. What made this especially significant during that era of *parvenu* social climbing was that she had been "exceedingly popular in society" and possessed "wide and distinguished social connections." The Wayside's simple, cultivated life lacking luxurious draperies and costly furniture, its unique guest list, her interest in the individual, "not his station or attainments," and her hearty invitations to the unfortunate to visit there as long as the experience benefited them demonstrated that in the Chicago area older wealth and patrician status were not incompatible with courageous, sacrificial reform leadership.[42]

Mrs. Lloyd led in making reform fashionable again among enlightened members of society, winning recruits as early as 1889 from Chicago's and the North Shore's fashionable set. Among these was the wealthy, gossipy Mrs. Lydia Coonley, later the wife of Professor Henry Augustus Ward, the eminent scientist. Mrs. Lloyd summoned her on one occasion to The Wayside with a crytic telegram, "Your dirt will keep, but the violets won't. Come immediately." The clergy at the Detroit Congress of Religion in 1900 were reconciled to the unorthodox religious training of the Lloyd sons when informed that "Mrs. Lloyd drives along the Sakonnet Road trailing all the beatitudes behind her." Such was the grace and manner of the altruistic Wayside that Prince Roger de Bourbon, the French pretender, was charmed by his entertainment there.[41]

The Lloyds represented "the highest ideal of the highest mutual relation" to Ellen Gates Starr, blue of the North Shore and Hull House resident. She "had never known a husband and wife who seemed so perfectly adjusted to each other and so mutually worthy of each other," despite complete difference in personalities. To her, on a "charming" drive with "The Master," in reply to her praise of Mrs. Lloyd, he replied, "Yes, it w'd be hard to find her beat," while expressing appreciation of how she so arranged matters that he never had "any disturbance" in his work from the numerous guests. It was, Miss Starr added, part of her "religion" to "believe that Mr. Lloyd's public work could never have been what it was and is but for the very elevated personal life behind it."[42]

Chapter XI

Trades Unions - Spring Valley

TRADES UNIONISM

AFTER 1888 Lloyd plunged energetically into social reform, un-inhibited by journalistic necessity or expectations of inherited wealth. He disseminated "The New Conscience" in a prophetic crusade for economic and social justice. He studied problem situations, attacked abuses and the combination movement in business, and championed organized labor in a relatively moderate campaign. In this manner he became the intellectual stimulator, guide, and spokesman of a rising demand for reform among the urban middle class, laborers, and farmers. As a religious liberal and associate of the ethical culture movement, he spoke for those religious elements that were the most friendly to organized labor, as Samuel Gompers observed.[1] While recognizing the need for new tactics and new institutional approaches by movements in behalf of the underprivileged, Lloyd frequently left organizational leadership to others but gave them intelligent, effective backing, as when he induced the *Chicago Tribune* to support Dr. Harriet C. B. Alexander of the Cook County Insane Asylum in her attempt to reform that horribly overcrowded institution.[2] He participated more directly in the trades union movement.

He stimulated its revival in the Middle West during 1888-93. His championship of the north Illinois coal miners demonstrated what élite leadership could achieve by assisting the discouraged wage-earners. The skill with which he related his philosophy to actualities in the course of this campaign won him and the wage-earners a wide hearing.

As he began Davidson persuaded him to lecture on "The Labor Problem" at the Farmington Summer School of Ethics, a continuation of the Concord School of Philosophy in the summer of 1889. This paved the way for subsequent presentation of his welfare philosophy to American philosophers and students of ethics in the East. Because of his brother David's premature death, Percival Chubb of the Fabian and New Fellowship societies, who had republished "The New Conscience" in London, presented Lloyd's lecture in his stead.[3]

Impelling him to test his social theory in action were the *Atlantic*'s and *Forum*'s rejections of his "Servitudes Not Contracts." That article discussed the Reading Railroad's "yellow dog contracts," and developed Thorold Rogers' thesis that unorganized workers could not make free contracts. This thrust at the prevailing freedom of contract shibboleth that anti-trades unionists currently invoked had elicited editorial allusions to "wild-eyed socialistic theories."[4]

Trades unionism and the Spring Valley tragedy described below provided capital opportunities to investigate industrial conditions and a competitive mining district and, while reporting the facts, to make humanitarian appeals to the public. On July 4, 1889, Lloyd spoke on invitation at the huge eight-hour demonstration at Cheltenham Beach, an amusement resort twelve miles south of Chicago, that the Chicago Trades and Labor Assembly staged. His previous eight hour speeches had stimulated a trades union revival in the city. At Cheltenham he spoke as the well-dressed Victorian clubman, from gray top hat to well-polished boots, to the brown-derby-hatted workers.

They cheered lustily as he identified shorter hours with the historic struggle against despotism. He praised the labor movement's attempt to broaden "political freedom into industrial freedom" and nurture thereby "a new, better civilization." To arrest "the decline" caused by business abuses and revive the "upward movement" of "progress" was trades unionism's unique mission. This embodied a "distinctly higher ideal than

that obeyed by modern society." Seeking to advance "morality
a step farther," apply brotherhood in industry, and extend "the
Golden Rule into the market" the labor movement was "the
most religious movement of the day," at "the forefront of civilization." By contrast "organized abuses" made the churches,
economists, universities, and political parties impotent. Although
the Lambeth Conference in Britain and the Evangelical Alliance
of America were silent on modern war, which he called "the
crime of crimes," "the British Trades Union Congress opposed
that together with child labor, mothers' labor, and unemployment. Trades unionism sought to prevent interclass hatred and
achieve social justice while resisting "taxation by capitalistic
trusts without consent."

While expounding "The New Conscience" Lloyd excoriated
those of old American stock who, by perverting justice, rigging
markets, corrupting legislatures, and abusing managerial responsibilities destroyed "Freedom" in "our innermost sanctu-
aries." The "materialistic and atheistical aspects of . . . modern
thought" trades unionism opposed as it did fanaticism, the Single
Tax, prohibition, Socialism, and Greenbackism, he said. By
practical steps as in Great Britain trades unions would establish
"industrial democracy," beginning with the eight-hour day. The
only "real obstacles" to that ultimate goal "lie in the hearts of
men." Its achievement would solve the labor problem, Lloyd
predicted.

This address made him the leading intellectual and favorite
orator of the midwestern labor movement. After the *Arbeiter
Zeitung* published it, the Rock Island trades unionists persuaded
him to repeat it at their Labor Day program. The *Chicago
Express* called Lloyd "a very Nineteenth Century Demos-
thenes."[5] Captain William P. Black, who had lost his lucrative
law practice because he had been counsel of the Haymarket
Anarchists, wrote Lloyd that his address was a "noble effort,
worthy of yourself." Its "dispassionate" analysis of trades
unionism was necessary to secure the support of "people of comparative intelligence and even moderate fairmindedness." *"The
slaves have never liberated themselves."* Black agreed that the

practical solution of the wage problem *"must* come" as the result of the wise counsels, fraternal aid, and earnest agitation "extended to the oppressed by their more fortunate brethren." The *Current* agreed. Black rejoiced that Lloyd, with means, leisure, and a sympathetic heart, had taken up labor's cause. "God bless you, in your work and labor of unselfish love," he said. Lloyd drew other liberals into a Gideon's band to aid the labor movement. I. Giles Lewis of Robert Stevenson & Company, wholesale druggists, promised help, remarking, "capital and brains seem everywhere combined in this country against the common people."[6]

After Labor Day Lloyd spoke frequently on the labor question in the Chicago area. Rejecting projects to colonize slum-dwellers in rural areas, he observed that many came originally from farms. He repeated his Cheltenham address on November 20 before a huge crowd at the Princess Opera House for the Ethical Culture Society. It was so enthusiastically acclaimed that the Socialist *Workman's Advocate* (New York) attempted a rebuttal. In "The Union For Ever," before the Chicago Nationalist Club, he championed trades unions eloquently, citing British support of the great London dockers' strike. He hailed citizens' contributions to aid Spring Valley miners as "breaking the drought of the human heart." Businessmen, he insisted, should see that their survival in a free economy could be secured by co-operating with trades unions in an industrial citizenship working for the general welfare, instead of becoming "Vassals of the Money Power," to which "Labor Power" was opposed. This was Lloyd's reply to the distant Major Huntington's blunt disbelief of the previous April that he or anyone else would succeed in solving "the problems that beset us" because the American people were "money-grubbers, money-worshippers, and tuft-hunters" and American institutions had been perverted "by the robbery of monopolies, the jobbery of politics, and the snobbery of social life" into "so many instruments of tyranny in the hands of the unscrupulous rich."[7]

SPRING VALLEY

When Lloyd first visited Spring Valley, September 3, 1889,

the lockout in that north Illinois mining town was four and a half months old. Chicago's Mayor Cregier and Congressman Frank Lawler had investigated it and collected money and food for relief. On August 22 the special commissioners appointed by Governor Joseph N. Fifer reported an illuminating analysis of that lockout and the north Illinois coal mine strike. The press had published sensational accounts of Spring Valley and solicited funds for its relief. Lloyd was at The Watch House when his attention was drawn to the episode by the *New York World*. Interest in aiding the labor movement and discovery that the President of the Spring Valley Coal Company was William M. Scott, a Gould lieutenant, led him to intervene.

The complex situation had been clarified but partially by the Commissioners' *Report*. Excessive north Illinois coal production and withdrawal of the southern Illinois mines from the annual conference of miners and operators of the competitive bituminous coal mining district had precipitated competitive coal price and wage reductions and the Spring Valley lockout and the north Illinois strike. Despite the miners' suffering the Special Commissioners reported that there were "no actual cases of starvation."[8]

Enlightened operators such as Colonel Wm. P. Rend, who had supported the annual conference, and Lyman J. Gage, the referee, made it clear during the arbitration elsewhere in the northern district that only a modest wage reduction of $7\frac{1}{2}$ per cent was justified. Rend urged that the operators recognize "a humanity line below which capital should not go in its relation to labor." Scott announced on August 22 a 60 per cent wage reduction after having previously reduced wages a third as terms for a settlement with his men.[9]

Lloyd went to Spring Valley immediately before Labor Day. He interviewed the miners and the Rev. John F. Power, priest of the Church of the Immaculate Conception, who backed the locked-out miners but urged him to "get the other side." After questioning the mining company's executives Lloyd concluded from "the reception and treatment accorded him that justice was not on their side." He espoused "the cause of the miners," thereby winning Power's admiration. He soon esteemed him as "a man of loftly ideals, disinterested, fearless; loving the truth, hating injustice, and filled with enthusiasm for the welfare of his fellow men."[10]

Lloyd's intervention defeated the "purpose of the lockout," vindicated the miners' rights, and became the turning point in the fortunes of the American mine-workers, who were developing a tradition of defeat after having been beaten in Hocking Valley and the anthracite coal fields."[11]

He discovered at Spring Valley that Scott had "boomed" the town, inducing an excessive influx of miners that facilitated wage reductions. Scott disrupted the District Operators Association by insisting that his miners accept four and a half times the agreed-upon wage reduction. Alleged nonpayment of dividends and company store bad debt accounts did not disguise his greater harshness to his employees in mines free from water and coal vein faults such as characterized those of nearby Peru, Streator, and Braidwood, where the operators adhered to the agreed policy.

Lloyd learned from Father Power about the mining company's $10,000 to $12,000 monthly profit when operating previously under the higher Conference wage scale, the $40,000 per annum net company store profits, and the $40,000 paid to the town site company for lots. Scott had invested these profits in expanding the mining company's land holdings. Power declared that his lying, "unscrupulousness and immorality," which the men knew, endangered public welfare. He believed that only the "merciless exposure and just criticism" of the press could prevent imposition of Scott's drastic wage reduction.[12] The *Tribune, Herald, Times,* and *Inter Ocean* declared journalistic war on him, and collected food and money, as did Lloyd. He asked the National Progressive Union of Miners to aid the north Illinois miners and persuaded President John McBride to go to Spring Valley.

When the late resumption of operations elsewhere in the northern district prevented miners from contributing to the relief of that town, Lloyd published "The Crisis at Spring

Valley" in the press. This reported malnutrition, begging, and starvation among school pupils. He proved that for four weeks the food distributed by the local relief committee had averaged in value but *eighty-four cents per person,* without which the miners' community would have starved. He reported excessive child mortality, the county doctor's refusal to treat miners' families, and absence of all but 250 adult miners because of search for work elsewhere. Medicines that Lloyd collected stemmed epidemics. Children's shoes and food that he and Cook County Agent John Foley sent alleviated much suffering.[13]

When Scott defended his wage reductions and attributed criticism of his management to "professional agitators and a partisan press," Lloyd persuaded the miners' union to reply in a scathing public letter to the Governor, offering to arbitrate or to work Scott's second and third veins at the Streator wage scale. The *Inter Ocean* then declared that the miners had won the argument and that Scott's real purpose was to destroy the Illinois miners' union.[14]

Father Power was "deeply grateful" for Lloyd's "masterly indictment of the real offenders in the great crime." If Scott's proposed Spring Valley wage scale were accepted, nearby operators would have had to reduce wages again, "and so reopen the whole wretched question. . . . More power to your elbow!" the priest said. The men's prolonged resistance, Lloyd's aid, contributed relief funds and supplies, press support, and the superintendent's offer to operate Scott's mines and pay him fifteen cents per ton forced him to moderate his wage reduction. Although double his first offer, his newly proposed scale was still lower than that of nearby Braidwood and specified termination of collective bargaining. Finally, the miners were stampeded back to work by false reports of a negotiated settlement and signed open shop contracts on November 12.[15]

After investigating the Spring Valley situation with great care, Lloyd was furious at Scott's methods and at the ruin of the town, whose "businessmen and other 'middle class' people," he wrote Power, should tell Scott and the world that "the miners' cause is their own." If they did, "much might be saved out of the wreck," and evicting of miners from company houses might be prevented. In resisting this, Chicago's Assistant Corporation Counsel, Clarence Darrow, "a zealous friend of the workingman," would help. Lloyd related the issue to the "scandalous" degradation of yeomanry into slummers" for which "there shall be a cure."[16]

He exposed Scott's mismanagement scathingly in "To Certain Rich Men," a sensational four-column letter to the *Chicago Herald*. This was a stroke of some import since Scott was an important Pennsylvania coal operator and Congressman. Spring Valley's tragedy became a national scandal after this piece's republication in the *New York Sun* and other eastern papers. In this letter Lloyd addressed himself to the leading owners of the Chicago and Northwestern Railroad and to the owners of the Spring Valley Coal Company, Chauncey M. Depew, Scott, the Vanderbilts, Marvin Hughitt, and N. K. Fairbanks of Chicago. Spring Valley, Lloyd disclosed, was a factor in the Northwestern's bid for cheap fuel as a means to transportation supremacy in the upper Mississippi Valley. He described the miners' meager earnings, the lockout's attempt to starve them into abandoning the union and selling their labor far below market value while a competing mine paid the former Conference scale, the mining company's defamation of its employees, and the suffering of the miners' families.

The public to whom Scott had appealed, Lloyd declared, would say that his methods were "conspiracy, gentlemen millionaires," a conspiracy to which the Northwestern would be a party if it accepted Scott's lower-priced coal after a settlement. Lloyd concluded this stinging castigation of antisocial entrepreneurship by demanding that the stewardship of wealth and general welfare principle be applied by Scott's backers if they avoid "the folly of your medieval exemplars whose castles now decorate a better civilization with their prophetic ruins."

In "The Crime of Spring Valley" the *Herald* remarked editorially that the verdict on the Scott mining associates must be "guilty." It declared that Lloyd's "arraignment" derived added force from his character, superb attainments, and "well-known philanthropy." His presentation of "the truth as to the Spring Valley scandal was one of the most powerful appeals for justice and one of the most eloquent denunciations of wrong which have come under the public eye for many a day. . . . There must be conspiracy laws for millionaires." The *Herald* endorsed Lloyd's declaration that social justice was essential to civilization's survival. It warned that "a Society which permits such inhuman outrages as that at Spring Valley is either asleep or in an advanced state of decay.""

The reception of "To Certain Rich Men" was all that Lloyd could have hoped for. The union officials thanked him for this "able and fearless exposition." McBride distributed a thousand copies at his national convention. Lloyd sent many copies to Power for "the church dignitaries," an attempt to win the Catholic hierarchy to labor's side. C. J. Devlin, General Manager of Scott's mining company, confessed to a banker friend of Lloyd's that the lockout had been "most iniquitous and entirely unwarranted." Prominent Chicagoans praised Lloyd's *Herald* letter emphatically. The *Boston Herald* termed it "magnificent." Howells wrote Lloyd that he had read the piece "with grief and rage," and hoped he could persuade an eastern publisher to issue an enlarged version. Liberals were warm in their praise. Single-Taxers were delighted. The New York press republished "To Certain Rich Men." The *Pittsburgh Post* declared that it cast significant oblique light upon Scott's Pennsylvania mining ventures. When Scott denied that he was blacklisting the miners' relief committee and union officials Lloyd replied in the press with a crushing exposure of his falsehood.

The *New York Sun* then buried Scott alive by disclosing that he solicited free passes from the New York Central on the ground that party differences were immaterial when it came to serving "corporate property." "Politically Mr. Scott is a back number, personally he is in a very unfortunate position before the American people," it observed.[18]

At a great Spring Valley miners' meeting Lloyd prophesied that the labor movement would "furnish a new brotherhood, a new civilization, and a new religion." He identified the miners' union with Lincoln, Emerson, Phillips, Mill, "and a host of others" in the struggle against "the fanaticism of modern trade." Strikes rightly instituted would receive public support, he promised, and congratulated the Convention of the Progressive Miners and Mine-Workers Union on its "unity of purpose" and pledged "hearty co-operation." That body voted its thanks for his interest "in the miners' cause generally, and the service he rendered the miners of Northern Illinois during the late conflict with the operators." His recommendations would "be carried out." Lloyd's publications on Spring Valley revolutionized "the attitude of the newspapers toward the working classes," the *Knights of Labor* observed. Eastern religious periodicals such as *Truth* asked their leaders to pray for the blacklisted Spring Valley miners.[19]

ANTI-BOURBONISM

Lloyd delighted Chicago laborers and Single-Taxers at a November Economic Conference with a "Dives and his Professors of Political Economy" introduction of Father Huntington, the Georgite New York Episcopalian priest. The Personal Rights League then invited him to preside at its Washington Birthday celebration. That powerful nonpartisan organization was fighting the nativist American Protective Association, Prohibition, political corruption, prolonged police brutality and infringement of civil liberties, food adulteration, and monopolistic combinations in transportation and utilities, in alliance with Swiss, German, Bohemian, and other labor unions in the Great Lakes area. That League had won a signal victory in 1888 when Judge M. F. Tuley ruled in the *Arbeiter Zeitung* case that Chicago's Mayor must dismiss police inspectors guilty of interfering with labor unions, arbitrary arrests, and prohibiting peaceful meetings. Lloyd had provoked great applause during his Mazzini lecture by denouncing Chicago's police for attempts at thought control.[20]

Lloyd opened the League's huge celebration as Chicago's leader of reform. With "What Washington Would Do Today" he attacked government by classes, special privilege, the

"Hydra" of industrial monopoly, "millionaire microbes, pestil-
ence germs of plutocracy . . . eating out the heart of our liberties," and the "real aliens" whose class legislation and scandals
in courts, politics, finance, and markets provoked mass discontent. Instant applause greeted his remark that in none of
these had a "foreigner" figured importantly. He contrasted "the
faith of the fathers" in the republic's ability to "absorb and
assimilate and ennoble" oppressed and poor immigrants with
the "Pacific Railroad Swindles, the Erie and Tweed rings," and
the starvation of Illinois miners.

Inspired by faith in "the Republic of Washington" the populace would overthrow plutocratic control and establish a new
order based upon brotherhood and a new sensitivity to social
wrongs. These "must be" corrected by social effort guided by
"the new conscience." "Consciousness of a new social power
for "the common good" and Washington's "love and sacrifice"
would inspire the newly oppressed poor and middle class to
defend the American heritage. Lloyd then aroused the throng
to "the most tremendous enthusiasm" by demanding protection for constitutional rights from police oppression.[21]

This stirring indictment of business and political "Bourbonism" and linking of Washington's ideals with "The New Conscience" confirmed Lloyd's leadership of Chicago's liberals and
wage-earners. General M. M. Trumbull thanked him and contrasted his courageous message with Dr. Tiffany's simultaneous
assertion before the Union League that what America needed
was "the quiet submissiveness of the Chinese to offset nihilism!"
Prime of Dwight delightedly hailed Lloyd's comparison of the
United States Senate to a railroad roundhouse. The *Chicago
Herald* declared that no more graphic characterization of the
evils of "trusts, monopolies, rings, combines, and other extortions of the money power . . . has been heard from press or
platform. . . . Every man interested in the public welfare"
should read and ponder it "seriously."[22]

A STRIKE OF MILLIONAIRES

Lloyd then published an enlarged history of Spring Valley as a sensational example of pathological entrepreneurship. Vividly written, it judged the record of the Scott group by the standards of "The New Conscience," which Lloyd applied to "undisputed facts" in coal mining where Scott had "supposed ethics had no jurisdiction." So he informed Davidson.[23] He entitled the book *A Strike of Millionaires Against Miners or the Story of Spring Valley,* Volume One of " 'Our Bad Wealth' Series," quoting Emerson's "It is high time OUR BAD WEALTH came to an end." The treatise was a product of the ethical revival and held "Captains of Industry" personally responsible for "what they do in managing the common labor," as Lloyd informed Professor Ely.[24]

The vivid narrative contrasted the Iroquois' destruction of the Illinois Indians at Starved Rock with Scott's lockout. It reviewed the press attempt to arouse public interest in and Father Power's solicitation of aid for the locked-out miners. Quotations from both sides of the negotiations between the Spring Valley Coal Company and its miners exposed the former's "campaign of slander" against them, its open-shop policy, and its postlockout blacklisting. Citation of the Special Commissioners' *Report* and Superintendent Dalzell's offer to lease the mines discredited Scott's claim that southern Illinois competition justified the lockout, his Draconian wage reduction, and open shop policy. Sarcastic chapter headings, viz., "Feed My Lambs," and withering contrasts between the Company's professions and its acts revealed his cynical hypocrisy. However, Lloyd erroneously attributed the prelockout "inter-state agreement" that had produced the annual conference exclusively to the miners' union, and forgot Colonel Rend again when he declared that "the workingman stands for the democratic principle in business" in opposition to "the business and railroad men" who illustrated "the oligarchic" and had killed the Conference.

If the attempt of the railroads to "partition" the bituminous coal business among themselves and "their business favorites" was accomplished by "the survival of the fittest," he declared, this would produce arbitrary control of the industry by a few railroad managers. "Only a fool can suppose that the republic

. . . will survive the continuance of such a system," he warned. What would be the result if the railroads reached out "for land monopoly and market monopoly" also? Upper-class contempt for and hatred of the workers he discovered in Governor Fifer's acceptance of his Attorney General's accusation that the starving Spring Valley miners got drunk and preferred to live on charity. The people had "lost their hold on their rulers" who were completely subservient to "the money power" that high public officials dared not "thwart," Lloyd charged. He warned that worse might yet be in store for wage-earners, consumers, and competitive businessmen.[25]

Like Henry O. Havemeyer of the "Sugar Trust" a decade later, Scott cared nothing for ethics in business. He ignored Lloyd's book and adhered to his previous managerial methods, despite the Winnetkan's hope to win him to a welfare management policy.[26] Lloyd's prolabor bias did not appeal to Scott.

In May 1890, before the Congressional Committee on Immigration, Lloyd repudiated the inference that the Spring Valley "trouble" had been caused by foreigners. He attributed it instead to "commercial war on the workingmen" and attacked Scott's resort to illicit contract immigration. He also objected vigorously to illicit contract immigration and to the suggestion that immigrants be excluded from America because of their supposed radical opinions, asserting that this would be un-American.[27] His testimony provoked scathing press criticism of Scott's methods as far east as Pittsburgh. The *New York Journal* then persuaded him to describe the continued suffering of the Spring Valley miners. Lloyd sent 750 copies of this statement to influential men. The *Chicago Herald* attributed to Spring Valley Mining Company executives "immorality and coercion of the women of the miners." However, Walter C. Wyma, a mutual friend, conveyed to Lloyd Manager Devlin's thanks for his championship of the miners, who appreciated his "labor of love!"[28]

A Strike of Millionaires appeared that same month. Most press reviews were favorable and criticized Scott. Some castigated the "grasping cruelty" of the existing industrial system, as the *Springfield Republican* expressed it. The *New York Commercial Advertiser* demanded that Scott present his defense quickly, since Lloyd's arraignment was "too worthy of respect to be treated with silent contempt." The *Burlington* (Iowa) *Hawkeye* declared that the book expressed the almost unanimous opinion of the north Illinois press, clergy, and civic leadership. The *Rock Islander* endorsed Lloyd's criticism of Governor Fifer, whose political career ended abruptly. Only the *Chicago Tribune* took exception to Lloyd's narrative and accused him of gross bias.

Magazines sympathetic to reform endorsed the book's definition of the issues that the Spring Valley episode illustrated. B. O. Flower, editor of *Arena,* later termed it "one of the pioneer works" that exposed the ruthless labor policies of great corporations. *Open Court* (Chicago) said that it made every citizen of "healthy morals" ashamed. Hugh O. Pentecost in *Twentieth Century* attributed the tragedy to "the social system" whereby railroad-controlled legislatures favored "man-starvers" owning coal mines. While complimenting Lloyd, *Dawn* reported New York press support of locked-out cloak-makers and Boston clerical backing of a building trades strike. *New Ideal* agreed with Salter that the Spring Valley lockout was "nefarious." *The Nationalist* praised the book.

In London *The Democrat* and *Commonwealth* stressed its grim contrast of original American republican principles with contemporary "millionaire senators, huge rings of unscrupulous capitalists, corrupt wire pullers, and terrible extremes of wealth and poverty." *Seed-Time* termed it the "most complete exposure of the tyranny and cruelty of capitalism" extant.[29]

In Illinois Judge Altgeld welcomed Lloyd's book. Father Power sent his complimentary copy to Bishop Spaulding of Peoria, after thanking Lloyd for publishing "our true story." The mass unrest, he observed realistically, resulted from draining the profits of farmers and workers into "the enormous fortunes of millionaires." Charles H. Ham was "profoundly impressed," and asked that a copy be sent to "Tommy" Morgan. *The Farmer's Voice* (Chicago) reported daily orders for the book. The newly organized United Mine Workers of America and the *Labor Tribune* thanked Lloyd for exposing Scott, as did his manager Devlin. The young economist F. W. Taussig of Harvard College informed Lloyd that his book's documents alone sufficed to damn Scott. Would Lloyd contribute to the *Quarterly Journal of Economics?*

This explains why *A Strike of Millionaires* went into a second edition despite a booksellers' boycott. During the great coal strike of 1894 the *Chicago Times* recalled that it had cheered "slaves" and warned "slave drivers" that the day would yet come when "these men could not be starved, robbed, and despoiled of the fruits of their exertions at the command of plutocrats." In 1900 the *New York Journal* declared that the anthracite coal strike of that year opposed the same "horrors" that Lloyd had described in 1890.[30]

Meanwhile, he kept in touch with the continuing tragedy of Spring Valley. In 1891 Scott attempted vainly to induce Bishop Spaulding to move Father Power elsewhere, so as to break the miners' resistance. In 1895 three hundred of Scott's miners offered to enter voluntarily into slavery to him if guaranteed comfortable houses, fuel, food, and serviceable clothing for themselves and families. In 1897, when food and clothing were still collected in Chicago for the starving Spring Valley miners, Lloyd recognized that his long campaign and exposures had had no effect whatever upon Scott's management. Not until the United Mine Workers' organizing campaign of 1899-1900 were that magnate's employees lifted from semistarvation to a living wage and by collective bargaining accorded a contractual voice in their compensation and working conditions.[31]

PROPHET

A Strike of Millionaires made Lloyd the publicist of the midwestern campaign for social justice. It drew him closer to Judge Altgeld, who followed his Spring Valley campaign with keen interest. After hearing Lloyd deliver "The New Independence" to the Ethical Culture Society in December 1890, Altgeld wrote him, "You have placed all lovers of justice under obligations to you by your remarkably able . . . address." He had followed his example by speaking repeatedly to labor gatherings. Lloyd spent a night at the Altgeld home and learned more of the views of the author of *Live Questions,* who advocated Australian ballot, court reform, penal reform, protective legislation for women in the garment industry, labor unions, the eight-hour day, and compulsory arbitration of industrial disputes. The two men sustained each other as advocates of social justice, social reform, and trades unionism.[32]

"The New Independence" was a significant elaboration of "The New Conscience," and attacked the power enterprisers of American business for duplicating Louis XIV's absolutism. Lloyd listed business abuses and asserted that the labor movement "is *our* chapter of the great historic uplift" that was forcing upon "the Money Power" the maxim "brothers instead of slaves." Contemporary workers, agrarians, and the cooperatives of Britain and America had the same objective, winning independence from industrial feudalism. Lloyd called the new Sherman Anti-Trust Act "The Anti-Trades Union Law" because of its quick perversion into judicial restraint of labor organizations. This was part of "a world-wide concert of action of a money power, crazy with greed, and fanatical to the hilt, to reenslave the working people," he cried in angry exaggeration. While this presaged future indulgence in extreme language in advocacy of reforms, it was provoked by the hostility of most American businessmen to labor organizations and by most enterprisers' desire to reap for themselves exclusively the wealth created by modern technology. The railroads, Lloyd said, led in this. His remedies, recognition of farmer, labor, and cooperative organizations, and government regulation of railroads were moderate, an application of his new liberalism.[33]

Altgeld's applause and ensuing collaboration were significant. Although he was a successful lawyer and judge, and a wealthy developer of Chicago "Loop" business rental real estate, he had followed Lloyd into the liberal-labor position that was becoming popular among advanced reformers and politicians in Britain and the United States. This explains why, as Governor of Illinois during 1893-94, he befriended the labor movement, supported social legislation, staffed his administration with liberals, radicals, and labor leaders, and opposed George M. Pullman, the midwestern railroads, and Grover Cleveland's growing conservatism.

Lloyd employed historical analogy in "The New Independence" and exhibited a keen appreciation of historical continuity and development. Like other early American rebels against formalism in social thought, he stressed historical development, the law, liberty, brotherhood, social ethics, the state's relation to the economy, and equalitarianism's impact upon the class structure. History justified to Lloyd an ethical and reformist perfectionism similar to Thomas Hill Green's. Lloyd cited historical persons and experience as perspective for problem analyses and to validate principles. Historicism, then, buttressed his repudiation of Darwinian determinism and Marxian materialism. It pointed up the role of prophetic vision and heroic leadership in achieving progress.

Derived from Lieber, Emerson, historical economics, Hegel, and Green, it became an instrument of great effectiveness in his hands. A scientific aspect of his thought was evident in his derivation from history of "laws" of social change and reform. The Positivist ethical utilitarianism that he espoused provided philosophic justification for this use of history. Hence, although he read history for enjoyment he valued it more as a practical resource to aid in problem solving, an attitude that later characterized John Dewey.[34]

Thus Lloyd emerged to prominence in 1890 as a leading reformer and the recognized prophet of a social-welfare, ethical philosophy designed to bring American democracy to grips effectively with the problems of the machine age. His other role as the patrician leader and chief intellectual of midwestern labor's growing demand for recognition and social justice brought him into direct touch with actualities. This enriched his original contributions to social ethics and emerging pragmatism and prepared him for the role of social critic in which he would exert great influence.

His championship of the Spring Valley mine-workers confirmed also the admiration with which midwestern farmers and
commercial interests serving them, such as Montgomery Ward
& Company, had long regarded him as the champion of western interests and economic justice for agriculture. Shortly before
publication of *A Strike of Millionaires,* that mail order company's organ, *Farmers' Voice,* completed editorially the agrarian portrait of him in glowing phrases that explained agriculturalists' continuing response to his leadership :

Many of our readers know of Henry D. Lloyd, the
scholar, and philosopher whose home is in Chicago, where
he is held in highest honor by all classes. . . . Some . . . give
admiration and respect on account of his social position,
brilliant literary genius, and singularly pure and beautiful
life, while others . . . reverence this divinely illuminated
man, for the helpful love he carries . . . to the lowly ones
whether poor in purse, sick in body or sorrowing in mind.
    Henry D. Lloyd is a just man. . . . He will tell the truth
where he loves. He will tell the truth where he hates.[35]

Chapter XII

 For Social Justice and

Urban Regeneration

LABOR'S CHAMPION

AFTER LLOYD HAD stimulated the trades union revival in the Chicago area in 1888 despite George Schilling's opposition, the American Federation of Labor made the eight-hour day its immediate objective. The carpenters' bid for this was scheduled for May 1, 1890, to be followed by the United Mine Workers. Lloyd and Judge R. S. Tuthill spoke at the Chicago carpenters' preliminary meeting, March 4. The former cited precedents set by London's County Council and dockers' strike and predicted, to the dismay of the (Chicago) *Economist*, that shorter hours would provide leisure ultimately for workers' afternoon cultural pursuits. At Grand Rapids he warned the furniture workers that if wage-earners did not use their liberties and political rights "they and America would lose them." Distinguished in manner, his brown hair sprinkled with gray, he made an indelible impression.' To the St. Louis Ethical Culture Society he predicted that the labor movement's higher ethical ideal would cure " the fanaticism of money making."

Significantly, on April 19 he exposed in the *Farmers' Voice* the secret attempts of some businessmen and the United States Adjutant General to mobilize the militia and police locally on May 1. While warning trades unionists that the eight-hour movement must "be studiously quiet" so as not to provoke police or militia intervention, he quoted ex-President Hayes's doubt that the labor question could be solved by reliance "upon a militia that think with bayonets in their hands." Then he spoke

with Samuel Gompers at Battery D, Chicago, for the eight-hour
day. A warm friendship ensued, fostered by mutual admiration
of Thorold Rogers. Lloyd, Judge Tuley, Darrow, and Otis
Favor of the Personal Rights League raised funds for the
carpenters, obtained press support, and arranged citizens' meetings to endorse their eight-hours strike, thereby checkmating the
employers' "Patriotic Club." With such assistance the carpenters
won the eight-hour day, as did the other building trades and
cigar-workers.² When invited by the latter, Lloyd aided an
abortive attempt in June to revive the United Labor Party in
order to secure repeal of anti-trades union statutes and prohibition of employers' use of private detectives.³

His leadership of the trades union revival was largely intellectual. He preached the philosophy of trades unionism, urged
study of advanced labor leadership of eastern cities and Great
Britain, and cited Lord Brasy's experienced friendship for labor
organizations. He addressed the striking steam-fitters and striking coopers. He encouraged strikes for recognition, eight hours,
and improved working conditions. He informed workers on
current issues, the British labor movement, social legislation, and
Australia's emerging welfare democracy. He and Gompers
appealed to Chicago workers to aid the coal miners' eight-hours
strike. He led the unions' fight for civil liberties and insisted that
labor must be effective politically.⁴

In November the French Consul in Chicago regarded Lloyd
as the best person to enlighten a French investigator on American labor organizations. Gompers persuaded him to write "Why
Workingmen Should Organize" for the *Souvenir* of the AFL's
annual convention. In that Lloyd declared that trades unions
were indispensable to civilization : "Only by organization can
workingmen prepare themselves to be Citizens of Industry . . .
which is their manifest destiny." He advocated voluntary arbitration of industrial disputes in the *Hand Book* of the Steam
and Hot Water Fitters Union. He urged that Chicago's printers
aid a nine-hour-day printers' strike in Germany. Via Typographical Union No. 16, he contributed money to aid striking

printers on the *Staats-Zeitung* and in Pittsburgh. He supplied data on the labor movement to Professor Ely.

Indicative of Lloyd's increased stature in the ethical movement was Professor Adams' invitation to lecture on the labor question at Ann Arbor's Summer School of Ethics. In 1890 he also presented "The Humanitarian View" at the Farmington School of Ethics on a series with John Dewey, Harris, and Salter, after a lecture course featuring T. H. Green. Lloyd also lectured at the Deerfield Summer School of History and Romance on the "Condition of Western Workingmen,"[5] insisting as did John Kells Ingram of Dublin that the needed reforms in business and labor relations were essentially ethical.

Lloyd presided at the gigantic Cavalry Armory meeting of the building trades and Trades Assembly, December 27, 1891, protesting against brutal police disruption of a Painters' Union meeting at Greif's Hall. He delivered the main address, knowing that Judge Altgeld had protested privately to the Chief of Police. That raid's brutality had violated every right of free men, he cried, and demanded that Mayor Cregier explain why the guilty police had not been indicted or punished. He warned Chicagoans alarmed by trades unionism that the alternatives were either a violent "French Revolution" or "an Anglo-Saxon revolution of peace, compromise and progress." In a brilliant metaphor he declared that if American citizens and workers used their inherited "rings of citizenship" they could "break the rings of boodlers, rings of politicians, rings of money power, street-car rings, gas rings, railroad rings, rings of monopoly," but warned that if citizens did not use their power they would lose it. Chicago's workers should show to the world at the "World's Fair" the "citizenship with which we vindicate our rights like freemen." Inspired by Lloyd and other speakers, the mass meeting demanded punishment of the guilty police, a municipal apology, and an end to such oppression.[6]

From his office as chief counsel of the Northwestern Railroad, Darrow complimented Lloyd on his address : "It was *great*. In logic & law it can not be disputed. It made me feel that I am a hypocrite & a slave and added to my resolution to make my term of servitude short. I am glad that you dare to say what is true & know so well how to say it."⁷ Carter Harrison endorsed the resolutions heartily. "Tommy" Morgan, Socialist leader, wrote Lloyd equal praise. As founder of the International Machinists Union, Morgan was an important leader in the AFL. He had induced the Trades Assembly to convoke the Armory meeting and to threaten independent political action. Although excluded from the Committee and speakers' list, he had kept silent there, but stressed the importance of independent political action by labor privately to Lloyd hoping that "the magic rings would imply that you do not overlook it."⁸

A few days later a prominent attorney described in the *Chicago Herald* the secret corruption fund that had persuaded the police to repress legitimate labor activities since the Haymarket riot.⁹ Organized labor supported Harrison's independent mayoral race in 1891, after which he was "counted out" despite his plurality. The next year the Chicago police made headlines by breaking up Socialist parades carrying the "Red Flag" and threatening Anarchist speakers in public meetings.

Lloyd's and Gompers' leadership, the activity of Morgan and Schilling, aid from sympathetic Chicago lawyers and judges, and the hard work of organization so strengthened trades unionism in Chicago that before the Greif's Hall raid some 262 to 300 unions with a claimed 150,000 membership existed in Cook County. This strength no aspiring political figure thereafter dared to ignore.¹⁰

During those same years Lloyd was active in the Chicago Sunset Club. Organized under Lyman Gage's aegis with W. W. Catlin, another banker, as secretary, it comprised business and professional men, financiers, labor leaders, and radicals. Debates on various aspects of the labor movement were staged after dinner at the Palmer House. There Lloyd, Darrow, Altgeld, Tuley, Tuthill, Trumbull, Bonney, Ham, Morgan, and other liberals and radicals opposed their opposites. Replacing Salter's Economic Conferences, the club bridged the class chasm dug by Haymarket. Indirectly it facilitated trades unionism.

There, on election eve, November 6, 1890, Lloyd debated

"Strikes and Lockouts" with R. H. Maxton, a building contractor, following an eight-course dinner including Pointe Canet and Sauterne. The members' diversity of dress ranging from "sack-coats, the mark of true democracy, cutaway coats, which incline more toward aristocracy, and Prince Albert coats" marking those "thoroughly au fait," symbolized the viewpoints present. Maxton denounced strikes as violent, socially injurious, and unbeneficial to workers, and would substitute arbitration for collective bargaining.

As a professed "striker for truth," running his fingers through graying hair still brushed in pompadour, Lloyd made an impassioned speech declaring that strikes and lockouts were "skirmishings of a great social war" in which the laborers might make mistakes but were "always on the right side." The Club's members shouted and stamped "the floor till their insteps ached" when he demanded that the public awaken "to the misery of the lower classes" (!) and called Jay Gould "the enemy of American liberty" for dismissing underpaid employees demanding collective bargaining. It was "excruciatingly funny," he said, that the boulevardier with a life expectancy of fifty-five years should accuse back-street labor leaders enjoying but twenty-eight. Wages should be based upon production costs, and "the real cost of production to the American citizen" should include no child labor, motherhood exempt from wage-earning, fatherhood with leisure, "and a manhood which should be allowed to cast a ballot as conscience alone dictated." During the discussion not an employer backed Maxton. A dozen members supported trades unions.[11] The Club and the St. Louis *Union-Record* published Lloyd's address, which he repeated with equal success before the Chicago Ethical Culture Society.

At the Sunset Club his subtle, witty criticisms of the *status quo* delighted the members and, when published, the liberals, workers, and farmers of the region. When invited to speak on "The Red Flag" program the next January, he declined. When asked for a paper on the subject, he expressed surprise that the Club was "expecting an article from me on 'the pet vanity' of bulls, Chicago policemen and millionaires." After citing C.

Osborne Ward's thesis that the red in the American flag represented "the poor, the slave, the workingmen," he defended the right of anyone "to fly the ancient red cap of the slave as a banner." America could afford "to tolerate the wildest dissents . . . on the chance of hearing the voice of a Christ or an Emerson." Policemen invading workers' homes to tear down the flag that was their "protest against the oppression of the weak by the strong" were rehearsing the folly of "the successful protestants who deny to others below them the right to protest."[12]

Equally appreciated was "The Milch Cow Fable" that he presented on Ladies Night, February 4, 1892. President Frances E. Willard of the Women's Christian Temperance Union presided at the discussion of "How Would You Uplift the Masses?" Jane Addams presented the social settlement as the agency to heal interclass antagonism. Disclaiming any ability to add to "the weight or force or eloquence" of the discussion, Lloyd described a "fresh milch cow" that had had the misfortune to attract "the attention of a Foreign Syndicate of Flies . . . traveling through the country in search of investments." Upon seeing it, the "Model Merchant" heading the "Syndicate" declared, "This is a sure thing." The syndicate included the cow in its "Trust" and drew dividends from "her circulating medium." When the cow began to run, members of the "Syndicate" addressed her after dinner on "questions of reform," congratulating themselves on employing "her otherwise undirected energies" and applying to her "the law of supply and demand." The cow stopped and began to roll, ignoring the alarmed Model Merchant's protest that she was "evidently a member of the Farmers' alliance" opposed to "honest currency" and "the obligations of contract." Completing the roll, she prevented the attempt of the "Syndicate" to withdraw to a better field for investment by crushing "the Flies."

Schilling wrote Lloyd afterward, "Your cow is a daisy & ought to be seen in every reform paper." He offered to introduce him to eastern labor leaders and pay half the cost of printing the fable, while attributing Mrs. Lloyd's good health to "the Milk from the cow." The fable appeared in the *Farmers' Voice*,

American Nonconformist and other Populist papers, labor press, *New Nation*, and daily press, wittily stimulating resurgent anti-monopolism.[13]

At the Club's fiftieth meeting the following December, Lloyd achieved his greatest triumph with a "letter" from "a new Mahatma, Mahatma Carnegie." Asserting that this had come "by invisible post," he presented it after Senator William A. Peffer of Kansas had denounced Carnegie's labor policy and employer use of private armies in labor disputes during a debate on "The Lessons of the Homestead Troubles." Carnegie announced in the "letter" his retirement from his earthly mission of "preaching the Gospel of Wealth" into the mountains. "Unlike Buddha, I have taken my boodle with me. I am tired of paying all the expenses of advertising a heaven which is the monopoly of the poor, as only they grow thin enough to pass through the eye of the needle. I am preparing the millionaire's paradise, . . . where their will shall be done as it has been on earth" and "the Almighty Dollar" would "have its Incarnation" as "the God of Wealth"—terms, net cash in advance." Founding libraries had trained him for this. Prayers to him "must be accompanied by remittances." Those rejecting Homestead with its "gutters of typhoid fever" as "Heaven," or who would "undo" the 100 per cent ad valorem duty on steel and "go after a strange God of another Golden Rule than mine, I, the dread Divinity of the Dollar . . . shall break in sunder" and send "my Cherubim and Seraphim with flaming Winchesters" to "drive them forth" and "lock them out of the Promised land." Lloyd broke off, declaring that the "letter" must have been forged by the Devil's agent. The members cheered until Catlin, the jolly chairman, adjourned the meeting amid laughter and more cheers for the caricature of Carnegie's "Gospel of Wealth" and his retreat to Skibo Castle while his General Manager Henry Clay Frick inflicted *sturm und drang* upon Homestead.[14]

Nearly two years earlier at a Chicago Press Club program on "The Absurdities of Nationalism," Lloyd had observed that "the discussion" of the social problem was on "in the parlor," the club, on the sidewalk, in the lecture-room, and even in the pulpit." Seeing "the evils which all see in the social system," he shared the "desire that fills all hearts to join in some move by which conditions might be improved and man restored to his better estate. The field is wider than that in which Garrison fought, and, as Socrates said . . . 'The venture is a glorious one.' " The *Daily News* concluded that Lloyd preferred to remain an individualist while seeing "much to admire" in Bellamy's utopianism.[15] To the Evanston Cosmopolitan Club in November 1891 he interpreted the social ferment optimistically as presaging "a moral revolution." His assertions that circumstances were analogous to conditions preceding earlier revolutions and that the "new theology" recognized "all men as co-operative" alarmed wealthy General Walter Newberry, who replied vigorously that education, self-improvement, and raising all to "genteel" standards were still valid for the wise and pure, and better than Bellamy's utopia.[16]

Rising unrest and growing popular apprehension of a "revolution" led Lloyd to study the accounts of Cromwell, Sir Harry Vane, and the Levellers in T. H. Green's lectures and J. R. Green's *Short History of England*. British press reviews of Ruskin's *Fors Clavigera,* IV, addressed to the trades unions, and James Bryce's assertion in *The American Commonwealth* of the priority of reform sentiment among the middle and humbler English classes confirmed a faith in trades unionism derived from study of the London dockers' strike.[17]

During May–June 1890 he privately defined "The Prophet" in social development as the creator because "he sees the ideal." That role he filled dramatically in the Middle West. Humanity, he predicted, would soon act "co-operatively in all lands" more swiftly along traditional "social curves" under the inspiration of such figures. Social love was basic and divine, a universal truth, but more than this was needed to achieve something other than benevolent autocracy. He reiterated that "The Vanderbilts and Rockefellers" as "the Fittest" correctly measured "the character of current civilization" and exhibited America as an uncivilized "cruel, selfish, carnivorous, short-sighted herd." Yet, geographic exploration and railroad building indicated that modern men could become a united brotherhood, guaranteeing individuality by "contest, competition, selection, survival" to the "disadvantage of sinister elements."[18]

His notebook jottings exhibited continuing faith in the perfectibility of man and manhood suffrage. State action on an international scale to solve the complex labor problem he thought was foreshadowed by a "revolution" in public opinion. That the people were ahead of the intellectuals he perceived in international May Day's contrast with Froude's old fashioned radicalism.[19]

DEVELOPING RADICALISM

While observing the swift rise of Bellamy's Nationalism into a middle-class mass movement, Lloyd continued his study of collectivism and other issues involved in the social problem. With Professor Ely he concluded that government ownership of railroads and other natural monopolies was probably the wisest policy. Then, after taking Will to Carlsbad for the cure from rheumatic fever in the summer of 1891, they went to London to outfit before returning home. Between visits to their tailor they went slumming in Whitechapel with Herbert Burrows, a young journalist active in the Social Democratic Federation and among "labor reformers and theosophists" who were working "for a new Heaven and a new earth." Burrows took them also to Salvation Army shelters, Mrs. Annie Besant's séances, and to Cradley to see the women making chains. The Lloyds interviewed Tom Mann and John Burns, leaders of the dockers' strike and exponents of mass unionism. They met the leaders of the Fabian Society, and with Burrows' help interviewed the Marxians, Friedrich Engels, Alfred Henry Wallace, and Hyndman.

Henry D. Lloyd discovered that a "large proportion of the officials in the Government service" were Socialists, particularly in the Colonial and Foreign offices. They worked "evenings and holidays" to "overthrow" their government while other Socialists were "making converts everywhere" among "all classes of English society." London "is the fermentingest place in the world," he concluded after returning to America with the English commissioners to the World's Fair.[20]

Unlike Darrow, Hale, and Howells, he had watched the Bellamy movement with little enthusiasm, and usually regarded the *New Nation* with contempt. The lines of influence between Lloyd and Bellamy flowed from Winnetka to Springfield, Massachusetts, as the former helped to subsidize the *New Nation* and Bureau of Nationalist Literature in harmony with his policy of aiding all reform movements that promised to contribute to a solution of the social problem. Lloyd entertained leading Nationalists Henry Legate and Eltweed Pomeroy during the World's Fair at Chicago. His *Wealth Against Commonwealth* of the following year exhibited but few traces of Bellamy's influence. However, that great utopian inscribed a copy of his edition of the *Fabian Essays* to the Winnetka reformer, who was subsequently invited to write the memorial sketch for a posthumous edition of *Equality*.[21]

The chief inspiration of Lloyd's continued interest in collectivism continued to be European. After returning from Carlsbad and London he analyzed Thomas Kirkup's *Inquiry into Socialism* (1888). Its assertion that because industry had become collective industrial rewards should be collective impressed him, since the few monopolized "individual development, freedom, security of property" which the "common man and philosophic man want." Yet, he reiterated his qualification of Mazzinian collectivism in a notebook, "never to surrender to collectivity . . . the right of opinion and expression, right to home, wife, etc., right to vote." The mean between individualism and collectivism is "the real solution," he believed. He applied to the social problem his liberal religious approach when he added that all material progress was "mere brutishness, unless it is equalized, spiritualized, made the broad stairway by which man may mount to greater liberty, goodness, equality, less poverty, labor and crime." Institutions permitting the few to monopolize the fruits of human effort embodied social treason, he noted. Collectivism was not new, "but we are on the eve of a great extension of it." The issue was "whether the people shall take hold of railroads, telegraphs, mines, etc." The "only new question" was, would government by consent be extended to property and the practice of popular election to the rulers of industry? This indicated a democratic socialism.[22]

Previously, fear that socialism might lead to despotism had restrained him from commitment to it, as the Marxian *The People* (New York), April 5, 1891, reported after he addressed the Chicago Ethical Culture Society. Continuing his analysis of Kirkup and socialism, Lloyd wrote, "Last great change. . . . But hopeless confusion, unless sternest clarification of thought concerning . . . 'right to think.' . . . Right thinking, speaking and doing, are progressively more perfectly realized by freedom than authority. Freedom is not freedom to do everything, but freedom to do right." These principles would check institutional fossilization and special interest-serving, and facilitate emancipation of thought, speech, and action in the economic realm and abolish class perquisities in employment.[23]

Instead of the Christian Church, which would be "first to go" in the great changes ahead, Lloyd preferred the "Real Church" of those who did the Lord's work, the immortality of children and society, and "the creation we see in progress," with each man a priest, each act worship, every wish a prayer, every good book a Bible. This Emersonian religiosity permeated his reform thought, helped to motivate his dedicated life, and clarified the religion of labor of "The New Conscience."[24]

To the Evanston Cosmopolitan Club in November 1891 he compared British ferment to Bellamy Nationalism. He defined Socialism vaguely as "sympathy, a community of interest . . . a better share of civilization and of life, a broader christianity." Inferring that *Looking Backward,* trades unionism, and the farmers alliance presaged a moral "revolution," he asked, "Can we make it an orderly reconstruction?" Eighteen months later on the train to Quincy he concluded that the Western world would be compelled to choose between further reform and "suicidal" revolution. The first alternative, promoted by new ethics, brotherhood, altruism, and welfare economics, he be-

lieved to be more probable. "Mankind is now quivering with its
purposes need add new institutions to the achievement of its
progressive movement." On a letter from Ignatius Donnelly, the
Minnesota antimonopolist, he jotted, "If we wait to be forced
by events we shall be astounded to find how much more radical
they are than our parlor Utopias." Before the Evanston Conference Club, in December 1891, he had upheld the feasibility of
government ownership of railroads. In January at the Ethical
Culture Society he indicted railroad "governments within
governments" so effectively that M. M. Kirkman, whose book
upheld private ownership, suggested that they agree to dis-
agree.[25]

The *Chicago Tribune*'s disclosure that western railroads
granted exclusive secret rates regularly to single grain buyers,
and that gross discriminations to the meat packers and the
Standard Oil demonstrated that government regulation was a
failure. Lloyd recalled how he and Sterne had vainly urged that
the Cullom Committee confer judicial powers on the Interstate
Commerce Commission. At Quincy in March 1893 he declared
that the railroad men were "the most powerful body in the
country," and that they and their business allies were leaders of
the combination movement. Then, at the National Anti-Trust
Conference in June, he advocated socialization of anthracite
coal carriers and mines as the solution for the "Trust Problem."
Presented in collaboration with General James B. Weaver and
Ignatius Donnelly, this disclosed publicly Lloyd's shift to radical
reform.[26]

Assisting Hull House

The Lloyds may have been present at the meeting in Mrs.
Lydia Coonley's La Salle Street home in the spring of 1889
when Jane Addams broached her project. As soon as Hull House
opened they joined others from the North Shore in assisting its
program. Henry D. Lloyd appreciated instantly that settlement's
potential for social reform. His sympathy and support contrasted
with Davidson's opposition, which sprang from fear that the
residents would lose their individuality. To Lloyd Hull House

institutionalized the altruism and brotherhood of "The New Conscience," Jane Addams agreed. Her serene humanitarianism, leadership, and stress upon ethical problems of urban life made her especially congenial to Chicago liberals, radicals, and labor leaders.

Miss Starr, her lieutenant, combined cultivation of love of beauty among slum children with a passion for social justice. She urged workingwomen to join trades unions; she picketed during strikes; she addressed the strikers. Julia Lathrop brought calm efficiency and a warm heart into cold-blooded "scientific" charities. Mrs. Alzina Stevens, a fiery Populist, helped the anti-sweatshop campaign.[27] The Lloyds entertained the Hull House residents regularly.

Henry D. Lloyd became chairman of the Literature Committee of the Arnold Toynbee Club at Hull House. Jane Addams invited him to speak as "by far the ablest person to do it" at the shirtmakers' first rally in November 1891. She asked him to lecture frequently at Hull House, that he negotiate with *Century* for an article series on the settlement to be written by the residents, and assist Mary E. Kenney, Boston labor organizer, to finance a co-operative garment factory nearby. Jane Addams wrote her admiration of him on the flyleaf of *Hull House Maps and Papers* that she sent hoping for his approval of that literary venture. She helped him in turn to plan the programs of the Labor, Co-operative, and Single-Tax congresses for the World's Fair Auxiliary. During the "hard times" that followed she confessed to him, "we are having an awful time with our feeble effort."[28]

With Miss Starr he developed a similar relationship. While inviting him to speak at the Settlement Congress on "The Relation of Settlements to the Labor Problem," she confided, "I want awfully to talk to you about something."[29]

As co-operating patrons, when Jane Addams' health broke in 1895 the Lloyds entertained her at The Watch House until November to ensure her recovery. She sought Henry D. Lloyd's suggestions wittily when she began to write for the magazines,[30] an unconscious tribute to his extraordinary sympathy and understanding of what her band of enlightened women were attempting to accomplish. He accepted the justice of feminism's campaign for equal rights and the suffrage as a matter of course.

Mrs. Florence Kelley became a very close friend of the Lloyds. As the Socialist divorcee daughter of Congressman William H. Kelley, an admirer of *A Strike of Millionaires,* and friend of his sister Caro, she interviewed Lloyd in January 1892. He helped her to find remunerative work assisting the Congressional "Special Investigation of the Slums of Great Cities" which, with Hull House surveys, produced the *Maps and Papers.* With high-spirited impatience she persuaded Chicago's Health Department to investigate local sweatshops and prosecute violators of municipal regulations. She berated Marshall Field, who refused to improve his garment industry management on the pretext that he could not, as she informed Lloyd, "deprive worthy widows of the chance of working at home with their children ! The only one I have yet found working for him earned *$9.37 in 13 weeks* and we fed her !" She wished that he "felt as warmly with the workingmen on the basis of personal contact" as he did "against the robbers in spite of the acquaintance of the most *decent* of them. . . . There is such urgent need of a leader now; and the men at the helm are such sorry steersmen."[31]

Lloyd and she helped Miss Kenney organize garment workers' mass meetings and to mobilize public support for their strikes. At the second meeting, May 8, 1892, Jenkin Lloyd Jones announced the alliance of leading clergy and others with the Trades Assembly in war upon Chicago sweatshops whose conditions, Mrs. Kelley demonstrated, were worse than those in New York's East Side. Dr. Bayard Holmes of the College of Physicians and Surgeons attributed many epidemics "on the boulevards" to their infected clothing. Garment workers' and cigar makers' spokesmen and Congressman Lawler voiced organized labor's and the general public's demands for reform. Lloyd's opening address contained an unforgettable parable on the cynical sweatshop "Good Samaritan" employer who exploited helpless women. Lloyd's remedy was the garment workers' union aided by other trades unionists, capitalists, and professional men.[32]

After Governor Altgeld's inauguration, Schilling, his Secretary of the Bureau of Labor Statistics, made Mrs. Kelley investigator of child labor. She compiled Eastern child labor laws and agitated for similar legislation in Illinois. She and Mary Kenney provided Hull House hospitality, a conducted tour of sweatshops, and a readable report for the General Assembly's commission on the employment of women and children in industry. Careful publicity facilitated introduction of a factory bill. Lloyd, Miss Kenney, and Mrs. Kelley staged a monster demonstration in support of this at Central Music Hall under Trades Assembly sponsorship, whose costs the Winnetkan defrayed. Boston and New York antitenement and antisweatshop leaders, Chicago clergy, professors Bemis, Albion Small, and John Leonard of the new University of Chicago, legislators, labor leaders, Hull House residents, women garment workers, and both Lloyds spoke. Denunciations of Chicago's sweatshops preceded the cheering, unanimous adoption of Henry D. Lloyd's resolutions. Then a legislative committee headed by him was appointed to present them to the General Assembly. They demanded a living wage, denounced Marshall Field & Company's leadership in the demoralization of the garment industry, asserted society's obligation to prevent industries from injuring the public welfare, demanded strong garment workers' unions, and requested tenement house legislation and statutory protection of women and children, in the garment industry.

Illinois was in the novice stage of social legislation when Lloyd took his committee to Springfield. It included Bishop Samuel Fellows and other prominent clergy, Dr. Holmes, Jane Addams, Mrs. Kelley, Miss Starr, Bemis, socially prominent women, and labor leaders.[33] As they arrived Chicago cloakmakers announced a 25 per cent wage reduction. The Illinois manufacturers opposed the Committee's draft factory bill so vigorously that Governor Altgeld informed Lloyd that more support was needed for its enactment. Mrs. Stevens and Lloyd persuaded Darrow, Chicago's Corporation Counsel, to come to Springfield. Together, with the co-operation of Mrs. Kelley, Miss Kenney, Schilling, and Altgeld they defeated the manufacturers' lobby. The measure became the Illinois Factory Act of 1893.

Altgeld appointed Mrs. Kelley Factory Inspector on Lloyd's recommendation. She sought his counsel, studied law at night, won admittance to the bar so as to enforce the law herself when lawyers boycotted it. For the next four years Lloyd was her confidant and inspirer. Mrs. Lloyd entertained her sons regularly at The Wayside and The Watch House.[34]

Mrs. Kelley advanced Henry D. Lloyd's education in the problem of poverty. They visited a tin can factory where they discovered a shelf occupied by young boys, with cut fingers tied with rags, removing defectives from a continuous procession of can lids, their eyes strained, their legs and backs crooked, their minds "stupefied and deadened." They also saw there a white-haired man, who for thirteen years had inspected "an endless procession of cans." Lloyd was "fascinated, horrified." The man was native born, literate, but after his ten-hour day "his eyes were too weary for reading."[35]

Altgeld and Amnesty

Governor Altgeld was much gratified at Lloyd's effective support of his gubernatorial campaign of 1892. During work for the Factory Act Lloyd also helped to unite the Amnesty Association, of which he was a vice-president, Hull House, liberals, labor unions, Polish Americans, and Chicago's Russian colony at a great mass meeting in opposition to the new extradition treaty with Russia because it provided for return of political refugees. He carried the protesting resolutions which Salter and Howells supported, to President Cleveland, whose rejection of them antagonized powerful liberal-labor Illinois Democrats.[36] Lloyd then helped to rally those same elements in behalf of a pardon for the imprisoned Haymarket Anarchists.

He and General Trumbull collaborated in a leaflet describing the Amnesty Association's work to counteract Judge Gary's article in *Century* that rallied conservatives against gubernatorial clemency. Darrow and Judges Tuley, Brown, and MacConnell also worked to counteract this article's effect upon the lawyers. Lyman Gage joined the Association. Lloyd went to Springfield on its committee to present a pardon petition bearing 60,000 signatures to Altgeld.

On June 26 he pardoned Fielden, Neebe, and Schwab, appending a review of the Anarchist case that criticized Gary and his article. This threw the gauntlet at the feet of his conservative admirers. Joseph Medill picked it up and threw it in the Governor's face with unprecedented abuse and misrepresentation of his motives. The conservative press then pilloried the courageous German-American who had predicted the storm. Lloyd defended him in a letter to the *Chicago Herald*. He drafted the Amnesty Association's congratulatory resolutions, complimenting Altgeld for breaking "the wheels of a judge-made revolution" that would deprive "the people" of their constitutional rights of freedom of speech and assemblage, introduce "class distinction in the administration of justice," and subject the public to police censorship. When the Governor's press conferences did not quiet the conservative outcry Mrs. Lloyd invited the Altgelds to "run away and hide" at The Wayside. Altgeld declined to turn tail on his attackers, but hinted that "it might not be long before the Altgelds took up their abode by the wayside."[37] Gary's worshipers never forgave him.

During 1895 the Lloyd group defended him from their attacks. General Trumbull replied in the *Arena* to Gary. When the Republicans nominated him for the appellate court in reply to Altgeld, Lloyd, Darrow, and Schilling rallied the disbanded Amnesty Association, contributed money, and circulated a speech of Lloyd's in an anti-Gary campaign. Lloyd attacked Gary as a monopolist and user of railroad passes in a letter to the Trades Assembly, which circulated 50,000 copies. Lloyd and Schilling distributed 50,000 copies of Altgeld's pardon statement. On election eve Lloyd published a formidable statement of the antimonopolist, labor, and social issues involved in the judicial election, since the laissez faire, antilabor Republicans

dominated the courts. Altgeld complimented him but regretted
that this could not "have been circulated a little earlier." However, the Democratic machine's refusal to nominate an able
man in opposition to Gary, and the hard times, enabled him to
win by a majority of 5,000.[38]

Darrow observed to Lloyd afterward : "The election might
have been worse but it shows how much there is to do." Frank
A. Stauber, a former Socialist who had been ousted once from
the Common Council because of his views, expressed his disgust
to Schilling at the workingmen's failure to defeat "the mur-
derer of five of their own !"[39]

THE WORLD'S LABOR CONGRESS

Lloyd's role in planning the World's Labor, Co-operative,
and Single-Tax congresses for the World's Columbian Exposition of 1893 widened his reform orientation and circle of friends
and brought him into association with leaders of the Exposition.
These Congresses were a part of Charles Bonney's "Congress of
World Thinkers" in every important area of intellectual, religious, and social activity that was held at the Art Institute on
Michigan Avenue. As secretary of the Program Committee and
chairman of the Literature Committee, Lloyd planned the program of the Labor Congress with advice from Ely and Stewart.
Its ambitious program covered every phase of the labor movement, and the problems of Negroes and Indians, the Single Tax,
Populism, and Fabianism. At the opening of that Congress his
"eminent services" were mentioned. He responded to Bonney
ironically but hopefully, after which his friends Burrows and
Clarke of London, a Professor Zacher of Berlin, and Victor
Delahaye of Paris replied in behalf of European labor and social
reform.

Lloyd had urged Bellamy to come but desisted with great
regret when that utopian whom he had planned to schedule as
"the most important feature" demanded an entire day for
Nationalism. Booker T. Washington, Principal of Tuskegee, at
Lloyd's insistence came despite his school's financial plight and
visited at The Wayside. There he met the Fabians, Clarke and

Burrows. Such entertaining, directing the Congress' program, and distributing labor literature occupied Lloyd from August 28 to Labor Day, when Samuel Gompers closed the Labor Congress with an address on Federation.

Almost every important American labor leader appeared on that Congress' program. George McNeill, Clarke, and Sidney Webb discussed the labor movement's philosophy. Women in industry and sweatshops were discussed by Jane Addams, Mrs. Grace Kelley, Grace Dodge, Professors Lucy Salmon and Katharine Coman of Vassar, Miss Florence Routledge, Rev. Anna G. Spencer, Beatrice Webb of London, and Mme. Hann Horany of Beirut. Zacher analyzed Germany's social insurance. Fabian Society activities were reported and its literature sold in the lobby. Senator Peffer and John Bascom developed legal aspects of labor disputes with emphasis upon Pinkerton detective activities. Detailed reports were made on the labor movement in each country represented.

Ely debated "Public Ownership of Agencies to Supply Public Needs" with Professor Edmund J. James and Laurence Gronlund. J. M. Sullivan of *Twentieth Century* described the Swiss referendum. John R. Commons advocated proportional representation. Adler and Salter discussed ethical aspects of labor problems. J. Keir Hardie and Sidney Webb described political objectives and methods of British labor. Lloyd presided at an interdenominational program where Archbishop Ireland, Rabbi G. Hirsch, some Protestant clergy, and W. D. P. Bliss, the Christian Socialist minister, discussed the churches' relation to the labor movement.

For American labor leaders the firsthand reporting of methods, programs, and achievements from European and Antipodean labor movements at the Labor Congress was profoundly stimulating. They discovered that democratic governments on those continents were socializing utilities, clearing slums, adopting labor legislation, and embarking upon government-owned railroads and telegraph at the instigation of trades unions that frequently participated directly in politics. Many non-Socialists carried home in America new conceptions of welfare democracy from the meetings.[40]

Lloyd's radical trend was quickened by the programs of the Labor, Co-operative, and Social Settlement congresses and by conversations with foreign delegates, some of whom he entertained. The Trades Assembly followed him in voting fraternal greetings to the labor movements of Europe and Australasia, and pledged Chicago labor to work for industrial democracy "in the spirit of international patriotism."[41]

Lloyd learned much from the World's Fair Auxiliary. He had insisted to Gage in advance that the educational exhibit be made "surpassingly good" as evidence of America's appreciation of intellectuality. He was impressed by the civic patriotism of the Fair's leaders, and their large scale co-operative achievement. He observed in the wage-earners' spontaneous response to the Fair the possibility of their elevation to "higher levels of social achievement." However, he realized that only "government auspices and the motive of public benefit" had made it possible to subordinate "the private and money-making" in organizing the Fair. So he informed Daniel Burnham, one of the chief architects. He hoped that the frequency of expositions augured eventual "disappearance of war."[42]

Simultaneously Lloyd was drawn into direct contact with industrial relations and unemployment. On an arbitration board in May he learned that the carpenters had been able to save individually but eight cents per day during the previous six years. In August he represented the Trades Assembly on a committee of twenty-five notables to devise work for the jobless. Carter Harrison placed him on the Mayor's Committee to plan "ways and means of caring for the unemployed," who had induced Lloyd to address them during the Labor Congress after their demonstration in the Loop. He discovered then the respectable, job-seeking character of many helpless victims of the economic crisis, the indifference of the wealthy to them, and the ineffectiveness of the Relief and Aid Association. Only the labor unions, saloons, and County Commissioners helped the unemployed. They slept under bushes and trees in Grant Park and on harbor docks while weather permitted. During cold weather they entered cheap lodging-houses or slept on police station floors, in saloons, and on City Hall floors.[43]

Lloyd's public championship of their cause made him an indispensable speaker at the huge Central Music Hall meeting, November 12, that W. T. Stead of the London *Review of Reviews* organized. He had remained after the Fair, a famous journalist who had exposed British aristocratic interest in the white slave trade, to interview the jobless and discover appalling conditions in the city. These ranged from unrestrained vice that shocked his experienced sensibilities to almost unbelievable municipal corruption. He launched a multilevel fight for reform, aided by the receptivity to new ideas fostered by the Fair.

At that unprecedented meeting Lloyd joined representatives of all elements on the stage. They applauded Stead's devout, dynamic appeal to provide for the unemployed, enter politics and capture municipal and state governments, and transform them into an "instrument of social and civic regeneration" after the example of the British "Lib-Labs." The great throng voted to establish a committee to organize a nonpartisan civic federation to unite all reform elements, labor, and the churches in cleaning up the city. Stead collected $200,000 for an experiment with work relief. He returned later to collaborate with civic leaders in accelerating municipal reform.

Lloyd assisted Stead's attempt in 1894 to defeat "the boodlers and their patrons" in the spring municipal election. This welded them together in an enduring transatlantic reform partnership. When Stead published his sensational *If Christ Came to Chicago,* and *Chicago Today, or the Labor War in America* Lloyd wrote him, "They are the most notable contributions of recent years to the social problem. They will do great good." The books applied the muck-raking technique that he had developed in his own earlier campaigns to social and industrial relations. Meanwhile, as labor disputes multiplied in the city the Industrial Committee of the new Chicago Civic Federation headed by Lyman Gage, President of the First National Bank, appointed Lloyd to a board of conciliation together with Jane

Addams, E. B. Butler and Professor C. R. Henderson of the University of Chicago, wealthy Arthur Ryerson, and three wage-earners."

It was evident to Gage, Burnham, Harrison, and Stead that Lloyd had developed a unique influence as labor's leading champion, as a practical worker for the underprivileged, and as the spokesman of advanced thought with its criticism of abuses and its emerging hope. As Altgeld's "brain truster" of 1893 his effectiveness was patent.

Chapter XIII

An Experiment with American
Fabianism : The Labor-Populist Alliance,
1893-1896

For Welfare Democracy

LLOYD WAS UNAMBITIOUS for political preferment despite his interest in political action as an instrument of reform. He was, as he informed Frances E. Willard in January 1892 when she attempted to persuade him to form a Prohibitionist-Farmers Alliance coalition, "a man without party."[1] Preoccupation with trades unionism blinded him as it did Samuel Gompers to Populism's professed friendship for the labor movement. Both men concluded erroneously that the Omaha Platform said nothing in July 1892 "of any value for the workingmen's movement—nothing in favor of trades unions and the Eight Hours Day." Yet Lloyd wrote Gompers that it was mutually advantageous for the laborers and farmers to be "allies," since the artisans had led "every great social change" that farmers had "also fed."[2] This Locofoco view had activated worker-farmer alliances earlier.

During 1893 Lloyd worked with Altgeld and Gompers. For the former he led the midwestern and Populist delegation at the National Anti-Trust Conference. After the Labor Congress Gompers invited him to address the AFL's annual convention in Chicago.

Slender, slightly above medium height, with a thoughtful, scholarly face, a mustache and wavy hair of iron gray, and

bespectacled, kindly, dark-blue eyes, Lloyd spoke earnestly to
the delegates on December 12, his voice filling Chicago's Common Council Chamber easily. His subject was "The Safety of
the Future Lies in Organized Labor."

He called upon the AFL to crusade for a "progressive," welfare democracy, the first time that this was formally proposed
in America and just as New Zealand's program was reaching a
climax. For realization of this, industrial democracy was indispensable, Lloyd declared, as the solution of "our irrepressible
conflict" with arbitrary business. The British Trades-Union
Congress had demanded nationalization of land and mines, a
labor party, and ultimately, the "principle of the collective
ownership and control of all the means of production. Democracy must be *progressive* or die," he cried. The unemployed
sleeping on the floors of the City Hall at night implied "that
the *general welfare* . . . is the object of society." Effective labor
organizations must institute "this *new democracy of human
welfare*" by political action, abolishing the contract system on
public work and directing "the co-ordinated labor of all" for
the general welfare. National and international labor conferences were necessary to achieve such a welfare democracy,
whereby poverty would be abolished. On May 1, 1901, "a grand
international constitutional convention" should draft "a new bill
of rights . . . to guide and inspire those who wish to live the life
of the commonwealth."

The applauding Convention approved Tommy Morgan's
motion to print 20,000 copies of Lloyd's address, of which he
took 2,000 for his literary bureau. Gompers distributed 5,000.
Judging from this and a Pittsburgh delegate's praise of Lloyd,
the AFL was most receptive to the Lloyd program, which combined limited socialization of the economy with antimonopoly
action and social legislation.

The excitement and enthusiasm that it engendered strengthened the AFL's radical wing. The Illinois Federation of Labor
had authorized recently an industrial conference to unite all
producers in "independent political action." Seizing the opportunity provided by Lloyd's address, Morgan secured unanimous

reference of the British Trades-Union Congress' political program to the AFL's member unions in a referendum. This implied a conditional endorsement of that combination of welfare legislation, Swiss initiative and referendum, municipalization of utilities, and nationalization of communications, railroads, and mines with "(10) the collective ownership by the people of all means of production and distribution." To Morgan, an English Socialist ever since girls had ridiculed a squint caused by an early accident, "Plank 10" was the major objective. Lloyd's address had mentioned it but did not endorse it. Excepting Swiss democracy, he favored the remainder of British labor's program.

Morgan's successful maneuver disclosed a powerful collectivist element within the AFL deriving from Bellamy, Populist ideas, Socialism, and the World's Labor Congress. The Convention referred Lloyd's proposed national and international labor congresses to the executive committee. Gompers was "impressed deeply" with Lloyd's address, as he wrote him in February, and wished to make the "most of" the project of an international Congress in 1901 as "the central idea."[3]

Governor Altgeld was also greatly impressed by the address. He wrote Lloyd, "It has the imprint of genius on every line. Accept my congratulations and go on with your work." Catlin agreed with Lloyd "fully." E. A. Moseley, Secretary of the Interstate Commerce Commission, wrote Lloyd of his "pleasure and delight" and insisted that to realize "your glorious paper's" goals labor must find leaders willing to become martyrs to its cause. S. F. Norton endorsed the address in the Populist *Chicago Sentinel*. President E. Benjamin Andrews of Brown University wrote Lloyd that his address "has just the right ring" and labor leaders should keep *"labor solid for labor"* politically. In Chicago the *Record* and the *Times* published the address, the latter with unqualified praise of Lloyd's attack upon private contracting of public works.[4] Thus, he won important converts and a hearing for his seminal, welfare democratic program, which he had formulated after correspondence earlier that year with Richard J. Seddon of the New Zealand Cabinet.[5]

Despite its radical character, contemporary trends made Lloyd's policy appear to be especially timely to the variegrated new liberals and radicals of that post-Panic winter. However, its general acceptance by reformers was prevented by unforeseen events and a schism within the labor movement. That was precipitated by the referendum on British labor's political program. However, the progressive trades unions in Illinois accepted Lloyd's and Stead's ideas. With these the gradualist Socialists led by Morgan were prepared to combine in the projected third party on condition that it endorse all the political program and allow them to agitate for a democratic Socialism. Factionalism and strong conservative elements made it impossible to unite the entire Illinois labor movement in behalf of either Lloyd's policy or the still more radical British labor program.

The first unforeseen event was the pathetic march of unemployed "armies" on Washington to petition for work relief that began early in 1894, initiated by "General" Jacob S. Coxey of Massilon, Ohio. These "Commonwealers" appeared to validate earlier fears that business excesses would precipitate a social upheaval. Some "armies" seized trains to secure transportation in a sensational defiance of law, order, and property rights. Federal courts and troops effectively dispersed Coxey's "Army" in Washington and made him ridiculous by arresting him for walking on the grass of Capitol Hill. However, crushing the "Commonweal" without providing unemployment relief or granting a redress of popular grievances intensified social unrest at a time when moderate westerners were antagonized by repeal of the Silver Purchase Act and scandalous enactment of the Wilson-Gorham tariff.[6]

Lloyd was completely opposed to the "Commonweal" and refused to address "General Kelley's army" in April in Chicago. Instead of a "physical" remedy for outrageous wrongs he declared that "America is at the verge of her Decline and Fall unless by political means we can remove both such causes and their results."[7]

His radical mood was intensified by the great coal strike in the central bituminous field for the "living wage." While operators with surplus stocks "cleaned up" at high prices, sensational press accounts of violence at the mines supported sheriffs' requests for militia. Governor Altgeld's General Order No. 7, written after consultation with Lloyd, declined to send militia at operators' requests unless local authorities demonstably could not maintain order. Altgeld denounced the Spring Valley Coal Company, which again imposed a lockout, as a "curse" and "expense to the State" when Lloyd showed him a letter from Father Power exposing the falsity of press reports of violence in Spring Valley. Its miners' wrongs, Lloyd wrote the Governor, "would almost justify them in recourse to revolution," but he opposed violence and urged that the Bureau of Labor Statistics enlighten the public on the matter. Despite doubt of the press's willingness to publish news unfavorable to the operators, Altgeld gladly instructed Schilling accordingly.[8]

Then Lloyd inexplicably criticized Altgeld by implication with an undiscriminating interview in the *Chicago Times,* June 17. In this Lloyd attacked state governors for sending militia to the mines and preventing union committees from coordinating the strike. Lloyd did not criticize Illinois miners for refusing to adhere to their Union's Columbus agreement with the operators. After asserting that labor organization would help miners, he declared that only the middle class could secure nationalization of the mines as the proper remedy for industrial strife. America, he prophesied, "is on the edge of a great historic and social change" comparable to "the coming of Christianity." Willis J. Abbot, the editor, observed that Lloyd's remedy was "more radical" than the miners' proposals but recognized his "warm sympathy, brilliant intellectuality, and absolute courage. No band of heartless monopolists or hireling legislators" could carry the nation "clean over the precipice," Abbot declared, and the public would not submit longer "to any ring."[9] Obviously, Lloyd was diverging from Altgeld's moderate welfare program that he had himself helped to shape.

To forestall organized labor's Industrial Conference, the Populists held another representing farm and labor organizations at Springfield on the eve of their May state convention.

That conclave proposed a farmer-labor party to support the Omaha Platform and the AFL political program excepting Plank 10. Organized labor awaited its own conference of July 2-4. After Chicago Typographia No. 9, a German local, named Lloyd as its representative, Morgan assured him that the Conference's importance was such that he should consent. Two hundred Cook County delegates representing all factions, including Wm. C. Pomeroy's "labor skates," planned to attend. M. M. Madden, President of the Federation, invited Lloyd to address the conference.[10]

Lloyd conceived of himself as its harmonizer. He drafted a flamboyant preamble invoking equalitarian and antimonopolist stereotypes and asserting a "sacred constitutional right" of "perpetual and peaceful revolution" to justify demanding institution of "the Co-operative Commonwealth," an objective borrowed from Gronlund. Lloyd drafted a platform that modified the AFL's proposed political program. He demanded revocation of all private franchises, no future "grants of public powers for private use," a genuine merit system, direct democracy, and government acquisition "of all such means of production and distribution, including land, *as the people elect to operate collectively for the use of all.*" If adopted and instituted, this Fabian program would have established progressively the welfare democracy that he had proposed to the AFL. Undoubtedly he had in view the mixed economy resting upon free enterprise that New Zealand was extending. Lloyd's program preceded the publication of Bellamy's edition of the *Fabian Essays* in America by four months. Making the extent of economic collectivization contingent upon popular referenda modified Plank 10 decisively, since the public could make this partial rather than complete as the Marxians desired. The draft platform was designed to appeal at Springfield to all but the conservative trades unionists and extreme Marxians.[11]

Organization of a labor-agrarian party committed to the Lloyd policy would forestall any resort to violence by the discontented. He intended, apparently, to create in Illinois a partial American equivalent of Keir Hardie's Independent

Labour Party of Great Britain, with whose founder he corresponded.

Lloyd drafted these documents as a strike of Pullman shopworkers widened into a sympathetic boycott of Pullman cars on the railroads by the rising American Railway Union led by Eugene V. Debs. This blow at the great Pullman monopoly, whose arbitrary factory management was widely known, was resented by the General Managers Association of the midwestern railroads. As a rate-fixing, strike-breaking body it attached Pullman cars to every train and determined to destroy the powerful ARU. Transportation paralysis threatened catastrophe to the cities.

On July 1 the Cook County delegates to the Industrial Conference approached Debs, who said that "as his assistants" they should "use what service" they could find to get to Springfield. "His heart would be with us," Madden informed Lloyd, who went with sixty others on a "scab" Wabash train to Decatur, whence an ARU train crew took them to the capital after considerable delay. As they arrived, Chicago Federal District Judge Peter S. Grosscup issued a sweeping injunction prohibiting the ARU from interfering in any way with railroad employees.[12] Attorney General Richard Olney had devised this injunction to defeat the boycott, while persuading President Cleveland to order troops from Fort Sheridan to Chicago without previously requesting Governor Altgeld to forestall expected violence.

That night Lloyd sat in Altgeld's office as he dealt with the unprecedented situation, and saw papers on the desk ordering the mobilization of all state militia companies and their dispatch to Chicago if its mayor appealed for aid in maintaining order. The next morning both men learned that federal troops had occupied Chicago as the injunction was served on Debs and his lieutenants, and then of the great mob outbreak that the regulars could not quell. Altgeld sent militia to Chicago and restored order.[13]

The Industrial Conference convened on July 3 in an excited, indignant mood, furious at federal intervention in the Pullman strike. Altgeld's telegraphed protest to Cleveland against the lack of prior consultation with the Illinois Governor kept most workingmen from deserting the Democratic party immediately. The Conference was torn by factional strife despite every incentive for united action. The United Mine-Workers, downstate cities, and Populists were well represented, as were the orthodox and progressive trades unionists, ARU, Single-Taxers, Knights, Socialists, and Anarchists. "Billy" Pomeroy and Morgan headed rival factions. Schilling represented Altgeld. W. H. Harvey, editor of the free-silver *Coin* and A. L. Maxwell, Populist state chairman, also attended.

Attacks on the Anarchists, who announced they no longer advocated armed force, and upon Pomeroy's attempt to "milk" the Cook County Clerk, and a bitter fight over the platform featured the sessions. Pomeroy was whitewashed of the corruption charge and rehabilitated himself by attacking the Socialists, who attempted vainly to insert Plank 10 into the proposed platform. That document contained the remainder of the proposed AFL political program, leading Populist demands, and the Single Tax. Schilling withdrew when Morgan proposed a substitute platform pledging the delegates never again to vote a major party ticket and combining Lloyd's draft preamble with the entire proposed AFL political program. Reciprocal attacks between Pomeroy, Maxwell, and Single-Tax leaders nearly disrupted the Conference. By exerting his utmost influence Lloyd secured adoption of his original modification of Plank 10 and a recommendation that a national convention be convoked to institute independent labor-farmer political action.

This completed the Springfield Platform, and merged politically independent trades unionists with the Populists, Socialists, some Single-Taxers, Prohibitionists, ARU men, and Knights in a temporary political alliance. The Platform resembled the program of the Fabian Society of which Lloyd was now a member and committed the coalition to campaign for his proposed welfare democracy. Overjoyed, the Morgan faction nominated him for the United States Senate but withdrew this with the understanding that if the Labor-Populist party won control of the General Assembly, he would be elected Senator.[14]

GOVERNMENT BY INJUNCTION?

Lloyd returned to Winnetka as the successful architect and leader of that radical coalition. Henry Latchford compared him to Sir George Grey, who had laid the foundations of New Zealand's welfare democracy, in his religious spirit and insistence that national welfare and morality depended upon "a just distribution of the good things of life," guided by the Golden Rule.[15] Certainly Lloyd had led in the organization of a left-wing Fabian movement of as yet undisclosed potentiality. The odds against its success were great that summer as he lectured at the Plymouth School of Applied Ethics, published *Wealth Against Commonwealth,* and learned of the arrest, condemnation, and sentencing of Debs and the ARU directors for contempt after they had ignored Judge Grosscup's injunction. Lloyd contributed toward their legal expenses at Mrs. Kelley's suggestion and wrote them sympathy and advice. Learning from Professor Bemis that railroad agents had incited the Chicago riots' vandalism, Lloyd concluded angrily that Cleveland's prorailroad intervention in the strike and the contempt proceedings against the ARU officials were unjustified.[16]

He said so when he, Darrow, Debs' attorney, and others debated "Strikes and Injunctions" at the Sunset Club. There, looking at federal judge William A. Wood, a guest, Lloyd stressed the increase in railroad power resulting from federal court injunctions in strike breaking. "Power is always progressive—for power," he declared. America's "social units have already been driven apart by unpunished injustice. To reunite them by force is impossible." Only the love, justice, mutual and equal service, and "reciprocal brotherliness" of "The New Conscience" could reunite the divided nation. Such was his reply to Lloyd W. Bowers, who had secured an injunction to break a recent strike on the Northern Pacific. Darrow backed Lloyd by demonstrating the Sherman Act's perversion into an antilabor instrument. The *Chicago Times* supported their stand, published Lloyd's remarks, and quoted an admission by Edwin Walker, the federal district attorney's special assistant, that the injunction method was designed to prevent railroad strikes.[17]

Thereafter, Lloyd repeatedly attacked the double standard of American jurisprudence that left unpunished the boycotts, lockouts, violence, other illegalities, and obstructions of inter-state commerce perpetrated by railroad managers and "Trust" executives. The "middle classes," he said, would find that tolera-tion of arbitrary, uncontrolled railway power, and of aid to "a few thousand plutocrats" who were depriving wage-earners of their rights would "boomerang" against themselves fatally.

At the great Battery D reception given Debs and his fellow ARU directors in Chicago after their release from Woodstock Jail in November 1895, Lloyd declared extravagantly that they were victims of "judicial lynch law" imposed by "the most dangerous tyranny that ever threatened" popular freedom. He wished them honored universally for their defiance of contempt of court as a substitute for the Constitution. In "Lessons of the Debs Case" in the *Coming Nation* he warned the reform world that there could not be "many more marches for us to make" in the "journey of disfranchisement of property, liberty, life itself." Thus he joined Darrow and Lyman Trumbull in defin-ing the injunction issue that liberals and radicals would agitate until passage of the Norris-LaGuardia Act.[18]

A DISCORDANT COALITION

From Woodstock jail in August 1894 Debs wrote Lloyd his appreciation of his aid and encouragement, and predicted "The People's Party will come into power with a resistless rush." While seething with indignation at the crushing of the ARU, Lloyd asserted in his notebook, "Monopoly forces the issue. . . . Sympathetic strikers C. C. S. S. Capable of self gov. in pol.— in ind." which would nationalize the railroads and "Trusts" by "condemnation." However, he predicted pessimistically to Stead, "In no event will the workingmen and farmers be allowed, no matter what their majority, to take control of the government." Reactionary elements had perpetrated the violence and attributed that to the populace : "in Chicago, I verily believe . . . it is their winning card." His bitterness was unassuaged by Gompers' silence after telegraphed urging that he convoke the national conference that the Springfield Conference had demanded. Instead, Gompers warned against subordinating trades unions to partisan politics. This was a body blow at Illinois Labor-Populism.[19]

Nevertheless, Lloyd labored *in absentia* during the summer to prevent disruption of the new coalition. His report on the Conference to Typographia No. 9 observed that although the Populists were "a middle class party" and that "a permanent union of the workingmen" with them "might prove . . . unnatural and unprofitable," a closer union of the industrial workers with the more enlightened of the farmers was necessary. The next convention would give radical workers "a greater majority." His support of the progressive unions and Socialists led the Pomeroy faction to withdraw into the background when the Chicago Trades Assembly's huge ratification meeting endorsed the Springfield Conference's actions.[20]

Wage reductions, growing unemployment, bitterness at the Pullman strike's defeat, and revelation of Olney's anti-ARU bias by the United States Strike Commission hearings confirmed the political independence of many normally Democratic workers. The *Chicago Times,* their favorite paper, criticized Cleveland's action against Debs and befriended the new party. Sincere Labor-Populists then defeated an attempt of the Pomeroy element, in alliance with the Hopkins-Sullivan Democratic "ring," to capture the Cook County People's Convention on August 19. The progressive unions named a ticket that endorsed the Springfield Platform at a subsequent Uhlich Hall Convention. There ARU director L. W. Rogers declared angrily that the new party's purpose was to "turn upside down the whole industrial system." Lloyd's modified Plank 10, which the orthodox Populists again opposed, was endorsed overwhelmingly.

He accepted nomination for Congress in the Seventh District by the Labor-Populists after urging by Abbott and Mrs. Kelley and compliments from the *Railway Times* and *Searchlight,* which called him "the peer of any statesman." Lloyd thought he could serve "the cause better without office" and regretted mention of his name for the Senate.[21] He believed that the third party would be a useful vehicle for expressing popular grievances and disseminating his welfare policy.

He developed an ardent attachment for Labor-Populism in early September during a weekend visit at the Mt. Lebanon Shaker Colony near Albany, New York. He and the Shakers, led by Eldress Anna White, greatly impressed each other. Before his arrival they had read "The New Conscience," which he had sent, and esteemed him "beyond" any other "outside worker." He was stirred by their efficient, cooperative productivity and the beauty of their cooperative life hallowed by social love and a vital religious spirit. Before the Self-Improvement Society he confessed to an inexpressible emotional experience and discovery of the high potentiality of communal life in "mental and spiritual aspirations" while the members performed "manual labor." There were, he declared, "no other people so susceptible" as the Shakers "to those clear burning truths that are for the redemption of humanity."

Thus, in the religious communitarianism of Mt. Lebanon, a type that he had hitherto scorned, Lloyd found practical validation of the altruist, equalitarian, ethical, and cooperative conceptions that were fundamental to his welfare philosophy. Had he not been predisposed by preceding events to a favorable view he might have detected evidence of decay in that six-thousand-acre community, where competition by commercial producers with its furniture was already felt and young recruits were insufficient to displace the tenant farmers. Instead, he accepted the stone factory, well-kept farms, and huge barns as evidence of impregnable prosperity and proof of the practicability of "The Co-operative Commonwealth." Thereafter he valued communitarian communities as having experimental and symbolic significance. He became the friend and counselor of "my beloved Mt. Lebanon," as he called it, although he envisaged no static utopia.[22]

His leadership of Illinois Labor-Populism now became permeated by evangelical fervor. He subsidized the *Chicago*

Searchlight. The ARU *Railway Times, Chicagoer Arbeiter Zeitung,* and *Age of Labor* followed his lead, although the influential *Eight-Hour Herald* withheld support from the county ticket. The *Chicago Times* advised the third party on tactics, attempted to unite its factions, and endorsed their chief candidates including Lloyd, who negotiated vainly with the Harrison estate for purchase of that paper. Its editor, Abbot, declared that public opinion was moving towards public ownership of all natural monopolies, the Ely formula that he wished to substitute for the Springfield Platform's Fabianism. Lloyd drew Darrow and Trumbull into the party's leadership. The trio joined Debs and Rogers in a formidable list of speakers that included Ignatius Donnelly, Governor Davis H. Waite of Colorado, and Father McGlynn. They attracted large crowds.

On October 6 at Central Music Hall, while Darrow presided, Trumbull and Lloyd set the tone of the campaign. Trumbull attributed the massive unrest to the concentration of wealth, and advocated middle-class-labor political action to remedy this by heavy inheritance taxes and curtailment of federal judicial power. Lloyd stated the philosophy of the movement, developing its similarity to the rising parties of the Left in Britain, France, Germany, and Australia, and to Jefferson's Virginia program of 1776. The international radical development he called "the great political fact of our times."

Instead of the dreaded social revolution, he cited *Wealth Against Commonwealth* to prove that a conservative revolution had actually occurred. "Campaign contributions" had delivered American governments on all levels into control of industrial monopoly, railroads, franchise interests, armor-plate contractors. Special legislation and abuse of the power of eminent domain had transformed popular government into an instrument for "the enrichment and aggrandizement of a few," which was now exempting railroad and "Trust" executives from "punishment for the crimes they are committing."

Labor-Populism's purpose, he declared, was a global "counter-revolution" to overthrow monopoly capitalism and governments of special privilege and establish ultimately the "co-operative commonwealth." This would re-establish industrial freedom as the public determined the extent of economic collectivism. Only the People's Party could accomplish this, because both major parties controlled by the "money power" surrendered individual liberties and states rights to "centralized corporate despotism." If placed in power this party would nationalize communications and railroads, municipalize utilities, establish postal savings, institute women's suffrage, and eliminate the "political corruption, boss rule, and boodle" produced by the "briberies of syndicates." Chicago must achieve "a great upward emancipation" by democratizing "collective industry" and realize Emerson's "the American idea." When freed from servitude to "syndicates" and possessed of a publically trained civil service, America would achieve the new democracy and remedy unemployment. Since the People's Party was also campaigning for this program in New York, Connecticut, and Wisconsin, he predicted that the next national Populist convention would endorse it.

The enthusiastic applause of the great audience expressed the radical temper of Illinois Labor-Populism. Lloyd's rhetorically brilliant address was republished with praise by Populist newspapers and also in the New York Fabian *Commonwealth,* there entitled "Revolution. The Evolution of Socialism." The *American Non-Conformist* circulated 10,000 copies as a pamphlet, as did the *Chicago Searchlight* in a brochure also containing Trumbull's address. Thus, Lloyd's redefinition of Populism as a combination of Jacksonian antimonopolism, "The New Conscience," and Fabianism received widespread publicity.[23]

This and his new book placed him among the "thought leaders" of the new radicalism of the Mauve Decade. He presented his welfare program during the autumn campaign to Populists in Iowa, Minnesota, and South Dakota, and in every part of Cook County, Illinois.

He helped to finance the donwstate campaign, but the hostility of the corn belt to Populism and the dissidence of the Single-Taxers doomed the legislative ticket there to defeat.

Henry George attacked Populism in Chicago a week after Lloyd's Central Music Hall address, and preached the Single Tax as the sole panacea for social problems. Despite his sympathy for "The New Conscience," he did not follow "The Maister" of The Wayside along a Fabian course. He detached the downstate Single-Taxers from the Labor-Populist movement and confirmed their opposition to Plank 10 during the AFL referendum. At the State Federation of Labor's Belleville Convention they aided Pomeroy in defeating it while praising Lloyd's work for labor and instructing the delegate to the AFL convention to support the rest of the "political programme" and independent political action. The Pomeroy faction returned to Chicago singing that they had "knocked" the Socialists "out with the Single Tax."[24]

Lloyd and Andrew Adair, leader of Chicago's printers, immediately urged that Labor-Populists unite in hostility to monopoly "from land to trusts." The *Times* castigated George's refusal to support Labor-Populism's immediately realizable objectives. Lloyd reminded the Single-Taxers that their Chicago leader, Andrew Z. White, endorsed the Springfield Platform. However, the discomfiture of Morgan's faction at Belleville made the Socialists more assertive. This antagonized Catholic workers. The Pomeroy faction nominated a competing ticket. Consequently, only sixty-eight unions in Cook County supported the Labor-Populists, who included only the progressive unions, ARU, a few Fabians, radical Single-Taxers, gradualist Socialists, and a handful of orthodox urban Populists.[25]

Lloyd led them in a remarkably able campaign. It concluded with a torchlight parade of 7,000 Labor-Populists led by their candidates, which invaded the Loop with flags and banners bearing quotations from Emerson, Lloyd, and George. Morgan's men wore red ribbons and scattered red fire as they marched. The parade was cheered continuously by sympathizers as it proceeded from the business district to the great ampitheatre of Tattersall's into which 15,000 crowded while 5,000 stood outside. There Lloyd, Darrow, Morgan, and the Methodist preacher of Pullman, the Rev. W. H. Carwardine, demanded

institution of "The Co-operative Commonwealth." Lloyd declared that the Springfield platform would apply to economic
life "The New Conscience" and "The New Self-Interest" demanded by *Wealth Against Commonwealth*.[26]

The huge, excited demonstration indicated a Labor-Populist
vote exceeding the 50,000 the *Times* had predicted. Officially
this could not be. The People's Party was denied election
judges. "The count" was made by the major parties. The
Republicans profited from the hard times, Cleveland's alienation
of labor, farmers, and tariff reformers, and his feud with Altgeld. The latter's radical anti-trust position, demand for municipalized electric lighting, hostility to Cleveland, and social
legislation kept many wage-earners loyal to him. Many discontented farmers, floating voters, and some workers turned
to the Republicans for relief as the G.O.P. swept the local and
Congressional elections. On election night Gompers wired
Cleveland that although the political upheaval might benefit
organized labor little, "the rebuke" of "your unwarranted assumption of unconstitutional authority and unwarrantable use
of the military power" to "crush" it "will . . . be appreciated
and remembered."

Although Lloyd polled 7,000 votes in the "fearfully conservative" Seventh Congressional District, every Congressional,
legislative, and county Labor-Populist candidate was defeated.
The official county Labor-Populist vote of 40,000 disappointed
him and the other leaders. It was a smaller proportion of the
poll than the United Labor Party received after Haymarket.
Undoubtedly, the corrupt "count" reduced the total by as
much as 25 per cent, if not more. If this were added Lloyd's
Labor-Populists polled almost a third of the strength of organized Labor in Cook County.[27] That measures the extent of
the radical protest that had been provoked by the depression,
the Armour-Field-Yerkes business régime, and Cleveland conservatism's favoritism to the "Trusts," Pullman, and the railroads.

However, the Cook County Labor-Populist campaign did
arouse interest. Abbot described in it the *Arena*. In Illinois

Lloyd helped to increase the official Populist vote from 22,000 in 1892 to 66,000 with the probability that unofficially it reached 100,000 in 1894. Nationally Populism received nearly a half million additional votes.[28] This resulted largely from the AFL referendum precipitated by Lloyd's Convention address and the enhanced social unrest that he helped to channel into a radical political attempt to overthrow "the system" of business and political power that he had long opposed.

LABOR-POPULISM *vs.* FREE SILVER

National Populist leaders were disappointed by the failure of their bid for sufficient labor support to win control of the House of Representatives. Herman E. Taubeneck of Illinois, Chairman of the National Executive Committee, and General James Baird Weaver decided to substitute a single-plank, free-silver platform for the Omaha and Springfield platforms, so as to draw silver inflationists into the People's Party. Those leaders were obligated for past financial support to the American Bimetallic League, to which the Springfield Platform was unacceptable.[29]

Taubeneck convoked a conference of Populist leaders at St. Louis in late December to consider his new strategy. Alerted in advance by Nationalist and radical friends in East and West, Lloyd warned the *American Non-Conformist,* "If the People's Party . . . is not a revolution, it is nothing." He attended with resolutions drafted by Lyman Trumbull for the purpose of defeating Taubeneck's attempt to dehorn the Populist bull. Fearful lest a general strike in retaliation for Judge William A. Wood's post election conviction of Debs *et al.* for contempt dissolve society because of the reactionary temper of "the plutes" and courts, Lloyd intended to commit the Conference to a broad redress of grievances and confine labor's resentment to political channels. The extremism of the wealthy would oblige the people to unite to support a radical remedy, he believed.

Supported at the Conference by George Howard Gibson, editor of *The* (Omaha) *Wealth Makers,* Thomas F. Byron, editor of the *Farmers' Tribune* (Des Moines), and many antimonopolists, Nationalists, and Labor-Populists, Lloyd secured the Trumbull resolutions' adoption by skillful appeals to liberal shibboleths and a common antimonopolism. The series extended the Omaha Platform to include statutory limitation of inherited wealth, prohibition of government by injunction, and government ownership of all monopolies "affecting the public interest." He returned home triumphant, having secured nationwide extension of the Labor-Populism, as leader of a powerful coalition of midwestern and southern Populists and eastern Nationalists.[30]

During the next three months he led the Chicago coalition in a municipal campaign. The opposition of the small orthodox Populist faction to Morgan's following made this difficult. Darrow was reluctant "to run another Socialist movement under the guise of 'The People's Party'," as he said. So was Willis Abbot. Lloyd believed that "a good budget of municipalizations and nationalizations" based upon Peffer's "Public Ownership of Public Utilities," would hold the Socialists in the party, get Socialists elsewhere to join, and make Chicago "the intellectual and political leader of this movement." He and Darrow sponsored a Chicago Radical Club that provided radical leaders of all types with social, educational, and political felowship. They reasserted their leadership in the Cook County Populist Central Committee.[31]

However, at the Denver AFL Convention in December the defeat of Plank 10 and independent political action after the proposed "political program" had won the craft unions' referendum, and revocation of the charter of Morgan's International Machinists' Union inflicted a decisive defeat upon the Socialists. Encouraged by John McBride, the new AFL President, to continue independent labor politics in behalf of the remainder of the political program that the Convention adopted, the progressive trades unions in Chicago organized a Trade and Labor Congress committed to Lloyd's policy and excluding the "fakirs." Until July 1896 it was the chief local support of Labor-Populism.[32] The orthodox Chicago Populists were encouraged by these developments to attempt to oust the embittered Socialists. Taubeneck and Weaver immediately revived their demand for a one-plank silver platform.

Lloyd called the AFL's rejection of Plank 10 a "national misfortune" because, as he wrote John Burns, "it is only on some such plain, general, radical proposition that the peculiarly difficult elements of our reform labor movement can be united" since American laborers lacked "the mutual confidence" in "progressive action" that characterized British labor. His support of Plank 10 was Lloyd's farthest left deviation during the Mauve Decade. He added hopefully that the municipal reform movement indicated an irresistible demand for municipalization of utilities. He predicted most unrealistically that the Populists would carry the country "before two more presidential elections" because the St. Louis Conference placed them on common ground with all reformers seeking "to improve municipal administration by collective effort. The public use of public powers, for the public benefit, so far and so fast as the public may demand" would prove to be irresistible, he claimed.[33]

He presented an adaptation of Burns's business municipal politics as a utopian fantasy, "The Parable of the Garden City," in a lecture to the Single Tax Club at Lake Forest University and elsewhere. This depicted Chicago's transformation into a model "Co-operative Commonwealth" by the spirit of "The Fair," which would emancipate women and found a co-operative Christian Socialist colony of unemployed in the suburbs whose superior economic efficiency would enable it to absorb the metropolis, other cities, and eventually the entire nation.[34]

Lloyd and Darrow led the discordant Labor-Populists in a novel but futile municipal campaign. Its radical platform, drafted by Lloyd, was designed to retain the Socialists' support but deny them control. It demanded twenty-year franchises for utilities subject to a gross receipts tax and eventual municipalization, slum clearance, home rule, municipal management of public works, municipalization of docks and markets, a merit system for the police, and endorsed the Omaha and Springfield platforms and public ownership of all monopolies. Dr. Bayard

Holmes, mayoral candidate, led this obvious bid for middle-class support. Lloyd hoped that his program would be adopted in other cities, and informed Keir Hardie that the silver faction in the People's Party was beaten. Thus he worked for the "unity of belief" essential to "unity of organization," which Mason A. Green of *Greater Boston Magazine* said was his distinctive contribution to the Populist "revolt."[35]

Lloyd dissociated Labor-Populism's Socialist trend from German Socialism whose "hard tone" and doctrine of the "class struggle" repelled him. He found inspiration instead in the Fabian Society and Albert Shaw's *Municipal Government in Great Britain*, as he admitted to President George A. Gates of Iowa College. Americans exhibited "less of a tendency towards Socialism" than any other "civilized nation," he stated to a journalist, and restricted his own proposals to "government ownership . . . of all monopolies." His condescension toward W. D. P. Bliss' impractical attempts to propagate undiluted Fabianism and rejection of his Christian Socialism indicates that he was still guided largely by empirical considerations and his own welfare policy. To Albert Shaw he wrote that the Chicago Labor-Populists were his "faithful disciples." A report to Clarke that the Labor-Populists were suffering from the "backwash of reaction" suggests that Lloyd was again motivated chiefly by education objectives in his political leadership.[36]

This was realistic. Although the city's mis-government and corruption were notorious the Populist program, which contained Stead's earlier proposals and initiated the movement to oust Yerkes and municipalize the utilities, alienated most middle-class, labor, and labor support.

A moderate good government movement organized by the Civic Federation in March attracted this instead. This capitalized upon protests against the Ogden Gas and Cosmopolitan Electric Light franchises that the Hopkins-Sullivan "ring" had voted itself and its business allies. The "Gas Trust," which would have to purchase the Ogden firm so as to continue its monopoly, covertly supported a Central Music Hall protest meeting on March 3 sponsored by the Civic Federation. This

meeting demanded revocation of the new franchises and elimination of the Common Council's "boodler ring." Lloyd spoke as
Chicago's leading authority on monopolies. He demanded repeal
of the ordinances because of their "infamous" method of enactment, but described carefully their provisions which would
produce lower rates, a $3\frac{1}{2}$ per cent. gross receipts tax, and municipal ownership on termination. Instead of confirming the "Gas
Trust's" monopoly, he urged endorsement of a policy of municipal ownership of utilities so as to enable Chicago to compete
more effectively with New York City for leadership. Neither this
nor his reference to Shaw's report on British municipalities
persuaded the Civic Federation to adopt his as the proper
remedy for "boodle."

Lloyd's address did enhance popular realism. The *Chicago
Dispatch* chortled at how he had upset "a Beautiful Pail of
Trust Milk." Even the Yerkes-controlled *Inter Ocean* conceded
the wisdom of municipalizing electric lighting. Lloyd's blunt
"It is privilege which is the father of boodle" was republished
with praise by *The Kingdom* and *The Cause*.[37] This bold stand
enhanced Lloyd's reputation for courageous criticism, realism,
and constructive thought. It established him among America's
leading radical municipal reformers.

This availed the faction-ridden Labor-Populists little. The
corrupt, bipartisan municipal ring was overturned instead by
the Civic Federation's aldermanic ticket, led by William Kent,
who would eventually learn the accuracy of Lloyd's and Stead's
identification of the business source of "boodle." Lloyd's Labor-
Populists suffered a humiliating defeat that was worsened by
a pre-election split between the Socialists and the orthodox
Populists. That was precipitated by the latter's insistence upon
fusion with the Democratic Hopkins-Sullivan "ring," the corrupt opposition to Altgeld, Populism, and Socialism.[38] Lloyd
had attempted to make bricks without straw with the usual
result.

The *National Watchman* organ of the Taubeneck-Weaver
leadership, rejoiced at his defeat. After calling his midwestern
antimonopolist supporters "Socialists" to justify revival of the

one-plank proposal, it declared that Socialism's disastrous defeat placed Taubeneck "on top" and would prevent further
broadening of the Omaha Platform. Thereafter, that journal
labored to disrupt the Labor-Populist coalition. Weaver secured Byron's dismissal from the *Farmer's Tribune.* The Chicago
Age and Searchlight repudiated Lloyd, calling him a Marxian.
Although progressive trades unionists retained control of the
Populist City Committee, Lloyd's local and national influence
in the People's Party was sedulously neutralized by Taubeneck.[39]

Lloyd remained undaunted. He wrote Morgan the following
summer that he would "never recede" from the Springfield
Platform and urged vainly that he remain in the People's
Party and cooperate in an attempt to commit the next national
convention to it. After reading Bliss's new *Handbook of
Socialism,* Lloyd wrote him graciously that this might "perhaps
compel me to do what I have not yet done—avow myself a confessed socialist." At the Battery D reception to Debs he
preached again the need for independent political action by
labor to win a redress of grievances and "industrial democracy."
Despite his praise of the ARU's hero and great popularity with
the throng, his brilliant elaboration of "The Co-operative Commonwealth" was "heard with respectful impatience" by workers who cheered his denunciation of Judge Wood and viewed
cordially his characteristic "light gray trousers," long "frock
coat," pince-nez glasses with gold chain, jeweled scarf pin, and
seal ring. Lloyd concluded privately that while predatory capitalists combined "spontaneously" the "retreating masses . . .
disunite spontaneously," and the first thing every labor reform
movement did was "to split, at least, into two."[40]

Yet, he stubbornly insisted upon independent political action
by labor, and that the labor movement and anti-Trust agitation
were "two wings of the same advance" to the Ethical Culture
Society. To this he added significantly, "I am not a state
socialist." This indicated again the tactical considerations which
had dictated his belief that Plank 10 was essential to an effective,
unified labor political movement.

From then until July 1896 he attempted to revive the Labor-

Populist alliance, with time off to judge the Chicago popular song contest with Hamlin Garland. The eastern Populists followed Lloyd's lead. They were impressed by his advocacy of public ownership of monopolies at the "United Front" Staten Island Conference the preceding summer. He reasserted his party leadership in Illinois. He subsidized the *Union Workman* (Chicago), which pushed Debs for the party's presidential nomination with the approval of many "reform" and labor journals while combating the one-plank silver movement that only seven of 275 exchanges favored. Lloyd renewed his liaison with Morgan. Charles B. Matthews, Empire State Populist leader, informed him of opposition to the Taubeneck policy elsewhere. Lloyd conferred with Debs, kept in touch with Victor Berger, whose Labor-Populist municipal ticket he had aided in 1895, and won the support of B. F. Fries, a Pennsylvania labor leader. In Illinois he regained the backing of Henry Vincent and Maxwell, orthodox Populists, by reminding them that Fisk, Gould, and Vanderbilt had been "the prototypes of all the procession of corrupters and oppressors that has followed." The resulting problems, he warned, could not be "cured by spinning wheel and ox team remedies."[41]

He informed Professor Ely that he was urging a political solution for social ills as the alternative "of revolution, which I do not expect, or of a rotting down which I think is already under way." The Populist leaders, he predicted, would surrender their party to the "Free Silverites." Ely declined his invitation to join Bellamy in a pamphlet to combat Taubeneck. He called the silver issue "most unfortunate for the cause of economic and social reform" and scorned the "sub-treasury" plank, but thought it possible to "switch" Populism "to more promising issues."[42]

Lloyd guessed acurately that Taubeneck and Weaver had "been flimflammed" by the American Bimetallic League and the silver Democrats. Unknown to him William Jennings Bryan induced Taubeneck to schedule the Populist National Convention to meet *after* that of the Democratic Party. Lloyd perceived immediately after Bryan's nomination that the Populists

were left "with the Hobson's choice" between fusing with the
Democrats on "the issue" with Bryan as joint candidate or of
naming their own ticket and attempting belatedly to develop
another. Taubeneck and Weaver altered the states' representation at the Populist convention so as to give the free-silver
states control."

Lloyd was reluctant to go to St. Louis at the head of the
Illinois delegation in opposition to a contesting Cook County
silver Populist group. Mrs. Kelley, Dr. Holmes, and Chicago
labor leaders persuaded him to attend with a view to separating
the "socialistic" wing of the People's Party (government ownership advocates, Nationalists, Debs's following, radical trades
unionists, Fabians, gradualist Socialists) from the silver Populists, who presumably would endorse Bryan and join the Democrats. Since both sides to the contest recognized its character
and alternative courses of action, the issue was decided at St.
Louis by those possessing control.

Recognizing that his side was maneuvred into the position
of "kickers," Lloyd determined to seek at St. Louis "the most
aggressive possible revision of the Omaha Platform," grafting
to it the Springfield Platform and St. Louis Conference resolutions." There, as a guest of N. O. Nelson, co-operator and profit-
sharing industrialist of Edwardsville, Illinois, he attempted to
rally his side behind either Debs or Coxey. He prepared a draft
platform demanding government ownership of all monopolies
"affecting the public interest," and an address appealing to
"middle-of-the-road" delegates not to repeat the Liberal Republican mistake of 1872. Then, when seated in the convention,
he was informed cynically by Senator William V. Allen of
Nebraska, permanent chairman and pro-Bryan leader, that he
"would never allow" him "to catch his eye to get the floor."
The packed Resolutions Committee "summarily squelched"
Lloyd's government ownership plank and, after presenting
the platform, moved the previous question to prevent debate.
Thus, the great business interests whom Lloyd's crusade for
social justice had challenged since 1888, via the agency of the
free-silver Bryan Populists, blocked his plan to carry the con-

vention for Labor-Populism and antimonopoly from the floor. Debs did not attend, and withdrew permission to present his name for the presidential nomination.

Lloyd sat helpless, deserted by Darrow who joined Schilling, who had gained a seat in the Illinois silver Populist delegation that received half the state's seats. Darrow and Schilling urged that fusion with the Democrats was the only feasible course. Lloyd was unable to unite a "middle-of-the-road" conference on a candidate and antimonopoly government ownership plank. Emerging, he forecast accurately the nomination of a southern man for Vice-President to prevent a complete Populist-Democrat fusion, but invited press ridicule with the gloomy prediction that Cleveland "will not leave the White House without serious trouble." After Bryan was nominated he remarked that Populism had entered "that bourne from which no reform party returns." Trembling with indignation, he told Nelson "The Cause is lost" that night. He withdrew from politics.

He predicted shrewdly that "a large percentage of the radical members of the party would go into one or another of the socialist parties" and most Populist journals would become "socialist." With this the *Appeal to Reason* agreed. Within four to eight years, Lloyd added, "the ideas and the men who went down here before the silver cyclone will reappear." The Republicans laughed at his equally accurate prophecy that the Populists would degenerate into "a mere vermiform appendix to the Democracy." He confessed to Ely and to Adair, editor of the *Union Workman,* that the convention had been "the most discouraging experience in my life." There was nothing left for the betrayed Populists to do, he told C. P. Somerby, but to work for an anticlass, nonproletarian "Socialism," in other words for the welfare democracy that he had proposed to the AFL in 1893. To the *Review of Reviews* he reported that the antimonopolist radicals had been the strongest element and might have carried the convention for an advanced platform had they had a carefully groomed candidate and adequate organization. Their leaders had not acted effectively because they feared that an irretrievable opportunity for uniting the "reform" forces might be lost.[45]

During the campaign he declined the Populist "middle-of-the-road" nomination for lieutenant-governor, but was kept on that ticket notwithstanding. He remained politically inactive at The Watch House, rejecting Darrow's and Mrs. Kelley's pleas to campaign for Altgeld. He did what he could to counteract Theodore Roosevelt's emotional, unfair attack upon Altgeld in *Forum* with a letter to the *New York Journal*. This exonerated Altgeld from all suspicion of anarchism and gave an eye-witness account of his loyal course during the Pullman Strike. Altgeld sent the Lloyds tickets for the speakers' platform at Cooper Union, where he replied to his eastern enemies. Henry D. Lloyd informed his Illinois following that the Governor's defeat would be a "great misfortune." Republication in Chicago of his *Journal* letter helped Altgeld's cause.

Lloyd attempted to awaken reformers everywhere from the delusion that the Democratic and Populist platforms were identical by letters to influential friends and a widely reported "smoke talk" at the Boston Twentieth Century Club. There he declared that the "silver-mining-millionaire" who had trumped up the silver issue was "the cow-bird of American politics," seeking to "take possession of the social reformers' nests . . . in order that he may use these reformatory movements to enrich himself at the expense of his dupes and victims." As the *Boston Daily Advertiser* observed after Bryan's defeat, "the witty and learned Fabian from Chicago" perceived that 50 per cent devaluation of the dollar would not smash the "Trusts," compel railroads to obey the ICC, prevent government by injunction, or stop use of "Pinkerton mercenaries." Boston reformers who had joined "the American Fabian Movement" only to be swept into the silver craze had failed to realize, as Lloyd had and the *Advertiser* observed, "the cow bird is several degrees more unscrupulous as well as more cunning than is the cuckoo."[46] In his speech, obviously, Lloyd had attempted to counteract also the effect of his exhumed *Chicago Tribune* free-silver editorials of 1877-78 that Altgeld was circulating in Illinois to counteract

Medill's journalism and the syndicated progold standard column of Professor A. Lawrence Laughlin.

Privately, Lloyd was convinced that only "the Co-operative Commonwealth in our time" could restore democratic liberties and opportunities. To Adair he had confessed that he might vote for Bryan as "the Knight of the Disinherited, like Ivanhoe, but he will not be the next President and I am content." Actually, he voted in bitter disillusionment for the Socialist Labor Party ticket, which he hated. Afterwards he began to seek other means to achieve fundamental reforms. For this his visit with Nelson at St. Louis and Edwardsville had prepared him.[47]

Chapter XIV

 Wealth against Commonwealth

PREPARATION : 1889–93

Lloyd's antitrust campaign after 1889 was the other wing of
his crusade for social justice. The first phase of his antitrust
agitation, aided by the activity of others, had produced the
American antitrust mind, which attempted to perpetuate the
competititive system by statutory prohibitions. Before the Sherman Law was enacted, however, Lloyd had moved obliquely
beyond his new liberalism into social welfare radicalism. As he
became a social rebel he related his antitrust investigations and
activity to his reform program. Intimate knowledge of the
motivations, methods, and justifications of combination promoters provoked him sometimes to invoke the new ethics hotly.
He cited pertinent legal penalties in a desire to bring them
individually to book. Skillful analyses of the combination movement carried him far beyond this. As he grasped at business
reality he realized that combinations derived partially from
economic imperatives. He foresaw that economic concentration
and the emerging oligopolistic economy must be made to function for the general welfare. To accomplish this became for him
and his circle a major objective, as when during the Labor-
Populist experiment he advanced from Ely's proposed socialization of natural monopolies to the St. Louis Conference demand
for government ownership of all monopolies.

Neither Lloyd nor Ely was a doctrinaire. Theory for them
derived from analysis of developing practicalities, and was intended to guide men to effective action. More than did Ely,

Lloyd engaged sporadically in antitrust activities of varied types. His greatest single contribution in this field was *Wealth Against Commonwealth*. It was the composite product of empirical economic analysis, applied ethics, and contrasting allusions to laissez faire and his welfare philosophy. It brought Lloyd dramatically into sharp clashes with John D. Rockefeller and aligned him openly against the Standard Oil, the most powerful industrial combination of the era.

Lloyd began work on this treatise after Ely, Mead, and Stewart convinced him that the "Trust Problem" ranked in importance with the labor problem. They perceived during 1888–89 that antitrust legislation exerted little restraint upon promoters of new business combinations,[1] whose activity did much to galvanize the farmers' alliances and precipitate "The Populist Revolt." Lloyd's continued interest in "the octopus," to investigate which he made repeated expeditions during his convalescence and formulation of his new social philosophy, made this persuasion easy. So did James Bryce's evaluation of the general problem in his *American Commonwealth*. That corroborated Lloyd's earlier analysis[2] and explained the Interstate Commerce Commission's inability to prevent the growth of industrial monopoly. This he had predicted in 1886 to Senator Cullom. Foreboding lest the "trusts" precipitate a violent social upheaval,[3] which was shared widely, also motivated his research. Simultaneous Congressional and New York Senate investigations of the "trusts" in 1888 provided new data and precipitated a popular antitrust campaign. After this A. B. Stickney's *The Railroad Problem* confirmed Lloyd's earlier assertion of the decisive relation of railroad favoritism to industrial monopoly.[4]

Interestingly, Lloyd declined to write articles on the sugar and copper combinations and the "trusts' " perversion of the courts for the *Atlantic* and *Forum* in 1888, although he worked with Henry F. Hudson of the *Pittsburgh Dispatch* to secure publication of the Congressional antitrust investigation's full proceedings.[5]

His decision to write a book on the Standard Oil followed

attendance at an ICC proceeding in a case arising from rebate payments to the Standard Oil on the independent refiner George Rice's oil shipments. Lloyd renewed friendships there with journalists, petroleum men, and editors as they appraised Rockefeller on the witness stand. He wrote a graphic memorandum entitled "Fanatic S. Oil." This quotes railroad attorneys' uncomplimentary comparisons of the forty-eight-year-old magnate with "a hawk," "a sharper," "a Keno King." To Lloyd he looked like a calculating, supercautious, false, hard, ruthless robber, who preferred a "lie" to the truth. Lloyd's Carlylian phrases seconded the quoted views of Rockefeller's carrier allies :

> He is . . . a depredator . . . not a worshipper of liberty . . . a Czar of plutocracy, a worshipper of his own Money Power over mankind. He will never sacrifice any of his plans for the restraints of law or patriotism or philanthropy. . . . His greed, rapacity, flow as a Universal solvent wherever they can, melting down into gold for him, private enterprise, public morals, judicial honor, legislative faith, gifts of nature. He will stop when he is stopped—not before. Not a tiger but a lynx. . . . a makeup like that of the "gentleman pirate" of romance, think cold ruthless. Knowing the outward forms of gentlemanliness, making with the eager accuracy of steel, a Robespierre of competition.[6]

This impression was indelible.

Lloyd did not believe that business piracy was limited to the Standard Oil. Learning a year earlier that Pennsylvania Railroad rate policies had obliged Lewis Emery, Jr. of Bradford to sell his refinery to the Standard Oil he had written him : "So, our leading railroad men are still in the brigand stage of development! Such men are the real anarchists of this country." Pleased that Emery retained his "independent attitude," he asked him for documents and pamphlets. "All such stuff is grist for my mill," Lloyd added.[7]

In May 1889 he determined to write a book on the "Trusts" featuring the Standard Oil as their "Father," a reference book for all "students of American liberty" that would illumine "every phase" of the " 'New Industry' " and the "moral, social, and industrial displacements and perversions that have followed from the appropriation by the strong and clever of the lion's share of the power and wealth created by modern machinery." After showing this prospectus to Salter he informed Charles B. Matthews, independent Buffalo refiner, that he would write "a full, and *absolutely and documentarily* accurate" history of Rockefeller's monopoly "as the most characteristic thing in our business civilization . . . the most threatening for the future."[8] Ethics, historicism, and antimonopolism constituted the tripod supporting Lloyd's research. To complete it and produce his book required five and a half years. He regarded it as Volume II of his "Bad Wealth Series," to which Stewart promised to contribute a volume but did not when the other subjects on the list attracted no authors.[9]

Lloyd gathered data from Senators, Congressmen, American and foreign officials, journalists, and independent oil men. He consulted and borrowed briefs, testimony, and pamphlets from Roger Sherman and George Shiras, Jr., similar attorneys of independents in Buffalo and Marietta, subscribed to a press clipping service, and followed leads intensively. Sherman, John Teagle, Emery, Rice, Matthews, and others posted him on current developments in petroleum and natural gas.[10] Lloyd's legal training and editorial experience stood him in good stead as he analyzed his findings.

When he could not corroborate deductions he omitted these from his narrative, viz., the Hepburn Committee proceedings' indication that the Standard Oil had originated in an alliance between the Rockefeller group and the Erie Ring. He analyzed the evidence and defense presented by Standard Oil spokesmen carefully, especially S. C. T. Dodd's *Combinations: Their Uses and Abuses, with A History of the Standard Oil Trust*. In the Congressional proceedings of 1888 he detected Dodd's doctoring of the record of the Buffalo conspiracy trial in which three

Standard Oil trustees and the chief executives of the Vacuum Oil Company had been accused of conspiring to blow up a competing refinery.

Lloyd interpreted the legislative background of the Sherman Act in the light of the wealthy, corporation-dominated, Republican-controlled United States Senate. He concluded as did the *New York World* that the statute would be employed primarily against labor. Material on the Standard Oil's activity in Europe was supplied by Scottish chemists and Imperial Privy Counciller Dr. Alfred von der Leyen of Charlottenburg, Germany. To him Lloyd observed that as "the first and worst" of American "trade combinations" the Standard Oil exhibited "in the most alarming form the culmination of the most evil tendencies of modern commercialism." Von der Leyen agreed, sent data, but declined Lloyd's invitation to contribute a chapter, "The Oil Trust in Europe," to the projected book.[11]

The treatise, as Lloyd described his first draft in 1891, presented the facts "relentlessly, . . . under the clear light of an ethical ray which the Captain of Industry fatuously thinks shines in his world only when he sits in his pew." To his mother Lloyd expressed revulsion from the "piles of filthy human greed and cruelty almost too nauseous to handle." Driven by a stern sense of duty, he was convinced that "men must understand the vices of our present system before they will be able to rise to a better."[12] He gathered statistics laboriously to test the Standard Oil's claim that it produced cheaper products than could competition. Articles by E. Benjamin Andrews, Sherman, and the *New York Commercial Bulletin* enabled him to demonstrate the reverse.[13]

In May 1893 he asked Sherman, A. E. Macomber, a Toledo attorney, and Adelbert Moot of Buffalo to read his third draft for accuracy and libel. This they did but refused fees. Sherman wrote Lloyd, *"Have no fears of your book!"* As attorney for the United States Pipeline Company, he valued the book especially for its bearing upon that firm's attempt to reach salt water. When Sherman attended the World's Fair he visited The Wayside.[14]

Howells, America's leading novelist, interested Harper & Brothers in Lloyd's new book. Lloyd wrote him that he had devoted "more than two years" working time to its preparation, "and the sky seems full of signs that the time for the appearance of such information has come." A full year elapsed before that publisher accepted the book after drastic compression, despite readers' warnings against antagonizing powerful interests, incurring libel suits, and excessive moralizing. Harper & Brothers accepted the revised manuscript after Howells took it again to the head of the firm, but on condition that Lloyd pay for the electroplates. Publication occurred in September 1894, after Lloyd's attorneys had verified the references and quotations and read the text for possible libel twice.[15] In the final revision he added analyses of the anthracite coal, milling, whiskey, and sugar "trusts," of the combination movement, and of related railroad rate discriminations. He appended the best up-to-date list of industrial combinations. This produced the most important treatise extant on the economics and social implications of the "trusts."

Before publication Lloyd wrote Salter that the book's preparation "has been a much more serious task than I dreamed. Facts are difficult things to harness." Professors Ely, John Bates Clark, and Jeremiah W. Jenks were eager to see the treatise. When acknowledging receipt of Ely's *Socialism and Social Reform*, Lloyd observed humorously, "The gun needs to be loaded carefully; the query uppermost in my mind is, which is going to be the most dangerous place, the front of it or behind?" Did he anticipate merely bitter conservative attacks or the libel suits that Harper & Brothers readers feared?[16]

THE BOOK

Wealth Against Commonwealth's appearance was a significant event. Although to some extent it was a tract for the times[17] it was more important as a product of the new economics and the ethical revival. These, as in the Ely school, were intimately interrelated. The book contributed significantly to "Progressive" and radical democratic thought, economic know-

ledge and theory, and the philosophy of progress and civilization. It exhibited indebtedness to the Jacksonian and Christian
Socialist traditions. It disclosed the antisocial character of the
amoral, predatory, speculator-promoter business oligarchy, and
anticipated Albert Schweitzer by pleading for a higher social
ethics to enable civilization to master the machine age. Lloyd
depicted monopoly capitalism as intensely coercive, subjecting
the people and institutions to the will of a minority holding
economic power.[18]

The book reiterated his demand that modern technology and
giant business serve the general welfare. It upheld competition's
claim to credit for technological innovation, in which it assigned
monopoly the cow bird status. Lloyd discovered that the Standard Oil's and other "trusts'" monopoly policies curtailed
production and employment. This John A. Hobson soon confirmed.[19] Lloyd's deduction that gigantic fortunes and the concentration of wealth and economic power in America derived
from monopoly profits John R. Commons had already established.[20]

To subdue monopoly capitalism with its power-hungry
"Caesars" and institutional imperialism Lloyd insisted that
democratic brotherhood be applied to the economy. This would
harmonize individualism with cooperative association and
democratic statism, and thus advance "progress." With brilliant
epigrams, vivid page and chapter headings, and striking anti-
theses he preached "The New Conscience" and his welfare
policy more brilliantly than ever. "The word of the day is that
we are about to civilize industry; to be safe liberty must be
complete on its industrial as well as on its political side." By
applying "co-operative" methods to monopoly Americans could
move upward to "a private life of new beauty . . . commoners,
travellers to Altruria." Not proletarianism nor an absolutist neo-
Hamiltonianism, but instead an elevated commonalty with
higher living standards, ethics, brotherhood, and cultural life
and impelled by a progressive dynamism reminiscent of the
Jacksonian era was Lloyd's objective. His text was replete with
allusions to and experiential testing of the dogmas of orthodox

economics and Social Darwinism and their professed exponents in "Big Business."

The book's intellectual richness had to be appreciated as well as its extraordinary revelations before it could be evaluated. Lloyd wrote it not for the populace like George's classic or for a frustrated middle class as did Bellamy. He intended that his book should convert an intellectual élite comprising clergy, journalists, publicists, and enlightened women into disciples of his welfare philosophy and practitioners of its principles. He expected approval by the Ely school. Lloyd's findings justified Populism's limited collectivism and its indictment of monopoly. The treatise was, therefore, more than "the classic of the American literature of exposure."[21] It loomed in 1894 on the far frontier of democracy as a multitowered fortress, emblazoned with new banners, foretelling the emergence of a cooperative, welfare, machine age democracy.

Readers during the Mauve Decade and Rooseveltian Era were especially impressed by the extraordinary exposures of the abuses of the railroads and the "trusts," and of their economic and political power. Without naming him, Lloyd convicted Rockefeller as the villain who had developed a new system of industrial monopoly with the decisive aid of illicit railroad favoritism and by ruthless, illicit, competitive methods. No reader who accepted Lloyd's truthful account of how that self-designated paladin of Christian and business ethics had euchred a widow out of her husband's independent lubricants factory, paying her a small fraction of its value, could regard him as other than a cad and a scoundrel. The Widow Backus episode clung to Rockefeller thereafter as the tar baby did to Brer Fox.[22]

The book opens with an extraordinary analysis of the world-wide combination movement. It describes railroad dominance of anthracite and bituminous coal mining, the "Whiskey Trust's" dynamiting of competitors' distilleries, corruption of officials, adulteration of products, the railroad-favored grain elevator combination that fixed wheat prices, and the millers', bakers', meat packers' and butchers' associations that exploited consumers and depressed farm produce prices. An episodic analysis of the history of the Standard Oil as the prototype of industrial monopoly follows, filling 350 pages. This contrasts the Rockefeller coterie's conflicting sworn statements on the same issues and their amoral business methods with their professed ethics and asserted regard for public welfare. No more graphic method could have been devised to portray their cynical perjury, occasional violence, hypocrisy, disregard for the oil regions' welfare, hostility to competitive enterprise. Amid sarcastic references to Social Darwinism's mechanistic "survival of the fittest" in the economy, Lloyd demonstrates that the oil magnates were personally responsible for the coup that imposed a callous monopoly upon a dynamic, speculative, competitive enterprise. He bared their defiance of railroad regulation, oil inspection, and antitrust legislation. He traced the Standard Oil's spreading tentacles into railroading, cottonseed oil, gas, traction, electric lighting, and high finance.

Although scholarly research has since discovered new materials that illumine further the Standard Oil's institutional history and competitive policies, careful comparison of Lloyd's account with the sources and subsequent studies establish its accuracy in describing the transportation bases of that giant monopoly. His assertion that prior to 1872 the Standard Oil secretly undermined competitive oil refining has been partially substantiated by discovery of covert Rockefeller alliances with Henry Harley's pipeline combination and Gould's Erie-Atlantic & Great Western railroad system.[23] The well-kept secret of the key role of this system and of the Lake Shore and Michigan Southern Railroad, both the Standard Oil's allies, in the nefarious South Improvement Company, for which Lloyd insisted the Rockefeller group were chiefly responsible, is now coming to light.[24]

He asserted correctly that during 1873–77 Rockefeller's policy was to achieve the refining monopoly and control of railroad transportation that that abortive coup attempted. Equally accurate was his thesis that the objective of the independent oil men was to recreate competition in the industry by smashing the Standard-trunkline railroad alliance while constructing pipelines to the sea. The Standard Oil monopoly, largely achieved by 1877 and perpetuated with incidental competition to 1894, *was* primarily the artificial result of special privilege conferred by and wrested from the railroads *plus* control of the gathering and subsequent trunk pipelines as Lloyd asserts. Preferential rates enjoyed since 1868, exclusive tank car service on the Erie and New York Central railroads after 1873, exclusive use of their oil docks in New York harbor, and the Pennsylvania Railroad's similar favoritism after 1877 *were* decisive advantages, in comparison with which Rockefeller business efficiency was secondary.

Lloyd erred, however, in attributing the system of secret railroad and pipeline drawbacks and rebates to the Standard Oil, although after 1868 it enjoyed larger, more extensive, and exclusive rate and service concessions on the northern trunklines. Some evidence indicates, as Lloyd implied, that these were secured in part by joint investments with railroad men, i.e., Amasa Stone of the Lake Shore's investment in the Standard Oil, and Rockefeller and Gould's investment in Harley's pipeline system.[25] The chapter "The Smokeless Rebate" discloses wide resort in 1894 to the Gould-originated practice of conferring exclusive rate favors upon a single shipper in a business, with consequent development of monopoly. The crucial influence of "The Smokeless Rebate" in extinguishing competition was indubitable, although patents, tariff favors, and other forms of government favoritism had similar results.

Explicit in Lloyd's narrative is a trenchant antimonopolism. "Industry and monopoly cannot live together. . . . Liberty and monopoly cannot live together . . . political brotherhood cannot survive where industrial brotherhood is denied," the epigrams sparkle. Lloyd also relates the age-old struggle for position, special privilege, and power to his era, conceding that the avaricious, corrupting *arrivistes* represented its regnant "spirit," and that the social energy of reform was weaker. He hoped so to invigorate the latter that it could initiate "times that may be." However, he bluntly applied Thorold Rogers' economic interpretation of history to explain how the "money power" had usurped mastery of the state, churches, schools, colleges, and the law : "The harmony of things insists that which is the source of power, wealth, and delight shall also be the rule of it."

Instead of surrendering to materialistic determinism, however, he demanded that "the people take their proper place in the seat of sovereignty," terminate "deceit, tyranny, and cruelty," overthrow dominant monopolistic and financial power, and institute "a well-ordered commonwealth of labor!" New applications of social love could achieve this and ensure that power held by officials in trust would not again be used to betray the general welfare. Instead of Adam Smith's reliance upon competing selfishnesses to institute economic harmonies, he proffered equalitarian mutual aid as the foundation of an effective welfare democracy that must control and administer its technology and institutions justly if it would preserve its freedom.

Only a "progressive" people could achieve this, and only after reformers had won the public to more enlightened principles and new loyalties, Lloyd claimed. By confronting monopoly's *de facto* displacement of humane democracy realistically an ethical, enlightened leadership could foster "the saving ferment" and "make all things new by bringing them nearer to the old ideals." After citing Emerson, Ruskin, Plato, Aristotle, the Christ, and George Sand to justify his position, Lloyd invoked Goethe to persuade reformers to create a new "spirit of the age." He redefined "the right" so that reformers and the democracy would be impelled to "do the right."

Wealth Against Commonwealth concluded with an appeal to the heart, confident that if the people "know, they will care," hate "evil," develop "new love of the good, new sympathy for the victims of power," and, by "enlarging its science . . . quicken the old into a new conscience. Democracy is not a lie. There live in the body of the commonalty the unexhausted virtue and the ever-refreshed strength which can rise equal to any problems of progress."[26]

CRITICISM AND EVALUATION

Lloyd expected that his book would rigorously "arouse public opinion and the transgressors themselves to the truth that moral laws must be embodied in institutions, customs." Like the great religious revivalists he intended to lead sinners to repentance by convicting them of their sins, and to salvation by winning them to his welfare theory and polity.[27] Compression of the text, with greater resort to the epigram, refined and developed Lloyd's ethical empiricism into a devastating weapon, although the years intervening before publication diminished his confidence in his ability to convert the Rockefellers and their imitators to business virtue. His applied ethics exploded complacency as it exposed business brigandage and invalidated Darwinist clichés, making promoter-speculator and monopolist claims to being "the fittest" ridiculous. The demonstration of their perversion of justice and defeat of the regulatory commissions stimulated impatience with the miniscule results of government regulation. It opened minds to consider the radical remedy of public ownership, which Lloyd hinted was more adequate to solve the problem of monopoly. Thus, he applied to the deficiencies of power entrepreneurship and public policy Green's axiom that the validity of professed principles was established in action.

The moral appeal of complete sincerity made this extremely effective, as Lloyd made his points with firm logic, wit, sarcasm, and irony. The restraint with which he depicted the fruits of business pathology carried conviction that a democratic welfare policy was necessary. Lloyd's muckraker disciples would lift their eyes also to gaze on the "Heavenly City" of a new conscience. The combination of irrefutable exposures with the assertion of old and new democratic principles placed him among the immortals of American liberalism.

Furthermore, the book repudiated "The Old Self Interest" of the Ricardian school. It offered instead the free individual who placed humanity first in his scale of economic values and resorted to voluntary association and governmental action to resolve problems resulting from excessive individualism. Lloyd insisted that the rehabilitation of individual and economic liberty so essential to further democratic advances must result from the progressive, experimental harmonization of individualism with social cooperation. These doctrines were pregnant with large implications for twentieth-century democracy.

Such was Lloyd's greatest book and its message for the Mauve Decade with its popular distress, frustrations, and upper crust *fin de siècle* cynicism, ostentatious luxury, and social climbing.

Certain aspects of the book subjected it to immediate criticism. The omission of names was regretted. Since Lloyd's motives for so doing were repeatedly impugned by Rockefeller spokesmen and apologists, the omission requires an explanation. Although Lloyd had named his characters in early drafts, when he sent his final version to Howells he stated that he omitted names "to avoid a 'damnable iteration'," and that these could be found in the references. He and his legal advisers knew that such omission was no defense if he made false statements injuring personal and business reputations in ways that did not serve the public interest. With his counsel's aid he established the accuracy of his statements and avoided malicious libel. Had he slandered or libeled the Rockefellers or other "trust" magnates and railroad managers, they would certainly have instituted litigation for damages. Fear of libel did not lead Lloyd to tone down his treatment prior to publication. As he informed Harper & Brothers, he presented his data so far as he could, not as "an assailant of 'monopolies'" but rather as a sympathizer with the victims of "a false gospel of wealth."[28] It required genuine courage and civic spirit for Harper & Brothers to publish the volume since it risked not only ill-advised, costly libel actions but also the danger of incurring the continuing business hostility of the railroads and the "trusts," whose magnates frequently demanded and enjoyed a Renaissance adulation from writers.

Much more important in establishing the book's caliber was its comprehensive analysis and interpretation of the recent revolution in business in the United States and Europe. Lloyd considered virtually all the external circumstances that produced monopolistic business giantism in America. In addition to transportation and governmental favoritism he concluded accurately that sheer weight of capital resources in control of high finance, as in Europe, could also produce it. This uncovered the key to the sudden revival of the combination movement that would occur after 1896. "Wall Street" rather than industrial power entrepreneurship would lead that spectacular second phase.

He did not feel obligated to analyze the inner, institutional imperatives within large enterprises that worked toward the same giantism, as he might have done fairly well in view of his experience in financial journalism. These aspects of the combination movement belonged to the as yet unborn field of institutional business history. He ignored this area of business experience except for exploding fallacious claims. His book, then, was a historical critique, accurate within the limits of his purposes, sources, and knowledge, but focusing largely upon external aspects of the combination movement, its anticompetitive business methodology, growth of monopoly, and ideological defenses. The low level of competitive ethics in the oil industry Lloyd attributed almost entirely and inaccurately to the Rockefeller group.

However, in identifying the stages in evolution of monopolistic forms, from corners to pools to "trusts" to mergers, he made an important contribution to economics. His portrayal of the role of special privilege in this development exhibited an unassailable grasp of the subject. Subsequent studies by Wm. Z. Ripley, Ida M. Tarbell, John T. Flynn, Hans Thorelli, and Arthur M. Johnson have demonstrated the soundness of this portion of his anlysis. Professor Oscar Handlin of Harvard University corroborates Lloyd's explanation of the basis of the Standard Oil monopoly with the assertion that from its origin to the end of Rockefeller's administration the Standard Oil depended primarily upon illegal, criminal conspiracies with the railroads for favors that placed its competitors at a decisive disadvantage. The *non sequiturs* in the Hidys' recent attempt to prove that Rockefeller's policy was to operate within the law, although he insisted upon policies that produced repeated court defeats and the Supreme Court decision of 1911,[29] lead to the same conclusion.

Some professional historians have elaborated upon monopoly capitalism's fatal implications for democracy, which *Wealth Against Commonwealth* developed, and also its discussion of how the railroads and "trusts" controlled political parties, courts, government, and intellectual life. Some economic historians are beginning to ask as Lloyd did, is business oligopoly compatible with democracy?

Certain exceptions must be taken, however, to his portrayal of the independent oil men, whom Standard Oil defenders accused indiscriminately of attempting business blackmail of the Rockefeller combination while seeking preferential rebates for themselves. Lloyd's account of the independents' courage, devotion to competition, opposition to railroad discrimination, antimonopolism, and resort to voluntary trade and business associations has been validated by comparison with the sources. His error in attributing the rebate system to Rockefeller has been noted above. The chapters on Toledo's experiment with municipal gas omit the prominent role of the real estate men wishing to boom that city with "free gas." His enthusiasm for municipalized utilities and his desire to depict the sins of the Standard led him, apparently, to overlook this and also the need for continuous exploration of gas territory that the municipality's managers neglected.[30]

Franklin B. Gowen's portrait as the shining knight of the antimonopolist crusade in Pennsylvania against the Standard Oil omits the fact that for years he had been head of the anthracite coal monopoly that the book exposed. Possibly this omission is attributable to Lloyd's admiration for Gowen's enlightened labor policy in the coal combination, his support of the ICC, his opposition to rebates and free passes, and his attempts to compete with the eastern trunklines for the oil traffic in cooperation with the Tidewater Petroleum Company's transmountain pipeline.[31]

Lloyd did give the Standard Oil men, other monopolists, and railroad men their day in court in his book. Of 649 footnotes and undocumented statements verified in an elaborate test of the book's accuracy, 200 derived from them. Lloyd regularly gave their defense when discussing episodes in which they figured.[32] In an attempt to achieve impartiality he had declined financial assistance proffered during his research by the independent petroleum men. Not a word in his correspondence, notebooks, and drafts of the book substantiates to the least degree that charge made subsequently by John D. Archbold and Allan Nevins that he attempted to blackmail the Standard Oil in writing it. Lloyd's character and independent means made that accusation ridiculous. Lord Macaulay was Lloyd's authority for describing such magnates and their literary defenders as "barbarians . . . from above."

Wealth Against Commonwealth was not completely accurate despite Lloyd's great care and the verifiability of almost all his factual statements. The inaccuracies are chiefly those pertinent to the larger aspects of his subject, and some significant omissions. The book was not a history of the "trusts." Rather it was an original and valuable analysis of monopolistic and railroad pathology and the implications of resulting concentrations of economic power for liberty, free enterprise, democracy, business, ethics, and the public welfare. While developing these considerations and his subtly presented welfare theory, Lloyd wrote as the leading publicist of both fields. The book's social philosophy and reform purposes colored its contributions to historical and economic knowledge and to theory. However, economists, free enterprisers, antitrust champions, advocates of government regulation or government ownership, agrarian and labor leaders, the Social Gospel clergy, and proponents of government honesty and efficiency found in it a mine of invaluable data and varying degrees of inspiration. This explains the book's continuing appeal to reform leadership during ensuing decades of conservative reaction and "Progressive" revival. Thus, while the book contained "the most powerful indictment of monopoly ever written" it became "the first great document of the new protest," as Harold U. Faulkner has said.[33]

Impact

Although popular antimonopolism had reached high tide

during 1890–93, it had divided into moderate and radical wings when the book appeared. Many antimonopolists were content to await the practical results of antitrust legislation. The more alert detected its ineffectiveness because of "Bourbon" control of law enforcement. Radical remedies proposed by the Populists and Labor-Populists and sporadic violence by Commonwealers and labor in 1894 precipitated a conservative reaction. Some new school economists began to desert Ely. Professor Jenks remarked in September that the antitrust laws' ineffectiveness necessitated acceptance of monopolistic price determination and an experimental policy of sanctioning industrial combinations subject to government inspection and publicity.[34] The effect of the fragmentation of the antitrust movement would be seen in Bryan's defeat in 1896 and the combination movement's subsequent revival.

Wealth Against Commonwealth aroused, stimulated, and eventually helped to reunite American antimonopolism. Within eighteen months after its appearance it provoked a wider discussion of economic problems than any book since *Progress and Poverty*. The book's appeal to reformers was enhanced by Latchford's glowing comparison of Lloyd with Sir George Grey and Lessing in the *Arena*. After four reprintings within a year, Lloyd could regard his book as successful. Yet, the 8,000 copies sold during its first decade did not compare with the distribution of George's and Bellamy's classics. Charles B. Spahr of *The Outlook* predicted accurately that *Wealth Against Commonwealth*'s intellectual brilliance would diminish its appeal to average Americans.[35]

The book's wide influence was attributable first to Lloyd's successful Emersonian bid for the support of an élite. Via the intellectuals, editors, clergy, and enlightened women who read and accepted the conclusions and ethical welfare philosophy of his book, Lloyd ultimately reached the "masses of the people," as he expected to do. Analysis of the reaction of different segments of the scholarly, literary, periodical, newspaper, legal, business, reform, agrarian, and labor communities in the United States, Great Britain, and Europe discloses that Lloyd's classic precipitated a revolution in opinion toward the combination movement.[36]

Ely, Andrews, Jenks, Clark, and other new school economists used the book in their classes but did not endorse government ownership of the "trusts." Ely sent Lloyd a list of economists who received complimentary copies. *Wealth Against Commonwealth* was not approved in other scholarly circles. Orthodox economists controlled the American Economic Association, whose journal did not review it, nor did other economics journals. In the *American Journal of Sociology,* Albion W. Small of the University of Chicago repudiated the equalization of rewards implied by the philosophy of the book but agreed with its hostility to special privilege monopoly and pseudo-aristocracy. The *Political Science Quarterly* declared that it was unscholarly, marked by excessive eloquence and denunciation, and lacked the needed dispassionate analysis of the oil trust's economic effects. However, President William Preston Johnston of Tulane University praised the book, expressing "a most profound hatred of the Vampyre Trusts." William T. Harris, United States Commissioner of Education, drew upon it for an article series and hoped it would lead to a "careful canvass" of monopoly problems.[37]

Howells wrote his highest praise to Lloyd predicting that future writers depicting "the evilest phase of the century" would use his book. This was more dramatic and fascinating and better than "any narrative that can be drawn from it." Mead said to an Old South Church good government rally that no book had affected him so profoundly in years. His very favorable review in the *New England Magazine* was reprinted in *Dawn* and circulated as a pamphlet, *Church, State, School, and Money.* It endorsed Lloyd's thesis that "the rising issue" of reform was with business' far-reaching social control. *Commonwealth* (Boston) said the book was a "most proper outrageous statement of truth," but criticized Lloyd's excessive rhetoric and "socialistic theories." *The Dial* declared that Lloyd had performed "a patriotic service." The editor of *Donahoe's Magazine* declared that his book supplied reformers with "a perfect arsenal of the very facts required."[38] Although the major literary monthlies refrained from comment, this explains why Latchford wrote Lloyd : "You have the game in your hand. . . . You are backed (and I can say it with confidence) by the deep-down convictions of all right-minded men & women who have known you (all newspaper men included) although they are afraid to come out for you."[39]

The journals of opinion divided on the merits of *Wealth Against Commonwealth*. In the *Review of Reviews* (New York) Shaw acknowledged Lloyd's mastery of his theme but feared his brilliance was "too overwhelming in its assault to command" the greatest influence. *The Outlook* declared that the book's appeal to "the intellectual classes" to rally "the antimonopoly forces" rested upon undisputed commercial facts.[40] By contrast, a vituperatively adverse review in the *Nation*, written by W. T. Scheide, a Standard Oil executive, determined the viewpoint of the *New York Evening Post, American Banker, The New York Times,* and the *New York Tribune*. This attack did not surprise Shaw, who knew of the *Nation's* "blacklist," which included Lloyd and Ely. Lloyd noted the reviewer's resort to *ad hominem* and ridicule, and that he was not a staff member of the *Nation*. The *Literary World* followed the latter in denouncing Lloyd as a "systematic socialist."[41]

Influential papers praising his book were the *Springfield Republican, Boston Herald, Boston Globe, Pittsburgh Dispatch, Brooklyn Standard-Union, Cincinnati Post,* and *New York World*. Even the conservative, pro-Yerkes Chicago *Inter Ocean* admitted that Lloyd's evidence was "overwhelming and convincing"! However, the *Chicago Tribune* ridiculed his allegedly Platonic "dreams" and depreciated the "trusts' " evil aspects. Many editors wrote Lloyd that he had performed a great public service and opened their columns to him. Hudson of the *Pittsburgh Post-Dispatch* wrote him that he had destroyed the Standard Oil's entire defense. George H. Warner of the *Hartford Courant* called his book "a master-work."[42]

Competitive businessmen welcomed the book. The Boston banker C. F. Dillaway urged that it be circulated widely, as did

Henry H. Dupree of Walpole Dye & Chemical Company and
Charles S. Bird of a large paper company. Some New York
businessmen converted other executives to Lloyd's views by circulating personal copies, and suggested a cheap edition for
businessmen.[43]

Independent petroleum men were enthusiastic at Lloyd's
revelations and interpretation of their position. Roger Sherman
persuaded United States Pipeline executives to circulate copies
widely in America and in Europe "to do missionary duty."
After receiving a copy Senator John J. Ingalls of Kansas was
much impressed. Sherman wrote Lloyd, " 'The Smokeless
Rebate' is as effective as it is great and unanswerable. . . . How
I would like to join in the coming crusade for Liberty!" The
Titusville *World* and *Bradford Record* propagated the book's
revelations, asserting they did not tell half the story. *The Paint,
Oil and Drug Reporter* praised its contribution to educating
the public on "the peril which threatens not only the commercial independence but independence of any sort in this
country." When the American Oil Works of Titusville sent
Lloyd a complimentary barrel of kerosene he insisted on paying
for it to keep free from "obligations to the Independents for
whom I have been glad to speak in my book."[44]

The most prominent of the many lawyers who praised it was
Louis D. Brandeis of Warren & Brandeis, Boston. He was profoundly impressed by its statement of facts, its depth, and
unique "method analysis," its demand for "a new theoretical
approach" to economic and political problems. He discussed its
implications with friends, and wrote Mead that it should be
rewritten in popular form naming names so as to destroy
popular admiration for "the Captains of the Trusts" and facilitate "progress against the trust phalanx." In 1911, after the
United States Supreme Court dissolved the Standard Oil of
New Jersey, Brandeis would state to the Senate Interstate
Commerce Committee that the decision confirmed "what everyone ought to have known" since publication of *Wealth Against
Commonwealth*. While lawyers from many cities wrote to Lloyd
during 1894–96 of their agreement and support, the *Virginia*

Law Register published "Trusts and Monopolies" criticizing the
Supreme Court "Sugar Trust" case decision. *Wealth Against
Commonwealth* was turning legal opinion against laissez faire.[45]

Reformers of many types responded enthusiastically. Hale of
Boston and Junius H. Browne and Byron Holt of New York
endorsed the book's social theory. *City and State* (Philadelphia)
praised its disclosure of corporation dominance in Pennsylvania
and termed it the most remarkable book of the generation.
Thomas R. Slicer of Buffalo's Liberal Club said, "I get so hot
over that I feel as Crusaders did when Peter the Hermit was
stirring their blood."[46]

Hull House residents enthusiastically marked Jane Addams'
copy "H. H." Mary Gooding, Brooklyn socialite and suffragist
supporter of Mayor Seth Low, ranked *Wealth Against
Commonwealth* with Darwin's *Origin of Species*. The *National
Single-Taxer* urged every subscriber to read it "before another
moon wanes. Great is the Enemy." The *Encyclopedia of Social
Reform* based articles on "Trusts" and "Plutocracy" upon it. S.
M. Jones's *The New Right* declared it to be "unanswerable."[47]

Most religious and ethical periodicals were profoundly
impressed by the book. When the *Methodist Review* (New
York) criticized it severely, the Rev. Columbus Bradford of St.
Louis rebuked it stingingly. The *Northwestern Christian Advocate* and *Methodist Herald* praised the book, as did *Christian
Register, Christian Nation, Unity,* and *Universalist.* The *Kingdom,* organ of the Brotherhood of the Kingdom, endorsed the
book, castigated Rockefeller's gifts to the University of Chicago,
and placed Lloyd on its editorial board. Bliss and George D.
Herron were strongly influenced by his book. The Rev. Heber
Newton of New York City declared it "the most damning indictment that could well be conceived" in the *Independent* in
1896. While praising it to Washington Gladden, John Bascom
declared that Rockefeller had "no right to endow a university."
The Cincinnati Methodist Ministerial Association demanded
that Lloyd's ethical principles be enforced in business. The leading Maine Universalist minister urged his friends to study the
book. Congregational and Presbyterian ministers accepted

Lloyd's leadership and invited him into their pulpits. The Rev. Leighton Willia ms of New York, Secretary of the Brotherhood of the Kingdom, became Lloyd's warm friend. Winning a great clerical following was among Lloyd's greatest achievements.[48]

The delight of agrarian leaders with his book enhanced his prominence as a Populist leader. Paul Van Dervoort, a Nebraska Populist, informed him that it would be "the Uncle Tom's Cabin of the New Revolution," a view that the Rev. Hale shared. The *American Nonconformist, Appeal to Reason,* and *Wealth Makers* recommended it warmly. California farmers' clubs cited it as justification for supporting an independent oil company against the Standard Oil and Southern Pacific Railroad. Moderate western farm journals appreciated the book's exposures of monopoly.[49]

Endorsements by the *American Federationist* and Swinton gave it standing in labor circles. Debs predicted it would exert "powerful influence in righting the social and industrial wrongs with which the Republic is afflicted." Socialist journals regarded the book as unanswerable, and for years excerpted it. The pro-labor Christian Socialist *American Fabian* hailed it as "impregnable."[50]

In the British Isles, whose critical opinion strongly influenced the American reading public, *Wealth Against Commonwealth*'s impact was greater than any American economic treatise since *Progress and Poverty*. Stead reviewed it favorably in the (London) *Review of Reviews* and discussed it incessantly with John Morley and others. He assured Lloyd that the value of "really great books such as yours" was discovered gradually. It won the respect of the British intelligentsia, which customarily depreciated American books. Bryce informed Lloyd that its subject, "of immense importance to your country . . . may become very important here, also." W. H. H. Lecky, historian of European morals, wrote Lloyd how impressed he was by the insight the book provided into American conditions. Charles Trevelyan informed him of how it interested him in American political parties, and was "most particularly anxious" to meet him. Lloyd granted permission to draw material from his treatise

for "a very savage" antimonopoly romance of the oil regions to
Morley Roberts, friend of Robert Louis Stevenson. Roberts
informed him of references to *Wealth Against Commonwealth*
in H. H. Champion's "Australian paper," and sent the novel's
manuscript to The Wayside for criticism. Youthful H. Wickham
Steed, in Paris preparing for a notable journalistic career, was
profoundly influenced by Lloyd's book. He persuaded Ida M.
Tarbell to read it there.[51]

John A. Hobson, wealthy Ruskinite and lecturer on economics, valued the book as "being by far the most powerful and
convincing exposure of the natural working of developed
Capitalism that has yet appeared." His *Evolution of Modern
Capitalism* soon corroborated Lloyd's general position. As the
best solution for the American "trust" problem he recommended "public control of transport" but recognized that
carriers might control the regulatory commissions as Lloyd indicated. In the *Progressive Review* of October 1896 Hobson's
extensive review of *Wealth Against Commonwealth* declared
that the most conservative appraisal of the facts it presented
established the Standard Oil's antisocial character. Hobson
reported that British economists, hard-headed businessmen, and
Socialists accepted "the general accuracy of this criticism" of
American monopolies while fearing their secret, illicit tyrannies.

Led by the *London Daily Chronicle*, the *Times, Edinburgh
Scotsman,* and *Dundee Advertiser* praised Lloyd's classic repeatedly. The *Chronicle* called him "one of the most prominent
and respected friends of labor and reform in America" and
castigated the "trust" promoters' criminal perversions of traditional self-help. Lloyd's appeal to public spirit and his attempt
to ensure that the community share the wealth that it helped to
create it declared to be "the true method of dealing with the
industrial problems of our day." The popular Socialist *Clarion*
and the YMCA's *Christian Million* published very favorable
reviews, while high praise of the book appeared in the trade
journals, *London Transport, Chemist and Druggist,* and *Food
and Sanitation.*[52] On the other hand, the *Saturday Review*
criticized Lloyd's unrestrained style, "obvious one-sidedness,"

and inconsistency in implying that unrestrained competition would be "the salvation of the oil industry" while exhibiting "Socialist tendencies." While asking for "the other side," it informed Britons they could be thankful they lived "under an effete monarchy."[53]

British reformers reacted with warm enthusiasm to the book. *Seed-Time* urged that the Fabian Society study it. *Fabian News* remarked that it confirmed Clarke's analysis of American industry while telling how a "silly, ignorant Democracy, help-less and uninstructed," was "governed by an exceedingly able aristocracy of wealth" while its monopolies "rake in their levies." *Labour Copartnership* urged that British cooperators "consolidate their enterprises beyond the possibility of domina-tion or extinction" by the "Trusts." The *Municipal Journal* termed Lloyd's indictment of them "unanswerable."[54] Finally, A. J. Wilson's fourteen-page article in *Investor's Review* stressed the "deep" import of Lloyd's treatise for businessmen and investors in American securities. He warned that none "can have the least confidence in the stability of anything American" and advised investors to unload their American railroad securities. He expressed vigorous antipathy to American "market monopoly" in the British Isles.[55] Thus Lloyd won his objectives and started a backfire in Great Britain that had repercussions in America. In 1902 Stead would ascribe to his book the odium attaching to American "trusts" in Britain, while reporting his reputation there.

Wealth Against Commonwealth exerted less influence on the Continent, least of all in France, whose venal journalists were "comfortably certain" there was no danger there from the Standard Oil. The treatise was reviewed at length in Holland by F. W. Wibaut, and was the basis of the embattled indepen-dent C. Bogaert's articles on the oil trade in *XXe Siècle* (Brussels). The *Frankfurter Zeitung und Handelsblatt* praised the book. Alfred von der Leyen wrote Lloyd his praise, reviewed the book exhaustively, and sent a list of German and Austrian journals that would do likewise. After copies were distributed by Emery among "high officials of the Empire" the German

Government forced the Standard Oil to abandon destructive local price-cutting and American independents enjoyed "good trade & fair prices."[56]

The book attracted attention in Canada, also. A Montreal tobacco manufacturer distributed copies, as did A. H. Drury of the Imperial Oil Company, Ltd., while cooperating with Emery's attempts to develop European markets before the Canadian independents surrendered to the Standard Oil. George Iles, wealthy Montreal hotel man, wrote Lloyd after reading his book that "the Standard Oil Trust's success had been built upon a thousand breaches of trust on the part of railroad managers . . . freedom has perished of sheer dishonesty, and the moneybags will lord it over us more and more boldly until the people rise to a wholesale killing. Your book will inevitably have an alleged 'answer'," he warned, "your evidence is too well massed and too damning to be passed by in silence."[57] They became warm friends.

Wealth Against Commonwealth thus enhanced Lloyd's prestige and greatly extended his influence as America's greatest antimonopolist exponent of the social welfare philosophy. Preparation of the book matured him as a business critic. Publication established him as the chief non-Marxian radical intellectual in the United States, and confirmed his position among the trans-Atlantic ethical leaders. He was recognized as an authority on business combinations on both sides of the Atlantic Ocean.

Chapter XV

The Standard Oil Counterattacks

INDIRECTION

PUBLICATION OF *Wealth Against Commonwealth* plunged Lloyd into a prolonged dramatic conflict with Rockefeller and the Standard Oil. He expected a counterattack from that quarter, since its detectives had shadowed him for years. Knowing its magnates' ruthless methods, he "expected to be *crushed*" by the Standard Oil executives. They did not accord him this honor, but employed indirect methods first and then officially impugned his accuracy and motives to discredit him and his book. Getting down to details would have necessitated embarrassing admissions, as Allan Nevins concedes, while insisting that Rockefeller and his organization should have made a direct, official reply to counteract the book's influence.[2]

A libel suit or suit for damages would have been ideal for such a purpose, had the book been vulnerable. If successful, either would have discredited it and vindicated S. C. T. Dodd's claim that his superiors were enlightened, public-spirited enterprisers. That litigation of this type was not instituted against Lloyd and Harper & Brothers by the Rockefeller coterie is strong *prima facie* evidence of the factual accuracy and public importance of the book. But, despite Rockefeller's and Nevins' denials, the Standard Oil did reply to it in repeated attempts to exonerate itself.

W. T. Scheide's attack upon it in the *Nation* opened the counterattack, as has been noted above.[3] Supposedly independent authorities on the "trusts" then followed suit.

During the World's Fair Ernest Levy von Halle had called at The Wayside while investigating American industrial combinations for the *Verein fur Social-Politik*. He received a copy of Lloyd's address to the National Anti-Trust Convention before calling at 26 Broadway to interview and receive documents from Standard Oil executives. As a historical economist he saw in combinations the working of the evolutionary process. In 1895 he published *Trusts or Industrial Combinations and Coalitions in the United States*. This was as friendly to the American combination movement as his article in *Uberwirtschaftlish Kartelle in Deutschland und in Ausland* was to the Deutsch-Amerikanische Petroleum Gesellschaft, the Standard Oil's Continental subsidiary with which he had formed a liaison before visiting America in 1893.[4]

Von Halle's *Trusts* called *Wealth Against Commonwealth* "a *chronique scandaleuse*" that did not even attempt to present both sides, although he accepted Lloyd's account of the Buffalo conspiracy case. The German's book was so biased that the *Chicago Evening Post* declared it "a side-wind reply" to Lloyd. The *New York Tribune* remarked that it was "sadly marred by some inexcusable errors of language and of fact." Von Halle's most ludicrous blunder was classifying Dodd, the Standard Oil's solicitor, and George Gunton, its secretly subsidized editor and lecturer, as "younger economists" teaching that combinations were "an unavoidable step in an organic development."[5]

Lloyd was prepared for the German's pro-"trust" stand. To Albert Shaw the Winnetkan associated von Halle's "acceptance of the Trusts as 'unavoidable' " with the attitude of "conventional economists toward what they call Facts, while leaving to persons really 'scientific' the work of study, protest and reform." He added that he had "scrupulously given any defense the trust has made."[6]

He joined Professor Laughlin in a Sunday symposium on von Halle's *Trusts* in the *Chicago Times-Herald*. Both criticized it severely. Lloyd ridiculed von Halle's assertion that publicity and government regulation would remedy the "trusts' " evils, since thirty years of that had not "stayed or softened the hands of the appropriating geniuses" or prevented government control from being transmuted into the "trusts' " control of the government. The real issue, he said, was whether their power had been "rightly got" and was "rightly held." "Moral sterility" prevented economists from producing a "commanding work" on that subject, and their avoidance of fundamental issues was "the gravest of intellectual errors." Invoking Darwinism to justify business combinations excluded them from the social sciences as being beyond control. "The science which classifies as 'unavoidable' the acts of men or society is a science of impotence, and its professors live up to it," Lloyd concluded emphatically. Spahr termed this review "admirable," and asked for more of "such things."[7]

So adverse was American reaction to von Halle's book that the Standard Oil made another attempt to discredit *Wealth Against Commonwealth*. Official silence in face of its ever wider acclaim was interpreted as a confession of guilt "all along the line."[8] Gunton, editor of the *Social Economist,* was selected as best qualified to attempt a rebuttal. In July 1895 he attacked the book in "The Integrity of Economic Literature,"[9] declaring that Lloyd's book was the "worst specimen of iconoclastic propaganda" against millionaires and "Big Business' emanating from "advocates of socialism, populism," etc. It was sponsored, he claimed, by unsuccessful competitors of giant business and substituted "demagogic misrepresentation" for "honest statement and interest in public welfare, undermining the integrity of economic literature." After repeating Dodd's defense of the "Trusts," Gunton declared that *Wealth Against Commonwealth* was one-sided and inaccurate, suppressing evidence favoring the Standard Oil, dishonest in analyzing litigation, and implied that monopoly corrupted the courts. He analyzed and rejected Lloyd's accounts of the Widow Backus episode, South Improvement Company, Samuel Van Syckel's experiences, and George Rice's misadventures. Gunton denied that the admittedly "scandalous" South Improvement Company had had "any real existence" and that the Standard had been responsible for it. He denied that the Backus Oil Company's valuation when

Rockefeller acquiried it should have been the capitalization of its net income, as Lloyd had asserted soundly, and stressed instead that magnate's offer to return the property to Mrs. Backus when she protested *post hoc* against his ruthlessness. As for the judicial vindication of Van Syckel's invention of continuous distillation, Gunton asserted there was "no such process in use anywhere in the world." Lloyd's account of Rice's long fight against the Standard he termed "a fine piece of revolution-creating literature," since that organization's executives were no worse than other businessmen. His only interest in the matter was his desire to defend "the integrity of economic literature." Lloyd was "one of the sworn enemies of man" whose book would "invalidate history and corrupt the morals of public thought and action" more "than could a hundred trusts."

Lloyd rated Gunton's article "an amazingly weak performance," but analyzed it exhaustively, making devastating marginal notations. He wrote beside Gunton's claim that the SIC had not done business "Ohio 79 for checks sent to S. Imp. Co. contracts signed rates raised & rebates Dodd," and "untrue" beside the erroneous claim that prominent Standard Oil men "were among those who procured the death of the South Improvement Company." Beside the attempt to exonerate the Standard in the Van Syckel litigation he noted, "They admitted it." Regarding the suppression of that individual's invention he noted, "Every monopoly does this. Monopoly can no more manage American property than despotism." His contempt for Gunton's falsification of the facts in Rice's suit against the Marietta railroad was scathing.

To Spahr, whom he asked to read Gunton's piece critically, he observed, "as to nearly every episode my version is the *adjudicated* one." The Standard Oil executives, he declared, were "anarchistic" in demanding that adverse court and regulatory commission acts and legislative inquiry findings "be overridden and nullified. . . . They recognize no law but their own. *The Outlook* has stood by my book so handsomely that I wish to make sure that no cloud rests upon your mind or Dr. Abbott's."[10] Spahr replied, "That George Gunton should fall foul of your book, would be so much additional testimony," and that the Standard "thinks itself bolstered up by such a supporter illustrates how easy it is to be transformed from a crank to an authority."

Lloyd consulted Sherman on the character of the independents whom Gunton traduced, asserting interestingly that it was "important to *the cause* (!) that the people be not allowed to be fooled into the belief that these things are not so." Sherman replied, "Gunton is simply a liar, and that is all you can say on the subject," and informed him that Gunton was paid by Standard Oil. Rice corroborated *Wealth Against Commonwealth*'s statement that the Marietta Railroad had discontinued payments of rebates on his oil shipments to the Standard only after federal judge J. Baxter so ordered. After consulting Ely, Lloyd drafted a careful rejoinder which Harpers termed "complete and effective."[12]

Mead placed this in the *Boston Herald*. Entitled "THE FIGHTER OF TRUSTS. HENRY D. LLOYD SCORES GUNTON'S DEFENSE OF STANDARD OILERS. MONOPOLY DENOUNCED AS BEING 'ECONOMIC IDOCY'," it appeared on the front page, October 23, 1895. Five columns rebutted Gunton's major criticisms with data drawn from the Rice, Van Syckel and Scofield, Shurmer & Teagle suits, disclosing that he had ignored contrary evidence and relied exclusively upon Standard executives' claims regarding the SIC. Rebutting the charge that he had omitted the Standard's side, he referred to his book's 200 quotations from the testimony of its executives, agents, and "railroad allies." The accuracy of Lloyd's reply to Gunton, whose charges were later reiterated by John D. Archbold, Nevins, and to some extent by the Hidys, has been established by careful comparison with the sources. Lloyd distributed his rebuttal widely. In a gay letter to Major Huntington about the rise of Chicago "Loop" real estate values, a visit to Ravinoaks, and the visit of the Ned Masons at The Wayside, he mentioned casually his answer "in the Boston Herald to the only considerable attempts to answer my book."[13]

Gunton replied in the *Herald* on December 16. He claimed

that he was a new type of economist that championed both industrial and labor combinations, while Lloyd was a narrow antimonopolist contributing to "the social insanity" that culminates in the "overthrow of existing institutions." After declaring that the SIC was "a myth" he said that John A. Hobson had written him confessing his error in treating it seriously.

Lloyd promptly asked Hobson for an explanation, and sought more data from Sherman on the SIC. Sherman replied that reliable sources indicated that Gunton was "an employee of the Standard Oil Trust." As for the SIC, nine of its thirteen organizers were afterward that organization's executives. The SIC's railroad contracts demonstrated that it had begun to do business.

Hobson replied from the Riviera that his letter to Gunton had been intended for publication in the *Social Economist* in reply to a review of his own book. He had written that all informed Englishmen believed that the charges against the SIC were "correct." "I am quite convinced that you are right," he informed Lloyd, "in your identification of the South Improvement Co. as the Standard Oil Co. . . . I should be the last person to underrate the value of the work you are doing or to be deceived by the loose (not to say dishonest) reasoning with which I am familiar in Mr. Gunton's writings. I am thoroughly with you in the fight against Monopolies."[14]

"I think I have Gunton on the hip," Lloyd wrote Mead jubilantly, enclosing a draft reply : "Am I within the record in what I say of Gunton's position? Is Gunton worth this?" If so, would Mead place it in the *Herald* "and order 500 copies for me" from the edition that "comes to the exchanges." Mead approved : "It is a very strong point. What a d——d liar and sneak this cuss is !"[15] The *Herald* published Lloyd's second rebuttal on February 1, 1896. This demanded that Gunton publish Hobson's letter in the *Social Economist* and resolve "the awkward question" that had arisen from what he had said it contained. Until he did so and could demonstrate thereby that "he can correctly describe so simple a thing as this letter 'just received' and lying before him," the public would "not attach

New York Liberal Club,

ROOMS, PLIMPTON HALL,

Junction of Ninth and Stuyvesant Streets.

New York, March 21, 1871.

Dear Sir:

      You are respectfully invited to attend the Eightieth Meeting of the **NEW YORK LIBERAL CLUB,** *to be held at its Rooms, Plimpton Hall, junction of Ninth and Stuyvesant Streets, on Friday Evening, March 24th, at 8 o'clock.*

Mr. HENRY D. LLOYD,

ASS. SEC. AMERICAN FREE-TRADE LEAGUE.

Will review the propositions advanced at a former meeting of the Club by Mr. Horace Greeley, in his reply to the Free-Trade Letter of John Stuart Mill.

      All interested in this question, are invited to attend,

      A full attendance of members is requested.

      By order of the Executive Committee,

D. T. Gardner,

Secretary.

N. B.—There will be an important business meeting of the Club on Wednesday evening, March 22d, 1871, to be held at the rooms. Every member is expected to be present, as the committee on By-Laws, etc., will present their report for adoption.

Invitation to the New York Liberal Club (courtesy State Historical Society, Wisconsin)

Henry D. Lloyd as an undergraduate at Columbia College, 1868 (courtesy Columbia University Library)

Henry D. Lloyd, 1872 (courtesy State Historical Society, Wisconsin)

Lieutenant Governor William Bross

William Bross, Moses Bross, William Bross Lloyd, and Jessie Bross Lloyd

*John Crilley Lloyd, Aaron Lloyd, William Bross Lloyd and
Henry D. Lloyd, 1879*

The Wayside, 1961

The Watch House before demolition, 1959

Jane Addams

Thomas J. Morgan

Henry D. Lloyd, 1897 (courtesy State Historical Society, Wisconsin)

Edward W. Bemis (courtesy State Historical Society, Wisconsin)

Henry D. Lloyd New Zealand, 1899

Golden Rule Park, Toledo

Reverend Edward Everett Hale (courtesy of the Boston Athenaeum)

The Miners' Triumverate: Henry D. Lloyd, John Mitchell, and Clarence Darrow (courtesy State Historical Society, Wisconsin)

much importance to his efforts to paint the black of the oil trust white, and the white of 'Wealth Against Commonwealth' black."

Gunton did not reply to this deft, crushing rejoinder. He did not publish Hobson's letter. Samuel Leavitt of the *Joliet News* wrote Lloyd his delight that he had "that fraud Gunton on the hip." Lloyd did not live to see Gunton installed as an economics professor at Columbia University, when it was discovered that he had received during fifteen years preceding $225,000 from the Standard Oil men plus half a million more to finance his journal.[16] This illustrated Lloyd's revelation of the "trusts' " attempts to control American intellectuals and higher learning in America.

Rockefeller Bids for Exoneration

Shortly after Lloyd silenced Gunton, the Standard Oil magnates attempted to secure religious and scholarly exoneration of their business methods. This was occasioned by the call at 26 Broadway of the Rev. Benjamin Fay Mills, influential Social Gospel evangelist, who previously had praised Lloyd's book. In April 1896 he inquired of Rockefeller what he had to say in reply to it. This synchronized with *The Outlook*'s demand that the oil monopolists publish their official defense if they had any. Rockefeller handed Mills on to Dodd and the Rev. Frederick T. Gates, his adviser on philanthropy, who scheduled him for a lecture at the University of Chicago. They went through *Wealth Against Commonwealth* with him and convinced him that its "charges" were "at least susceptible of reasonable explanation, and possibly, of disproof." The Standard's policy, they said blandly, was "never to deny or attempt to disprove charges" made against it "in a public manner." All that "trust's" actions had been "from any reasonable business standpoint—thoroughly moral." To prove this they would consent to "a reasonable investigation" by a committee of qualified clergy and economists "of the charges made" by this book against the Standard and its methods. Rockefeller approved.

At his ":very urgent request" Mills invited leading Social Gospel clergy and certain new school economists to constitute this committee, conveying Rockefeller's assurances to them that all "the charges made against the Standard Oil Co., of various forms of immorality, are unfounded and false." They were invited to visit 26 Broadway where Rockefeller and Dodd "will be glad to take their own time and put all the facilities of their office at your disposal—for your investigation of the serious charges made against them," Mills said. Lyman Abbott, Hale, Josiah Strong, General Secretary of the Evangelical Alliance, Graham Taylor of the Chicago Commons, Spahr, Thomas Hall, Gladden, Leighton Williams, Herron, James H. Ecob, and President George A. Gates of Iowa College were the Social Gospelers invited. Ely, Commons, and Jenks were the economists. Mills invited them to meet in New York together at a convenient with "others suggested by any of you," when the group "could hear what the Company would be glad to state."[17]

Those men had informed Lloyd previously of their satisfaction with his replies to Gunton. Herron forwarded his invitation from Mills to Lloyd asking him to keep it "confidential" but to "take such action as the case seems to need. . . . It seems to me a case of the most transcendent gullibility of modern times." Herron informed Mills that the "sole consideration" on which he would consent to sit on the committee was "that Mr. Lloyd be present to lead" the inquiry; the "idea of a company of Christian gentlemen coming together to receive the bland assurance of the attorney of the Standard Oil Co., is so transparently absurd that I can hardly believe the written words before my eyes."[18] Spahr, Strong and Williams also informed Lloyd of the "oil trust's" invitation.

This, he informed Gladden, Mead, and Ely, offered an opportunity "to strike some very effective blows." Would they criticize draft alternative replies to Mills that he enclosed? Spahr had assured him the invitees "would appreciate that the church would simply be further smirched by such a ridiculous procedure as the proposed investigation" and that any reply to Lloyd's book "must be addressed to the public."[19] Lloyd prepared two draft replies to Mills. In draft "A" he said he was "entirely ready to meet Rockefeller anywhere and at any time" before the committee "stipulating only that the unreversed findings of the courts, . . . and of the Interstate Commerce Commission, as given in my book, be accepted . . . as conclusive of the facts covered by them unless the Oil Trust can show that they—the findings—are incorrectly reported by me." Since the Standard's executives had testified that they kept no books or records, "the only proper place to investigate was among the public records." If the committee met at 26 Broadway he would attend "provided the meetings are public" and he was free to discuss afterward its "conclusions . . . and all the facts concerning the matter." In draft "B" he said "the whole thing seems almost like *opéra bouffe* to me." How could a single committee meeting resolve the complex situations that had occupied the best legal talent for years? Gates must be especially qualified to pass judgment on his sponsor's business method, he added sarcastically.[20]

Spahr "chuckled over B" and handed "A over to Dr. Abbott just in time to change his reply to Mills and Rockefeller." Mead shared "A" with Hale, and expressed amazement to Lloyd at "the request of John the Baptist for trial by 'divines.' One wonders if he considers ecclesiastical courts of higher jurisdiction than the civil. . . . It would be 'nuts' to have you actually inside the ring, . . . with free right to ask any questions you like, and talk about it afterwards as much as you please. Speed the day."[21] Spahr might have asked also why Rockefeller sought exoneration in this manner if his methods were as ethical and legal as he had always claimed.

Lloyd sent "A" to each invitee, and to Abbott a detailed review of Standard Oil propaganda, noting its subsidized newspapers, "literary bureau," and *Social Economist*. "The Oil Trust" had no defense to make other than that which it "has already unsuccessfully offered," Lloyd asserted; the real issue should be to determine the validity of the "adjudicated decisions" on which the charges against the Oil Trust rested. Abbott should observe that the dissolution of it ordered by New York courts was only nominal. The Rockefeller group's success "for so many years" in its "callous and cynical indifference to the public will" and its maintenance of "the position of a law-breaker, is to me . . . a demonstration that in these matters there is not yet any such thing as an American people," Lloyd concluded.[22]

Abbott replied that he would have "no confidence in the result of my investigation" of the Standard "even if I had abundant leisure to make it." He declined to join the committee. Strong informed Mills that the inquiry "would be worse than useless" but wished to "be there to see" if Lloyd attended. Ely demanded that a competent attorney conduct the inquiry and that he be allowed to bring witnesses from Ohio. Gladden warned Mills that clergymen of limited practical knowledge were incompetent to "undertake to reverse or even to review" court actions, ICC rulings, and legislative investigations. As for "the *advocatus diabioli,* we might know before hand what he would say." If Lloyd and competent lawyers conducted the inquiry in public, employing cross-examination, "some useful results might be secured" and he would "gladly assist, in the french sense." Commons would attend if Jenks did, who said he would if the inquiry were thorough and no farce."[23]

After receiving these replies from Mills, Rockefeller hastily dropped the scheme. If he wanted a fair investigation, he would have accepted Ely's, Jenks's, and Gladden's stipulations, permitted the committee to retain a qualified attorney, and held the sessions in Lloyd's presence, according him opportunity to comment. Rockefeller's rejection of these conditions spoke volumes to the informed, among whom were the most influential new school economists and Social Gospel leaders. This was indirect corroboration of *Wealth Against Commonwealth* with a vengeance! Rockefeller and Dodd had measured Lloyd's metal accurately during his exchanges with Gunton. By refusing to meet him face to face, Rockefeller confessed covertly the inadequacy of his own armor and his moral guilt in the very field in which he posed as the paladin of virtue.

After seeing Mills at Toledo, Herron reported to Lloyd that that evangelist had been "taken in" by "the piety and seeming fairness" of Dodd and Gates, and was still convinced "that the

Standard folks are not as bad as painted." Herron urged Lloyd to combat further Standard attempts "to try this game of fairness and piety" on the clergy. Lloyd immediately sent copies of *Wealth Against Commonwealth* to long lists of ministers supplied by Gladden, Strong, and Hale. He canvassed with Mills "the particular points made by the Oil Trust people," sent him his *Herald* replies to Gunton, and warned him that a minister seeking to apply Christ's gospel to business needed not only to be "harmless as a dove but wise as a serpent." After Mills invited him to visit him at Fort Edward, near Lake George, Lloyd sent him a commentary on the statements that Gates and Dodd had made to him. "The simple issue of monopoly is the main point," Lloyd observed, but the "trust" magnates' control of the markets and of social, religious, political, and educational life presented "a question as great as any . . . which have made the previous crises of history." The world never submitted to "the power to make both sides of its bargains. . . . No glitter of wealth or personality in those who hold this anti-social power will deter the people from making good their rights."[24]

Mills replied that Rockefeller's proposal had been "so honorable" that he could not refuse to send the invitations although he knew he would be misunderstood. "Personally, I did not need any testimony regarding the evils of monopoly" and "have not changed my public addresses on account of my conference in N.Y." Lloyd was delighted that "the Philistines" led by Rockefeller, "the incarnate spirit of our age of gold," had not deceived him. Could the Millses visit at The Watch House?[25]

The incident, excluded from public view as it was, greatly enhanced Lloyd's prestige among forward-looking clergy, economists, and journals of opinion. After Rockefeller's refusal to face him before a committee of inquiry of his own devising, all subsequent attempts to apply the customary Standard Oil rationale and methods to invalidate Lloyd's book were ridiculous.

Mills persuaded Lloyd to address a "confidential conference" of reform clergy, professors, and sympathizers at Fort Edwards that summer, and cancelled his own engagement to lecture at the University of Chicago.[26] This initiated a series of Fort Edwards summer conferences between clerical and lay reformers, who were determined to enforce social justice in the business system. Lloyd became an important leader of this upper circle of influential reformers. Thus, from their struggle for the adherence of the Social Gospel clergy, new economists, and upper level social reform to their respective systems, he emerged the victor over Rockefeller.

Lloyd's Victory

Defense of his book involved Lloyd in frequent controversies. In March 1897 he crossed swords with Dodd and Gunton in the *Independent*'s symposium, "The Question of Trusts," to which Ely and Clark and De Leon contributed. Most contributors assumed that the "trusts" were permanent despite their illegalities, which Lloyd, Clark, and Ely described. De Leon hailed these organizations as ultimately beneficial to the proletariat, and declared that the "middle class" were attempting to destroy them. Ely urged abolition of tariff privileges and public ownership of natural monopolies.

The sharpest clash occurred between Lloyd and Dodd, whose sponsors would rival J. P. Morgan for leadership in the reviving combination movement. Lloyd reviewed Standard Oil publicity and history scathingly, arguing that its executives had enriched themselves by monopoly prices rather than superior managerial genius. He alluded pointedly to Dodd's earlier admission that the Standard paid a "bonus" (bribery!) to railroad officials to secure rate favors. Dodd attempted to discredit Lloyd's book by charging that he suppressed important facts and by repeating Gunton's *ad hominem* attacks. Lloyd was "a leading Socialist," he charged. While denying that the Standard's success sprang from exclusive freight-rate favors, Dodd claimed for it and all large corporations lower rates than competitors received because of their larger shipments. He misrepresented Alexander J. Cassatt's testimony before the Hepburn Committee, the records of the Van Syckel case, and

Buffalo conspiracy case. He denied that the Standard Oil was then enjoying widespread rate favors, the existence of which the United States Commissioner of Corporations subsequently demonstrated (1906) to have been so extensive as to confer upon it "monopolistic control," Lloyd's main thesis.

Editorially, the *Independent* discriminated between "good Trusts" that passed their economies on to the public in reduced prices and "bad" combinations perpetrating "serious abuses." For remedies it proposed publicity, abolition of rebates, tariff reduction, and prohibition of stock-watering. Implicit in this was "the rule of reason" that Dodd had devised earlier which the Supreme Court would eventually promulgate in 1911.[27]

To his sister Caro the Winnetkan remarked, "Rather peculiar is it not that Gunton and Dodd can not bring forward one specimen of the suppressed facts they allege?" Adelbert Moot complimented Lloyd's "clear and timely" contribution as rendering the "country a real service." To Moritz Pinner, aged German-American antislavery figure, Lloyd compared the Standard Oil men to the antebellum proslavery leaders in their attempt to discredit "any kind of reform."[23]

In August the defense of the "trusts" by ex-Governor Roswell P. Flower of New York, banker and Standard Oil men's stock market leader, provoked the *New York Journal* into publishing its own symposium. Lloyd contributed to this "Trial of the Trusts by Public Discussion." So did Dodd; Senator John P. Jones; Benjamin H. Butterworth, Commissioner of Patents; Thomas Murphy; and John Brisben Walker, editor of *Cosmopolitan*. Lloyd, Jones, Butterworth, and Walker condemned the great combinations. Lloyd carried the burden of the antitrust case. He riddled Flower's assertion that business combinations' greater efficiency reduced prices and gave better service. He cited a recent rate increase on grain on the eastern trunklines, and the "poorest and most expensive telegraph service of any civilized country" supplied by Western Union. The "trusts'" concentrating market power was the real issue, Lloyd declared. To that the American would never submit. Flower was opposing the public opinion that backed the antitrust laws and the New

York courts' dissolution of the oil and sugar trusts, he added. Dodd argued in an attempted *reductio ad absurdum* that antitrust law enforcement would injure farmers and labor, or "the poorer manufacturers," rather than the wealthy and powerful. Such legislation was an attempt "to destroy business," and enforcement would produce chaos. "Long live Anarchy and Nihilism," Dodd cried.[29]

When the *Chicago Times-Herald* in November 1898 endorsed the *Social Economist*'s attack upon George Rice, Lloyd informed it that it had been completely misled by Gunton, declaring that his earlier falsification of Hobson's letter had placed him "entirely outside the pale of controversy with gentlemen." By citing ICC and federal court records, he established the reliability of his book's account of Rice's struggle against the Standard Oil.[30]

When the *New York Evening Post* asserted in September 1899 that *Wealth Against Commonwealth*'s great influence rested upon improbable "if not false accusations" lacking insufficient evidence to sustain a jury verdict, the amused *Brooklyn Citizen* observed, "Trusts must be in a bad way, indeed, for argument to justify their existence when . . . the 'Evening Post' bogs, flounders and falsifies so pitiably in defense of them." Lloyd's reputation was "not made by inaccuracies," and his book's revelations were "grossly and criminally libellous" if untrue. Yet, "none of the persons inculpated ever attempted to vindicate their characters by proceeding against Mr. Lloyd."

He wrote courteously to the *Post,* admitting that mathematically it was possible that all the courts, judges, and investigators had erred in their "verdicts" and the testimony cross-examined by them might be mistaken. If so, his book "must fall with them for it is built on them." However, he called public attention to the "dramatic fact" of a redistribution of its wealth that was still proceeding "by methods . . . pronounced by every organ of constitutional investigation a democratic people could use to be illegal and sometimes criminal," and that the people "were standing paralyzed." Would the *Post*'s wealthy constituency recognize that "our good wealth will commit the greatest mistake ever made in history by any people if it allowed its interests to be confounded in the public mind with the interests of . . . 'the truly dangerous classes'," whom Governor Roosevelt described in "the days when his pen was mightier than his sword" as " 'our criminal rich' "?

William Lloyd Garrison complimented his reply to "the stupid article that called it out" as did Josiah Strong. George Iles wrote Lloyd, "Wasn't it nuts to see the Evening Post publish your card without note or comment? I credit this to the admirable restraint you displayed in maintaining your ground." Gladden asked him in mock astonishment : "How could you be so cruel to the innocent?" Lloyd chortled to Bowles, who reprinted his reply to the *Post*, "When these Philistines attack me, the Lord almost puts them in my hands."[31]

During the previous December Carroll D. Wright had placed *Wealth Against Commonwealth* at the head of a list of recommended books for the United States Industrial Commission to study. Professor Jenks, its expert, borrowed materials from Lloyd.[32] Standard Oil executives then attempted to counteract the prestige of his book and the testimony of independent oil men by rebuttals and successful pressure on the secretary of the Commission to edit Rice's testimony. During the stormy hearings President M. L. Lockwood of the American Anti-Trust League drew heavily upon *Wealth Against Commonwealth* when attacking the "system of railway discriminations which has made this great curse, the Standard Oil monopoly, a possibility."

Archbold, head of the Standard, then declared to the Commission that Rice had attempted business blackmail against his organization and that Lloyd was "open" to the "suspicion" of seeking to share it, since his book was "cunning fiction made up entirely on one-sided testimony and dressed for sale," and was "one of the most untruthful, distorted compilations that was ever inflicted upon a suffering public." While minimizing, ridiculing, and repudiating court decisions adverse to the Standard Oil, he presented letters from railway executives stating that it no longer received rebates.[33]

While absent in the Antipodes, Lloyd was invited to testify

before the Commission on the "Trust Problem." Not until
April 1900 did he see Archbold's attack in the *Preliminary Report* that had been written subject to his pressure via Senator
Boies Penrose of Pennsylvania. Lloyd had not been anxious to
appear before the Commission, although he wanted what he
called Rockefeller's "preposterous statements" rebutted. Jenks
informed him that he could reply to Archbold by affidavit.
Although Willis Abbot advised him not to do so because the
Democratic Party National Committee intended to discredit
the report, Lloyd replied in the final *Report*.

His affidavit presented a remarkable summary of the theses
and factual basis of *Wealth Against Commonwealth*'s analysis
of the Standard Oil. It cited documentary evidence supporting
passages that Archbold, Dodd, and Gunton attacked, supported
Rice's testimony with elaborate citations, and asserted that no
critic had proved that it omitted or quoted inaccurately any
important fact on the record or that it had failed to present the
nature of the defense or that the author had "in any case gone
beyond the record." Railroad discriminations favoring the
Standard in all parts of America, Lloyd declared, had been the
chief issue litigated before the ICC, which in March 1898 had
discovered such extensive underbilling of Standard tank cars in
Massachusetts that half the shipments were carried "free." Proof
that similar rigging of freight rates in the Standard Oil's favor
existed elsewhere in America and Canada preceded a challenge
to Archbold to produce one "iota of fact" justifying his insinuation that Lloyd had attempted literary blackmail of it in writing his book. The Standard Oil's method was to insist that the
public allow it to nullify court decisions years afterward and
accept its new version of the matters so settled, while it continued to defy courts and legislatures, he declared. His crushing
affidavit posed a crucial test as to whether or not citizens,
scholars and statesmen would accept adjudicated evidence of
business law-breaking. Lloyd used *ex parte* statements from
both sides to the litigation that his book analyzed, but adhered
to the rulings of courts and regulatory commissions. This vindication of the book's accuracy enhanced his reputation and

influence as the leading authority on monopolistic business organizations. He handed copies of the affidavit to the press, which gave it wide publicity.[34] The Industrial Commission's final report stressed his evidence on freight rate discriminations favoring Standard Oil.

Before this he had learned of Archbold's savage, secret attack upon himself to R. Heber Newton. Replying to his expressed surprise at the People's Institute's Conference on Trusts that the Standard Oil had not brought a libel suit against Lloyd, Archbold had referred Newton to Gunton and charged that Lloyd had avoided this by omitting the names of Standard Oil men from his book. Archbold declared it to be "absolutely untruthful," one-sided, and motivated by "sensationalism to sell" and a "meaner and more mercenary" motive "than this." Lloyd replied to Newton that Archbold knew that omission of names was no safeguard. They had been omitted to avoid appearance of personal antagonism so that the public attention might be concentrated "on the evil behind the obnoxious persons who were enriching themselves by it." As for Archbold's accusation of having attempted blackmail, Lloyd remarked, "If my life does not speak for itself, my lips would not be witnesses worth hearing; but I will point out how perfectly absurd the charge is on the very face of it." Was not this "contemptible as an exhibition of the moral and intellectual pauperism" of the Standard Oil's defense? Its executives "ought to be in the penitentiary. Civil equality in this country is at an end, and the public is at an end, if we enforce our laws only against the poor and not against the rich."

To Lloyd's great satisfaction, Newton replied that he recognized "the force of all you have said. Your answer to the imputation of my Standard friend is complete. . . . Of course I did not credit" his charge. Newton had learned from Marietta, Ohio, of Rice's excellent reputation, which Archbold had virulently assailed to him also, and that Lloyd's account of Rice's experiences with the Standard and the Marietta Railroad were correct.[35]

After publication of Lloyd's affidavit in the Industrial Commission's *Final Report,* the Standard Oil men let him strictly alone. Only after he had left the field of reform on his shield would Rockefeller and his successors attempt again to make head against *Wealth Against Commonwealth*'s analysis of the origins, illicit and pathologic business methods, and antisocial policies of their monopolistic organization. They recognised, as some more recent scholars have forgotten, that Lloyd's extraordinary success in shattering the Standard Oil's apologia had been the essential preliminary to popular and official determination to enforce the antitrust laws and revive the competitive economy. Lloyd's victory over Rockefeller, which Ida Tarbell consolidated, ranked therefore among his greatest achievements. It explains also why the Standard Oil, since publication of his book, "had come to represent to the American public the personification" of the hated "trusts."[36]

Chapter XVI

Cosmopolitan "Fighter of Trusts,"
1893-1903

Antitrust Leadership

Repeated antitrust activity enhanced Lloyd's reputation despite his radical position. Of medium height, slender, graying, and of limited stamina, he became the great "Fighter of Trusts." Employing dynamic ethical and value terms and ironic allusions evoking the strongly positive, popular emotive responses essential[1] to remedial action, Lloyd was a brilliant, charming, insistent moralist.[2] He would elevate all mankind to high standards of right living and social action in a state of free, cooperative, economic and social virtue. Following Green, he demanded that Americans validate their principles in action[3] and learn thereby how to promote social progress wisely. Like John Dewey he urged them to abandon evil, which both defined as lawlessness, selfishness, baseness, degeneration,[4] to which Lloyd added hypocrisy, betrayal of trust, and favoritism.

When Governor Altgeld appointed him head of the Illinois delegation to the National Anti-Trust Conference at Chicago, June 5-6, 1893, he was given his first opportunity for practical antitrust leadership nationally. He accepted "if there is to be no 'baby-talk'," and asked Altgeld to appoint Darrow, Hubbard, and Mrs. Stevens alternates. He did so and telegraphed, *"Fire away."* Lloyd and Ignatius Donnelly convoked a preliminary conclave of the "faithful," and persuaded them to attempt to confine the agenda to "the *coal* combination" as "the illustration" of all "the Trusts" and even more than the Standard Oil "a part of the railway problem." The conclave approved

Lloyd's prepared address and heavily documented "Summary of Facts."[5]

The drastic remedy for coal and railroad monopoly that Lloyd presented to the Conference in his address, "Cornering Our Coal," was so popular with the delegates that they adopted the document as their address to the public. After describing how the combined anthracite carriers dispossessed efficient, independent operators and created "artificial winter" for consumers while exploiting labor, he presented a sevenfold remedy for "the trust problem." All "trusts" should be administered for "the public good" subject to pitiless publicity, and federal and state governments should enforce the principle : "no private use of public powers." Municipal coal yards should sell coal at cost to the poor. States must resort to eminent domain to regain coal land ownership and expropriate the railroads since regulation had failed, while leasing coal lands to private operators via competitive bidding. Finally, the taxing power should be employed fully "to decentralize wealth." Presented before the Panic and Lloyd's AFL address, this speech invoked the general welfare principle and Ely's socialization of natural monopolies as bases for the mixed economy of their proposed welfare state.[6]

The Resolutions Committee's moderate report omitted government ownership of mines and railroads, which Lloyd and General James B. Weaver urged. When the Conference preferred this report to Lloyd's government ownership program by a narrow majority, the radical minority withdrew. Lloyd returned home while delegates from thirteen western states held a rump conference. This adopted his speech as *its* public address and his radical resolutions as *the* platform. Thus, a year before the Springfield Conference he had rallied western anti-monopolists to government ownership of mines and railroads and social taxation. The metropolitan press ignored his address until Henry R. Legate gave it to the *Boston Daily Traveller*, whence it was copied by the *New Nation, Halifax Herald*, and other newspapers.[7]

In March 1894 Lloyd recommended a popular boycott of

"trust" products in the *American Federationist*. Since a return to laissez faire was impossible and no monopolist in control of the market ever made "commodities cheap," "only the new conscience can emancipate" by destroying conditions favoring monopoly.[8] Before publication of *Wealth Against Commonwealth* he declared in the *Chicago Daily News* that America's "crucial fitness . . . to survive" depended upon applying "Americanism" or "the golden rule" to monopoly as "the central problem" rather that "socialism."[9] To this Emersonian or Social Gospel method the Springfield Platform's Fabian program presumably gave substance.

Lloyd assumed that the problem was basically intellectual, that is, how to persuade the public to recognize the abuses, the private collectivism, and the undemocratic aspects of monopoly power, and that correct principles must be adopted and implemented experimentally. His tremendous knowledge, sanguine temperament, and welfare philosophy led him to press for a radical remedy since his earlier, moderate regulatory policy had proved ineffective. This stand separated him from the moderates. Yet, his radicalism pointed up the problem while his incessant agitation stimulated a reconsideration of business and political ethics and popular determination to accomplish their reform. His extremism, therefore, prodded the cautiously indignant to moderate remedial action.

In December 1894 he debated "The Trust Problem" at the Buffalo Liberal Club with Wm. H. Gratwick, a Social Darwinist lawyer. Before that unsympathetic audience Lloyd discussed "The Uses and Abuses of Corporations." That important address drew upon "Obstacles to Social Progress," which he had presented at the Plymouth Summer School of Applied Ethics, where he had conferred with Andrews, Clark, and Simeon Patton.[10]

At Buffalo Lloyd attacked uncritical fears of reform and depicted monopoly's challenge to consumers, laborers, farmers, competitive business, and democracy. He buried the "economists of the pigeonhole" with Emerson's " 'The scholar who defends monopoly is a traitor'." Cheaper products could not justify monopoly when this necessitated surrender of government "virtue," the citizen's "independence," and "market freedom," he cried. "Ten-ply millionaires" did not result from lowering prices below the competitive level. "The true American knows that power without control cannot be trusted."

Unrestrained power of great corporations over production, prices, and the distribution of wealth was "plain English of the 'uses and abuses of corporations'." In almost Marxian terms, Lloyd warned, "the country that begins by producing million-aires will end by reducing every one else to the proletariat. There can be no middle class." He depicted the great power en-terprisers' control of the party system and government, as in the New York State Constitutional Convention where President J. H. Choate, the Standard Oil's attorney, had stacked the committees so that the "trust" issue could not be brought to a vote! The monopolists' precarious position drove them to at-tempt to control Congress, courts, government executives, press, schools, colleges, and social leadership. "Education is as fatal to a monopolist as to a priest; he must dominate it," Lloyd said. Better wit, "world-wide discussion of market ethics," a suitable terminology to describe monopolistic pathology, and insistence upon rendering "service due for service" were needed to cope effectively with monopoly power. Its origin he attributed to perversion of government functions to serve privilege. Ordinary practitioners of current unethical business methods would recog-nize that the "great business criminals" were no worse than themselves. This position Lloyd would reverse later. He de-manded reform of increasingly collectivist business management by subordinating it to "social self-interest." Reformers must help the people to utilize "the new powers to which they have grown while they slept."[11] For courageous, perceptive candor on the subject this address had few contemporary parallels. The valid-ity of its analysis of monopolistic power and its abuses has been established by Thomas C. Cochran and William Miller, *The Age of Enterprise*.[12]

Yet, during the debate that followed, six members of the Club, including the editor of the *Buffalo Express*, supported

Gratwick's insistence that Social Darwinism in business was superior to applied Christianity.[13]

During 1894-97 Lloyd developed a dual method in attacking the "trusts." While he led Labor-Populism to demand socialization of all monopolies, in his nonpolitical writing and lecturing he appealed to the "intelligent" middle class to terminate monopoly's "despotism." At Boston Twentieth Century Club's "Smoke Talk," January 12, 1895, he repeated his Buffalo address and urged prevention of the loss of liberties in nonmarket areas, i.e., prohibition of utilization of troops and injunctions in industrial disputes. During the discussion Baxter, Legate, and Harry Lloyd, a prominent local labor leader, supported his stand. The Boston press reported the "deep impression" that Lloyd made on influential Bostonians. Professor Albert Bushnell Hart, the *Herald* remarked, had corroborated Lloyd's condemnation of Cleveland's suppression of the Pullman strike in *Forum*.[14]

Several days earlier that paper had published an interview with Lloyd, who had charged that Cleveland's administration illustrated the control of political "rings" by campaign contributions from "syndicates of capitalists." Olney had used his office as Attorney General, he said accurately, "to promote the interests of great railroad corporations, and not suppress trusts, some of which are known to have been large contributors." Judicial opinions arising from the Pullman Strike were "but the expressions in legal phraseology of the philosophy" of union-smashing by a combination of the federal government with powerful corporations. However, Lloyd detected "the beginning of a new era" in the municipal reform movement led by the Rev. Charles Parkhurst of New York. The demand for regulation of utilities was "an intermediate step towards public ownership," which could transform cities into ideal communities when combined with municipal reform, resistance to business encroachments upon civil liberties, and purging of vicious competitive methods. After this and his "Smoke Talk" the *Buffalo Express* reversed itself, remarking : "Mr. Lloyd is doing an excellent work in analyzing the subject of trusts . . . and is attracting wide attention every day and it is a good sign."[15]

At "The Hub" he was lionized by authors, journalists, and intellectuals, and elected to the Twentieth Century Club. Mrs. James T. Field entertained him at her salon. Liberal and reformist Boston admired his intellectual realism, courageous attack upon abuses, and demand for fundamental reforms. He expressed his enjoyment of this experience graciously to Mrs. Field :

> When I told Mr. Howells about my time in Boston, and of my gratification in finding that good form and reform could meet there on an equal footing, he took it entirely as a matter of course. Boston, he said, "has always led in the thinking of America, and is doing so still." . . . Boston made me feel at home. Its courtesy and sympathy nowhere wore a franker and more agreeable face than that I met in your agreeable salon."[16]

ANTI-STANDARD AT HOME AND ABROAD

During 1897-1902 he developed an aggressive opposition to the Standard Oil, only a part of which can be attributed to its repeated attacks upon *Wealth Against Commonwealth* and himself.

He sympathized with the Pennsylvania independent oil men's attempts to compete with that monopoly in America and overseas, and kept in touch with Roger Sherman, who fought the United States Pipeline's legal battles. He drew upon Hudson; Emery, Jr.; Rice; N. M. Allen, a retired Titusville journalist; H. M. Young of the *Star and Kansan;* Canadians; Englishmen; Scotchmen; and von der Leyen for data on the world petroleum trade. He proffered advice to Emery, informed Sherman of the Rockefeller-Mills episode, and warned him that unless the independents took "very radical legal and political action" to support their "commercial contests" with the Standard Oil it would soon be too late. "Unless these Trust men can be brought to justice every competitor will be at the mercy of their loaded dice. Tweed, all-powerful as he seemed, was brought to justice. Why not Rockefeller?" he asked.[17]

Sherman agreed that " a vigorous effort should be made to contest the great underlying question in the courts." Even if defeated there "we could make the Standard Trust such an object lesson for the world to gaze upon as would produce results."[18] Encouraged by Lloyd, he persuaded the independents to unite in the Pure Oil Company. He was preparing a comprehensive criminal suit under the Sherman Act against the Standard Oil of New Jersey executives when he died of angina in the Astor House, New York, on September 19, 1897.[19] With this event passed the last opportunity, dependent as it was upon Sherman's matchless knowledge of the oil industry and his extraordinary legal talent, to bring the responsible heads of the Standard Oil to account in the courts.

During those same years Lloyd persuaded Bowles; Willis Abbot; W. V. Benthuysen, an editor of Pulitzer's *World;* Eliot Lord of the *Boston Traveller;* Baxter of the *Boston Herald;* and the *Boston Globe* staff to give sympathetic publicity to the Pennsylvania independents' activities. Van Benthuysen was grateful to him for "tips" on the Standard Oil and the antisocial methods of "Big Business." As early as 1894 Lloyd had persuaded Mead, Bowles, Lord, Baxter, and Mary Kenney to rally the Boston press to resist a Standard Oil attempt to combine the eight Boston gas companies. They remained unmerged but under Standard Oil control until they attracted Brandeis' interest after 1900.[20] This, and the exposures in Lloyd's book so stung the Standard Oil group that Patrick C. Boyle denounced his Twentieth Century "Smoke Talk" in the *Oil City Derrick* and declared that he should be hanged. Lloyd replied in the Titusville *World* that such a "reply" from "our lawless wealth" simmered down to "our will and greed are the only law."[21]

Personal ties enhanced Lloyd's influence during these contests. During the summer of 1896 he sailed with his sons in their new boat across to Block Island to call upon the entire Sherman family who were vacationing there.[22] After informing Roger Sherman that the Deutsche-Amerikanische had just purchased

Herr Ploth, distributor for American independents, he remarked angrily that the latter like "all the other victims of the trusts are not radical enough. Our industrial usurpers . . . push their adventure to its furtherest" utilizing every "political power as well as every industrial one to the utmost." Unless the public could "show as much radicalism and diligence in the cause of equality and right, as the other side show in aggrandizing themselves, we need look for nothing but a continuance of our present defeats." He followed local business and municipal contests with the Standard Oil closely, exchanging data with Bowles, Macomber, and the *Star and Kansan* on such episodes.[23]

While he was distressed when an independent firm or municipal gas enterprise surrendered to that monopoly, he discriminated between public and private aspects. When the Pure Oil Company after competing with difficulty with the Standard, was arranging in 1902 "for a division of territory, especially in Europe, and a chance to live," he wrote Ida Tarbell, "They cannot be blamed. It is only from the public that the public has a right to demand public spirit."[24]

He played a similar role in the British flashpoint controversy, in which Scottish shale-oil refiners, certain public men, and London journalists campaigned to persuade Parliament to raise the legal flashpoint on kerosene to protect consumers. Since the Anglo-American Oil Company, Ltd., the Standard Oil subsidiary, was the largest distributor of illuminating oil there, this precipitated a bitter attack upon its business methods. Enjoying close ties with the Conservative Party and reluctant to lose a large market for the "export oil" that could not be sold in most of the United States, that "trust" fought back. Lloyd's reputation as the leading authority on the Standard Oil facilitated his cooperation with the British reformers, who became his friends.

The controversy originated with the demand of Scottish shale-oil refiners in 1892 that the flashpoint be raised above 73°F. (Abel). Tests in Edinburgh and Glasgow disclosed that "Royal Daylight," Anglo-American's ordinary brand of kerosene, flashed at 69°F. (Abel) and ignited at 108°F., dangerously low

temperatures. The Scottish refiners claimed they marketed no
kerosene with a flashpoint lower that 100°F. The relation of
serious fires in London and other cities to use of "Royal Daylight" was declared to be obvious. A trade journal's account of
the tests precipitated a sensation. Lord Rosebery's Cabinet,
prodded by H. H. Asquith, son-in-law of a Scottish refiner,
secured a Select Committee of the Commons to investigate.
This he persuaded Lord Salisbury's Cabinet later to continue.[25]
Begun in 1894, the inquiry lasted four years, during which
British chemists led by Lord Kelvin clashed with Standard Oil
chemists led by Professor Charles Frederick Chandler of Columbia University.

Wealth Against Commonwealth was the British reformers'
reference book during their campaign. On invitation Lloyd contributed "An American View of the Petroleum Question" to
the (London) *Chemical Trade Journal,* October, 1896. This
stung the British by declaring that the "export oil" which the
Standard imported there "is as explosive in a hot room or on
a hot day as dynamite," scattering death by "explicit" governmental permission. Although American newspapers regularly
exposed the "encroachments of the Oil Trust and other trusts
upon the liberties and prosperity of the people," no English
paper or weekly except the trade journals discussed the subject.
As for the Standard Oil's attempt to attribute the fires to defective lamps, Lloyd recommended sarcastically that "the Flash
Test of their wits, not to say conscience, should be raised as well
as that of the refuse oil they are defending."[26]

Cecil Henry News, editor of *Food and Sanitation,* republished this with stinging criticism of "the hypocritical scoun-
drels" of "the American oil gang." He wrote Lloyd, "It was
just what I wanted, and said what I am not allowed to say."
He wished his publishers would allow him to "get Rockey in
the Law Courts over here and worry him a bit." News ham-
mered at the Standard and informed Lloyd that its "Specifically
Refined Safe Oil" flashed at "76°F."[27]

Lloyd must have been shocked when he was informed by
Lewis Emery, Jr., that 73°F. (Abel) oil was "certainly a good

and safe burning oil, if it is actually 73 Abel," which Germany and American states that had no legal flashpoint used. Emery assumed that the oil complained of in Britain was below that standard, but remarked that the British "will have to take their medicine" if their government refused to enforce or raise it.[28] Lloyd continued to throw his influence behind the British campaign for a higher flashpoint to ensure marketing of a safe quality product, an impartial opposition to substandard products of whatever source. To Lecky he wrote that Britain "is still more subservient to the Oil Trust than we of America." D. R. Steuart of Broxburn, Scotland, informed him that "a certain clique of scientific men" in London were attempting "to prevent a scandal" and screen "our immaculate government officials and experts," who have "simply been bought up."

During the 1896 hearings before the Petroleum Committee Professor Chandler's equivocation provoked the contempt of its first chairman, Alex Ure. In February 1897 Lloyd sent a long memorandum on the matter to Stead, the *London Chronicle,* other British papers, and the reformer Samuel Plimsoll, who was campaigning to prevent "a landing of the American Armada of trusts upon British shores." His efforts, Lloyd remarked dryly to Stead, were "a little late." That memo and succeeding communications on the "Trusts" to British papers suggested to Stead his *Americanization of the World.*[29]

The memo also enlisted the *Chronicle*'s support for the higher flashpoint. Fear of American "trusts" spread rapidly among British industrialists. A North England manufacturer and M.P. informed George D. Herron that "if American trusts kept on gaining power as they are at present" he would become "the rankest kind of socialist." *Food and Sanitation* for February 1897 quoted Lloyd on Iowa's successful fight against a low flashpoint, and advocated 100°F. (Abel). Then Lloyd persuaded the illustrated weekly *London* to join the *Chronicle* and London *Star* in demanding the higher flashpoint. *The Deadly Seventy-Three Degrees* published by the *Star* aroused the *Investor's Review,* which demanded that the fire insurance companies look into the matter.[30]

Lloyd's October interview in the *Star,* illustrated by his portrait, appeared also in the *Morning Leader*. It featured him as the international authority on "the ways of the Standard Oil Trust." He reported the dismissal of Professor Bemis from the University of Chicago, the Standard Oil executives' widening field of investments, and Senator Marcus A. Hanna's advice to the Ohio Attorney-General David K. Watson to leave that firm alone. Rockefeller, Lloyd said, was a man of Napoleonic daring but "utterly unscrupulous as to means." What was Britain going to do about "the octopus"? In America it "never succeeded in forcing on us the refuse explosive article that is being sold in England by the Trust. . . . Your Select Committee is a farce." He dared Englishmen to "set us an example," keeping in mind that export oil in New York was 3d. a gallon and sold in London at 7d. "When is the English people going to begin?"[31]

Testimony from coroners and county councils strengthened the case for the higher flashpoint before the Petroleum Committee. The Rothschilds began selling 100°F. (Abel) oil at the same price as "Royal Daylight," while the *Star, London, Ethical World,* and *Labour Leader* kept up a steady fire. Salisbury reappointed the Select Committee, which voted finally by a narrow majority for a 100°F. (Abel) flashpoint as Lord Kelvin recommended. Influential friends of the Lloyds such as Arthur G. Symonds and William Mather worked for the bill's passage. The *Star* fictionalized *Wealth Against Commonwealth*'s account of the Buffalo conspiracy case, quoting Lloyd's devastating epigram, "The Oil Trust is explosive at one end and evangelical at the other." His letters to Earl Grey, Clem Edwards, F. Brocklehurst, and the Manchester *Courier* enlisted support for the measure.

Not even discovery that the Standard Oil was manufacturing "opinion" by petition campaigns among oil dealers or lurid anti-Standard propaganda won Home Office support. In August 1898 Mather informed Lloyd that the matter had probably "been burked" because the Standard posed as a vested interest under attack. The Anglo-American shunted responsibility for explosions and fires upon allegedly defective lamps, and pressured the Home Office and Conservative Party. This defeated the Petroleum Bill. The Boer War distracted attention from the issue until a new series of fires traced to an Anglo-American "Tea Rose Oil" revived public indignation and precipitated an acrimonious Parliamentary debate in 1902. American state legislation providing a higher flashpoint and effective inspection was called pointedly to the Home Secretary's attention. Not even this induced the Conservative Cabinet to act. The agitation remained fruitless during the remainder of Lloyd's life.[32]

It did plant enduring stereotypes on the power and nature of the American "trusts" in British minds. When Ida Tarbell's *History of the Standard Oil* appeared, the *Star* related how it kept on its salary list in Britain "the expert advisers" upon which M.P.'s relied.[33] The episode illustrated the cooperation of American with British reformers. Especially significant were the techniques that Lloyd employed in mobilizing British leadership and popular support in that attempt to oblige the Anglo-American to conduct its business with due regard for consumer and community welfare.

ANTITRUST PUBLICIST

Lloyd's reputation in Europe as a leading authority upon American "trusts," high finance, and politics was confirmed by articles in *Investor's Review, Progressive Review,* and *Social Praxis* (Berlin). In the former, on January 30, 1896, and a year later in the *Progressive Review,* he analyzed President Cleveland's bond sales to sustain the American monetary system. While depicting the bitter controversies that this incident precipitated, he repeated Pulitzer's charges of Treasury and Presidential favoritism to the Morgan syndicate. The issue, he declared, lay between a diffused, democratic power and "concentrated money power" dependent upon government favor. "The folly and fraud of the silver movement" had enabled "the money interest" and "a hundred companies of the most dangerous marauders that ever plundered a civilization" to pose as the public's defenders.

In *Sociale Praxis,* June 24, 1897, he declared that the holding company's appearance was precipitating an "undisguised revolt" of the American urban middle class, many of whom were prepared to demand government ownership because of the revival of the combination movement. There and in the *Progressive Review* he reviewed the sugar scandal of the Dingley Tariff, exposing the "Sugar Trust's" manipulation of Congress and Senatorial speculation in its stock. He reported also the "violent, popular irritation" provoked "by the peculiar helplessness of the people under our system." While stressing the power of high finance and such political "bosses" as Senator Thomas C. Platt, he noted that public indignation had prevented the Republican Illinois Legislature from depriving municipalities of control of utilities, and that federal court decisions indicated an inclination to check the combination movement.[34] The articles presented an invaluable portrayal of McKinley conservatism and enhanced the realism of European thought about America. Lloyd's subsequent correspondence with Stead, H. W. Massingham, Mather, and Symonds disseminated additional information in Liberal circles on the combination trend in America.[35]

During these same years Lloyd labored incessantly to enlighten the American public on the implications of the combination movement, which would produce 318 industrial "trusts" by 1904. As early as October 23, 1895, he predicted in the *New York World* that instead of reverting to the discredited medieval system of government regulation the United States would move "to higher ground" as New Zealand democracy was doing. His "Suffer Little Children" in *The* (Chicago) *Public* disclosed how monopoly transmuted the health and energy of youth into dividends and asserted that vast private fortunes and the public welfare could not coexist. In the *Boston Herald* he declared, "The greatest idiots of our times are the men who fancy that they can continue to take fabulous wealth out of the social product and escape social control." "Radical changes in our institutions" were needed to facilitate the enforcement of existing laws, which were sufficient "to knock every one of these trust monopolies in the head if public opinion would only energize it."[36]

Privately, however, he assured influential men that he was no bitter-end foe of either combinations or capital. To Simon Sterne he wrote that he discriminated between "an attack upon capital and one upon the abuses of capital," and that capital was made more secure by the exposure and correction of abuses.[37] To Congressman Frederick H. Gillett of Massachusetts he distinguished between inevitable business combination, whose pioneers he termed "pioneers in our commercial evolution," and "arbitrary power in the market." That was intolerable, he said. For this the remedy was "expropriation" and every important "trust" magnate should be "in one of our penitentiaries because of his illicit acts." However, the power of wealth had so developed that its possessors hardly needed to combine formally, as was illustrated by certain Boston utilities controlled by "our old friends, the Oil Trust men."[38]

While appreciating the technologic and administrative advantages of business combination, and urging moderates to work for moderate reforms, Lloyd advocated government ownership as an effective means of preventing monopolistic abuses and rule by a wealthy oligarchy. Later he conceded that "the right of combination . . . is not to be taken away," but argued that it should "be always under public control," and in some cases under public ownership as in New Zealand.[39]

He kept well informed on contemporary business methods and developments. Learning of Yerkes' "repudiation of his contracts and his assassination of the Stock Exchange," Lloyd told A. O. Slaughter, a Chicago private banker, that "you and the few men like you . . . Chicago bankers and brokers ought to send Yerkes back to his penitentiary. We let the meanest men 'work us and our institutions' . . . until they get to be Caesars, and then we find that the only law they recognize is that of their own accursed greed or money and power." Slaughter refused to fight the powerful Yerkes but expressed vigorous antipathy to such promoters of industrial combinations as Judge W. H. Moore.[40]

Samuel Bowles and Boston journalists briefed Lloyd on the West End Railway's attempt in "The Hub" to extend its traction monopoly to gas, telephones, and electricity. To William Kent he termed this a significant illustration of how "Bad Wealth" prayed upon legitimate wealth, prejudicing the security of both and antagonizing the public."

This correspondence raised an interesting question. Lloyd's objectives were still a redress of grievances by correction of specific abuses and the operation of modern technology and business for the general welfare. This he would accomplish by correction of a dangerous concentration of wealth and overthrow of arbitrary economic and political power. However, his proposal of a radical, welfare policy to the underprivileged and a more moderate policy to the moderates suggests opportunism and an illogical straddle. Preoccupation with practical ends and his eclecticism explain this partially. Like other public men and intellectuals of the Mauve Decade he wavered between moderate and radical measures. Few reformers except the single-minded George and Bellamy committed themselves entirely to either course. While acting sometimes as a Fabian Socialist, Lloyd exhibited on other occasions the new liberal's moderation and discrimination. This dualism explains partially his simultaneous Labor-Populist leadership and continuing influence upon the urban middle class. The same dualism appeared in his agitation for both socialization of monopolies and social legislation. He knew that his radical antitrust and welfare program frightened moderates into awareness of the monopoly problem and to demand moderate reforms. He encouraged them to do so within the existing framework of business and politics. Thus, his activity fostered obliquely the revival on a broader front of the seminal Progressivism of his journalistic years.

As an antitrust publicist he was influential during the McKinley Era. Ely received from him the latest data on European policies toward the oil and sugar "trusts." Joseph French Johnson of Wharton School and David Kinley of the University of Illinois accepted his thesis that a "trust" might rest upon sheer weight of capital resources. Ely asked him to criticize a Ph.D. dissertation on the Standard Oil, a deft compliment. Johnson, who had eaten "Sunday Turkey" at The Wayside, accepted his view that the combination movement was actuated by "deeper springs" than price fluctuations. Ely and Henry C. Adams agreed with Lloyd that the decisive factor fostering the early "trusts" had been railroad discriminations. Taussig taught Franklin D. Roosevelt at Harvard that monopoly price control was the prime objective of the "trusts." Adams and Kinley would soon be presidents of their universities. Jenks, as expert for the United States Industrial Commission, asked for a loan of Lloyd's large collection on the "trusts" and that he name half a dozen reliable men to testify on the Standard Oil.[42]

Occasionally Lloyd miscued as an antitrust analyst. During October 1898 he learned of ex-Governor Flower's statement that the new "Federal Steel Trust" would include the Rockefeller-owned Mesabi Iron Range, and that its integration would achieve the lowest production costs while preventing workers from playing member firms off against each other. Lloyd concluded hastily that Rockefeller had become a major factor in steel, with a stock market coup in prospect analogous to earlier oil exchange manipulations. He immediately alerted Social Gospel friends. Mills, however, consulted a Mr. Moody who was in the "trust business." He objected to Lloyd's deductions, alluding witheringly to "would-be business reformers." When so informed Lloyd concluded that Moody was a defender of the "trusts" like L. Z. Leiter who, although agreeing that legitimate wealth should separate publicly "from the criminal rich like the men of most of the trusts," invested in their highly profitable enterprises. Lloyd warned Mills that Moody resembled the moderates who had afflicted Mazzini and betrayed "progressive movements from the inside." He warned Massingham and Mather in England that the Federal Steel would probably reduce wages in an attempt to overpower its English competitors. This accurate forecast alarmed Mather, an iron master and Liberal who was knighted for his services to Britain.

In this hair-trigger attempt to mobilize his supporters Lloyd made several errors. Rockefeller and the Mesabi were not included in that combination. If Lloyd had verified Flower's reported statement, as the caution of his *Tribune* editorship would have dictated, he would have learned that Morgan & Company organized the Federal Steel.[43]

His information was somewhat more reliable on the Standard Oil magnates' raid on copper. In October 1898 he informed the *Investor's Review* of "furious speculation in copper stocks in Boston" and press reports that Rockefeller was attempting to corner the copper market, which he was disposed to believe. A year later he met Clarence W. Barron of the *Boston News Letter*, who had distributed copies of Lloyd's classic to inform friends of "the methods of Standard Oil" which he considered "a great menace to our free institutions." Barron and Richard Heard, a Boston businessman, supplied Lloyd "inside" data on H. H. Rogers' market seizure of the Boston & Montana Company preliminary to launching the Amalgamated Copper Company. This the *Boston Herald* confirmed.

"I believe in fighting for every inch of the ground," he wrote Arthur G. Symonds of Chelsea regarding the rising combination movement that was led by the rival Morgan and Standard Oil men, "and I believe also that the turning point, which must be found somewheres, should be as far as possible this side of ruin. It is for this reason that I thoroughly disbelieve in the policy of some socialists of letting everything drift into the hands of the trusts with the idea that we can then by a *coup d'économie* change masters from monopolist to democracy. Just as we are about to shake ourselves for this grand transformation, we may find, too late, that the process of preparation has annihilated us."[44]

Lloyd was greatly interested in the attempt of Frank S. Monnett, Ohio Attorney General, to enforce the Ohio Supreme Court's decree ordering the Standard Oil Company of Ohio to withdraw from the Standard Oil Trust, which had since been transformed into a community of interest dominated by a holding company, the Standard Oil of New Jersey. After instituting contempt proceedings against the Ohio Standard before that court, Monnett initiated *quo warranto* proceedings to void the Ohio charters of other Standard subsidiaries. This litigation precipitated a national sensation when the Ohio Standard burned sixteen boxes of its records after receiving a subpoena to produce its books. Then the company officers denied having burned them but refused to produce them on the ground that to do so might incriminate them.

In 1899 the sensation heightened when George Rice, Monnett's adviser, charged that Standard Oil sources had offered the Attorney General $400,000 to put the *quo warranto* suits to sleep. This Monnett confirmed, and filed a supplemental complaint relative to it in the Supreme Court. When he attempted to take testimony on this a single Justice ordered him to desist. Lloyd telegraphed Monnett to defy this order, promising to sit in jail with him as long as he was "obliged to serve in confinement for contempt." Monnett replied that the Standard had also attempted to bribe his predecessor, David K. Watson, to get him to discontinue the original state antitrust suit against it, but did not defy the Justice.

The litigation dragged on until late in 1900. After McKinley's re-election the Ohio Supreme Court returned an evenly divided decision on Monnett's contempt petition, which technically rejected it. Monnett's successor abandoned the other suits, and the Standard won a victory. Only its great political influence in Ohio can explain why that Court declined to take testimony on the Attorney General's allegation that the defendant in the *quo warranto* cases had attempted to bribe him. Lloyd arranged to have Monnett speak to the Boston Twentieth Century Club and the New York People's Institute.[45]

In 1899 a widely publicized passage on the Standard Oil in *The New Right* by Mayor S. M. Jones of Toledo alarmed Lloyd. Jones said that the Standard Oil men differed from other businessmen only in having been more successful in the currently unscrupulous competitive game, a position that Lloyd had expressed previously. He now asked Jones if his kind-heartedness had not made him "a little too indulgent toward our old enemy, the oil trust," since most American businessmen had been forced into "unscrupulous methods" by "a few (business) radicals." This revived and broadened the thesis as to the influence of the Standard Oil upon railroad rate policies and com-

petitive methods in the petroleum industry that he had enunci-
ated in *Wealth Against Commonwealth.* Jones, he added, was
condoning the activities of men who "as the adjudicated re-
ords show, ought to be in the penitentiary. I cannot see much
hope of a moral revival in a community which lets its big criminals go unpunished, but religiously puts all its little thieves in
jail." Competition was "the normal" condition of the petroleum
industry, he said, in contradiction to his proposed socialization
of all monopolies.

Jones adhered to his position. Had Lloyd read *The New
Right* carefully, he would have discovered that it endorsed
Wealth Against Commonwealth's portrayal of illicit Standard
Oil methods. Meanwhile, James Creelman of the *New York
Journal* wrote Lloyd of his agreement that "the whole trust
structure rests upon a system of favoritism."[46]

Lloyd continued behind-the-scenes mobilization of public
opinion against the "trusts." He tipped Van Benthuysen on
recent Standard Oil price increases. He aided him in a comprehensive investigation of that organization's activities. When need
for funds and fear of Rockefeller, who had denounced Lloyd's
earlier lecture there bitterly to a trustee, obliged The People's
Institute to cancel Monnett's speaking appointment, Van Benthuysen invited Lloyd to help the *New York World* list the instances in which free speech had been "squelched" by the Standard Oil and men crucified by it on account of their opinions.[47]

Lloyd did not attend the Anti-Trust Conference of the
Chicago Civic Federation during mid-September 1899. He was
not invited by the sponsors, whose views were less advanced
than his. Such friends as Professor Adams, Bemis, Kinley,
Byron Holt and "Tommy" Morgan attended, however. Politicians such as Bryan dominated the proceedings. Gunton spoke
and was booed vociferously by the galleries.[48] The American
Anti-Trust League had held its own Anti-Trust Conference
there the next February, when the speakers revived some of
Lloyd's program of 1893, viz., use of eminent domain to nationalize the railroads and telegraph. Like Ely, some demanded
abolition of tariff protection for "trusts." *Wealth Against Com-*

monwealth was the delegates' handbook in what was essentially an antidiscrimination gathering. Lloyd was cited repeatedly as the leading authority. Preparation of his books on Antipodean Democracy prevented his attendance, but the League's officers had conferred with him in advance on how to secure "immediate practical action against the trusts." W. B. Martin, National Secretary, informed him : "Your writings have been a stimulus and encouragement . . . for many years in the battle against plutocracy." President Lockwood, a Pennsylvania Congressman and independent oil man, drew upon *Wealth Against Commonwealth* heavily for the League's pamphlets.[4]

Lloyd's influence was apparent in the antitrust phase of the Democratic Presidential campaign of 1900, some of which was attributable to his friend Willis Abbot, the Democratic National Committee's Press Chief, who distributed articles based on his book to the press.[50]

With such allies as John Graham Brooks, influential reformer and lecturer, and John Bates Clark, who was about to publish his *Control of Trusts,* Lloyd's pioneer work of exposure, analysis, protest, and reform leadership in the field was almost complete. "Single-handed" he had "started out . . . to fight the Trusts" two decades earlier. By this time, as Helen Winslow observed in her *Literary Boston,* he had "won thinking men and women to his side, until he no longer fights alone, but has a brave army of followers."[51] He continued to participate in the antitrust agitation, however. From Berlin in 1901 he informed the *Independent* that European business could not prevent a widely feared "capitalistic conquest of Europe by America."[52] When abroad the next year, he concluded that international "trusts" presented American reformers with their greatest problem. He rejected Sidney Webb's view that they led inevitably to Socialism, and deduced instead that they tended toward what would now be recognized as Fascism. He noted Morgan's attempt to control the literary monthlies.[53]

Lloyd kept in view the growing concentration of power produced by the combination movement. Neither denunciation nor criminal punishment of its promoters and the "trusts'" executives, nor mere "government ownership" would solve the problem, he said. "Through their usurpations, violations, etc., these men have become the masters of *us*," he wrote Bemis. "If we buy them out, we but worsen our position. . . . No reform will be a real reform that does not destroy the *present predominance* of this property and its owners. The very utmost I would leave them, either by expropriation or taxation, would be enough to maintain their living on its present scale . . . anything short of this will also like all our half reforms prove still less practical."[54] This resembled the Fabian program.

In 1900 *The* (Philadelphia) *Conservator* observed that something must be done since the combination movement threatened "to overflow everything right and left." Would that be accomplished "by the people acting through their government or by . . . some other method?" the Tolstoian editor Horace L. Traubel asked, conceding that "Lloyd has been both prophet and historian" in describing the movement's past and predicting its future course.

As Theodore Roosevelt identified his administration during 1901-3 with the antitrust agitation, Lloyd observed its "phenomenal" increase in strength. As yet, he said, the public did "not know what to do," although the railroads were being combined into six great systems that would operate "under a single will" (Morgan's). Convinced that the chief problem was the "centralization of industrial power" in which "railroad centralization" was "foremost," he predicted that on this "point" the "social struggle will probably" be focused. America would have to choose between consolidation "for public motives" or for "private motives."[55]

He was alarmed when he learned that Ida Tarbell was interviewing H. H. Rogers in preparation for a history of the Standard Oil. Lloyd warned Congressman T. W. Phillips and James W. Lee of the Pure Oil that she might be unduly influenced, and asked James W. M. Lewlin, an attorney, to orient her properly. She interviewed Lloyd after his return from Europe in 1902. He loaned her certified copies of Mrs. Backus' affidavits. He called her attention to continued railroad favoritism to the

Standard Oil and its destruction of its records to "conceal evidence of violation of law" as Archbold had admitted to the Industrial Commission. Rockefeller and his associates incarnated "the most dangerous tendencies in modern life." Lloyd informed her that Emerson had said, "We want justice with heart of steel to fight down the proud. . . . The Scholar who defends monopoly is a traitor." The writers' function was "to keep the conscience of mankind," he warned. If coercion of them continued, it would not be long "before we all shall have to have patrons again."[56] He loaned her his notes, entertained her at The Watch House, and persuaded Emery, Rice, and Matthews to relate their business experiences to her. He persuaded Mrs. Roger Sherman to give her access to her late husband's papers. She put him on *McClure's* "complimentary list" and wrote him after her interview at The Watch House, "I shall never forget your wonderful home."

Ida Tarbell's *History of the Standard Oil* evinced his ethical influence. So heavily indebted was it to his earlier study otherwise that some readers charged her with extensive plagiarism. Lloyd's chief concern had been that she have full access to the sources and not be a Standard spokeswoman. As her treatise appeared serially in *McClure's* it exonerated him from the charge of exaggeration in his own book. Like it, her *History* contributed importantly to the ethical revival that influenced the Progressive Era so decisively.[57] His guidance and behind-the-scenes assistance to her was therefore an important contribution to the orientation of the dawning "Muckrake Era" that followed his pioneer journalism and the eighties so closely in its antimonopolism, techniques, and moral appeal.

Chapter XVII

 Champion of Academic Freedom

ELY

Wealth Against Commonwealth declared that the new American "mercantile aristocracy" had acquired dominant power in "State, Church, and School." Validation by recent events alarmed Washington Gladden, leader of the Social Gospel movement whose "Tainted Money," *The Outlook,* November 2, 1895, warned educational institutions against accepting benefactions from "wealth unrighteously acquired" since this necessitated defense by recipients of predatory business. Lyman Abbott endorsed this "as irrefutable." Lloyd's friend Henry C. Adams had been ousted from Cornell University by the Gould group. Chicago police interference with laborers' freedom of assemblage and speech had paralleled pressure upon himself to conform to socially approved views, briefing him further on the social control that business pressure, intolerance of heterodox opinions, spectacular philanthropy, and Social Darwinism were imposing upon the American mind.

When Ely intimated to him in February 1893 that Professor Edward W. Bemis was on the verge of dismissal from the University of Chicago because of his reform activity and public ownership publications, Lloyd replied: "I am sorry to, hear about Bemis, but it is inevitable . . . We had better talk quick and talk to the mark before the chains that are coming are clamped to our tongues." In May 1894 the *Chicago Times* said that Bemis was "one of the few eminent economists and sociologists whose theories are practical and applicable to existing conditions."[1]

Ely was the greatest academic victim marked for destruction by frightened reactionaries. Lloyd wrote him admiringly in March 1894 that he was one of the heralds of a great new era. When at the Johns Hopkins University Ely had been attacked repeatedly by conservative papers and the *Nation*. The first platform of the American Economic Association, which he had helped to draft, advocated state and church intervention in the economy. As leader of the new school he was America's most influential economist. At the University of Wisconsin after 1892, as Director of the School of Economics, Political Science, and History, he subjected socialism to adverse criticism while advocating public ownership of natural monopolies and cultivating labor leaders to facilitate the scholarly investigation of labor problems. Lloyd depreciated a savage *New York Evening Post* attack on him during February-March 1894 as coming from the "impotent" organ "of the New York consolidators of the people's wealth."

Ely's studies of labor, socialism, and monopolies also offended Oliver E. Wells, State Superintendent of Public Instruction, an *ex officio* Regent of the University. After the Pullman strike he attacked Ely in the *Nation* as a "Socialist," fomenter of strikes, and for "seeming moral justification of attacks on life and property." Godkin demanded Ely's expulsion from Wisconsin because he was "a practical ethical socialist." The Chicago *Inter Ocean, Indianapolis News,* and certain Milwaukee papers seconded this demand. Wisconsin's Board of Regents appointed a committee to investigate the charges. David Kinley organized Ely's defense with the aid of Frederick Jackson Turner and William A. Scott. Albert Shaw's *Review of Reviews*, the Baltimore *Sun*, and *Washington News* defended Ely and the new school economists.

"On investigation, the charges preferred by Superintendent Wells entirely broke down," President Charles E. Adams of the University of Wisconsin informed Carl Schurz. Wells had to retract. The committee report exonerated Ely and unflinchingly dedicated the University to academic freedom in a classical statement that is mounted in bronze on a huge boulder before Bascom Hall. "Madison roared with laughter" at Well's and Godkin's humiliation. Ely's trial, however, "sent a chill through political economists everywhere." Only "the opening move in the conspiracy has been scotched," the *Boston Daily Advertiser* warned.[2]

Lloyd remained at The Watch House correcting the proofs of *Wealth Against Commonwealth* during that trial. As architect of Labor-Populism he could have been of no help to Ely, but continued to collect data on infringements of academic freedom.

BEMIS

The attack on Ely had been an attempt to intimidate the new economists, as Kinley and others were aware. Despite Lloyd's scorn for "economists," he always exempted that school from his meaning of the term. He admired Ely. Albert Shaw, Ely's former student, was his close friend. He knew that the new school's rise had precipitated bitter strife in the universities, that Ely and Sumner were at odds. The Ely group found it difficult to secure positions and to publish because of conservative economists' insistence upon orthodoxy,[3] a limitation upon academic freedom that has developed occasionally in other scholarly fields since then. The situation was aggravated by the conservative reaction of the mid-nineties. Powerful business interests were antagonized by scholarly demands for regulation or socialization of segments of the economy to further the general welfare or eliminate monopoly.

This occurred when administrators were attempting to raise large sums for new graduate schools and building programs, but coincided with the inclination of publicly detested power enterprisers and speculators to give large sums to colleges and universities in accord with the "Gospel of Wealth." Some benefactors, like Mrs. Leland Stanford, believed that the faculty of a university so favored should reflect the views of the donor on public matters.[4] Railroad and business interests controlling state legislatures believed that professors should support the *status quo*. Some campus and off-campus conservatives agreed that supposedly "radical" professors should be ousted from their chairs. This the *Boston Advertiser* charged. So the well-informed Ely and Lloyd believed.[5] Beginning with Ely's trial, unprecedented attacks upon new economists and liberal sociologists ensued.

The dismissal of Professor Bemis from the University of Chicago was determined secretly after Ely's acquittal.[6] He was among the more prominent of Ely's former students. Lloyd was Bemis' most important nonacademic adviser during the ensuing controversy. This brought the Winnetkan again into open conflict with Rockefeller and also with his new university, five months before the Mill-Rockefeller imbroglio developed.

Bemis was a University Extension Associate Professor of Political Economy on tenure, an Amherst alumnus. He was an authority on co-operatives, municipal utilities, and labor. In December 1890 ex-President Hayes had complimented him in his diary for recommending state regulation and control to solve problems resulting from unrestricted competition.[7] Bemis joined Chicago's Department of Political Economy in 1892 as representative of the New School when President William Rainey Harper failed to get Ely for Head. To induce Bemis to leave Northwestern University, Harper gave him a permanent appointment. During his first year he devoted two thirds of his time to extension, the remainder to campus teaching, which was to be increased. Among his courses was "The State as an Agent for Social Amelioration." He ranked third in the Department, of which Professor Laughlin was head.[8]

Despite his scholarly reputation, successful teaching, and popularity with the campus students, Bemis was shifted to the Department of Social Science in April 1894 and dismissed the following year. Responsibility for this was shared by Laughlin, certain utility interests, and the University's administration, which feared that Bemis' publications and off-campus civic activities were jeopardizing the prospects of the new university. Laughlin was hostile to all new economists, zealous for the

University's development, and opposed to Bemis' public activities. He determined to oust him from his Department and the university.

Bemis had antagonized the gas industry with his *Municipal Ownership of Gas in the United States*. Waldon Clark, general superintendent of the United Gas Improvement Company, a Standard Oil subsidiary that held stock in thirty-five municipal gas companies, informed him in 1893 that the gas industry executives had decided that he "must be put down" because he advocated municipal ownership. Lloyd knew that Bemis advised the Chicago opposition to the local "Gas Trust" and had accompanied proponents of a "model" eventual municipal ownership franchise, which he had helped to draft, to present it to the legislature. When President Harper applied for a reduction of gas rates that "trust's" president rudely declined, waving the press account of Bemis' activities in his face.[9]

During the summer of 1893 Bemis came under Lloyd's influence and participated in the antisweatshop agitation. Bemis persuaded the University's Toynbee Club to distribute Fabian tracts and imitate the Fabian Society's lectures for wage-earners. He consulted Lloyd about Clark's attacks and informed him that he was subject to pressure at the University to cease making public statements on reform and social problems. Both men knew undoubtedly that the Standard Oil magnates were investing heavily in gas and other municipal utilities, although Bemis did not know that Clark's Company was Standard controlled until March, 1895. Lloyd told Bemis that "keeping back of *all* one's views is a sign of weakness." They exchanged bibliographic data. Their wives became friends. Bemis became a leader in the Lloyd circle.[10]

In August 1893 Harper proposed to Laughlin that the distinction between Bemis' extension and campus teaching be eliminated. Mindful of Yale College's tradition and interested in continuing the new economics at the University, the President was attempting to strengthen his position. Laughlin objected, depreciated Bemis' caliber, and demanded that his campus course on labor be transferred to Social Science, which would debar Bemis from a permanent place in Political Economy for which campus teaching was essential. That summer Clark informed Bemis : "If we can't convert you we are going to down you. We can't stand your writing. It means millions to us."[11]

Harper found himself entangled in the system of departmental administration that he had instituted. Heads administered their departments individually with virtually complete power. They constituted the University Senate. When Laughlin invoked his authority, Harper acquiesced, probably because of the strong local pressure from the "Gas Trust." On April 3, 1894, the Trustees of the University voted to transfer Bemis to Social Science "in case he remains with the University," an obvious attempt to force him to leave. Bemis continued as Extension Associate Professor of Political Economy, but was ranked third in the faculty of Social Science, where his campus courses were listed. He was *persona non grata* to the "strongly conservative and capitalistic" influences dominant in the University.[12]

Harper then suggested that he relocate elsewhere :

> Instead of the opportunity becoming better for work on your part in the University proper, the doors seem to be closing. I am persuaded that in the long run you can do better in another institution, *because of the peculiar circumstances here,* a better and more satisfactory work. (Italics added).

Bemis showed the letter to Ely, who informed Lloyd. Bemis' son recalls visits to his home by the University's business manager, who attempted to persuade the professor to moderate his views and desist from reform activities. The visits terminated in an ultimatum.

Harper's expansion program necessitated a cordial *rapport* with philanthropic but conservative Chicago businessmen and good relations with Rockefeller, the University's founder. The opposition of Ely, Bemis' sponsor, and of Lloyd, his friend, to

Rockefeller, the Standard Oil, the "trusts," and exploitive public utilities was well known. Harper had to choose where he would stand. His letter to Bemis revealed his decision.[13]

That professor remained at the University while Ely attempted to relocate him, and did not moderate his position on economic issues or desist from reform activity. At Kimball Hall on the campus that spring he arraigned railroad management policies before a cheering audience of workers and advocated effective government regulation. In the *Chicago Times* he declared that Chicagoans would vote, if opportunity arose, for municipalization of gas and electricity, franchise taxes on other utilities, and state income and inheritance taxes, the latter derived from Lloyd's program. Bemis favored strong labor unions and compulsory arbitration of industrial disputes. In *The Outlook* he stated that fair-minded people gave "moral support to the striking coal miners."

A University trustee told him that the ARU men were "positive criminals" during the Pullman strike. Bemis then addressed a public protest meeting against government by injunction. The University was dominated by anti-labor sentiment. Professors Laughlin and E. R. von Holst supported George M. Pullman in the *Journal of Political Economy*.[14] At Chicago's fashionable First Presbyterian Church Bemis pleaded for a realistic view of the Pullman strike. After having urged Debs not to impose the Pullman boycott, he believed that while condemning the great strike he could urge that the railroads be "law abiding" instead of defying the ICC and Sherman Act and corrupting tax assessors and legislators. Immediately after he said this, President Marvin Hughitt of the Northwestern Railroad arose and declared it "an outrage" that "a man in your position should dare to come here and imply that the railroads cannot come into court with clean hands." He protested vigorously to the University's President and trustees. Learning of Harper's disapproval of his speech, Bemis informed him of his earlier attempt to prevent the boycott.[15]

Harper replied stingingly on July 28 that the speech had caused him great "annoyance. It is hardly safe for me to venture into any of the Chicago clubs. I propose that during the remainder of your connection with the university you exercise great care in public utterances about questions that are agitating the minds of the people." Laughlin wrote Harper that Bemis' speech "has been a last straw to some good friends" and . . .

> he is making very hard the establishment of a great railway interest in the University. I know you have done what seemed best to stop him; and Small has told me regretfully how he somehow spoiled your arrangement; but, in my opinion, the duty to the good name of the University now transcends any softheartedness to an individual. I do not see how we can escape ourselves except by letting the public know that he goes because we do not regard him as up to the standard of the University in ability and scientific methods. . . . You probably know that he told Small that his hold on the working-classes was so strong that the University dare not drop him,—or something of that purport. I believe you will find the extension men of my opinion—certainly Mr. Butler.[16]

Harper was disinclined to retain Bemis because of business and conservative professorial pressure. A frank interest in putative benefactions to the University might be inferred from Laughlin's and Von Holst's attacks on the Pullman strike in the *Journal of Political Economy*. After *Wealth Against Commonwealth* appeared that September Bemis' activity in the Lloyd circle was still more unpalatable to Rockefeller. That magnate threatened to withhold further gifts because certain professors at the University seemed to be "sympathizing" with the Pullman "strikers." This threat and Chicago businessmen's attacks upon Bemis impelled Harper and the University trustees to dismiss him despite his professorial tenure. Only professors on temporary appointment, according to the University's regulations, could be released at the termination of their appointments

if they exercised "the right of free expression in such a way as
to do . . . the University serious injury.""

In the autumn of 1894 in the *Chicago Searchlight* he
published an article favoring municipalization of utilities. In
December, at Minneapolis he told the National Convention for
Good City Government how a corporation had voted $100,000
to buy the Chicago Common Council." During Christmas week
the University's Trustees voted his dismissal, and planned to
keep this secret with the understanding that Harper would
persuade him to leave voluntarily. In this manner they
attempted to escape the odium of dismissing a professor on
tenure who was popular in liberal and radical reform and labor
circles, and whose scholarly reputation was unassailable.

Bemis consulted Small on the quality of his work. That
sociologist said he was entirely "competent" and his courses
suitable to social science. However, his participation in "so
many phases of public questions" including the moderate Civic
Federation was injuring the Department and the University.
Small had himself postponed taking up reform in his classes, he
said, and instead lectured upon transcendental philosophy "so
as to be as far as possible from these reform movements and
establish the scientific character of my department." Bemis
inferred that Small was jealous of his public prominence and
"afraid of the trustees & of the flings of Laughlin. Harper is left
free under the pressure of the trustees & moneyed men & of
Laughlin to go back on all his pledges to 'stand by' me which
he solemnly made before I ventured to come," he informed
Ely."

Harper waited until March to notify Bemis of the trustees'
action. He attributed this to Bemis' opposition to the franchise
applications of Chicago utilities and to his First Presbyterian
Church address." He warned Bemis that if he publicized this
explanation or fought back he would never find another
academic position. Lacking an alternative position, Bemis was
obliged to sign a secret "Memorandum of Agreement" promising Harper his undated resignation, which the President would
not date until he secured a position elsewhere not later than

January 1, 1896, and to accept an interim assignment to extension teaching exclusively. For this Bemis would receive only his
course fees. This "Agreement" resembled a characteristic
Standard Oil method of dealing with crushed competitors.[21]

Retaining this "Memorandum," Harper omitted Bemis' name
from the list of faculty resignations. On June 30, without
naming Bemis, he justified the secret dismissal of him obliquely
with a statement, "The Public Work of Professors." The social
scientist, he declared, should teach his subject and its principles
"and not his opinions. . . . He must stand above party lines,
and be independent of party affiliations [!]" While Harper
inconsistently denied that this "in any way restricted the
liberty" of the "professors in the declaration of their opinions,
or in the performance of their duties as free citizens," he
announced that if any professor confounded "personal privilege
with official duty" and mistook "popular pleading for scientific
thought" they should forfeit their chairs.[22]

Bemis' dismissal could not be kept secret. Lloyd informed
Lyman Abbott that in the presence of the President of the
Chicago Gas Company Harper had rebuked Bemis for his
publications and teaching and that the latter was being crowded
out of the University because of his antimonopolism. *The Outlook* remained silent after Harper wrote Abbot the University's
view. On May 18 in *The Public* Lloyd attributed Bemis' dismissal to his advocacy of municipalized gas, and alluded to
four economists who had been either warned, silenced, or dismissed at the behest of offended business. "Overgrown wealth,"
he said, "cannot afford to allow the academic discussion of
opinion it deems hostile to its pecuniary interests." On his
advice Bemis did not hand Harper the undated resignation
called for in the secret "Memorandum." His service at the
University was terminated at the close of the summer quarter.[23]
Bemis' Chicago friends were furious. They sought Ely's support
for an attack on the University of Chicago.

Before this Lloyd had stepped dramatically into the controversy in a vigorous attempt to vindicate Bemis and checkmate a general purge of professors. At the Iowa College

Commencement, June 12, he spoke with great charm and literary skill on "The Scholar in Contemporary Practical Questions." Direct, felicitous, permeated with "the noblest ethical and Christian ideals" as President Gates reported afterward, he pleaded for academic freedom for scholars advocating general welfare policies and attacked great enterprisers for nullifying such legislation. Although he was himself a radical advocate of municipalized utilities and social legislation, Lloyd spoke in a semidetached manner of the class prejudices of businessmen who coerced professors proposing such policies, alluding to Waldon Clark's attempt to silence Bemis. Deftly Lloyd upheld the wisdom of according freedom of teaching, publication, and reform activity to professors. He observed pointedly that reactionary enterprisers were provoking an extreme radical opposition similar to what southern slaveholders had invited after rejecting compensated emancipation. Lloyd asked that scholars seek the social solution that would free the next century from fear of a mass revolt and "Reign of Terror." In behalf of that solution he preached again "The New Conscience," welfare economics, and the "religion of progress," disclosing thereby the .conservative purpose that still actuated his reform activity. He stressed mankind's creative power and the potentiality of social cooperation based on the Golden Rule. Afterward Gates called him one of the finest men he had ever met."

Having failed to raise money for an endowed chair for Bemis at Wisconsin, Ely informed Lloyd there was no prospect "for academic work" for him "unless private persons provide the means;" $500 for a course of lectures by him at Madison "would help to retain him in the university world." Lloyd replied that the best procedure would be to get Bemis "out of the way first" before castigating the University of Chicago. He contributed $100 toward the lectures and pledged to renew this for three years. He recommended Bemis to Iowa College, offering to pay his salary. Lloyd offered $800 to Northwestern University toward Bemis' salary if he was called there. President

Henry Wade Rogers replied that his trustees objected because of the situation at the University of Chicago.[25]

Lloyd also wrote to Rev. Leighton Williams, a University of Chicago trustee, remarking, "The Bemis case fits into a multitude of circumstances evidencing that the 'Bad Wealth' of our country is bent on controlling the mind as well as the markets of the people."[26] He determined to force publication of the reasons for Bemis' dismissal and to discuss the matter. He rallied journalists and magazine editors, clergy and religious journals. The *Northwestern Christian Advocate* and *Chicago Daily News* declared in July that Bemis' dismissal derived from his hostility to the "trusts" and that the "atmosphere of the Chicago university is not congenial to those who refuse to muzzle their consciences." An inspired press story replied that Bemis resigned because of a difference in views with Laughlin. The *Springfield Republican* demanded that the University publish its explanation lest the public conclude that it was "striving to place the stamp of authority upon a perverted economic system" and coloring the truth to suit the antecedents of its endowment.[27]

By mid-August 1895, 180 of 200 newspapers editorializing on the matter attributed Bemis' dismissal to his hostility to monopoly. The *Boston Herald* concluded that Harper and his aides were "gagged" and the University of Chicago was losing its reputation "of being an institution where freedom of opinion is allowed and the truth is accepted." The Baptist *Standard* (Chicago) then insisted that Harper speak authoritatively on the matter. Laughlin wrote him from Vienna that "a full statement should be made" to the public. The Bemis affair thus became a *cause célèbre*. Because of *Wealth Against Commonwealth*'s influence many editors attributed the dismissal to the Standard Oil.[28]

As the *Standard* published an inspired disclaimer that Rockefeller interfered with appointments or dismissals at the University and asserted that "the enforced resignation" derived from other, unstated causes, Bemis handed a statement of why he had been dismissed to Lloyd for criticism. Ely, Abbot, and Kinley advised publication, and Lloyd urged him to fight "the

Universities." In *The Outlook* Lyman Abbott, who had been consulted during the statement's drafting, declared: "The money power is not to be permitted to control our great universities, or their teaching. . . . It is impossible to maintain freedom of research and teaching without touching what are called 'burning questions.' . . . Freedom of teaching, in our judgment, is absolutely essential to the higher life of our universities, and colleges; to their vitality, their progress, and their integrity." The *Boston Transcript* observed that the issue was the "liberty to teach the truth freely on vital subjects" at Chicago rather than accepting "limitations imposed by its principal benefactor."[29]

At the University of Chicago's October Convocation Harper denied that "from the beginning of the university" there ever had been "an occasion for condemning the utterances of any professor upon any subject, nor has any objection been taken to the teachings of a professor," nor had any wealthy donor "ever uttered a syllable or written a word of criticism of any theory advocated by any professor." The University's policy was to appoint men of different views to the same department, he announced as he appointed a conservative economist to fill Bemis' place.[30]

Bemis replied to Harper in the *Chicago Chronicle,* October 9, 1895, as the press announced that he would lecture at the University of Illinois and had been appointed associate editor of *Biblioteca Sacra.* Lloyd regretted that his statement was not more aggressive, but informed him, "Harper will never answer you and will never forgive you. . . . If you make any further statement . . . write it with a sledge hammer."[31] In reply to Harper's published imputation and private assertion that he had been dismissed for incompetence, Bemis mentioned his call to Chicago on tenure and contrasted Hughitt's and Harper's criticism of his First Presbyterian Church address with the latter's assertion that Chicago professors had never been criticized for any utterance. Bemis concluded with a ringing denunciation of the "benumbing influence of a certain class of actual or hoped-for endowments" as "a great danger confronting some of the best institutions," documenting this with statements by a trustee and Harper.[32]

Public Opinion republished this beside Harper's Convocation statement. In siding with Bemis, *The Kingdom* remarked, "No candid reader . . . can fail to see clearly on which side the right of this controversy lies." The *Chicago Chronicle* added, "The Chicago university knows on which side its bread is buttered. Let us pour Standard Oil upon troubled waters." The *Springfield Republican* declared that Harper's statement was "an evasion," and Bemis' facts, "if true," should provoke "the profoundest indignation." The *Boston Herald* reminded Harper of the academic freedom in British and German Universities.[33]

The pro-Yerkes *Chicago Journal* asked, however, what businessman would retain a subordinate whose speeches "interfered with the financial stability of his establishment. The 'pursuit of truth' is not the object of university teaching. The duty of the professor who accepts the money of a university for his work is to teach established truth." The *Detroit News* agreed, accusing Bemis of a radicalism "inconsistent with that slow and orderly development of thought represented in all our institutions of learning."[34]

City and State predicted: "The world is going to know whether Truth in Chicago university (or any university, college, or school) must wear a tag, especially a rich man's tag, and especially the tag of that stripe of rich man; whether monopolists and trust-lords who levy tribute upon cities and states and nations for their own aggrandizement are to have their way in closing the mouths of those whose teachings do not please them because they interfere with their peculiar style of money-getting." The Des Moines First Baptist Church forum concluded that Bemis' statement was correct, after hearing speakers condemn "the policy of great institutions receiving endowments from monopolies" since "the doctrines taught must be tainted under the circumstances."[35]

Preceded by Small's denial in the *American Journal of Sociology* that Bemis had been gagged and public interest was involved, Harper, Small, and the Head of the Extension

Division replied jointly to Bemis. They attacked his extension teaching, termed him an unsuccessful instructor given a year's notice because he was unadapted for the regular staff, and denied that he had been dismissed because of outside pressure. If he hadn't chosen "to play the martyr," he would still be lecturing since the University had offered to continue his extension work to January 1, 1896. In no other university in America, Harper asserted, was freedom of teaching "more untrammeled." The University distributed this circular widely. Gunton's *Social Economist* baldly stated the Standard Oil view: "Why should an institution pay a professor to teach social doctrines which are contrary to the concensus of opinions of the faculty, the supporters of the institution, and of the general community?" *City and State* concluded, however, that the Harper-Small-Butler statement was "open to serious drawbacks."[37]

When the circular appeared on October 20, Bemis handed a long rebuttal to the press. While defending his extension teaching's quality and record effectively, he demonstrated that he had taught on the campus also where his graduate classes' enrollment during his last quarter at the University averaged more than many full professors'. He quoted a glowing letter of recommendation by John Bates Clark and Harper's warning to himself against protesting against dismissal. He quoted also Small's objection that he had been identified excessively with reform movements.[38] In rebuttal Harper replied on October 22 attributing Bemis' dismissal to the need to balance the budget of the Extension Department, despite Bemis' earlier disclosure that his extension fees had totalled $3,600 of the $5,626 he had received from the University. In the "Statement of the President," June 30, 1895, Harper had reported that the University could not supply the demand for extension courses.[39]

At this juncture Lloyd re-entered the controversy. Before the Boston Twentieth Century Club he repeated "The Scholar in Contemporary Practical Questions," carrying the issue to the intellectual capital of America and citing successive attempts of the "trusts" to blacklist professors. The *Boston Globe* then

published an interview with him headlined, "Bemis' Friend."
In this Lloyd declared there was "a deep interest in the Bemis
case in Boston and Cambridge, as well as in university circles
all over the country." The talk of Bemis' alleged "incompetence" deceived none. Lloyd said Boston papers should
publish his First Presbyterian Church address and inform "The
Hub" what Harper's administration considered "dangerous and
unsafe." Had the gas magnates that threatened Bemis and
pressured Harper protested also against that speech? The presidents of Harvard, Massachusetts Institute of Technology, and
Brown said bolder things. None could make Americans believe
that Bemis would have been dismissed if he had keep silent on
vital contemporary problems. "The question is whether the
administration" at Chicago "was not under the duress of that
gratitude which is 'a lively sense of favors to come.'" The
University of Chicago's administration must snap its "fingers in
the face of great monopolists hovering round with germinating
endowments." Bostonians could count on Bemis, "a lover of
truth and resolute about it."[40] This confirmed the impression
made in "The Hub" by the *Arena*'s and *New England
Magazine*'s condemnations of the University of Chicago.

Republication of this interview in Chicago papers, Mrs.
Coonley wrote Lloyd, carried conviction "everywhere" except
among extreme conservatives. His intervention defeated Harper's
attempt to win over the *Boston Herald*,[41] and rallied embattled
antimonopolists to the side of the harassed new economists and
academic freedom.

Then, while his new university was attacked from coast to
coast, Rockefeller gave it $1,000,000 to endowment and
$2,000,000 conditionally if that were matched by others. This
was his response to the trustees' request for $5,000,000. It was
a resounding gesture of confidence in Harper and implied
approval of Bemis' dismissal.[42] Harper announced a university
holiday. Faculty and students assembled and sang songs praising their benefactor. The Vice-President of the trustees intoned,
"There was a man sent from God whose name was John."
Laughlin added that it could not be said of Rockefeller that he

accumulated his fortune "by methods which interfered with the accumulations of others."[43]

Disgusted, Lloyd asked Ely to reply to him. Ely replied that brave men doing good work in the universities needed support from informed laymen until their work would eventually tell : "The great thing is to support and sustain them in every way. It is going to be hard work, and . . . will take a long time, to cultivate the right disposition in the general public, and to incalculate sound views."[44] Lloyd answered Laughlin in the press on November 10 with a short review of the judicial evidence on illicit railroad rate favoritism to the Standard Oil at its competitors' expense. Lloyd then asked, "if this manner of accumulating millions by the help of unlawful contracts to ruin all other operators is not an interference with the accumulations of others, what is the 'scientific' name for it and for the kind of political economy which commends it for imitation to the young men and women of the country?"[45]

This resounding rebuke of the cult of the donor on the Midway campus was published widely. The *Dubuque Telegraph* observed, "Laughlin may be a good magnet to attract donations to the University, but he is not a good man to teach political economy." The *Detroit News* demanded that the University "declare frankly" that it could not justify "Mr. Rockefeller's illegal acts." The *Philadelphia Inquirer* said, "The amazement with which a good many people viewed the discharge of Professor Bemis is not likely to be lessened by the extraordinary and wholly false assertion of Professor Laughlin, and by the influence of such teachings as are already shown in the songs of Chicago's undergraduates." The *Illinois State Register* concluded that "the Standard Oil regards the Chicago college as part of its sandbagging business."[46]

Bemis was fortunate that he had Ely's backing and Lloyd's guidance and powerful influence behind his appeal to public opinion to sustain academic freedom and professors' right to full citizenship. Gratified by Bemis' thanks for silencing Laughlin, Lloyd was much pleased with the *Boston Standard*'s vigorous support.[47]

Bemis vindicated his reputation as a teacher and scholar. His lectures at the University of Illinois impressed President Draper. At the University of Wisconsin his lectures on money were reported as far away as the *Indianapolis Sentinel,* drew large student audiences, and made "a most favorable impression." At the conclusion he was "heartily cheered." *The Cardinal* referred to "his very successful course." Ely was much gratified, and wrote Lloyd, "Bemis is a strong man, and he is going to prove it conclusively, in spite of all the University of Chicago can do."[48] Bemis also delivered a lecture series at Syracuse, which Ely arranged and Lloyd and others quietly financed as they had the previous ones despite Harper's protests. Fortunately for Ely, his university's trustees, who didn't want to quarrel with the University of Chicago, did not discover that he had stated at the National Education Association Convention that Harper had remarked to him, as Bemis quoted in his first public statement, "It is all very well to sympathize with the working man, but we get our money from those on the other side and we can't afford to offend them." When a similar series by Bemis was suggested to Mt. Holyoke College, the president sent marked copies of the *Mt. Holyoke Monthly Magazine* describing gifts from alumnae at the University of Chicago and of a skating rink donated by Rockefeller.[49]

Lloyd reported this to Bowles as proof of the "terrorism" that large endowments and Harper were inflicting upon economists. He had heard Bemis' "class *applaud* him" at Madison. Bowles replied : "It is well to make much of his case and seek to arouse public sentiment against the dictation of the monopolists in the management of our higher educational institutions. The agitation has already done good."[50] Bemis remarked subsequently that Lloyd had been his "adviser in all the contests with the University of Chicago and in all the public statements which I prepared, . . . and he did more than anyone else, I think, to keep up my courage for the work at the time when I really needed it."[51]

For Academic Freedom

Although Walter P. Metzger concludes after describing the Ely trial that there was no general conspiracy of business to intimidate professors into becoming defenders of the *status quo,*[52] Bemis, Lloyd, Ely, and many of their allies and supporters believed that that was being attempted. That trio administered a severe lesson to the University of Chicago with the cooperation of the universities of Illinois and Wisconsin. Some of the University of Chicago Trustees remained unconvinced. When E. Benjamin Andrews was dismissed from Brown for having supported Bryan in 1896, Ford W. Peck declared that trustees should exclude "unsound financial doctrines" and "anything of a dangerous doctrine" from their institutions. Not until 1899 did the University of Chicago perfect a formula relieving it of responsibility for the public utterances of its professors, which presumably enabled them to engage in civic activity without losing their chairs.[53]

Lloyd, Willis Abbot, and Bemis formed an influential triumvirate in the campaign for academic freedom. Bemis' fight greatly interested Governor Altgeld, who determined to develop a graduate school free from tutelage to "Big Business" at the University of Illinois. He learned in 1896 that the professorial participation in public affairs to which Harper and Laughlin objected was that in behalf of the underprivileged, since Laughlin campaigned for McKinley and attacked the Governor publicly, and contributed anonymously a gold standard column to the *Chicago Times-Herald*. In 1897 he defended private ownership of utilities in the *Independent*. Altgeld called him "the handy hired man" of "the great schemers of the world."[54]

In the *Progressive Review*, February, 1897, Lloyd declared that it had become impossible for American economists to support bimetallism as British professors were doing, and none in the rich eastern universities said or wrote anything "that could help the people in their mortal struggle with *nouveaux riches.*"[55] His friends kept him informed of infringements of academic freedom. Paul Tyner of Denver reported that the local traction magnate had obliged the Chancellor of Denver University to drop his "agitation in favor of public ownership of municipal monopolies." Bemis wrote that a pledged contributor to his *City Monopolies* withdrew when the technical school hiring him stipulated that he say "nothing whatever of a *sociological* character."[56]

With Bowles the Winnetkan watched the "Brown University Scandal" with keen interest. Rockefeller withheld a gift of a million there until the trustees ousted President Andrews, a bimetallist and critic of the Standard Oil, despite protests from the faculty, alumni, and the presidents of Harvard, Columbia, and Johns Hopkins. When Brown's trustees selected Rockefeller's pastor as the new president to secure the anticipated gift the *Springfield Republican* attacked this action editorially in "For Truth or Endowment." Lloyd asked Bowles to persuade Charles Eliot not to attend the appointee's installation "in that cesspool," detailed the scandal to Morley Roberts, and asked him to write a book about it.[57]

The episode led George H. Shibley, Secretary of the Chicago Civic Union, to sponsor a bill at Springfield to ensure academic freedom in the universities. The years 1899–1900 witnessed the climax of the conservative attempt to eliminate social critics from institutions of higher learning. During the spring of 1899 Syracuse University ousted John R. Commons, Ely's student and a well-known liberal economist and sociologist. He had offended by sponsoring Bemis' lectures there, whereupon the Chancellor added John D. Archbold to the Board of Trustees and asked Commons to moderate his views. When this was ineffective the trustees abolished his professorship. Commons was informed of this three months later and told that college presidents "had agreed that no person with radical tendencies should be appointed to their faculties."[58]

At Kansas State College academic freedom was denied first by the Populists and then by the Republicans after election victories. The former, in 1897, installed a new Board that appointed to the faculty Bemis and Frank Parsons, reformer and former teacher at the Boston University Law School. Both favored socialization of natural monopolies as did Thomas E. Will, the new president. They embarked upon a "fearless" search for truth. After Herron spoke there the *Kansas City Journal* declared war on the College. Then a Republican election triumph produced a new Board of Regents. In July 1899 it ousted the president and four professors, including Bemis and Parsons, at a time when Lloyd, Bemis, and Bowles were publishing the misdeeds of the Massachusetts State Gas Commission and planning a book on the Boston West End Railway's influence on the municipal government.

When Bemis' "Academic Freedom" appeared in the *Independent* after this *dénouement,* Lloyd distributed it on both sides of the Atlantic. Its evidence of coercion of professors and graduate students by conservative administrators more than justified the quoted alarm of British universities at the infringements upon academic freedom in America.[59] Both men championed academic freedom in part because they desired to secure a place in higher education for criticism and analytical study of the *status quo,* and for consideration of remedial measures proposed by advocates of a new democracy. But like the businessmen on the Board of Trustees of Trinity College, Durham, North Carolina, who upheld Professor John Spencer Bassett against the popular majority after he challenged regional racial mores,[60] they understood the functional role of academic freedom in a free society.

In July 1899 the National Conference on Social and Political Reform at Buffalo voted to remedy the infringements on academic freedom of economists and sociologists by establishing at Boston an "American College of Social Science" to be staffed by the purgees, and assisted by Herron and Willis Abbot. Nearly $20,000 was subscribed toward endowing the "College." Aided by Ely, Bemis, and John Bascom, Lloyd helped to divert the abortive project into a Bureau of Economic Research with "chairs of investigation" for Bemis and Commons, as "a center of information on the various monopoly and other questions" that institutions of higher education "do not venture to handle." As treasurer he contributed to its budget. Most of the funds came from Shibley, who dominated its program. Eventually Commons was called by Ely to the University of Wisconsin. Bemis became Director of the Municipal Water Works under Mayor Tom L. Johnson of Cleveland.[61]

The debate on academic freedom continued. Abbot reviewed the experiences of the liberal and radical social scientists in "Plutocracy's Training Schools" for *Social Forum,* quoting a Northwestern University trustee's assertion that a professor "must of necessity be an advocate, in harmony with the conclusions of the powers that be, with the . . . main purpose of the institution, and with the teachings of his co-laborers."[62] Abbot debated the issue with Albion Small in the October *Arena.* Small decried protests against violations of academic freedom, and censored the "intellectual sans cullotes" of the Reform Conference and heterodox social scientists. Those he declared to be unentitled to that privilege, but said that it had not been denied to any social scientist "in the interest of wealth." Abbot compared his to the proslavery professors' stand on the slavery question, and criticized the University of Chicago's ruling that professors must dissociate their public statements on controversial issues from the University. The all-important question was how to remedy the "widespread tendency in American colleges to abridge academic freedom," he declared.[63]

Lloyd was angered by Herron's resignation under pressure from Iowa College. In 1895 he had met him and President Gates when he delivered the Commencement Address there and admired them as "great men." Gates fought for years against businessmen whom Herron's radicalism antagonized to keep him on the faculty. Lloyd's "New Conscience" and *Wealth Against Commonwealth* influenced them profoundly.

Lloyd described the American Book Company's textbook monopoly to Gates, who published *A Foe of American Schools* in 1897 exposing it. The pamphlet precipitated a sensation, and was republished in *The Kingdom*. After attempting to enjoin the sale the American Book Company sued Gates and the Kingdom Publishing Company twice each for $100,000 damages. As Treasurer of their Defense Fund, Lloyd announced that he would receive contributions. The suits' issue, he said, was "one of the most momentous that can ever be presented to the American people." He raised a substantial sum from Chicago and Boston friends, and from Ginn & Company and Rand McNally & Company, business rivals of the plaintiff." On Lloyd's invitation Clarence Darrow joined the defense counsel in Minneapolis, where the suit against the Kingdom Company was tried. Melville Stone excluded news of it from Associated Press wires.

Darrow and his associates proved *The Kingdom*'s innocence of libel on fourteen of fifteen counts by establishing the bribery and corrupt practices perpetrated by the American Book Company in marketing its textbooks. They lost on the fifteenth, the technical question of whether or not the pamphlet was privileged, because The Kingdom Publishing Company had sold 1,000 copies to Ginn. The ABC claimed plausibly but inaccurately that a business rival had inspired publication of the pamphlet, against which the inability of a key witness to testify led to the court's ruling that the pamphlet was unprivileged. On that count The Kingdom Company was found guilty and ordered to pay $7,500 damages. It suspended publication.

Evidence of the ABC's unethical influence upon teachers and school administrators adduced during the trial aroused much interest in the Minneapolis area. More important for the publishing business was defeat of ABC's claim to the status of professional man or tradesman under the law of libel. If it had been sustained in this, the muckraking movement that Lloyd had launched would have been severely handicapped. Darrow signally defeated the textbook monopoly's attempt to secure legal protection from exposure of its illicit and unethical methods. Mead declared there was "no more infamous trust in the country than this, whose corrupting influence is penetrating our educational circles everywhere."[65]

During that trial Lloyd welcomed Herron's attempt to persuade Protestants to attack contemporary problems, and corresponded with the Rev. J. Stitt Wilson, Herron's associate in the Social Crusade. Although Lloyd regarded Herron as "a consecrated soul of the new order that is coming," he rejected his "attempted renaissance of Christ" who, he believed, was "of value only as a symbolical figure illustrating the possibilities of humanity." Lloyd believèd "the inspiration of the future will come from the vision to the people that there is in every one of them a possible Christ." As a Christian Socialist Herron expanded "The New Conscience" and copied Lloyd in exposing social evils in sensational lectures in Chicago during 1898–1900. This precipitated his forced resignation from Iowa College despite the support of Grinnell and enlightened press protests "against muzzling professors."[66]

Lloyd published his disgust at Herron's surrender of the endowment the Rands had set up for him to Iowa College in the *Social Gospel*. That action precipitated wide discussion of the ethics of acceptance by "colleges, churches, and moral reform institutions, of money accumulated by questionable business methods." The *Boston Herald* discussed the need for a liberal university, although, as the *American Fabian* observed, purgees were primarily economists and theologians.[67]

In mid-November 1899, Abbot attempted to place Commons and another purgee in the University of Nebraska where "we Bryanites" controlled the Regents. "I think," he informed Lloyd, "since 'academic freedom' is denied us we will take a hand at reorganizing colleges when we get control." Conceding it to be unethical and "not the golden rule" to do so, since other professors must be ousted to make places for the purgees, he remarked "But we have to fight with the weapons of barbarians after all."

When Henry Wade Rogers was ousted from Northwestern University in 1900 because he opposed imperialism, *The Public* listed five leading victims of the conservative purge that had occurred since 1894, Bemis, Will, Andrews, Herron, "and now Rogers for standing by the declaration of independence." The time "cannot be far off," Louis F. Post predicted, "when college educators will clearly understand that if they wish to hold their chairs they must suppress all opinions which do not harmonize with the partisan or sordid interests of the plutocratic college bosses."[68]

Lloyd sketched sardonically lectures on the problem for the University of Chicago during the spring of 1902. This prospectus exhibited opposition to the limitations that conservatism and institutional promotion imposed upon academic freedom and the social sciences. Lloyd wished to discuss the "regressive" influence of endowments from antisocial and conservative enterprisers on private institutions and of large campaign contributions and political control upon state institutions. He included the methods by which donors' fortunes were acquired, the "History of Eight Centuries of Warfare Waged by Institutions of Learning against the discoveries and reforms of the creators of Civilization," classical economics as "the Bulwark of Social Injustice," effects of faculty inbreeding, and the relation of student preoccupation with books and sports to "the decay of courage, faith, the creative instinct and capacity for leadership." This searing performance the Midway campus did not experience, but as an intended course in academic realism Lloyd's plan was unique.[69]

Wayne MacVeagh, wealthy civic-minded Philadelphia attorney of Morgan & Company and other great interests, invited him to discuss together the effect of large benefactions upon the caliber of the universities. Subsequently, MacVeagh urged him to publish an article "in one of the leading reviews" on the theme "the evil influence of restitution when disguised as charity,"[70] demonstrating "the undesirableness of our very rich men making gifts to furnish free reading or free education." This would be "of very great practical advantage," since "the public conscience is very likely to be debauched by these gifts," MacVeagh said. These oblique thrusts at Carnegie and Rockefeller impinged pointedly upon their spectacular practice of "The Stewardship of Wealth." Privately, MacVeagh agreed with Lloyd's circle and Gladden's following on the necessity of academic freedom, which they helped to make possible by educating public opinion on that issue of such vital importance to twentieth-century democracy.

Chapter XVIII

Co-operation : Utopia or Practical Solution for the Social Problem

UTOPIANISM

AFTER LABOR-POPULISM'S COLLAPSE Lloyd turned to the co-operative movement as the reform with the greatest potentiality for advancing the objectives of his welfare philosophy. As early as 1886 he had learned from "Bert" Stewart of the Knights of Labor co-operatives. Stimulated by the World's Congress of Co-operation during the World's Fair, his circle had studied British co-operatives. While leading Labor-Populism he corresponded with J. A. Wayland and George Howard Gibson, who were promoting farmers' co-operatives and utopian communities in Kansas and Nebraska. Early in 1896 Alonzo Wardell, a Topeka Populist, had persuaded Lloyd's circle to join in convoking a National Co-operative Congress at St. Louis during the Populist National Convention. From this there emerged the American Co-operative Union and the Brotherhood of the Co-operative Commonwealth.[1]

Lloyd was elected to the Board of Directors and the Executive Committee of the American Co-operative Union. There he was associated with Nelson, the Edwardsville, Illinois, co-operator, and James Rhodes, editor of the *American Co-operative News,* organ of New England's rival Co-operative Union of America. While on the Board of the American Co-operative Union, Lloyd witnessed a suicidal debate between the political anti-monopolists who wished to expand "co-operation" to include government ownership of monopolies and those attempting to restrict the program to Rochdale co-operatives.[2]

He was also interested in the revival of communitarianism. This was fostered by Bellamy's classic and the transoceanic literary utopianism that it stimulated. To the discontented urban middle class, frustrated Populists, and defeated trades unionists, it offered escape from monopoly and unemployment. After the World's Fair Lloyd's lecture, "No Mean City," presented an urban utopian remedy. A successful communitarian suburb recruited from the unemployed, and equipped with a progressive school would absorb and then rebuild Chicago into a park city with the best cultural facilities and deep channel passage to the ocean. His visit to Mt. Lebanon had convinced him of the efficacy of communitarianism. He discussed with Kansas Populists the feasibility of founding a model "co-operative commonwealth" colony.

He was keenly interested in Wayland's Ruskin Colony in Tennessee. Perhaps he agreed with Herron that if such communities were "rightly initiated" and federated "we may have one key to the situation." Herron drew him into planning the Christian Commonwealth Colony with Gibson, that was soon planted in Georgia. Although he was skeptical as to its doctrinal basis, Lloyd confessed to Gibson in December 1895 that he, too, was tempted to settle in some such community. Although he believed that his "place" was to continue his current reform work, he regarded the communitarian movement as "the most religious manifestation of our day," which might develop a civilizing role similar to that of the medieval monasteries during "the troublous anarchy I fear is coming."[3]

The communitarians shared his foreboding of imminent social disaster. Some Maine Socialists proposed to save America from "its impending doom" by colonizing western states with Socialists of all types under a "non-partisan Brotherhood of the Co-operative Commonwealth." Lloyd contributed liberally to its treasury, but warned against forsaking the ballot and sidetracking the Rochdale system.[4] He remained a pluralist in reform tactics.

The B.C.C. was organized after the National Co-operative Congress. A referendum unanimously elected Lloyd President, made N. W. Lermond of Thomaston, Me., Secretary, and Wayland's *Coming Nation* the organ. Lloyd declined the presidency, but fostered the communitarian spirit with a lecture, "A Day with William Morris," at the Chicago Art Institute, to the gratification of the Director, W. M. R. French. He signed a B.C.C. circular with Debs that proposed a new social order based upon brotherhood. Soon the B.C.C. claimed 1,200 members and $29,500 pledged. It founded Equality Colony on Puget Sound, an event that Lloyd compared sanguinely with the Free-Soiler colonization of Kansas. However, the B.C.C. did not achieve a projected federation of communitarian colonies.[5]

Former American Railway Union members were infected by the communitarian idea also. Debs invited Lloyd to be his "colony organizer." The ARU Chicago Convention in June 1897 produced the Social Democracy committed to this method of capturing a western state for Socialism. Lloyd withdrew when a merger with the B.C.C. was rejected. He refused to associate with the Social Democracy as it turned to political Socialism, whose prospects he depreciated.[6]

In *New Time* (Chicago) he advocated both Rochdale co-operatives and communitarian colonies. He asked that journal to report regularly on co-operative movements "in this country and abroad," including the co-operative European "people's banks" described by Henry Wolff. Recognizing that the American co-operative movement was "very weak," he desired that it "be made a considerable force in the American reform movement." A "larger number of co-operative societies and communities like that at Ruskin, Tenn. in vigorous and healthful operation . . . might do something for the new liberty, if the crisis came, like that which was done by the New England towns" during the American Revolution.[7] Although he believed that the antitrust campaign was "the most important work" and predicted that co-operatives would be unable to supplant the "trusts," he supported Charles G. Boring's National Congress of Voluntary Co-operation and aided and counseled many communitarian colonies.[8]

Shortly after he walked out of the Social Democracy Convention he laid the cornerstone of the "Ruskin College of the New Economy" at Ruskin Colony, of which the *New York Herald* published his account. His prepared address, "The New Political Economy," was deeply religious, transcendental, imbued with hope and the spirit of martyrdom. He preached "The New Conscience" that would extend brotherhood into the working world. Each reformer and laborer would become "a creator," enabling the masses to overcome their wealthy rulers and create "the Messianic democracy of a self-redeeming people." To this he dedicated the "first Socialist College in the World."[9] After returning to The Watch House he concluded that Ruskin Colony's fate was "doubtful." In the *Coming Nation,* admitting that the Ruskinites had made mistakes in their "Co-operative Life," and asserting that the "colony idea" was "a solution" for the social problem, he declared that every successful voluntary cooperation advanced "the day of social co-operation." Let all "save our attacks for the common enemy, and spare the mistakes of our friends," he urged, "I did not lose my faith in the experiment, or my hope." He represented Ruskin Colony at the Third International Co-operative Congress at Delft, Holland, in September.[10]

APPRAISING CHRISTIAN SOCIALISM IN INDUSTRY

Nelson claimed credit later for Lloyd's attendance at Delft. He supplied him with letters of introduction to George Holyoake, the aged English Christian Socialist, and other important European cooperators. The B.C.C. and National Congress of Voluntary Co-operation also named Lloyd their delegate. Samuel Gompers asked him to question Tom Mann and other English labor leaders about the English co-operatives for the AFL.[11]

Lloyd was profoundly influenced by the Delft Congress. There he discovered in the co-operative movement, rather than in Continental democratic Socialism which he had intended to investigate afterward, the movement of greatest significance for American reform. He enjoyed the unique entertainment provided by the J. C. Van Markens, influential sponsors of the Dutch co-operatives. The delegates met in the Gemeenschap in Agneta Park among landscaped gardens and lawns encircling a lake and the village of Mr. Van Marken's employees, with whom he shared his publishing profits. That enterpriser staged a Venetian Fête, its rainbow arc over the lake converted into a semicircle of fire at night when a Vandyke cordon of fire stretched around its banks, a fire engine played, and the Gemeenschap was illuminated. Madame Van Marken's luncheon, the first day, amused the delegates with "Consommé Co-operatif," and "Fruits du Succès," while "Cotellettes d'Agneau, à la Wolff" edified admirers of *People's Banks*. All were charmed by the Van Markens' garden party the next evening. A peak of hilarity was reached at the last night's banquet at the Hague, when Madame Kerdyk's cook, anxious to please the British, served "Bloated Potatoes" and "Savage Duck."

As Honorary President on the second day Lloyd received many inquiries about Ruskin Colony and American co-operatives. After learning of English profit-sharing and labor copartnership industry, he decided to study them immediately. Henry Vivian of the Labour Association and Thomas Blandford of the Productive Co-operation Association, Ltd., copartnership leaders of London, promised to escort him. They insisted that true co-operation demanded that wage-earners share not only in the profits but also in the ownership and management of the businesses where they worked. While recalling that this derived from Christian Socialism, Lloyd learned that the English Rochdale co-operators opposed labor copartnership but operated productive enterprises to supply their wholesale organization. This schism in the British co-operative movement was discussed earnestly at Delft, where the Continental Socialist delegates supported copartnership. No other country "had anything to report like Ruskin," Lloyd wrote home, although possible communities were discussed and the Sunderland consumers co-operative had founded a small colony. He predicted in the *Coming Nation* "a notable communistic development in the near future" among European co-operators.[12]

He hurried with Vivian to England to attend "The Midland Co-operative Festival" sponsored by Earl Grey at Rugby, the day after the Congress adjourned. After examining the exhibits and hearing reports on co-operative farming, Lloyd charmed everybody at a "tea in the Eagle Assembly Room" by remarking that he had "learned more of co-operation that day" than during "the whole of the time he had been away from America."[13] He and Vivian traveled together to Kettering and Leicester, strongholds of co-operation and copartnership, where E. Owen Greening conducted them through copartnership factories. Lloyd peered into homes erected on Equity Road for wage-earners of the copartnership Equity Shoe Factory by Leicester co-operative builders. He inspected the copartnership publishing company that printed *Labour Copartnership,* organ of the movement. He attended a copartnership meeting at Co-operative Hall, Kettering, where he was impressed by the speakers' moral idealism. He had read the strictures on co-partnership in Beatrice Potter Webb's *The Co-operative Movement* and Benjamin Jones' *Productive Co-operation.* He discovered that the Wholesale's factories were copying the patterns developed by the Huddersfield copartnership textile factory, with which they competed.

As Lloyd and Vivian attended co-operative meetings they became warm friends. Vivian remarked later, "We got on famously together. Lloyd was a delightful companion, who would strike up friendly relations with the most humble and obscure working men at our Conferences and draw out the simple story of their lives." Lloyd formed an equally firm friendship with Blandford, who accompanied him on the Irish tour and impressed him with his complete "devotion to the cause."

Lloyd drew upon his knowledge of business and finance in analyzing his findings. That the Hepden Bridge Fustian works in Yorkshire could borrow capital at 4 per cent and was refusing subscriptions to its stock he regarded as proof of efficiency. The absence of class antagonism or jealousy of employers among copartnership workers nullified Mrs. Webb's strictures. He concluded that copartnership labor was creating "Socialism with no state help" by capitalizing itself. He determined to let the facts determine the relative merits of copartnership and Wholesale's factories, which did profess "some principles of justice for labor." But the notebook entry, "C. W. are capitalist & proud of it, temporary phase of parvenus," disclosed where his sympathies lay. Frequently years of failure preceded the co-operatives' success, he discovered, which was an "Answer to Jane Addams."[14]

He contrasted copartnership's method and faith in "home rule, local self gov. private initiative & industrial dem." with Socialism's belief in "centralization & political initiative." *"Both are right,"* he concluded. "There will be some industries nationalisable i.e. R.R. Some must remain municipal; some co-operational & coop. Boot & Shoe." In copartnership enterprises workers were "able to borrow, able to anticipate markets &c.," achieving Socialism's ultimate goal and proving that capitalistic ability was "no monopoly of middle class."[15] He criticized himself for not having discovered copartnership earlier :

> While we are reading our Ruskin & Carlyle & sighing for the abolition of the cash nexus, & dreaming blissful dreams of the C. C. & applauding the speakers who give some new perfection of varnish to the demand that business should be humanized & here, almost silently . . . millions of workingmen organized Business with motives of Equity & Unity all & all for each. Good Halls & Other Education, libraries, songs, eloquence, the laughing of the people.[16]

The British co-operative movement, he concluded, "must be given its place as the most important social movement of our times," because it envisaged a "thoroughgoing program of a complete social reconstruction." No other "surpasses it in radicalism, no other approaches it in achievement, neither in its number of adherents nor solidarity of resources, in men, minds and money." Christian Socialist sympathies led him to deduce, erroneously, that leadership in this was passing to the copartnership wing, which "alone speaks that democratic invitation . . . which in human history has been the only thing that as never been turned back, nor silenced."[17] There he discovered validation of the Christian Socialist brotherhood conception and ethical principles and of his own faith in man's creative collectivity.

During Lloyd's English tour George Thompson, Ruskinite trustee of St. George's Guild, discussed with him "the Master's principles," regaled him with co-operative anecdotes, and escorted him through William Thomson & Sons, whose profit-sharing had transferred control to the employees. Sidney Ball entertained him at St. John's College, Oxford. George Pitt, a Ruskinite, praised Ruskin Colony's "College of the New Economy." At Manchester, after calling upon the *Co-operative News* and Co-operative Union, Lloyd visited with and charmed the entire William Mather family. "My wife and daughters have enjoyed days of intellectual refreshment they will not forget," the iron master wrote him afterward, "Dorothy was exuberant in her expressions of attachment to you, & to be liked by 'sweet seventeen' you will admit is to belong to the select few of mankind!"[18]

In Ireland Lloyd and Blandford inspected co-operative creameries and the Doneraile People's Bank. At Dublin Lloyd visited the famous Positivist, Professor John Kells Ingram. He won the respect of Horace Plunkett, Ireland's great agricultural reformer, and of R. A. Anderson, Secretary of the Irish Agricultural Organization Society, whose effective technical aid of the peasantry impressed him. Anderson wrote afterward, "we do not often meet with such intelligent sympathy as yours in the work we have in hand."[19] Lloyd and Blandford also inspected the Glasgow area's co-operative and copartnership enterprises.

Their tour ended in London, where Lloyd investigated the co-operative movement, Labour Association, and Productive Co-operative Association Ltd. At Brighton he formed a warm

friendship with G. J. Holyoake, the noted cooperator. He studied the co-operatives' recreational program, visited the Royal
Arsenal Co-operative Society at Woolwich, and was present at
the opening of its Lakeland Road branch. He won the friendship of George A. Livesey of the South Metropolitan Gas
Company, whose profit-sharing program placed workingmen on
the Board of Directors.[20] Admiration for *Wealth Against Commonwealth* opened doors and facilitated inquiries as it had at
Delft. Lloyd made new friends during his tour of the Isles.
After his return home, L. C. Gray, Secretary of the Manchester
Co-operative Union, sent him confidential data on British co-
operation, and Blandford, Vivian, Wolff, J. M. Ludlow, and
Holyoake wrote to him frequently.

Two interviews in the London press disseminated his views.
In "The Outlook in the United States" in the *New Age,* the
editor complimented his "fine culture, deep thought, and earnest nature" and knowledge of the "social problem," remarking
that as a "competent economist and distinguished journalist"
"in any company he would be accounted a man of distinction."
Lloyd predicted accurately in that interview Seth Low's victory
over Henry George and Tammany, that American labor would
not organize an independent political party, that American
business would not allow "the gold standard to be disturbed,"
and that America would fight for the Monroe Doctrine if necessary.[21]

In London, Lloyd called upon William Clarke, Arthur C.
Symonds, and A. J. Wilson, who informed Clarke afterward
that he looked to men like Lloyd "for the future of the United
States." "I should call the blushes to your face if I were to tell
the many kind things said of you by friends here," Clarke wrote
Lloyd.[22]

Lloyd wrote up his findings quickly in a modest volume aided
by the latest reports of British and Irish co-operators, photographs sent by Blandford, and his and Vivian's critical reading
of the manuscript and proofs. Lloyd hoped that the book would
arouse sufficient interest to enable both men to lecture in

America the following year. Harpers published it on the same terms as *Wealth Against Commonwealth*.[23] It was a characteristic Lloyd contribution to American reform.

Entitled *Labor Copartnership*,[24] it presented an illustrated report by a "Democratic Traveler" on co-operation in the United Kingdom. It replied to Mrs. Webb's attacks upon copartnership, encouraged its leaders, sought to inspire American wage-earners and reformers to introduce it, and attempted to stimulate American co-operatives generally. Lloyd told Americans copartnership was "a path of voluntary effort by which the pick of the people might begin their march to self-employment and self-government pioneering for the rest of us."[25] Publication was preceded by H. Paul Douglass' article on Christian Socialism's contribution to the co-operative movement in the *American Co-operative News,* and Bliss's *Encyclopedia.* In April 1898, also, Lloyd had championed co-operatives in "As Others See Us" in *Labour Copartnership,* corroborating the business capacity of laborers that British professors and "literary reformers" decried and predicting that "in the Twenty-First Century" co-operators and Socialists would be divisions of the same crusade, moving toward "the administration of industry under public motive."[26]

Admitting that British copartnership was controversial, he attempted an impartial account. After reporting the Delft Congress he devoted disproportionate space to co-operative farming, despite its bad financial record, because he believed that dairy co-operatives had an important future. There followed a valuable account of the Irish co-operative creameries, people's banks, and co-operative marketing and purchasing of supplies by the peasantry, attributed appropriately to Plunkett's leadership. Careful analyses of British consumers' co-operatives, copartnership, and profit-sharing enterprises followed. Copartnership was compared favorably with the English Co-operative Wholesale Society's "productive co-operation." Lloyd awarded the palm for efficiency and enlightened attitudes toward copartnership and profit-sharing to the Scottish Wholesale Society.

Eye-witness descriptions, factual presentation, apparent impartiality, and restrained analyses were convincing. Lloyd stressed copartnership's ultimate objectives : "to frame a new economic system" and "make a new economic man." Copartnership firms' labor policies were superior to those of the ECWS factories, he reported, while the happy brotherhood of the former was in harmony with the Golden Rule so essential to a new democracy. Because of copartnership's 16 per cent annual increase in business volume during the depression he prophesied that in industry soon and in agriculture eventually it would usher in the ideal society.

Lloyd's utopian hopes thus found focus in copartnership, which he asserted had "successfully institutionalized the Golden Rule in business." Americans' talent for co-operation in industry would lead to "much grander accomplishment" than Britain's, he predicted, while co-operation would find expression "partly" in "the establishment of new communities" which, when federated, might achieve independence from the "trusts." What copartnership needed in America was "not philanthropy, but leadership initiative" such as Holyoake, Ludlow, Plunkett, and Van Marken provided.

Labor Copartnership was thus a report and a skillful plea for introduction into the United States of Christian Socialism in industry. It also favored consumers' co-operatives and communitarian colonies. Lloyd appealed to trades unionists to institute copartnership and to capitalists to engage in profit-sharing such as Nicholas Paine Gilman was advocating. Thus he published his departure from the polity of the English Fabians.

Lloyd's account of Irish agricultural co-operatives was soon verified by Plunkett's *Ireland and the New Century*. However, British co-operative farming did not become the cure for land monopoly and landlordism that Lloyd anticipated. Despite its current vigor and success, copartnership did not supplant British private enterprise. Preference for the ideal led Lloyd to minimize the danger of private, nonlabor investment in such enterprises and to exaggerate the labor copartnership aspect. Subsequent competition from the ECWS, the influence of private investment, and the effects of World War I would so retard copartnership that many of such factories would be acquired by the ECWS. Others were liquidated. As early as 1897, furthermore, British municipal Socialism overshadowed both copartnership and ECWS factories. Lloyd did vindicate copartnership from the charge of sweating labor and established the ability of elected shop committees to develop managerial standards essential to large-scale production. His friendly account was valuable for its appreciation of copartnership's social and ethical idealism. Democratically managed producers associations were not directly opposed to community interests, despite Mrs. Webb's objections.[27]

The treatise was well received on both sides of the Atlantic. Professor Charles Zeublin of the University of Chicago rated it the most important economics book of 1898. While the *Social Democratic Herald* (Belleville) attacked it as contradictory to Socialism, the *Chicago Post* praised it because it was "a blow to state socialism and a practical argument for individualism and private enterprise in the labor world." The *New York Journal* called it a work of "good omen" and published Lloyd's summary of foreign copartnership successes. Similar praise was voiced by the *Chicago Times-Herald, Brooklyn Eagle, Springfield Republican,* and *New York Herald.* Samuel Bowles invited American laborers to study this "most encouraging word that has lately come from the industrial world." The *Boston Transcript* warned, however, that leadership was needed before American co-operatives could be developed successfully. The *New York Evening Post* prophesied that the "millenium," if it did arrive, would more probably "come by the road followed by Mr. Plunkett, the Liveseys," and copartnership.[28]

Thus, after economic depression and acute social unrest, the appearance of Lloyd's hopeful book appealed to enlightened conservatives, the independent press, and non-Socialist reformers. Gladden, *The Kingdom, Chicago Commons, The Dial, The Conservator,* and the *Social Gospel* praised it highly, although the *Christian Register* regarded Lloyd's claims for copartnership skeptically. Washington Gladden in *The Outlook* predicted that his volume would encourage "all who have hope for industrial democracy." *Bookman* and *Harper's Weekly* praised it for leaving "inference to the reader." *New England Magazine* declared that it described "the most pregnant and promising work now going on in the whole industrial world." *The Cause* called it "the book of the year to those who are seeking light." Ernest H. Crosby, in the *American Federationist,* told trades unionists it was "high time" they organized copartnership industries.[29] Lloyd had developed further Flower's technique of reporting overseas reform movements. His example suggested that others might find practical solutions for American problems in successful foreign experiments.

The *London Chronicle* also stressed the pertinence of co-partnership for American reform. This gratified Lloyd immensely. The London *Review of Reviews* termed the book one "which all students of social and economic questions should possess." Holyoake praised it in *Labour Copartnership* as did Vivian discriminatingly, while welcoming the criticism and suggestions of "one of our best friends and helpers." Vivian was pleased that Lloyd said that "our central principle is the worker's share in control and not his share in profits." After depreciating the scope and importance of copartnership the *Fabian News,* however, reiterated the Webbs' assertion that it was "merely a glorified form of profit-sharing and unlikely to revolutionize industry," since the workers' contribution to "share capital" was relatively small and at times only a minority of workers participated. The reviewer claimed erroneously that the ECWS paid wages 15 per cent to 20 per cent higher than their competitors as tantamount to profit-sharing. That was news to Henry Vivian.[30] In the Antipodes the *New Zealand Times* and *Christ Church Press* declared that *Labor Copartnership* showed the way to reform.[31]

Influential Americans wrote Lloyd how favorably they were impressed by his latest book. Among these were Horace White; Graham Taylor; E. B. Permain, a Boston stock broker; Professor Charles N. Zeublin of the University of Chicago; Charles B. Spahr; and Professor John H. Gray of Northwestern University. Helen MacDowell declared it "the most hopeful sign of the times." Jane Addams expressed her admiration and thanks, and said, "I feel a stirring of old faiths." Lloyd was much gratified by reviews by N. P. Gilman, the *Literary World,* and the *Conservator,* and the favorable notice in the American *Review of Reviews.* Frank Parsons commended the book "as the latest and best word on the most hopeful movement of our time."[32] It aroused great enthusiasm among co-operators. The Secretary-Treasurer of the American Section, The International Co-operative Alliance, wrote Lloyd that it was "performing a mighty work," provoking inquiries on how "to put farms, workshops, factories, etc. on a profit-sharing basis."[33]

Carroll D. Wright called the Industrial Commission's attention to it, and urged that its inquiry be broadened to include "industrial copartnership." Lloyd wrote Albert Shaw that if he read the "chapter on Kettering the world will never look the same to you again." However, F. W. Taussig at Harvard University wrote Lloyd that copartnership in America "will have a slow and uncertain development." Lloyd presented a copy to Booker T. Washington, hoping to persuade him to promote southern Negroes' co-operatives and copartnership.

After Earl Grey of Northumberland sent Lloyd the badge commemorating a co-operators' visit to his seat at Bowick, Harpers published an English edition. George Livesey declared it the *"best* account" extant of its subject. Wolff thanked Lloyd for his treatment of co-operative banking and promised to defend profit-sharing from co-operators' criticism. The book persuaded the *London Chronicle* to support co-partnership. Anderson of the IAOS wrote his appreciation.[34] The book involved Lloyd in a dispute with John Burns, who opposed profit-sharing and claimed that it had increased the accident rate in Livesey's company. Lloyd replied to him that universal profit-sharing would hasten "the triumph of democracy" and such copartnership would train future industrial executives and workers for "a democracy of socialistic industry."[35] Lloyd confirmed thus his variance from the Webbs' viewpoint. He con-

fided to Livesey his pluralistic, non-Marxian theory of progress
in explanation of his multilevel reform activity :

> My theory of progress is that it must proceed along a
> great number of different lines simultaneously. There will
> never be a single solution for the ills of society, nor a single
> model for a social organization. I do not call myself a
> socialist in any sectarian sense, but even if I did, I cannot
> see why such efforts as yours would not be welcome. Any-
> thing, it seems to me, that raises the general level of intelli-
> gence, independence and morale helps the whole body.[36]

His tour and book elevated him in the United Kingdom to the
position of counselor and constructive critic of the co-operatives.
He informed Blandford that English co-operators and American
reformers were too faint-hearted toward co-operative farming.
He advised Wolff to found a people's bank periodical and become interested in Irish rural co-operatives. He joined the
Labour Association that propagandized the Continent in behalf
of copartnership. He contributed an article on Ruskin Colony to
the *Copartnership Yearbook* and posted Livesey on the adoption of profit-sharing in America.[37]

Lloyd surrendered his royalties on a special English edition
of his book to further "the cause," and asked Vivian to have
it translated into French and German to counteract Mrs. Webb's
book. When he learned that Sidney Webb had been "com-
misioned to write the history of English Co-operation" he
termed that "a disaster." Webb, he wrote Vivian, had "no real
ear for the true music of the co-operative movement" and that
his projected history of co-operatives "will serve to stereotype"
his views "forever in the minds of readers." The Webbs, intellectual leaders of the Fabian Society, he thought were "immensely overrated."[38] Lloyd planned later a comprehensive
study of British and Continental co-operatives to counteract
Sidney Webb's treatise. That Fabian's preference for great
capitalistic organization disqualified him as a historian of
English cooperation, he believed. In 1902 he reported to Holy-

oake how he had discovered "the trail of that serpent," the ECWS, "everywhere—in Switzerland, Germany Denmark." Hadn't Judge Thomas Hughes erred "in dropping the fight" in the Co-operative Congresses "against its centralizing and commercializing influence"? Wasn't it curious that the wealth created by Robert Owen's idealism was "now strangulating the idealism?"[10]

Lloyd's relation to the British co-operators paralleled that which he had developed toward the American independent oil men. Beginning as a sympathetic investigator, he progressed to intimate friend, counselor, and ardent advocate. Just as he burned only "independent oil" at The Wayside and The Watch House, he secured from English copartnership people a "suit of heavy stuff, suitable for cold weather" and cloth for a "spring overcoat." When lecturing on European co-operatives in America he wore his "co-operative suit," symbolizing his faith in the movement's ideals and practicality.

American Co-operator

Nelson and Lloyd became advisers of the scattered American co-operatives after attending International Co-operative Congresses. Nelson maintained that the best way to introduce copartnership was to multiply consumers' co-operatives. In 1898 New England possessed the only active federation of these, which elsewhere experienced a scattered growth. Consumers' co-operatives existed in the Galveston, Texas, Johnson County, Kansas, and Cerro Gordo, Iowa, areas, as well as in Upper Michigan, Rhode Island, New Jersey, upstate New York, and Boston. Farmers' co-operative insurance associations were widespread. Co-operative dairies of New England and Scandinavian origin were developing rapidly in the upper Mississippi Valley. Profit-sharing was beginning, led by Nelson's plumbing supply company at Edwardsville, Illinois, where the employees operated the Leclaire Co-operative Society.[40] Inadequate financial support, however, precipitated Rhodes' resignation from the editorship of the *American Co-operative News*. Then John Graham Brooks, Parsons, Hiram Vrooman of Baltimore, and

Bradford Peck of Lewiston entered the movement and provided needed leadership.[41]

Lloyd asked Gompers to invite Vivian and Blandford to address the next AFL convention, but its rules now excluded non-union speakers. When he suggested that his friends lecture in the United States under AFL sponsorship Gompers declined because of uncertainties produced by the Spanish-American War.[42] However, inspired by Lloyd's book "Tommy" Morgan persuaded the Chicago Socialist Labor Party to establish the Chicago Co-operative Trading Society and co-operative store in the "Socialist Temple," and attempted to convert the Jews to co-operation, after Lloyd convinced him there was "no *necessary* antagonism between Voluntary Labor Copartnership and the political movement of Socialism." He warned Morgan that a successful co-operative movement must be built from the ground up and directed by the members. The "most profitable" work for the disinterested reformer, he said, "is in the work of information and encouragement."[43]

He stimulated Graham Taylor and Jane Addams to attempt co-operatives.[44] Agitate, educate, and encourage Lloyd did. He scattered copies of his new book widely. He encouraged James Farrell, President of Typographical Union No. 6, New York, in co-operative gardening for unemployed union members. He urged that they study Wolff's *People's Banks*. In *The Union Signal* he declared, "Cooperation has won the right to be accounted the most important social movement of our times outside politics," and urged that the W.C.T.U. Publishing Association be transformed into a copartnership enterprise. He recommended profit-sharing to the Chicago Tribune Company and Illinois Central Railroad.[45]

He lectured constantly on co-operation, never admitting publicly as he did to himself privately the contradiction between the conceptions underlying consumers' co-operation and copartnership. In November 1898 he astonished Chicago's People's University Club with statistics of co-operative successes in the United Kingdom. Two years later at Faneuil Hall, Boston, he developed the co-operative movement's potentiality for reform.

In 1902 at Plymouth Church, Rochester, he told how the European workers transformed themselves from hirelings to partners in business by copartnership.[46]

While urging its importance, he declared that "in America as in Great Britain and on the Continent" it could "go on" only "by the help of men of means, culture, and good-will, men well-to-do in good deeds as well as in title deeds." Perhaps, as he expressed his élitist theory of reform, he recalled Simon Sterne's advocacy of co-operatives at Cooper Union when he was a freshman at Columbia College. At the People's Institute from the same rostrum in December 1901 he described European co-operatives so vividly that the *New York Journal* headlined its report, "Co-operation Holds a Utopia in Store." Tremendous applause greeted his account of Bradford Peck's gift of his Lewiston department store to his employees' co-operative, and Lloyd's allusion to his copartnership suit : "I consider myself the best dressed man in New York tonight."[47]

His book provoked more than 200 letters from all parts of the United States to James Rhodes, seeking assistance for experiments. He sought help from Lloyd, who replied, "I am very much inclined to think our evolution has possibly gone beyond the point where" it would "be opportune" to "play the part of an American Plunkett." He would, however, finance an educational campaign.[48] Despite communitarianism's diminishing momentum, as Ruskin Colony and then the Christian Commonwealth Colony disintegrated, Lloyd learned that "a rapid growth of interest on all sides in co-operation" was developing in California, Denver, Chicago, and Boston. "When the next pinch comes, we shall see action along a great many lines," he predicted.[49]

As a temporary resident in Boston that autumn he helped to launch "The Workers' Co-operative Association" to provide work for the unemployed. At a great Faneuil Hall meeting in December 1900 he cited the Irish Agricultural Organization Society as the model method of stimulating co-operatives and producing a complete economicosocial transformation in a few generations. This produced the Co-Workers Fraternity, a Boston application of Plunkett's technique in 1901. Lloyd, Peck, Parsons, Flower, J. Pickering Putnam, Hiram Vrooman, Willis Abbot, Professor Elmer Gates of Washington, Charles E. Lund, Secretary of the Co-operative Association of America, and Carl Vrooman, a regent of Kansas State Agricultural College, were the incorporators. As a "trust" in the interest of the people, the Fraternity owned 90 per cent of the capital stock of the Co-operative Association of America that Peck had organized, proposed to establish liberal schools and colleges, and protected the "honesty and integrity" of the co-operative movement. "The college organization" then acquired 90 per cent of the stock of the Massachusetts Co-operative Association, planned an ambitious program of consumers' and wholesalers' co-operation backed by an educational campaign, and assumed management of Peck's former department store at Lewiston. Vrooman, the President, induced Ralph Albertson, a founder of Christian Commonwealth Colony and former editor of the *Social Gospel,* to head the Co-operative Association of America and edit *The American Co-operator.*

Lloyd's role in this was that of inspirer and collaborator. He served on the literary committee of the Co-Workers Fraternity during 1902-03. He was its delegate to the International Co-operative Congress in 1902. Preoccupied with writing and further overseas investigations, he left the work of organization to Vrooman, Parsons, and Albertson.[50]

He was unable to persuade the AFL to take an active interest in co-operation, which Gompers rejected finally as inconsistent with trades unionism. This narrow view provoked Lloyd to write Vivian indignantly : "It is hard to be patient with such asininity. I have ordered some things sent to him from your association direct, which I trust may help to give a proper color to the matter in his brain."[51] The Co-Workers Fraternity, he wrote Vivian, was "an honest and legitimate experiment," and compared Peck to Robert Owen. To Rhodes he confided his faith that ultimately the American people would "start" and "move," but "when" and in what direction in the co-operative field were "mysteries . . . but that they will do both in their own good time I feel sure." Jane Addams, he reported, believed that "the private organization of business" was "so unscrupulous and complete that cooperation can not encounter it and live."

He admitted that economic conditions had changed vastly since the first founding of co-operatives. He added, "I am quite prepared to believe that the American business man is about to overrun and conquer Europe." Their "wonderful" successes had produced a "sort of exaltation" imbued with the "expectation of sudden developments of great fortunes and luck in America." It would take "a generation or two to sober down." Meanwhile, "we must do what we can, and you certainly have done and are doing a noble work."[52]

This sincere compliment did not allay Rhodes' resentment at being excluded from the directorship of the Co-Workers Fraternity. When Lloyd declined to help finance a delegate to the next International Congress because of commitments to the Lewiston co-operatives and the Co-Workers Fraternity, and was cool to the Workingmen's College at Lawrence, Massachusetts, Rhodes attacked him in print. Lloyd remarked to Vrooman that a sincere co-operator should not imperil the vigorous movement developing in New England.[53]

In 1900 Lloyd had informed Vivian that the co-operatives were "on the point of taking a real start in America. . . . Of course we shall make a great many mistakes, but I have confidence that we shall issue in a more advanced development." A year later he concluded that business giantism and agricultural mechanization would defeat copartnership and prevent co-operatives from gaining the ascendancy. What the remedy for America's problems would be he confessed he could not predict.[54] He turned again to welfare democracy as the more effective method of achieving fundamental reforms. A great expansion of the cooperative movement was, however, just beyond the horizon. To this his agitation for copartnership and support of consumers cooperatives made an undoubted contribution.

Chapter XIX

 Importer of Antipodean Democracy

"To Altruria"

LLOYD SOON WIDENED his investigations to include Antipodean democracy. His circle had begun its study of New Zealand and Australasian "progressive" legislation in March 1893 before studying the British co-operatives. "Dick" Seddon, Minister for Public Works at Wellington, sent Lloyd data that he cited in "The Safety of the Future Lies in Organized Labor" before the American Federation of Labor when he first presented his welfare polity formally. In 1894 he began to correspond with Edward Tregear and Robert Strout, other New Zealand Cabinet members. He shared data on the Australian state railways with Ely, and regarded the Antipodes as illustrative of the welfare democracy that he wished to establish in the United States.[1]

Thereafter his following cultivated interest in the Antipodes among Chicago trades unionists. Willis Abbot asked in the *Chicago Times* why New Zealand reforms could not be introduced into America. Knowledge of these furnished an experiential basis for a portion of the Springfield Platform. During 1895-96 the *Eight-Hour Herald* published "Special Correspondence from the Antipodes" containing labor news and reports on Premier Seddon's policies, including the compulsory arbitration of industrial disputes. The *Union Workman* discussed William Pember Reeves' "The Toiler's Paradise" in *Westminster Review* for December, 1895. Then, after McKinley's victory, Frank Parsons discussed "Compulsory Arbitration" in the *Arena* and Bliss's *Encyclopedia of Social Reform* supplied New Zealand data to reformers.[2]

During Lloyd's tour of the United Kingdom in 1897 he read Reeves's article in the *National Review* on New Zealand compulsory arbitration, which he had introduced when Minister of Labour at Wellington. He was now New Zealand's Agent General at Westminster. His article provoked long, favorable comment in *The Co-operative News,* and undoubtedly revived Lloyd's interest in New Zealand.[3]

Labor Copartnership's favorable reception convinced him that he had developed an effective technique for stimulating American reform. In 1896, as he knew, most business executives had viewed "Social Theorists" with undisguised impatience. " 'An able and upright manufacturer' " declared then that religious, sentimental, ethical, philanthropic, and humanitarian considerations were inapplicable to management-labor relations.[4] Emerging general welfare considerations such as the living wage, industrial democracy, and social legislation had been submerged by the McKinley reaction and rejected by the Illinois Supreme Court in *Ritchie* v. *The People.* Lloyd became convinced that the future prospect of reform was blighted unless Americans could be convinced of the practicality of individual reforms by knowledge of successful experiments elsewhere. In October 1898 he wrote to E. B. Watson of Detroit :

> If the American people could be roused to the point of naturalizing all the reforms that have been successfully instituted in different parts of the world in town government, national socialism, and in the voluntary field of cooperation, we should have a very nearly ideal Utopia, right here and now.

He wanted to see the things that "the common people, with no theoretical socialism impelling them" had done, "which our leaders here tell us cannot be done."[5]

While lecturing to the Brotherhood of the Kingdom at Marlborough Lloyd had met Hugh H. Lusk, New Zealand consul in

New York City. They became friends. After entertaining him
at The Watch House, Lloyd determined to investigate Antipodean democracy and possibly the Dutch East Indies and the
Philippines. Aided by Lusk and Reeves he briefed himself on
New Zealand and received letters of introduction from them,
Van Marken, and others from labor leaders, journalists, economists, and British and American reformers. He became an enthusiastic admirer of Sir George Grey.[6]

He explained to Lockwood why he was making that expensive
journey. He was almost convinced, he said, "that a political
remedy for the situation of things in this country is beyond
our reach . . . until we have in some way effected an economic
readjustment" that would correct simultaneously the "maldistribution of wealth" and "a corresponding maldistribution of
political power" concentrated in "a very rich class." Illogically,
because this required political action, he thought this might be
secured by "reforms in progressive taxation, government ownership, land restoration, co-operation, &c., which are now being
pushed with such success in New Zealand and England. I
think we are bound to make the effort, and I am going over
to New Zealand in a few weeks to make a study of Antipodal
democracy on the spot," he wrote.[7]

Following John R. Commons' suggestion Lloyd persuaded
Carroll D. Wright to appoint him a representative of the United
States Bureau of Labor Statistics without pay to gather Australasian "labor facts." Horace Plunkett encouraged him. Lloyd
volunteered to gather documentary materials for Arthur T.
Hadley of Yale, whom he now regarded as "by far the most
dangerous of the Bourbon economists," undoubtedly to re-
orient him. He offered to gather data for Debs also.[8]

Henry D. Lloyd and Will left Chicago on January 6, 1899, in
search of "democratic novelties," after having failed to persuade
Willis Abbot to accompany them. In the Hawaiian Islands they
investigated the Ewa Plantation communitarian community.
The New York Times reported their landing in Wellington,
February 2, in "a regular Noah's ark rain." They presented
Lusk's letter of introduction to Chief Justice Sir Robert Stout,

"the most . . . cultivated radical in the Southern Hemisphere," and were put up at the Wellington Club.[9]

The *New Zealand Times* announced that Henry D. Lloyd would report officially to Wright and publish his observations "in adequate permanent form. It remains for time to show if we can sustain our reputation under the probe and lens of such a critical expert analyst of men and methods." He came, Lloyd said, to study "the political democracy of the foremost civilised country in the world, if by civilised we mean . . . an ability to use the common resources for the common good."[10] This opened doors everywhere.

New Zealand was completing its great era of internal reform when the Lloyds landed. Sir George Grey's pioneering statesmanship, and ideas derived from Henry George, Bellamy, Reeves's articles on historical utopias, and the *Fabian Essays* had given focus to popular grievances, revolutionized public opinion on taxation and land policy, and stimulated attempts to overthrow the "squattocracy." Land-hungry farm laborers, the unemployed, and trades unionists had turned to the Liberal Party as it revived Grey's program. The "Progressive" Liberal-Labor coalition gained control of Parliament and, led by Premiers John Ballance and "Dick" Seddon, during 1891-95 enacted a remarkable series of reforms. Building upon earlier "state trading," viz., state-owned railways, telegraph, postal savings banks, and state life insurance, and inspired by Reeves, Minister of Labour and the Cabinet's idea man, the "Progressives" perfected a labor code. This legalized trades unions, established protective safeguards, and instituted voluntary conciliation and compulsory arbitration of industrial disputes. Simultaneously, John ("Jock") McKenzie, a former squatter's shepherd become Minister of Agriculture, expanded the policy of repossessing and subdividing large estates into small, profitable leaseholds let to Crown tenants for 999 years. Women were enfranchised. In March 1898 Seddon inaugurated old age pensions, completing the "Progressive" attempt to elevate the populace via a general welfare policy resting upon a mixed "state-trading"-private-enterprise economy.

When the Lloyds arrived Reeves was in London. Tregear had replaced him in the Labour ministry, and Stout had become Chief Justice. "Our Dick" Seddon, who had risen from prospector in the gold mining districts to the premiership while but partly "civilized" was "a jolly, good-tempered despot" who kept his party in power until 1906. A return of prosperity gilded the new welfare democracy with materialistic success. Rising revenues enabled the Treasury to carry the increased indebtedness with ease."

The Lloyds' investigation was an arduous but highly enjoyable experience. Henry D. Lloyd found the first fortnight of "interviewing labor leaders, ministers of departments, country squires," and his "attempt to digest all the departments of a national government in 'twenty minutes for refreshments' a good deal of a strain." On February 12 he conferred with the Minister of Education and with Joseph G. Ward, Minister of Railways, who escorted him through the locomotive shops while informing him that operating policy was to reduce rates when profits rose above 3 per cent. A streetcar driver told him that with the best meat at five to six cents a pound, an unmarried worker could live on the equivalent of $3.75 a week and enjoy "the best of joints." Lloyd found that "Jock" McKenzie and Edward Tregear, Reeves' successor as Minister of Labour and author of the definitive book on the Maoris, were the most interesting Cabinet members.

Wellington charmed the Lloyds. They walked frequently in the city that was "hillier (and holier) that San Francisco." Large palms studded the streets and heliotrope bloomed "all year round," some "eight feet tall." Sir Robert Stout entertained them, introducing them to Thomas Larkin, an authority on Australia.

After Seddon instructed his subordinates to facilitate their tour of the Islands, McKenzie directed the Assistant Surveyor General to supply needed documents on the land "systems" and appointed a Department official to accompany the Lloyds on visits to "The Village Settlements." John Riggs, Parliamentary Librarian, presented Henry D. Lloyd with "a walking stick."[12]

Official co-operation, letters of introduction, advance copies of his books, and the Lloyds' geniality facilited their inquiry. They sailed on coastal steamers to ports on South Island and traveled inland. At Christchurch reviews of *Labor Copartnership* in the local papers before their arrival and an interview after they landed that appeared in the *Press* provoked "great curiosity." They were put up at both clubs.

After attending the Arbitration Court they traveled by railway 'bird-cage car" with side aisles protected by wire railings to examine the Temuka "village settlements." A three-day coaching trip carried them over the former Cheviot estate of "Ready Money Robinson," which McKenzie had taken at tax valuation and subdivided. Accompanied by J. R. March, Superintendent of Village Settlements, they saw thriving new farms "buttressed with golden stacks of grain as big as the barns" and "prosperous towns" where five years earlier there had been a manor house and 84,000 acres supporting 80,000 sheep. Here was a precedent applicable to American railroad land grants, Lloyd informed the *Lyttleton Times*.[13]

In late February they almost reached fiordlike Milford Sound on the southeast coast by taking the first steamer up Lake Te Anau, but a heavy storm prevented hiking over the pass. They returned to Dunedin, then drove north to Mt. Cook, "King of the New Zealand Alps." That surpassed any mountain that Henry D. Lloyd had seen except the Matterhorn. After climbing the Tasman Glacier and the "enchanted" Hochstetter Ice Falls, they drove south to Lake Wanatka beneath Mt. Aspiring, and thence to Te Anau. They carried packs over the pass to Milford Sound, whose scenery they found indescribable. The *Lyttleton Times* published their praise of "the Switzerland of the Australian colonies."[14]

While touring South Island Henry D. Lloyd was repeatedly interviewed. The "settlements" on the Cheviot, he informed the *Christchurch Press,* possessed a situation and climate superior to that of Colorado, but while crop yields were extraordinary some farms were too small. When inspecting the Arrohenna Village he predicted that New Zealanders' future progress would "be slow" because its "enlightened measures" would prevent discontent. The *Temuka Leader* replied : "The people have tasted the fruits of progressive legislation and mean to have more of it." However, Lloyd's prescience was sound. Leslie Lipson attributes the complacency of subsequent New Zealand generations to their successful welfare democracy.[15] In that interview Lloyd maintained that American conditions were "the darkness which precedes the brighter day" whose advent was impeded by courts, monopoly control, and difficulties of constitutional amendment. The *Leader* replied that the capitalists' dominance of the United States approached "the despotism pictured in 'Caesar's Column,' and justified Mr. Stead's assertion that America is more despotic that Russia." Such papers noted Lloyd's part ownership of the *Chicago Tribune* but stressed his activity as antimonopolist, publicist, social investigator, and author. Their reports of his praise of the land settlement policy, compulsory arbitration, and old age pensions endeared him to "Progressive Party" leaders, while descriptions of his interrogations of farmers in the "settlements" and his preference for leasehold tenure evoked popular admiration.[16]

Will wrote his mother that New Zealand was "the most truly Christian country of the earth," since the people "seem to think the Golden Rule is worthy of practical application . . . on all sides of life" in contrast with "other countries" whose people "rush to business Monday and violate every tenet" of Christianity.[17]

During leisure moments Henry D. Lloyd read and rejected the analysis of Wilhelm Wagner and Walt Whitman in E. Carpenter's *Angel Wings,* after comparing it with Wm. M. Salter's essay on Walt Whitman. He challenged Carpenter's acceptance of Wagner's thesis that the "folk" are the "true inventors," thereby questioning the assumption that had motivated his New Zealand journey. Reviving his élitist theory, he repudiated Tolstoian anarchism as nonsensical. He concluded that "the real inventors" arising "among the people" should be given every opportunity to separate from them to create an "aristocracy" of talent analogous to the emergence of a "plutocracy" in a business society. Instead of Carpenter's theory of art as emotional expression he preferred a conception of art as *"creation"* leading from "stage to stage along the reaches of the higher life," whose highest form "is the creation of a new man by himself." He rejected Carpenter's assertion that the new democratic art should not be luxurious. Instead, "complexity" must be the key axiom of democratic art.[18]

Contact with New Zealand statesman and inspection of the fruits of their reforms precipitated the completion of Lloyd's theory of progress inspired and led by inventors in every field, creating a new man while they created a new life. What he discovered provided dramatic experiential justification of his faith in human brotherhood's creative power and in the possibility of social justice achieved by democratic redistribution of wealth and broadening of opportunity.

From Christchurch the party traveled south to the newly subdivided Waihahahi Estate in Waimate, where Lloyd was chosen "scrutineer" by acclamation. After the land board's examination of the applicants and the balloting, he drew the ballots from the boxes and announced the recipients of the new leasehold farms.[19]

For four weeks after this, the Lloyds roamed the partly settled North Island by steamer, rail, stage, and Maori canoe. After having their coach ferried on Maori canoes over the swift Waikato draining Lake Taupo, they penetrated the hot spring, geyser, "floating earth" region in the Island's center, which was shaken continually by earthquakes. They traveled around it to sleep at Takaanu on its southern shore, and rode thence to Pipiriki on the Whanganui River. Paddled upstream by four Maoris, they were enchanted by "the bush's" ferns, the evergreen trees reaching hundreds of feet above them, and the Maori's songs. They camped for a night near a Maori village, where Henry D. Lloyd questioned the natives. They said, "The missionaries taught us to lift our eyes in prayer; while we prayed they stole the ground under our feet." On North Island as in Hawaii, he observed, "some of the very richest people are the descendants of the missionaries, and land is usually their principal possession."[20]

A steamboat took them from Pipiriki to Cook Strait and then to Wellington. After a week of further inquiries, document collecting, and entertainment by officials they sailed for Sydney. Lloyd had won the enduring friendship of the New Zealanders. The *Lyttleton Times* was especially impressed by his quiet, gentle, "courtly manner," combined with an "intense fervid fighting spirit" activated by hatred of evil and love of mankind. Judge J. G. Findlay wrote him afterward of how "your visit . . showed us a type of homo Americanus that has somehow raised our idea of the whole American people." Tregear added : "I feel more drawn toward your great Nation by having had the honor of meeting and knowing you than would have been otherwise possible."[21]

The Lloyds landed at Sydney, April 27, during the campaign for Australian federation. They entrained immediately for Adelaide, where they began investigations that took them from state to state as far north as Brisbane. The premiers did their best to aid them. At Adelaide they studied the state railroad, compulsory arbitration system, and old age pensions. In South Australia and New South Wales the Lloyds learned of the disastrous effects of subsidizing co-operative communities of unemployed. Henry D. Lloyd approved of South Australia's rejection of an application for subsidy of Roman Catholic parochial schools as a victory for public education essential to the "modern State." He commended consumers' co-operatives and copartnership enterprises. At the Leongatta state farm for unemployed in Victoria the Lloyds were welcomed by a government investigating board. What he learned of such experiments apparently terminated Henry D. Lloyd's interest in communitarianism, since he ceased to advocate or support it afterwards. At Brisbane he inquired into the feasibility of cultivating sugar cane with white labor. Departments of agriculture there, at Melbourne, and at Wellington, he learned, were encouraging farm produce exports with agricultural credit resembling the American Populists' subtreasury plan.[22]

On May 23 the Lloyds boarded the R.M.S. *Warrimoo* at
Sydney for Honolulu, and won the respect of the colonial first-
class passenger list by being loyal Americans "without being
offensive." After the steamer left Honolulu for Vancouver the
passengers elected Henry D. Lloyd chairman of the "Warrimoo
Theatre of Varieties." Professor Sydney B. J. Skertchly, Queensland state geologist, drafted a memorandum for him on the im-
practicability of white labor in the tropics in opposition to a
Hawaiian sugar syndicate agent's claim. Because of interest in
the Lloyds' desire to reach Cambridge, Massachusetts, in time
for "Hal's" Commencement, Captain William Hay broke the
steaming record from Sydney to Vancouver. This enabled them
to catch the first eastbound Imperial Limited on the Canadian
Pacific Railroad.

The *New York World* featured the Lloyds' "record-breaking
run." The *Montreal Gazette* obtained a front page story of
Henry D. Lloyd's views on Australian Federation, which had
been voted during the voyage. He charmed Canadians when he
said "he liked Australia, but he fell in love with New Zealand,
where he found the finest Anglo-Saxon people in the world."
Father and son arrived in Cambridge in a blaze of newspaper
publicity, reunited with their family, watched "Hal" graduate
with honors, and enjoyed the most remarkable Class Day in
many years.[23] Embarrassed by the publicity given to his return
journey, Henry D. Lloyd wrote Bowles : "I hope the absurd
performances of the Boston papers have not persuaded you
that I am merely a globe-trotting fakir." Skertchly wrote him
humorously of how the Chicago tin-plate people attempted to
squeeze him and his Queensland associates out of control of
their tin mine, before going on to New York and London in
search of more congenial backing.[24]

REPORT ON THE ANTIPODES

Having investigated Antipodean democracy, Lloyd returned
with faith restored in the efficacy of the welfare polity which
he had first advocated. Lloyd was soon at work at The Watch
House, as the *Boston Herald* syndicated two interviews with

him on Australia and Hawaii. Walter Hines Page induced him to write an article for the *Atlantic*. He reported informally to Wright, and sent Australasian documents to Arthur T. Hadley, newly elected President of Yale University. He wrote Reeves how charmed he was with New Zealand. Letters poured in from New Zealand officials and friends. They were delighted with his account of compulsory arbitration in the *Herald*, marked copies of which he had sent, and were gratified that he had overcome the opposition of Australian labor leaders and Socialists to federation by arguing when in Australia that federal union in America had advanced democracy. While reporting the weakness of Australasian labor and co-operative movements in *Labour Co-Partnership*, he expressed grief at Thomas Blandford's sudden passing.[25]

The *New Zealand Times* agreed with Lloyd's *Herald* statement that the "Progressive" reforms had resulted from practical steps taken by a democratic people to solve practical problems. His enthusiasm for these measures increased the determination of officials and political leaders "to give them a fair trial," Judge Findlay declared later after becoming Attorney General.[26]

At The Watch House Lloyd wrote quickly a small volume on compulsory arbitration in New Zealand and articles on that colony for the *Atlantic, Outlook,* and *Ainslee's.* Then the arrival of Reeves and three Australian Agents-General to attend a Commercial Congress at Washington stimulated further interest in the Antipodes. Frank Parsons was gratified when Lloyd declared that New Zealand's progressive land reforms and income taxes had stopped "absolutely" the "accumulation of wealth in a few hands."[27] Shortly after the Lloyds settled for the winter at Beacon Street, Boston, Reeves's party visited them.

Reeves described the New Zealand Arbitration Act to the Twentieth Century Club, and Lloyd persuaded the *Herald* to publish a long interview with him on the day that Admiral George Dewey was welcomed tumultuously at "The Hub." After President McKinley received the four Agents-General, they returned to Boston and were honored at Harvard at a luncheon given by President Charles Eliot. Lloyd handed

Reeves the manuscript of his new book, which he read critically en route to London. Reeves wrote the introduction to it and his New Zealand friends sent photographs and data for a second, more general treatise. J. A. Wayland wrote Lloyd, meanwhile, that his *Atlantic* and *Ainslee's* articles on New Zealand were having "an immense effect in awakening interest in the way that that country had solved the problem."[28]

A Country Without Strikes[29] combated Carroll D. Wright's and Gompers' opposition to compulsory arbitration. Engagingly written, it rated this policy "one of the most original pieces of work done in modern times." After an eye-witness account of the Arbitration Court's session at Christchurch, a detailed review of the law's effect in successive industries and in abolition of the sweatshop enabled readers to appraise it. Lloyd declared that compulsory arbitration was a victory for social ethics in an area of anarchic strife. This reversed his previous attitude toward a reform that Altgeld, Lyman Abbott, Bemis, Gronlund, and Parsons had advocated in America. The book demonstrated that New Zealand trades unions benefited and industry prospered under the new policy, to which industrialists were increasingly favorable. Reeves, the originator, was an important "social inventor," Lloyd declared. Conciliation and compulsory arbitration lifted "civilization a stage" by humanizing industrial relations and enforcing the living wage. The New Zealand reforms enforced "the doctrines of Carlyle and Ruskin and all the great poets," making industrialists and laborers public servants and "social functionaries," realizing the loftiest doctrines of the "religion of labor and love" while achieving a just distribution of wealth. Lloyd seized upon the opportunity presented to preach his social gospel and exaggerated for effect the change in status of employers and workers wrought by the Arbitration Act. The book appeared in May 1900, three years after the American Federation of Labor's bitter opposition to the Erdman Arbitration Bill.[30]

Lloyd's third book attracted unusual interest. His preceding articles and press reviews and the Reeves party's public statements had created the impression that New Zealand had solved its problems better than America. George Iles wrote to Lloyd enthusiastically from his Park Avenue Hotel that the book might so arouse the public "on both sides of the Atlantic that New Zealand shall soon cease to stand alone in compulsory arbitration." President Gates called the book "glorious." R. Heber Newton praised it. Anne Withington of Dennison House called it "simply immense." Professors Gray and Zeublin used it in their university classes. Horace White wrote Lloyd that it was "the most suggestive work" on industrial disputes that he had read and declared in the *New York Evening Post* that compulsory arbitration was the legal remedy for strikes. The *Nation* added that America owed Lloyd a "debt of gratitude," but asked what would happen to compulsory arbitration during a depression.[31] Drawing upon Lloyd's book and articles the *Age of Reason* disseminated the new gospel widely among its 65,000 subscribers. The press welcomed the book as the first adequate treatment of the compulsory arbitration system, while a revival of industrial strife led the *New York World, New York Journal, Boston Transcript, Illinois State Register,* and *Tacoma News* to demand its institution. The *Buffalo Express* published letters from New Zealand describing the Arbitration Court and supported a compulsory arbitration bill at Albany.

Some papers were more cautious. While the *Springfield Republican* declared that "the possibility of its successful trial elsewhere" was undoubted, it observed that the reform was still experimental in New Zealand. The *Chicago Tribune* stated that that colony's policy was not necessarily "practicable here or in any European country" despite its consistency with "notable tendencies of thought on both sides of the water." Preserved Smith asked Lloyd if New Zealand conditions might not have to be reproduced if the experiment were to succeed elsewhere.[32]

The Outlook welcomed Lloyd's influential support for that reform. *The Dial* said it provided "the only rational promise for a . . . just decision of class controversies." John A. Ryan stressed the "morality of compulsory arbitration" in the *Catholic World,* and asked "Why should it not be tried here in America?" Although the *National Single Taxer* raised individualist objections, *Social Gospel* declared that Lloyd's books "bring gladness and courage to every reader."[33]

Antipodean press reviews strongly commended Lloyd's accuracy and impartial analysis. The British press expressed a friendly interest in his report, while stressing the experimental status of the New Zealand Arbitration Act. However, the *Fabian News* asked him to send his book to Lord Rosebery, leader of the Liberal Party.[34]

Lloyd had begun agitation for compulsory arbitration in the United States before his book appeared with a terse, illustrated article in the *New York Herald,* March 25, 1900, entitled "Unique Among Peoples—A Country Without 'Strikes'." He sent the Missouri Commissioner of Labor the New Zealand statute and data on its operation to promote adoption of that policy there, terming it "the greatest advance that has been made in the science of government in modern times." He preferred the term "State arbitration." In Boston Conrad Reno, an attorney, founded the Industrial Courts League to agitate for "Industrial Courts." After Justice Marcus A. Knowleton stated that New Zealand's policy would solve industrial strife, he presented a bill to institute it to the legislature. This bill was defective. Before a select committee Lloyd opposed its prohibition of strikes while leaving lockouts legal and providing for appeals to the Massachusetts Supreme Court. He demanded amendment of the Massachusetts Constitution to authorize an arbitration court.[35]

In the summer of 1900 he published *Newest England: Notes of a Democratic Traveller in New England, with some Australian Comparisons.*[36] After reading the manuscript Reeves had predicted it would "be of immense value," confessing that he had dreamed of writing "a similar book . . . but while I have been dreaming you have been working and I congratulate you with all my heart." So stimulated, he began work on his monumental *State Experiments in Australia and New Zealand,* which he published two years later. Impressively illustrated and brilliantly written, *Newest England* was the most constructive of Lloyd's books. Its demonstration of the practicability of a general welfare policy established him as the leading publicist of this phase of the democratic revival. It combined a traveler's narrative with analyses of all aspects of New Zealand democracy and its Australian parallels and was based upon personal observation and official documents. The presentation was singular felicitous and lacked the biting irony and moralizing of *Wealth Against Commonwealth*. The chapter on arbitration and the realistic eyewitness descriptions of Antipodean democracy are historically important. Permeating the narrative was the personality of "The Meister" of The Wayside, gay, cultivated, cosmopolitan, widely read, but interested, humane, understanding of persons and problems, the knightly champion of social justice and welfare democracy.

Newest England established the indigenous character of New Zealand's "Progressive" program, which it attributed to a democratic revolt against monopoly and concentrated wealth uninspired by systematic social theory. The origins and institution of the land settlement policy, however, are ascribed too exclusively to McKenzie. The discussion of the progressive income and inheritance taxes, measures that Lloyd had long advocated, is excellent. Few readers forgot his description of the New Zealand land policy, the balloting at Waimati or of the new farming settlements. Admission of the failure of government-sponsored co-operatives and communities of unemployed betokened intellectual integrity! He said the Australasians were leading "a renaissance of democracy" with an experimental leadership that was "saving the commonwealth of the whole world." Antipodean example should guide American reformers "in our struggle with the gentlemen in whose legs I have tried to keep my teeth ever since . . . I put myself forward in the Atlantic twenty years ago," he informed Major Huntington.[37]

Explicitly and implicitly Lloyd projected his narrative against American experience with railroad discrimination, the "trusts," antilabor management policies, industrial warfare, land engrossment, and concentration of wealth and economic power. While describing the nondiscriminatory operation of Antipodean state railways, whose policy was maximum stimulation of economic growth and receptivity to public criticism, he observed, "There are no railroad wreckers in the boards of directors." He contrasted the contracting of construction to workers' co-operatives with Gould's perpetuation of Credit Mobilier methods. The account of New Zealand labor legislation contrasted with its absence in Illinois. As if in anticipation of future New Deal crisis leadership, he described government intervention in the Bank of New Zealand after the panic of 1893, pumping in new capital and putting government representatives on the directorate. Long-term and short-term credit extended to New Zealand and South Australian farmers, which he reported, anticipated future United States farm policy.

For comprehensive, glowing, constructive suggestivity to a perplexed continental republic grappling ineffectively with a myriad of problems *Newest England* was unequalled. New Zealand's reforms, Lloyd asserted, were "A Substitute for a French Revolution." As he wrote to Holyoake they were a "successful experiment in revolution by political methods" with "an important message for the people in . . . America at this crisis. Why should we not be . . . successful in the application of laboratory procedure in the wider theatre of social politics?"[38] Privately, he feared the New Zealand program might fail because it had "not gone far enough." Because it presented brilliantly a far-reaching, albeit alien polity as an adequate solution for inescapable American issues, *Newest England* provoked widespread comment and much controversy. Its influence matched *Wealth Against Commonwealth*'s and pointed toward twentieth century development of an American welfare democracy.

The Outlook's review asserted a few months before Theodore Roosevelt became President that the New Zealand rèforms destroyed "plutocracy at the top and . . . a proletariat at the bottom" by abolishing "the classes" and unifying them "in one true brotherhood," thereby attaining the "democracy of the future." The *Arena* ranked Lloyd as the New World's ablest author of "solid, practical, and vital literature of social democracy." In *The Public,* the single taxer Louis F. Post attacked

New Zealand's "Government & Company, Unlimited," and saw in Lloyd's emphasis upon compulsory arbitration a penchant for "patchwork legislation instead of radical reform." Even more antagonized, the *Nation* reverted to its former hostility to Lloyd and accused him of championing a Jacobinical régime.[39]

The press divided similarly. The *New York Sun* accepted Lloyd's thesis that New Zealand was the world's experimental station for advanced legislation. The *New York Journal* acknowledged that colony's leadership "in the actual movement" whereby the middle class would "absorb all the other classes." The *Springfield Republican* accepted Australasian primacy in political and economic innovation on "lines known . . . as 'populism'." The *Boston Herald* thought the New Zealand Public Trustee for administering estates was needed in America. Ella Wheeler Wilcox widely syndicated newspaper articles based on *Newest England.* The *Helena Independent* urged western miners to study it, and the *Kansas Populist* rejoiced that Populism was now vindicated. The *Chicago Record, Pittsburgh Commercial Gazette,* and *San Francisco Star* reacted favorably.[40]

The *Nation's* lead was followed by the *New York Tribune* and *Philadelphia Bulletin* in hostile, sarcastic reviews. While urging Americans to welcome and study the New Zealand experiments, the *Rochester Post-Express* warned that Lloyd assumed too readily the "absolute success" of "paternalism in government." The *Chicago Tribune* warned that he was an advocate but urged "every advanced thinker" to read the book, and predicted that New Zealand policies would have "a distinct and valuable influence in guiding Americans in the solution of these same problems, though under radically different conditions."[41]

Thus Lloyd precipitated a farflung debate on the suitability of Antipodean welfare democracy for America. As the *Boston Transcript* observed : "It was a brilliant bit of controversial tactics, while all the world is discussing the great social questions, to make the trip to New Zealand and study the reforms . . . in actual operation."[42]

In Great Britain, where Sidney Webb had urged Lloyd to describe Australasian democracy for Americans, the *Fabian News* asked every "Fabian, every other Socialist, who cares to know what the State can do when it really represents the people organized to help themselves" to read *Newest England* "at once." The *Manchester Guardian* accepted Lloyd's conclusion that New Zealand's prosperity sprang primarily from its essentially "regulative . . . bold new departure in legislation." The *London Daily Mail* declared that his book supplied what thoughtful Englishmen had wanted since the appearance of Charles Dilke's *Problems of Greater Britain,* "a clear and unprejudiced account of the New Zealand experiments." Although marred occasionally by "excessive enthusiasm," it made "a contribution of the greatest value, in its bearing upon the social problem of the old country." The *London Daily News* agreed.[42]

Antipodean newspapers expressed emphatic appreciation. The *Christchurch Press* declared that all New Zealand Progressives "must have a copy, for in it they make their journey 'to the stars'." It discriminated between Lloyd's "judicial" analyses and the "sanguine temperament and intense interest in social evolution" that had made him "see the innovations of the last ten years . . . in a very favorable light." The *Brisbane Worker* recommended that a copy be placed "into the hands of every thinking man and woman in Australia, especially in Queensland."[44]

Premier Seddon expressed "most heartfelt gratitude" to Lloyd for *Newest England*'s appreciation of his Government's attempts "to raise and improve the condition of the majority of the colonists" and for the respect that this would secure the colony abroad. No other "guest has carried away more warm esteem and liking than yourself," he added. Remarking that he had never read a better book on social conditions, Judge Findlay added, "Your fine approval of John McKenzie pleases the people here immensely." Reeves congratulated Lloyd, thanking him "for *the* book, the one great Apolgia for our Party and our ten years' work."[45] Yet, careful verification of Lloyd's factual statements and analyses discloses an extraordinary accuracy, which is corroborated by Reeves's great classic of 1902 and J. B. Condliffe's *The Welfare State in New Zealand.*[46] Because of their wide appeal and influence, Lloyd's two books on the Antipodes made him not simply "an Atlantic man" but rather a transoceanic reformer whose influence reached from Adelaide and Wellington to America, the United Kingdom, and the European Continent.

DEFENDER OF THE ANTIPODES

After publication of Lloyd's two books, Edward Tregear was swamped with inquiries from America about the conciliation boards and arbitration court. Other New Zealand officials received voluminous requests for information on the functioning of other Seddon policies. As the *Lyttleton Times* remarked this was a "strong testimony to the power of Mr. Lloyd's books."[47] This vogue for New Zealand alarmed old-fashioned American liberals and conservatives. The *New York Evening Post* attacked *Newest England,* December 18, 1900, claiming that New Zealand's reforms had caused an annual emigration of 2 per cent since 1890. Since Lloyd had asserted in the *New York World* that compulsory arbitration would have prevented the anthracite coal strike of that year, and his admirers were agitating from coast to coast for adoption of various Antipodean reforms, he was obliged to reply. This involved him in a prolonged controversy with the *Evening Post* and *Nation* on the solvency, wisdom, justice, and effectiveness of Antipodean democratic statism.

Simultaneously, Reeves was obliged to counteract the London *Times*'s criticisms of the Seddon government. He and Lloyd drew upon the statistics of New Zealand's development to repel the conservative counter attack, although each wished that Seddon and Ward were less extravagant in their borrowing.

Urged on by Bemis, his father, and Mortimer Johnson, Lloyd demonstrated in the *Post,* December 29, that during 1892-98 the Seddon government had naturalized more immigrants than any other Australasian colony, and that the large New Zealand debt earned a net income annually above interest charges from its investment in state enterprises. New Zealand bonds sold in London at a premium of from 3½ per cent to 10 per cent. To George Iles he ridiculed the *Post*'s garbling of New Zealand statistics. Spahr rejoiced that his *riposte* left "nothing to be desired except the single leg to support the *Post*'s dignity."[48] In August 1901 Lloyd joined Reeves in exposing a cabled canard to the *London Daily Mail* reporting that Seddon had turned against the Arbitration Act that was syndicated to American paper's before his denial reached London. Lloyd wrote Bowles that "the enemy" was financing circulation of the false report to lesser newspapers, and quoted Seddon's reassurance to his Parliament in another letter to the *Evening Post*.[49]

A more sweeping *Evening Post* and *Nation* attack upon Antipodean democracy, based upon the conservative T. Grattan Gray's *Australia Old and New,* predicted an early repeal by Seddon's government of compulsory arbitration and old age pensions. When the *Chicago Record-Herald* cited Gray to counteract Lloyd's influence in the Middle West, he replied with crushing facts on October 22, 1901. In the *Evening Post* of December 7, 1901, he replied to its attack in a letter to the editor from the Pacific Coast, where he was lecturing. This letter described New Zealand's financial situation and economic development, exploding the misrepresentations and prediction that Seddon's policies would precipitate the colony's ruin that the *Sydney Herald, London Times,* London *Economist* and *Edinburgh Scotsman* circulated. He attributed the attack to the "taint of socialism" in the colony debt's investment in state enterprise that earned a net profit, and contrasted the premium on New Zealand bonds with the eight points below par of United Kingdom bonds. Headlined "New Zealand Defended," this was an effective rejoinder.[50]

He sent hundreds of marked copies of this to American friends and reformers. Having informed Seddon that he would defend New Zealand credit, he wrote Sir Joseph G. Ward that the sedulous attempts to discredit New Zealand policies rested upon the assertion the colony was experiencing "a severe economic and political reaction" that would necessitate repeal of progressive" reforms. He was keeping the public "fully informed as to the real facts," Lloyd said, and needed the fullest and latest information. "It is a real pleasure for me to do this work, for I love New Zealanders and New Zealand institutions." Its officials sent the latest reports.[51] Reeves assisted with a letter to the *Boston Herald* vindicating the colony's credit. Tregear refuted Gray in the *New York Evening Post.* The *New York Journal* published Lloyd's assertion that American capitalists were distributing "manufactured" attacks on New Zealand to the press to oppose "the tide of reform thought which is sweeping through the land to-day." He sent "New Zealand Defended" to the *Star and Kansan* as material "to answer the lying fakes."[52]

His lectures in the Rocky Mountain and Pacific States for the University Association of Chicago stimulated growing interest in New Zealand. He precipitated a debate in California on Antipodean democracy that William E. Smythe, founder of the National Irrigation Congress and an editor of the *Land of Sunshine Magazine,* continued. Disseminating Lloyd's account, he agitated for adoption of New Zealand's socialization of utilities to break California's land and irrigation monopolies. Lloyd reported to Reeves that Pacific Coast interest "in your experiment is very great."[53]

In July 1902, when the Victoria Royal Commission reported favorably on New Zealand compulsory arbitration, the *Evening Post* reported this respectfully. *The Outlook* observed that Lloyd's report was now vindicated. The Boston Life Underwriters' Association heard him assert that "American opinion about New Zealand is rapidly changing."[54] At the National Civic Federation Conference on Arbitration at Chicago Lusk had carried the torch in December 1900 for New Zealand, and nearly every speaker discussed compulsory arbitration.[55] Of the agitation for that reform Lloyd was the recognised prophet. Aiding him were Lusk, W. Stainsby, Chief of the New Jersey Bureau of Labor, Justice Knowleton, and Justice W. P. Potter of the Pennsylvania Supreme Court. Judge Tuley of Chicago endorsed the reform but predicted the courts would declare it unconstitutional.[56]

Lloyd upheld compulsory arbitration as the only means of reconciling labor and capital against Bishop Henry Codman Potter, who relied upon public opinion, and Charles Francis Adams, who demanded boards of investigation, in the *New York Journal* September 24, 1901 symposium. Lloyd demanded the employment of arbitration courts as productive of greater justice when collective bargaining failed. The dangers involved were "largely imaginary," and the public would demand this remedy after it had "suffered enough." This argument was conclusive for men as remote as Govnor Teats, a Tacoma attorney, and E. W. Harris of the *Greenville* (Texas) *Herald.*[57]

During the great anthracite coal strike of 1902 the *Boston Transcript* and other papers demanded compulsory arbitration to prevent future catastrophic strikes. Lloyd elaborated its advantages before the National Geographic Society, Washington, D.C., and in the *Boston Globe,* describing New South Wales' adoption of that policy. His "Australasian Cures for 'Coal Wars' " in the November *Atlantic* maintained that the measure was consistent with "Anglo-Saxon liberty," having elevated trades unionism to responsibility in the Antipodes. Alluding to the anthracite operators' rejection of voluntary arbitration the *Springfield Republican* declared that America would have to try tentative steps after New Zealand's example "to cope with the fast deepening and very threatening labor problem." The *New Orleans Picayune* emphatically endorsed compulsory arbitration.[58]

Settlement of the anthracite strike diminished the demand for immediate adoption of this reform, as Charles Francis Adams argued that compulsory investigation and publicity were more consistent with American traditions. However, the *Trenton Times* expounded the message of *A Country Without Strikes* in a dozen editorials. *The Pilgrim* declared that in New Zealand there could have been no anthracite coal strike, and cited Lloyd's "notable services" in familiarizing the public with the Arbitration Act's operation.[59]

In 1902, also, Reeves gave New Zealand's reforms full coverage in his comprehensive treatise, whose circulation and favorable reviewing Lloyd furthered. Aided by new data from Wellington he kept his lectures, newspaper statements, and articles abreast of developments. Critical analyses of New Zealand compulsory arbitration by Albert Métin, André Siegfried, Judge A. B. Backhouse, the Victoria Royal Commission, and Victor S. Clark's 1903 investigation for the United States Bureau of Labor Statistics substantiated his account of its effectiveness. Ex-Senator Richard F. Pettigrew, "Mark" Hanna's foe, traveled "with and by" *Newest England*. Only Lloyd's books, articles, and newspaper statements achieved a general circulation, however. To these and his supporters in many areas must be ascribed the vogue for Antipodean democracy that characterized the "Progressive Mind" and created a favorable climate of opinion for welfare reform measures during the "Era of Theodore Roosevelt." Thomas E. Watson of Georgia, the President's new friend, declared that *Newest England* is one of the *great* books." Professors Jenks and Clark utilized Lloyd's New Zealand books in their college classes. Students at the University of Nebraska and Earlham College studied them and debated compulsory arbitration. Ely compiled a bibliography on arbitration. Lloyd lectured successfully on compulsory arbitration at Allegheny College.[60] In London William Clarke and Hobson endorsed the reform.

During 1903 Lloyd defended New Zealand vigorously from American detractors. In *Boyce's Weekly,* the *Sunday School Times,* and *Good Housekeeping* he supported Seddon's régime, describing New Zealand's system of social security for labor, religious, and feminine readers. Irked by the attacks of Hugo Mayer of Harvard on New Zealand welfare democracy, he asked Sir Joseph Ward, Minister of Commerce at Wellington, to prepare a comprehensive statement of that system's operation. This he would give "influential circulation in America." It would support his writing, he said, which was motivated *"not alone for the sake of New Zealand, but for the sake of the ideas of reform in which New Zealand has taken the lead and which I hope to see acclimitized in America, and indeed, throughout the whole world."* He distributed Reeves's articles and statements in the American press.[61]

From Wellington Tregear conveyed Premier Seddon's "very kindest regards . . . and his fervent hopes for the success of Compulsory Arbitration in the States." Tregear's "may you have health and strength to carry on the heavy fight" encouraged Lloyd to persist in the campaign whereby, he believed, America might be revitalized.[62]

Despite the opposition of Gompers and many employers' associations he knew that this cause was gaining ground. Some believed as he did that it was the alternative to "compulsory spoliation." He persuaded John Mitchell that that policy was successful and beneficial to trades unions in the Antipodes.

Lloyd spoke incessantly in its behalf. His articles received wide publicity. Mitchell conceded that compulsory arbitration was feasible in America in the restricted field of transportation. Albert Brandt's foreman in Trenton, an influential leader in the International Typographical Union, espoused the policy after reading *A Country Without Strikes.* Students in universities and colleges debated the policy's merits and wrote to Lloyd for data. He predicted to Reeves that the anthracite coal strike arbitration of 1902-1903 would advance the reform's prospects.[63]

Lloyd erred in this prediction, as the adamant opposition of the *United Mine Workers Journal* indicated.[64] He acknowledged regretfully the opposition of most trades unionists to the reform.[65] His premature death removed compulsory arbitration's leading advocate from the scene when middle class interest in it was rising rapidly.

His agitation undoubtedly popularized voluntary arbitration as an effective method of resolving industrial strife and expedited development of the Conciliation Service of the United States Department of Labor. Of greater importance was his success in winning respectability in American thought for general welfare policies by vindicating the practical success of Antipodean democracy. This enhanced his reputation as the leading publicist of the "new democracy."

Chapter XX

Dean of American Reform During the McKinley Era

Toward Man the Creator

Lloyd's immediate sphere of reform activity after "The Battle of the Standards" continued to be the Chicago area until 1899. Defeat at the St. Louis Populist Convention had smashed the political instrument he had fashioned to achieve the "Co-operative Commonwealth." Freed from the dilemmas that confront the social prophet who attempts to merge moral idealism with political ideas, he witnessed the fragmentation of the radical movement. Debs's seizure of the tradition of independent radical political action was made possible within a year partially by Lloyd's disillusionment with third party politics. Discouraged by the failure of the populace to rally decisively to his political movement after *Wealth Against Commonwealth* exposures he castigated the Populists for having been "tricked and bulldozed and betrayed at St. Louis into supporting Bryan," and criticized them for lacking "some common article of faith." Ineffectiveness of reform would continue, he predicted, until "the leaders" drilled "their followers" in "a definite and symmetrical body of truths" that would provide "a common standard by which they can act together without leaders."[1]

He forgot the common antimonopolism that had held the Populists together and also the Fabians' warning that America would achieve its reform by pragmatic, piecemeal methods.[2] He was so discouraged after the 1896 election that he doubted it

424

was "possible to carry on democracy by means of . . . party government," since existing methods of campaigning and voting prevented expression of the people's "real will." As he turned to the co-operative movement he remarked, "political methods are an antiquated and inefficient means of . . . effectuating democracy."[3]

Ely warned him successfully after McKinley's victory against attempting to "do something" with the Socialist Labor Party, and promised to formulate an antimonopolist program supporting "every measure" advancing "equality of opportunity" and increased "opportunities for the masses." At Ely's suggestion Lloyd cultivated Governor-elect Hazen S. Pingree of Detroit. Ely's influence explains partially Lloyd's refusal to lead in organizing the "new Socialist Party" which Victor Berger advocated in February 1897 while a guest at The Wayside. Lloyd sent copies of Herbert W. Casson's demand for nonpolitical propaganda by "evolutionary Socialists" to Bellamy, Debs, Parsons, Morgan, Prestonia Mann of the *American Fabian* of which he was a contributing editor, and Berger. Only the Marxians Berger and Morgan differed. The future, Lloyd told Berger, lay with "American Socialism. What is the use in voting? They will do the counting. And we can't shoot. They own all the guns."[4]

A month earlier, in the *Progressive Review,* Lloyd had informed British New Liberals and Socialists that Americans "never will" accept the class struggle. He conceded, however, that the divided non-Marxian American radicals were "the most distracted and helpless body of political Radicalism in the world today, and the most uncertain element in America Political Arithmetic."[5] In Chicago he declared that an "ethical renaissance" was essential to extend democratic collectivism in the urban world. He criticized Populist moderates' attempts to combat abuses of "the syndicates and plutocrats" with halfway measures.[6] Disillusioned he turned away from politics to work as a publicist and leader, inspirer, and participant in an astonishing number of nonpolitical reform movements.

Soon after McKinley's victory Lloyd proposed a nonpolitical

conference representing all reform elements to coordinate future activities. This produced an immediate meeting and successive informal and formal national reform conferences. By assistance to numerous causes, his information bureau, and the social program of The Wayside and The Watch House, Lloyd enhanced the *camaradarie*[7] and an *esprit de corps* that enabled reform during the McKinley era to lay the foundations of the "Progressive Era." His leadership in the antitrust, co-operative, and compulsory arbitration movements and his campaign for academic freedom gave continuity to radical reform while broadening its field of action and widening his influence.

Radical reform's short-lived utopianism and continuing pluralism, which he shared, were reminiscent of the Age of Jackson. However the continuing influence of trades unionism, the ethical movement, Christian Socialism, Fabianism, and Antipodean welfare democracy, which he represented, plus his welfare theory, Ely's new economics, and Ward's sociology grafted a complex ideology and program upon the simple idealism and evangelical humanitarianism of the earlier epoch. This was made evident by Bliss' *Encyclopaedia,* to which Lloyd's circle contributed with candid realism.

Reform shifted its focus swiftly after 1896 to the urban world. There a swelling middle-class protest seized the leadership and attacked with moderate, dynamic pragmatism the corruption, poverty, and public utility abuses of the cities. Lloyd agreed with Bemis that only in large cities were "consistently radical economic and social views" expressed freely. Debs's gathering of rump Populists, Fabians, and gradualist Socialists into his Social Democracy soon left Lloyd with a mixed constituency of new type liberals, humanitarians, Social Gospel clergy and social settlement residents, and nonpolitical, non-Marxian radicals. Among these his influence was enhanced by the early passing of Bellamy and Henry George. While reform relied more than ever upon formal organization, Lloyd's achievements and influence transcended institutional limits and appealed to the younger leaders who began to attack urban and national problems.

During the twilight of Altgeld's administration in Illinois Lloyd advocated municipal ownership of traction in a symposium for the Illinois Bureau of Labor Statistics. Then Governor John R. Tanner's inauguration restricted the sphere of reform activity abruptly to Chicago. He deleted Lloyd's proposal from that report. The Illinois Supreme Court had invalidated the eight hour day for women section of the Factory Act in *Ritchie* v. *The People*. Tanner appointed a convicted violator of that law to enforce the remnant as Factory Inspector. Altgeld's temporary retirement and subsequent preoccupation with local issues symbolized the changed situation.[8]

In December 1896 Lloyd convoked a Hull-House Social and Economic Conference to stimulate reform. Gladden, Ernest Crosby, John Dewey, and Charles Henderson of the University of Chicago, Boring, Graham Taylor, Edward O. Brown, and William Douglas of the Chicago Theological Seminary discussed Tolstoian theories, the Social Gospel, Fabianism, co-operation, the Single Tax, social and business ethics, and education's relation to social reform. Lloyd proposed "The Money of the New Conscience," urging that "the money of justice" be based upon a weighted commodity index, a proposal that derived partially from Ruskin and Simon Newcomb. Taylor, the Chairman, called it "eminently constructive." All who heard Lloyd were "impressed by the force of his thought, the grace of his style, and the stir of his spirit," the *Chicago Advance* reported. He considered the social problem essentially metaphysical, a position that gratified Dewey.[9]

Lloyd expanded his monetary reform proposal in the *Chicago Chronicle* and replied to a *New York Evening Post* attack on his speech. Although monetary reform alone could not accomplish social reform, he said, "the real need is for a social program of co-operation and anti-monopoly," of which "a better money would be" an aspect. In the emergency clearinghouse certificates issued during financial panics he perceived accurately "the germ of the currency of the future." He cited the Isle of Guernsey's financing of a market house with paper currency, the Populist subtreasury plan, and Tsarist agricultural credit as precedents for a commodity-based currency. Gold was invariably the money of monopoly, he said, but the "coinage of commodities" would "give the poor man a chance" and prevent panics. This proposal foreshadowed the Federal Reserve Banks' elastic currency based primarily upon commercial paper, and provoked much comment. He urged his commodity dollar plan repeatedly thereafter.[10]

The manuscript of this Hull House address is replete with citations to Jevons, Kinley, Wolff, and Ruskin. Maximum production was the major object of a sound credit system, Lloyd argued. The solution of the "money question" must rest upon enforcement of the Golden Rule in social relations, assist labor to command the living wage and the farmer "living prices for his product," and destroy monopoly in finance. This was the economic justice that labor and agrarian radicals had sought during the preceding generation to achieve via monetary reform. Lloyd also proposed the insurance of bank deposits by clearing houses or a national agency similar to the later FDIC. If adopted locally his monetary system would make Chicago the business leader of the world. This address modified Lloyd's Labor-Populist collectivism. While still favoring municipalization of utilities, the graduated income tax, government regulation, and "conquest of selfishness by the new conscience," he would "rescue the individual" by guaranteeing him "the open career." This would realize the "ideal of all human progress" by combining individual liberty with "the divine way" of voluntary brotherhood based upon "the Golden Rule of the cooperators." To Ely he ranked monetary reform with labor and trusts in importance because "the money institutions of society are as crude and cruel as any other of the economic institutions, and . . . have been as thoroughly usurped for the benefit of the few as the other forms of industrial control." Monetary reform should be "kept to the fore as an indispensable part of the social program," he asserted. He was so opposed to bimetallism that he distributed Edward Atkinson's gold standard pamphlets and wrote him, "I am perfectly willing to hold your knives while you stab the free silver folly."[11]

Early in 1897 Lloyd and Hull House joined the Municipal Voters' League in stimulating popular protests in Chicago against Yerkes' and the "Gas Trust's" attempts to secure fifty-year legislative extensions of their franchises. Lloyd addressed a gigantic anti-Humphrey Bill mass meeting sponsored by Hull House. He wrote a pamphlet against Yerkes' proposal and served on the Anti-Humphrey Bill Committee of the Chicago Federation of Labor after persuading it to co-operate after William Kent's antipathy for trades unions antagonized it. Lloyd drafted the resolutions which, when presented at the special legislative session supported by the Civic Federation, other societies, and Mayor Carter H. Harrison, II, defeated the "Eternal Monopoly Bills." Unfortunately, the Allen Bill satisfactory to Yerkes was corruptly enacted after those delegations returned home. That act authorized a referendum on municipal utility franchise renewals, and transferred back to Chicago the struggle between the utilities and the citizenry. As the Voters' League continued to purge the Common Council, Lloyd advised Kent on tactics against the dangerous, wealthy "bribe givers" whom Pingree termed "our dangerous classes." Growing support for municipal ownership emerged, led by Altgeld and then by John M. Harlan.[12]

During 1895 Lloyd had been apprehensive of an inevitable revolution if the "intolerable" monopoly trend continued. To Steuart in Scotland he wrote cynically after McKinley's victory, "civilization is a humbug pretending that its actions are dictated by some nobler motives."[13] However, a "Manuscript of 1896"[14] completed during the anti-Yerkes protest revealed a softening in mood. Lloyd still believed the populace would have to break "the stewards of power" if driven to extremes. Yet, he expressed there an optimistic faith in society's ability to create the world in which its members wished to live. The manuscript developed his Emersonian-Positivist religious thought further and harmonized it with his social theory, wavering between Labor-Populist collectivism and the Golden Rule voluntarism of "The Money of the New Conscience." Their interacting contribution to "the social curve of progress" he soon asserted to William T. Harris,[15]

During 1895-97 Lloyd also attempted to assimilate the religious spirit to reform as an indispensable dynamic, beginning with the Debs reception at Battery D. There he announced that "the religion of self-sacrifice" must be the "religion of the Co-operative Commonwealth." He informed Bliss that "if the new religion adequate for the age is to be developed the old term 'Christ-Church' must be discarded." A spirit of universal brotherhood was "budding," particularly "in business," he concluded after re-examining the theories of Ingram and the London Positivists. This trend would produce a great expansion of religion, and "is the keynote of our times. I am full of hope, nothing seems dark," he wrote to Mills.

After addressing the Detroit Conference of Applied Christian Workers and Social Reformers in 1895, he wrote to another friend, "I put God and Man in one class, and draw no dividing line between them. This . . . has gradually grown . . . spontaneously, in me into a firm faith and a very inspiring one."[16]

He began a "Bible of the Co-operative Commonwealth" including "Only the Social," substituting the "Epic of Progress. From Brothers to Plutocrats to . . . Utopia" for the "primitive idea of finding inspired authority and divine ideal." Christ was "the Shakespeare of Ethics" but not "the Son of God," Lloyd asserted. It is essential "to our religious and secular progress to recognise that his teachings, or those attributed to him" contain mistakes and "are not necessarily true for our time." Yet, "his teachings were the generalization of the best social experience of centuries, and are the sure clue to the solution of our present social problem. . . . I see that the new relations of humanity must be on a religious basis. But it must be a broader and newer basis that that of Christianity."[17]

Permeating this "Manuscript of 1896" was an ardent faith in man's divine creative power, which Lloyd had conceived during 1888. This he developed. To his theory of creative intelligence he assimilated Emersonian, Fabian, cooperative, feminist, mass union, and progressive education conceptions. A "Summary of New Forces at work to produce the New Era" exhibits these :

> The new woman. The new child.
> The new man—the laborer.
> *The new democracy—without politics.*
> The new industry—collective.
> The new religion—*man the redeemer.*
> The new nation—the internation.
> The new political economy—*of production for use,* of other self-interest, new money, new land held by use.
> The new Church—of the deed.
> *The new education—of Fit Fabricando Faber—of doing while learning and learning by doing, of school and livelihood woven into one web.*

To this Lloyd added, "The consent of the governed is the political realization of *this divinity of democracy—the creative will of the people* which is to be substituted for the old God."[18] Thus he produced the sociology of a secular, liberal religion that developed the progressive potentialities of Emersonian social love, the Golden Rule, brotherhood, and "Man the Creator" which he assimilated to Darwinian evolution. This was his reply to the deterministic Social Darwinism of Benjamin Kidd's *Social Evolution,* although Lloyd welcomed its stress upon altruism. Regarding "God" as the greatest of historical fictions, his completed religious faith was rational, liberal, fraternal, transcendental and collectivist, Positivist, humane, and Western. It cultivated the community of workers, demanded social justice based upon a balance between individualism and collectivism, and envisaged the mixed economy of the Co-operative Commonwealth. For this it offered a broad rationale. Its worldwide extension as a classless society based upon the religion of work would bring a progressive peace, Lloyd prophesied. Opposed to the Oriental mysticism and "self-surrender of the Asiatic mind" embodied in Christianity with its "morbid and unnatural" estimate of man as "a degraded, lost, sinful being," it offered "hope and enthusiasm" that man could achieve heaven on earth by giving primacy to "collective self-interest."

Thus, in man's creative heart, mind, and conscience Lloyd

discovered "The Godhead" that would advance civilization and achieve welfare democracy based upon Golden Rule ethics, but no static utopia. "It would show that the Republic, the school, society, were unceasing evolution . . . that the real division is between Radicals or Progressives, and Conservatives." He attributed to mankind collectively the perfectibility, divinity, and creative power that Emerson and Rudolph Maeterlinck reserved for the individual. He discovered in the labor movement the mass power and social intelligence that would overthrow industrial privilege, institute a generally beneficial redress of grievances, and institute welfare democracy. The treatise completed the development of Lloyd's unique social philosophy, and enlarges our understanding of his Labor-Populist leadership and the social objectives of *Wealth Against Commonwealth*. The manuscript was written *two years before* he discovered in the co-operatives the institutional manifestations of "Man the Creator," and *four years before* he saw it functioning in the Antipodes. He sought to implement its objectives persistently thereafter by writing, lecturing, practical reforms, and seeking validation of his program in overseas democracies. The potential that "Man the Creator" possessed for future Progressivism became apparent in 1906 when an edited version, published by Jane Addams and Anne Withington in *Man the Social Creator*, received much acclaim..

A Golden Rule Disciple

During 1896-97 Lloyd acquired an unusual disciple. This was President Samuel M. Jones of the Acme Sucker Rod Company, Toledo, Ohio, a manufacturer of oil well machinery and an admirer of *Wealth Against Commonwealth*. They had met in 1893 and again at the Hull House Conference of December 1896. Their friendship strengthened when Lloyd lectured in Toledo early in 1897 on a series with Jane Addams and Gladden. Lloyd aroused the admiration of the *Toledo Evening News* with "Uses and Abuses of Corporations," and learned that Jones was President of the Western Oil Men's Association. After inventing improved oil well machinery he had rented an abandoned factory, staffed it with the unemployed, and begun operations, posting the Golden Rule as shop rules. He paid the highest wages for the eight-hour day in Toledo, granted a week's summer vacation with pay, provided picnics for his entire force and their families, served luncheons at cost at his plant in "Golden Rule Hall," and transformed a nearby vacant property into "Golden Rule Park." There a band organized by his employees provided music on Sundays.[19]

Lloyd's lecture aided Jones's attempt to defeat the Toledo Traction Company's proposed comprehensive franchise extension on terms disadvantageous to the city. After Lloyd's departure he defeated Republican "Boss" Guy G. Major, a Hanna lieutenant, and was nominated for Mayor. During the campaign Lloyd advised him on the ethical and democratic significance of the movement for a new municipal democracy led by Albert Shaw, Parkhurst, and Pingree. In *Wealth Against Commonwealth* Jones found justification for his policies. It had inspired his Company's novel "Golden Rule" management. He now demanded traction franchises in the public interest, eventual municipal ownership, courted the wage-earners, repudiated the "machine," advocated nonpartisan municipal government, cultural development of the city, and application of the Golden Rule in municipal affairs. Although opposed by the "organization" he won by a majority of 500 votes and telegraphed Lloyd jubilantly, "I am elected in spite of six hundred saloons the traction co. and the devil."[20]

Lloyd answered with an admonitory, congratulatory letter, to which Jones replied significantly : "I have no other purpose than to use the larger field of opportunity in just the way that you suggest, feeling confident that I can do more along these lines. Yes a thousand times more than I can by devoting myself to the business of reducing taxation for a lot of rich tax dodgers. . . . I have a larger conception . . . that will explain what I understand by 'good government'; it is expressed in the word "Brotherhood.""[21] Thus inspired and coached, Jones soon became the leader of the Civic Revival in Ohio.

To Albert Shaw Lloyd wrote of him as he did to Spahr and

Stead : "I want you to become interested in him. If 'we 'uns' are ever going to accomplish anything . . . we must back each other up as faithfully as the other side do in their 'blind pools' and unconscious class conspiracies." Those editors hailed the Toledoan as a new type mayor. As "Golden Rule" Jones, he introduced the eight-hour day for municipal employees and the merit system into the police force. Thanking Lloyd wittily for the favorable publicity, he sought practical suggestions from "you and other kindred spirits."[22]

Lloyd introduced him at the second Crosbyside Conference of Social Gospel clergy and lay reformers in June in an old-fashioned hotel on Lake George. "Big, bluff, strong, warm-hearted" Jones impressed Eltweed Pomeroy, the secretary, as a simple man of action displaying the zeal of a new convert to reform. Jones was initiated there into America's upper reform leadership, and achieved fame as a courageous practitioner of the new ethics and municipal general welfare policies. He became Lloyd's most noted disciple in public life during the McKinley era. Jones evinced his indebtedness to "The Maister" in his *The New Right* and *Letters of Love and Labor* as the century closed.[23]

Dean of Reform

In the "Journal" of that Conference of approximately thirty men and women, Pomeroy also described Lloyd. The sessions were attended by eminent figures invited by Lloyd, Crosby, and President Gates : university presidents Andrews and Smart; professors Ross, Jenks, Seligman, Ely, Kinley, Henry C. Adams, Graham Taylor, Felix Adler, and Jessie Macy; John A. Hobson of London, Bellamy, Henry George, Howells, Nelson, *The Outlook's* editorial staff, Pomeroy, Abbot, Darrow, Jane Addams, Robert Woods, Frances Willard, Gompers, Carroll D. Wright, Edward King, Salter, Stead, Prestonia Mann, and a squadron of Social Gospel clergy. B. Fay Mills's hospitality and genial wit drew the different elements together.

As the most potent personality present, Lloyd was compared with him by Pomeroy, a businessman and practical reformer.

The lines of Mills' face and figure are horizontal, broad; the lines of Lloyd's are vertical, lofty. He is the most picturesque man here with his seamed melancholy face and warm, quiet, gentle manners and the soft pressure in hand-shake of his delicate, taper-fingered hand so different from Mills' strong grasp. His dress and demeanor are so unobtrusive as to be distinctive; you do not know but feel that he is well-dressed. His language is picturesque, poetic, imaginative, illuminative. His thought is keen, incisive, and so sympathetic and sensitive to all wrongs as at times to be almost bitter and revolutionary against the wrong-doers. He is pre-eminently a lovable man. He is as delicate, as fragile, as beautiful as a Sevres vase, as intense and as musical as a violin strung ready for the master's hand, as sympathetic as a woman. His sensitiveness is his weak point as his feelings for others would at times make him almost cruel in avenging their wrongs. The social conscience is overdeveloped in him.

Lloyd and the Rev. Ernest H. Crosby, a handsome, tall, traveled, cultured mystic and sentimentalist who was America's leading Tolstoian, had planned the program.[24]

Lloyd opened the meeting with a quietly delivered but very moving address that greatly impressed Jenks and many others who did not accept all his radical position. Later, after the discussion of many reform movements, he reported on Ruskin Colony and Parsons explained Debs' colonization plan. During the program devoted to "My Philosophy of Life," Lloyd's "wonderfully spiritual address" presented his "Man the Creator" religious philosophy with its promise of industrial democracy and industrial peace. He feared, he said, recurring to a theme he had developed earlier, that there would not be a revolution in America, meaning, of course, the constitutional, peaceful Anglo-Saxon reorganization that he sought. His discussion of "The Morality of the New Conscience" was also well received. After the Conference he was continued as chairman of the committee to arrange a third annual conference and left for Sakonnet the dean of American reformers.[25]

Yet, he and Kinley were dissatisfied. The Conference had been dominated by believers in "panaceas," Kinley observed, some so zealous that they did not exhibit "the true spirit of reform." Lloyd did not schedule another Crosbyside Conference, despite Pomeroy's protests.[26] With his aid, however, he arranged later for the National Conference of Social and Political Reform at Buffalo in 1899.

The Crosbyside conferences strengthened his ties with the Social Gospelers. So did his role in the Mills-Rockefeller affair and his support of *The Kingdom* during its litigation with the American Book Company. Leighton Williams persuaded him to address the Marlborough sessions of the Brotherhood of the Kingdom in New York in 1898, 1900, and annually thereafter. The Union Reform League elected Lloyd its first president in January, 1899. This he declined, but accepted the ranking vice-presidency of the Social Reform Union which the League was entitled after reorganization at the Buffalo Conference.[27] Then, in recognition of his standing as an authority on radical movements, the editors of the *Encyclopaedia Britannica* persuaded him to contribute an article on "Anarchism."

POTTER-ROCKEFELLER

Lloyd's friendship with Williams made him privy to a scandal involving the Tabernacle Baptist Church of New York City. Most of this episode, which made headlines during 1896-98, is beyond this study's purview. It is significant for this study because of its contemporaneity with Rockefeller's attempt to secure clerical and new school economists' exoneration of his business methods in the Mills-Rockefeller episode, and because this second imbroglio quickly aligned Lloyd with Rockefeller's opponents and clarified his attitude towards that magnate further.

The episode began in 1893, when Rockefeller and other benefactors withdrew support from the Tabernacle Church after charges of immorality were made against its pastor, the

Rev. D. C. Potter, by his new subordinate, J. W. Putnam, who aired his accusations in public print but declined to present them to the church's investigating committee. Potter sued him for libel during which an attempt to assassinate the former failed. Putnam was given another pulpit by the New York Baptist City Mission Society, to which Rockefeller assigned his Tabernacle Church mortgages. That Society foreclosed the mortgages and employed private detectives to oust Potter.

Williams attacked the ouster in a sermon to Potter's church, attributing it to the desire of powerful men to crush its pastor. He denounced the methods employed by the Mission Society. Rockefeller then persuaded Mrs. Potter to attempt to divorce her husband. This Potter defeated. He won libel suits against leading metropolitan newspapers, and also a court order awarding him repossession of the Tabernacle Church.

He was condemned, however, by a Committee of a Council of the New York City Baptist Churches after unfair investigation of Putnam's charges, as its manuscript minutes and stenographic report reveal. Instead of confining itself to Putnam's charge of immorality, that Committee investigated Potter's administration of his Church also. Despite Williams' repeated protests, it declined to follow customary procedures in taking and weighing evidence, and dispensed with legal safeguards. Admitting much hearsay, the Committee exhibited marked animus against Potter and put him in the position of having to disprove the charges against him. The burden of proof should have rested upon his detractors. The Committee's majority declined to hear or receive a statement and documents offered by Potter in his defense or to enter them on the record. Testimony indicated that Rockefeller's desire to protect his private reputation, and the majority's wish to avoid alienating a powerful, generous benefactor and prevent a public scandal involving him motivated its determination to accord Potter less than justice. A subcommittee of seven ministers had heard Mrs. Charles Williams's confession that disclosed the reason for Rockefeller's animus toward Potter.

Potter had employed the New York Chief of Police on the

latter's initiative as an intermediary in an offer to surrender to
Rockefeller certain documents impugning his character if the
persecution of himself was stopped. The Police Chief reported
later that the negotiation had failed, but declined to return the
documents, saying he had destroyed them.

Potter secured other affidavits, as from a Rev. Dr. Boyd, recently removed to St. Louis, and Miss J. S. Ross, Tabernacle
Church pastor's assistant. She had witnessed episodes corroborating Potter's eyewitness experience which, according to him,
had led to the ruin of himself and his Church. It was to Boyd
that Rockefeller had confessed the episode after Potter had
taken him to him. During the "trial" every effort was made by
hostile witnesses to destroy the characters of Boyd and Ross and
to protect Rockefeller's reputation.

After a fictitious Committee plurality found against Potter,
a minority led by Williams, a trustee of the University of
Chicago, protested vigorously. He jeopardized his directorate
of Amity House, by declaring that Potter was grossly wronged.
He had maintained consistently during the "trial" that Potter
was entitled to justice irrespective of the effect upon Rockefeller's
benefactions. His minority's powerful dissent declared the
so-called majority's report unjust, unsubstantiated, and the result of indefensible procedures. When the City Mission Society
offered to pay $19,000 damages to Potter and Miss Ross, if they
would sign a legal release of claims against it and Rockefeller,
it admitted where the right in the matter lay.[28]

As Williams informed him of it, the episode enlightened
Lloyd on hitherto undisclosed aspects of Rockefeller's character. As Lloyd learned from Potter and Williams of the inward-
ness of the affair, he informed friends of it. He warned the wife
of the editor of *Ford's Christian Repository,* a year before the
contest between the Tabernacle Church and Mission Society
reached a climax, that "a terrible scandal is all ready to break
out in New York in Baptist circles which . . . convinces people
. . . that a man who is rotten on one side of his nature is pretty
sure to be rotten on some other."[29] He urged the *American
Fabian* to prepare for the sudden bursting of a " 'Diamond-

Necklace' " affair! He asked Bowles to prepare to discuss in the *Springfield Republican* all its bearings and inner history. "In its social and political implications," Lloyd said, "it is much more important" than the Beecher scandal since "it involves the richest and most powerful man in the United States, *and the woman part of it is the least important.*" When the press publicized the struggle he sought Roger Sherman's advice for Potter, informing that attorney that there was "a tremendous sensation underneath" the "Rockefeller-Potter racket in New York."[30]

Bowles investigated but concluded that the *Republican* could not lead in exploiting this. Lloyd said he had not expected it to do so, but was anxious that when the matter became public his paper should "make up its mind with full knowledge." However, "what is portentously and universally and eternally important is the fact that a rich and guilty man can use all the resources of the courts, church, press, and society to crush an innocent and poor man. That we cannot tolerate."[31]

During Potter's "trial," March to May 1897, Lloyd noted the *Independent*'s sympathy with the attempt "to break" him and asserted that New York papers should give the matter "a great deal more attention" instead of bowing "to a cowardly fear of money on the other side. We were not given our country by that sort of spirit, and we cannot keep it so," he warned Williams. "If this moves on to the consummation which is now promised an opportunity will have been lost for the salvation of this country which may never recur."

To Bowles, who had editorialized on the subject, he emphasized the "opportunity to strike a blow at the most dangerous enemy the American people have to-day if delivered as it can be by shrewd and yet brave men." This "might easily be crippling. I rest this belief of mine on the opinion that the reputation which the chief person concerned holds with the body of the people for sanctity and generosity is today one of the strongest bulwarks of the whole system of monopoly and the tyrannical use of concentrated wealth." Lloyd asked *The Outlook* and *New York World* to give greater attention to the episode. He referred

Arthur Brisbane to Williams for information demonstrating "that there never was a case involving interests so great in which the risk of publication was so slight." Brisbane was deaf to his urging that publication of the facts would render Rockefeller "completely helpless."[32]

Lyman Abbott was willing to publish the entire story. However, Boyd broke his promise of full support to Potter and declined to tell what he knew. "Without that the Explosion would have wrecked only the journal," Spahr informed Lloyd. Having come to the Adirondacks while Lloyd was in Britain, when Potter's lawyer attempted to serve a summons on him Boyd evaded him and returned to St. Louis.[33] Although Lloyd learned of the charge of immorality made against Potter during the "trial," he knew that Boyd pronounced him "entirely trustworthy and unquestionably moral" on the strength of personal acquaintance. Williams informed him that the "trial's" disclosures confirmed "earlier impressions."

Lloyd was stunned by the Committee majority's verdict against Potter. Williams sent him the minority report and observed :

> It would be impossible in a letter to describe adequately the series of outrages perpetrated in this Council and the injustice of its findings in the face of the evidence presented. We are at a loss what to say or what to do. It seems of comparatively little moment that even the majority were forced to relinquish the charges of adultery and the charge of attending questionable resorts for immoral purposes, as well as the most serious and specific charge of dishonesty in respect to the Denike Fund. Nor do we take much comfort in the fact that the 1300 pages of evidence taken . . . are in our possession and should thoroughly disprove to any fair-minded man the charges against Dr. Potter. For who can we get to read the evidence or in what way can a summary be brought before the public.[34]

Would Lloyd do this?

He gathered voluminous data on the subject. After studying it he decided adversely, *as he certainly would not have done had he entertained a personal animus against Rockefeller.* Lloyd had helped to finance Potter's defense and publication funds, and now provided him anonymously a modest weekly stipend.

At the Marlborough Conference of August 1898 he urged vainly that Williams protest to the Baptist Conference against the New York City Baptist Church Council's action. In November he told Williams that *"the only effective"* protest had to *"come from the representative of the Church, which has been the chief victim of this outrage,"* and that the man wo made it would be *"even a more sacrificial personage than Potter himself."*[35] Confessing that he had thought of being "the Zola of this story," his judgment was that "for the sake of the truth" the matter had to be "dealt with from within the province where the occurrences originated and where the actors reside, and by those whose duty and position give them not only a right to speak but the duty not to remain silent." If the protesting clergy published "the truth . . . the whole case for the people against the wrongdoers acquires a new strength, because the wrongdoer is exposed in a new field, on a new issue, and by a new hand. Surely, there are persons in the church to defend the church and its Christianity in such an awful episode as this!"[36] Neither Williams nor the protesting minority accepted this pointed challenge, although the Tabernacle Church published an account of the episode three years later that was just to Potter. As son of a clergyman Lloyd appreciated the issues involved.

The flagrant abuse of Rockefeller power in the Baptist Church of New York City corroborated emphatically *Wealth Against Commonwealth*'s assertion that giant monopoly was gaining control of the churches. Vigorous clerical exposure of and opposition to this episode might have destroyed that magnate's hold on the Baptists and discredited his monopolistic industrial system that his reputation for piety was sanctifying for so many Christians.

However, the causes and character of the episode became known inevitably to the Social Gospel clergy and leading lay reformers. Williams was Secretary of the Brotherhood of the Kingdom of the Baptist Church. Although he was a trustee of the University of Chicago he and his family long resented the injustice to Potter. His widow gave the author of this treatise the complete manuscript record of the "trial" so that the truth about it might at long last be told. Although Lloyd dissuaded Lee Meriwether, St. Louis' influential political reformer, from fictionalizing the Potter-Rockefeller episode, he told Morley Roberts of London that the subject was a good theme for a book! Lloyd undoubtedly talked of the episode to members of his circle at The Wayside and The Watch House. The spread of the inside knowledge of why Potter was ruined influenced the upper reform world's appraisal of Rockefeller, the Standard Oil, the "trusts," and the concentration of economic power in the United States. The same knowledge, to the informed, validated *Wealth Against Commonwealth*'s analysis of Rockefeller and the Standard Oil. To Lloyd it completed his appraisal of that powerful magnate.

While perusing the "trial" record, Lloyd asked Williams if he had correctly detected in Miss Ross's testimony evidence that she had seen the same "commission of a crime by a great man," such as Potter had witnessed, "and had been persecuted ever since. . . . Is publication of the facts to be expected?" he asked pointedly.[37]

REFORM MISCELLANY

In May 1898 he joined the agitation for the release of the republican prisoners in the Kingdom of Italy because of a telegram from Mrs. Dario Papa, former Fidella Dinsmore of Boston and wife of an Italian Republican, to the Twentieth Century Club. Lloyd joined Howells, Mead, Hale, and others in organizing Boston and national Italian Prisoners Aid committees. He wrote to the *Transcript* to support Mrs. Papa's agitation. He asked Massingham to reply in the *London Daily Chronicle* to W. J. Stillman, who opposed the movement. He recruited a

Chicago committee and introduced Mrs. Papa to Lillian Wald and Mary McDowell of Henry Street Settlement. He sent her money before leaving for New Zealand. He expressed to Minna Smith of D. C. Heath & Company his fury at wealthy mid-westerners who refused to aid this humanitarian relief of the Italian prisoners. "They are restrained by that very shrewd timidity of capitalism and society which knows perfectly well that any agitation anywhere for right has in it possibilities of danger to them in their wrongholds. . . . Franklin MacVeagh, as fine, cultured, enlightened a man as lives . . . laughs at the suggestion that he should join and says he will write me some day why he does not. I know why." While he was in the Antipodes the agitation obliged the Italian government to release the prisoners. This victory enhanced the transAtlantic rapport between reformers.[28]

During the same years Lloyd enthusiastically supported Theodore Gilman's proposal of a national clearing-house currency as a means of checking the concentration of wealth and of shifting the center of world finance from London to New York City. He asked Byron L. Smith of the Northern Trust Company to present the plan to Chicago bankers. He circulated Gilman's books and pamphlets, and persuaded Shibley, Willis Abbot, and Van Benthuysen to confer with Gilman. The plan was presented to Lyman Gage, Secretary of the Treasury, and was included in the Republican platform of 1900. After the panic of 1907, Congress authorized an emergency clearing-house currency and a temporary national currency based upon commercial paper for issuance during future panics, embodying portions of Gilman's and Lloyd's plans for currency reform.[39]

More time-consuming was the Direct Legislation movement. Although this had interested Lloyd for years, he did not participate in it until the McKinley era. Eltweed Pomeroy, who was made editor of the *Direct Legislation Record* during the St. Louis Populist convention in 1896, persuaded him to endorse DL early in 1897. Previously Lloyd had regarded the Swiss referendum with reservations because legislation could be exempted from it. J. Ramsey MacDonald and the Fabian Society informed him that Swiss labor legislation rarely survived it. Lloyd had feared that the public could not prevent the referendum from being controlled by "wealth and monopoly." After Pomeroy converted him, Lloyd still believed there was ample political machinery for the public to "put an end to privileges and monopolies" if it understood "the economic question." He contributed to the Direct Legislation League organized at St. Louis, July 21, 1896, believing that DL was "a most promising means of destroying corrupt legislation, establishing real self-government, and opening the door to every true reform." He wrote in *New Time* after returning from Australasia that as the ideal method of restoring popular control "initiative and referendum must be supported by every true believer in free government" in the symposium where Lyman Abbott made his famous statement, "the remedy for the evils of democracy is more democracy."[40]

While he did not believe DL was the most important reform of the moment, Lloyd circulated its literature, cultivated Pomeroy, subscribed to a Swiss newspaper, and assisted the *Record*. The agitation developed strong DL sentiment in the upper Mississippi Valley and Far West, while retaining organized labor's support. After South Dakota and Utah adopted DL the Democrats endorsed it. Fifty-two state constitutional amendments authorizing use of the referendum were voted upon in 1900. During the next summer Lloyd informed Professor Stephen Bauer in Zurich that "the Swiss ideas of direct legislation by the people are making more progress among the Americans than any other political novelties." He investigated DL in Switzerland. He persuaded Pomeroy to send DL literature to Henry George Ell, its New Zealand MP advocate.[41]

"The Winnetka System" of DL that Lloyd had instituted in his village in 1896 received wide attention when Shibley organized the National Non-Partisan Federation for Majority Rule in Cities in 1902 to secure its general adoption by municipalities. As a member of its Advisory Council Lloyd had the Federation's literature sent to influential men in America and Britain and informed Shibley of Winnetka's defeat of a "foreign gas company." He supported Boston trades unionists' abortive plea for a DL constitutional amendment in Massachusetts. In Illinois the Referendum League joined Pomeroy in campaigning for compulsory state and local DL after securing an advisory referendum act. In 1902 the electorate there favored both by a three to one majority. DL was regarded by Lloyd, Pomeroy, and Shibley as essential to the realization of needed reforms and establishment of the new democracy.[42] Lloyd's advocacy of it and of a national clearing-house currency illustrated further the dualism of his reform technique that became evident simultaneously in the anti-trust campaign.

He was more active in the movement for the municipal ownership of utilities, which he had asserted was *the* solution for Chicago's traction problem in the suppressed portion of the Illinois Bureau of Labor Statistics' *Report* for 1896. Bliss's *Encyclopedia* gave impetus to the MO movement. As America's leading authority on municipal problems, Albert Shaw declared that the rapidly growing demand for MO was no abstraction agitated by malcontents but was essential to enable weak, corrupt city governments to resist powerful corporate interests, which, in the traction field, were attempting from coast to coast "to break down honest and able municipal governments" to obtain fifty-year franchise extensions. Bemis edited a book on municipalization of utilities.[43]

Lloyd carried the campaign into New York City. He asked Pulitzer to oppose the attempt to have the subways constructed by private enterprise. In February 1898 he debated affirmatively and radically "Is the Growing Demand for Public Control of Franchises Justified" before the New York Nineteenth Century Club with Mayor Josiah Quincy of Boston and Professor T. G. Robertson of Cambridge University.

With graceful realism, Lloyd informed that fashionable, unreceptive audience that the control of power was the real issue. This had resolved itself, he said, into a raid by "the criminal rich" upon legitimate enterprise, a "war of the rich upon the rich." The abuses perpetrated by "Our Bad Wealth" made municipalization inevitable, Lloyd declared, quoting Wayne

MacVeagh's "The Black Flag of the corruptionist is far more to be feared than the Red Flag of the anarchist." Citizens rebelling against abuses perpetrated by private administrators of public functions demanded MO in repudiation of polite society's "fin de siècle" mood, "blue with talk of degeneration in religion, democracy, society" and "the indispensable Boss." In the rising urban democracy "men of substance" reasserted the social validity of "the Golden Rule" and the supremacy of the public will over "the public opinion of money," whose control of regulatory commissions and attorneys-general must be broken or Americans would sing "their Recessional hymn." Men must learn again that "Democracy is Religion," and elevate civic spirit to control social development. "Therefore the watchword of politics of a self-governing people must be that government is best which governs most," Lloyd asserted in contradiction of a fundamental dogma of his and Jefferson's social philosophies. This suggested extreme collectivism which Quincy combated vigorously."

He counseled Meriwether's Missouri campaign for socialization of natural monopolies. He advised the National Municipal League that it should add MO to its program, since "honest government" was superficial as an issue compared with that "between those who believe that the institutions of social service which are democratic in their use must be democratic in their administration, and those who hold to the theory of laissez faire and vested rights to private ownership of public property. . . . The house will never be run rightly until the real owner, the public, asserts its ownership."" Since the success of British municipalized utilities demonstrated their practicability, Lloyd did not flinch when conservatives call this "Municipal Socialism." His friends agreed that civic ethics and welfare demanded it. MO was supported by many who simply wanted better service, more reasonable rates, and an end to utility-wrought corruption. His friend Jones was re-elected Mayor of Toledo in 1898 with his help on an MO platform. Eighty per cent of New York voters approved municipalized subways. Mayor Phelan of San Francisco and Mayor McVicker in Des Moines were elected on MO platforms. In Chicago the issue between Altgeld and Harrison was immediate or ultimate MO. The movement's support by many new civic leaders indicated that it was not exclusively the work of radicals. Pingree denied that MO was necessarily socialistic or that it would lead to general socialization of business. Shaw had disseminated information upon European municipalizations for years with significant effect upon public thought and action in the utilities field as the *Boston Herald* observed.[46]

From Jingo to Anti-Imperialist

Toward foreign affairs Lloyd exhibited obvious inconsistencies while working for a better, more peaceful world. Like some of the agrarian Populists he exhibited jingoism in behalf of liberal principles and the Monroe Doctrine. He also exhibited friendship for Britain and a short-lived imperialistic tendency, which he reversed quickly. During the war scare precipitated by the clash of American and British diplomacy over the Venezuelan boundary late in 1895, Robert W. Patterson asked him for an unrestricted statement on "our duty to England and Venezuela" for the *Chicago Tribune*. Lloyd replied in a statement endorsing Richard Olney's application of the Monroe Doctrine to the dispute, gave Cleveland's plan for a settlement qualified support, and exhibited respect for British susceptibilities. The real issue, he said, was between "monarchy and republic." America was bound to repel the threat of force implied in Lord Salisbury's refusal to arbitrate with Venezuela. Washington should keep Britain steadily "in the wrong," await the report of the presidential commission, and if this upheld Venezuelan claims ask Britain to arbitrate while reminding its Cabinet that the United States enforced the Monroe Doctrine.[47]

When Tommy Morgan reproached him, he replied that unless either Venezuela or England backed down "the English are going to fire on an American Republic. What then shall we do? Talk about the Brotherhood of Man, and say Fie!? I am no war-lover, nor British-hater, but if the United States are not a *missionary of liberty* they are nothing." He would extend the

Monroe Doctrine "to the defense of every Republic in Europe or America" and aid all people who wanted to establish republics! "What's the use of moaning about the Cooperative Commonwealth if we won't stand by the Republic?" he asked. Morgan replied that Harvard professors and wage-earners opposed Theodore Roosevelt's saber-rattling. Although Salter agreed with Lloyd, Zueblin asked if his *Tribune* letter was a "bluff or a satire? Are we very dull or have you been dining with the jingoists?" reminding him that a democratic monarchy was preferable to the aristocratic Venezuelan republic and that British "political radicalism has been restrained by the progress of social radicalism."[48]

Lloyd was neither jingo nor imperialist in 1895. To Stead he wrote that there was no popular imperialism behind Olney's intervention in the dispute. He insisted that arbitration would satisfy American opinion and avoid armed conflict that might follow a commission report favoring Venezuela. In a letter to the *London Daily Chronicle* he made a very strong case for arbitration, stating that American opinion asked no other settlement. This aided Massingham's attempt to oblige Salisbury to consent to it.[49] The successful arbitration that ensued laid the basis for the Anglo-American *rapprochement* that ensued under John Hay, with such significant effect upon world history.

However, Lloyd was swept off his feet by the humanitarian jingoism precipitated by the destruction of the battleship *Maine* at Havana, February 15, 1898. Unlike Tolstoian Darrow he did not regard patriotism as a "crime." *"Cuba Libre"* awakened memories of Holland's wars with Spain. As toastmaster at the Chicago Holland Society's banquet on April 18 after McKinley's war message to Congress, he remarked: "We want no Spanish soil, but the American flag must wave for a period over the spot where the bodies of the men of the Maine lie abandoned in the mud of Havana harbor." He proposed a bellicose toast "to William of Orange, who struck the first great blow at Spanish despotism, and to William of the United States" who would strike "the last blow," before securing adoption of resolutions demanding Cuban emancipation from "Spanish tyranny." "While peace becomes a nation, the war is holy that conquers despotism that peace may reign," the Society voted.[50]

While supporting the war, Lloyd soon learned that it muzzled "all reformers." To Albert Bushnell Hart of Harvard University he called Spain "the hyena of nations." He demanded that the war be financed by taxing the wealthy. He regarded President Eliot's, Professor Norton's, and Wm. Lloyd Garrison's opposition to the war "inexplicable." Junius Henry Brown's attitude he dubbed " 'copperheady' to the last degree." Anticipating Kipling's "Take Up the White Man's Burden," he asserted to Moritz Pinner that it would be a "great prelude to the fraternalization of the races to have *all* the inferior nations under the great protectorate of the greater one" despite imperialism's faithlessness and lust that would "darken the counsels of justice at home." Invoking "social evolution" to justify this, he declared it "an idle dream that *we* should progress from perfection to perfection while the Chinese ossified, and the Cubans and Phillipine people were disemboweled, and I am content to wake from it."[51]

He was awakened from outright imperialism by the "embalmed beef" scandal. Learning that it involved Secretary of War Russell B. Alger, whose liaison with the "Big Four" beef monopoly made dysentery in the army more disgusting, he demanded hotly that Samuel Bowles and the *Chicago Tribune* "open upon that jobber and traitor and drive him from public life." He informed Bowles of the War Department's blundering "black powder" contract with Winchester Arms. The *Springfield Republican* denounced both scandals indignantly. Lloyd's assertion that Alger used "his place to make money for others" at the nation's expense was believed widely. "I am proud to say that I hate Alger," he wrote hotly, and told Bowles of Alger's liaison with Diamond Match and western timber thieves. Yet, despite the press's hostility, Alger was subsequently elected United States Senator.[52]

Lloyd then advanced to anti-imperialism. He asked Bowles to read Hobson's article on imperialism in the *Contemporary*

Review as "most admirable ammunition to demolish McKinley's babble about trade following the flag," since the piece was based upon "the ethical and social point of view, which as Ruskin long pointed out, can alone give the true economic vision." Intercourse with Boston friends who were exposing "The Large Policy" of McKinley's administration confirmed his return to anti-imperialism. "Our war for humanity has unmasked itself as a war for coaling stations" and trading opportunities, he informed Howells, who was unwavering in opposition to it.[53]

He recommended Rees's *Sir George Grey* to Franklin Mac-Veagh, who had advocated overseas expansion at the Chicago Literary Club while Marshall Field nodded approval. "Chicago is swept off its feet by the 'expansion craze' and businessmen are parroting the cry that American production has outrun American consumption and we must seek markets for the surplus abroad," Lloyd informed Huntington. However, he did not see how America could permit the Phillipines to "float back into the hands of Spain." He predicted to Symonds that "Americans will never give up the Philippines to any . . . but the Phillipinos." "Our imperialism as a great danger," he wrote to F. Brocklehurst of Lancashire, and predicted that the Americans and British would regain control of their governments and set examples of enlightened treatment of "dependent peoples."[54]

His absence in Australasia prevented his participating in the early anti-imperialist agitation. At Christchurch in February 1899 he viewed American involvement in world affairs with complacency. Any policy tending to unite the world was beneficial, he said, while conceding that the war had "set back" the American social reform movement seriously.[55] When he returned to America, Aguinaldo's Filipino insurrection was arousing the Anti-Imperialist League's sympathy. Lloyd approved of Edward Atkinson's attempt to send its pamphlets to Manila and of the protest against military maladministration in Cuba. He subscribed to the *Anti-Imperialist* and wrote Atkinson that he was doing "good work." However, he regarded the agitation as doomed to failure because of the domination of "the money power" that precipitated an inevitable "imperialization of the

Republic," as he remarked to F. W. Gookin. Privately, he favored dominion status for the Philippines.[56]

His wife's illness prevented his participation, despite Pomeroy's urging that he attend, in the debate on imperialism at the National Conference of Political and Social Reform at Buffalo, June 28-July 4, 1899, whose "Call" he had signed. He had been scheduled to speak on "The New Conscience."[57] His reform circle continued to seek his counsel, co-operation, and financial aid after the Conference adjourned. As Chicago's leading authority on the labor problem he helped to plan the United States Commission's exhibit on American labor for the Paris Exposition of 1900. Skill in leading, inspiring, rallying support for, and coordinating successive agitations confirmed his role as dean of American reform. His influence upon British and Antipodean reform movements, publicists, and statesmen bulked large in America's overseas contribution to the burgeoning Empire of Reform.

As Henry George and Bellamy passed from the scene in the United States, it was evident that he had won the position of greatest influence among advanced thinkers and practical reformers. This was due to his incessant campaigning and to his philosophy of "Man the Creator," which verbalized the assumption of all non-Marxian radicals and moderates that during that dynamic era mankind could build for itself a better world based upon the ethical principles and equalitarian assumptions of the Christian and secular liberal traditions. This Lloyd related, more successfully than any other leader, to an unprecedented range of reform movements.

Chapter XXI

The Lloyds in Boston

RECRUIT FOR "THE YANKEE REFORMERS"

THE LLOYDS' TIES with Boston dated from Henry D. Lloyd's free-trader years and Jessie Bross's visits there before their marriage. Lloyd's membership in the Twentieth Century Club and the *Herald*'s support of his defense of Bemis and exchange with Gunton in 1895 indicated his standing there. In 1897 he aided the Citizens' Committee on Municipal Ownership of Street Railways led by Mead and Hale. He reproached Mayor Quincy because of the West End Railway's encroachment on the Common and Public Garden. In 1898 he planned a book with Bemis and Parsons to show how Boston was robbed "to death by franchises, subways, consolidations." He encouraged the *Springfield Republican*'s defense of the press from Moorfield Storey's attack on "yellowism." Obviously, he did not curry favor with the "Brahmins."[1]

The publicity given to his Australasian journey and his views on the Antipodes made him a celebrity there before he settled at 141 Beacon Street in October 1899. He invited a request to assist the "Yankee Reformers" when he sent them copies of his interview in the *Springfield Republican* on Antipodean state experiments. President Eliot's luncheon for Reeves's party, the Lloyds' guests, gave them standing at Harvard, where they were acquainted with eminent professors. Robert Treat Paine consulted Henry D. Lloyd on "the trusts" and persuaded him to speak at the Wells Memorial Institute for Workingmen. A deer hunt on the Lloyd family property in the Adirondacks, and

452

pleasant evenings at the Hales's listening to readings of James Russell Lowell's verse, rested him from writing.

Respect for constituted authority in business and finance and intellectual orthodoxy were not indispensable for social acceptance, although Barron had had to resign the financial editorship of the *Transcript* recently because he criticized Henry Villard's railroad entrepreneurship.[2] The friendship of the Sylvester Baxters, Hales, Fields, Meads, William Wilsons, and Mrs. Lucy Cleghorn of Concord enlivened the Lloyds' first year in "The Hub." Frank Parsons gave the boys a punching bag whose noisy welcome annoyed their father. Annie Fields drew Henry D. Lloyd into the tenement house reform movement "in order to make you feel completely one of us!"[3] He also assisted the co-operatives and advocated improved rapid transit and workingmen's housing *à la* New Zealand.

During November 1899 Willis Abbot introduced him to George Fred Williams, state Democratic Party leader and Bryanite antimonopolist. Williams entertained Lloyd at lunch before calling. Lloyd welcomed him heartily, liked him, and gave him a copy of his New Zealand report to Carroll D. Wright and wanted to see him again but did not return his call because of press of work on his books. Like the radical Democrats of Illinois, Williams advocated DL and MO and believed that he and Lloyd were close to "the border line between the Socialistic and Democratic camps." He welcomed the latter's advice on policy problems.[4] This was not surprising. On election eve 1896 Lloyd had decried the single gold standard at the Twentieth Century Club. When the *Herald* implied that he spoke there like a "fanatic," the *Boston Advertiser* had demurred in a most complimentary description of his manner, character, and standing as a respected Fabian.[5]

Lloyd attended the organization meeting of the Boston Authors' Club. In February 1900 Thomas Wentworth Higginson listed him among the charter members. When he did not attend the next meetings, Higginson invited him to talk to the Round Table Club "on some aspect of the social question." If this provoked "some difference of opinion, so much the better,"

That Club's membership was drawn from the First Families and leading educators, including Mrs. Alice Freeman Palmer.[6] Walter Hines Page's sponsorship, Lloyd's prominence as a publicist, social reformer, and "Fighter of Trusts," his status as a Chicago clubman, support of the Anti-Imperialist League, and Mrs. Lloyd's social standing explain this unprecedented reception.

Lloyd had lectured recently on Washington Gladden's nationally known series, on which Grover Cleveland also appeared.[7] After he presented "A Substitute for the French Revolution" to the New York Social Reform Club, the People's Institute at Cooper Union had to wait a year to schedule Lloyd. During his first year in Boston he addressed the Phillips Brooks Club, the Twentieth Century Club, Lincoln House Men's Club, Boston Society of Arts and Crafts, Workingmen's Political League, Union for Industrial Progress, and trades unionists at Pierce's Hall.[8]

His new books, articles, and lecturing made literary news. The *Transcript* announced that Robert Louis Stevenson ranked him with Howells and Henry James among "the few masters of English in this country." Lloyd's publications suggested to Stevenson a novel "with a trust magnate for the central character." E. H. Clement, the *Transcript*'s editor, was a kindred spirit, sharing Lloyd's antipathy to militarism, high finance, and monopolistic combinations. He told him how Barron's *Boston News-Letter* disclosed "just in advance" what "the enemy"—great financial and business interests—were planning. After receiving from Baxter the "Boa Constrictor Trust" pamphlet about New Hampshire's lumber monopoly, Lloyd observed wryly, "Massachusetts policy is directed by its rich men and rich men do not interfere with each other's piracies."[9]

He won Brandeis' warm friendship by advising him, Edward A. Filene, and Parsons during an attempt to secure a revision of gas and electric rates. Although 626 business firms signed the petition requesting this, the *Herald* and *Globe* ignored the document when they discovered there was "no syndicate" behind the matter. Lucia Ames Mead asked Lloyd to address a Faneuil

Hall demonstration in behalf of an "honest" spring election. Bolton Hall sought to interest him in reproducing Pingree's gardens for the unemployed.[10]

In July 1900 Lloyd wrote Huntington from The Watch House of his eagerness to return to Winnetka. Conceding that he had "in some ways" had "a pleasant time" in Boston, "the ink stains on my fingers, and reputation, may have had something to do with that, but I shall never willingly become a Bostonian. I should not want to leave Chicago to go to any theatre smaller than it." As he gossiped of Fred Mason's successful coup in "his Mexican railway ventures" and Mrs. Mason's "brilliant" participation in " 'the 400' set in New York," he intimated that there was a certain validity to Mrs. Wirt Dexter's assertion that "the Bostonian always begins to suspect something to be wrong if he feels himself warm," and to Oliver Herford's reference to Boston as " 'an abandoned farm'." The "situation" of American reform he described as "desperate beyond belief." Only excesses by "the gentlemen on the other side" would make it possible to unite "the people" for effective action, he said. As for the Lloyds :

> Our chronicles are brief. Will, who lost a year by accompanying me to Australia, is in the Law School; Hal, who always speaks with delight of your kindness to him, is studying medicine; Demarest—you remember my brother —enters Harvard next September; Jack is only 14 years old and makes no news; Mrs. Lloyd has no gray hairs. I am a badger,—and 53. My calendar is like a telescope; as it grows it brings nearer the objects of contemplation, and no figure it shows is dearer, my Major, than yours.[11]

Mrs. Lloyd's illness canceled plans to return to The Wayside. The family returned to Boston, to reside for three years at 95 Mt. Vernon Street, expecting each spring to return to Winnetka the next autumn.

During the Boer War Lloyd attempted to mobilize opinion

in behalf of the South African republics as Altgeld was doing in Chicago, and to persuade the State Department to support them. He suggested to Melville Stone, Bowles, and Van Benthuysen that the pro-British slant of the news be corrected. He kept in close touch with the London anti-imperialists Clarke, Hobson, and Wilson, who opposed that war. On Mead's solicitation in January 1900 Lloyd presented in the *Herald* the pro-Boer views of British Liberals who rallied around Massingham and Stead. He agreed with them that Britain should have arbitrated its quarrel with the Transvaal, and warned that the new Anglo-American entente might draw the United States into war with Russia while extending the exploitation of American resources by the British ruling class. This piece expressed current opinion that supported the Boers although America was conquering the Phillippines and couldn't protest. Clement called Lloyd's statement "superb, leaving nothing uncovered, as solid as it is inspiring." The *Herald* followed Lloyd in condemning the Boer War *and* the Philippine campaign. He encouraged Pulitzer's *World* to tap reliable sources of South African news.

The Lloyds attended the gigantic Boston pro-Boer meeting, which demanded vociferously American diplomatic intervention to persuade Britain to abandon the war. This and similar gatherings in New York and Chicago were ignored by the State Department, which needed the Anglo-American entente during the Boxer uprising in China.[12]

A Temporary Bostonian

Despite ill health Mrs. Lloyd transferred to the Lloyds' Boston home the gaiety and democracy of The Wayside and The Watch House. Table talk featured the Boer War, amid parental rejoicing at the Afrikanders' victories and the boys' announcements of British successes that provoked witty rejoinders. With the Hales, Meads, Baxters, Clements, Robert A. Wood, Anne Dennison, Parsons, Anne Withington, and visitors as frequent guests the Lloyds' home continued to be a social center of reform.[13]

This Lillian Whiting declared in "Eminent Residents of Boston" in the Chicago *Inter Ocean* was "a re-enforcement of the best traditions of Boston life . . . created by such men and women as Garrison, Lydia Maria Child, Wendell Phillips, Whittier, Professor Benjamin Pierce, Agassiz, Mrs. Mary Hemenway, Dr. Howe, Lucy Stone and others . . . a re-enforcement of the nobleness that they communicated to the social atmosphere. Henry D. Lloyd is in constant demand" as "one of the most able and brilliant speakers of the day . . . communicating impulse and stimulus in every direction for the betterment of humanity. As a thinker, a writer and a lecturer, he is one of the pre-eminent forces of the age. And the private and personal life of Mr. and Mrs. Lloyd offers an ideal illustration of what one might term that of the Christian capitalist."[14]

Boston was understandably amused, however, when *Book Chat* reported that, despite the "social democracy" of the Lloyd household, Will had informed his father that he intended to become a corporation attorney.[15]

Mrs. Lloyd's ill health, personality, and social activity were disclosed in a rare note from her to Caroline Stallbohm:

Mr. Lloyd went away Monday, and I packed his trunk twice, and doing the least little thing seems to upset me in the most exasperating way. Driven by my complete good-for-nothingness, I took a Turkish bath Tuesday, and stayed in bed all the afternoon until 4:30, when I dressed for Mrs. Dewey's reception. Edith Church sent her carriage for me, and we had a nice time going out. In the evening came Jack's lesson, and then I went to bed but not to sleep until after 2 o'clock in the morning. . . .

Mr. Lloyd comes home tonight, and you will be delighted to know that he has permitted Jack to go to the football game at New Haven with Will tomorrow . . . I am spending all my strength and no little of my money on fitting the 4 boys, who go, with a lunch worthy of the victory I hope Harvard may have, but I am afraid she wont. . . . Mrs. Charlie Davis slept in Mr. Lloyd's room last night,

Oakman in the study, and Lucy Cleghorn in Billy's room, and Grace in your room. . . . I do not get as strong as I wish, although I am really a great deal better. . . . I think you would say so if you knew what I did yesterday. I went down to the market, etc., did some errands, then took David in the afternoon to ride, went to Cambridge in the evening. Very naturally this morning I feel tuckered, although a whole bottle of champagne (it was only half a pint, dear) gave me a better sleep than I have had for a week.

With love to your Mother, Minnie and her husband and children.[16]

That autumn of 1900 Abbot and Williams persuaded Lloyd to support "The Great Commoner." While Abbot issued releases quoting *Wealth Against Commonwealth* from Democratic National Headquarters, Lloyd delivered "Uses and Abuses of Corporations" again at the Twentieth Century Club. The radicals rallied around Bryan in the hope that he could overthrow McKinleyism. Lloyd had learned from Altgeld that Bryan was "in truth more progressive" that his public statements, and on "Government Ownership," the referendum, and other issues was "as advanced . . . as we need him to be." Altgeld added that Bryan was "much more of a radical than Lincoln was" and if sentiment warranted "any aggressive step in economic political or social legislation he would encourage it." Reassured, Lloyd joined Higginson, Mead, Gamaliel Bradford, and ex-Governor Boutwell in speaking at a Bryan Club rally early in November. Yet, his insistence upon the secrecy of the ballot in a society dominated "by corporate monopoly and wealth" foiled the *Globe*'s attempt to learn how he would vote.[17] In 1902 his "literary bureau" distributed *The Commoner*.

Consultations with Parsons on "the cause of good government" in Massachusetts and aiding the co-operative movement consumed Lloyd's spare time preliminary to another European tour of investigation. He remained long enough to stand with Mrs. Lloyd and 20,000 Bostonians on the Common, December

31, to hear Hale proclaim the new century under Twentieth Century Club auspices. "We were proud for Boston, the people, the occasion and ourselves that the approach of the new century had such a Herald ! . . . I shall be back in May, and hope to find our first American cooperator and democrat still successfully defying the selection he read so well this morning from the Ninetieth Psalm—the third !" Lloyd wrote him New Year's morning.[18]

Since his wife's ill health continued, he ordered Miss Stallbohm to catalogue his Wayside library and bring to Mt. Vernon Street the books needed for his work. Thus, he established his "working environment" in his Boston home, happy that Mrs. Lloyd could sit up twice daily.[19]

As the leading exponent of the "New Democracy," he spoke and lectured constantly. On nearly all forums and lecture series in the East he spoke on New Zealand democracy, co-operation, corporation abuses, municipal ownership, Emerson, Morris, and "The Message of Culture." He conducted a "more vigorous campaign" for "much-needed reform." In January 1902 he spoke at the Rochester Labor Lyceum, delivered four lectures to the Philadelphia Ethical Culture Society, and debated "Wealth and Commonwealth" at the Philadelphia Contemporary Club with Joseph Wharton of Bethlehem Steel and W. U. Hensel. While Wharton claimed that the door was still open to the dollar a day laborer "to become wealthy as Carnegie did," Lloyd predicted confidently the collapse of "the present capitalistic regime and the rise of an era of workingmen's co-operation." He then carried the New Zealand gospel to Lynn, Northampton, Springfield, and Providence.[20]

As the reform movement revived, he joined the executive council of the National League for Promoting Public Ownership of Monopolies with Flower, George Gates, Parsons, and Thomas E. Will. Pomeroy consulted him about the DL agitation, as did Shibley about the Bureau of Economic Research and the National Federation for Majority Rule. Lockwood of the Anti-Trust League conferred with him. As Lloyd advised Reno on the compulsory arbitration agitation in Massachusetts, Margaret Morley provoked other requests for guidance with her complimentary "Natural History of a Social Reformer" in the *Transcript*.[21]

Mead persuaded Lloyd to address the Lake Mohonk International Arbitration Conference and drew him into the peace movement, in which he became an influential figure. Charmed by his New Zealand lectures at Los Angeles, Mrs. Caroline W. Severence sent Lloyd cards of introduction to Mrs. Charles G. Ames, Rev. Charles Dole, and other Bostonians. Grateful for her sponsorship and promising to present them, he replied that the optimistic "well-to-do as everywhere" were turning to "those who can amuse them with the sweet languors of culture."[22]

In this sphere he cultivated an interest in reform when he discussed "Is Personal Development the Best Social Policy?" before the Browning Society. There he urged wittily the need for the reciprocal stimulation of leaders and people so as to ensure fullest individual and cultural development. He predicted the rise of a new religion, new politics, and a new economics in opposition to Oriental religion and Tolstoianism. He recommended a new creed of work, full production, and creativity stressing youth, efficiency, kindliness, and patriotism. Thus he expanded "Man the Creator" to include cultural democracy in opposition to snobbery, dilletantism, and pseudo-aristocratic aestheticism. A year later Helen M. Winslow featured him in *Literary Boston of Today*.[23]

After aiding the abortive attempt to introduce DL into Massachusetts by constitutional amendment, he went abroad in 1902 on another investigating tour. Afterward he became engrossed in the great anthracite coal strike and the subsequent arbitration. Then the Lloyds returned to The Wayside in March 1903.

Henry D. Lloyd returned to Boston two weeks later to testify before a legislative committee, when he wrote home, "I have made up my mind that *if* I had been born in Boston I should have loved it." In April the Visiting Committee on Philosophy at Harvard invited him "as one of those interested in Emerson's personality and teaching and most associated in public thought" with him to assist in raising the building fund to construct Emerson Hall. It was eighteen years since Lloyd had given his wife a "set of Emerson" in appreciation of her "sweet guidance" which had led him "to know and love the greatest of American minds and hearts,"[24] as he expressed it then.

During the Emerson Centennial in July, after declining to head Chicago's celebration he lectured on "Emerson's Wit and Humor" in the Free Religious Association's Emerson Centennial Memorial School at Concord and Boston with Mead, Hale, President Jacob G. Shurman of Cornell University, Moorfield Storey, leading professional philosophers, Wm. Roscoe Thayer, Wm. M. Salter, Garrison, Mrs. Julia Ward Howe, and other Emersonians. The *Herald*'s praise of his lecture and an appreciative letter from Edith Emerson Forbes indicated the impression he had made. Perhaps because he loved Emerson, he loved Boston after all.[25]

RIPENING THEORY AND INFLUENCE

Lloyd's writing and lecturing during those years stressed the feasibility and need for a pragmatic, eclectic, and gradually developing welfare democracy. In "The Twentieth Century in New Applications of Democracy," *Christian World,* January, 1901, he almost forecast the Age of Insull and its sequel by predicting the rapid emergence of an electric age dominated by "a score of men." This would provoke such middle-class "social alarm" as to precipitate an evolutionary "social revolution" extending equalitarianism from politics to industry, when all would become capitalists and co-operators, working less than eight hours daily, with leisure "to be democrats." Rapid transit would transform cities into dispersed suburbia and people would be "educated back to the soil." Although imperialism would create rival Russian and American empires, "the peace of the world" would eventually destroy imperialism itself. Lloyd's chief reform interest had shifted from the Standard Oil and the "trusts" to the larger issue of world-wide socioeconomic change.[26]

A year later he discussed "New Forms and New Uses of Democracy" with Woodrow Wilson, Grover Cleveland, and

Henry J. Ford in *Problems of Modern Democracy,* a Book-lovers Library home reading course. There Lloyd termed Antipodean welfare democracy "a deliberate exploitation of both capitalists and proletariat by the middle class which means to be itself 'the fittest that survives'." He reported that Swiss state capitalism and direct legislation were elevating wage-earners and strengthening agrarian democracy.[27] As early as 1898 he had concluded that trades unionism offered "no social solution."[28] Because of Gompers' rejection of co-operation and compulsory arbitration, Lloyd cultivated the middle class's interests in overseas democratic "novelties" and attempted to turn its burgeoning reform spirit toward his welfare democratic goal. He had become the American equivalent of the late nineteenth-century British Radicals.

"Socialism" as a term of usage in America was still employed loosely to designate all advocates of drastic extensions of government authority into economic fields. It had been fashionable among liberal intellectuals, reformers, and the urban middle class to read utopian romances, Christian Socialist, Fabian, and other Socialist tracts, to avow sympathy with collectivist programs, to predict a vague social revolution, and to dub oneself "Socialist," all of which Lloyd had done periodically. Such was the so-called "middle-class socialism" of the turn of the century.

Actually Lloyd's "Socialism" of 1899 was an ideologic and policy straddle, more a modified Emersoniamism than Fabian. This he disclosed in the Fairhope, Alabama, single tax colony's *Courier,* September 15, and again privately that autumn. Declaring himself not "a sectarian Socialist," and uninterested in labels or "intricacies of creeds," he rejected proletarianism and Marxism's demand for a completely collectivized economy, defined "Socialism" in non-Marxian terms, and adhered to his earlier thesis of a necessary equilibrium between individualism and society. He opposed an "odium solilogicum," he said. He regarded a free, competitive economy as "entirely consistent with public and private morality and welfare." "Socialism" should permit individual initiative and business pioneering, but after a quarter century's profiting from this in a special field the community should "step in and appropriate and administer." His welfare democracy was to be achieved by interaction between individualism, association, and statism, and by application of "mercy, justice, and the common good" to "the fields of modern wealth." Citing Emerson, he anticipated much of Sweden's "The Middle Way" as the best economy, and alluded to "the money power" as "a tight fit for the facts." He demanded compulsory arbitration so as to subordinate to the public good it and the labor movement that was alarming Governor Theodore Roosevelt. Realistic reform must achieve democracy united instead of international proletarianism. Lloyd's semicollectivist welfare democracy according to the Marxist Daniel DeLeon was "the true historic democracy of America." He classified Lloyd as "an empiricist" lacking in understanding of Socialism, favoring ownership by the individual of "his necessary means of production" as in New Zealand except in restricted areas of government economic activity.[29]

In his role of the non-Marxian gentleman radical, Lloyd contributed significantly to "the revolutionary change in American thought . . . from an individualist to a collectivist basis" that occurred between 1865 and 1914. Philosophically, he had furthered the shift in intellectual America's allegiance from Spencer to pragmatism,[30] while sharing in the passing metaphysical interest in Kant, Comte, Hegel, and Green. He adhered to his theory that "progress" proceeded "along a great number of different lines simultaneously." However, he substituted middle-class welfare radicalism for the Locofoco producer radicalism that had underpinned his Labor-Populist Fabianism.

Fearing "a plutocratic revolution which will bind us in a worse than Roman rigidity until we break apart by a sort of decay," he impressed businessmen, professional men, journalists, clergy, and others with the need to counteract this by reform.[31] Fear lest the corporation oligarchy entrench itself permanently explains his savage hostility to "the Captain Kids" of giant business and high finance, and his preference

for expropriation to destroy their *"present predominance."*
Yet, since he would have left them sufficient to continue their
scales of living, for a radical he was exceptionally kind to millionaires.

He told Alfred Russel Wallace that a book on "Social Selection" was needed to counteract Darwinism's "depressive and destructive effects on social effort" and reveal how "the institutional variations of society have been produced." A systematic
Reform Darwinism would give "scientific sanction to the pro-
cesses of reform, and revolution, and a scientific place to the
idealizing faculty." Sobered by the swift subsidence of the
massive popular unrest during the late nineties, he recognized
that "our work, instead of being, as I supposed, political, is still
educational. We have no party in this country to call together
but we shall have to educate one."[32] This was after the organization of the Socialist party and disclosed his preference for a
radical interclass political alignment. While touring New Zealand he concluded that "the indirect method is often the most
direct. Don't turn people upside down to start with . . . get them
into the new position gradually and gently." After further
analysis of overseas and American trends he concluded, san-
guinely, "the cooperative commonwealth is evolving under our
eyes" and the people "as yet unconsciously are building for
themselves a better social body and soul."[33]

Since he believed that not more than 10 per cent of the
public effectively promoted reform, he studied the historic reform minorities such as the English Levellers and Diggers and
cited them repeatedly in his lectures. He predicted to Stephen
Bauer in 1901 that, despite temporary subsidence of American
reform activity, there would soon occur a "great awakening"
preceded by "a religious excitement of the first order." The
secular excitement precipitated by the Muckrakers began the
next year.[34] He consulted Edward Owen Greening of the Agricultural and Horticultural Association, Ltd. in England in 1901
on the wisdom of attempting another radical third party based
upon a modified Springfield platform, co-operatives, and mediation in the Boer War, but was advised that English attempts

to fuse co-operation with radical political action had been un-successful.[35]

He succeeded in winning a respectful sympathetic hearing for his program, however. In 1890 the Western Unitarians had re-garded him as excessively partisan in championing organized labor and attacking "trusts." A decade later ministers' institutes praised "Uses and Abuses of Corporations" because his "fair handling of the whole question" contrasted with Debs's bias. The increasing numbers of clergy who took up his demand for social justice contrasted with the few, i.e., Bishop O. I. Hunting-ton of Syracuse and founder of the Church Association for the Advancement of the Interests of Labor, who had welcomed *A Strike of Millionaires'* contribution to a necessary revolution in social policy. Lloyd's discussion of "Christianizing of the retail trade" at the Marlborough Conference in 1895 had won him the undying friendship of Leighton Williams. Lloyd's earlier, stinging epigram in "The New Independence," "our popular parsons preach to the rich and at the poor," became increasingly inapplicable after 1900.[36]

Friendship with other influential, socially minded clergy, his later books, and reputation as the great champion of social justice and welfare democracy made Lloyd the leading lay in-spirer of the Protestant Social Gospel as Ely withdrew from ac-tive association with it. As Lloyd's clerical friends brought their influence to bear upon business and social problems he jotted a manuscript note : "Pulpit is beginning to find its voice and will free its mind upon a great robber when he is safely dead." Many clergy and editors of denominational journals consulted him on problems of the urban-industrial age. As Charles A. Roberts wrote him in 1897 : "What a great state is Illinois when even her legislators are merchantable ! But 'the sun do move,' else the ministers would not preach *Wealth Against Commonwealth.*"[37]

While residing in Boston Lloyd kept in touch with Chicago and western reformers against the day of his return home. Jane Addams and Jenkin Lloyd Jones consulted him frequently. He corresponded with Altgeld, "Tommy" Morgan, liberal bankers, and William Kent. He continued to inspire Mayor Jones of Toledo and Smythe's California movement.

Lloyd helped to organize the National Social and Political Reform Conference at Detroit, June 28-July 5, 1901. However, Mrs. Lloyd's illness made it impossible for him to deliver his scheduled address, "American Ideals Abroad." Many delegates greatly "missed" him, as a hostile press campaign precipitated last minute withdrawals of many "respectable" liberals and authors. Responsible delegates secured adoption of a statement of principles and objectives. An Address to the public developed themes that Lloyd had long popularized, antimonopolism, and opposition to concentrated wealth, political corruption, and "the money power." Afterward, Bemis suggested to him that more good might be accomplished by returning to "private and comparatively small assemblies" of reform leaders.[38]

During that same summer Lloyd and Parsons joined David J. Lewis, a Cumberland, Maryland, attorney in organizing the National Public Ownership League in an attempt to unite liberal and radical Democrats on nationalization of the railroads. By following Lloyd's strategy Lewis expected to write a public ownership plank in the next Democratic national platform. The new League's activity, the MO movement, and the influence of Lewis F. Post and Willis Abbot persuaded Bryan that public ownership was an issue of mounting popularity that he could champion.[39] Radical, non-Marxian reform achieved a powerful position thereby in the Democratic party as Roosevelt rose to power.

Cosmopolitan Investigator

Lloyd's cosmopolitan activity continued during his residence in Boston. Hobson replaced Clarke as his leading London correspondent. Stead consulted Lloyd before writing *The Americanization of the World, or the Trend of the Twentieth Century* depicting the future role of powerful, ruthless American "trusts." The object was "to wake up John Bull, and I think that it will give him fits to have it rubbed into him that Uncle Sam is beating him hands down," he wrote Lloyd, who sent his latest articles and suggested "reference to the development of the Negro race." For this Stead was grateful.[40]

Stead asked for an appraisal of President Roosevelt. He was stunned by Lloyd's warning that the ex-Rough Rider was more emotional than intellectual and lacking in sympathy for "the new music of humanity that you and I would like to hear from the orchestra of the history of our times. He is probably an admirable instrument for the 'Americanization of the world,' commercial and military." Recollection of his jingoism and antipathy to Altgeld diminished Lloyd's appreciation of Roosevelt's contribution to civil service and municipal reform and his repugnance for business buccaneering. Alarmed, Stead warned Lloyd that "you in America have everything in your own hands if only you don't give way to Napoleonism." He consulted him on preparation of *The Money Kings of the Modern World,* and was informed that American anti-Trust sentiment was as strong as ever.[41]

From his European investigations of 1901-2 Lloyd hoped to complete the "salad of all the good ideas of Europe and Australasia" that America should accept and then "start where they have stopped" rather than exhaust itself in empire-building.[42]

From Swiss democracy, "the Alpine glow" he called it, he hoped to learn how democracy developed when untouched by "plutocracy." He was sponsored in his initial investigation by Holyoake, who introduced him to French co-operators and Socialists as "a Socialist and Cooperative explorer."[43]

Lloyd began his Swiss investigations in January 1901 after preliminary study, consultation with Baxter, Catlin, and Storey, and assurance of *The Outlook*'s desire for articles on Swiss democracy and British co-operatives. Advised by Professor C. L. Borgeaud of the University of Geneva, he studied in the State Library at Berne before travelling in the cantons. Professor Bauer of Basle helped him, for a consideration. Switzerland's relevance for America Lloyd stated to Borgeaud, "The problem is to establish those conditions of comparative economic equality which alone render democracy possible. You have it; we have lost it. We must regain it or lose more."[44]

He then investigated state policies, the Social Democratic parties, and co-operatives of the German Empire, Belgium, and France. In Berlin the American Consul-General aided him, as did von der Leyen, Professor G. Cohn of Goettingen University, and Edwin T. Hayn of the *Chicago Record*. He interviewed Karl Kautsky and Ferdinand August Bebel, the Social Democratic leaders; Edward Bernstein, the "revisionist Socialist" whose views were akin to those of the Fabians; Hugo Poetsch, editor of *Vorwarts;* Theodor Mommsen, historian of the Roman world, and Herr Theodor Barth, editor of *Die Nation* and spokesman of the National Liberal tradition. Lloyd then went to Brussells where he attended Parliament and introduced American friends to Lalla Vandervelde, leader of the Belgian Socialists. In Paris he interviewed Charles Gide, called upon Émile Zola and Georges Clemenceau, and visited Le Maison Leclaire, famous for profit-sharing.[45]

Three weeks in London brought him up to date on British thought and trends. The vacationing Sidney Webb sent him to his town house at 41 Grosvenor Road for the latest Fabian publications and data on workingmen's housing. Vivian showed him a plan "for co-operative house building." Holyoake was delighted to "see again such a cosmopolitan wanderer to whom so many movements are indebted." Lloyd visited Reeves and enjoyed his comparison of the March weather with "New Zealand frozen lamb!" Tom Mann sought his views upon American labor and Socialism and "the SDF. ILP. Anarchist & Trade Union Movement in this country." Hyndman predicted to Lloyd that "trusts will bring us Socialism quickly." A. J. Wilson entertained Lloyd at lunch. John Macdonnell, clerk of the London County Council, had him in for tea.

Stead's interview with Lloyd, "Why Not New-Zealandize Great Britain," in *Review of Reviews* reported his endorsement of *The Americanization of the World*. Lloyd, he said, was no Socialist. They agreed that the Liberals would discover in Antipodean democracy policies to counteract the Conservatives' attempt to "Americanise the Constitution." Appearing during a schism in the Liberal Party, this pointed the way emphatically to reunion and a return to power. Lloyd's repeated conferences with John Burns and his influence with Liberal M.P.'s such as Mather, and upon Stead, Clarke, Hobson, Wilson, G. O. Trevelyan, and Massingham contributed undoubtedly to this result. His reputation as the only reformer in the United States "whom everybody trusted" reinforced their respect for his books and views.

From Samuel R. Gardiner and other historians he learned more of the history of English radicalism. He dined at the Devonshire Club with Sir George Trevelyan and breakfasted with John M. Robertson, a Fabian. He saw all his friends, and quizzed Professor Alfred Marshall on economic theory.[46] He planned to visit Plunkett in Dublin but Mrs. Lloyd's second attack of typhoid obliged him to cancel all engagements and sail to Boston from Liverpool, after having discussed "The Americanization of Europe" for the *Chicago Record*.

Soon after he landed, he reported British and German Socialist dread of American "trusts" in the *Boston Herald*. At the Twentieth Century Club he discussed the threatened conquest of Europe by American "trusts," Swiss democracy, Belgian Socialism, and Milan's co-operatives. The German Socialists, he predicted, might precipitate "sensational development at any time. Gentlemen, it only calls for vision to see that a glorious destiny awaits the human race." This, the *Congregationalist and Christian World* observed, was "sober truth," while Lillian Whiting reported his enthusiasm for Swiss democracy and Belgian co-operatives to the Chicago *Inter Ocean*.[47]

That European tour enhanced his interest in the American labor problem. Then Herbert N. Casson's book on trades unions provoked him to remark, as if he were simon-pure middle class, that the trades union movement was about to be betrayed by its leaders. "They may have been seduced by the capitalist into the belief that the two great trusts,—the Labor Trust and the Trust of Capital—can unite in a common depredation on the public." He interpreted the recent meeting of "Mark" Hanna's National Civic Federation at New York as an attempt also "to feudalize labor" and informed Casson "The worst demagogues in history are the capitalists like Chamberlain and Carnegie who manipulate the mob to the destruction of liberty, justice, prosperity, and all the other real conservatisms."[46]

Despite Mrs. Lloyd's ill health, Lloyd left in March 1902 for the Continent with Professor and Mrs. William James on the *Ivernia*. James wrote Charles Eliot Norton afterward that Lloyd was "one of the most 'winning' men it was ever my fortune to know.[49] The reformer enjoyed the experience of learning more of his religious views, soon to be presented formally at Edinburgh.

Lloyd discovered "some 'hot stuff'" at Rome where Parliament was considering a compulsory arbitration bill, and was escorted on a tour of north Italy by Signor Carlo Contini, authority on co-operatives and arbitration.[50] He then investigated virtually all phases of Swiss life, democracy, policies, and institutions. He visited the Landesgemeinde of Glaris and sent home books and pamphlets. Swiss Democracy he regarded as the counterfoil of great power imperialism and industrial monopoly, more democratic than New Zealand because by DL it had "taken possession of the monopolies and changed them from instruments of private profit to public servants . . . on a national scale," while municipalizing utilities and establishing cantonal banks. As he compiled a bibliography for reference Miss Stallbohm sent data on his "causes in his wake."[51]

At Berlin, Ambassador Andrew D. White entertained him. Karl Kautsky welcomed him and reviewed his New Zealand books and *Wealth Against Commonwealth* in *Die Neue Zeit*. Via Brussels, Liége, Hamburg, and Copenhagen Lloyd traveled to England. Disgusted at the International Co-operative Congress's omission of subjects in his fields of interest from its program, he did not attend, returning home "a raving American," as he informed Bowles, because of Europeans' indifference to the United States despite its importance to them. "Europe holds no initiative in the ideas or the work of reform," he added, as he turned to confront a major crisis in American industrial relations. His Boston residence and inquiries abroad enabled him to contribute, as a cosmopolitan social reformer, to its solution in a unique manner. A warm note of his to William James warmed "my gizzard much," that professor replied, "What your true philosopher needs is *praise*."[52]

Chapter XXII

"The People's Attorney" and The Anthracite Coal Strike Arbitration

ROOSEVELT'S COUP

While returning from abroad in mid-summer 1902, Lloyd drafted a radical "Program for Reforms."[1] This expanded conservation from forests to water power, minerals, land, children, unemployed men and machines, luxury, monopolistic restrictions, and peace. It specified immediate study of the history of franchises and monopolies, and envisaged schools "for all ages" and occupations. It would advance "Progress" by enforcing "the right of the full development of every individual for *all* individuals." Anticipating the Civilian Conservation Corps of 1933 Lloyd proposed "an industrial militia out of the unemployed on the roads, forests and swamps, places of infection, etc." Via "Direct Legislation"[2] he would democratize "industrial powers by nationalization, municipalization," and finance this by "taxing luxury out of existence relentlessly." Private capital could make "public improvements" with a maximum 5 per cent profit. He would require "immediate registration of all citizens" and property, and restrict transfers to property registered for taxation. He concluded: "Immediate imprisonment of all the monopolists under the commercial laws. Such a Program demands the Ironsides spirit—Cromwell's."

Only a sanguine American reformer of Calvinist nurture whose collectivist tendencies had been so intensified by study of Swiss democracy as to blind him to the limitations on statism imposed by American constitutionalism could have conceived it possible to arouse the public to impose this program "immediately" upon America and thereby overthrow the dominant corporation oligarchy. Under the influence of Fabianism, Continental Social Democracy, and New Zealand and Swiss welfare policies Lloyd stepped farther across the threshhold of Socialist thought. However, although reckless methods of promoters of the second phase of the combination movement in the American economy provoked inevitable opposition, this did not necessarily portend a sudden transition to a far-reaching collectivism.

Lloyd landed at Boston during the great anthracite coal strike in east Pennsylvania. The Boston press, Pulitzer's *World,* the *New York Journal,* and other papers featured it as a struggle between a hated "trust" and its oppressed miners and consumers while coal stocks diminished, prices rose, and consumers faced a "famine." The feudal management of the mines, its cynical exploitation of immigrant labor, and the character of the Morgan controlled combination now sensationally exposed, have been validated since by Eliot Jones's and William J. Walsh's excellent monographs.[3]

John Mitchell, the United Mine-Workers' President, became a popular hero as he led the strike for recognition, higher wages, an eight-hour day, and control of the mines checkweighmen. He had been a miner in Spring Valley and a parishioner of Father Power when Lloyd wrote "To Certain Rich Men" and *A Strike of Millionaires.*[4]

Lloyd had investigated and exposed repeatedly the anthracite coal combination. Morgan's reorganized "trust" had developed effective market control accompanied by characteristic stockwatering. It had absorbed the large, independent Temple Iron Company. Lloyd's prominence as America's leading non-Marxian radical and chief inspirer of the anti-Trust movement drew him inevitably into the attempt to settle the strike. As early as 1896, when replying to the *Financial Chronicle*'s praise of that combination, the *Springfield Republican* had remarked that if Americans had to choose between eliminating competition in anthracite coal for the benefit of "the wealthy and powerful few" and its suppression "in the interest of all" the Socialists would "command . . . the more numerous following."[5] In 1893 Lloyd had demanded nationalization of coal mines as early as the National Anti-Trust Conference.

He recognized in 1902 that the UMW's strike challenged directly the allied seven anthracite railroads led by the Reading, New Jersey Central, Lehigh, and Erie, the Pennsylvania Coal Company, and the Temple Iron Company. These corporations were held together by intercorporate stockholdings, perpetual leases, and voting trusts giving the Morgan house control. George F. Baer, President of the Reading, New Jersey Central, and Temple Iron companies was official head of the "trust." During the preceding strike of 1900 Lloyd had demanded mines nationalization plus compulsory arbitration,[6] only to have Senator Hanna arrange a compromise settlement.

The 1902 strike had been precipitated by the "trust's" refusal to recognize and bargain collectively with the UMW, which in the central bituminous field had recently won recognition and the living wage. "There can not be two masters in the management of the business," the reactionary Baer replied to Mitchell. During the prestrike dispute Mitchell had forced discussion of the UMW's demands in the National Civic Federation. Baer had rejected arbitration there as he did also Hanna's attempts to negotiate a settlement. To Mitchell's proposal for arbitration by Archbishop Ireland, Bishop Potter, and a third figure, he had replied sarcastically :

Anthracite mining is a business, and not a religious, sentimental, or academic proposition. The laws organizing the companies I represent in express terms impose the business management on the president and the directors. I could not if I would delegate this business management to even so highly a respectable a body as the Civic Federation, nor can I call to my aid as experts in the mixed problem of business and philanthropy the eminent prelates you have named.[7]

As one railroad president observed, anthracite coal mining needed "an entirely different type" of executive who was "intellectually competent to do business" on the basis of "systematic recognition" of the UMW. When President Roosevelt sent Carroll D. Wright to investigate and propose arbitration, Baer rejected this also.[8]

A prolonged shutdown, operators' profiteering, and a developing "coal famine" ensued. John R. Commons, Bishop Samuel Fallows, and John Graham Brooks visited the anthracite districts and counteracted operator-inspired news with the aid of the *New York World* and *New York Journal*. Virtually the entire press demanded federal intervention. Ex-President Cleveland and William Randolph Hearst demanded prosecution of the anthracite carriers under the Sherman Act. Baer antagonized the press and public further by his arrogant reply to a Wilkes-Barre citizen who urged him to terminate the strike:

> I beg of you not to be discouraged. The rights and interests of the laboring man will be protected and cared for—not by the labor agitators, but by the Christian man to whom God in His infinite wisdom has given the control of the property interests of the country, and upon the successful management of which so much depends.

Pilloried as "the pious pirate" head of a "thieving trust" by Hearst's *Journal,* Baer was *the* typical "trust" magnate.[9] Thus, the issue was personalized by the press before Lloyd entered the debate, after a fashion that he had established some years earlier.

Anthracite prices were $30 a ton in New York when Hearst telegraphed him at Sakonnet, August 21, asking him to serve on a mediation committee to secure a "speedy and peaceful settlement." In a *Journal* symposium Lloyd demanded emergency nationalization of the coal carriers and mines backed by martial law if coal was not being produced by September 1. This stand Ernest Crosby and Jacob A. Riis supported, as did some leading newspapers tentatively. The *Central* (Chicago) *Law Journal* declared that the mines could be seized legally via condemnation proceedings by Pennsylvania, but Senator Matthew Quay's rule there made that impossible. Governor Wm. A. Stone advocated compulsory arbitration, however.[10]

Influential New Yorkers consulted Lloyd on how to settle the strike. Although he predicted that Roosevelt "Will not storm *this* hill" after writing "Australian Cures for Coal Wars" for the November *Atlantic,* he telegraphed the President demanding "Publicity and Prevention," "T. R.'s" favorite remedy for industrial strife. The *Boston Transcript,* John Bates Clark, and thousands of influential citizens demanded compulsory arbitration as a permanent policy. George H. Warner asked Lloyd to brief Roosevelt on the New Zealand Arbitration Act![11]

"T. R." secured an epochial arbitration *after* Attorney General Philander C. Knox informed him that he lacked power to intervene and antitrust proceedings were "improper," and *after* Wright's mediation failed. Determined to curb the great business combinations and restrain national labor organizations, and alarmed lest inaction alienate the electorate, Roosevelt forced Morgan's hand. After a secret, abortive White House Conference that enhanced Mitchell's prestige as the obdurate operators demanded military intervention, the President informed his Cabinet of secret military preparations to seize and operate the mines. Presidential letters to Robert Bacon, Morgan's favorite partner, depicted the danger of rioting if settlement of the strike were delayed. Elihu Root, Secretary of War, persuaded Morgan "unofficially" to propose investigation by a presidential commission.

"T. R." turned this limited concession into a spectacular victory for presidential authority and public opinion. "Arbitration" was carefully avoided and "recognition" of the UMW was prohibited in Morgan's "proposal," whose stipulated commission was to be stacked in the operators' favor. Acceptance obliged Roosevelt to appoint to it an east Pennsylvania federal judge, an expert mining engineer, an experienced anthracite operator, two others presumably sympathetic with management, and an "eminent sociologist." Unable to add a trades unionist to the

Commission as Mitchell demanded, he persuaded Bacon and the operators to allow him to appoint Edgar E. Clark, Grand Chief of the Brotherhood of the Railway Conductors, as the "eminent sociologist"! Roosevelt then assumed control of the Commission. After appointing Lloyd's stalwart friends Carroll D. Wright, Recorder, and E. A. Moseley, Assistant Recorder, he elevated Wright to the Commission. The other Commissioners were Judge George Gray of Wilmington, Chairman, Bishop John L. Spaulding of Peoria (a Baltimore patrician but Father Power's loyal superior), Thomas A. Watkins as the mining operator, General John M. Wilson from the Cuban military government and E. W. Parker, chief statistician of the Coal Division, United States Geological Survey, as the expert mining engineer. A majority of four were federal officials. Spaulding understood the situation in mining districts. Moseley, long indignant at the railroads' defiance of the Interstate Commerce Commission of which he was Secretary, became Recorder. By instructing the Commission to investigate and "pass upon the questions in controversy" and their causes, Roosevelt virtually ordered it to arbitrate the dispute and return an award. Baer and Mitchell accepted the Commission. Presidential investigation was now very close to compulsory arbitration that November.

Roosevelt's skillful but complicated coup gratified the public enormously by reopening the mines, and virtually insured the Republican party's victory in 1902 and Roosevelt's re-election. So Henry Cabot Lodge assured him. It was evident to all that Roosevelt had moved the White House back from 1 Wall Street to Pennsylvania Avenue, while launching the United States upon "a novel sphere of action."[12]

Lloyd was not sure, at first, that the Commission could make an acceptable award in view of Morgan's stipulations, and was misled by these into misreading the import of Roosevelt's appointments. After fearing a tie decision Lloyd was greatly relieved by Wright's elevation to it.

THE MINERS' ATTORNEY

Instead of crusading for introduction of Swiss democracy into the United States that autumn, Lloyd had first advised the Hearst Syndicated on issues involved in the strike and then gone into the anthracite coal regions in early October to see "this other great Strike of Millionaires against Miners." He advised the district union leaders to stand firm for arbitration or a negotiated settlement during "T. R.'s" pressure to return to work prior to the coup. After contributing to the miners' relief fund and presenting Father Power's letter of introduction to Mitchell he volunteered at his own expense to assist in money-raising, "defending the union," preparing press releases, or "getting ready your case for the proposed arbitration—anything, command me." He became an unpaid member of Mitchell's staff. During a flying visit into the Middle West he attended the Detroit Coal Conference and investigated public sentiment at Toledo and Cleveland and the views of Mayors S. M. Jones and Tom L. Johnson. Thrilled by the experience, he sat on the stage at the UMW Convention at Wilkes-Barre as it voted to accept the Commission and the strike.[13]

"A Boston Gentleman" then published in the *Transcript* a vivid, eyewitness account of that democratic event with warm appreciation of Mitchell's leadership. Lloyd witnessed the reopening of several mines, observing that some operators declined to rehire union officers. At Mitchell's headquarters he learned that the UMW still had $1,000,000 in its treasury to assist the displaced miners and finance its share of the arbitration. Never before had a labor union in America survived so long a contest with such prestige, strength, and public backing.[14]

Walter Weyl and the Rev. Peter Roberts, author of a book on anthracite coal mining, were congenial associates on Mitchell's staff. They gathered data so energetically that Lloyd became convinced that "no labor arbitration has ever seen the cause of the workmen presented as this will be." He and Weyl collected a dozen experts, including Commons, whom they put to work "on every conceivable phase of the case." Lloyd entertained Mitchell at dinner. He enjoyed being "on the inside of things." He secured the latest reports of British arbitrations. He encouraged his semi-invalid wife with daily letters.

Learning of the operators' and anthracite railroads' high-priced legal talent, Mitchell concluded that he needed a man of greater skill and reputation as UMW counsel than Weyl, a professional statistician. Lloyd suggested Darrow for chief counsel. When en route to Will's wedding to Miss Lola Maverick in San Antonio, he said a decisive word to Darrow in Chicago, backed by Mitchell's urgent telegram. As leader of Altgeld's following and independent candidate for the Illinois General Assembly on a municipal ownership platform, Darrow consented. He was then elected by a tremendous majority. Learning at San Antonio of his acceptance, Lloyd telegraphed him and Mitchell: "Congratulate both when bad men combine the good must associate." He also telegraphed the district UMW presidents to arrange that the Commission encounter crippled miners and children and underaged child mine-workers on its tour of the mines.

Back at Wilkes-Barre before Darrow arrived, he drew Mitchell into regular evening walks to combat his insomnia and "worrying at night." After Lloyd convinced him that a plea for collective bargaining would forestall the operators' plan to exploit the strike's violent incidents, Mitchell added him to the miners' counsel. Darrow and Lloyd explored the mines and examined documents and witnesses together.[15]

Lloyd was cheered by news from "Hal" at Harvard Medical School, "Demmie working hard at crew" in Harvard College, and "Jack" tutoring for college entrance examinations. Keenly interested in their desire for a football victory over Yale, he wrote his wife : "You can take great comfort in your sons. They are noble boys, and they love their Mother."[16]

The Commission agreed with the public and the miners that it was an arbitration tribunal and adopted customary procedures. The record would be the basis of an award. Toward the close of protracted hearings, formal court procedure was "gradually lessened" so as "to arrive at the truth with the least possible amount of obstruction.'"" Lloyd confided to a notebook that the anthracite "trust" should fix prices "to pay living wages," recognize trades unions, reduce transportation rates and coal prices, and pay the carriers the same compensation as other railroads receive. "We . . . ask this Commission . . . to square the exercise of monopoly powers with the good of all concerned," the miners, operators, "transporter and the public." The coal carriers would be unable to "play" with this Commission as the other railroads had "with the ISCC and even with Congress," he predicted.[18]

THE MINERS' CASE

The Commission toured the mining districts after hearing opening statements from the parties to the arbitration: the anthracite carriers and their coal operating companies (the "trust"), independent operators, organized miners whom Mitchell and his staff represented, and the unorganized miners whose attorneys were paid by the "trust." The Commission reconvened at Scranton in the Superior Court Chamber to hear the organized miners' testimony in support of demands that Mitchell had presented at Wilkes-Barre. Immediately before these hearings began, the press gave wide circulation to the declaration of President Eliot of Harvard "the strike breaker is a good type of American hero." In an equally well-circulated rebuttal, Lloyd compared the "scab" to the "Tory" of the American Revolution. "Men like President Eliot, . . . however honest they may be," he said, "are holding the hands of the defenceless masses while capitalism robs them of the only thing they have left—union."[19]

Lloyd, Darrow, Mitchell, and the UMW staff knew that they faced the "fight of their lives." Lloyd was proud of representing workingmen in an arbitration in "my *first* case." Scranton hotels were filled with operators' attorneys, led by Baer and Wayne MacVeagh, Morgan's representative. "The Tory is always the same," Lloyd wrote to his wife. Baer illustrated this with so unreasonable a reply to the organized miners' demands that the *Boston Transcript* quoted President Eliot's "the oper-

ators are in an inhuman state of mind." Baer's claim that the
UMW had no standing before the Commission it termed Pick-
wickian.[20] The Commission agreed with him, however. To win
recognition of the UMW as the miners' agent became necessarily a major objective of the organized miners' representatives.
Furthermore, Mitchell, Darrow, Lloyd, and four lawyer
assistants were restricted to presentation of the case for the
union miners as individuals. They were opposed by "twenty-five
of the country's ablest lawyers" representing the operators in
the "trust," the independents, and the nonunion miners.[21]

Darrow presented 241 witnesses in developing the union
miners' case. Lloyd helped prepare them to testify. He contributed largely to "planning and executing our campaign." Alert
to the human aspects of industrial problems, he persuaded
Darrow and Mitchell to schedule "some of the breaker
children" who picked slate from the coal in the dusty breakers
for the witness stand, and "some of the miners' wives to tell
how the wife & mother holds her family together, brings up the
children, always has something for the man's dinner pail on
$35 a month."[22] He worked late at night and arose at 4:30 A.M.
since Mitchell's counsel had to make their case against "every
company separately." He rested briefly during the noon hour,
but attended morning and afternoon sessions daily.

Mitchell's formal statement and testimony made recognition
of the United Mine Workers their fourth objective, while
demonstrating the UMW's democracy and responsibility. He
documented demands for higher wages, shorter hours, and
improved working conditions by adverse comparisons of housing, child labor, and wages in the anthracite districts with those
of the bituminous fields where the UMW had established higher
standards by collective bargaining; $600 a year should be the
minimum wage of anthracite mine workers, he said. His witty
and shrewd answers to emotional, unfair questioning during
cross-examination while presenting new evidence delighted the
spectators. Replying to MacVeagh's query whether the strike
had not inflicted serious losses upon the mining companies,
Mitchell demonstrated that despite five months' idleness they

could work as many days in 1902 as they did in 1901. When asked if a wage increase would not fall upon the "poor," he replied that it should be taken from profits and "put on the bowed backs of the rich." Quizzed as to a fair return on capital by the Lackawanna Railroad's attorney, he replied that its net earnings were 26 per cent per annum. Such poise won MacVeagh's compliment, "You are the best witness for yourself, Mr. Mitchell, that I ever confronted," and Lloyd's remark, "Yes, because for one thing he is a good man."[23]

Lloyd wrote home jubilantly : "Mitchell is a wonder. He was cross-examined today by Wayne MacVeagh, and he . . . threw him . . . down time after time. Even the Commission sometimes so far forgot themselves as to join in the laugh." Soon he added : "This case grows intensely interesting. We had a miner who began work at 8. He had *no* books in the house and never studied arithmetic. . . . No more stirring case could ever come."[24] His reputation with the Commission was revealed by Moseley's report that the Commissioners were impressed "tremendously" by Mitchell's opening statement. "It must have been edited by Mr. Lloyd," one remarked. "No," Bishop Spaulding replied, "that is impossible. It contains four split infinitives." Horace White wrote Lloyd how glad he was "that Mr. Mitchell has so good an adviser as yourself," and complimented his *Atlantic* article.[25]

Darrow presented sensational evidence, beginning with Roberts' testimony on the operators' antiunion activities. Then followed testimony of practicing physicians and health officials on miners' occupational diseases that defeated the operators' hope of securing a favorable award.[26]

Consequently, MacVeagh began secret overtures on November 16 to Mitchell, Darrow, and Lloyd, and asked the Commission to approve of a voluntary settlement. The Commissioners were agreeable. Darrow suggested that they adjourn to December 3 but remain in town, and predicted a negotiated settlement of most issues at stake. The Commissioners assented, and ruled that "as a commission of conciliation" it would welcome "agreed-upon statements" eliminating as many points "from the controversy as you may deem best." The final settlement had to be a Commission award. Although MacVeagh pressed for a complete, privately negotiated settlement, Darrow adhered to this instruction.[27]

Lloyd was delighted at the prospect of a settlement that would hasten his return to "my real work on my books. We are to have something better than arbitration,—conciliation," he informed his wife. At first he believed a complete agreement possible, with substantial gains for the miners. Then, when the negotiations in Washington were on the verge of complete success immediately before Thanksgiving, Baer called them off, treating MacVeaugh, Mitchell, Darrow, and Lloyd, who had gone to Washington to confer and see the President, to a telegraphed "taste of Baerism." Carroll D. Wright handed the press an account of the negotiations and a copy of the cancelled "Tentative Agreement." Its publication together with a statement by Darrow and Lloyd enhanced the UMW's prestige. The *Hartford Courant, Springfield Republican, Boston Herald,* and *Boston Post* approved of the course of the union miners' trio during the "mediation." MacVeagh's attempts to revive negotiations were defeated by Baer's desire for personal vindication.[28]

During the interim Moseley introduced Lloyd to the Department of Justice official who was secretly gathering data on the anthracite "trust." He conferred with Brandeis and the United States District Attorney in New York City, and secured comparative rate data from the ICC.[29] On Thanksgiving, Walter S. Wyman of the conservative Chicago Union League Club wrote Lloyd that " the cause" was "to be congratulated in having the counsel of one with such intelligence and heart as I have known in your voice. . . . I have taken great satisfaction in your recognition and wish to contribute one of the jewels for the crown." When the hearings resumed amid operators' embarrassment the *Coal Trade Journal* criticized MacVeagh's attempt and demanded "Lasting peace, not simply an early settlement."[30]

At Lloyd's insistence Darrow let the miners, their wives and children, subordinate mine-workers, and the priests of the regions present the irrefutable facts of long hours, low wages, poverty, conscienceless exploitation of child labor, the dismissals of union officers. This parade of the humble provided the dramatic, heart-stirring climax of the hearings. It established the facts of substandard housing and the elastic cars for filling which miners were paid. It exhibited contract miners receiving from $200 to $280 a year. It proved Coxe & Company's dismissal of all UMW officers. It presented a mine-worker receiving from 81 cents to $15 a fortnight, whose wife took in washing and sewing and had no new dress for eight years. It described the maintenance workers' thirteen-and-a-half-hour shift. It proved the miners' inability to keep their children in school after eleven years of age, the miners' sobriety and peaceable behaviour, the incredible low wages paid their daughters at nearby silk mills, the inability of the miners to support their families. It exposed the faked photographs in *Everybody's* and *Colliers* falsifying conditions in the anthracite districts during the strike. These disclosures provoked indignant comments from the Commissioners.[31]

Darrow and Lloyd exposed the companies' refusal to compensate for accidental deaths of mine-workers and insistence that their minor children assume their debts. They put tiny, nine-year-old Andrew Chippie on the witness stand. He told of how he had been held liable by Markle & Company for his deceased father's back rent ($88.17), after his accidental death in the mine, when he went to work on the breakers although younger than the legal age limit. When he exhibited the due statement of the balance owed that he received instead of his pay of 40 cents a day for his first fortnight's work, every adult in the Court Room shed angry, sympathetic tears.[32]

Lloyd had Andrew Chippie's photograph taken holding that due bill, and sold copies for his benefit to the Commissioners, spectators, and the press, which reproduced it as evidence of the operators' inhumanity. When Chairman Judge Gray purchased a lot of toys for Andy, Lloyd wrote home, "We are going to wind up our case in a blaze of glory." Judge Gray asked that the minimum adequate standard of living in the anthracite districts be determined after listening to the breaker boys' testimony. He demanded indignantly, after hearing a ten-year-old miner's daughter describe her five-and-a-quarter-cents per hour pay for a twelve-hour silk factory day, that the district factory inspector explain why the Pennsylvania child labor act was violated so flagrantly. Darrow exposed the false wage statements submitted by the Lehigh and Pennsylvania coal companies in attempts to shift the blame for the silk mill girls' employment to their miner fathers.[33]

Despite operators' vehement protests, Darrow then persuaded the Commission to allow Lloyd to present a carefully prepared documentary history of the anthracite "Trust"[34] as an analysis of the relations of the miners to the anthracite railroads. The public received this comprehensive account of the "Trust's" origins, character, and business methods with much gratification. In preparation of this Lloyd had enjoyed Brandeis' collaboration. The monopoly's antiunion policy, control of the Pennsylvania coal and iron police, engrossing of coal, and timber lands, interlocking directorates, subsidiaries, past punishment of operators granting the union's demands with treble freight rate increases and Morgan's conquest of the combination Lloyd established fully. Then, looking at the Commission, he observed that the president of the Temple Iron Company two years before had been Thomas H. Watkins. He might have been even more cutting had Commissioner Watkins not stated previously that he had transferred his Temple Iron Company stock to his former partner in Simpson & Watkins that it had absorbed. This close did Lloyd come to declaring outright that Morgan & Company had wangled the appointment to the Commission of a recent key executive in the "trust" as the price of acquiescence in presidential intervention in the strike.

After Lloyd exposed "excessive over-capitalization" of the "trust's" coal lands, he attempted to demonstrate that large profits justified the union miners' wage demands. Judge Gray ruled, after a heated colloquy between Darrow and operators' counsel, that the Commission assumed the operators "are able to pay fair wages . . . If they cannot pay fair wages, they had better go out of business." Lloyd acquiesced because this ruling committed the Commission to "the principle of the living wage" and set a precedent for future arbitrations! He offered to demonstrate that the anthracite carriers' discriminatory and exorbitant freight rates proved that wages and working conditions in the mines were "the result, not of natural economic forces . . . but of the unnatural combination produced by force and the violation of law." This, he declared, was the key to the wages problem, and would expose the "trust's" extraordinary power from whose effects the Commission should give the largest relief possible. Although it ruled that this was beyond its jurisdiction, Gray added that if inquiry into freight rates became essential to its award it would not "hesitate to turn to any source of information that may enlighten our pathway."

Lloyd was jubilant at his success in committing the Commission to the living wage. "The most advanced socialist could hardly ask for more," he wrote his wife. In his notebook he added: "An advanced & self protected public must now make public utilities out of these private utilities." The real issue in the Arbitration to him was between oligarchic and democratic power.

He and Darrow made their point indirectly with the testimony of John C. Haddock, President of the Lincoln Coal Company, the only remaining truly independent operating firm. As Haddock described his long fight against the combination's control of anthracite shipments and its discriminatory, exorbitant rates, Darrow asked Lloyd, "Did you get the history of this last effort in there?" Lloyd replied, "Yes." Whereupon Gray remarked, "I thought so."[35] Samuel Gompers, the union miners' last witness, greatly impressed the Commission and operators' counsel by demonstrating the beneficial effects of collective bargaining and the trade unions' fidelity to their trade agreements.[36]

The skilful presentation of the union miners' case received strong support from the independent press, for which Lloyd's public relations work at Mitchell's headquarters was partially responsible. Horace White literally gave him "the run of the *New York Evening Post.*" The weary reformer, who was "wrestling hard with lumbago," was encouraged by the *Boston*

Transcript's declaration that the living conditions of the miners were "a discredit to the country."[37]

FOR A TRADE AGREEMENT

He celebrated Christmas with his family at The Wayside. Then he sent Mrs. Lloyd south to Pass Christian to convalesce from a recent illness. He assured Signor Contini that America's "practical genius" for "short cuts in any impasse" sustained his courage "in the decidedly depressing circumstances of our present social condition," after relating how Roosevelt had secretly forced the operators to arbitrate by threat of seizure and operation of the mines. The people would quickly "finish" the "monopolies and capitalism" when "they set to work," he prophesied. While thanking Mather for data on British arbitrations, he asserted that the coal companies' bitter-end "irresponsible" opposition illustrated the dangerous "spirit of absolutism."[38]

At Darrow's request he invited Brandeis to make the argument for the union miners "at the close of the hearing." Lloyd preferred that his own participation in the legal presentation should "be more on lines of social economics." As associate editor in charge of "Co-operation, Arbitration and Social Reform" for the new *Boyce's Weekly* (Chicago), he placed his views and the latest news on such subjects before the trades unionists. His first piece, "In Favor of the Miners," presented the union miners' cause sympathetically and asserted that the Arbitration established a precedent for a permanent national industrial court.[39]

In Philadelphia, where the Commission held its post-holiday hearings, the testimony for the nonunion miners and the operators consumed five and a half weeks. Darrow and the other practicing attorneys on Mitchell's staff cross-examined hundreds of witnesses. Left initially with nothing to do in the Federal Court Room but write letters to his wife and articles for *Boyce's Weekly*, Lloyd lectured locally and along the coast as far north as Maine. This eased a personal financial stringency arising from the Chicago Tribune Company's passing of successive quarterly dividends, as it attempted to out-Hearst the new *Chicago*

Herald and the *Chicago American* despite protests from the minority stockholders.[40]

He was soon informed that he would present a portion of the organized miners' final argument. He had great difficulty in sleeping in the noisy Colonial Hotel. "I wish I were through this job here," he wrote to Mrs. Lloyd, "I can't really see that I am doing any good—or not much and I can't bear to think of the time of which so little is left slipping by with my own work undone."[41] He admired Darrow's courtroom ascendancy: "He is a wonderful fellow, absolutely tireless, more brilliant by far than I had thought." Lloyd noted a difference in Judge Gray's manner, suggesting that he had lunched at the White House. "We are correspondingly hopeful," he added.[42]

Darrow exposed skillfully the inconsistency of the operators' attempts to discredit the UMW while denying that the Commission could adjudicate the issue of recognition. His cross-examining so discredited hostile witnesses that Mitchell returned to the Cincinnati UMW headquarters. When Mitchell's universal popularity led to talk of running him for President of the United States on the Democratic ticket, Roosevelt assured him secretly not to worry about the Arbitration award.

Lloyd's assignment to union recognition and the trade agreement in the final argument originated with the Commission's refusal to inquire into freight rates and monopoly. This prevented him from making the "sociological" argument for which he was exceptionally qualified. It was impossible to use Brandeis to develop comparative freight rates.[43]

Lloyd and Darrow were lionized by Philadelphia liberals and enjoyed it. Most unusual was a dinner in honor of the Commission and the opposing counsel at the Clover Leaf Club, where the members gave them a customary unmerciful chaffing as they rose to speak. Although two Commissioners abandoned their speeches because lack of wit to ride out the gale of cat-calls and impromptu chorus-singing, Lloyd and Darrow were so charmed that they talked of organizing a similar club in Chicago. The James Dodges entertained Lloyd repeatedly, as did old Philadelphia abolitionist families. Horace Traubel and

he discovered a mutual admiration for Wendell Phillips. Lloyd
was accorded a fortnight's membership in the Union League
Club at the instance of a leading anti-imperialist.[44]

Learning from John Graham Brooks that the Commission's
award "will be more in our favor than generally anticipated,"
he informed Mitchell that he could "pull" a series of newspapers ranging from the *Springfield Republican* to the *Chicago
Tribune* in the UMW's behalf.[45] He was ready for the argument
on February 9, his spirits bolstered by Mrs. Lloyd's note re-
proving his lack of confidence. He followed Daniel J. McCarthy,
a lawyer after a quarter century's work in the mines, who
pleaded ably for better working conditions.

Encouraged by his sister Mrs. Madeleine Lloyd Goodrich's
presence, Lloyd presented an eloquent, closely reasoned plea
for a trade agreement that received much favorable press comment. Gray interrupted his criticism of scabs in a dramatic
colloquoy that Traubel long remembered. They, Lloyd said,
violated their "moral duty" to assist in the "elevation of their
own class and of society at large." Collective bargaining, he
declared, would introduce "industrial peace" into the industry.
He depicted its existence in New Zealand and the role of voluntary arbitration in American industrial disputes. After
stressing the UMW's observance of its contractual obligations,
he claimed for the miners "equal participation in initiating,
framing, consummating, interpreting, modifying, and annulling
the contracts by which we labour and live." Collective bargaining was true industrial democracy, the solution for "industrial
warfare" in harmony with the "instinctive, universal spirit of
democracy, the greatest social fact of our day." Recognition of
the UMW would bring peace, stability, enhanced profits, and
general well-being to the anthracite districts, their dependent
industries and the public. It would complete the defeat of
absolutism in the industry.[46]

As Lloyd concluded amid an ovation from the entire court
room, Baer turned to Darrow in humorous anxiety, "Darrow,
are there any more Chicago men coming on here to make
speeches?" After the adjournment he remarked, "Mr. Lloyd,

you are considerable of an optimist." The other defense attorney congratulated him, as did Darrow. "Unexpectedly triumphant," Lloyd telegraphed home. Samuel Bowles telegraphed commendation, congratulations, and "love" and published Lloyd's entire argument with his portrait in the *Springfield Republican* as did *Boyce's Weekly*. The *Chicago Tribune* endorsed his demand for an annual trade agreement as a "permanent remedy."

The *New York American* declared in agreement with Lloyd that "The Scab is justly despised." "Nurture the Unions," the *Portsmouth Herald* declared.⁴⁷ Lloyd's triumph consolidated public opinion's change from hostility to support of collective bargaining which his championship, the new economics, and the logic of events had helped to accomplish. Traubel wrote him : "You did the big thing which I expected you to do. I found the real America at last born in my delayed life. . . . You have stood for me as a chief figure in the drama. . . . You have added cubits to your stature. I am always at your service." Bishop Spaulding called Lloyd's plea *"the* gem of the whole proceeding."⁴⁸

Lloyd then withstood Baer's withering, sarcastic rebuttal, which invoked Social Darwinism while attacking the UMW as a monopoly and excoriating the National Civic Federation's abortive intervention in the strike. Baer lampooned reformers, upheld individualism in business, ridiculed socialism, and dubbed Lloyd "the distinguished literary philanthropist from Chicago." New Zealand conciliation and compulsory arbitration he called "another Paradise Lost." He defended industrial monopoly as sound in theory, beneficial to all in practice.⁴⁹

Lloyd was gratified that his own argument "proved so nearly a complete statement of our case" that it became almost "a syllabus" of Darrow's long, brilliant summation of the organized miners' case. This Lloyd termed "very good, great on child labor." It won the Commission's "undivided interest and admiration" and "quite carried away" many "of the *capitalist* women," he informed his wife. Turning to him, Darrow alluded gracefully to Baer's attack : "Your day, Mr. Lloyd, and mine will

come some day and there will be no Baers to dispute with us."
Darrow exposed the opposing counsel's bitter spirit and reliance
upon antiquated "theory" as he invited the Commission's attention to the real issues : higher wages, shorter hours, fair treatment, union recognition. After provoking the audience repeatedly to laughter and enthusiastic applause he declared, "the
biggest breaker is Mr. Baer himself" and closed with a brilliant
eulogium of Mitchell.⁵⁰

A POPULAR VICTORY

After final adjournment Lloyd, Mitchell, and Darrow left
for Chicago to attend a huge Auditorium "Reception" in their
honor, to which the eagerness of the Altgeld Democrats to nominate Darrow for Mayor gave a political overtone. Although the
trio arrived in Chicago amid "a real old-fashioned snow-storm"
Lloyd caught the first Northwestern train for Winnetka. He
arrived there at "half past ten" to find The Wayside "bright
with lights in the parlor and violets in the bedroom, and roses
everywhere," and a letter from his wife. "Was I lonesome," he
wrote her.⁵¹

Chicago hailed the trio on February 16, 1903, as "men who
have done themselves honor in support of a righteous cause"
and who had "pilloried the wrong." Despite drifted streets and
below-zero weather 5,000 enthusiastic liberals and laborers
crowded the Auditorium. Lloyd hailed Mitchell there as victor
in a contest greater than the Pullman strike, and Darrow as
"that rare bird, a lawyer whose first love is love of justice" as the
throng applauded every sentence. That Roosevelt had given
America arbitration, backed by threat of Federal seizure of the
mines, as the solution for catastrophic industrial strife, Lloyd
declared was "the most novel, the boldest, the greatest stroke
of recent statesmanship." Mitchell's defeat of the attempt to
exterminate trades unions in "the first real uprising of the
American people against the monopolists" had shown how to
deal with monopoly. Darrow spoke without preparation for
ninety minutes to the throng's complete satisfaction and Lloyd's
admiration and secret envy. After this masterly description of

the strike's issues and the great Arbitration, Mitchell's direct, unpretentious review of the miners' cause and victory won almost equal acclaim.[52]

Chicago was gratified with Lloyd's address. Salter said to him the next morning, "Bravo! It was fine. In fact, it was a fine meeting all round. Darrow seemed in a more genial mood than usual, and Mitchell much impressed me by his manliness and straight-forwardness and simplicity." The conservative *Chicago Journal,* however, attacked Lloyd's address as "the most demagogic of all and unworthy of a gentleman of his character, wealth, and education" because of its eulogy of Debs and criticism of Cleveland's handling of the Pullman strike. Lloyd asked his wife to reread his speech in "the most judicial vein" to discover "if you think it deserves these reproaches."[53] The Associated Press and eastern papers featured his contrast between Roosevelt's and Cleveland's methods of settling great industrial disputes. When the *New York Evening Post* declared that Altgeld had refused to send militia to Chicago during the great riots of 1894 and asked pointedly what could be the legal basis for federal seizure and operation of the coal mines, Lloyd replied with the *Springfield Republican's* support that he had witnessed Altgeld's command of the Illinois militia and his determination to prevent interruption of the public peace and transportation. As for the mines, any public official could institute equity proceedings for federal railroad receiverships, or invoke the Sherman Act "which expressly authorizes the seizure of coal mines and railroads, parties to an unlawful combination." Section 6 of that statute, which he invoked, had not yet been tested in the courts, but they have approved since then temporary emergency federal seizures and operation of national industries. Many lawyers agreed with Lloyd's position in 1903.[54]

He persuaded Darrow not to enter the Chicago mayoral race, and instead to introduce some social legislation bills in the General Assembly.[55]

Lloyd was gratified by the Strike Commission's award on March 23, 1903. "The men have not got all they ought to have had, but they certainly have won a notable victory," he wrote Moseley, who sent copies to his friends and officials in America, Australasia, and Europe for him. Darrow, however, wrote Lloyd bitterly that it was "a most cowardly document." The *United Mine Workers Journal* called it "a good decision," conceding "every proposition" in the UMW's platform but collective bargaining, "and that is provided for in such a way that it must naturally follow in a short time."[56] President Roosevelt declared publicly that "no Government document of recent years marks a more important piece of work better done" than the Commission's *Report.* He thanked the Commissioners for averting "a great national calamity" and for their service to the nation. The award and accompanying report were generally approved. They brought to a climax the public discussion of the labor problem that the great strike had stimulated.[57]

The award was more generous in some ways to the miners than the abortive secret agreement of the preceding November. It granted 10 per cent increase in pay and reduction of the work day to nine hours. Additional pay increases accrued from rulings that contract miners pay the checkweighmen, that cars of standard size be used, and that miners might employ the check docking bosses inspecting the coal for impurities. A sliding scale was instituted that increased wages 1 per cent for each five cents above $4.50 per ton of standard grade above pea in New York City. Denial of employment could not be based upon union membership or nonmembership. Elevation of the minimum age limit was strongly recommended, as was abolition of the coal and iron police. The award established a joint operator-miner Conciliation Board, secured UMW grant of autonomy to the anthracite districts in its organization, and by establishment of colliery and company grievance committees opened the door for eventual collective bargaining. The Commission recommended establishment of federal and state commissions for compulsory investigation of industrial disputes, in which Lloyd's influence was also evident. Although the Commission hoped that collective bargaining would ensue at the expiration of the award after three years, it did not materialize fully until

1916 after successive extensions of the award. Until that date anthracite miners' wages remained 25 per cent below those of the unionized bituminous fields. However, in 1912 Mitchell would describe the improvement in the anthracite miners' condition resulting from the award and subsequent union activity as tantamount "almost to a revolution." Its approval of collective bargaining and the defeat inflicted upon Morgan's "Coal Trust" gave a decided stimulus to trades unionism generally.[58]

In *Boyce's Weekly* Lloyd declared that the business world had paid $50,000,000 for "a lesson in what the best and most practical methods are in modern civilization," although "the very class" to which it was of "the most vital importance" was busy belittling it. "The parasites of the minority who do not know how to use their hands" should pray "that social disputes should always be ended by reason. A greater victory" in the race's social history had not been won. Moseley remarked to him, "While it fell short of being all that was expected the award is the greatest step forward that has been made in my recollection or time." This was the verdict of the *Review of Reviews. The Outlook* declared the award "the most important event in the industrial history of the past quarter century." As Father Walsh has demonstrated, it was a "remarkable and substantial victory" for the miners.[59]

Mitchell acknowledged frankly his great debt to Lloyd, which no financial reimbursement "will ever liquidate." Lloyd refused his offer of repayment of expenses plus the bills charged to his account by UMW staff at the Colonial Hotel. He was glad to contribute all this to the miners, whom he had admired ever since "I saw their heroism and suffering at Spring Valley." The UMW's funds "come out of very scanty purses," he added, and "is destined for the support of a movement much higher than merely the increase" of its members' wages. If needed again he would "respond to any call" without compensation, and in the future would not decline expenses.[60]

To Reeves and Sir J. G. Ward Lloyd attributed the Arbitration and the award justly to "the initiative and inspiration derived from the laws of your country." He predicted accurately that it would lead to demand for arbitration as a regular government function, but twelve years later the United States Supreme Court invalidated state compulsory arbitration. Subsequently, the great strikes of 1946 induced important midwestern newspapers to revive Lloyd's demand for this. In the interim the recurrence of catastrophic strikes obliged national administrations to resort to emergency seizures of the industries afflicted as Roosevelt had threatened to do in 1902. It was evident then that his intervention in the strike and the Arbitration Commission's work had been made possible by Lloyd's campaign for compulsory arbitration and federal action.[61]

Chapter XXIII

 A Pragmatic Test for Debs

RETURN TO WINNETKA

THREE CONTINENTS knew Lloyd as America's beloved radical in 1903, its "second Wendell Phillips." Mead reminded Gladden that Tarbell's *History of the Standard Oil* repeated *Wealth Against Commonwealth,* and called for "another muscular chapter from your own 'Tainted Money.' A democracy that can read such revelations and go on making such things the corner-stones of the nurseries of its youth is damned." Upon both wings of the progressives of the new era, whether Brandeis' and Bryan's attempt to revitalize competition and individualism or Lyman Abbott's demand for a paternalistic, positive state staffed by an educated élite, Lloyd's thought and reform activity exerted great influence.[1] While he had long believed it possible to develop individualism and collectivism simultaneously as interacting forces in human progress, he now stressed also the expansion of governmental regulatory and economic activity under the influence of recent study of the Antipodes and of Europe.

So he led the reform world, cultivated, fatigued, delicate, graying, the friend of each attempt to lighten men's burdens, interested in every "fighter against wrong." "Human nature" should exhibit "the nobleness of the seeker" after social righteousness if it would survive the strain of modern life. "Progress seems slow but I never grow faint-hearted," he wrote Pinner.[2] Had his wife been well she would have ordained the rest that his mother vainly urged him to take after the Arbitration. Instead, he forgot his injunction to a Pennsylvania spinster Socialist : "reformers sometimes forget that their business is not to sacrifice themselves." He had experienced additional strain in January from his father's opposition to Caro's Socialist husband.

During the Arbitration, Lloyd's tender letters to his wife expressed his appreciation of her encouragement, as he encouraged her long convalescence tenderly and with cheery news of their four sons. While she rested after Christmas at Pass Christian they longed together for The Wayside, "a sweet place, and *full of love*," which she opened by telegram for his return to Chicago for the Auditorium Reception.³ He wrote from there of their Winnetka friends and his arduous schedule in a manner disclosing the candor of their love :

> Tonight I dined with the (Rev. C. H.) Ames's. First of everything said Mrs. A. tell us how Mrs. Lloyd is. Mrs. Lloyd is very dear in this house. She is too precious a woman to let out of this world. Don't you think I had a pretty good dinner? . . . Beloved darling, it warmed my old heart to hear the Ameses talk *of you*.

> This is "my busy day." I have to get ready an article for the Booklovers' Magazine, one for Boyce's Weekly, prepare the scheme of a new talk on Compulsory Arbitration for Meadville, and write a letter to The Nation in reply to an attack; have Earnest and Tala Mie for dinner—at their initiative; go to see President Eliot in the afternoon . . . and take the 9.20 Eve train for Meadville. How's that for the day of rest?⁴

Cheered by his wife's ship's clock, he gathered pussy willows against her homecoming. He invited guests from Chicago for Sunday dinner before lecturing on "The New Democracy" at the Ethical Culture Society. In Hubbard Woods he gathered strength from the returning spring and refreshed his Emersonian love of nature. He advised "Demmie" not to work for the

Tribune and, with Alfred Cowles, protested vainly to Robert Patterson against its expensive new building. He was concerned at "Jack's headaches" and after his "coal argument" on Beacon Hill looked "him over carefully." At Cambridge he breakfasted with "Hal," interviewed "Jack's" tutors, helped him with "Caesar," and dined with his three sons there at "the Touraine," which "Hal" said did "the cockles of his heart good."[5] The elevator that he installed at The Wayside for Mrs. Lloyd symbolized his devotion. Lecture and article fees, and reletting his Lake County farm helped his budget. He subdivided his Woodlawn property at 63rd Street, Chicago, but labor troubles checked the building boom and obliged him to wait longer to terminate his "Forty Years in the Financial Wilderness" as he termed his speculation.[6]

In Winnetka he resumed his village leadership. The citizens persuaded him to permit erection of a bath house on his shore property. Encouraged by the success of the municipal electric light plant, Independent party leaders desiring a municipal gas plant conferred with him and launched a four-year campaign that succeeded when Will underwrote the bonds for the village's third successful MO venture. Lloyd and Judge Thomas G. Windes were members of the Advisory Council of The National Federation for Majority Rule that propagated "The Winnetka System—the Lloyd System." Many other members were Lloyd's co-workers in other fields. The *American Federationist* told how he had defeated a forty-year gas franchise in 1898 and of Winnetka's insistence on a referendum on all franchises.[7]

Despite fatigue he was eager to strike for reform while public opinion was receptive because of the Arbitration. His Pennsylvania friends won a higher minimum age for miners. As Jane Addams helped him and Darrow to secure an Illinois Child Labor Act modeled on the Massachusetts statute, he attacked child labor as "race murder" in *Boyce's Weekly*.[8] He was unimpressed by the National Civic Federation's campaign to incorporate trades unions that Brandeis favored, but wondered what their new power presaged. He was troubled by occasional broken contracts and violence but helped the Chicago Federation of

Labor reply to James J. Hill's attack on the labor movement. He dreaded the day when giant labor combinations might be managed by men copying the methods of those who looted great business corporations. He was indignant at West Virginia officials' mistreatment of "Mother" Jones and other UMW organizers. He regarded the public interest as paramount in industrial relations. He had impressed Brandeis with the need to establish industrial democracy by introducing him to arbitrary management and periodic unemployment in the anthracite coal industry during the Arbitration.[9]

AN INVITATION

During the Arbitration's first fortnight an invitation from Algie M. Simon, editor of the *International Socialist Review*, to join the Socialist Party had obliged Lloyd to confront the dichotomy between individualism and collectivism in his thought. In August 1902 on solicitation he had contributed his customary $10 to any reform movement to the Pennsylvania Socialists' anthracite coal region organizing campaign. The Socialist vote increased 210 per cent in Massachusetts and to 400,000 nationally that November in the wake of the great coal strike. Simons extended the same invitation to Darrow, which "Tommy" Morgan renewed to both men in February.[10] In 1899 Lloyd had subsidized his Chicago mayoral campaign, while subscribing to Wayland's *Appeal to Reason* and *The Labour Leader*. Although taking exceptions to Morgan's mayoral platform, he had deemed it extremely important that "so radical an element" should "have the freest opportunity" to present "its views." Yet he did not join Debs's party.[11]

During his 1901 Swiss tour, Lloyd had again straddled the individualist vs. collectivist issue. He regarded the test of collectivist policy as "does it give every individual the best chance and guarantee?" since "perfecting of the individual" was the "consummation of democracy." Swiss democracy indicated that diffusion and popularization of power, and "individualism, initiative," and concentration of responsibility combined with "decentralized local home rule" was the formula that would produce "the best leaders" and advance the general welfare."[12] His 1902 continental tour obliged him to study again Socialism's applicability to America, partially because Hamilton Holt of the *Independent* asked him to represent the Socialists in his symposium, "The Concentration of Wealth." In that contribution Lloyd characteristically based Socialism upon the general welfare principle, restricting desirable collectivism to collective aspects of the economy, excluding agriculture as Debs did not. He termed international organization for peace Socialist in disregard of the Liberals' activity in that field. His position contrasted vividly, however, with the Social Darwinism of James J. Hill and William Graham Sumner, the simple antimonopolism expressed by Bryan, Commons, and Crosby, and John Bates Clark's modified individualism.[13]

Lloyd read G. A. Kleene's article on Socialist thought while discussing this subject with Signor Contini in Italy. In the light of Kleene's analysis he admitted to himself that he was "certainly not a socialist—but a democrat," because he rejected proletarianism. The middle class, he believed, "will survive and will furnish the human material of the new order" in which the proletariat would "be at the bottom" as "of this." Democracy "refused to admit that the proletariat is the public." He did not believe that the proletariat could unite or by itself accomplish reforms. The "New Theory of Democracy" required individual dedication to the community and society's obligation to make life *"worth living for the individual."* He predicted that capitalistic methods would be surpassed in wealth creation by "intensive, democratic, home ruling, co-operative methods," while maintaining that it is more practical to enlist the sympathy and co-operation "of the better classes" in reform. Yet he believed that when the people realized that they created their only sure "heaven," they would "wake up with a feverish energy to the work of reform."

Judging from Swiss experience, he believed that Socialism "must be half cooperative and the other half democratic." He was, he realized, "a democrat in politics and a socialist in industry," provided that home rule counteracted "central rule," a position that Contini accepted out of compassion for the workers. Socialism, Lloyd concluded, was "the religion that is to be." Although his position deviated significantly from contemporary Socialist schools, he sent his photograph to John Spargo's *Socialist Illustrated Yearbook*.[14] His thesis that progress resulted from interaction of the individual and society, his fear of a tyrannical collectivism, his apprehension lest new labor leaders adopt "Robber Baron" methods, and his insistence that monopoly did not lead necessarily to Socialism differentiated him from Debs, Fabianism, and Continental Socialism. Lloyd insisted upon combining brotherhood, secularism, democracy, and collectivism with Christian and Positivist ethical altruism and individualism in *a radical general welfare system* to be accomplished with the aid of the wage-earners. Of this he was the acknowledged "prophet."

His position was markedly similar to what L. T. Hobhouse would define subsequently as "Liberal Socialism." That, Hobhouse says, must be democratic, "come from below," result from society's quest for social justice and "better organization of mutual aid," and "make its account with the individual." It "must be founded on liberty, and make not for the suppression but for the development of personality." To this Lloyd, like the Fabians, added a democratic élite of talent. Although a contradiction in terms, "Liberal Socialism" best designates Lloyd's thought and program, which anticipated Clement Atlee's welfare democracy of 1945-49 with its limited state capitalism "in the field of socially created values."[15]

Yet, its partial agreement with Debsian Socialism explains why Lloyd and Darrow considered the Simons-Morgan invitation seriously. Lloyd's constant agitation, exposures, and welfare democratic proposals had made many discontented Americans susceptible to Socialism. To him, if not to Darrow, the invitation presented the question of whether he should join and attempt to commit Debs's following to his own system or abandon that and accept Debs's doctrinaire revisionism in order to develop political power sufficient to institute drastic reforms. After the Arbitration Hobson advised Lloyd that reform could be expedited by allying the radicals with the Socialists, if the latter would co-operate. This Lloyd had attempted in 1894.

Advanced American thought justified either alternative. In November 1902 *The Outlook* agreed with Herbert Spencer that the trend toward Socialism was "irresistible" but declared that this was "essentially beneficial" as evolution to a higher "state of society." In February 1903 Lloyd had predicted early railroad nationalization in an article for *Booklovers' Magazine.*[16] As he studied the Socialist Party platform and publications, Morgan urged him to become a member at large and avoid local factionalism so as to achieve greater influence "perhaps" than Debs or Herron.

At that time the Maine and Massachusetts Socialists invited Lloyd to present their coal mines nationalization petitions to their legislative committees in a deft move to commit him to their party. He consented, confessing to George Fred Williams that he was "moving towards the socialistic party" because of Bryan's "immovable" opposition to MO. Wouldn't it be wiser to join, reform, and employ the Socialist Party to attack economic problems, he asked. He believed that his "experience" with the Populists justified this! The *Appeal to Reason*'s circulation boom convinced him that "a Socialist boom" was developing. "No wonder the people are turning to a party that has some principle and every courage," he wrote his wife, obviously impressed by its demand for nationalization of mines. "I feel as if the time were coming when every one ought to find some political means of trying to work out our salvation," he added.[17]

"My coal argument," he informed her, "presents the history of the monopoly movement in an appalling way." At Augusta he was applauded warmly after presenting it. On Beacon Hill the next afternoon he spoke for 80,000 petitioners to the Committee on Federal Relations in a hearing conducted by Henry Legate. After portraying the anthracite "trust's" abuses and illegalities Lloyd demanded its immediate nationalization under the Sherman Act or federal receiverships for the mines. The content, scope, force, and radicalism of "the argument" made an important contribution to the literature of protest. Legate praised it highly, sending "most hearty remembrances" to Mrs. Lloyd.[18] Maine and Massachusetts papers reported his argument lengthily.

The alarmed *Boston Journal* called Lloyd "a sincere Socialist," eager for government seizure of all property like the Paris Communards. Even if all Socialists were as charming as he "we might find a better Socialism than the highwayman's," Frank Munsey said. Lloyd replied that Senator George F. Edmunds and other Massachusetts lawyers advocated "summary seizure and forfeiture" under the Sherman Act to remedy monopoly. Denying that his proposal originated with the Socialists he remarked, "Nor am I one of them, as yet, though now that you mention it I think I will join them." The *Journal* entitled this rebuttal "The Unsocial Ventures of a Social Reformer and Esteemed Fellow-Sinner," pairing it with an editorial, "Little Talk With Our Convert." Lloyd confounded "insolvency," the reason for railroad receiverships, "with confiscation," Munsey said. Competition would cure coal and labor "trusts." Morgan's business combinations and diffusion of stock ownership was "more rational and effective than Mr. Lloyd's socialism." Lloyd replied in *Boyce's Weekly,* March 25, that he proposed a "strictly legal procedure." To Mrs. Lloyd he remarked, "The men on the other side are the revolutionaries."[19]

DECLINATION

He wished to "see" if "this socialist movement has really the makings in it of an *American policy*. We must find some political remedy." The Socialists' leadership in the mines nationalization agitation convinced him that "they are the only party really possessed of the principles of progress. Don't you think the Socialists ought to be helped by those who believe in the real thing," since they had the only adequate municipal and national platform, could not be "sold out," were democratically organized, and were well oriented "in economic principles"? he asked his wife.[20] She asked in reply if Roosevelt didn't merit support. He answered undiscerningly, depicting him as dominated by "boundless ambition . . . physically brave but morally, as ambitions men always must be weak," who "has flinched and not played the strenuous part" on the tariff, civil service, franchise taxes, and who "unquestionably surrendered to the great monopolies." Yet, during 1902-3 Roosevelt had struck repeatedly at Morgan combinations and begun to undercut the Standard Oil's privileged position on the railways. Lloyd was repelled, apparently, by the President's refusal to seize the anthracite mines and his appointment of Watkins to the Arbitration Commission.[21]

Work on the Arbitration and presentation of the Socialists' mines nationalization petitions had isolated Lloyd from the "Progressive" revival. He was tempted to join Debs, contrary though this was to the logic of his thought and his wife's advice. In March he preached the "co-operative commonwealth" to the Chicago Society for Ethical Culture. He studied the possibility of capturing the Socialist party for his welfare policy. Darrow "faithfully and devotedly" urged him to join and reap "the glory of coming out first." He would "jump in next" if the water "is not too cold. . . . I think we must all come to it." This nearly decided Lloyd's course. To Charles L. Fox's urging he replied, "Almost thou persuadest me to be a socialist." He asked William Mailly, the National Secretary, for the requirements of members at large, and of Bowles, "Do you forbid the bans?" Bowles replied the Socialists would probably not gain great political power while the radical Democrats would enjoy "increasing influence." Yet, "if you must join any party, I should say that the Socialist party is the one where you belong."[22]

After reading Millerand's *La République* and defending himself from the accusation of being a "revolutionary," he addressed the Chicago Socialist Convention of March 28. He attempted to win it for peaceful, democratic, nonconfiscatory institution of an economic collectivism limited by the majority will, and for the conservation policies and social legislation of his 1902 "Program of Reforms." These, he said, "only a socialized political economy can afford." He refrained from endorsing proletarianism. "True individualism" could be realized only by "citizenship rights in free social enterprise," he cried. His program would emancipate the people from "poverty, ignorance, monopoly" and open "to every man the closed doors of opportunity" by establishing "that everything is the property of every body, that each is the steward for his brother and his neighbor of all that he is and has." From that latter radical, partially Communist statement he rebounded quickly. The fumes of radical oratory had carried him to his farthest left.

Yet his great concern was actually for the American middle class, including farmers and clerks, which was unable to secure a redress of grievances from the major political parties. "These unorganized millions can organize only through the Socialist party," he concluded. He intended, *if* he joined it, to transform it into the instrument for the salvation of this great element, which had lost control of the Republic during the "status revolution" of the "Gilded Age," as Professor Richard· Hofstadter describes it so aptly. In his March 15, 1903 notebook, while preparing this address, he had written, *"Anti-Class Struggle."*[23] Three and a half weeks later he insisted that the individual must be the "off-set of centralization" while the "common welfare" remained civilization's goal.

On April 29, although he assented unqualifiedly to its "practical program," he objected vigorously as an American antimonopolist to Mailly against the doctrines of class struggle and proletarianism in the Socialist party membership application form, expressing thereby the anti-Marxist position of the genuine American radical. Did his objections disqualify him, he asked. "The present social contest," instead of being "one between the capitalists and the working class" was "a contest between the people" and their depredators, he urged, and the "people" and the "working class are certainly not, according to present usage, convertible terms." Although the farmers were not workers, their support was essential to any movement "that overthrows *the monopolies.*" Those joining the Socialist party in "considerable numbers" were "apparently excluded from it by terminology." Lloyd did not wish to join only to be "incontinently 'fired' " out of the party. "My understanding of the true 'class consciousness' is anti-class consciousness. I stand for the people and for the extinction of all tendencies that create 'class'—whether a capitalist class or a working class. Mr. Thomas J. Morgan tells me that these difficulties of mine are no obstacle to my joining the party. I am in entire sympathy with its practical work, and I think my socialistic theory is as sweeping as anyone's could be."[24]

He learned soon that Jacksonian antimonopolism and radical middle class equalitarianism were incompatible with Debsian Socialism. While awaiting a reply he sought advice from Gompers, Commons, Salter, Pomeroy, Ely, and Symonds. He informed Mitchell that he was seriously considering "whether my duty does not call me to join the socialist party" as the "only organization" comprehending "the whole problem—national and international—in its program. . . . What do you think?"[25]

Regarding these doctrinal difficulties he conferred with Simon, who resorted to flagrant equivocation, grouping farmers with the "working class" since they owned only part of their means of production and excluding enterprisers from the "capitalist class," which he classified as *rentier*. He urged that Lloyd join the party in Illinois, although he was certainly a *rentier*. Yet, the National Committee ruled that any state or local organization should expel members refusing to conform to the national constitution and platform from which Lloyd insisted upon deviating. He possessed a copy of that rule![26]

While awaiting his friends' replies, Lloyd and Mrs. Lloyd held a great reception for Will and Lola that introduced them to Chicago and North Shore Society. Lloyd was also lionized by Mrs. Lydia A. Coonley-Ward, who drew him into the social life of Chicago's artistic, literary, and intellectual communities. He attended the writers' and artists' "Klein Stube Katzen jammerjunst lerfest" and reception for President Charles Eliot in Winnetka, where they chatted pleasantly. Neither mentioned their public exchange on the "scab." Lloyd was disgusted at Mrs. Ward's social climbing in London, however.[27]

Before the Massachusetts Reform Club he debated nationalization of the anthracite railroads and mines on May 15 with John Graham Brooks and Gamaliel Bradford. While lending him data and briefing him on the Elkins Act, Mosley had remarked in advance on the ICC's inability to bring Morgan's combination to book. "The supposed regulation is only a farce," he said, and supervision to prevent extortion, unjust treatment, discrimination . . . has never been tried." Like Lloyd he attributed the rise of great monopolies to railroad favoritism. He preferred strong regulation.[28] Lloyd's "The Failure of Railroad Regulation" presented conclusive evidence of continuing railroad discriminations, analyzed recent combinations, depicted concomitant stock market rigging, and described managerial perjury before the ICC. This graphic account matched Commissioner Charles Prouty's report on the railroads' defeat of regulation to the American Economic Association. Alluding to the "Coal Trust's" defiance of the ICC, Lloyd quoted a coal carrier executive's description of helpless consumers as "whipped dogs." Current demands for railroad nationalization and utility municipalization Lloyd called "the first breath of a new spring of democracy" that was turning "to the greatest of their instruments—the state. . . . The remedy for the shortages of democracy is more democracy."

After the unprecedented ovation accorded to Lloyd's address, Brooks pleaded for another attempt at regulation. Bradford warned against government operation in an era dominated by the spoils system. Less government in business he cried, which gratified the *New York Sun* immensely. Brooks admitted to Lloyd afterward that he had stated correctly "the real question" which "is whether we can get rid of our debauch of private privilege . . . under any system of 'control'."[29]

Most of Lloyd's friends advised against joining the Socialists. All agreed that he would diminish his influence greatly by doing so. Mitchell replied that he could "render greater service outside of any political organization," with which Commons agreed while warning against the Socialist party's opposition to effective trades unionism and inevitable opposition to Lloyd's views. Ely urged him to think about the matter six months longer. Symonds reported the untrustworthy character of "Kier Hardie & Co." from London.[30] Lloyd had informed Pomeroy that he was ready to "turn now" despite personal antipathy to "the ever lasting 'proletariat' and 'class-consciousness' slang of the sectarian socialists." He wanted to organize effective counter action against the high tide of the business combination movement, and proposed another private conference of reform leaders to draft a platform "we could work together on." Pomeroy agreed that such a conference would be useful, and differed from Nelson, who said, "Any sort of Socialism and any program that a majority decides on is good enough for me." Pomeroy insisted that since Lloyd's proper sphere was in the "realm of thought," he should not repeat William Morris' disasterous attempt to lead a political Socialist movement.[31]

Meanwhile, Lloyd reviewed Kropotkin and concluded that Socialism must be "the movement of the whole people." Unless "our social revolution is to be an outburst of blind, animal fury, it will not be initiated by any one of the proletariat," he observed. He would combine all elements in an intelligent anti-monopolism against "the *great* capitalists who are monopolists." "In the pulsations of progress" he thought "the next beat may be to gather" workers already enjoying "place, education, hope, purpose, possibility, powers" of which their forefathers never dreamed into "the new collectivity." From the larger individualism, "larger than K. Marx and Engels dreamed of, there will be built a larger socialism than they dreamed of." "May be" offset "will be" in that statement, and "pulsations of progress" was a far cry from Marxian determinism. Lloyd's antimonopolism was socialistic only in its democratic semicollectivism and conceptions of brotherhood and economic justice. He would have left competitive economic activity in industry, farming, real estate, commerce, and commercial banking in private hands, operating with the aid of impartially government-owned mines, railroads, utilities, and industrial monopolies financed by government credit. Such a mixed economy was successful in the Antipodes and Switzerland.[32] Since Lloyd held that it should be instituted and operated by the middle class in behalf of the general welfare such a policy was *Radical* rather than truly Socialist in character.

Unless he was permitted to enter the Socialist party as the champion of this policy, he was bound by his logic and that party's rules to reject the Simons-Morgan invitation. He then subjected Simons' assurances and Deb's leadership to the pragmatic test.

In a letter to the editor in the *Chicago Tribune,* June 1, Lloyd opposed the Common Council's proposed twenty-five-year franchise renewal. He cited London's municipalized electric tram lines' more efficient, cheaper service and declared that only "immediate municipal ownership" could defeat "our ruling families' " attempt to perpetuate "a permanent tribute of millions a year" derived from the five-cent fare. All should rally "to guarantee to the community cheap transit, decent transit, democratic transit under public motives, for the public good." He asked Morgan, "Is not the socialist party the natural champion of the public in this matter?" He wrote Debs that it was an "ideal opportunity for Socialist propaganda and for the enlargement of Socialist influence by . . . the union of progressive radicals of all schools in a practical work." Thinking that they might do as he suggested, he drafted a non-Marxian, anti-monopolist statement, "Why I Join the Socialists," "tho with many misgivings because of their largely antiquated" thought and "most unpractical spirit." Nowhere else had he found "principles or organization that even approach the hem of our problems," he informed Salter. He wrote Louis F. Post that he would return from Sakonnet if "any work could be done in uniting the unions, socialists, single-taxers, in a practical campaign." He invited Debs and Morgan to lead in a campaign for a traction municipal ownership referendum in Chicago as the solution for its "most serious problem."[33]

Lloyd was stunned when Simon replied that the Socialist party was uninterested in the Chicago traction question. Debs termed it of local significance only, and believed such a coalition impossible. Morgan wrote that support from the city's Socialist organization depended upon its reorganization.

Debs's and Simons' replies Lloyd termed "simply incomprehensible." Forwarding these to Morgan he left his draft state-

ment incomplete and remarked indignantly : "Do you wonder
that I and I believe hundreds of thousands of other citizens,
ripe for action, can not see how we are to accomplish anything
by joining a party so led?"

Unavailingly, J. Ramsay MacDonald wrote Lloyd from London that the Socialist idea is "the only illuminating idea in
practical politics" and asked him to "start an American socialist
movement." Lloyd wrote-to Bemis, *"I have little confidence in a
class movement, even if it be in so good a cause as labor."*[34]

During the short remainder of his life, the *Chicago Socialist*
and Socialist party organizer in the city opposed Lloyd's leadership. He kept the Socialist party membership application card
unsigned in his files. Debs, to Lloyd, had failed the pragmatic
test of relating his movement to vital local problems, immediate
needs, and the actual socioeconomic structure. Lloyd's June 1
Chicago Tribune letter suggested that he might himself be persuaded to essay the leadership of radical reform on the Chicago
traction issue instead.

Chapter XXIV

 For Urban Welfare Democracy

RADICAL PRACTICALITY

DURING THE spring and summer of 1903, Lloyd worked hard for specific reforms on many levels. Mazzini's "the progress of all under the leadership of the wisest and best" was his goal, he informed Bemis. He scorned timid liberals' rejection of compulsory arbitration. He described New Zealand's old-age pensions in *Good Housekeeping*. He gathered more data on monopolistic practices and political corruption. While reflecting upon the newly discovered atomic energy, he was not stampeded into pessimistic determinism as was Henry Adams.[1] Instead, he praised "Golden Rule" Jones's statement of the municipal welfare theory. He welcomed the *Chicago Chronicle*'s warning that ruthless men might pre-empt the fruits of a collectivist régime. While publishing his "coal argument" in *The Pilgrim* and *The National Progress,* he exposed the courts as thoroughly as Lincoln Steffens was doing to the party "bosses" in *McClure's.* In *Boyce's Weekly* Lloyd called the United States Supreme Court "that fast friend of the vested interest," depicting its judicial nullification of social reforms, the federal income tax, and Interstate Commerce Act.[2]

Lloyd had observed to Ida Tarbell in May that the great combinations were "still pursuing precisely the same tactics" as before despite exposures and attempts at regulation, that the ICC still reported railroad rebates favoring the largest shippers and destruction of railroad freight rate collection records "to conceal the evidence of violation of law." In *Boyce's Weekly* he reported local outbursts of public indignation against abuses and widespread popular restlessness, clouds on the horizon that would compel Roosevelt to continue along the path of strenuous reform.[3]

Lloyd drew upon Gustav Le Bon's *Psychology of the Crowd* that summer in warning wage-earners against demagogic cultivation of the mob spirit by "spokesmen of the rich," such as Cecil Rhodes the imperialist who had rekindled "race hatred" and "all but corrupted the public opinion of Christendom." Decent persons, he said, should cultivate "a self respect" insulating them from appeals to "primal instincts" in behalf of power lusts and unscrupulous avarice.[4] He adapted William James's *Varieties of Religious Experience* to "Man the Creator." Differing with James's assertion that "the interest of the individual" is the pivot of religious life, Lloyd informed *Boyce's Weekly* readers that the greatest religious fact was the evolution from "the God of Creation to the Man who creates." The truly religious made "it his principal task to create happiness for others. . . . 'Salvation' is the religious name for the same thing for which socialism and democracy is the economic name."

After speaking at the New York Conference of Religion, he represented the AFL at the Detroit National Epworth League Conference on the program, "The Church and the Industrial Masses." While privately regarding the Epworth Leaguers "as certainly religious Choctaws," he presented "The Religion of Labor" to them as the extension of "the Kingdom of God" into "the unevangelized territory of trade, commerce, and industry." John Wesley, he reminded them, had not been "looking for endowments" when he attacked the slave trade and those who ground down the poor. Men "can be religiously free only if they are economically free," he declared, as in New Zealand and Switzerland in contrast with New England "Christian capitalists" who killed child labor bills at Atlanta. As the "collective Messiah" the "whole people" should make the Sermon on the Mount "a campaign document—as it was meant to be." "Democracy and Christianity" could socialize "the doing of good" in "the free democratic republic" and thus eliminate evils perpetrated by predatory wealth.[5] Permeated by faith in man's basic goodness and creative power, this speech ranked among the most confident religiosocial manifestos of the Progressive Era as it fostered Methodism's growing interest in the Social Gospel.

Lloyd attempted to advance world peace and disarmament in *Boyce's Weekly* during April and May. He proposed that the United States as the strongest nation unilaterally outlaw and boycott any belligerent. This would "compel the disarmament of Europe in ninety days" because of its dependence upon American food, stop the competitive armaments race that "is hurrying us down into an abyss of despotism, bankruptcy, and extermination," and usher in "the Golden Year." While thus anticipating the post-World War I view of the Nye Committee and many historians, Lloyd urged also that, if leading nations did not unite in "immediate and universal disarmament" at the next international peace conference, America should announce that it would go "on a war footing beyond anything ever known before" and thereby bludgeon the others into disarmament and peace.[6]

Like others he underestimated the complex obstacles presented by the international anarchy to the peace movement. He could not foresee that the Neutrality Act during 1931-41 would actually strengthen aggressor nations or that America's short-lived atomic bomb monopoly of 1945-47 would not oblige the Soviet Union to support the Baruch Plan. However, America's post-1918 experiments with naval disarmament, outlawry of war, and a unilateral boycott of belligerents indicate Lloyd's originality.

During the spring of 1903 he came to grips again with the equally refractory southern race problem. As a *Chicago Tribune* editor and afterwards, he had campaigned for Negro landed proprietorship, visited Hampton and other Negro colleges, financed scholarship students in them, become a warm friend of Booker T. Washington, and met W. E. B. Du Bois of Atlanta University, brilliant leader of the young Negro intellectuals. He had persuaded James D. Corrothers, his scholarship student at Bennett College, to remain in America to lead his people and appeal to "the American heart" by preaching, prose writing, and the poetry that won Howell's recognition and popular acclaim. To his Hampton scholarship student Lloyd wrote enthusiastically, "Hampton and Tuskegee are the best schools in the United States." His friend Sir William Mather introduced General Armstrong's and Booker T. Washington's methods at Garden College, Khartoum. Lloyd also interested Stead in the American Negro.[7]

In March 1903 Lloyd wrote Du Bois of his deep interest in his articles on the Negro, terming the race problem "the most critical one now before the American people, equalling, if not surpassing, in immediate and remote influence the question of the trusts." He complimented President Hadley in May for remarking in the Dodge Lectures upon "the error of those who today believe that political rights can be permanently withheld from the negro after he shall have achieved . . . industrial responsibility and independence."[8]

Lloyd distributed Richard P. Hallowell's pamphlet on Negro suffrage. In exchange he was introduced to *The Guardian's* editors, with whose opposition to new "Jim Crow" Southern state constitutions he sympathized. He was alarmed by the lynching and violence of the southern post-Populist reaction, and feared that "two more civil wars" might arise from race relations and sectional antagonism. Where were the "large men" able to develop the "large remedies" needed, he asked. He pressed his views upon a fellow Fabian, John C. Reed, an Atlanta attorney, who dissented vigorously. Yet Lloyd sympathized with the predicament of Southern white people. He held that the race problem "should be taken up by the whole nation." He warned that Northern trades unionism might be defeated by Southern Negro disfranchisement and subordination via a mass migration northward of discontented Southern colored people. Southern attempts to govern disenfranchised Negroes would fail, he predicted unrealistically. He ranked among the influential "spiritual descendants of the abolitionists" who, as the *Atlantic* observed, demanded cultivation of "Negro self-respect" and training in self-government.[9]

During that summer of 1903, Willis Abbot rested at The Watch House and discussed reform problems with the Lloyds. Waldo Abbot, Coe Kelley, T. W. Phillips, Jr., his sister, and other teen-agers sailed with "Demmie" and "Jack." After mornings at work on his book on Switzerland, Henry D. Lloyd sailed with them. He collected photographs, engravings, and paintings, and considered purchasing a Washington by Charles Willson Peale, which he identified with the aid of N. S. Prichard of the Boston Museum of Fine Arts.

He should have taken a complete vacation. He was "very tired" during the Epworth League Convention. Thankful for his wife's affectionate encouragement, he replied, "I am altogether happy in loving you, and being loved." Worried about her health, he was relieved when he received her letter at Winnetka. There he found Will's Halwayside "scrumpled-up and as pretty as a picture in and out."[10]

I.M.O. and ――――

During July 21-22 he conferred with Jane Addams, labor leaders, Municipal Voters' League officers, leaders of the Municipal Ownership Delegates Convention, and Referendum League officials on the traction problem. Walter L. Fisher of the Voters' League advised against "*immediate* municipalization." "The situation" in Chicago "is tremendously complicated and delicate," Lloyd informed his wife. After Debs's and Simon's rejection of his proposal, the traction problem challenged him to vindicate his reform judgment. Following publication of his *Chicago Tribune* letter the trades unionists, Single-Taxers, and radical reformers had organized the Delegates' Convention and placed him on the steering committee.[11]

The situation had changed since he had helped to defeat the Humphrey Bill. Yerkes had fled to London after a prolonged contest with the Voters' League, leaving the Union Traction Company to the allied Widener-Elkins group, Morgan & Company, and the Whitney-Standard Oil New York utility combination. The City Railway Company, in which the Field and Kent fortunes were heavily invested, co-operated with the new syndicate. As the Voters' League purged the Common Council, Mayor Carter Harrison II had fought for the city's "rights." William Kent studied British municipalizations as Lloyd had done, and became convinced likewise that only municipalization could demolish the alliance between the traction companies and vicious political elements. Kent intended also to municipalize gas lighting where an equally corrupt utility-political coalition persisted.

The Chicago MO movement threw down the gauntlet before the powerful eastern financial interests, who picked it up. They had no intention of abdicating before resurgent urban democracy. Thus, Chicago's purification politically and its business emancipation were both at stake as the allied traction companies sought franchise renewals with the least possible concessions to the municipality.

Harrison demanded uniform twenty-year traction franchise extensions, providing optional MO by purchase after ten years, improved service including the underground trolley, and waiver of the corruptly procured Ninety-Nine Year Act of 1865 upon which franchises in the heart of the city rested. The new Public Opinion Act of Illinois made advisory referenda mandatory upon petition. In the April 1902 referendum 80 per cent of the voters had demanded municipalization of traction and lighting. Early in 1903 the Mayor, Council, Illinois and Chicago Federations of Labor, Referendum League, and civic organizations had secured the Mueller Act authorizing municipalization of utilities subject to referenda. Chicago then re-elected Harrison for a fourth term.[12]

Chicago's insistence upon municipalized traction derived from genuine grievances. Yerkes' buccaneering had alienated most friends of honest government from the utilities, as had the Chicago City Railway's average 44.63 per cent annual profit during 1883-1901 upon its heavily watered stock. The traction companies' stubbornly poor service, refusal to install improvements, and 450 per cent overcapitalization of their combined net property value of $26,684,908 explained the public's attitude. Bion Arnold, Chicago's consulting engineer, reported that an investment of $70,000,000 would provide a first-class electric traction system *plus* a downtown subway. The Voters' League was determined, also, to force local high finance and corporation management to abandon Yerkes' demoralizing methods.[13]

On July 31, 1903, the traction franchises on most streets expired after Harrison defeated their renewal. Instead of surrendering those of its lines to the municipality, the Union Traction Company resorted to a federal receivership installed by Judge Grosscup on petition of the Guaranty Trust Company, a Morgan ally and nonresident stockholder. This postponed adjudication of the Ninety-Nine Year Act. Grosscup's instructions to the receiver upheld its validity and subsequent franchises based upon it under the Fourteenth Amendment. Harrison's policy was wrecked. With great difficulty he secured temporary operating permits from the Common Council for the companies for streets with lapsed franchises. Grosscup then enjoined the receiver from paying municipal taxes. This almost precipitated a violent explosion. Some Chicagoans knew that he was a stockholder in the Matoon Street Railway.[14]

A demand for immediate municipal ownership crystallized swiftly among the elements schooled by the Lloyd group and *The Public*. More moderate college graduates, businessmen, and property holders concluded that "they could not clean up the traction question without at least" MO authorization. They knew that the eastern syndicate was attempting to unify and monopolize all utilities in each field in many cities. The Municipal Ownership League, Referendum League, Teachers' Federation, Federation of Labor, and Single-Taxers supported the IMO movement, guided by *The Public* and Rev. Jenkin Lloyd Jones.

Lloyd was the most influential leader of this coalition. His real estate in the city gave him a personal interest in cheap, efficient traction. The Lloyds' city apartment, "The Pickwick," made him technically a resident.[15] On June 28, after returning to Sakonnet, he was invited by the Municipal Ownership Delegates' Convention to lead the fight against further franchise extensions. Gompers and Daniel C. Cruice of the Referendum

League urged him to accept this call. Jane Addams invited him to make Hull House his headquarters for conferences. She said, "the fight is worth making," although George E. Hooker of the *Chicago Tribune* and Hull House warned that the Delegates' Convention was not very representative. Lloyd arrived as *The Public* attacked Grosscup for "wresting powers of local self-government" from Chicago. This late July situation made it impossible to confine the immediate municipal ownership movement initially to a "still hunt," as Lloyd had advised. Yet, a corps of "Ironside men" was recruited, propaganda prepared, and a "plan of campaign developed before showing a head, or saying a word." However, Darrow's and Schilling's adherence to the City Hall and Socialist aloofness prevented development of a labor-liberal-radical-Socialist-IMO united front.

During intensive conferences Lloyd accepted the movement's leadership. He determined that "nothing but Municipal Ownership" should result from the crisis. "It is likely to be a memorable struggle," he wrote Shibley, soliciting suggestions, "It will be all the monopolies against one municipality."[16] That decision shortened Lloyd's life by a decade, and deprived the Empire of Reform of his leadership at a time when his fearless, realistic radicalism was very influential. He drew into IMO some influential figures, such as C. L. Bonney the traction expert, who tendered "hearty co-operation." Determined to prevent IMO from becoming "a class movement," Lloyd invited others of "rank and means" to contribute money and their names. He consulted Bemis on how to exploit MO's endorsement by the League of American Municipalities and the National Municipal League. His strategy was to mobilize public opinion to defeat any Council attempt to issue franchise extensions and to oblige it to institute IMO.[17] To accomplish this the movement had first to win a referendum approving resort to the Mueller Act and an IMO referendum under it by a three-fifths majority. Acquisition of the companies' property and unexpired franchises had to be financed, although Chicago had borrowed to its statutory debt limit. The Ninety-Nine Year Act had to be adjudicated. These were formidable obstacles.

George Schilling promptly wrote Lloyd that Harrison preferred his own policy. His administration feared that the city's welfare would be "slaughtered" by "unreasonable fanatics on one side insisting on the impossible" and "the alert gray wolves on the other side who are ever ready to strike a blow for predatory interests at the most opportune time." Schilling argued that the public could not be held in line for IMO during a five-year contest. George Sikes, author of *The Street Railway Situation in Chicago,* believed IMO was "crazy." He urged that Lloyd support Harrison's policy so as to accomplish MO "as soon" as possible.[18]

Lloyd concluded that Schilling erred. Commons and "Bert" Stewart agreed. Lloyd secured legal advice from Frank Parsons and Chicago attorneys. He began intensive research on the traction problem. Returning to The Watch House with documentary materials, he drafted a manual on the case for IMO. He desired a municipalized traction system with modern equipment and a single city-wide fare, instead of the three to six fares with no transfers charged by the companies. This was practicable, as Detroit demonstrated. Although he knew the caliber of the opposition, he wrote enthusiastically to Bemis : "If this Chicago fight goes forward, . . . it will be the greatest thing yet. It will be all the monopolies against one municipality."[19]

Charles Zueblin, Secretary of the American League for Civic Improvement, pledged assistance. Other MO men sympathetic with Lloyd's objectives felt that the municipality's financial interests would be served best by Harrison's policy, which would terminate all franchises simultaneously at a future date.

Although convinced, correctly, that the courts would uphold the Ninety-Nine Year Act, Lloyd was satisfied with "the general features of the program of our Committee." After completing the first draft of his pamphlet, cheered on by Willis Abbot and Henry George, Jr., he entrained for Chicago a fortnight before Labor Day as Hearst's *Chicago Examiner* broke with Harrison because of the issuance of a temporary operating permit to the City Railway Company. It came out forcefully for IMO.[20]

Lloyd made Hull House his headquarters. He embarked upon

an arduous schedule of research, recruiting influential liberals, speaking, and conferring with Cruice, Morgan, and Miss Haley of the Federation of Teachers. The Delegates' Convention authorized the Labor Day circulation of Mueller Act referendum petitions and supporting district meetings as Lloyd recommended. When the *Chicago Socialist* attacked him for "indifference to the subject of Municipal Ownership of the kind now advocated," this did not dampen his enthusiasm. Stimulated by participation again in public affairs and eager to demonstrate Direct Legislation's usefulness in instituting MO he enjoyed fighting once more against monopoly power and high finance with a popular following. He seemed years younger to friends at Hull House.[21]

The Labor Day petition campaign was highly successful. The Mueller Act referendum was scheduled eventually for April 4, 1904, when the city voted overwhelmingly for (1) local adoption of that Act; (2) that the municipality proceed immediately under it to municipalize traction; and (3) that no franchises be granted pending this. As the *New York Herald* remarked, no more "sweeping victory" could have been desired for Lloyd's IMO strategy.[22] His victory, however, was posthumous.

After Labor Day he took the Hull House residents gaily to inspect the Zion City utopia, whose leader was making a fortune by exploiting its inhabitants. This he depicted to Anne Withington of Boston, adding a new resident's impression of Hull House. He rated it "the best club in Chicago" with its "free association of men and woman under the same roof," its "bountiful" table, its "only enclosed court of greenery" in Chicago. He reported "a well-developed plot" in the Council "to place the city permanently under the traction monopoly . . . under pretence of municipal ownership." He doubted that the "people can be aroused," partially because humble folk "do not dare to express themselves. . . . 'Because the great capitalists are all interlocked'," as the Athenaeum's janitor informed him. Containing warm compliments for Jane Addams and Anne Withington, the letter exhibited his gay, cultivated, realistic, and courageous spirit.[23]

To Jane Addams he revealed his mastery of "the difficult art of comradeship." At Hull House he created "a new fascination for serious things," such as the changing American attitude toward the Negro implied by increasing acceptance of the reconstructed Southern caste system. He predicted the gravest consequences if Americans permitted "the rights of the humblest to be invaded," and declared that winning new liberties was "essential to retaining our old liberties." She learned that he was an accomplished student of Italian literature, an admirer of Dante, a sympathizer with the new Italy and Italian immigrants in America. Together they remarked upon "the hard places into which the friends of labor unions are often brought when they sympathize with the ultimate objects of a strike but disapprove of methods employed during it."[24]

Privately he refused to "despair of Democracy." The earlier organizations of the "Robber Barons" were "compelling the organization of the people, everywhere," he observed. History "may be accuratey defined as the gradual recognition . . . of the social wit, and its institutionalization by the social will." Democracy "is first, a necessity of human life, enforced by the mechanical pressures of society, and its success is, second, a certainty in the nature of things. The vices organize first, the virtues organize last, but best." Those profiting by "injustice, special privilege, monopoly, excessive wealth" were "always going about declaring democracy to be a failure." Such attacks were "the instinctive voice of the social robber." This was an issue in the Chicago traction as he analyzed it.[25]

Nelson of Leclaire saw him "gay and joking" at the big Hull House table. Lloyd had "gained in spirits by the transition . . . to constructive work." He wrote of his enjoyment of the social settlement and "my own work" to "The Missus." However, he confessed to Caro that he had "not seemed to be quite up to par since coming west." This he blamed upon "the weather—with its Chicago trimmings of dust, smoke and noise." Brandeis sent his briefs on the Boston "subway cases" and related traction pamphlets. Lloyd acknowledged those appreciatively. "I wish we had your valiant help in the struggle coming on here." He persuaded Pomeroy, Shibley, Abbot, and other national MO leaders to speak in Chicago. He warned Caro that the situation was "ominous. We are up against the 'Money Power' with no such advantage of sectional and geographic limitations as helped the antagonists of the Slave Power." Friends in the financial district told him that the eastern syndicate promised funds to modernize the traction service in return for new franchises.[26]

Lloyd led IMO strategy planning to prevent another Morgan coup, and rushed his traction pamphlet to the printer. He convoked the Delegates' Convention to meet September 19 at Athenaeum Hall immediately before the Federation of Labor meeting, after drafting a "Traction Emergency Call" with Miss Haley and others. This document demanded referenda upon proposed franchises, an early Mueller Act referendum, no interim grants to traction companies, and adjudication of existing franchise rights. Lloyd's group issued a circular letter declaring "that another franchise grant in Chicago will be a death blow to Municipal Ownership elsewhere." This asserted that the companies' profits were paid chiefly to eastern capitalists and the Union Traction Company's plans to raise new capital would enlarge this tribute. The Mueller Act referendum position was "merely the opening gun of the fight."[27]

On the evening of the 18th Lloyd developed a cold and headache. He slept at "The Pickwick" until dinner the next day, before attending the Delegates' Convention to secure adoption of the Emergency Call." "I had to," he wrote Mrs. Lloyd before sleeping twelve more hours at their apartment. Awakening, he added, "I am all right. . . . the cold has 'set' in my bronchial region, and nothing now remains but to wear it out." Praising her devotion to others' happiness, he said, "I have to go to the Federation of Labor to speak and after that I think I shall go to the Halfwayside, and probably stay over Monday for a good rest."[28] To speak to the Federation after the cold settled in his bronchial tubes was gambling with Fate.

Convinced that his presence at the Federation was necessary, he sat on its stage in his overcoat with Miss Addams. After Miss

Haley secured the "Call's" adoption he asked the Federation for mass support of its presentation at the Council meeting, September 28. He warned that unless the Mueller Act was adopted quickly and its authority exercised Chicago's traction lines would be unified by a syndicate allied with the "Gas Trust" in a New York-Philadelphia-controlled monopoly. He invoked "No Monopoly" again to rally equalitarian democracy against special privilege. Barney Berlin, the Socialist, renewed his attack upon the IMO movement, arguing that capitalist combinations expedited proletarian control of all means of production. Ignoring him, the Federation voted mass presentation of the "Emergency Call."[29]

Simultaneously, Toledoans supported Mayor Jones's veto of a twenty-five-year traction franchise extension by a similar demonstration. This occupied the City Hall as the Council laid on the table the proposal to enact the ordinance over the veto, while red fire burned in the corridor and glass doors gave way before crowd pressure. This incident alarmed Chicago conservatives with the prospect of a similar episode when Lloyd should present the "Call."[30] Mayor Harrison announced that the citizenry would be welcome at that Council meeting, where the Federation of Labor would learn that the aldermen would ignore IMO. He denied "that a perpetual franchise shall be granted in any way to a syndicate or the present companies." The Council leader promised that MO would be provided for in any franchise extensions. Neither statement satisfied the demand for IMO via the Mueller Act.[31]

Lloyd would have tolerated no violence had he led the mass demonstration on September 28. What he could have achieved had he presented the monster referendum petition and "Emergency Call" cannot be determined.

Far ahead of schedule "The Grim Reaper" called him to new fields of reform on September 28. Chilled, he had ridden in an open street car after the Federation meeting to take the Northwestern train to Winnetka. His daughter-in-law did not prevent his returning to Chicago. Willis Abbot found him ill two days later at "The Pickwick," and summoned a doctor who discovered that Lloyd had pneumonia. Fatigued, prematurely aged by unremitting labor for reform, the underprivileged, and the welfare democracy of his dreams, he grew worse rapidly. He had been in excellent health the preceding summer, his wife said later. However, he had not recuperated fully after the coal strike arbitration. The IMO campaign had encroached upon his seaside vacation. When he contracted pneumonia, its course was more rapid than it would otherwise have been.

Mrs. Lloyd and his other sons arrived on the 26th, bringing "the fresh air of Sakonnet." During two days of alternating delirium and sanity Lloyd fought the unfinished traction fight. He admitted that he had attended the Delegates' Convention and Federation against his better judgment. "But I'd do it again," he told his wife. Exposure after the second meeting had caused the pneumonia, he believed. He asked Will to publish his traction pamphlet. Exhilarated by news of the Toledo demonstration, he rejoiced that Americans still possessed the spirit to "fight when it is required." In Philadelphia after an arbitration session he had remarked to Traubel : "When the hour strikes, and you happen to be on the spot you can't do anything else but offer yourself for the sacrifice." On Monday morning after a day of agony repressed, he handed the IMO torch to his wife and Will as the morning sun topped the trees, Jessie's name on his lips.[32]

ASSOCIATES' APPRAISAL

"A genial, gentle, kindly man . . . and yet a warrior of the higher type and of terrible effective blade," the *Union Labor Advocate* called him. As his widow and Will assumed leadership of the IMO movement, his disciples, associates, and friends picked up the torches of his other causes. On the evening of September 28 a huge throng of laborers and reformers crowded the City Hall Council gallery, lobby, and corridors in silent tribute to IMO's fallen leader, whom they regarded as one of America's "first citizens." The Delegates' Convention made "the movement a memorial" to him. Reformers, laborers, men of means, and radicals combined in hot resentment at the "wrongs and indignities" heaped upon the city by the traction companies in a crusade to terminate their corrupt dominance. Few forgot the concluding chapter of Lloyd's posthumous pamphlet, which cited London's example to justify the fight to overthrow "the latest feudalism" and achieve a comprehensive municipal welfare policy in "this war between the trusts and the towns, of one monopoly against all the municipalities—New York against the whole country."[33]

Lloyd's ashes were buried beneath the autumn leaves south of The Wayside. His cremation prevented a spontaneous mass demonstration of the humble and socially enlightened at his bier such as had honored Henry George. Instead, a memorial service in Lloyd's honor was held at the Auditorium, November 29. It was sponsored by the AFL, UMW, United Turner Societies, Chicago Federation of Labor, Village Council of Winnetka, Municipal Ownership Delegates' Convention, Hull-House, Chicago Commons, Henry George Association, Typographical Union No. 16, and the Carpenters' District Council. Socialist organizations were notably lacking.

This Memorial Meeting was a national tribute. Lloyd had won the love and respect of all levels in the transoceanic Empire of Reform. Five thousand persons admitted by ticket to the Auditorium included those of all political beliefs, those "devoted to public good along widely varying lines; scholars, jurists, lawyers," popular leaders from Chicago and "distant cities," delegations from reform organizations Lloyd had worked with, officers of the UMW's anthracite districts, trades unionists, Chicago's liberal judges and reform aldermen, Social Gospel clergy, Franklin MacVeagh, Louis F. Post, Willis Abbot, social settlement house residents, women doctors, teachers, socially prominent women led by Mrs. Charles Henrotin, Single-Taxers, Thomas J. Morgan's following, and the IMO leaders.

After hearing the massed German Singing Societies 500 strong John Mitchell, Judge Edward F. Dunne, Mayor S. M. Jones, Edwin D. Mead, Darrow, and Mayor Tom L. Johnson of Cleveland addressed the throng. Mitchell described Lloyd's uncompensated labors for the miners. Mayor Jones declared that Lloyd's "Golden Rule" philosophy offered "the only hope . . . for the realization of the American ideal of equality." Jane Addams confessed her discipleship of Lloyd's ethical thought, and stressed the vital importance of his passion for "social righteousness," his fact-finding techniques, his far-sighted leadership in "the delicate process of social adjustment and reconstruction" and his desire for an honest, socially responsible labor movement. She emphasized the importance of his propagation of information about the policies of advanced overseas democracies, and of his emphasis upon the paramountcy of the public welfare in industrial disputes. After alluding to Count Tolstoi who had once wanted to bring Lloyd, Henry George, and Howells together to concert measures to advance "the regeneration of degenerate humanity," Darrow ranked Lloyd with that Russian reformer and with Altgeld. He called him an incorruptible, radical, fearless socialist scholar aristocrat who dared to condemn existing evils and champion the common man. Tom Johnson declared his discipleship of Lloyd's antimonopolism as did Mead, and predicted the success of the intermunicipal MO campaign.

While the Memorial Meeting became "a consecration in the municipal ownership work" that Lloyd left unfinished, as *The Public* observed, it symbolized to the Empire of Reform the vital, complex contribution that America's greatest radical had made during three decades to the reorientation of thought and policy to cope with the problems of the Great Society. In distant Wellington the New Zealand Parliament, on Premier Seddon's motion, voted its appreciation of his championship of industrial peace, democracy, and labor's welfare, and of his favorable analyses of that colony's welfare polity.[34] There and in London the New Liberals, Progressives, and labor leaders mourned his passing.

Bibliography

The extensive typed bibliography of the primary and secondary sources consulted in preparation of this biography has been placed in the Library of Congress for the convenience of scholars. The code letters for manuscript collections cited in the Notes are listed here.

MANUSCRIPTS CITED

Library of Congress

JA Jane Addams Papers
ACSCP Anthracite Coal Strike Commission Proceedings, I–LVI
AC Andrew Carnegie Papers
WJB William Jennings Bryan Papers
JAG James A. Garfield Papers
WQG Walter Q. Gresham Papers
MM Manton Marble Papers
RO Richard Olney Papers
LFP Louis Freeland Post Papers
TR Theodore Roosevelt Papers
CS Carl Schurz Papers
LT Lyman Trumbull Papers
DAWLC David A. Wells Papers

State Historical Society of Wisconsin

DDL Daniel DeLeon Papers
RTE Richard T. Ely Papers
BSF Bishop Samuel Fallows Papers
LPM Henry Demarest Lloyd Papers
SLP Socialist Labor Party Papers

Chicago Historical Society
  CHS Manuscripts

Rutherford B. Hayes Memorial
  RBH Rutherford B. Hayes Papers

Illinois Historical Society
  GAS George A. Schilling Papers

Columbia University Library
  CC Columbiana Collection
  CUARecs Columbia University Alumni Office Records

Harvard University Library
  WDH William Dean Howells Papers
  CSH Charles Sumner Papers

University of Chicago Library
  TJM Thomas J. Morgan Papers

University of Kansas Library
  JBW J. B. Watkins & Company Papers

University of Michigan Library
  JAL Joseph A. Labadie Papers

Yale University Library
  TD Thomas Davidson Papers, by permission of Charles Bakewell
  ATH Arthur Twining Hadley Papers, by permission of Morris
    Hadley
  WK William Kent Papers, by permission of Mrs. William Kent and
    Sherman Kent
  FP Frank Parsons Papers
  RS Roger Sherman Papers

Oberlin College Library
  JDC Jacob D. Cox Papers

McCormick Agricultural Library
   MHM McCormick Harvesting Machine Company Papers

Massachusetts Historical Society
   EAA Edward A. Atkinson Papers

Minnesota Historical Society
   ID Ignatius Donnelly Papers

New York Public Library

   RRB Richard Rogers Bowker Papers
   FC Ford Collection
   HG Henry George Papers
   PG Parke Godwin Papers
   HG Horace Greeley Papers
   SS Simon Sterne Papers
   DAW David A. Wells Papers

Ohio Archeological and Historical Society
   WG Washington Gladden Papers

Rochester Public Library
   PO'R Peter O'Reilly Papers

Papers in Private Hands
The Lloyd family at Winnetka, Illinois
   WB William Bross Papers
   LPW Henry D. Lloyd Papers and Library
   CSL Caroline Stallbohm Papers

American Federation of Labor, Washington, D.C.
   AFL Archives

Mrs. S. P. Capen, Buffalo, New York
   CDW Carroll D. Wright Papers

Conrad Godwin-Goddard, Roslyn, Long Island, N. Y.
   WCB William Cullen Bryant Papers

George Davis Herron, New Orleans, Louisiana
GDH George D. Herron Papers

Clara W. Hill, Brighton, Massachusetts
EDM Edwin D. Mead Papers

Hull House, Chicago
HHA Archives and Records

Philip Jordan, Miami, Ohio
WMS William MacIntyre Salter Papers

Harry Barnard Kletsky, Chicago
HDLS MS. Henry D. Lloyd, "Summary of Facts submitted before the Anti-Monopoly Convention recently held in Chicago"

Society for Ethical Culture of Chicago
SEEC-MB Minute Books, I–II (1883–1904)

Margaret Winfield Stewart, Washington, D.C.
ES Ethelbert Stewart Papers

Francis B. Thurber
FBT Francis B. Thurber Papers

University of Chicago
UC-BT Minutes of the Board of Trustees, 1892–1896
UC-POF President's Office Files, 1892–1896

Women's Christian Temperance Union, Evanston, Illinois
FEW Frances E. Willard Papers

Mrs. Nellie W. Williams has given to the author certain items from
DLW Rev. D. Leighton Williams Papers

Notes

CHAPTER I

[1]LPM, C. Lloyd to H. D. Lloyd, January 12, 1894; LPW, M. C. Lloyd to HDL, two undated notes, September 18, 1900; MS enclosure, HDL to James T. White & Company, February 10, 1900, (Courtesy of J. T. White & Company); Caro Lloyd, *Henry Demarest Lloyd, 1847–1903*, I (New York, 1912), 5.

[2]LPW, pencil and ink MSS (n.d.) by A. Lloyd, MS biography for *National Cyclopedia of American Biography;* LPM, MSS by John Crilley Lloyd; W. V. Brownlee, "History of the Dutch Reformed Church," *History of all the Religious Denominations in the United States* (Harrisburg, 1848), pp. 219–223; C. Lloyd, *op. cit.,* 1, 7.

[3]E. T. Corwin, "History of the Reformed Church, Dutch," *American Church History Series,* VIII (New York, 1895), 194–195, 208; Leonard W. Bacon, *History of American Christianity, (Ibid.,* XIII) (1907), 134, 328–329.

[4]Arthur C. Cole, *Era of the Civil War (Centennial History of Illinois,* III, Springfield, 1919), pp. 1–5, 12–16, 29, 54.

[5]Kenneth S. Latourette, *History of the Expansion of Christianity,* IV (New York, 1941), 391–392.

[6]Cole, *op. cit., pp.* 124–178; Frederick Jackson Turner, *The United States, 1830–1850,* edited by Avery Craven (New York, 1937), pp. 125, 320–322; W. V. Pooley, *The Settlement of Illinois from 1830 to 1850* (Madison, 1908), pp. 639–651; William Nisbet Chambers, *Old Bullion Benton* (Boston, 1956), p. 31.

[7]LPM, MS "Notebook by Henry Demarest Lloyd Pekin Tazewell"; Cole, *op. cit.,* pp. 233–236; Turner, *op. cit.,* pp. 320–322.

[8]Cole, *op. cit.,* pp. 245–250; Latourette, *loc. cit.;* Bacon, *loc. cit.*

[9]C. Lloyd, *op. cit.,* I, 8–12; J. F. Richmond, *New York and Its Insti-*

531

tutions, 1608–1871 (New York, 1871), p. 108; Royal Cortissoz, *The Life of Whitelaw Reid,* I (New York, 1921), 231.

[10] LPM, J. B. Wallace to HDL, June 21, 1894; C. S. Straus, *Under Four Administrations From Cleveland to Taft* (Boston, 1922), pp. 22–23; Richmond, *op. cit.,* pp. 132–138; Arthur Charles Cole, *The Irrepressible Conflict, 1850–1865 (History of American Life,* VII) (New York, 1934), pp. 344–349; Alexander C. Flick, editor, *History of the State of New York,* VII (New York, 1935), 129–131; C. Lloyd, *op. cit.,* 1, 12, 16.

[11] LPM, HDL's MSS student notebooks; *The Columbiad,* II, No. 1 (New York, February, 1865), III (April, 1866); Straus, *op. cit.,* pp. 26–27; Allan Nevins, *Hamilton Fish* (New York, 1936), pp. 96–98; John Howard Van Ameringe, *History of Columbia University, 1754–1904* (New York, 1904), pp. 130–143

[12] LPM, MS note on English theme, MS "Halusis"; CC, MS "Minute-Book of the Class of 1867," December 22, 1864, March 10, 1865; *Columbiad,* III (April, 1866); Samuel Appleton Blatchford, *A True History of The Class of 1867 of Columbia College* (New York, 1867), pp. 69–71, 94.

[13] Frank Friedel, *Francis Lieber* (Baton Rouge, 1947), pp. 367–369; *Reminiscences, Addresses, and Essays by Francis Lieber,* I (Philadelphia, 1881), 34–36.

[14] LPM, for the original MSS.

[15] *Columbiad,* III (April 1866).

[16] CC, MS "Minute-Book of the Class of 1867," March 10, 1865, April 6, 9, 10–20, 26, 1866; LPM, MS "Special Plea," May 2, 1866, MS Minutes of Court Martial, Class of '67 correspondence with Barnard, N. Fish to HDL, January 1, 1868; Blatchford, *op. cit.,* pp. 36–75.

[17] LPM, MSS "Valedictory," "Classical Studies"; CC, Leaflet "Class '67," Program, "Class Day '67" MS "Minute-Book," April 12, October 19, November 6, 1866, March 22, 1867; *Columbiad,* III, No. 1 (April, 1866).

[18] LPM, MS "Soda and Society."

[19] *Ibid.,* N. Fish to HDL, January 1, 5, 15, 1868, HDL to Fish, January 3, 10, 1868.

[20] CUARecs; Straus, *op. cit.,* pp. 29–31.

CHAPTER II

[1] LPM, Barnard to Field, May 1, 1869.

[2] *Ibid.,* HDL to H. F. Keenan, June 24, 1872.

[3]*Harper's Weekly*, XV (New York, May 27, 1871), 474–475; *New York Evening Post*, semiweekly, July 20, 1869.

[4]*Ibid.*, semiweekly, May 25, 1869; John Foord, *The Life and Public Services of Simon Sterne* (New York, 1903), pp. 3–4, 35–54.

[5]Howard K. Beale, *The Critical Year* (New York, 1930), pp. 287–295; WCB, Sterne to Bryant, November 3, 1865; Foord, *op. cit.*, 72–73.

[6]Francis Lieber, *Notes on Fallacies Peculiar to American Protectionists* (New York, 1869); Parke Godwin, *A Biography of William Cullen Bryant*, II (New York, 1883); Allan Nevins, *The New York Evening Post* (New York, 1922), pp. 100–365; WCB, clipping, *San Francisco Bulletin*, December 21, 1871.

[7]*Free-Trader*, II (New York, March, 1869), 136–139, 145; EAA, Sands to Atkinson, March 10, 1869; Walter Barrett, *The Old Merchants of New York City*, I (New York, 1863), 25, 99.

[8]*New York Tribune*, July 28, 1869, May 9, 1870; *New York Evening Post*, semiweekly, April 6, May 14, 21, 1869; Kate McKean, *Manual of Social Sciences: Being a Condensation of the "Principles of Social Science" by H. C. Carey* (Philadelphia, 1872); *Chicago Tribune*, June 28, 1879, interview with Hamilton Fish.

[9]Cf. *New York Tribune*, May 29–November 27, 1869.

[10]Robert Ronald Ferleger, *David A. Wells and the American Revenue System, 1865–1870* (New York, 1942), pp. 127–152; Harold Francis Williamson, *Edward Atkinson. The Biography of an American Liberal, 1827–1905* (Boston, 1934), pp. 64–71.

[11]WCB, Bryant to R. Johnson, January 19, 1868; *Free-Trade Tracts*, I, XXXIII, XXXVI (New York, 1865–1867); *The League*, I (New York, June, 1867), 2–3, II (December, 1868), 91; PO'R, Henry O'Reilly, MS "Confidential Inter-Communication—Railroads and Telegraphs," R. E. Fenton to H. O'Reilly, September 27, 1867; Lee Benson, *Merchants-Farmers-Railroads: Railroad Regulation and New York Politics, 1850–1887* (Cambridge, 1955), pp. 18–20; John Morley, *Life of Richard Cobden*, (one volume, edition, London, 1908), 144, 249, 290, 295, 299.

[12]EAA, C. Nordhoff to Atkinson, January 27, 1869; DAWLC, December 11, 1869, American Free-Trade League circular; *New York Evening Post*, semiweekly, January 1, 8, 12, 15, 19, 21, 26, 1869; *Free-Trader*, II (December, 1868, January, February, 1869), 91, 112, 129; EAA, Sands to Atkinson, March 29, 1869; *New York Evening Post*, semiweekly, November 19, 23, 1869.

[13]*Some Account of the American Free-Trade League and of its Purposes* (New York, 1869), p. 7.

[14]EAA, Sands to Atkinson, February 13, March 1, 8, 10, 16, 18, April 21, 1869; *Some Account of the Free-Trade League,* pp. 1–2; *New York Evening Post,* semiweekly, April 6, 23, May 4, 14, 1869.

[15]*Cincinnati Daily Gazette,* January 1, 1867, October 22, 1869; Ohio State Board of Agriculture, *Twenty-First Annual Report, 1866* (Columbus, 1867), pp. 70–75, 190–191, *Twenty-Third Annual Report, 1868,* pp. 62–63; *New York Evening Post,* June 4, 1869; Roeliff Brinkerhoff, *Recollections of a Lifetime* (Cincinnati, 1900), pp. 190–196.

[16]LPM, Brinkerhoff to C. L. Withington, January 4, 1904; *Free-Trader,* III (July, August, November, 1869), 18, 43–44; *Die Freihandels-Bund an seine Subscribenten und das Publikum* (New York, 1869), pp. 1–7.

[17]*New York Evening Post,* semiweekly, May 29, June 1, 18, 25, July 9, 23, 27, October 19, 1869; DAWLC, E. L. Godkin to Wells, July 14, 1869; *New York Tribune,* July 19, August 13, 23, September 2, November 17, 1869.

[18]CHS, Gardner Brewer to Sumner, July 7, 1865.

[19]LPM, HDL to D. D. Lloyd, March 17, 1871; *The Political Writings of Richard Cobden* (two volumes, London, 1868).

[20]LPM, MS "H. D. L. Private" Notebook.

[21]LPM, W. Reid to HDL, October 20, 1870; *Free-Trader,* III (May, 1870), 201; *New York Evening Post,* March 18, 1870.

[22]*Free-Trader,* II (May, 1869), 167, III (September, December, 1869, April, 1870), 57, 114–115, 179.

[23]Quoted, Nevins, *Evening Post,* pp. 361–363.

[24]*Ibid.,* p. 393; *New York Evening Post,* semiweekly, April 26, June 17, 1870; Nevins, *Fish,* pp. 272–289; David Barr Chidsey, *The Gentleman from New York: A Life of Roscoe Conkling* (New Haven, 1935), pp. 142–150.

[25]EAA, H. Adams to Atkinson, February 1, 1869.

[26]CS, Sands to Schurz, November 10, 1870, italics added.

[27]Brinkerhoff, *op. cit.,* pp. 205–206.

[28]DAWLC, C. H. Marshall, A. Pell, and Sands to Wells, November 23, 1870; *New York Evening Post,* semiweekly, July 5, 1870; *Free-Trader,* IV (December, 1870), 118, 122, 130; *New York Tribune,* November 29, 1870.

[29]HG, Greeley to Colfax, October 6, 1870; Brinkerhoff, *op. cit.,* pp. 209–211.

[30]LPM, HDL to D. D. Lloyd, March 13, 17, 1871; CS, Godkin to

Schurz, April 5, 1871, Schurz to Godkin, March 31, 1871; *Free-Trader,* IV (May, 1871), 215.

³¹*Ibid.,* IV (April, 1871), 193; *New York Daily Bulletin,* January 21, 28, 31, 1871.

³²William Dudley Foulke, *A Hoosier Autobiography* (New York, 1922), 15; LPM, Greeley to HDL, April 2, 1871; *New York Tribune,* March 28, 1871; *New York Evening Post,* April 18, 1871; *New York World,* March 25, 1871; *Free-Trader,* IV (May, 1871), 209–211.

³³LPM, Greeley to HDL, February 15, 17, 28, 1871, Lieber to HDL, March 2, 11, April 12, November 18, 27, 1871; *New York Evening Post,* February 18, April 14, October 7, 1871.

³⁴Pp. 53–55.

³⁵*New York World,* May 10, 1871; *New York Tribune,* May 13, 17, 1871; LPM, MS petition to Beecher, February 1872, M. C. Lloyd to HDL, May 17, 1871, correspondence with Voorhis, Hewitt, Beecher; Henry Ward Beecher, *Libraries and Public Reading Rooms . . . in the Cooper Union Hall, Monday Evening, April 22d, 1872* (New York, 1872).

³⁶*New York Tribune,* January 22, 1871; *New York Times,* June 28, 1871.

³⁷*New York Evening Post,* September 5, 1871; WCB, J. Hay to M. Godwin, September 6, 1871; LPM, HDL to Mr. Hodgskin, October 1872, MS agreement, "Ballot-Box Guard," October, 1871.

CHAPTER III

¹*Nation,* XIV (February 1, 1872), 68–69; *People's Pictorial Tax-Payer,* I (New York, March, 1872), 21.

²*Ibid.,* I (February, 1872), 11; William B. Hesseltine, *Ulysses S. Grant, Politician* (New York, 1935), pp. 252–253, 263; Grace J. Clarke, *George W. Julian* (Indianapolis, 1923), pp. 311–312, 321–336.

³EAA, Grosvenor to Atkinson, December 21, 1871, January 13, 1872, Sands to Atkinson, January 4, 1872, Atkinson to Grosvenor, December, 1872; JDC, Grosvenor to Cox, January 19, 1872, Sands to Cox, May 14, 1872.

⁴MM, Grosvenor to Marble, November 8, 1871; *New York Evening Post,* December 23, 1871.

⁵*Ibid.,* December 21, 1871; EAA, Grosvenor to Atkinson, December 21, 1871.

536   *Henry Demarest Lloyd and the Empire of Reform*

⁶Earl D. Ross, *The Liberal Republican Movement* (New York, 1919), pp. 10–11.

⁷*Tax-Payer,* I (February, March, April, 1872); LPM, HDL to Sterne, January 18, 1872, Grosvenor to HDL, February 1, 1872, I. R. Walsh to S. T. K. Prime, February 3, 1872, Prime to HDL, February 4, 1872, H. White to HDL, February 3, 1872; EAA, HDL to Atkinson, February 7, 1872.

⁸*Ibid.; Tax-Payer,* I (March, 1872), 21, 25.

⁹EAA, Grosvenor to Atkinson, February 3, 6, 14, 1872; JDC, Garfield to Cox, February 20, 1872; *Tax-Payer,* I (March, 1872), 21, 25.

¹⁰*Tax-Payer,* I (March, 1872), 20, 28–29, (April, 1872), 35, 41; Ross, *op. cit.,* pp. 51–52; LT, Trumbull to H. White, April 24, 27, 1872; CS, A. Belmont to Schurz, April 1, 1872, M. Marble to Schurz, April 23, 30, 1872; JDC, Garfield to Cox, March 30, 1872, Bowles to Wells, March 25, 1872, in Wells to Cox, March 27, 1872.

¹¹HG, Cox to Greeley, July 17, 1869; JDC, Bowles to Wells, March 25, 1872, Cox to Grosvenor, March 23, 1872, Grosvenor to Cox, March 25, 1872, Cox to Wells, March 16, 1872; CS, Belmont to Schurz, April 1, 1872; *New York Tribune,* March 16, 26, 30, April 2, 5, 30, 1872; John Bigelow, *Retrospections of an Active Life,* IV (New York, 1910), 570–571; *Nation,* XIV (New York, April 4, 1872), 209; Claude M. Fuess, *Carl Schurz Reformer* (New York, 1952), p. 185.

¹²CS, Cox to Schurz, April 5, 1872; EAA, Cox to Atkinson, April 11, 1872; Grosvenor to Atkinson, April 22, 1872.

¹³JDC, K. Cox to J. D. Cox, April 7, 1872; *New York Tribune,* March 30, April 13, 1872; *Nation,* XIV (April 18, 1872), 249.

¹⁴LPM, Lieber to HDL, April 23, 1872; RRB, HDL to Bowker, April 22, 1872; EAA, W. U. O'Dwyer to HDL, April 19, 1872; DAWLC, G. W. Curtis to Wells, April 23, 1872; PG, Curtis to Godwin, March 27, 1872; *Independent,* XXIV (New York, April 4, 1872), 3; *Nation,* XIV (April 25, 1872), 265.

¹⁵*New York Evening Post,* May 1, 1872; *New York Tribune,* May 2, 1872; *Chicago Tribune,* April 30, 1872; Henry Watterson, *"Marse Henry," An Autobiography,* I (New York, 1919), 243.

¹⁶*New York Tribune,* May 3, 1872.

¹⁷CS, Belmont to Schurz, April 1, 1872; MM, Marble to Wells, April 30, [1872].

¹⁸*New York Evening Post,* April 29, May 1, 1872; *New York Tribune,* March 16, April 28–30, May 1–3, 1872; Watterson, *op. cit.,* pp. 243–244; Fuess, *op. cit.,* p. 187; *Nation,* XIV (May 9, 1872), 303.

[19]*New York Evening Post,* April 29, May 1, 1872; *New York Tribune,* April 28–30, May 1, 1872.

[20]*Ibid.,* April 29, 1872. Cf. *Nation,* XIV (May 30, 1872), 345.

[21]*New York Tribune,* April 26, 1872; Chester McArthur Destler, *American Radicalism, 1865–1901* (New London, 1946), pp. 50–60.

[22]CS, O. H. Pollock to Schurz, May 2, 1872; *New York Tribune,* May 1, 2, 1872; *New York World,* May 2, 3, 1872; Ross, *op. cit.,* pp. 89–90.

[23]LPM, circular, Cincinnati, May 2, 1872; *New York Tribune,* May 3, 1872; *Nation,* XIV (May 9, 1872), 303; Ross, *op. cit.,* pp. 91–92.

[24]*New York Evening Post,* May 3, 1872; *New York Tribune,* May 1–3, 1872; *Nation,* XIV (May 9, 1872), 303; Fuess, *op. cit.,* pp. 188–189.

[25]LPM, HDL to Keenan, June 14, July 12, 1872, D. D. Lloyd to Keenan, May 8, 1872.

[26]*Nation,* XIV (May 9, 1872), 297, 303; *New York Tribune,* May 3, 4, 8, 10, 31, 1872; Ross, *op. cit.,* pp. 96–103; CS, Schurz to Godkin, November 23, 1872, Schurz to Sands, May 9, 1872; JDC, C. F. Cox to Cox, May 3, 1872, Sands to Cox, May 14, 1872, Cox to Sands, May 10, 1872.

[27]JAG, Cox to Garfield, May 10, 1872, Cox to A. Cox, May 6, 1872; EAA, E. W. Kittridge to Atkinson, May 4, 1872; *New York Tribune,* May 6, June 25, 1872; *Cincinnati Gazette,* May 4, 1872.

[28]WB, William Bross MS Diary, May 3, 1872; Ross, *op. cit.,* p. 110; *Independent,* May 9, 1872; *New York Times,* May 4, 1872.

[29]*New York Evening Post,* May 2, 4, 1872.

[30]LPM, telegrams HDL or Sands to D. D. Lloyd and Wm. O. McDowell, May 9–11, 1872, Sands to Minturn, May 9, 1872, Wells to Sands, May 10, 1872, Cox to Sands, May 9, 1872, Atkinson to Sands, May 10, 1872; JDC, Sands to Cox, May 9, 10, 14, 1872; EAA, Sands to Atkinson, May 10, 13, 1872.

[31]LPW, Atkinson to Sands, May 10, 1872; EAA, Grosvenor to Atkinson, May 12, 1872, Atkinson to Grosvenor, May 11, 14, 1872, Sands to Atkinson, May 22, 1872; CS, Schurz to Sands, May 9, 1872, Sands to Schurz, May 14, 1872.

[32]CS, Schurz to Greeley, May 6, 9, 18, 1872, Greeley to Schurz, May 8, 17, 1872, Reid to Schurz, May 27, 29, 1872, Grosvenor to Schurz, May 22, 26, 1872; DAWLC, Reid to Bowles, May 26, 1872; *Nation,* XIV (May 23, 1872), 304, 329.

[33]DAWLC, Bowles to Wells, May 28, 1872.

[34]*New York Evening Post,* May 30, 31, 1872; *Chicago Tribune,* May

28, 1872; *New York Tribune,* May 31, 1872; Ross, *op. cit.,* pp. 112–114; LPM, leaflet, "Call for a Free Trade Meeting."

[35]JDC, Sands to Cox, May 31, June 1, 1872; Ross, *op cit.,* pp. 118–120.

[36]LPM, HDL to Keenan, May 23, July 12, *n.d.,* 1872; EAA, Wells to Atkinson on reverse of Storey to Wells, May 28, 1872, HDL to Atkinson, June 4, 1872.

[37]CS, T. F. Randolph to Schurz, June 2, 1872, HDL to Schurz, June 6, 1872, Schurz to Grosvenor, June 5, 1872, H. White to Schurz, June 8, 12, 1872; LT, HDL draft "Invitation to Conference;" JDC, HDL to Cox, June 3, 4, 1872: *New York Tribune,* June 14, 1872; PG, Schurz to P. Godwin, May 28, 1872.

[38]*Ibid.,* HDL to Cox, June 3, 1872; CS, Randolph to Schurz, June 7, 1872; LPM, HDL to Keenan, *n.d.;* EAA, Godwin to Atkinson, May 29, 1872; *Chicago Tribune,* June 17, 1872: *Nation,* XIV (June 6, 1872), 365.

[39]CS, HDL to Schurz, June 17, 20, 1872, Randolph to Schurz, June 19, 1872; *New York Herald,* June 21, 1872; *Corning Graphic,* October 3, 1877; *New York Tribune,* June 18, 1872; *Brooklyn Daily Eagle,* June 18, 1872.

[40]CS, Schurz to Godwin, June 23, 1872; JDC, Cox to J. Lynch, July 11, 1872; *New York Tribune,* June 21, 22, 24, 25, 1872; *New York Herald,* June 21, 22, 1872; *Nation,* XIV (June 27, 1872), 413, 416; *New York Evening Post,* June 21, 22, 1872; *Independent,* XXIV (New York, June 27, 1872), 4; *Golden Age,* II (New York, June 29, 1872), 4–5: *Chicago Tribune,* June 25, 1872.

[41]*Atlantic Monthly,* XXXI (May, 1873), 650.

CHAPTER IV

[1]LPM, HDL to Keenan, [May], June 24, July 12, 1872, D. D. Lloyd to Keenan, July 2, 1872; LPW, Keenan to Mrs. H. D. Lloyd, October 1, 1903.

[2]*Ibid.,* HDL to Keenan, July 23, 1872; Woodford Clayton, *History of Bergen and Passaic Counties, New Jersey* (Philadelphia, 1882), p. 358.

[3]LPM, HDL to Keenan, June 24, July 2, 3, 4, 5, 8, 10, 12, 24, 1872.

[4]*Ibid.,* HDL to Keenan, June 25, July 8, 12, 1872; *Nation,* XIV (June 27, 1872), 416; EAA, S. L. Taylor to Atkinson, June 24, 1872.

[5]LPM, HDL to Keenan, July 6, 8, 10, 15, 19, 24, 1872; *Independent,* XXIV (August 15, 1872), 4.

⁶LPM, HDL to Keenan, July 15, 24, 1872.

⁷*Ibid.*, HDL to Keenan, July 24, 1872.

⁸"William Bross," *Western Monthly,* I (Chicago, June, 1869), 329–330; Charles A. Yount, *William Bross, 1813–1890* (Lake Forest, 1940), pp. 11–16; Philip Kinsley, *The Chicago Tribune. Its First Hundred Years,* II, *1865–1880* (Chicago, 1945), pp. 4, 9, 136–139.

⁹WB, Bross MS Diary, February 21–28, July 22, 1872; Frederick Francis Cook, *Bygone Days in Chicago* (Chicago, 1910), pp. 341–344; Bessie Pierce, editor, *As Others See Chicago. Impressions of Visitors, 1673–1933* (Chicago, 1933), p. 211.

¹⁰CHS, Annie Hitchcock to Mrs. Jewett, December 8, 1871; TD, circular, "The Philosophical Society of Chicago"; Mrs. William Blair, "Out of the Past," Caroline Kirkland, *Chicago Yesterdays* (Chicago, 1919), p. 85; WB, Bross MS Diary, January 3, 18, April 29, July 1, December 7–10, 1872; "William Bross," *loc. cit.,* p. 328.

¹¹LPM, HDL to Keenan, August 25, 28, September 19, 1872; DAWLC, I. H. Osborne to Wells, November 9, 1872.

¹²LPM, HDL to Keenan, August 25, 1872.

¹³*Ibid.*, HDL to Keenan, September 3, 4, 9, *n.d.*, 24, 1872.

¹⁴*Ibid.*, HDL to Keenan, *n.d.*, September 24, October 3, 1872.

¹⁵LPM, HDL to Keenan, October 14, *n.d.*, 1872; Everett Chamberlain, *Chicago and Its Suburbs* (Chicago, 1874), p. 268.

¹⁶LPM, HDL to Keenan, October 14, 1872.

¹⁷*Ibid.*, HDL to Keenan, October 29, 1872.

¹⁸*Ibid.*, HDL to Keenan, October 31, June 4, 1874; DAWLC, H. White to Wells, October 29, 1871; *Chicago Tribune,* November 17, 1872; Chamberlain, *op. cit.,* pp. 254–265; A. T. Andreas, *History of Chicago,* III (Chicago, 1886), 695.

¹⁹Cf. *Harper's Weekly,* XV (February 25, 1871), 163.

²⁰*Chicago Tribune,* November 10, 1872.

²¹November 17, 24, 1872.

²²LPM, Lewes to HDL, March 19, 1873; Estelling Bennett, "The Story of Society in Chicago," *Chicago Magazine,* September 11, 1911, pp. 543–549.

²³LPM, Bryant to Fairbanks, November 14, 1872.

²⁴*Ibid.*, HDL to Keenan, *n.d.;* Louise deKoven Bowen, *Growing Up With A City* (New York, 1926), p. 42.

²⁵LPM, HDL to Keenan, *n.d.;* WB, Bross MS Diary, August 11–13, 1875, August 27, 1878; Andreas, *op. cit.,* III, 429–430.

²⁶*Chicago Tribune,* February 2, 1873.

²⁷*Ibid.*, February 2, March 23, April 21, June 9, 22, 1873.

[28]LPM, HDL to M. C. Lloyd, *n.d.,* February [10], [14], 1873.

[29]*Ibid.,* HDL to Keenan, June 12, 23, [24], September 4, 1873.

[30]*Chicago Tribune,* June 1, 21, 1873.

[31]*Ibid.,* December 14, 21, 28, 1873.

[32]*Ibid.,* December 28, 1873, supplement.

[33]WB, Bross MS Diary, September 14, 1873.

[34]LPM, HDL to Keenan, October 31, November 28, 1873; *Chicago Tribune,* December 22, 25, 1873.

[35]WB, Bross MS Diary, December 5, 11, 17, 24, 25, 1873; LPM, wedding invitation, Charles Wendt to C. L. Withington, December 20, 1907; *Chicago Times,* December 26, 1873.

CHAPTER V

[1]WB, Bross MS Diary, December 26, 28, 29, 1873, January 6, 12, 13, 1874.

[2]*Ibid.,* January 6, 15, 16, 23, 1874.

[3]LPW, J. B. Lloyd to Keenan, [October 28, 1874], HDL to Keenan, June 12, 1874.

[4]Tyler Dennett, *John Hay* (New York, 1934), pp. 95–142.

[5]WB, Bross MS Diary, January 4, March 17, August 28, 1874; "William Bross," *loc. cit.,* p. 328; F. Cyril James, *The Growth of Chicago Banks,* I (New York, 1938), 350–352, 429.

[6]LPM, HDL to Keenan, February 11, 1878.

[7]*Ibid.;* Bross MS Diary, January 1, 23, 1875; *Memorials of the Chicago Literary Club,* I (Chicago, 1913), 13; Frederick William Gookin, *The Chicago Literary Club* (Chicago, 1926), pp. 1–60, 270; *Henry Demarest Lloyd, In Memoriam* [Chicago, 1903], p.4; Edward Osgood Brown, "The Chicago Literary Club," *Papers of the Bibliographical Society of America,* XI, No. 1 (January, 1917), 93–96.

[8]LPM, printed announcements, C. W. Wendte to C. L. Withington, July 20, 1907; *Chicago Tribune,* June 16, 1874.

[9]*Ibid.,* March 1, 29, 30, September 20, November 16, 1874, February 24, 1875, circular, "The Sunday Lecture Society."

[10]*Ibid.,* May 1, 8, 1876.

[11]LPM, bulletin of the Society, August 1876, HDL to H. B. Mason, December 31, 1898, HDL to A. B. Mason, December 8, 1896.

[12]*Ibid.,* circulars, clippings, and bulletin; DAWLC, Prime to Wells, February 25, 1875.

[13]LPM, HDL to Keenan, June 12, 1875, February 11, 1878, HDL to Huntington, July 20, 1888, Prime to HDL, November 18, 1895.

[14]*Ibid.,* HDL to Keenan, March 31, June 12, 1875; WB, Bross MS

Diary, October 30–September 1876; *Chicago Tribune,* October 20, 1880.

¹⁵Diary, June 15, 1874.

¹⁶LPM, HDL to Keenan, February 11, 1878.

¹⁷*Chicago Tribune,* 1873–November 7, 1874; Kinsley,˙*op. cit.,* II, 193–207.

¹⁸*Ibid.,* II, 187, 202; WB, Bross MS Diary, 1875–85; *Chicago Tribune,* February 2, April 21, June 1, 1873.

¹⁹*Ibid.,* February 28, 1874; Kinsley, *op. cit.,* II, 192–196.

²⁰*Chicago Tribune,* April 11, 1874; Joseph Fort Newton, *David Swing* (Chicago, 1909), pp. 58–94.

²¹*Ibid.,* pp. 98–112; *Chicago Tribune,* March 1, 3, 21, 29, April 30, May 6–16, October 19–24, November 1, 1874; A. T. Andreas, *History of Chicago,* III (Chicago, 1886), 802–804, 827.

²²LPM, HDL to Keenan, October 28, 1874; *Chicago Tribune,* March 29–October 5, 1874; Kinsley, *op. cit.,* pp. 183–204.

²³*Chicago Tribune,* March 25–27, 30, September 13, 27, October 11, November 1, 8, 1874.

²⁴*Ibid.,* October 11, 1874.

²⁵*Ibid.,* November 9, 1874; Andreas, *op. cit.,* III, 695–696, 827.

²⁶LPM, W. S. Jevons to HDL, December 19, 1874, HDL to Keenan, October 28, 1874; *Chicago Tribune,* October–November 24, 1874.

²⁷JAG, Medill to Garfield, April 17, 1872; *Chicago Tribune,* November 10, 1874.

²⁸LPM, HDL to Huntington, July 7, 1900.

²⁹*Ibid.,* MS Fragment of Lloyd's plans, W. M. Taylor to HDL, December 15, 1874, HDL to D. D. Lloyd, April 18, 1875, May 23, 1876, W. T. Felton to D. D. Lloyd, June 3, 1875, W. T. Felton to HDL, June 5, 1875.

³⁰*Ibid.,* MS plan for the *Chicago Daily News,* J. E. Scripps to HDL, May 27, June 2, 1876, HDL to J. C. Lloyd, *n.d.,* P. R. Meggy to C. L. Withington, April 28, 1908, Melville E. Stone to C. L. Withington, January 2, 1906, J. C. Lloyd to C. L. Withington, *n.d.,* Meggy to I. W. Ostrander, *n.d.;* Melville E. Stone, *Fifty Years a Journalist* (New York, 1921), pp. 51–64.

³¹*Ibid.,* pp. 44–45, 63–65, 77, 101.

³²LPM, letters to HDL from N. C. Perkins, February 15, 1881, C. S. Darrow, May 14, 1889, E. G. Bell, August 8, 1889, Bowles, January 21, 23, February 4, 1891, W. R. Burke, June 25, July 10, 14, 1894.

³³RRB, HDL to Bowker, November 20, 1875.

³⁴A. B. Stickney, *The Railway Problem* (St. Paul, 1891); Robert E,

542   *Henry Demarest Lloyd and the Empire of Reform*

Riegel, *Story of the Western Railroads* (New York, 1926), pp. 223–228.

[35]*Chicago Tribune,* November 29, 1874, February 22, March 27, 1875; Charles H. Baker, *Life of William Taylor Baker* (New York, 1908), p. 112.

[36]*Chicago Tribune,* December 13, 16, 24, 27, 1874, February 7, March 5, 10, 11, 27, 1875, July 5, November 11, 14, 1877, September 28, 1879, March 27, November 24, 1880.

[37]*Ibid.,* December 19, 1884; *Current,* II (Chicago, October, 1884), 226, IX (December 24, 1887), 58–59.

[38]*Chicago Tribune,* July 30, December 14, 19, 27, 1887, January 14, 18, February 19, 1878; LPM, HDL to Keenan, February 11, 1878.

[39]*Chicago Tribune,* January 8, February 2, 27, April 3, 1875, August 18, December 20, 28, 1877, *et seq.*

[40]*Ibid.,* December 13, 23, 1874, February 28, 1875, July 8, 1877, January 17, 21, 1880; WB, Bross MS Diary, October 1879, Cf. Homer Hoyt, *One Hundred Years of Land Values in Chicago* (Chicago, 1933), p. 125; Agnes M. Johansen to Chester McA. Destler, August 12, 1942.

[41]*Chicago Tribune,* January 1, 1875, January 1, 1880.

[42]LPM, Robert Patterson to HDL, December 8, 1895.

[43]Destler, *American Radicalism,* Ch. IV.

[44]DAW, Cox to Wells, February 28, 1878.

[45]WB, Bross MS Diary, December 13, 1877, January 15, 1878; *Chicago Tribune,* July 13, 1877–February 10, 1879; LPM, E. Suess to HDL, March 3, 1878.

[46]*Chicago Tribune,* July 6, November 7, 20, 21, 26, December 3, 20, 31, 1877, January 9, 10, 12, 1878; *Nation,* XXXII (March 10, 1881), 160.

[47]*Ibid.,* February 4, 1881, quoting *Des Moines Register.*

[48]*Chicago Tribune,* January 20, 25, February 19, 1879, April 3, December 9, 1884; LPM, W. G. Eggleston to C. L. Withington, May 12, 1909; Harry Barnard, *Eagle Forgotten. The Life of John Peter Altgeld* (Indianapolis, 1938), pp. 356–357; Davis Rich Dewey, *Financial History of the United States* (New York and London, 1931), pp. 407–408.

CHAPTER VI

[1]*Free-Trader,* IV (February, 1871), 162; *Charles Francis Adams, 1836–1915: An Autobiography* (Boston, 1916), pp. 172–175, 184–195.

[2]*Proceedings of the Special Committee on Railroads Appointed under a Resolution of the Assembly to Investigate Alleged Abuses in the Management of Railroads Chartered by the State of New York* (Six volumes, New York, 1879), cited hereafter as Hepburn Proceedings; Foord, *op. cit.*, pp. 183–198; Lee Benson, *op. cit.*, Ch. VI.

[3]*Chicago Tribune,* November 1, 1874, February 6, 1875, July 10, 20, 1877.

[4]*Ibid.*, July 19–31, August 4, 1877; Allan Nevins, *The Emergence of Modern America, 1865–1878 (History of American Life,* VIII) (New York, 1928), pp. 395–391.

[5]Elwin W. Sigmund, "Railroad Strikers in Court," *Journal of the Illinois State Historical Society,* XLIX (Springfield, Summer, 1956), 190–209.

[6]*Chicago Tribune,* November 4, December 20, 21, 1877, *et seq.*

[7]*Ibid.*, November 3, 5, December 3, 1877.

[8]*Ibid.*, January 23, February 8, 1878, January 1, 1881, May 11, 1884; LPM, Fink to Lloyd, April 4, 1881.

[9]*Chicago Tribune,* November 26, 1879.

[10]*Ibid.*, September 26, October 4, November 26, 27, 28, 1879, January 20, 1880, Charles Francis Adams, *The Federation of the Railroad System* (Boston, 1880), pp. 7–9; Edward Gross Campbell, *The Reorganization of the American Railroad System, 1893–1900* (New York, 1938), p. 146; Benson, *op. cit.*, p. 141.

[11]*Chicago Tribune,* November 26, 29, December 3, 1879; LPM, HDL to Fink, December 28, 1880.

[12]*Chicago Tribune,* October 4, November 20, 28, 29, 1879.

[13]*Ibid.*, November 28, 29, 1879.

[14]Eliot Jones, *Principles of Railroad Transportation* (New York, 1931), p. 62; Thomas Cochran and William Miller, *The Age of Enterprise* (New York, 1942), pp. 155–162.

[15]Benson, *op. cit.*, pp. 150–152.

[16]LPM, HDL to Mrs. H. D. Lloyd, April 21, 1903; C. Lloyd, *op. cit.*, I, 53; Kinsley, *op. cit.*, II, 332.

[17]*Chicago Tribune,* November 20, 1879, January 23, 1880.

[18]*Ibid.*, November 28, December 2, 1879, March 2, 1880.

[19]*Ibid.*, November 23, 26, 30, December 6, 13, 1879, January 7, 27, 1880.

[20]*Ibid.*, December 6, 19, 20, 1879, January 20, February 2, 3, 1880.

[21]Adams, *Federation, passim.*

[22]*Chicago Tribune,* January 28, 29, March 13, 1880; Hepburn *Proceedings, passim.*

[23]Benson, *op. cit.*, pp. 132–155; LPM, HDL to Sterne, September 23, December 20, 1879; *Chicago Tribune*, January 28, March 13, 1880.

[24]*Ibid.*, January 23, February 7, 19, March 3, 6, 1880.

[25]*Ibid.*, December 29, 31, 1880, January 7, 21, 1881, January 8, February 21, March 3, 6, 31, 1882, April 4, 1884; John C. Cochran, *Railroad Leaders, 1845–1890* (Cambridge, 1953), p. 186.

[26]*Ibid.*, pp. 185–189; *Chicago Tribune*, March 2, 1880, April 4, 1881, October 1, 1882, October 24, December 15, 1883, April 4, 12, 1884.

[27]*Ibid.*, March 17, 1880, August 18, 1882, January 14, 1883, April 4, November 11, 21, 1884; Select Committee on Interstate Commerce, 49 Congress, 1 Sess., *Senate Report 46*, I (Washington, 1886), 188–189.

[28]LPM, H. H. Gorringe to HDL, December 8, 1881, C. A. Spofford to HDL, July 18, [1881]; *Chicago Tribune*, July 12, 14, 17, 18, 19, 1881; *Duluth Tribune*, July 19, 1881; James Blaine Hedges, *Henry Villard and the Railways of the Northwest* (New Haven, 1930), pp. 105–106, 295–300.

[29]*Chicago Tribune*, September 1–10, October 6, 12, 14, 18, 1883; Bross MS Diary, September 1, 1883; LPW, clipping *Seattle Daily Times* from a Salt Lake City newspaper, October 18, 1901, Cochran, *op. cit.*, pp. 112, 186. Henry Villard, *Memoirs*, II (Boston, 1904), 309–312; Henry George, *Social Problems* (New York, 1886), p. 68.

[30]*Chicago Tribune*, September 28, October 1, 3, 1883.

[31]*Ibid.*, October 4, 7, 8, 13, 1883; Stuart Daggett, *Chapters on the History of the Southern Pacific* (New York, 1922), pp. 140–316.

[32]*Chicago Tribune*, January 24, 1881.

[33]*Ibid.*, December 25, 27, 28, 1883; *Radical Review*, I (Chicago, December 29, 1883), 1.

[34]*Chicago Tribune*, December 25, 27, 28, 29, 1883.

[35]*Ibid.*, February 20, 1883; *Hartford Courant*, March 21, 1883; *The Current*, I (Chicago, January 5, 1884), 34. Lloyd listed his sources, published shortly before, and did not cite Julian's essays while presenting a different account. Cf. Robert S. Henry, "The Railroad Land Grant Legend in American History Texts," *Mississippi Valley Historical Review*, XXXII (September 1945), 180, for discussion of the map.

[36]LPM, Van Wyck to HDL, May 7, 1884; *Chicago Tribune*, May 23, 1884, January 9, 1885; Marie U. Harmer & James L. Sellers,

"Charles H. Van Wyck," *Nebraska History Magazine,* XII (Lincoln, July–December, 1929), 205–346.

[37]*Chicago Tribune,* January 10, April 10, May 23, 24, 1884.

[38]Ellis Paxon Oberholtzer, *A History of the United States since the Civil War,* IV (New York, 1931), 189–210.

[39]*Chicago Tribune,* December 11, 16, 20, 1884, January 2, 3, 10, 1885; Oberholtzer, *op. cit.,* IV, 337–341, 619–623.

[40]*Chicago Tribune,* January 2, 10, 12, 1885; JBW, HDL to Van Wyck, January 22, 1885, by courtesy of Professor Paul W. Gates.

[41]LPM, MS draft, HDL to S. M. Cullom, December 10, 1886; John D. Clark, *The Federal Trust Policy* (Baltimore, 1931), pp. 17–18; Riegel, *op. cit.,* pp. 292–293.

CHAPTER VII

[1]Vernon Louis Parrington, *The Beginnings of Critical Realism in America, 1860–1920 (Main Currents in American Thought,* III) (New York, 1930), pp. 284–285.

[2]LPM, Jevons to HDL, December 19, November 17, 1881, Small Notebook 1881; Joseph Dorfman, *The Economic Mind in American Civilization,* III, *1865–1918* (New York, 1949), 83–85, 165–166; Helen Merrell Lynd, *England in the Eighteen-Eighties. Toward a Social Basis for Freedom* (New York, 1945), p. 105. Richard Horstadter, *Social Darwinism in American Thought* (Philadelphia, 1944), pp. 99, 144.

[3]LPM, Small Notebook July 1877 A.

[4]*Ibid.,* Small Notebook A 1879; James A. Froude, *Caesar* (New York, 1879).

[5]*Ibid.,* Clarke to HDL, January 8, 1894, HDL to W. C. Eggleston, December 27, 1890, HDL to Henry B. Fay, December 31, 1898; *Chicago Tribune,* March 17, 1883.

[6]*Ibid.,* Small Notebook 1881; Dorfman, *op. cit.,* III, 89–91.

[7]LPM, Small Notebook 1881.

[8]*Ibid.,* Small Notebook 1881, 1883 Notebook; Hofstadter, *op. cit.,* p. 125.

[9]LPM, 1883 Notebook.

[10]LPW, G. Shiras, Jr., to HDL, December 26, 1879, R. Sherman to HDL, January 2, 1880.

[11]XLVII (March, 1881), 317–334; LPW, E. G. Patterson to HDL, January 31, 1880; LPM, W. D. Howells to HDL, December 6, 1880, HDL to Huntington, July 7, 1900.

[12]*Chicago Tribune,* December 31, 1880.

[13]Cf. Chester McArthur Destler, "The Standard Oil, Child of the Erie Ring, 1868–1872," *Mississippi Valley Historical Review,* XXXIII (June, 1946, March, 1947), 89–114, 621–628; Arthur Menzies Johnson, *Development of American Petroleum Pipelines* (Ithaca, 1956), pp. 14, 28; Hans B. Thorelli, *The Federal Antitrust Policy* (Baltimore, 1955), pp. 91–96; Allan Nevins, *John D. Rockefeller,* I (New York, 1940), 53–59; Harold F. Williamson and Arnold R. Daum, *The American Petroleum Industry 1859–1899, The Age of Illumination* (Evanston, 1959), pp. 343–551, for an objective analysis of Lloyd's subject.

[14]LPM, T. P. Fowler to HDL, May 31, 1881, Patterson to HDL, February 22, 1881, Sherman to HDL, March 21, 1881; EM, Peters to HDL, February 23, 1881; *National Anti-Monopoly League, Specimen Monopolies (n.d.);* Frederick Emory Haynes, *Third Party Movements since the Civil War* (Iowa City, 1916), p. 147.

[15]Clark, *op. cit.,* p. 17; Thorelli, *op. cit.,* pp. 134–159.

[16]*Chicago Tribune,* January 14, 16, 17, 19, 30, 1881; *Current,* II (July 5, 1884), 2; Ida M. Tarbell, *The Nationalizing of Business, 1878–1898 (History of American Life,* IX) (New York, 1936), 36–39.

[17]LPM, J. B. Aldrich to HDL, April 24, 1883; *Atlantic Monthly,* L (July, 1882), 69–82; Frank A. Fetter, "The Early History of Political Economy in the United States," *Proceedings of the American Philosophical Society,* LXXXVII, No. 1 (Philadelphia, July, 1943), 59–60.

[18](New York, 1885); LPM, Fowler to HDL, July 17, 1882, Thurber to HDL, June 20, 1882, Gorringe to HDL, *n.d.; Independent,* XXXIX (June 22, 1882), 11; FBT, HDL to Thurber, June 23, 1882 (courtesy of Lee Benson); *Springfield Republican,* June 24, 1882.

[19]Henry D. Lloyd, "Political Economy and the Goulds," *Nation,* XXXIV (June 29, 1882), 543; *Springfield Republican,* July 7, 1882; *The New York Times,* July 2, 1882; *New York Evening Post,* June 20, 1882; *Current,* II (September, 27, December 6, 1884), 194, 353–354; Parrington, *op. cit.,* pp. 154–168; Ernest Crosby, "The Dangerous Classes," *North American Review,* CXXXVI (New York, March, 1883), 353–354.

[20]*Chicago Tribune,* November 4, 1883.

[21]"Making Bread Dear," *North American Review,* CXXXVI (August, 1883), 118–136; LPM, C. Partridge to HDL, May 8, 1883, J. N. Jewett to HDL, August 16, 1883; *Nation,* XXXV (September 14, 1882), 214–215.

²²Cambridge *Independent Press,* September 29, 1883; *Pall Mall Gazette,* September 13, 1883; *Springfield Republican,* July 21, 1883; *Boston Daily Advertiser,* July 19, 1883; *Philadelphia Daily Ledger,* July 24, 1883.

²³CXXVII (October, 1883), 372–387; LPM, Hutchinson to HDL, April 29, May 3, 1888, HDL to Hutchinson, May 2, 1888.

²⁴Henry D. Lloyd, *Lords of Industry* (New York, 1910), pp. 142–146.

²⁵LPM, Clarke to HDL, May 23, 1883, June 15, July 8, October 22, 1884, Swinton to HDL, December 25, 1884; TD, Clarke to David-son, June 12, 1882; *Bradstreet's,* IX (New York, May 24, 1884), 326–327; *Age of Steel,* IV (St. Louis, May 24, 1884), 649; *Current,* II (September 27, 1884), 1.

²⁶*Chicago Tribune,* January 2, October 10, December 2, 10, 21, 25, 1879, January 22, 27, 1880, September 3, 1883; Lynd, *op. cit.,* pp. 132–139.

²⁷*Chicago Tribune,* December 30, 1882, March 19, 1883, December 27, 1884.

²⁸*Chicago Tribune,* January 28, February 1, 9, 1880, May 17, 1884; William A. Russ, Jr., "Godkin Looks at Western Agrarianism: A Case Study," *Agricultural History,* XIX (October, 1945), 233–242.

²⁹*Chicago Tribune,* March 9, 1880, January 20, 1881, April 14, 1884.

³⁰*Ibid.,* August 13, 1882.

³¹*Ibid.,* January 6, 1881, January 6, 1883, November 20, 1884.

³²*Ibid.,* April 5, 1884; John A. Ise, *United States Forest Policy* (New Haven, 1920); Flick, *op. cit.,* X (1935), 275.

³³*Chicago Tribune,* December 30, 1882, January 1, 21, 1883.

³⁴*Ibid.,* January 21, February 23, March 4, 1880, January 7, 1883.

³⁵*Ibid.,* January 6, December 23, 27, 28, 1882, January 6–27, 1883.

³⁶*Ibid.,* February 22, 1881, August 17, December 22, 31, 1882, January 23, February 11, September 14, 1883; FBT (Courtesy of Lee Benson, by permission), HDL to Thurber, February 11, 1884; *Justice,* Nos. 43–101 (New York, May 19, 1883–June 28, 1884); *Radical Review,* II (July 12, 1884), 6–7.

CHAPTER VIII

¹WB, Bross MS Diary, November 13, December 9, 1875, January 18, February 2, April 10, 1876, January 10, 1882, March 17, 1885; TD, M. LeB. Goddard to Davidson, February 2, 1881, August 9, 1883; LPM, J. B. Lloyd to Keenan, October 27, 1874; *Chicago Tribune,* October 9, December 28, 1883; LPW, HDL to Mrs. H. D. Lloyd, hereafter JBL, November 7, 1902.

²LPM, A. S. Richardson to JBL, *n.d.;* WB, Bross MS Diary, September 7, 1874, January 18, February 2, 1876, April 11, June 5, 1878, August 4, 1880, November 16–30, 1882, April 20, 1884; *Chicago Tribune,* October 20, 1880, "Fall Days" by "HDL."

³*Chicago Tribune,* May 7–November 7, 1884; LPM, M. LeB. Goddard to HDL, July 24, 1884, Wm. Clarke to HDL, October 22, 1884; TD, Clarke to Davidson, December 12, 1884; *Radical Review,* II (July 12, 1884), 7–8; C. Lloyd, *op. cit.,* I, 73–74.

⁴*Chicago Tribune,* November 17, December 3, 17, 1884, January 11, 16, 1885; JBW, HDL to Van Wyck, January 22, 1885.

⁵LPM, MS 1885 Notebook.

⁶*Chicago Tribune,* October 30, 1879, January 19, 1885.

⁷*Ibid.,* October 30, 1879, January 11, 19, February 29, March 7, 21, 22, 29, 1880, September 1, December 18, 1882, April 8, 1884; LPW, MS "Pullman," Bowker to HDL, February 12, 1884, corrected galley proof "Pullman"; Almont Lindsey, *The Pullman Strike* (Chicago, 1942), pp. 38–39

⁸*Chicago Tribune,* October 3, 1884, February 14, 1885; LPM, Stewart to HDL, September 15, December 14, 15, 23, 1884, enclosure, February 6, 1885, November 27, 1886.

⁹*Ibid.,* A. White to H. C. Adams, January 15, 1885, Clarke to HDL, October 22, 1884, February 2, 1885; LPW, HDL to "My Dear Mother," *n.d.*

¹⁰*Chicago Tribune,* December 6, 1884, January 20, 26, 27, 30, 31, February 4–21, 1885.

¹¹WB, Bross MS Diary, February 24, 28, March 3, 1885; LPM, C Heurotin to Prince de Caraman, March 14, 1885.

¹²*Ibid.,* S. Strickland to HDL, January 12, 1896, T. Hooker to HDL, June 5, 1885; WB, Bross MS Diary, June 1, 9, July 12, 27, 1885.

¹³LPM, HDL to JBL, August 7, 1885, Clarke to HDL, May 23, 1883, January 8, 1884; TD, Clarke to Davidson, January 13, 1884; Beatrice Webb, *My Apprenticeship* (London, 1926), pp. 173–174; Helen Merrell Lynd, *England in the Eighteen-Eighties* (London, 1945), pp. 133–143, 389–397; M. Beer, *History of British Socialism,* II (London, 1921), 246–277.

¹⁴LPM, HDL to JBL, August 1, 7, 1885, T. P. O'Connor to T. Harrington, August 6, 1885; Webb, *op. cit.,* pp. 176–177.

¹⁵LPM, HDL to JBL, August 5, 7, 1885; C. Lloyd, *op. cit.,* I, 76–77; Hesketh Pearson, *G. B. S.* (New York, 1942), pp. 77, 79, 154.

¹⁶LPM, HDL to JBL, August 12, 22, 28, 1885.

¹⁷*Ibid.,* HDL to JBL, September 2, 1885.

[18]*Ibid.*, HDL to JBL, September 5, 1885; LPW, HDL to Huntington, July 20, 1888, undated MS beginning "The history of man . . ."

[19]WB, Bross MS Diary, October 13, 1885; LPM, Mead to HDL, October 30, 1885; LPW, HDL to Salter, October 30, 1885; Mildred Howells, editor, *Life in Letters of William Dean Howells,* I (New York, 1928), 415.

[20]LPW, HDL to Salter and note, Salter to Mead, October 30, 1885; *Radical Review,* I (November 17, 1883), 1–2.

[21]LPW, W. E. Barnes to HDL, December 1, 1885; LPM, Mary Salter to HDL, May 6, [1886]; *Age of Steel,* XLV (January 2, 1886), 15; *John Swinton's Paper,* February 14, 1886.

[22]LPW, HDL to Swinton, June 8, 1886.

[23]*Ibid.*, MS excerpt *Report, 1886,* Illinois Bureau of Labor Statistics; LPM, Stewart to HDL, November 27, 1886; *Knights of Labor,* I (August 19, 1886), 2.

[24]LPW, HDL to Adams, December 6, 1886. C. Lloyd, *op. cit.,* I, 109–112, the typed LPM, Notebook G *(n.d.),* pp. 69–73, except as indicative of Lloyd's thought in 1886. This is an obvious interpolation. It is not written in Lloyd's style, and proffers a Guild Socialism that he never advocated or mentioned elsewhere and was based upon the fad for medievalism that he rejected. *Ibid.*, MS Notebook 18, p. 17. Lloyd did not employ such phrases as "capitalistic slave-drivers" or advocate "confiscation with workhouse relief" for railroad investors.

[25]LPM, Adams to HDL, November 18, 1886; *Knights of Labor,* I, (Chicago, October 23, 1886), 8–9, (November 13, 1886) (November 27, 1886, 8–9; *John Swinton's Paper,* IV, October 17, 1886, May 1, 29, 1887; *Chicago Herald,* January 4, 1892; Barnard, *op. cit.,* pp. 118–120.

[26]LPM, HDL to Barry, October 15, 1886; Henry J. Carmen, Henry David, and Paul H. Guthrie, editors, *The Path I Trod: The Autobiography of Terence V. Powderly* (New York, 1940), pp. 145–161.

[27]LPM, Stewart to HDL, November 27, 1886, January 14, 1887; ES, HDL to Stewart, December 23, 1886.

[28]*Ibid.*, HDL to Stewart, April 14, 1887, Stewart to HDL, April 15, 1887; *Knights of Labor,* II (May 7, 1887), 1.

[29]LPM, HDL to A. S. Brunswick, August 28, 1887, Swinton to Lloyd, August 26, 1887, Stewart to C. Stallbohm, September 20, 1909; ES, HDL to Stewart, August 26, 1887.

[30]*Knights of Labor,* II (May 7, 1887), 1.

[31]September 25, 1887.

[32]August 6, 1887.

[33]ATH, MS "Notes on Industrial Legislation"; Curtis W. Garrison, editor, "Conversations with Rutherford B. Hayes," *Mississippi Valley Historical Review,* XXV (December, 1938), 379.

[34]VI (September 4, 1886), 145; WB, Bross MS Diary, July 24, 1886; LPM, H. C. Adams to HDL, November 18, 1886; Henry David, *History of the Haymarket Affair* (New York, 1936), p. 396, says that in 1887 "Lloyd was in many respects one of the most able and admirable men of his time."

[35]MS Notebook, quoted, C. Lloyd, *op. cit.,* I, 91–92.

[36]Lloyd did not attend Gage's meeting, but otherwise cf. *Ibid.,* p. 90, quoting MS 1889 Notebook; David, *op. cit.,* pp. 433–434.

[37]HG, George to Oglesby, November 5, 1887; GAS, Ingersoll to Schilling, November 3, 4, 1887; Howells, *Life in Letters,* I, 398–413: David, *op. cit.,* pp. 400–402.

[38]LPM, HDL to Stewart, October 21, 1887; Wm. M. Salter, *What Shall Be Done With The Anarchists* (Chicago, 1887); Wm. M. Salter, *The Cure for Anarchy* (Chicago, [1887]).

[39]C. Lloyd, *op. cit.,* p. 93; LPM, A. Fischer to HDL & Salter, November 4, 1887.

[40]*Chicago Tribune,* November 10, 1887.

[41]*Ibid.;* LPM, MS "Petition, for the Pardoning of the Anarchists," November 8, 1887, MS notes on Haymarket trial, November 1887, HDL to A. Lloyd, November 10, 1887; *Labor Enquirer* (Chicago), November 14, 1887; David, *op. cit.,* pp. 440–445.

[42]*Ibid.,* Mrs. J. D. Altberger to C. L. Withington, *n.d.; Chicago Tribune,* November 10, 1887.

[43]LPM, HDL to A. Lloyd, November 10, 1887.

[44]WB, Bross MS Diary, November 10, 11, 1887; *Knights of Labor,* II (November 19, 1887), 8; David, *op. cit.,* p. 467; Joseph Buchanan, *The Story of a Labor Agitator* (New York, 1903), pp. 417–422.

[45]CSL, signed MS "Let the People's Voice Be Heard," November 11, 1887; C. Lloyd, *op. cit.,* I, 98.

[46]LPM, Hunt to HDL, November 14, 1887; Frederic C. Howe, *Confessions of a Reformer* (New York, 1925), pp. 113–116.

[47]LPM, E. M. Heurotin to HDL, November 28, 1887, Clarke to HDL, December 13, 1887, Mead to HDL, November 21, 1887, Ham to HDL, December 13, 1887; Howells, *Life in Letters,* I, 333, 398–399, 407–408.

[48]ES, HDL to Stewart, August 26, 1887; *Knights of Labor,* II (November 19, 1887), 8.

⁴⁹ES, Stewart to HDL, October 8, 1887, HDL to Stewart, October 31, 1887.

⁵⁰LPM, typed MS, *n.d.*

⁵¹LPW, MS "Anarchists"; *Chicago Herald,* January 3, 1888.

⁵²*Ibid.,* Robert Patterson to HDL, December 31, 1887.

⁵³*Ibid.,* Darrow to HDL, January 4, 1888, Ham to HDL, January 7, 1888, Stewart to HDL, January 12, 1888, Hunt to HDL, January 12, 1888, S. C. Moseley to JBL, February 3, 1888; *Liberty,* XIV (November, 1903), 5–6.

CHAPTER IX

¹LPW, HDL to Huntington, July 20, 1888.

²*Ibid.,* HDL to Swinton, June 8, 1886.

³WB, MS Bross Diary, February 25, March 11, 27, August 26, 1886.

⁴*The Works of John Ruskin,* XVII (London, 1905), lxxi–cxi; Lynd, *op. cit.,* pp. 218–219, 222–229, 368; John A. Hobson, *John Ruskin, Social Reformer* (Boston, 1898), pp. vi, 193–194.

⁵Webb, *op. cit.,* pp. 218–249; W. D. P. Bliss, editor, *Encyclopedia of Social Reform* (New York, 1897), pp. 182, 1209–1210; Lynd, *op. cit.,* pp. 53, 63.

⁶"The American Scholar," "The Divinity School Address," "New England Reformers," "Nature," "Man The Reformer," "Politics," "History," were Emerson's essays that influenced Lloyd most, and must be read together with his editorials, essays, and books to ascertain their influence upon him. Cf. LPM, Small Notebook (transcript) F–3. For Emerson's personality, which influenced him directly, Ralph L. Rusk, *The Life of Ralph Waldo Emerson* (New York, 1949). David W. Noble, *The Paradox of Progressive Thought* (Minneapolis, 1958), pp. 145–156; Daniel Aaron, *Men of Good Hope* (New York, 1951), pp. 152, 170.

⁷LPM, Mary G. Salter to HDL, May 16, 1886; MS Catalogue, Henry D. Lloyd private library, Winnetka.

⁸(Chicago, 1884), pp. 31–34; Cf. J. M. Whiteson, *The Reaction of Ethics upon Economics* (1888), quoted in Bliss, *op. cit.,* p. 896.

⁹LPM, MS Notes and Notebooks, Small Notebook, pp. C2–5, Card Notes, p. 146; William James, *A Pluralistic Universe* (New York, 1909), pp. 263–264.

¹⁰LPM, MS Notebooks, 1886–1887. I am indebted to Professor Charles L. Stevenson and to C. D. Broad, *Five Types of Ethical Theory* (New York, 1950), pp. 104–121, for clarification of this phase of Lloyd's intellectual development.

[11]LPM, Adler to HDL, December 19, 1887.

[12]*Ibid.,* MS Notebook VII, p. 163.

[13]*Ibid.,* MS Notebook 1883. Cf. F. O. Matthiesson, *American Renaissance* (New York, 1941), pp. 42–45, 58.

[14]Thomas Hill Green, *Prolegomena to Ethics* (London, 1883); R. L. Nettleship, editor, *Works of Thomas Hill Green* (three volumes, London, 1886–1888), II, 350–362, 416–417, 428; LPM, MS Notebook XVIII (1890); D. C. Somervell, *English Thought in the Nineteenth Century* (London, 1929), pp. 197–198; Noble, *op. cit.,* pp. 148–151, quoting and analyzing Lloyd, *Man the Social Creator* (1906), p. 179.

[15]LPM, MS Notebook 1886, pp. 1–7; Noble, *op. cit.,* pp. 144–145.

[16]LPM, MS Notebook 1886, pp. 3–4, 8.

[17]*Ibid.,* MS 1887 Small Notebook, pp. 1–2, 26.

[18]*Ibid.,* pp. 1–2, 6, 9, 11, 18, MS Notebook XIX, MS Card Notes, pp. 30–31, and 143, which cite Ward, American Economic Association, Vol. 10, n. 3, Supplement, p. 84.

[19]LPM, MS Notebook 1887, pp. 13–14, 22, 26, MS Notebook 17, December 1889.

[20]*Ibid.,* Notebook XVIII, p. 6.

[21]*Ibid.,* Small Notebook 1887, pp. 6–28.

[22]*Ibid.,* pp. 35, 37, 40–41, Notebook XVIII, p. 16.

[23]*Ibid.,* Small Notebook 19, p. 10, Notebook 8, pp. 18–20.

[24]*Ibid.,* Small Notebook 1887, pp. 30, 42.

[25]*Ibid.,* Notebook IX (1888), 2, 7, 13–14.

[26]Allan Nevins, *Grover Cleveland* (New York, 1933), p. 379; Chester McA. Destler, "Agricultural Readjustment and Agrarian Unrest in Illinois, 1880–1896," *Agricultural History,* XXI (Washington, April, 1947), 104–116; Destler, "The Opposition of American Businessmen to Social Control during the 'Gilded Age,'" *Mississippi Valley Historical Review,* XXXIX (March, 1953), 641–672.

[27]*Chicago Herald,* January 4–5, 1892; Claudius O. Johnson, *Carter Henry Harrison I* (Chicago, 1928), pp. 183–185.

[28]Stone, *op. cit.,* p. 118; *Chicago Times,* May 27, 1894; Carter H. Harrison, *Stormy Years* (Indianapolis, 1895), pp. 110–112.

[29]*Chicago Tribune,* April 6, 1890, January 1, 1891; *Chicago Times,* May 27, 1894.

[30]WK, MS "Chicago." Italics added.

[31]LPM, HDL to Salter, April 17, 1891, July 14, 1895; *St. Louis Republic,* April 7, 1890; Willis J. Abbot, *Watching the World Go By*

(Boston, 1933), pp. 61–63; Elmer Ellis, *Mr. Dooley's America. A Life of Finley Peter Dunne* (New York, 1941), pp. 16–52.

³²*Hull-House Maps and Papers. A Presentation of Nationalities and Wages in a Congested District of Chicago . . . By Residents of Hull-House* (New York, 1895), pp. 3–33; *The Land of the Dollar* in Pierce, *As Others See Chicago,* pp. 399–400.

³³*Chicago Tribune,* January 27, 1891.

³⁴Mrs. Florence Kelley, "I Go to Work," *Survey Graphic,* XVIII (New York, June 1, 1927), 273.

³⁵Garrison, *op. cit.,* pp. 379–380; Howells, *op. cit.,* I, 411, 413–414; Charles Richard Williams, editor, *Diary and Letters of Rutherford B. Hayes,* IV (Columbus, 1922–1926), 261–262, 348, 367, 378.

³⁶TD, Clarke to Davidson, June 12, 1882; Thomas Davidson, *Education as World-Building* (Cambridge, 1925), pp. xx–xxi; Davidson, *Education of the Wage-Earners* (Boston, 1904), p. 12; *Ethical World,* III (London, July, 1890), 91–95.

³⁷LPM, R. L. Stevenson to G. Iles, December 14, 1887.

³⁸Henry D. Lloyd, *The New Conscience* (London, third edition, 1893), pp. 5, 11, 13–15, 18; Frederick Lewis Allen, *The Great Pierpont Morgan* (New York, 1949), p. 77.

³⁹Lloyd, *New Conscience,* pp. 1, 16, 18–22; LPM, Salter to HDL, February 6, 1888, Buchanan to HDL, February 6, 1888; *Labor Enquirer,* February 11, 1888; WB, Bross MS Diary, February 8, 1888; *Chicago Times,* February 5, 1888; *Ethical Record,* I (April, 1888), 31–32.

⁴⁰LPM, A. T. Rice to HDL, April 20, May 28, 1888.

⁴¹*Ibid.,* D. D. Lloyd to HDL, September 21, 1888, G. E. Adams to HDL, September 21, 1888; *The* (New York) *Standard,* September 22, 1888; *Chicago Tribune,* September 8, 1888; *Pittsburgh Telegraph,* September 27, 1888.

⁴²LPM, Clarke to HDL, December 22, 1888, January 25, April 3, December 30, 1889; *Ethical Record,* III (April, 1890), 56–57.

⁴³LPM, Altgeld to HDL, June 3, 1890; RTE, HDL to Ely, *n.d.;* GAS, Schilling to Mrs. Parsons, December 1, 1893.

⁴⁴"The Settlement as a Factor in the Labor Movement," *Hull-House Maps and Papers,* pp. 183, 200–201, 203.

CHAPTER X

¹LPM, Small Notebook F–4 (1888–89).

²TD, Salter to Davidson, April 5, 1888; *Ethical Record,* I (July,

1888), 60–61, III (April, 1890), 61; *Labor Enquirer,* April 7, May 6, 26, 1888.

³LPM, Mead to HDL, March 22, 1888, Davidson to HDL, October 11, November 14, 27, 1888, HDL to Davidson, October 19, November 23, 1888; TD, HDL to Davidson, August 10, 1888, February 5, 1889; Davidson, *Education as World Building,* pp. v, xxvi, 1–5, 12, 15–20; C. M. Bakewell, MS "Glenmore" (Courtesy of Professor Bakewell); "Laurence Gronlund," *Social Science,* I, No. 9 (New York, August 31, 1887), 3; Ralph Barton Perry, *The Thought and Character of William James,* I (Boston, 1935), chs. XLVI–XLVII.

⁴LPM, HDL to Swinton, November 30, 1888, Davidson to HDL, January 13, 1889; C. Lloyd, *op. cit.,* I, 120; LPW, Mrs. Delano Goddard MS Journal (copy) February 20, 1873.

⁵LPM, MS Notebook IX, 1.

⁶*Ibid.,* MS pp. 5–6, 8.

⁷*Ibid.,* Notebook IX, 19–23, Notebook 1888; TD, HDL to Davidson, November 23, 1888.

⁸LPM, MS Cards and Notebooks, 1888–1903, pp. 60–61, Notebook IX, 8; William Clarke, editor, *Essays: Selected from the Writings, Literary, Political, and Religious, of Joseph Mazzini* (London, 1888), p. vii, 2, 46.

⁹LPM, Notebook IX, 11–12, 18, XII, 9–10, MS Cards & Notebooks, p. 69; Noble, *op. cit.,* p. 148, for misquotation.

¹⁰LPM, MS Notebook IX, pp. 19–22.

¹¹*Ibid.,* pp. 24–31.

¹²*Ibid.,* pp. 34–36, 38–39.

¹³*Ibid.,* pp. 39–40.

¹⁴*Ibid.,* Stewart to HDL, September 7, 1888, *The Herald* to HDL, October 29, 1888, Detwiler to HDL, September 6, 19, October 13, 27, 1888.

¹⁵LPM; Clarke, *op. cit.,* p. vii; *New Statesman and Nation,* New Series, XXX (London, December 29, 1945), 442; E. E. Hales, *Mazzini and the Secret Societies* (London, 1956); *The Leader,* No. 11 (Chicago, March 2, 1889), 126; Henry D. Lloyd, *Mazzini and Other Essays* (New York, 1910), pp. 1–41.

¹⁶IX (February, 1889), 258–260, "The Real History of the People."

¹⁷S. T., "An Open Letter to Henry D. Lloyd," *America,* I (Chicago, February 28, 1889), 3–4.

¹⁸LPW, Mrs. A. C. Lloyd to HDL, *n.d.*

¹⁹WB, Bross MS Diary, May 20, June 8, April 23, 1878, April 12, 1879, May 1, 1889.

20LPM, HDL to Mrs. A. C. Lloyd, March 27, 1891.

21LPW, MS "Letter to Winship," M. F. Prouty to HDL, March 2, 1887, HDL to Prouty, March 5, 1887, MS "Statement of Taxes Aug. 17, 1887, Winnetka Village," R. S. Moth to HDL, August 9, 1889, January 14, 1890; *To The Winnetka Improvement Society* [1883]; *Public Schools of Winnetka. Annual Report, June 30, 1898.*

22WB, Bross MS Diary, April 12, 1882.

23*Ibid.,* July 3, 4, 1879, July 3, August 4, 1880, February 27, 1881, June 12, July 4, 1882, January 11, February 19, 1883; LPM, J. B. Lloyd to C. Lloyd, January 10, 1904; Henriette Greenebaum Frank and Amalie Hofer Jerome, *Annals of the Chicago Woman's Club for the First Forty Years* (Chicago, 1916), p. 39.

24WB, Bross MS Diary, February 27, May 3, 1881, March 24, 1882, April 30, May 12, 19, August 31, 1883, August 14, October 16–20, 1884, July 6, 1886; *To The Winnetka Improvement Society.*

25WB, Bross MS Diary, March 17, 1885; Yount, *op. cit.,* pp. 28–29.

26WB, Bross to "My Dear Grand-Son," February 24, 1876, Bross MS Diary, February 24, 1875, August 1, 1878, October 18, 1881, May 29, 30, 1883.

27*Ibid.,* May–August, 1886.

28LPM, Huntington, Kirkland, March 29, 1888, HDL to Huntington, July 20, 1888, HDL to Kirkland, *n.d.*

29MS Wm. L. Garrison to J. B. Lloyd, February 16, 1888, in Ralph W. Emerson, *Natural History of the Intellect* (Boston, 1893), in Henry D. Lloyd private library, Winnetka residence. Mrs. Goddard wrote Davidson, TD, October 3, 1888, that the Lloyds "showed every sign of prosperity."

30Cf. Henry Russell, *Hitchcock, Rhode Island Houses* (two volumes, Providence, 1939).

31LPM, S. Strickland to HDL, January 12, 1896; TD, HDL to Davidson, February 5, 1889, October 9, 1891.

32LPM, Hale to HDL, August 2, 1890.

33*Ibid.,* HDL to Ely, August 3, 1896, Foster to HDL, April 1, 1897, J. D. Pearce to C. L. Withington, October 23, 1907; *Chicago Evening Post,* September 5, 1894; *Boston Globe,* September 29, 1903.

34LPM, HDL to S. Bowles, June 24, 1899, HDL to Bemis, June 27, 1900, Latchford to HDL, October 5, 1894; "Morley, Margaret Warner," *Dictionary of American Biography,* XIII (New York, 1934), 193; C. Lloyd, *op. cit.,* I, 177.

35LPM, Darrow to HDL, April 23, [1896], N. Kelley to Mrs. C. L.

Withington, *n.d.;* CSL, HDL to Stallbohm, July 11, 1897; MS N. Kelley to C. M. Destler, May 18, 1940; *Boston Globe,* August 29, 1897.

[36]Interview with T. W. Phillips, Jr., Butler, Pa., December 4, 1945; LPM, Helen Dana to HDL, September 14, 1900; LPW, Abbot to HDL, August 20, 1903.

[37]LPM, H. Campbell to HDL, December 22, 1893, HDL to Bemis, June 20, 1900.

[38]Probate Court, Cook County, Illinois, *Record of Wills,* X, 278–283.

[39]The Tribune Company passed some dividends during 1902–3 when it was attempting to out-Hearst the *Chicago Herald.*

[40]LPW, March 24, 1904.

[41]MS N. Kelley to CMD, May 18, 1940; *Springfield Republican,* December 30, 1904; Marian Depew, "Living Out a Theory," *St. Paul Pioneer Press,* July 4, 1897; Henry Latchford, "A Social Reformer," *Arena,* X (Boston, October, 1894), 583.

[42]Depew, *op. cit.;* Columbus Bradford, " 'Over the Tea-Cups' with Henry D. Lloyd," *Unity,* III (Chicago, April 14, 1904), 107; Latchford, *op. cit.,* p. 583; *St. Paul Pioneer Press,* July 4, 1897.

[43]LPM, Prince Roger de Bourbon to JBL, April 4, 1895; CSL, HDL to Stallbohm, November 23, 1900; *Springfield Republican,* December 30, 1904.

[44]LPM, E. G. Starr to JBL, September 30, 1903.

CHAPTER XI

[1]George E. Mowry, *The Era of Theodore Roosevelt, 1900–1912 (New American Nation Series)* (New York, 1958), p. 25.

[2]LPM, Dr. Alexander to HDL, May 31, 1889, February 7, 1890.

[3]*Ibid.,* Davidson to HDL, February 9, June 5, 1889, Salter to HDL, July 17, 1889, Chubb to HDL, August 1, 1889.

[4]*Ibid.,* MS.

[5]*Ibid.,* L. Hartmann to HDL, March 14, 1889, J. S. Gallager to HDL, June 12, 1889; *Chicago Express,* September 21, 1889; Henry D. Lloyd, *Men the Workers* (New York, 1909), pp. 3–44; *Rock Islander,* August 10, September 7, 1889.

[6]LPM, Black to HDL, July 6, 1889, Lewis to HDL, September 20, [1889].

[7]*Ibid.,* undated clippings; LPW, MS, and HDL to Salter, October 18, 1889, Huntington to HDL, April 17, 1889; New York *Workman's Advocate,* November 30, 1889; *Nationalist,* II (Boston, January, 1890), 78; Lloyd, *Men the Workers,* pp. 45–76.

[8]J. M. Gould and Fred H. Wines, *Report of the Coal-Miners' Strike and Lock-Out in Northern Illinois* (Springfield, 1889), pp. 10–22.

[9]USM, "Testimony taken in the Arbitration . . . in the Northern Illinois District at Chicago, . . . July 24, 1889"; Gould and Wines, *op. cit.*, pp. 5–24.

[10]LPM, Power to J. Mitchell [autumn, 1903].

[11]Elsie Gluck, *John Mitchell* (New York, 1929), p. 19.

[12]LPM, Power to HDL, October 8, 1889.

[13]*Ibid.*, T. Brady to HDL, October 7, 1889, Hamilton to HDL, September 20, 1889, J. Foley to HDL, September 20, 1889, MS report of Relief Committee, McBride to HDL, September 23, 1889; *Chicago Tribune*, September 29, 1889; *Rock Islander*, October 12, 1889.

[14]Henry D. Lloyd, *A Strike of Millionaires Against Miners or the Story of Spring Valley* (Chicago, 1890), pp. 271–280, 348–371; LPM, Brady to HDL, October 7, 1889, W. Scaife to HDL, October 10, 1899, A. D. Bourke and Brady to Scott, *n.d.*

[15]*Ibid.*, Power to HDL, October 11, 13, 25, 1889, HDL to Power, October 17, November 2, 3, 1889, Power to HDL, October 13, 25, 1889, Scott to Devlin, November 2, 1889.

[16]*Ibid.*, HDL to Power, November 2, 3, 1889, HDL to Salter, October 18, 1889.

[17]*Chicago Herald*, November 13, 1889.

[18]*New York Sun*, December 16, 21, 1889; *Pittsburgh Post*, December 15, 1889; LPM, Power & McCall to HDL, December 2, 1889, C. Furbish to HDL, November 20, 1889, M. R. Kulther to HDL, November 28, 1889, S. Baxter to Mead, December 2, 1889, Howells to HDL, December 4, 1889, H. Hill to HDL, December 6, 1889; USM, [T. F. McNulty] to HDL, November 27, 1889.

[19]LPM, McCall to HDL, December 6, 1889, Scrapbook II, clipping dated Indianapolis, December 19, and *Knights of Labor*, December 28, 1889; *Truth* (Buffalo), December 29, 1889; *Chicago Herald*, December 14, 1889.

[20]LPW, MS "Mr. Henry D. Lloyd introducing Father Huntington, Madison St. Theatre," November, 1889, Schilling to HDL, January 20, 1890; *Chicago Herald*, January 19, 1890; *Chicago Tribune*, January 16, 1890; A. M. Johnson, *American Petroleum Pipelines*, p. 74; Willis J. Abbot, *Carter H. Harrison* (New York, 1895), p. 193.

[21]*Chicago Times*, February 23, 1890; Lloyd, *Lords*, pp. 159–176.

[22]LPW, Furbish to HDL, February 23, 1890, Prime to HDL, February 22, 1890, note from Trumbull; *Chicago Herald*, February 24, 1890.

[23]LPM, HDL to S. Bowles, January 14, 1890; TD, HDL to Davidson, January 30, 1891.

[24]RTE, HDL to Ely, August 27, 1890.

[25]Lloyd, *Strike,* pp. 141–223.

[26]Cf. United States Industrial Commission, *Preliminary Report on Trusts and Combinations,* I (Washington, 1900), 118; LPW, HDL to M. Pinner, December 17, 1897, HDL to Power, August 19, 1890.

[27]House of Representatives Reports, 51 Congress, 2 Session, Volume 2886, p. 611; *Pittsburgh Commercial Gazette,* May 28, 1890.

[28]LPM, HDL to W. Hawthorne, August 18, 1890, Hawthorne to HDL, August 24, 1890, H. W. Seymour to HDL, August 26, 1890, W. C. Wyma to HDL, August 28, 1890.

[29]Lloyd, *Strike,* 2d edition, pp. 269–298; LPM, HDL to Bowles, June 14, 1890; *Springfield Republican,* May 26, 1890; B. O. Flower, *Progressive Men, Women and Movements of the Past Twenty-Five Years* (Boston, 1914), p. 135; *Chicago Tribune,* May 24, 1890; *Open Court,* LV (July 31, 1890), 2429; Hugh O. Pentecost, "The Address. A Case of Starvation," *Twentieth Century,* IV (New York, June 12, 1890), 10–12; *Dawn,* VII (July–August, 1890), 160; *New Ideal,* III (Boston, August, 1890), 469; *Nationalist,* III (August, 1890), 54; *Seed-Time,* No. 6 (London, October, 1890), 1; *The Democrat* (London), July 1, 1890, pp. 164–165; *Commonwealth* (London), August 2, 1890.

[30]LPM, Taussig to HDL, July 12, 1890, Power to HDL, May 16, 1890, C. J. Devlin to Gookin, July 17, 1890, Ham to HDL, June 10, 1890, L. C. Hubbard to HDL, August 16, 1890, Scaife to HDL, May 20, 1890, E. Howells to HDL, June 6, 1890, O'Malley to HDL, June 12, 1890; *Chicago Times,* June 17, 1894; *New York Journal,* September 19, 1900.

[31]LPW, HDL to Pinner, December 17, 1897, Power to HDL, March 18, 30, 1891, HDL to Power, March 25, 1891; *Commonwealth,* II (New York), No. 29 (July 20, 1895), 18.

[32]LPW, Altgeld to HDL, June 3, December 7, 1890, Latchford to HDL, November 28, 1889, December 7, 1890; Barnard, *op. cit.,* p. 130; John Peter Altgeld, *Live Questions* (Chicago, 1890).

[33]LPM, MS, December 7, 1890; *Chicago Evening News,* December 8, 1890; Lloyd, *Workers,* pp. 131–155.

[34]Morton White, *Social Thought in America: The Revolt from Formalism* (New York, new edition, 1957), pp. 52–55, and *passim.*

[35]November 23, 1889.

CHAPTER XII

[1]*Chicago Herald,* March 5, 1890; *Grand Rapids Telegram,* March 31, 1890; *Economist,* March 15, 1890.

[2]LPM, Wm. Ralph to HDL, April 14, 1890, Favor to HDL, April 10, May 3, 8, 1890, Darrow to HDL, April 28, 1890.

[3]*Ibid.,* Power to HDL, June 9, 1890, clipping dated June 8, 1890.

[4]*Ibid.,* Burke to HDL, December 23, 1890, A. H. Brown to HDL, January 9, 15, 25, 1892; LPW, MS "Eight Hours Day."

[5]LPM, "Deerfield Summer School of History and Romance, . . . 1890," Announcement, "School of Applied Ethics, Summer Session," Adams to HDL, April 2, 1891, E. Brecwardt to HDL, November 12, 1890, E. de Billy to HDL, April 11, August 11, October 27, 1891, Gompers to HDL, October 13, 1891; William Knight, editor, *Memorials of Thomas Davidson* (London, 1907), pp. 55–57; H. D. Lloyd, "Why Workingmen Should Organize," *Souvenir of the American Federation of Labor,* December 14, 1891 *(n.d.).*

[6]LPM, MS "Free Speech and Assemblage;" *Chicago Tribune,* December 18, 1891.

[7]LPM, Darrow to HDL, December 28, 1891.

[8]*Ibid.,* Morgan to HDL, December 29, 1891, January 5, 6, 1892; TJM, Morgan to the Officers and Members of the International Machinists Union, February 10, 1896.

[9]*Chicago Herald,* January 4, 1892.

[10]*Chicago Tribune,* August 30, 1891; *Rights of Labor* (Chicago), February 7, 1891; Wm. C. Pomeroy, *Official Labor Gazette 1892* (Chicago, 1892), pp. 15–29, 33, 47.

[11]"Strikes and Lockouts," Chicago Sunset Club, *Twenty-Third Meeting* (Chicago, 1890), pp. 1–5; *Chicago Times,* November 7, 1890; *Union Record* (St. Louis), December 6, 1890.

[12]W. W. Catlin, *Echoes of the Sunset Club* (Chicago, 1890), p. 205.

[13]Chicago Sunset Club, *Meetings 1891–1892* (Chicago, 1892), pp. 110–123; *Chicago Herald,* February 5, 1892; LPM, Schilling to HDL, February 8, 1892; *New Nation,* II (February 13, 1892), 106.

[14]LPW, MS "The Deification of Carnegie;" Sunset Club, *Meetings of 1892–1893* (Chicago, 1893), p. 23.

[15]March 3, 1890.

[16]*Evanston Press,* November 7, 1891.

[17]LPM, MS Notebook XIX, 1, 4.

[18]*Ibid.,* MS Notebooks XVIII, 15, XIX, 9.

[19]*Ibid.*, MS Notebooks XVIII, 18.

[20]*Ibid.*, HDL to Huntington, October. 2, 1891, HDL to Davidson, October 9, 1891.

[21]*Ibid.*, Bellamy to HDL, February 11, 1892, HDL to C. Lloyd, November 7, 1893, December 5, 1896, HDL to F. Bellamy, November 12, 1898, F. Bellamy to HDL, March 13, 1899.

[22]*Ibid.*, MS Small Notebook D, pp. 2–5, MS Card Notes, p. 79.

[23]*Ibid.*, MS Small Notebook E, pp. 2–3.

[24]*Ibid.*, pp. 1–2; Aaron, *op. cit.*, p. 170.

[25]LPM, MS note on reverse of L. J. Duncan to HDL, March 17, 1893, MS note on reverse of Donnelly to HDL, March 31, 1893, Kirkman to HDL, February 1, 1892; *Evanston Press,* November 7, December 19, 1891; *Chicago Herald,* February 1, 1892; Lynd, *op. cit.*, pp. 278–296; R. C. K. Ensor, *England 1870–1914* (London, 1936), p. 334.

[26]*Chicago Tribune,* March 7, April 16, 1892, June 7, 1893; *Quincy Journal,* March 23, 1893; ID, HDL to Donnelly, May 28, 1891; LPW, HDL to Sterne, January 7, 1891; LPM, MS "Summary of Facts submitted by Henry D. Lloyd before the Anti-Monopoly Convention recently held in Chicago."

[27]Jane Addams, *Twenty Years at Hull-House* (New York, 1910), pp. 89–90; Raymond C. Ginger, *Altgeld's America* (New York, 1958), pp. 113–142.

[28]LPM, Starr to HDL, October 21, 1891, Addams to HDL, November 18, December 15, 1891, January 2, December 15, 26, 1892, December 1, 1894; Addams, *Twenty Years,* pp. 181–182.

[29]LPM, Starr to HDL, May 23, 1893.

[30]*Ibid.*, Anne Withington to HDL, November 16, 1896, Addams to HDL, February 10, 1896.

[31]*Ibid.*, F. Kelley to HDL, January 4, June 30, November 28, 1892.

[32]*Chicago Herald,* May 9, 1892; James Weber Linn, *Jane Addams* (New York, 1937), pp. 114–115.

[33]LPM, M. E. Kenney to HDL, April 19, 1892; *Chicago Tribune,* February 20, 1893; Florence Kelley, "I Go to Work," *Survey Graphic,* XVIII (June 1, 1927), 271–274, 301; Latchford, *op. cit.*, p. 583.

[34]LPM, Darrow to HDL, May 17, 1893, Stevens to HDL, May 22, 30, 1893, Kelley to HDL, July 13, August 20, October 10, 1893, October 31, 1894; Interview with Dr. Alice Hamilton, Hadlyme, Conn., December 13, 1944; Ginger, *op. cit.*, pp. 133–135.

[35]Florence Kelley, *Modern Industry in Relation to the Family, Health, Education Morality* (New York, 1914), pp. 102–103.

[36]LPM, Altgeld to HDL, May 24, 1892; BSF, HDL to S. Fallows, April 2, 1894; Harvey Wish, "The Administration of Governor John Peter Altgeld" (unpublished Ph. D. dissertation, Northwestern University, 1936), pp. 38–39 n.; *Chicago Herald*, April 24, 1893; *New Age* (London), March 11, 1897.

[37]LPM, Mrs. Altgeld to Mrs. H. D. Lloyd, July 14, 1893, Darrow to HDL, April 26, 1893, C. Bury to HDL, May 31, 1893, Morgan to HDL, July 21, 1893; *Chicago Herald,* June 27, July 7, 10, 1893; Barnard, *op. cit.,* pp. 183–259; David, *op. cit.,* pp. 487–501.

[38]LPM, Altgeld to HDL, November 7, 1893, Darrow to HDL, July 10, October 6, 12, 1893, Schilling to HDL, August 15, 1893, *An Exposure of Judge Gary by Henry D. Lloyd* [Chicago, 1893].

[39]GAS, Darrow to Lloyd, November 9, 1893, Stauber to Schilling, November 8, 1893.

[40]*Daily Columbian* (Chicago), August 28–September 4, 1893; *Chicago Times,* August 29–September 4, 1893; *Programme of the Labor Congress, August 29–September 4, 1893* (Chicago, 1893); LPM, HDL to Bowles, March 15, 1893, HDL to E. Pomeroy, May 26, 1893, Pomeroy to HDL, May 31, 1893; LPW, B. T. Washington to HDL, August 12–29, 1893; AFL, HDL to Gompers, February 18, 1891.

[41]C. Lloyd, *op. cit.,* I, 163.

[42]LPW, HDL to Burnham, March 26, 1895; LPM, HDL to Gage, November 29, 1892.

[43]*Ibid.,* J. Cogswell to HDL, June 14, 1893, undated MS on wages, E. J. Lindholm to HDL, August 23, 1893, MS "September 24, 1893," Gallagher & McCormack to HDL, August 29, 1893, C. E. Harrison to HDL, August 25, 1893; *Chicago Searchlight,* August 2, 1894; *Chicago Times,* August 29, 30, September 1, 1893; W. T. Stead, *If Christ Came to Chicago* (London, 1894), pp. 3–15, 125–127, 147.

[44]LPM, Stead to HDL, November 11, 1893, January 17, 30, 1894, R. M. Easley to HDL, May 12, 1894; LPW, HDL to Stead, August 21, 1895; Frederick Whyte, *The Life of W. T. Stead,* II (London, 1925), 40; W. T. Stead, "My First Visit to America," *Review of Reviews,* IX (London, January–June, 1894), 414–417.

CHAPTER XIII

[1]FEW, HDL to Willard, October 29, 1891, February 1, 1892; LPM, Willard to HDL, January 28, 1892.

[2]AFL, HDL to Gompers, July 10, 1892; John D. Hicks, *The Populist Revolt* (Minneapolis, 1931), pp. 443–444; Samuel Gompers, "Organized Labor in the Campaign," *North American Review,* CLV (July, 1892), 92–95.

[3]Italics added. Lloyd, *Men the Workers,* pp. 77–99; Eugene Staley, *History of the Illinois State Federation of Labor* (Chicago, 1930), pp. 111–112; *Chicago Tribune,* December 12, 1893; LPM, MS "Gompers," n.d., Gompers to HDL, November 1, 1893.

[4]*Ibid.,* Altgeld to HDL, December 26, 1893, Moseley to HDL, December 28, 1893, Andrews to HDL, February 13, 1894; *Chicago Times,* December 14, 1893; *Chicago Sentinel,* December 28, 1893.

[5]LPM, Seddon to HDL, March 22, 1893.

[6]*Ibid.,* W. S. Brackett to HDL, May 1, 1893, Gus Mohme to HDL, January 10, 1894; Donald L. McMurray, *Coxey's Army* (Boston, 1929), pp. 268–283.

[7]LPM, HDL to A. E. Gans, April 27, 1894.

[8]LPW, Altgeld to HDL, May 11, 1894, J. F. Powers to HDL, May 30, 1894, Altgeld to HDL, June 6, 12 and enclosure, 1894; GAS, HDL to Altgeld, June 2, 1894; WQG, R. U. Johnson to Gresham, July 24, 1894.

[9]*Chicago Times,* June 17, 1894; Illinois Bureau of Labor Statistics, *Eighth Biennial Report, 1894* (Springfield, 1895), pp. 435–462.

[10]LPM, Morgan to C. L. Withington, July 31, 1905, Madden to HDL, June 27, 1894; *Eight-Hour Herald,* May 10, 1894; Destler, *American Radicalism,* pp. 169–170.

[11]LPM. Italics added.

[12]LPW, Morgan to Withington, July 31, 1904, Madden to HDL, June 27, July 1, 1894; *Chicago Times,* May 15, 17, June 16–July 14, 1894; Lindsey, *op. cit.,* pp. 90–144; *Illinois State Register,* July 3, 1894.

[13]Henry D. Lloyd to the editor, *New York Journal,* October 18, 1896; *Report of the Chicago Strike of June–July 1894 by the United States Strike Commission* (Washington, D.C., 1895); Lindsey, *op. cit.,* Ch. IX; Barnard, *op. cit.,* pp. 291–311.

[14]*Illinois State Register,* July 3–6, 1894; *Eight-Hour Herald,* July 10, 1894; Staley, *op. cit.,* pp. 114–117.

[15]Latchford, *op. cit.,* pp. 577–589.

[16]LPM, Debs to HDL, July 24, August 15, 1894; Mrs. Kelley to HDL, July 18, August 1, 1894; *The Cause* (Philadelphia), III, No. 1 (January 1897), 2; Lindsey, *op. cit.,* pp. 215–216.

[17]Chicago Sunset Club, "Strikes and Injunctions," *Seventy-Fifth Meet-*

ing, October 25, 1894 (Chicago, 1894); *Chicago Times,* October 26, 1894.

[18]*American Non-Conformist,* November 28, 1895; *Chicago Chronicle,* November 23, 1895; Lloyd, *Men the Workers,* pp. 172–185.

[19]LPW, MS note, HDL to Stead, August 21, 1894; LPM, HDL to Gompers, July 30, August 14, 1894; JAL, Gompers to Labadie, September 13, 1894; *American Federationist,* I (New York, October, 1894), 172, 182.

[20]*Chicago Arbeiter Zeitung,* August 2, 1894.

[21]LPM, HDL to Maxwell, August 30, 1894, W. R. Burke to HDL, July 14, 1894, Abbot to HDL, September 1, 1894, Mrs. Kelley to HDL, August 13, 1894, Maxwell to HDL, August 14, 1894; Destler, *American Radicalism,* pp. 183–192.

[22]LPM, MS "Shaker Impressions of Henry D. Lloyd"; LPW, HDL to "Sister Catherine," January 13, 1896; S. I. S., "Brief Report of the Self-Improvement Society of Mt. Lebanon, N. Y.," *The Manifesto,* XXIV (Mt. Lebanon, October, 1894), 242–243; *Chicago Evening Post,* September 5, 1894; Marguerite F. Melcher, *The Shaker Adventure* (Princeton, 1941).

[23]*Chicago Tribune,* October 7, 1894; *Chicago Record,* October 8, 1894, compared Lloyd as "a man of substance, a scholar and a philanthropist" with August Bebel and Karl Liebknecht, leaders of the German Social Democrats; Destler, *American Radicalism,* pp. 213–221.

[24]*Ibid.,* pp. 200–202.

[25]*Chicago Times,* October 12, 14, 1894.

[26]Destler, *American Radicalism,* pp. 204–205.

[27]*Ibid.,* pp. 209–211; AFL, Gompers to Cleveland, November 7, 1894. By courtesy of Raymond C. Ginger.

[28]Destler, *American Radicalism,* pp. 208–209; Hicks, *op. cit.,* pp. 337–338.

[29]Destler, *American Radicalism,* pp. 226–228.

[30]LPW, HDL to C. A. Powers, December 16, 1894; *Western Rural,* LIII (Chicago, January 10, 1895), 17; *Chicago Searchlight,* January 24, 1895.

[31]LPM, HDL to Darrow, November 23, 1894, Darrow to HDL, November 22, 1894, circular letter from R. H. Howe, November 13, 1894.

[32]TJM, MS "Report of R. Pohle"; *American Federationist,* I (February, 1895), 286, II (March, 1895), 17; Staley, *op. cit.,* p. 127.

[33]LPW, HDL to Burns, February 6, 1895; *Boston Herald,* January 12,

1895; *Chicago Times,* January 15, 1895; *Chicago Searchlight,* January 24, 1895.

[34]Lloyd, *Mazzini,* pp. 201–232; *Chicago Evening Post,* March 27, 1895.

[35]LPW, HDL to E. Benjamin Andrews, February 19, 1895; LPM, Green to HDL, February 3, 1895; *Labour Leader* (London), May 4, 1895.

[36]LPW, MS draft platform, HDL to ?, February 16, 1895; LPM HDL to Gates, May 23, 1895, Clark to HDL, April 4, 1895, HDL to Bliss, May 4, August 5, 1895, HDL to Albert Shaw, April 6, 1895, HDL to Morgan, July 11, 1895; MS pencil note in Albert Shaw, *Municipal Government in Great Britain* (London, 1890), in Lloyd private library; Howard H. Quint, *The Forging of American Socialism* (Columbia, 1953), pp. 109–126.

[27]LPW, MS "Municipal Ownership Speech," March 3, 1895, Chicago *Inter Ocean,* March 5, 1895; *Chicago Dispatch,* March 4, 1895; *The Cause,* April, 1895, in LPM, Scrapbook, III.

[38]Destler, *American Radicalism,* pp. 250–251.

[39]*Ibid.,* pp. 251–254; *National Watchman,* April 12, 1895.

[40]LPM, HDL to Bliss, August 5, 1895, HDL to Morgan, September 13, 1895; Lloyd, *Men the Workers,* pp. 185–194; *Chicago Chronicle,* November 23, 1895.

[41]*Ibid.,* January 6, 1896; LPM, HDL to Maxwell, March 6, 1896, Vincent to HDL, June 1, 1896, Fries to HDL, March 21, 1896, T. I. Kidd to HDL, April 6, 1896, Matthews to HDL, December 7, 1895, Debs to HDL, February 1, 1896, Adair to HDL, December 16, 1895, Darrow to HDL, January 29, 1896; *Union Workman* (Chicago), January 4, 25, May 30, 1896.

[42]LPM, HDL to Ely, March 14, April 2, 6, May 28, 1896, Ely to HDL, June 2, 1896.

[43]*Ibid.,* HDL to H. I. Grimes, July 10, 1896; *St. Louis Post-Dispatch,* January 18, 19, 1896.

[44]LPM, HDL to Holmes, July 13, 1896, Holmes to HDL, July 11, 1896, Mrs. Kelley to HDL, June 18, 1896.

[45]*Ibid.,* Adair to HDL, July 16, 1896, Debs to HDL, July 25, 1896, MS "Speech before the Peoples Party Convention at St. Louis, July 1896," HDL to Ely, August 3, 1896; LPW, HDL to Adair, October 10, 1896; N. O. Nelson, "Henry D. Lloyd," clipping, Scrapbook I; *Chicago Tribune,* July 26, 1896; *Appeal to Reason* (Girard, Kansas), August 1, 1896; Henry D. Lloyd, "The Populists

at St. Louis," *Review of Reviews,* XIV (New York, September, 1896), 296–303.

⁴⁶Lloyd detected behind the cries of alarmed men of property interested motives that he described in the (London) *Progressive Review,* I (October, November, 1896), 75–77, 117–132. Cf. LPM, Abbot to HDL, October 12, 13, 1896, Mrs. Kelley to HDL, October 1, 15, 1896; *New York Journal,* October 18, 1896; *Chicago Times-Herald,* November 3, 1896; *Chicago Labor Advocate,* October 24, 1896; *Boston Advertiser,* October 27, November 17, 1896.

⁴⁷LPM, HDL to Adair, October 10, 1896, HDL to Wharton Barker, *n.d.*

CHAPTER XIV

¹Jeremiah W. Jenks, "Capitalistic Monopolies and Their Relations to the State," *Political Science Quarterly,* IX (New York, September, 1894), 486–509; Hans B. Thorelli, *The Federal Antitrust Policy,* p. 141.

²II (third edition, New York, 1907), 855–857.

³Henry D. Lloyd, *Wealth Against Commonwealth* (New York, 1894), Chs. XXXIV–XXXV; Richard Hofstadter, *The Age of Reform* (New York, 1955), pp. 91–93, 141; LPM, HDL to Cullom, December 10, 1886.

⁴*Passim.*

⁵LPW, Hudson to HDL, June 25, 1883, Rice to HDL, January 8, 1888.

⁶*Ibid.,* Pencil MS. November 26, 1887, "Fanatic S. oil."

⁷RS, HDL to Emery, December 14, 1887.

⁸LPM, MS "Sins of a Trust. March 6, 1889," HDL to Matthews, May 20, 1889, italics added; LPW, HDL to Salter, August 30, 1894.

⁹LPM, HDL to Stewart, October 17, 1890, Stewart to HDL, October 29, December 12, 1890.

¹⁰LPM and LPW contain extensive correspondence with these and others arising from Lloyd's research.

¹¹Destler, *American Radicalism,* p. 150, n. 44; Lloyd, *Wealth,* pp. 66 ff for footnote references to Dodd's *Combinations;* LPM, C. M. Pepper to HDL, August 23, 1888, von der Leyen to C. L. Withington, "My Personal Relationship with Mr. Henry D. Lloyd"; LPW, HDL to von der Leyen, November 19, 1891, January 7, 1892.

¹²*Ibid.,* HDL to M. C. Lloyd, March 27, 1891; TD, HDL to David-

son, January 30, 1891; LPW, HDL to R. Sherman, May 23, 1893.

[13]Lloyd, *Wealth,* pp. 430–431 note; Roger Sherman, "The Standard Oil Trust: The Gospel of Greed," *Forum,* XIII (New York, July, 1892), 613–614; LPW, HDL to Matthews, April 28, 1892; LPM, HDL to G. Rice, November 20, 1891.

[14]RS, Sherman to HDL, May 15, 1893, June 2, 1894; LPW, HDL to Sherman, May 23, 1893, Macomber to HDL, April 28, 1893, Moot to HDL, April 16, 1894; LPM, Sherman to HDL, July 29, 1893, Moot to HDL, May 15, 1894.

[15]*Ibid.,* Howells to HDL, May 21, 1893; LPW, HDL to Howells, May 20, 1893, HDL to Mr. Harper, May 20, 1893, Harper & Brothers to HDL, June 6, 16, July 13, 1893, and enclosures, HDL to Harper & Brothers, July 17, 1893, July 9, 25, 1894, Harper & Brothers to HDL, October 24, December 22, 1893, March 23, 1894, Sherman to HDL, April 30, June 8, 1894, Moot to HDL, April 16, 1894, Macomber to HDL, June 2, August 31, 1894; Howells, *op. cit.,* II, 46.

[16]LPM, HDL to Ely, January 12, 1894; LPW, HDL to Salter, August 20, 1894.

[17]Hicks, *op. cit.,* p. 322.

[18]Destler, *American Radicalism,* p. 159 and n. 87.

[19]*Evolution of Modern Capitalism* (London, 1895), pp. 149–151.

[20]*Distribution of Wealth* (New York, 1893).

[21]Robert E. Spiller, Willard Thorpe, and Henry Canby, *Literary History of the United States,* II (New York, 1948), 980.

[22]Other data indicate that the analysis of this episode in my *American Radicalism,* pp. 148–149 and n. 38 is too generous to Rockefeller. Cf. John D. Rockefeller, *Random Reminiscences of Men and Events* (New York, 1909), pp. 96–107, for affidavits procured *after* Mrs. Backus' death *from* her relatives to contradict her affidavits in Standard Oil Company vs. Scofield, Skurmer & Teagle and to counteract Lloyd's account based upon them. Cf. Ida M. Tarbell, *History of the Standard Oil Company,* I (New York, 1905), 203–206.

[23]Destler, 'Standard Oil: Child of the Erie Ring," *loc. cit.;* Williamson and Daum, *The American Petroleum Industry,* pp. 303–306.

[24]JAG, J. H. Devereux to James A. Garfield, April 19, 1872, a letter unused by Williamson and Daum, *op. cit.,* pp. 346–352, but which modifies their position drastically.

[25]*Supra* n. 23; Arthur M. Johnson, *Development of American Petroleum Pipelines,* p. 14 and *passim.*

[26]Pp. 535–536.

[27]LPW, MS fragment of third draft.

[28]LPM, for successive drafts and MS description.

[29]Oscar Handlin, "Capitalism, Power and the Historians," *New England Quarterly,* XXVII (Brunswick, March, 1955), 102–106; Ralph W. and Muriel E. Hidy, *Pioneering in Big Business, 1882–1911. History of Standard Oil Company* (New Jersey) (New York, 1955), *passim.*

[30]Destler, *American Radicalism,* Ch. VI.

[31]Cf. Marvin W. Schlegel, *Ruler of the Reading: The Life of Franklin B. Gowen* (Harrisburg, 1947).

[32]Destler, *American Radicalism,* Ch. VII, for a full report.

[33]Lloyd, *Wealth,* p. 510; Harold U. Faulkner, *American Political and Social History* (New York, 1948), pp. 529, 625.

[34]*Supra* n. 1.

[35]LPM, Spahr to HDL, October 13, 1894; Latchford, *op. cit.,* pp. 577–589. Spahr was not qualified to appraise Lloyd's handling of the Widow Backus episode, which he depreciated.

[36]LPM, MS "Inscription" appended to first draft; Columbus Bradford, " 'Over the Tea-Cups' with Henry D. Lloyd," *Unity,* April 14, 1904, pp. 107–108.

[37]LPM, Wm. P. Johnston to HDL, May 11, 1895, Clark to Iles, October 19, 1894, Jenks to HDL, May 1, 1894, Ely to HDL, February 22, 1898, Harris to HDL, December 12, 1895, December 11, 1897; *Political Science Quarterly,* IX (March, 1895), 185; Small, "Private Business is a Public Trust," *American Journal of Sociology,* I (November, 1895), 276–289.

[38]LPM, P. O'Neill Larkin to HDL, October 17, 1894; Howells, *Life,* II, 54–55; "Editor's Table," *New England Magazine,* XIX (Boston, November, 1895), 380–384; Edwin D. Mead, *Church, State, School and Money* (Boston, 1895); *Donahue's Magazine* (Boston), January, 1895, pp. 71–74; *Commonwealth* (Boston), February 9, 1895; *Dial,* XVIII (October 16, 1894), 320–332.

[39]LPM, Latchford to HDL, October 5, 1894.

[40]*Review of Reviews,* X (November, 1894), 571; *Outlook,* LI (New York, April 6, 1895), 565–566.

[41]*Nation,* LIX (November 8, 1894), 207, 348; *American Banker* (New York), November 21, 1894; *The New York Times,* December 20, 1894; *New York Evening Post,* November 10, 1894; *New York Tribune,* April 15, 1895; Nevins, *Rockefeller,* II, 338–339; Richard T. Ely, *Ground Under Our Feet* (New York, 1938), pp. 221–222;

Literary World, November 3, 1894; LPM, Sherman to HDL, January 11, 1895.

⁴²*Ibid.,* G. H. Warner to HDL, October 23, 1894, Abbot to HDL, n.d., C. F. Mosher to HDL, September 18, 1895; *Springfield Republican,* October 12, 1894; *Boston Herald,* December 2, 1894; *Chicago Tribune,* October 27, 1894; *Pittsburgh Dispatch,* October 30, 1894; *Brooklyn Standard-Union,* November 3, 1894; *Chicago Inter Ocean,* May 9, 1896; *Boston Globe,* October 14, 1894.

⁴³LPM, Dillaway to Pearmain, March 8, 1895, H. D. Dupee to HDL, March 12, 1896, J. Lloyd to HDL, n.d.

⁴⁴*Ibid.,* Rice to HDL, October 12, 1894, Emery Jr., to HDL, March 23, 1896, Sherman to HDL, September 14, October 28, 1894; *Titusville World,* October 27, 1894, February 9, 23, 1895; *Bradford Daily Record,* November 26, 1894; LPW, HDL to Westgate, August 5, 1895; *Paint, Oil and Drug Review,* XIV (Chicago, December 19, 1894), 10.

⁴⁵LPM, Brandeis to Mead, November 9, 1894, Bryan to HDL, June 24, November 16, 1895; Alpheus Thomas Mason, *Brandeis* (New York, 1946), p. 141; Alpheus T. Mason, *Brandeis Lawyer and Judge in the Modern State* (Princeton, 1936), pp. 27, 115–119; Senate Resolution 98, 62 Congress, December 14, 1911, Volume I, p. 1163, for which citation I am indebted to Professor Mason.

⁴⁶LPM, Browne to HDL, October 29, 1894, Holt to HDL, October 5, 13, 1894, Slicer to HDL, n.d.; *City and State,* I (Philadelphia, September 12, 1895), 2, II (June 4, 1896), 2.

⁴⁷LPM, Mrs. Kelley to J. B. Lloyd, October 31, 1894, J. Addams to HDL, December 1, 1894, Mary Gooding to Mrs. Lloyd, May 6, 1895; *National Single-Taxer,* VII (New York, March 17, 1897), 10; Bliss, *Encyclopedia,* pp. 1013–1016, 1285, 1346–1348; Samuel M. Jones, *The New Right* (New York, 1899), p. 256.

⁴⁸*The Cause,* II (Philadelphia, May, November, 1896), 33–34, 66; LPM, C. Bradford to *Methodist Review,* January 15, 1895, and for correspondence with Gladden, Williams, Herron, and Bliss; *Methodist Review,* January–February, 1895; *Independent,* XLVIII (December 31, 1896), 1786–1787; *Northwestern Christian Advocate* (Chicago), October 31, 1894, p. 8; *Christian Register,* LXXIV (Boston, March 21, 1895), 186; *The Kingdom,* VII (Minneapolis, February 1, 1895), 674, VIII (June 7, 1895), 120–121; *Universalist,* July 18, 1896; *Christian Nation* (New York), April 18, 1896.

⁴⁹LPM, Van Deervoort to HDL, January 7, 1895; *Wealth Makers* (Lincoln), February 14, March 14, May 16, 1895; *American Non-*

conformist, December 12, 1895; *Appeal to Reason,* May 2, 1896; *Southwestern Farmer* (Witchita), October 9, 1896.

[50]*American Federationist,* I (December 1894), 212–213; *Chicagoer Arbeiter Zeitung,* October 9, 1894; *American Fabian,* I (February, 1895), 8; *Commonwealth,* II (New York, October 12, 19, 1895); *St. Louis Labor,* January 6, 1895; LPM, Debs to HDL, December 10, 1894.

[51]LPW, Stead to HDL, July 28, 1894, November 5, 1895, Bryce to HDL, March 28, 1895, HDL to Lecky, June 12, 1895, Roberts to HDL, May 5, 1896, C. Trevelyan to HDL, March 17, 1896; WDH, HDL to Howells, February 5, 1895; Ida M. Tarbell, *All in the Day's Work* (New York, 1939), p. 204.

[52]John A. Hobson, *The Evolution of Modern Capitalism* (London, 1895), pp. 131–138; LPW, Hobson to HDL, February 22, 1895; *London Chronicle,* November 5, December 14, 1895, August 5, 1896; *The Times,* November 29, 1894; *Dundee Advertiser,* December 13, 1894; *Edinburgh Scotsman,* May 3, 1895; London *Clarion,* January 12, 1895; *London Transport,* December 28, 1894; *Christian Million* (London), December 20, 1894; *Progressive Review,* I (October, 1896), 88–92. Thirty-three British newspapers and magazines reviewed *Wealth Against Commonwealth.*

[53]Clipping, LPM, *Wealth Against Commonwealth* Scrapbook, II.

[54]*Labour Copartnership,* III (London, March, 1897), 41–42; *Seed-Time,* No. 27 (London, January, 1896), 1–4; *Fabian News,* VI (London, September, 1896), 26; *Municipal Journal* (London), September 3, 1896.

[55]LIII (London, September, 1897), 140–154.

[56]LPM, H. Sparling to HDL, March 26, 1895, Sherman to HDL, January 5, 1895, von der Leyen to HDL, January 30, 1895, C. Bogaerts to HDL, March 13, 1899; LPW, complimentary copy, F. W. Wibaut, *"Business. Wealth Against Commonwealth. door Henry D. Lloyd." Overgedrukt wit de Kroniek van 14, 21 en 28 November, 5, 12, 19, 26 December 1897 (n.p., n.d.).*

[57]LPW, Drury to HDL, November 8, 1894, Iles to HDL, October 15, 1894.

CHAPTER XV

[1]Caro Lloyd, *Henry Demarest Lloyd, 1847–1903, op. cit.,* I, 206.

[2]Nevins, *Rockefeller,* II, 339–340; *Toronto Globe,* September 17, 1897.

[3]*Supra* p. 000.

⁴Ernst Levy von Halle, *Trusts or Industrial Combinations and Coalitions in the United States* (New York, 1895); von Halle, "Industrielle Unternehmer-und Unternehmungsverbaende in den Vereinigten Staaten von Nordamerika," *Ueber wirtschaftliche Kartelle in Deutschland und in Ausland (Schriften des Verein fuer Socialpolitik,* LX) (Leipzig, 1894), 98–200.

⁵LPM, Schilling to HDL, July 27, 1893; *New York Tribune,* April 15, 1895; *Chicago Evening Post,* March 23, 1895; von Halle, *Trusts,* pp. xiv, 12 n.1, 76, 117.

⁶LPW, HDL to Shaw, April 6, 1895.

⁷April 15, 1895; LPM, Spahr to HDL, May 3, 1895.

⁸Nevins, *Rockefeller,* II, 340.

⁹IX, 11–25; Destler, "Opposition," p. 652; LPM, Jenks to HDL, November 20, 1895; Commons, *Labour,* II, 302–304; Nevins, *Rockefeller,* II, 141–142.

¹⁰LPM, annotated copy, Gunton's article; LPW, HDL to Spahr, July 22, 1895.

¹¹*Ibid.,* Spahr to HDL, July 29, 1895.

¹²Italics added. RS, HDL to Sherman, September 10, 1895, Sherman to HDL, December 30, 1895; LPM, Sherman to HDL, September 16, 1895, HDL to Sherman, September 19, October 10, 1895, Rice to HDL, October 21, 1895, HDL to Ely, October 6, 1895, copy of note from Charlton T. Lewis.

¹³*Ibid.,* HDL to Huntington, December 11, 1895; RS, Sherman to HDL, December 30, 1898.

¹⁴LPW, Hobson to HDL, January 8, 1896.

¹⁵LPM, HDL to Mead, *n.d.,* Mead to HDL, January 31, 1896.

¹⁶*Ibid.,* J. R. Commons to HDL, May 18, [1896], Leavitt to HDL, February 25, 1896; *Chicago Sunday American,* January 14, 1906.

¹⁷LPM, Mills to E. E. Hale, April 21, 1896; LPW, Spahr to HDL, April 24, 1896.

¹⁸LPW, Herron to HDL, April 25, 1896, Strong to HDL, May 11, 1896.

¹⁹*Ibid.,* HDL to Mead, Gladden, Ely, April 28, 1896; LPW, Spahr to HDL, April 24, 1896.

²⁰*Ibid.,* MSS drafts "A" and "B," April 28, 1896.

²¹*Ibid.,* Spahr to HDL, May 2, 1896, Mead to HDL, April 30, 1896.

²²*Ibid.,* HDL to Abbott, May 7, 1896. Contrast with Nevins, *Rockefeller,* II, 339–340.

²³LPW, Abbott to HDL, May 19, 1896, Strong to HDL, May 11, 1896, Ely to HDL, enclosure, May 1, 1896, Gladden to HDL, April

30, 1896, Commons to HDL, May 18, 1896, Jenks to HDL, May 22, 1896.

²⁴*Ibid.*, Herron to HDL, May 15, 1896, HDL to Mills, May 12, 21, 1896.

²⁵*Ibid.*, HDL to Mills, June 3, 1896, Mills to HDL, June 1, 1896.

²⁶*Ibid.*, Mills to HDL, July 2, October 2, 1896.

²⁷XLIX (March 4, 1897), 266–268, 278–279; United States Department of the Interior, *Report on the Transportation of Petroleum* (Washington, 1906), pp. xx–xxvii, 1, and *passim.*

²⁸RS, HDL to Sherman, March 12, 1897; LPM, Sherman to HDL, March 19, 1897, Moot to HDL, March 20, 1897, HDL to C. Lloyd, March 17, 1897.

²⁹*New York Journal*, August 25, 1897; Arthur Pound & Samuel Taylor Moore, editors, *More They Told Barron* (New York, 1931), pp. 48, 79.

³⁰LPW, HDL to H. H. Kohlsaat, December 2, 1898; *Chicago Times-Herald*, November 22, December 5, 1898; *Social Economist*, XV (New York, November, 1898), 322 ff.

³¹LPM, Iles to HDL, October 6, 1899, Garrison to HDL, October 5, 1899, Strong to HDL, October 10, 1899, HDL to Bowles, October 5, 1899, Gladden to HDL, October 12, 1899, H. White to HDL, October 10, 12, 1899; *New York Evening Post*, September 18, 26, 1899; *Brooklyn Citizen*, September 20, 1899; *Nation*, LXIX (September 21, 1899), 218–219.

³²LPW, HDL to Wright, January 5, 1898; Hearings of the Industrial Commission, Testimony of the Honorable Carroll D. Wright, p. 40, December 15, 1898.

³³United States Industrial Commission, *Report*, I (Washington, 1900), 391, 559; John R. Commons, *Myself* (New York, 1934), pp. 76–79; Nevins, *Rockefeller*, II, 500; M. L. Lockwood, "Standard Oil Methods Exposed," *The Anti-Trust Bulletin*, I (New York), No. 1 (August, 1899), 1–8.

³⁴LPM, HDL to Jenks, March 1, 1900, B. Holt to HDL, March 3, 1900, R. H. Newton to HDL, February 24, 1900; LPW, S. S. Mehard to HDL, June 28, 1900; Industrial Commission, *Report*, XIII (1901), cxviii–cxxii, 639–646.

³⁵LPM, Moton to HDL, February 24, 1900, HDL to Newton, March 6, 1900, Newton to HDL, March 13, 1900, C. Lloyd, *op. cit.*, I, 228.

³⁶George E. Mowry, *The Era of Theodore Roosevelt, 1900–1912*, pp. 82–83.

CHAPTER XVI

[1]Charles Leslie Stevenson, "The Emotive Meaning of Ethical Terms," *Mind,* XLVI, New Series, No. 181, 20–23.

[2]Charles L. Stevenson, *Ethics and Language* (New Haven, 1944), pp. 242–252.

[3]Cf. Green, *Prolegomena,* p. 342.

[4]John Dewey, *Outlines of a Critical Theory of Ethics* (Ann Arbor, 1891).

[5]LPM, Altgeld to HDL, June 3, 1894, Wm. L. Doze to HDL, *n.d.,* May 25, 1893, Donnelly to HDL, May 30, 1893, Schilling to HDL, May 25, June 1, 1893; GAS, MS "Summary of Facts;" ID, Lloyd to Donnelly, May 28, 1893; "Anti-Trust Conference at Chicago," *New Nation,* II (June 17, 1893), 305; Richard T. Ely, *Problems of Today* (New York, 1890), pp. 106–139.

[6]*New Nation,* III (June 17, 1893), 300–306.

[7]*Ibid.,* p. 305; LPM, HDL to Ely, October 1, 1893; *Chicago Tribune,* June 6, 7, 1893.

[8]I (March, 1894), 4.

[9]September 5, 1894.

[10]LPM, H. C. Adams to HDL, January 1, 1894.

[11]Lloyd, *Lords,* pp. 177–213.

[12]New York, 1942.

[13]*Buffalo Express,* December 23, 1894; LPM, C. G. Carig to HDL, December 26, 1894.

[14]Cf. Lindsey, *op. cit.,* pp. 149–327.

[15]January 14, 1895; LPW, HDL to R. Sherman, July 18, 1895.

[16]MS. Henry D. Lloyd to Mrs. Field, February 7, 1896 (Courtesy of the Henry E. Huntington Library and Art Gallery).

[17]RS, HDL to Sherman, February 5, 21, 1895, April 2, July 13, 1896, February 17, 1897; LPW, Sherman to HDL, July 16, October 27, 1896.

[18]LPM, Sherman to HDL, February 25, 1895.

[19]LPW, Sherman to HDL, February 2, 1897, Emery to HDL, March 23, 1898.

[20]LPM, Van Benthuysen to HDL, September 15, 1899, HDL to Bowles, November 27, 1894, Bowles to HDL, December 3, 1894, HDL to *Boston Post,* November 27, 1894; LPW, HDL to Mead, November 27, 1894; Mason, *Brandeis,* p. 126.

[21]LPW, HDL to F. F. Murray, December 19, 1895.

[22]RS, HDL to Sherman, August 6, 1896, MS Diary 1896, August 5–8,

[23]*Ibid.,* HDL to Sherman, August 6, 1896; LPM, HDL to Young, December 13, 1897, HDL to Macomber, February 1, 1897, HDL to Bowles, August 12, December 6, 1898; Ida M. Tarbell, *History of the Standard Oil Company* (New York, 1905), II, 177.

[24]LPW, HDL to Tarbell, May 6, 1902.

[25]LPM, R. Donald to HDL, March 10, 1897; "The Flash-Point of Oils," *Glasgow Oil and Trade Review, Supplement,* July 7, 1894, p. 3; *Report of the Select Committee on Petroleum, Parliamentary Papers, Reports of Committees, 1894, XIV* (London, 1894), 6.

[26]LPM, C. H. News to HDL, July 12, 1896; *Chemical Trade Journal,* XIX (Manchester, October 3, 1896), 213.

[27]LPM, News to HDL, October 7, 1896; *Food and Sanitation,* VII (London, October 24, 1896), 513, and later numbers.

[28]LPM, Sherman to HDL, October 29, 1896.

[29]*Ibid.,* Steuart to HDL, March 15, 1897, Stead to HDL, October 12, 1901; LPW, HDL to Stead, February 5, 1897, and enclosure, April 1, 1897, MS "Subservience to the Oil Trust in Great Britain," January 5, 1897; *Report and Minutes of Evidence, Select Committee on Petroleum, Parliamentary Papers, 1896, XII (1896),* 484–497, *ibid., 1898,* XI (1898), xl; Richard Heathcote Heindel, *The American Impact on Great Britain, 1898–1904* (Philadelphia, 1940), p. 146.

[30]LPM, Herron to HDL, January 21, 1897, Donald to HDL, March 10, 1897; LPW, HDL to D. R. Steuart, February 26, 1897; *Investor's Review,* No. LIII (September, 1897), 140–141; *London Daily Chronicle,* February 20, 1897.

[31]*The Star,* October 27, 1897.

[32]LPM and LPW for correspondence with British Liberals; *Parliamentary Debates, Fourth Series,* CV (1902), 718, CXVI (1903), 452, 1218, 1623; *Parliamentary Papers, 1898,* XI, *Report of the Petroleum Committee,* viii–xi; *Labour Leader,* X (June 25, 1898), 213; *Ethical World,* June 24, 1898; *Daily Messenger* (Paris), March 4, 1899; *Star,* September 22, 23, 1898; Hendel, *op. cit.,* p. 185.

[33]*Star,* March 23, 1905.

[34]*Investor's Review,* No. XXVI (January 30, April 1896), 218–220, 358–361; *Progressive Review,* I (January, 1897), 358–361, II (September, 1897), 551–555; Henry D. Lloyd, "Die Trust in Nord-Amerika," *Sociale Praxis,* VI (Berlin), 941–947; Lloyd, *Lords,* pp. 214–223; F. W. Taussig, *Tariff History of the United States* (New York, 1923), pp. 348–352.

[35]Cf. Wm. T. Stead, *The Americanization of the World, or The Trend of the Twentieth Century* (London, 1902), pp. 144–145.

[36]LPW, MS "Danger of Great Fortunes," MS "Suffer Little Children"; LPM, Brisbane to HDL, November 2, 1896; *Boston Herald,* October 24–25, 1895.

[37]LPM, HDL to Sterne, October 6, 1895.

[38]LPM, HDL to Gillett, November 30, 1896.

[39]*Ibid.,* HDL to E. F. Adams, August 17, 1899; LPW, HDL to E. L. Shuman, May 16, 1896.

[40]*Ibid.,* HDL to Slaughter, September 6, 1896, Slaughter to HDL, October 14, 1896.

[41]WK, HDL to Wm. Kent, March 26, 1898.

[42]LPW, Ely to HDL, March 23, 1898, HDL to Ely, March 17, 1899, HDL to Kinley, November 2, 1899, Kinley to HDL, November 13, 1899; LPM, Jenks to HDL, February 28, 1899, HDL to Johnson, October 19, December 3, 1898, November 9, 1899; *Springfield Republican,* August 25, 1899; Daniel R. Fusfield, *The Economic Thought of Franklin D. Roosevelt* (New York, 1956), pp. 22–23.

[43]LPM, HDL to E. E. Hale, October 11, 1898, HDL to Mills, November 10, 1898, Mills to HDL, November 5, 1898, HDL to Mather, October 11, 1898; LPW, HDL to H. W. Massingham, December 27, 1898; Ida M. Tarbell, *Elbert H. Gary* (New York, 1926), pp. 90–98.

[44]LPM, Barron to HDL, September 9, 15, 1899; LPW, HDL to Symonds, December 29, 1898, Barron to HDL, December 15, 1899, Heard to HDL, December 18, 1899; *Boston Herald,* December 24, 1899; Arthur Pound & Samuel Taylor Moore, *More They Told Barron,* pp. 47–48.

[45]Monnett, *Report to the Governor for 1899* (Columbus, 1899), p. 41, which Nevins, *Rockefeller,* I, 252–253 ignores. Thomas Beer, *Hanna* (1929), pp. 304–325, whose validation of Lloyd's assertion that eastern high finance controlled the Republican Party is ignored by Hidys, *op. cit.,* pp. 644–646; LPM and LPW for Lloyd–Monnett correspondence, 1898–1900; LPM, HDL to S. Bowles, November 11, 1899; Industrial Commission, *Report,* I, 99–100; *The Public,* III (Chicago, October 20, 1900), 437.

[46]LPM, HDL to Jones, August 7, 1899; Samuel M. Jones, *The New Right,* 59–61, 256; LPW, HDL to Pomeroy, January 3, 1900.

[47]LPM, Van Benthuysen to HDL, September 29, December 27, 29, 1899; LPW, Bemis to HDL, March 28, 1900.

[48]*Chicago Conference on Trusts, . . . September 13–16, 1899* (Chicago, 1900).

[49]*Official Report of the National Anti-Trust Conference Held February 12–14, 1900, in . . . Chicago* (Chicago, 1900); LPW, H. B. Martin to HDL, February 26, 1900, Lockwood to HDL, August 2, 1899, April 25, 1900, Bemis to HDL, March 3, 1900; *Anti-Trust Bulletin,* I, No. 1 (August, 1899).

[50]LPM, Abbot to HDL, January 3, 1900: *National Democrat,* III (Washington), July 3, 1900.

[51]Clark, *Control of Trusts* (New York, 1901); Helen M. Winslow, *Literary Boston Today* (Boston, 1903), p. 378.

[52]Lloyd, "The Next World Power," *Independent,* LIII (May 16, 1901), 1111–1112.

[53]LPM, MS Notebooks, X, 29, XI, 41–46; LPW, HDL to Bemis, February 21, 1902.

[54]LPM, HDL to Bemis, August 28, 1901.

[55]*Ibid.,* HDL to H. W. Chaplin, March 31, 1903; *Conservator,* XI, No. 2 (April, 1900), 1–2; Henry D. Lloyd, "Railway Consolidation. A Radical View," *Booklovers Magazine,* April, 1903, p. 391.

[56]LPM, T. W. Phillips to HDL, December 30, 1901, HDL to Tarbell, May 6, 1902, Mrs. A. S. Sherman to HDL, March 12, 1902; LPW, Tarbell to HDL, March 28, 1902, Tarbell to Stallbohm, April 4, 1902, J. W. Lee to HDL, December 30, 1901.

[57]RS, Mrs. Sherman to HDL, December 16, 21, 23, 1901, March 2, 1902, HDL to Mrs. Sherman, December 19, 1901, Tarbell to Mrs. Sherman, March 9, 11, June 23, 1903; CS, HDL to Stallbohm, October 21, 24, 1902; LPW, Tarbell to HDL, September 29, November 17, 1902, April 15, 1903; LPM, HDL to Tarbell, November 19, 1902, April 11, 1903, Emery to HDL, March 10, 25, April 9, 1903, Mrs. Sherman to HDL, January 21, 1902, Rice to HDL, January 26, 1902; *Boston Herald,* September 31, 1903; H. Wickham Steed, *Through Thirty Years, 1892–1922,* I (London, 1924), 47–48; Tarbell, *Day's Work,* pp. 204, 231–233.

CHAPTER XVII

[1]LPM, L. F. Abbott to James Cunningham (copy), March 13, 1896, HDL to Ely, January 12, February 19, 1893, March 3, 1894, Bemis to HDL, May 27, 1893; *Chicago Times,* May 14, 1894.

[2]CS, C. K. Adams to Schurz, September 14, 1895; JAL, Ely to Labadie, September 18, 1894, and enclosure; LPM, Ely to HDL,

March 2, 1894, HDL to Ely, March 3, 1894; *Nation,* LIX (July 12, 19, 1894), 27, 41–42; *Public Opinion,* XVII (New York, August 16, September 27, 1894), 462–463, 617–618; Richard Hofstadter and Walter P. Metzger, *The Development of Academic Freedom in the United States* (New York, 1955), pp. 425–427; Dorfman, *Economic Mind,* III, 161–164, 256–257; Joseph Dorfman, *Thorstein Veblen and His America* (New York, 1934), pp. 109–110.

³Dorfman, *Economic Mind,* III, 206–212; Ely, *Ground,* pp. 149 ff.

⁴Hofstadter and Metzger, *op. cit.,* pp. 437–444.

⁵*Public Opinion,* XVII (September 27, 1894), 217–218.

⁶Hofstadter and Metzger, *op. cit.,* pp. 427–430.

⁷Williams, *op. cit.,* IV, 622.

⁸University of Chicago, *Annual Register, 1892–1893* (Chicago, 1893), pp. 12, 40–41.

⁹UC-POP, Laughlin to Harper, August 31, 1893; UC-BT, I, April 3, 1894; Dorfman, *Veblen,* pp. 64–79; LPM, Bemis to HDL, March 27, 1893; RTE, D. Kinley to Ely, February 27, 1895, Bemis to Ely, June 2, 1894.

¹⁰LPM, Bemis to HDL, October 9, December 21, 1893.

¹¹UC-POF, "J. Laurence Laughlin File," Laughlin to W. R. Harper, August 31, 1893; LPM, Bemis to HDL, May 27, 1893; *Public Opinion,* XIX (October 17, 1895), 489.

¹²UC-BT, I, April 3, 1894; University of Chicago, *Annual Register. July 1893 to July 1894,* pp. 58–63; RTE, L. Williams to Ely, February 13, 1895.

¹³"Statement by Bemis," *Public Opinion,* XIX (October 17, 1895), 489; Interview with Walter S. Bemis, August 27, 1942.

¹⁴LPM, Bemis to HDL, June 10, 1894; Wish, *op. cit.,* pp. 218–219; *Chicago Times,* May 8, 13, 14, 1894.

¹⁵UC-POF, "E. W. Bemis File," Bemis to Harper, July 23, 1894; *Public Opinion,* XIX (October 17, 1895), 489; *Chicago Chronicle,* October 9, 1895; Hofstadter and Metzger, *op. cit.,* p. 426 n. 46.

¹⁶UC-POF, Harper to Bemis, July 26, 1894, Laughlin to Harper, August 6, 1894, *Public Opinion,* XIX (October 17, 1895), 489.

¹⁷University of Chicago, *The President's Report, 1892–1902* (Chicago, 1903), p. xxii; RTE, D. Kinley to Ely, February 27, 1895, Bemis to Ely, June 28, 1895.

¹⁸Henry D. Lloyd, "Plutocracy," Bliss, *Encyclopedia,* p. 1035; LPM, Bemis to HDL on reverse of HDL to Bemis, December 1, 1894.

¹⁹RTE, Bemis to Ely, January 12, 1895.

[20]Bemis letter in Upton Sinclair, *The Goose-Step* (Pasadena, 1923), pp. 244–245.

[21]RTE, Bemis to Ely, March 15, 1895; UC-POF, "E. W. Bemis File," for MS "Memorandum of Agreement."

[22]University of Chicago, *Quarterly Calendar,* IV (August, 1895), 11, 14.

[23]UC-POF, "Bemis File," L. Abbott to Harper, February 26, March 15, 1895.

[24]Lloyd, *Mazzini,* pp. 147–189; LPM, Gates to G. Warner, June 15, 1895.

[25]LPM, Ely to HDL, June 17, 23, 1895, Bemis to HDL, July 9, 1895, H. W. Rogers to HDL, July 17, 1895, G. A. Gates to HDL, November 9, 1895.

[26]LPW, HDL to Williams, July 25, 1895.

[27]LPM, Bemis to HDL, July 9, 1895; *Springfield Republican,* July 28, 1895.

[28]UC-POF, "Bemis File," clipping from *Boston Herald* in J. S. Dickerson to Harper, August 30, 1894, Laughlin to Harper, September 8, 1895.

[29]LPM, Bemis to HDL, August 27, September 16, 19, October 5, 1895; *Chicago Chronicle,* September 20, 1895; *Public Opinion,* XIX (September 5, 1895), 297.

[30]*Ibid.,* XIX (October 17, 1895), 488–489; *Chicago Chronicle,* October 9, 1895.

[31]LPW, HDL to Bemis, October 8, 1895.

[32]*Chicago Chronicle,* October 9, 1895.

[33]*Public Opinion,* XIX (October 17, 1895), 411, 488–489; *The Kingdom,* VII (Minneapolis, October 11, 1895), 410–411.

[34]*Public Opinion,* XIX (October 17, 1895), 489–490; *Union Workman,* October 19, 1895.

[35]I (October 31, 1895), 3.

[36]*Union Workman,* October 19, 1895.

[37]UC-POF, "Bemis File," undated MS, J. C. Rand to Harper, October 19, 1895; *Chicago Chronicle,* October 19, 1895; *Public Opinion,* XIX (October 17, 1895), 490, (November 7, 1895), 582.

[38]*Ibid.; Chicago Chronicle,* October 19, 1895.

[39]*Ibid.,* October 23, 1895; University of Chicago, *Quarterly Calendar,* IV (August, 1895), 17.

[40]*Boston Globe,* October 26, 1895.

[41]LPM, L. A. Coonley to Mead, November 1, 1895, Bemis to HDL, November 6, 1895; UC-POF, Small to Harper, *n.d.*

[42]*Chicago Chronicle,* November 3, 1895.

[43]*Ibid.; Chicago Tribune,* November 10, 1895.

[44]LPM, Ely to HDL, November 9, 1895.

[45]*Chicago Tribune,* November 10, 1895.

[46]RS, HDL to Sherman, November 25, 1895; *Springfield Republican,* November 15, 1895; *Dubuque Telegraph,* November 13, 1895; *Illinois State Register,* November 5, 1895; *Public Opinion,* XIX (December 26, 1895), 849.

[47]LPM, Bemis to HDL, November 10, 1895; *Boston Standard,* January 22, 1896.

[48]LPW, Ely to HDL, November 29, 1895; *The Cardinal,* December 5, 1895; *The Kingdom,* VIII (September 20, 1895), 576.

[49]LPW, Bemis to HDL, December 8, 1895, HDL to Bowles, December 24, 30, 1895, HDL to Ely, December 21, 1895; RTE, Ely to HDL, December 24, 1895.

[50]LPM, Bowles to HDL, January 4, 1896, HDL to Bowles, December 31, 1895.

[51]*Ibid.,* Bemis to C. L. Withington, August 30, 1906.

[52]Hofstadter & Metzger, *op. cit.,* pp. 420–451.

[53]University of Chicago, *President's Report, 1892–1902,* p. xxi; *The Public,* I, No. 32 (November 12, 1898), 2.

[54]Barnard, *op. cit.,* pp. 135–139.

[55]I (February, 1897), 418–420.

[56]LPM, HDL to Bemis, December 24, 1895; LPW, Bemis to HDL, December 7, 1895.

[57]LPW, HDL to M. Roberts, August 23, 1899, HDL to Bowles, September 15, 1899; LPM, HDL to Bowles, September 26, 1899; *Springfield Republican,* September 15, 1899.

[58]John R. Commons, *Myself,* pp. 58; *Social Forum,* I (Chicago, February, 1899), 25.

[59]LPM, HDL to Mrs. Diggs, November 26, 1898, HDL to Bemis, December 17, 1897, February 17, May 4, 1898, Bemis to HDL, November 15, 1898; *American Fabian,* IV, No. 9 (September, 1898), 7; *Social Gospel,* II, No. 7 (July, 1899), 19; Bemis, "Academic Freedom," *Independent,* LI (August 17, 1899), 2195–2199.

[60]Hofstadter & Metzger, *op. cit.,* pp. 446–449.

[61]WG, Bemis to Gladden, January 10, April 12, 1900; LPM, HDL to Ely, July 19, 1899, Bemis to HDL, July 26, 1899, HDL to Bemis, October 15, 1899; LPW, Shibley to HDL, September 26, October 11, 1899, Commons to HDL, October 10, 1899, Bemis to HDL, October 18, 1899, February 1, 3, April 12, 1900; Willis J. Abbot,

"Academic Freedom, II," *Arena,* XXII (October, 1899), 478–480.
[62]I (September, 1899), 133.
[63]XXII (October, 1899), 463–481.
[64]LPW, for extensive correspondence during 1896–1898 on the subject and exhibits of testimony; *The Kingdom,* X (January 27, 1898), *passim;* Isàbel Smith Gates, *The Life of George Augustus Gates* (Boston, 1915), pp. 23–24.
[65]*Supra* n. 64; LPM, Head to HDL, October 22, 1898; FP, MS "Dr. Gates & the American Book Co.," leaflet: "An Important Law Question"; *The Kingdom,* X (June 30, 1898), 731.
[66]LPW, HDL to R. Proctor, April 10, 1897; LPM, Herron to HDL, July 25, 1895, March 31, 1898; Bliss, *op. cit.,* p. 259; *The Public,* I (December 17, 1898, February 25, April 1, 1899); *Marshalltown Times-Republican,* June 26, 1899; GDH, L. F. Berry to C. Rand, September 27, 1899, C. Rand to D. W. Norris, June 29, 1899.
[67]V, No. 10 (December, 1899), 5; *Boston Herald,* May 17, 27, 1900; LPM, Herron to HDL, December 18, 1899; *Social Forum,* I (November, 1899), 177–180, 201; *Social Gospel,* No. 22 (November, 1899), Supplement, No. 23 (December, 1899).
[68]LPM, W. J. Abbot to HDL, November 15, 1899; *The Public,* III (June 16, 1900), 145.
[69]LPW, MS.
[70]LPM, MacVeagh to HDL, April 28, 1902.

CHAPTER XVIII

[1]LPM, S. McLallin to HDL, November 15, 1893, HDL to Wayland, April 5, 1894, I. C. Fales to HDL, January 21, 1896; *Commonwealth,* II, No. 50 (December 14, 1895), 19–20; *Coming Nation,* August 1, 1896.
[2]*Ibid.;* LPM, Wardell to HDL, March 5, 16, 31, 1897, Fales to HDL, August 4, September 9, 1896, January 31, 1897; *Coming Nation,* August 1, 1896; *American Co-operative News,* I (Cambridge, February, 1897), 158; Colston Estey Warne, *The Consumers' Co-operative Movement in Illinois* (Chicago, 1926), p. 22.
[3]LPM, Annie L. Diggs to HDL, September 17, 27, 1895, HDL to Mrs. Diggs, September 23, 1895, G. H. Gibson to HDL, December 6, 1895, HDL to Gibson, December 18, 1895, Herron to HDL, January 13, 1896, Wayland to HDL, letters 1894–1895; Lloyd, *Mazzini,* pp. 201–232.
[4]LPM, G. E. Pelton to HDL, May 22, 1895, Lermond to HDL, April

580   *Henry Demarest Lloyd and the Empire of Reform*

4, 25, July 6, 16, 1896; *Union Workman*, No. 34 (May 30, 1896), 4–5; *Commonwealth*, II, No. 50 (December 14, 1895), 19–20.

[5]LPM, Pelton to HDL, December 14, 1897, Lermond to HDL, September 21, 1896, August 31, November 26, 1897, F. Parsons to HDL, December 12, 1896, n.d., French to HDL, March 23, 1897; *Coming Nation*, June 27, 1896, July 3, 1897, November 28, 1896.

[6]LPM, Debs to HDL, July 10, 1897, HDL to I. A. Hourwich, July 21, 1897; *Wisconsin Vorwaerts* (Milwaukee), April 30, 1897; *Coming Nation*, July 3, 1897; *Social Democrat* (Terre Haute), July 1, 1897.

[7]I, No. 16 (July, 1897), 59, quoted in *Coming Nation*, July 17, 1897.

[8]LPW, HDL to Pomeroy, March 6, 1897; LPM, Boring to HDL, June 24, July 27, 1897.

[9]*Ibid.*, A. S. Edwards to HDL, May 24, 1897, MS "The New Political Economy"; *American Fabian*, III No. 4 (April, 1897), 1–3; *New York Herald*, June 20, 1896; *Coming Nation*, July 3, 1897, 4,000 extra copies of which were sold. Edwards issued the address in pamphlet form also. LPM, Edwards to HDL, August 3, 1897.

[10]LPM, Edwards to HDL, July 28, August 20, 1897; CS, HDL to Stallbohm, July 11, 1897; *Coming Nation*, July 31, 1897.

[11]LPM, F. Parsons *et al.* to HDL, August 25, 1897, Gompers to HDL, October 2, 1897; LPW, HDL to Parsons, August 13, 30, 1897.

[12]October 16, 1897; George J. Holyoake, "The Dutch International Congress," II, IV, *The Co-operative News*, XXVIII (Manchester, September 25, October 2, 16, 1897), 1090, 1114, 1159; *Bulletin du Congrès 1897. Publication Officielle du Troisième Congrès de l'Alliance Co-operative Internationale. Angetapark prés Delft, 15–17 Septembre*, No. 4 (Delft, 1897), pp. 9–10.

[13]*Co-operative News*, XXVIII (September 25, 1897), 1081–1083.

[14]LPM, MS 1897 Notebook, pp. 204–208, 211, 214, 219–222.

[15]*Ibid.*, p. 222, 225–227.

[16]*Ibid.*, p. 230.

[17]*Ibid.*, pp. 234–236.

[18]LPM, Mather to HDL, April 19, 1894, October 25, 1897, Thomson to HDL, September 20, October 20, 1897, Blandford to HDL, September 27, 1897, S. Ball to HDL, October 4, 1897, Pitt to HDL, October 20, 1897.

[19]*Ibid.*, Anderson to HDL, October 22, 1897, Latchford to HDL, December 27, 1898.

[20]LPM, Holyoake to HDL, October 20, 1897, HDL to T. G. Arnold,

November 19, 1897; *Co-operative News,* XXVIII (October 9, 1897), 1131; *Woolwich Pioneer,* April 15, 1913.

[21]October 28, 1897, p. 52.

[22]LPM, Clarke to HDL, November 18, 1897.

[23]LPW, MS corrected by Vivian, HDL to Blandford, December 23, 1897, April 30, May 12, 1898, Blandford to HDL, April 18, May 1898, Vivian to HDL, January 19, 1898; LPM, Harper & Brothers to HDL, February 24, May 4, September 23, 1898.

[24]New York, 1898.

[25]LPM, clipping, letter to editor, *Book News* (New York), December, 1898.

[26]IV (London, April, 1898), 54–55; *American Co-operative News,* I (May, 1897), 218–220.

[27]Cf. Beatrice Potter, *The Co-operative Movement in Great Britain* (London, 1891), pp. 117–169; Sidney Webb, *The Consumers' Co-operative Movement* (London, 1921), pp. 446–447; Horace Plunkett, *Ireland in the New Century* (London, 1904).

[28]LPM, Zeublin to HDL, September 22, 1898; *Boston Transcript,* September 14, 1898; *Chicago Post,* November 8, 1898; *Springfield Republican,* September 11, 1898; *Brooklyn Eagle,* August 28, 1898; *New York Herald,* September 11, 1898; *New York Journal,* August 27, 1898; *New York Evening Post,* October 8, 1898; *Chicago Times-Herald,* August 27, 1898; *Social Democratic Herald,* February 4, 1899; *American Journal of Sociology,* IV (March, 1899), 687–691.

[29]B. O. Flower, *Progressive Men, Women, and Movements of the Past Twenty-Five Years* (Boston, 1914), p. 136; *New England Magazine,* New Ser. XIX (November, 1898), 391–392; *The Dial,* XXVI (January 1, 1899), 2–3; *Social Gospel,* I (October, 1898); *The Cause,* V, No. 1 (January, 1898), 2–3; *The Kingdom,* X (December 8, 1898), 159–160; Washington Gladden, "Social Progress of the English People," *Outlook,* LX (December 24, 1898), 1002–1004; *Harper's Weekly,* XLII (September 24, 1898), 945; *American Federationist,* V (November, 1898), 172.

[30]LPM, Vivian to HDL, December 20, 1898, HDL to Wm. Clarke, December 27, 1898; *London Daily Chronicle,* December 5, 1898; *Review of Reviews,* XVIII (October 15, 1898), 415; *Labour Co-partnership,* IV (October, 1898), 165–168, V (January, March, 1899), 35, 130–136; *Fabian News,* VIII, No. 9 (November, 1898), 35.

[31]*New Zealand Times,* February 27, 1899; *Christchurch Press,* February 25, 1899.

[32]LPM, Spahr to HDL, September 14, 1898, MacDowell to HDL, October 2, 1898, Zeublin to HDL, September 22, 1898, Taylor to HDL, September 21, 1898, J. Addams to HDL, October 18, 1899, Gray to HDL, October 29, 1898, Parsons to HDL, November 2, 1898, HDL to Traubel, December 13, 1898, White to HDL, September 24, 1898; LPW, HDL to A. Shaw, November 10, 1898.

[33]*Ibid.,* J. Rhodes to HDL, January 1, 1898.

[34]LPW, HDL to Wright, November 10, 1898, HDL to A. Shaw, November 10, 1898; CDW, MS Testimony of Hon. Carroll D. Wright before the United States Industrial Commission (Thursday, December 15, 1898); LPM, HDL to T. J. Morgan, November 5, 1898, Taussig to HDL, November 27, 1898, B. T. Washington to HDL, November 25, 1898, HDL to Earl Grey, November 22, 1898, Wolff to HDL, December 5, 1898, Livesey to HDL, January 23, 1899, Anderson to HDL, October 5, 1898.

[35]*Ibid.,* HDL to Burns, January 5, 1899.

[36]*Ibid.,* HDL to Livesey, January 3, 1900.

[37]*Ibid.,* HDL to Blandford, September 12, 1898, HDL to Wolff, November 22, 1898, HDL to G. Livesey, November 5, 1898.

[38]LPW, HDL to Vivian, June 2, 14, August 7, November 6, December 18, 1901; LPM, Vivian to HDL, December 3, 1901.

[39]*Ibid.,* HDL to Holyoake, July 29, 1902, HDL to Vivian, February 21, 1898.

[40]LPM, Stewart to HDL, September 14, November 16, 1898; E. W. Bemis, "Report on Co-operation in the United States," *Report of the International Co-operative Alliance* (London, 1895), pp. 376–381; Bemis, "Co-operative Distribution," *Bulletin of the Department of Labor, No. 6, September 1896* (Washington, 1896), pp. 610–655; *American Co-operative News,* I–II (July 1896—June 1897), *passim,* III, No. 4 (October, 1898), 7; Warne, *op. cit.,* pp. 20–22; Bliss, *op. cit.,* pp. 366–380, 786; Fred T. Shannon, *The Farmer's Last Frontier, 1860–1897 (Economic History of the United States,* V) (New York, 1945), pp. 267, 332–336.

[41]*American Co-operative News,* III (August, 1898), 4; Flower, *op. cit.,* p. 141.

[42]LPM, Gompers to HDL, November 13, 1897, March 15, 1898.

[43]*Ibid.,* HDL to Morgan, November 5, 1898, Morgan to HDL, October 18, December 29, 1898.

[44]*Ibid.,* Taylor to HDL, September 21, 1898.

⁴⁵*Ibid.,* HDL to Farrell, November 11, 1898, HDL to Cristopel, November 2, 1898, HDL to Stuyvesant Fish, November 11, 1898, HDL to Vivian, November 17, 1898; H. D. Lloyd, "Co-operation," *Union Signal,* XXIV (December 28, 1898), 4 (p. 792).

⁴⁶LPW, MS "Co-operation"; *Chicago Times-Herald,* November 21, 1898; *Rochester Union-Advertiser,* January 25, 1902.

⁴⁷*New York Journal,* December 21, 1901; *Union Signal, loc. cit.*

⁴⁸LPW, HDL to Rhodes, August 11, 1899; LPM, Rhodes to HDL, August 14, 1899.

⁴⁹*Ibid.,* HDL to E. F. Adams, July 18, November 17, 1899; LPW, "The Big Five" of Denver to HDL, March 6, 1901; *Social Gospel,* II, No. 6 (June, 1899), 29–30; *Brotherhood,* New Ser. VII, No. 5 (London, September, November, 1899), 76–77, 109; *American Co-operative News,* III, No. 6 (January, 1899), 7.

⁵⁰LPW, Vrooman to HDL, April 30, June 16, August 14, September 20, 1902, HDL to F. Parsons, March 31, 1902, Bowles to HDL, February 9, 1900; *Brotherhood,* New Ser. X, No. 3 (July, 1902), 33; *Flower, op. cit.,* p. 141; *Boston Herald,* December 5, 1900; *Boston Budget,* February 9, 1902.

⁵¹LPW, HDL to Vivian, January 4, 1900.

⁵²*Ibid.,* HDL to Vivian, December 4, 1900, December 18, 1901, HDL to Vrooman, May 22, 1902, HDL to Rhodes, May 22, June 14, 26, 1901.

⁵³*Ibid.,* HDL to Rhodes, May 22, 1902, HDL to Vrooman, May 22, 1902.

⁵⁴*Ibid.,* HDL to Vivian, January 4, 1900, HDL to Pinner, August 18, 1901.

CHAPTER XIX

¹LPW, Seddon to HDL, March 22, 1893; LPM, Stout to HDL, March 22, 1894, Tregear to HDL, April 25, 1894, HDL to Ely, October 1, 1893; Lloyd, *Men the Workers,* 81–84.

²*Eight-Hour Herald,* November 30, 1895; *Chicago Times,* April 10, 1894; *People's Party Paper,* June 1, 1894; *Union Workman,* January 25, 1896; W. A. P. Bliss, *Encyclopedia,* pp. 85–86, 932–938; *Arena,* XVI (March, 1897), 663–676.

³XXVIII (November 27, 1897), 1305; *Fabian News,* VII, No. 9 (November, 1897), 33–34.

⁴C. R. Henderson, "Business Men and Social Theorists," *American Journal of Sociology,* I (January, 1896), 387.

⁵LPW, HDL to Watson, October 19, 1898.

⁶LPM, Lusk to HDL, September 19, October 14, 21, November 9, 23, 1898, HDL to Lusk, November 10, 23, 1898, Reeves to Robert Donald, November 23, 1898, HDL to Zeublin, October 26, 1898; *American Fabian,* IV, No. 5 (May, 1898), 7.

⁷LPM, HDL to Lockwood, November 23, 1898.

⁸*Ibid.,* Commons to HDL, November 17, 1898, HDL to Hadley, December 13, 1898, Hadley to HDL, December 19, 1898, Wright to HDL, December 31, 1898, Plunkett to HDL, December 8, 1898; LPW, HDL to Wright, November 10, 1898.

⁹LPM, Abbot to HDL, December 7, 1898, E. C. Rhodes to HDL, April 18, 1899; *Sheridan Road* (Winnetka) *News-Letter,* March 25, 1899; *Chicago Record,* January 14, 19, 1899; *New York Times,* March 19, 1899; Henry D. Lloyd, *Newest England* (New York, 1900), p. 130.

¹⁰February 10, 1899; *Sheridan Road News-Letter,* March 25, 1899.

¹¹J. B. Condliffe, *The Welfare State in New Zealand* (London, 1959), pp. 207–211, 236, 243–244, 279–298; Leslie Lipson, *The Politics of Equality* (Chicago, 1948); Horace Belshaw, editor, *New Zealand* (Berkeley, 1947), pp. 89–95, 182–183; J. Holland Rose *et al.,* editors, *The Cambridge History of the British Empire,* VII, Part II, *New Zealand* (New York and Cambridge, 1933), 171–198; William Pember Reeves, *State Experiments in Australia and New Zealand* (Two volumes, London, 1902); A. Métin, *Socialisme sans Doctrines* (Paris, 1901).

¹²LPM, Stout to HDL, February 13, 1899, A. Baride to HDL, February 14, 1899, Tregear to HDL, February 17, 1899, Riggs to HDL, February 17, 1899; *Sheridan Road News-Letter,* March 25, April 23, 1899.

¹³February 21, 24, 25, 1899; *Christchurch Press,* February 20–28, 1899; LPW, Bristed to HDL, February 15, 1899; Reeves, *op. cit.,* I, 277; *Sheridan Road News-Letter,* April 23, 1899.

¹⁴March 27, 1899; *Sheridan Road News-Letter,* April 29, 1899; *Otago Daily Times,* February 27, March 1, 1899; *Christchurch Press,* February 28, 1899; LPM, R. J. Seddon to HDL, February 28, 1899; LPW, S. F. Witumke to "Dear Beattie," February 22, 1899.

¹⁵*Temuka Leader,* February 23, 1899; *Otago Daily Times,* March 1, 1899; Lipson, *op. cit.,* Ch. XV; Rose, *op. cit.,* pp. 161–199.

¹⁶*Omaru Mail,* March 6, 1899; *Otago Daily Times,* March 1, 1899.

¹⁷LPM, undated clipping from *Sheridan Road News-Letter.*

¹⁸LPW, MS New Zealand Notebook, p. 89.

[19]LPM, H. C. March to HDL, March 11, 1899; *New Zealand Times,* March 30, 1899; *Christchurch Press,* March 29, 1899.

[20]LPW, HDL to J. B. Lloyd, April 15, 17, 1899.

[21]LPM, Tregear to HDL, April 7, 1899, Findlay to HDL, May 13, 1899; *Lyttleton Times,* September 14, 1912.

[22]LPM, Memorandum, May 2, 1899, chief Secretary, Adelaide, to Heads of Departments, J. Ross to HDL, May 9, 1899, A. C. Casiner to HDL, May 16, 1899, W. Mather to Mrs. H. D. Lloyd, May 3, 1899; *The* (Sydney) *Daily Telegraph,* April 27, 1899; *South Australian Register,* May 2, 1899; *The* (Melbourne) *Age,* May 5, 10, 1899; *Sydney Morning Herald,* May 15, 1899; Lloyd, *Newest England,* pp. 221–226.

[23]LPW, Skertchly to HDL, June 16, 1899, Van Benthuysen to HDL, June 19, 1899; *Montreal Gazette,* June 23, 1899.

[24]LPM, HDL to Bowles, June 24, 1899, Skertchly to HDL, July 22, 1899.

[25]V (October, 1899), 171; *Boston Herald,* June 27, 1899; *Springfield Republican,* July 21, 1899; LPW, HDL to Wright, October 18, 1899; LPM, Page to HDL, June 25, 1899, Hadley to HDL, July 8, 1899, Reeves to HDL, July 3, 1899.

[26]*Ibid.,* Findlay to C. L. Withington, June 14, 1907; *New Zealand Times,* September 6, 1899.

[27]LPM, Parsons to HDL, September 13, 1899; H. D. Lloyd, "New Zealand Newest England," *Atlantic,* LXXXIV (December, 1899), 789–794; Lloyd, "A Visit to the Compulsory Arbitration Court of New Zealand," *Outlook,* LXIII (December 9, 1899), 877–879; Lloyd, "Some New Zealand Scenes," *Ainslee's,* IV (New York, January, 1900), 752–759.

[28]LPM, Reeves to HDL, *n.d.,* HDL to S. Baxter, October 3, 1899; LPW, Reeves to HDL, July 3, September 16, December 2, 1899, HDL to Wright, October 18, 1899, Wayland to HDL, May 5, 1900, *Boston Herald,* October 11, 15, 1899; *Boston Transcript,* October 9, 1899.

[29](New York, 1900).

[30]*Eight-Hour Herald,* VI (February 16, 1897), 4; Samuel Gompers, *Seventy Years of Life and Labour* (London, [1926]), II, 134–139.

[31]*Nation,* LXXI (July 12, 1900), 38–39; *Coming Nation,* January 6, February 24, April 14, 1900; LPW, Wayland to HDL, May 5, 1900, Iles to HDL, May 8, 1900, Gray to HDL, October 13, 1900, Gates to HDL, October 11, 1900, H. White to HDL, May 26, 31, July

14, 1900, Newton to HDL, July 3, 1900; LPM, A. Withington to HDL, December 21, 1898; *New York Evening Post,* May 31, 1900.

³²LPM, P. Smith to HDL, October 28, 1900; *New York World,* May 18, 1900; *New York Journal,* May 31, 1900; *Chicago Tribune,* May 29, 1900; *Springfield Republican,* May 13, 1900; *Boston Transcript,* May 17, 1900; *Illinois State Register,* July 1, 1900; *Buffalo Express,* March 20, 1900; *Tacoma Ledger,* June 13, 1900.

³³No. 33, New Ser. 4 (November, 1900), 31–32; *Dial,* XXVII (June 1, 1900), 437; *Catholic World,* LXXII (November, 1900), 145–157.

³⁴XIV (February, 1901), 47; *New Zealand Times,* June 16, 1900; *Lyttleton Times,* June 11, 1900; *Auckland Weekly News,* June 29, 1900; *Melbourne Age,* March 16, 1901; *London Daily Chronicle,* July 28, 1900; *Glasgow Herald,* December 18, 1900.

³⁵LPM, Reno to HDL, November 16, December 18, 1899; LPW, "Industrial Court League, Industrial Courts to Administer Industrial Justice," an undated clipping containing Lloyd's testimony of March 12, 1902, Reno to HDL, *n.d.; Boston Herald,* January 24, 1902, *Boston Globe,* February 14, 1902; *Boston Transcript,* March 5, 1902; *New York World,* September 30, 1900; N. P. Knowleton, "Legislation and Judicial Decision," *Yale Law Journal,* XI (December, 1901), 11–16.

³⁶(New York, 1900).

³⁷LPM, HDL to Huntington, July 7, 1900, Reeves to HDL, September 20, 1900.

³⁸*Ibid.,* HDL to Holyoake, November 29, 1900; LPM, Van Benthuysen to HDL, November 27, 1900; LPM, HDL to A. Lloyd, December 9, 1900.

³⁹*Outlook,* LXVII (February 16, 1901), 390–399; *Arena,* XXVI (July, 1901), 100–105; *Public,* III (January 12, 1901), 629–632; *Nation,* LXXII (April 18, 1901), 322.

⁴⁰*New York World,* February 10, 1901; *New York Journal,* January 8, 1901; *Kansas Populist,* January 24, 1902; *Springfield Republican,* December 19, 1900; *Helena Independent,* June 9, 1901.

⁴¹*New York Tribune,* March 17, 1901, supplement; *Philadelphia Bulletin,* December 11, 1900; *Rochester Post-Express,* April 30, 1901; *Chicago Tribune,* November 21, 1901.

⁴²March 20, 1901.

⁴³*London Daily News,* June 13, 1901; *London Daily Mail,* April 9, 1901; *Fabian News,* XV (August, 1901), 23–24; *Manchester Guardian,* March 5, 1901.

⁴⁴*Christchurch Press,* November 27, 1901; *Lyttleton Times,* February

18, 1901; LPW, undated clippings, *Adelaide Herald,* January 5, 1901.

[45]LPW, Seddon to HDL, March 21, 1901, Reeves to HDL, November 8, 1900; LPM, Findlay to HDL, January 19, 1901.

[46]*Supra* n. 11.

[47]February 20, 1901; LPW, J. Maclay to HDL, June 9, 1900. Reeves seriously considered Lloyd's suggestion that he return to Wellington, re-enter the Cabinet, and "restrain" Seddon.

[48]LPM, Johnson to HDL, December 19, 1900, Bemis to HDL, December 28, 1900, A. Lloyd to HDL, December 19, 1900, HDL to Iles, December 26, 1900; Spahr to HDL, January 2, 1901; *New York World,* September 30, 1900.

[49]*New York Evening Post,* August 20, 23, 30, 1901; *London Daily Mail,* August 7, 1901; LPM, HDL to Bowles, August 20, 1901.

[50]*Ibid.,* Reeves to HDL, January 3, 1902, and enclosure; LPW, HDL to H. White, December 3, 1901; *Chicago Record-Herald,* October 22, 1901; *New York Evening Post,* September 26, October 3, December 7, 1901; *Nation,* LXXII (October 3, 1901), 259–260.

[51]LPM, HDL to Ward, November 11, 1901; LPW, HDL to Stallbohm, *n.d.*

[52]*Ibid.,* Reeves to HDL, January 3, 1902, and enclosure; LPW, HDL to Young, January 28, 1902; *Boston Herald,* December 30, 1901; *New York Evening Post,* February 8, 1902; *New York Journal,* January 10, 1902.

[53]LPM, correspondence with Smythe, 1901–3, HDL to E. H. James, October 14, 1901, HDL to Ely, October 22, 1901, H. Fuller to HDL, October 18, 1901; LPW, HDL to Reeves, November 5, 1901, HDL to Ely, October 18, 1901; *Land of Sunshine,* XIV (Los Angeles, May, 1901), 512; "Henry Demarest Lloyd. A Student of Institutions," *Out West,* XVI (Los Angeles, May, 1902), 542–543; William E. Smythe, "Socialism and Construction," *ibid.,* p. 539.

[54]*New York Evening Post,* July 26, 1902; *Outlook,* LXXI (August 9, 1902), 902–903.

[55]*Chicago Tribune,* December 18, 1900.

[56]LPM, Tuley to HDL, September 22, 1901, Lusk to HDL, November 6, 1900, May 24, 1901, Potter to HDL, December 22, 1900.

[57]Cf. *Boston Transcript,* October 16, 1901.

[58]LPW, HDL to Stallbohm, October 14, 21, 1902; *Boston Globe,* October 12, 1902; *Washington Times,* March 19, 1902; *New Orleans Picayune,* October 30, 1902; *Springfield Republican,*

November 2, 1902; H. D. Lloyd, "Australasian Cures for Coal Wars," *Atlantic,* XC (November, 1902), 667–676.

⁵⁹LPW, A. W. Wisehart to HDL, December 29, 1902; WG, Taylor to Gladden, October 29, 1902; W. J. Abbot, "The Coal Strike Arbitration," *The Pilgrim,* V (Battle Creek, December, 1902), 4.

⁶⁰LPW, HDL to J. B. Lloyd, November 24, 1902, February 23, 1903, Wayland to HDL, March 26, 1902, reports selling 90,000 copies of "New Zealand in a Nutshell" based on Lloyd's books, HDL to Reeves, April 4, 1902; LPM, T. E. Watson to HDL, August 11, 1902; C. Vann Woodward, *Tom Watson* (New York, 1938), p. 307; Nicholas P. Gilman, *Methods of Industrial Peace* (Boston, 1904), pp. 364–408.

⁶¹LPW, HDL to Sir J. G. Ward, March 31, 1903, italics added, HDL to Reeves, April 20, 1903; LPM, HDL to Bowles, May 3, 1903; H. D. Lloyd, "The Abolition of Poverty," *Good Housekeeping,* I (Springfield, Mass.), September, 1903, 216–220; *Boyce's Weekly* (Chicago), February 4, 1903; H. D. Lloyd, "New 'Song of the Shirt,'" *Sunday School Times* (Philadelphia), March 21, 1903, p. 15.

⁶²LPW, Tregear to HDL, July 21, 1903.

⁶³*Ibid.,* J. R. Meek to HDL, February 24, 1903, HDL to Ely, July 29, 1903, HDL to Reeves, April 4, 1903, HDL to J. Mitchell, May 12, 1903, A. Brandt to HDL, June 26, 1903; LPM, MS New Notebook I, Mitchell to HDL, May 7, 1903, E. P. Trueblood to HDL, February 2, 1902; John Mitchell, *Organized Labor* (New York, 1903), pp. 337–344; *Washington* (D.C.) *Times,* September 21, 1902; *Springfield Republican,* November 2, 1902; *Binghamton Herald,* November 10, 1902; *Boston Transcript,* November 5, 1902.

⁶⁴*United Mine Workers Journal,* February 26, 1903, p. 4; *The Outlook,* LXXXV (August 15, 1903), 915; Jane Addams, "Henry Demarest Lloyd, His Passion for a Better Social Order," *Chicago Teachers' Federation Bulletin,* January 29, 1904.

CHAPTER XX

¹LPM, HDL to Skillman, October 7, 1895; LPW, HDL to Adair, October 10, 1896; LPW, HDL to Rogers, October 26, 1896.

²LPM, F. E. Russell to HDL, *n.d.*

³*Ibid.,* HDL to A. Lloyd, November 31, 1896; LPW, HDL to Pomeroy, January 25, 1897.

⁴LPM, HDL to Ely, November 4, 13, 1896, Ely to HDL, November

12, 17, 1896, Bellamy to HDL, December 5, 1896, Morgan to HDL, December 4, 1896, Berger to HDL, January 11; February 3, 1897, Debs to HDL, December 12, 1896, H. S. Pingree to HDL, December 30, 1897; *American Fabian,* III, No. 7 (July, 1897), 2.

⁵I (January, 1897), 360–361.

⁶LPM, HDL to J. H. Ferris, June 13, 1897.

⁷Brand Whitlock, *Forty Years Of It* (New York, 1914), pp. 222–223.

⁸LPW, HDL to E. H. James, December 30, 1897; Linn, *op. cit.,* p. 154; Wish, *op. cit.,* p. 243; LPW, Schilling to HDL, "Suppressed Part of the Ninth Biennial Report of the Bureau of Labor Statistics of Illinois," *Social Forum,* II (April, 1900), 135–137.

⁹LPM, J. G. Stevenson to HDL, December 22, 1896; *Hull-House Bulletin,* I, No. 7 (Chicago, December 1, 1896), 2; *Chicago Commons,* I (Chicago, December 1896), 2–11; *Chicago Advance,* December 17, 1896.

¹⁰*Chicago Chronicle,* January 10, 1897; *New York Evening Post,* December 16, 26, 1896.

¹¹EA, HDL to Atkinson, December 3, 1897; LPW, MS "Money of the New Conscience," HDL to Ely, January 25, 1897.

¹²*Ibid.,* HDL to Shaw, April 23, 1897; LPM, J. Addams to HDL, March 23, 1897, Salter to HDL, April 3, 6, 1897, A. P. Stevens to HDL, March 25, 1897, G. E. Hooker to HDL, March 13, 1897; WK, HDL to Kent, March 26, 1898, "Resolutions adopted . . . December 11, 1895"; *The Public,* I, No. 37 (December 17, 1898), 12; Harrison, *op. cit.,* pp. 113, 137–150.

¹³LPW, HDL to Steuart, November 14, 1896.

¹⁴LPM.

¹⁵*Ibid.,* HDL to Harris, December 17, 1897.

¹⁶*Ibid.,* HDL to Mills, November 30, 1895, HDL to Bliss, August 3, 5, 1896; LPW, HDL to J. B. Wood, December 24, 1895.

¹⁷LPM, HDL to Gibson, February 5, 17, 1896; MS inside Fiske's *Myths and Myth-Makers* in Lloyd personal library at Winnetka.

¹⁸Italics added.

¹⁹LPM, Jones to HDL, December 14, 26, 1896, January 10, 19, February 1, 5, 15, 1897, J. J. Lawless to HDL, February 13, 1897; Ernest Crosby, *Golden Rule Jones Mayor of Toledo* (Chicago, 1906), p. 7.

²⁰*Ibid.,* pp. 7–18; LPM, HDL to Jones, March 23, 1897, Jones to HDL, March 25, 1897, telegram, Jones to HDL, April 6, 1897.

²¹LPM, Jones to HDL, April 16, 1897, James H. Rodabaugh, "Samuel

M. Jones," *Historical Society of Northwestern Ohio Bulletin,* XIV (January, 1943), 25–27.

²²LPW, HDL to Stead, April 7, 1897, HDL to Shaw, April 7, 23, 1897; LPM, Jones to HDL, April 28, 1897.

²³LPW, MS "Journal of the Lake George Conference, June 24–30, 1897"; SMJ, HDL *et al.* to Jones, May 5, 1897; S. M. Jones, *Letters of Love and Labor,* I–II (Toledo, 1900, 1901); Jones, *New Right, passim.*

²⁴LPW, MS "Journal"; C. Lloyd, *op. cit.,* II, 47–49; Crosby, *op. cit.,* pp. 49–50.

²⁵LPW, MS "Journal," K. L. Maltby to HDL, July 24, 1897; *New Time,* I (August, 1897); C. Lloyd, *op. cit.,* II, 50–52.

²⁶LPM, Kinley to HDL, March 5, 1898, Pomeroy to HDL, February 25, 1898.

²⁷*Ibid.,* Editors of *Encyclopedia Britannica* to HDL, December 7, 1897, June 6, 1901, Williams to HDL, May 31, July 2, 1898, June 27, July 24, 1899, May 15, 1900, June 12, 1903, Bliss to HDL, January 10, July 18, 1899; Henry F. May, *Protestant Churches and Industrial America* (New York, 1949), pp. 191–192.

²⁸DLW, MS Minutes, Tabernacle Baptist Church Committee, MS Stenographic Report of Testimony, Investigating Committee, Council of New York Baptist Church, December 20, 1897–June 23, 1897, MS Minutes "Matter of Potter, New York June 20, 1898, Council at North Baptist Church," Potter to Williams, February 7, 1897, MS "The Christian Panoply. . . . January 17th, by Rev. Leighton Williams"; LPW, MS majority report of Investigating Committee, which Williams notes was adopted by 26 to 19 with 14 absentees that were added to the majority to make it 43, circulars issued by the Tabernacle Church, leaflet of June 27, 1898 by Williams *et al.; New York Herald,* August 30, 1898; *New York Tribune,* October 21, 1898; *The New York Times,* October 18, 1898; Interview with Mrs. Nellie W. Williams, February 11, 1937; George F. Roesch, Justice, Fourth Judicial District Court of New York City, *Decision in D. C. Potter and J. S. Ross vs. New York Baptist Mission Society et al.* (1897); *Short Sketches of Seven Suits at Law and a Violated Agreement. The Tabernacle Church to the Southern New York Baptist Association* (New York, 1901); Leighton Williams *et al., Protest Against the Course of Findings of the Tabernacle Council . . . June 27, 1897, as Irregular, Unjust, and Not a Final Settlement* (New York, 1898).

²⁹LPW, HDL to Mrs. S. R. Ford, September 8, 1896.

³⁰LPM, HDL to Bowles, January 25, 1897, HDL to P. Mann, January 25, 1897.

³¹RS, HDL to Sherman, February 17, 23, 1897; LPM, HDL to Bowles, February 26, 1897.

³²*Ibid.*, HDL to Bowles, March 9, 1897; LPW, HDL to Williams, March 6, 1897, HDL to Brisbane, April 23, May 19, 25, 29, 1897.

³³*Ibid.*, Williams to HDL, December 4, 1897; LPM, Spahr to HDL, April 23, 1897; DLW, Potter to Williams, February 7, 1897.

³⁴LPW, Williams to HDL, July 2, 1898, HDL to "My Dear Friend," December 25, 1897, February 17, 1898, HDL to Bemis, May 16, 1898.

³⁵*Ibid.*, HDL to Williams, November 5, 1898, January 1, 1899, Williams to HDL, August 15, November 12, 1898, Potter to HDL, September 24, 1898; LPM, Williams to HDL, January 27, 1899.

³⁶LPW, HDL to Williams, November 26, 1898.

³⁷*Ibid.*, HDL to Williams, July 25, 1899, HDL to Meriwether, November 26, December 28, 1898, January 1, 1899, HDL to Roberts, August 23, 1899.

³⁸*Ibid.*, HDL to M. Smith, November 26, December 13, 1898, HDL to Mrs. Papa, October 26, November 23, 1898; LPM, Howells to HDL, July 9, 1898, Mrs. Papa to HDL, October 5, November 12, 1898, Fidelio Papa to JBL, July 16, 1899, M. Smith to HDL, August 17, October 4, 1898, HDL to Massingham, October 17, 1898, Morgan to HDL, November 12, 1898; *Boston Transcript,* October 13, 1898.

³⁹LPM, HDL to Gilman, eleven letters, October 19, 1898–December 25, 1899, Gilman to HDL, seven letters, October 24, 1898–November 16, 1899.

⁴⁰*Ibid.*, HDL to Pomeroy, November 12, 1895, Parsons to HDL, January 1, March 6, May 18, 1897; LPW, HDL to Pomeroy, November 12, December 28, 1895, January 19, 24, March 6, 9, 1897, Pomeroy to HDL, January 5, 1897; *New Time,* I (November, 1897), 287; *Direct Legislation Record,* III, No. 2 (March, 1896), 15, No. 4 (September, 1896), 25–26; *Coming Nation,* August 1, 1896.

⁴¹*Ibid.*, VII (December, 1900), 59, VIII (September, 1901), 43, 45; *Social Gospel,* No. 37, New Ser. No. 8 (March, 1901), 43, No. 9 (April, 1901), 33–34; LPM, Pomeroy to HDL, February 25, 1898, August 2, 1901, HDL to Pomeroy, January 3, 1900; LPW, HDL to Pomeroy, June 21, September 13, October 26, 1901, HDL to Bauer, July 12, 1901.

⁴²LPM, Shibley to HDL, January 25, 1902, HDL to Shibley, January 28, 1902, Pomeroy to HDL, September 2, 1902; LPW, HDL to Pomeroy, September 17, 1902, HDL to Shibley, March 31, 1903; SF, D. L. Cruice to S. Fallows, August 1, 1902; *Direct Legislation Record*, IV (June, 1902), 29–30, 33; *The Outlook,* LXXII (November 15, 1902), 618.

⁴³W. D. P. Bliss, *Encyclopedia,* pp. 649–652, 905, 1293–1294; *Independent,* LXIV (May 6, 1897), 569–578.

⁴⁴LPW, MS "Municipal Ownership," HDL to Pulitzer, January 1, 1898; *Brooklyn Standard-Union,* February 11, 1898.

⁴⁵*Ibid.,* HDL to Woodruff, October 22, 1898; LPM, Meriwether to HDL, October 9, 1898, March 21, 1900.

⁴⁶*Boston Herald,* January 28, May 21, 1900; *Brooklyn Daily Eagle,* May 9, 1898; *Social Gospel,* II, No. 6 (June, 1899), 19–20; *Social Forum,* II (January, 1900), 20–24.

⁴⁷LPM, Patterson to HDL, December 22, 1895; *Chicago Tribune,* December 24, 1895.

⁴⁸LPM, HDL to Morgan, December 30, 1894, Morgan to HDL, January 10, 1896, Zeublin to HDL, January 1, 1896, Salter to HDL, January 2, 1896.

⁴⁹LPW, HDL to Stead, January 1895, HDL to Roberts, May 22, 1896; *London Daily Chronicle,* January 28, 1896.

⁵⁰*Chicago Tribune,* April 19, 1898.

⁵¹LPM, A. Shaw to HDL, May 9, 1898, HDL to Hart, May 12, 1898; LPW, HDL to Blandford, April 30, 1898, HDL to Senator J. K. Jones, May 7, 1898, HDL to Pinner, June 15, 1898; *Lyttleton Times,* February 21, 1899.

⁵²LPM, HDL to Bowles, June 18, 20, July 20, August 12, 25, 27, September 10, 1898; LPM, HDL to Bowles, September 3, 1898.

⁵³LPM, HDL to Bowles, October 18, 1898; Howells, *op. cit.,* II, 96.

⁵⁴LPM, HDL to Bowles, November 23, 1898, HDL to Huntington, Thanksgiving, 1898; LPW, HDL to Brocklehurst, January 5, 1899, HDL to A G. Symonds, December 29, 1898.

⁵⁵*Lyttleton Times,* February 21, 1899.

⁵⁶LPM, HDL to Gookin, March 1, 1900; EA, HDL to Atkinson, July 24, November 11, 1899.

⁵⁷*Ibid.,* Waterman to HDL, March 26, 1899, Pomeroy to HDL, June 27, 1899; LPW, HDL to Pomeroy, December 8, 1898; *New York Sun,* March 16, 1899; *Buffalo Commercial,* June 23, 1899; *Direct Legislation Record,* VI, No. 3 (July, 1899), Special Number, pp. 34–64.

CHAPTER XXI

[1] LPM, Parsons to HDL, February 19, 1897, February 24, 1898; LPW, HDL to Shaw, February 15, 1897, HDL to Bemis, February 17, May 4, 1898, HDL to Bowles, December 13, 1898.

[2] LPM, Paine, Jr., to HDL, October 11, 1899, HDL to Hale, November 1, 11, 1899, J. C. Lloyd to HDL, November 1, 1899.

[3] LPW, Annie Fields to HDL, November 20, 1899, JBL to Parsons, March 1, 1900; LPM, A. Fields to HDL, January 25, 1900, J. Pickering to HDL, November 15, 1898; *Boston Herald,* March 9, 1900.

[4] LPW, Williams to HDL, November 4, 6, 1899, February 18, 1903, Abbot to HDL, February 27, 1900; LPM, HDL to Williams, March 1, 1903.

[5] October 27, 1896.

[6] LPW, Higginson to HDL, February 26, 1900; *Boston Herald,* January 7, 1900.

[7] LPM, Gladden to HDL, October 2, 13, 1898.

[8] *Ibid.,* L. L. Lincoln to HDL, February 1900, Foster to HDL, February 3, 1900, Lincoln House Men's Club Program, January 26, 1900; LPW, Mead to HDL, January 6, 1900; *Boston Transcript,* January 5, May 9, 1900.

[9] *Ibid.,* February 7, 1900; LPW, Clement to HDL, March 1, 1900.

[10] *Ibid.,* Coxe & Co. to HDL, March 20, 1900, HDL to Parsons, March 23, 1900, HDL to Baxter, August 22, 1900; LPM, L. A. Mead to HDL, *n.d.,* B. Hall to HDL, *n.d.*

[11] *Ibid.,* HDL to Huntington, July 7, 1900.

[12] *Ibid.,* HDL to R. H. Van Schaak, October 17, 1899, HDL to Bowles, September 20, October 5, 1899, HDL to Van Benthuysen, October 7, 1900, Clement to HDL, January 9, 1900; LPW, Mead to HDL, January 5, 9, 1900, Bowles to HDL, December 16, 1899, Van Benthuysen to HDL, October 7, 1899, January 31, 1900, March 15, 1902; *Boston Herald,* January 9, 22, 31, 1900; *Illinois Staats-Zeitung,* June 6, 1900; John R. Ferguson, *American Diplomacy and the Boer War* (Philadelphia, 1939); Howells, *op. cit.,* II, 121.

[13] LPM, HDL to Hale, November 11, 1899, HDL to Mrs. Altberger, February 16, 1900; LPW, J. B. Lloyd to Parsons, March 1, 1900, HDL to Baxter, August 22, 1900.

[14] December 16, 1900.

[15] December, 1900.

[16]CSL, Mrs. H. D. Lloyd to Stallbohm, November 23, 1900.

[17]LPW, HDL to Altgeld, August 11, 1899, Altgeld to HDL, August 2, 17, 1899; *Boston Herald,* October 25, 1900; *Boston Globe,* November 2, 1900.

[18]LPM, HDL to Hale, January 1, 1901; LPW, Parsons to HDL, November 9, 1900.

[19]CSL, HDL to Stallbohm, June 19, 1901.

[20]*Rochester Herald,* January 8, 1902; *Philadelphia North American,* January 8, 1902; *Philadelphia Public Ledger,* January 15, 1902; *Springfield Republican,* January 30, 1902.

[21]November 9, 1901; LPW, Wendte to HDL, August 16, 1901; Sidney Fine, *Laissez Faire and the General-Welfare State (University of Michigan Publications, History and Political Science,* XXII), (Ann Arbor, 1956), pp. 339–346, for a succinct appraisal of Lloyd's position.

[22]LPW, Mrs. Severance to HDL, December 6, 1901, HDL to Mrs. Severance, January 2, 1902; LPM, H. Holcome to HDL, October 31, 1901, B. F. Trueblood to Dr. Watson, April 1, 1902; E. D. Mead, "Boston Memories of Fifty Years," Elizabeth M. Herlthy, *Fifty Years of Boston, 1880–1930* (Boston, 1932), pp. 31–33.

[23](Boston, 1903), pp. 378–391; Lloyd, *Mazzini,* pp. 190–200.

[24]LPM, HDL to JBL, September 27, 1885, G. B. Dorr to HDL, April 16, 1903; LPW, HDL to JBL, March 12, 1903.

[25]LPM, "The Emerson Centennial. Memorial School at Concord and Boston, July 13–31, 1903"; Mead, *op. cit.,* p. 33; LPW, E. E. Forbes to HDL, July 23, 1903; *Boston Transcript,* June 11, 1903; *Boston Herald,* July 24, 1903; Lloyd, *Mazzini,* pp. 71–100. Cf. LPM, Charles Eliot to HDL, August 10, 24, 1901, for the former's earlier refusal to accept Lloyd's Chicago real estate as endowment for a school to apply "the principles of manual training in the field of agriculture" because such a school "does not appear to be part of a university's work."

[26]C. Lloyd, *op. cit.,* I, 307–308.

[27]Handbook I, Pt. I, 81–90, Pt. II, pp. 95–96.

[28]LPW, HDL to Symonds, December 29, 1898.

[29]*Fairhope Courier,* September 15, 1899; LPM, MS 1899–1902 notebooks, HDL to Gookin, March 9, 1900, Mrs. Kelley to HDL, October 14, 1900; *The People,* January 13, 1901.

[30]*The Times Literary Supplement,* September 15, 1945, p. 441.

[31]LPW, HDL to Gilman, June 27, 1900, HDL to Livesey, January 3, 1900.

[32]*Ibid.,* HDL to *Wallace,* November 13, 1901, HDL to H. B. Fay, March 10, 1898.

[33]LPM, MS New Zealand notebook; LPW, HDL to Holyoake, July 29, 1902; Margaret Morley, *loc. cit.*

[34]*Ibid.,* HDL to Bauer, July 12, 1901.

[35]LPM, Greening to HDL, September 16, 1901.

[36]*Ibid.,* I. O. Huntington to HDL, March 3, 1891, T. R. Slicer to HDL, June 17, 1898; *Unity,* May 7, 1890; *Quincy Journal,* March 23, 1898.

[37]LPM, Roberts to HDL, June 5, 1897, MS note.

[38]LPW, Bemis to HDL, July 1, 1901, HDL to Pomeroy, June 21, 1901; SF, J. M. Darwin to Fallows, February 6, 1901; *Social Gospel,* No. 41, New Ser. 12 (July, 1901), 41.

[39]LPW, Lewis to HDL, July 5, 1901; LFP, Bryan to Post, November 12, 1904; Fine, *op. cit.,* p. 339.

[40]LPM, Stead to HDL, October 12, 1901, HDL to Stead, November 2, 1902.

[41]*Ibid.,* HDL to Stead, November 2, 1901, Stead to HDL, January 18, March 15, 1902; LPW, Stead to HDL, November 13, December 14, 1901, HDL to Stead, June 30, 1902.

[42]*Ibid.,* HDL to Pinner, August 18, 1901, HDL to Borgeaud, December 13, 1900.

[43]*Ibid.,* HDL to Mrs. Lloyd, *n.d.;* LPM, Holyoake to de Boyve, January 1, 1901.

[44]*Ibid.,* Borgeaud to HDL, December 24, 1900, HDL to Burgeaud, February 7, 1901, Bauer to HDL, February 16, 24, March 6, 1901; LPM, Catlin to HDL, December 18, 1900, HDL to Bauer, February 17, 1901.

[45]*Ibid.,* MS Swiss and German Notebook, Kautsky to HDL, March 7, 1901, Bebel to HDL, March 8, 10, 1901, Kautsky to HDL, March 7, 1901, von der Leyen to HDL, March 28, 1901; LPW, Vandervelde to HDL, March 20, 1901, A. Lamperière to HDL, *n.d.*

[46]LPM, C. Lloyd to HDL quoting J. Burns, *n.d.,* S. Webb to HDL, April 1, 16, 1901, HDL to Clarke, April 11, 1901, Wilson to HDL, April 12, 1901, Mann to HDL, April 14, 1901, Hyndman to HDL, April 19, 1901, Robertson to HDL, April 18, 1901; LPW, HDL to Reeves, April 8, 15, 1901, Plunkett to HDL, April 10, 1901; CSL, Holyoake to HDL, April 10, 1901; *Review of Reviews,* XXII (London, May 15, 1901), pp. 494–497.

[47]*Boston Herald,* May 3, 1901; Chicago *Inter Ocean,* July 7, 1901; *Direct Legislation Record,* IX, No. 1 (March, 1902), 14–16; LPM,

clipping, A. Chesterfield, "From Day to Day," *Congregationalist and Christian World*.

⁴⁸LPM, HDL to Casson, December 19, 1901.

⁴⁹Henry James, editor, *Letters of William James*, II (Boston, 1920), 166.

⁵⁰LPM, HDL to his parents, May 4, 1902; LPW, HDL to Stallbohm, *n.d.*

⁵¹*Ibid.*, R. W. Weeks to HDL, May 2, 1902, MS Notebooks B (1901), II, Swiss Nos. 1 & 2 (May, 1902), VII Swiss 4, VIII Swiss 5; H. D. Lloyd, *A Sovereign People. A Study of Swiss Democracy*, edited by John A. Hobson (New York, 1907), pp. 47–56.

⁵²LPW, A. D. White to HDL, June 7, 1902, James to HDL, September 2, 1902, Heinrich Brauen to HDL, June 7, August 11, 1902, HDL to Stallbohm, May 11, 26, 1902, and *n.d.*, K. Kautsky to HDL, January 11, 1902, HDL to Holyoake, July 29, 1902, HDL to Vrooman, July 29, 1902; LPM, W. Dieu to HDL, June 22, 1902, HDL to Bowles, July 14, 1902.

CHAPTER XXII

¹LPM, MS 1902 Notebook II, p. 35.

²Abbot assured Lloyd that the fight for DL "is as good as won."

³Eliot Jones, *The Anthracite Coal Combination in the United States* (Cambridge, 1914); William J. Walsh, *The United Mine Workers of America as an Economic and Social Force in the Anthracite Territory* (Washington, 1931).

⁴Elsie Gluck, *John Mitchell* (New York, 1929), pp. 4–26.

⁵February 7, 1896. Cf. *New York World*, January 23, 30, February 3, 1896.

⁶*Ibid.*, September 16, 1900; *The Public*, III (October 13, 1900), 423–424.

⁷Herbert Croly, *Marcus Alonzo Hanna* (New York, 1912), pp. 393–396; Carroll D. Wright, "Report to the President on the Anthracite Strike, June 20, 1902," *Bulletin of the Department of Labor* (Washington, 1902), pp. 1186–1187.

⁸*Ibid.*, p. 1153; Gluck, *op. cit.*, pp. 106–107.

⁹Cf. C. Lloyd, *op. cit.*, II, opposite p. 190.

¹⁰Mowry, *op. cit.*, p. 135 and n. 24; LPM, *American & Journal* to HDL, August 21, 1902.

¹¹*Ibid.*, HDL to T. Roosevelt, telegram, *n.d.*, HDL to Bowles, *n.d.*, Warner to HDL, September 29, 1902; *Boston Transcript*, October 14, 1902.

[12]TR, for scores of letters related to the background and creation of the Commission, viz., TR to Attorney General, June 26, 1902, TR to Quay, September 27, 1902, TR to H. C. Lodge, September 27, 30, October 7, 17, 1902, Lodge to TR, October 1, 20, 1902, Mitchell to TR, October 1, 8, 11, 16, 21, 1902, TR to Hanna, October 3, 5, 16, 1902, TR to Bacon, October 5, 7, 1902, Wright to TR, October 6, 1902, TR to J. P. Morgan, October 16, 1902, TR to Governor Murray Crane, October 22, 1902, P. C. Knox to TR, October 10, 1902, G. B. Cortelyou to Mitchell, October 14, 1902, MS Memorandum, October 16, 1902, Roosevelt to the Anthracite Strike Commission, October 23, 1902, George Gray to Roosevelt, October 24, 1902; *Boston Transcript,* October 6, 10, 11, 14, 16, 1902; Philip C. Jessup, *Elihu Root,* I (New York, 1938), 273–276; *Bookman,* XVI (December, 1902), 403–404; *Outlook,* LXXII (September 20, October 11, 18, 1902), 141, 345–347, 381; *Hartford Courant,* October 18, 1902.

[13]LPM, C. J. Mar to HDL, August 29, 1902, HDL to Mitchell, October 14, 1902; LPW, HDL to J. B. Lloyd, October 9, 10, 1902, HDL to Power, September 17, 1902, Power to HDL, September 20, 1902, September 18 MS Notebook; *Springfield Republican,* November 19, 1902.

[14]*Boston Transcript,* October 22, 24, 25, November 11, 12, 1902; LPW, HDL to JBL, November 4, 1902; LPM, HDL to Mitchell, October 14, 1902.

[15]LPW, HDL to Mitchell, October 30, 1903, HDL to JBL, October 14–November 23, 1902; LPM, Weyl to HDL, October 29, 1902; CSL, HDL to Stallbohm, November 6, 9, 1902.

[16]LPW, HDL to JBL, October 14, December 12, 1902.

[17]Walter Weyl, "The Award of the Anthracite Strike Commission," *Review of Reviews,* XXVII (April, 1903), 461–462.

[18]LPW, October 3, 1902 MS Notebook, pp. 31–35.

[19]*Washington Times,* November 12, 1902. Cf. *Boston Transcript,* October 30, November 6, 20, 1902, for the AFL Convention's censure of President Eliot.

[20]LPW, HDL to JBL, November 12, 13, 1902; *Boston Transcript,* November 13, 1902.

[21]ACSCP; Anthracite Coal Strike Commission, *Report* (Washington, 1903), p. 17; *Boston Transcript,* November 15, 1902; *Outlook,* LXXII (November, 15, 1902), 620.

[22]LPW, HDL to JBL, November 13, 1902.

[23]*Ibid.,* HDL to JBL, November 15, 1902; ACSC, *Report,* pp. 39–41;

ACSCP, II, 9–709, IV, 321, V, 608, VI, 709; *Boston Transcript,* November 18, 1902.

[24]LPW, HDL to JBL, November 12, 14, 15, 1902.

[25]*Ibid.,* HDL to JBL, November 15, 1902; LPM, White to HDL, November 18, 1903.

[26]ACSCP, VI, 760–773, VII, 830–940, VIII, 1014–1029.

[27]*Ibid.,* VIII, 1052–1053, IX, 1056–1068; *Boston Transcript,* November 22, 1902.

[28]LPW, HDL to JBL, November 16–18, 22, 25, 28, December 3, 5, 1902, Cortelyou to Moseley, November 25, 1902, HDL to Mitchell, November 27, 1902; *Hartford Courant,* November 27, 1902.

[29]LPW, HDL to Moseley, November 28, 30, 1902, HDL to JBL, December 2, 1902, HDL to Brandeis, December 3, 1902, MS October 3, 1902 Notebook.

[30]LPM, Wyman to HDL, November 26, 1902; *Scranton Republican,* December 5, 1902.

[31]ACSCP, X, 1080 to XII, 1574.

[32]*Ibid.,* XV, 1952–1994, XIII, 1619–1632, XIV, 1844–1852; LPW, HDL to JBL, December 4, 10, 1902.

[33]*Ibid.,* HDL to JBL, December 8–16, 1902; ACSCP, XIII, 1585, XVII, 2205–2209, XX, 2848–2879, XXI, 3000–3003, 3008–3015, XXII, 3162–3192; *Scranton Republican,* December 16, 1902.

[34]ACSCP, XX, 2928–2930.

[35]*Ibid.,* XX, 2928–3007, 3086–3090; LPW, MS October 3, 1902 Notebook, HDL to JBL, December 15, 1902, HDL to Brandeis, December 16, 1902, January 29, 1903; *Scranton Republican,* December 17, 1902. For Simpkins & Watkins' absorption by the Temple Iron Company, see 226 *U. S. Reports* (Rochester, 1913), 324–373, U. S. Appellant *v.* Reading Company *et al.; Who's Who in America, 1903–1905* (Chicago), p. 156; Jones, *Coal Combination,* pp. 74–78, 80.

[36]ACSCP, XXI, 3090, 3098–3161; LPW, MS October 1902 Notebook, HDL to JBL, December 13–15, 1902; LPM, HDL to Gompers, January 30, 1903.

[37]LPW, HDL to JBL, December 18, 1902; *Boston Transcript,* December 13, 1902.

[38]LPM, HDL to Contini, December 30, 1902, HDL to Mather, January 1, 1903.

[39]*Ibid.,* HDL to Brandeis, December 31, 1902; LPW, W. D. Boyce to HDL, December 6, 1902; *Boyce's Weekly,* January 7, 1903.

⁴⁰LPM, Abbot to HDL, June 14, 1900; LPW, HDL to JBL, January 7, 8, 10, 11, 16, 20, 1903; *Boston Transcript,* December 15, 1902.

⁴¹LPW, HDL to JBL, January 13, 14, 1903.

⁴²*Ibid.,* HDL to JBL, January 6–14, 1903.

⁴³*Ibid.,* HDL to JBL, January 18, 23, 24, 27, 1903, HDL to Mitchell, January 24–30, 1903, Mitchell to HDL, January 25–28, 1903; LPM, HDL to Brandeis, January 29, 1903; Gluck, *op. cit.,* p. 154.

⁴⁴LPW, HDL to JBL, January 16, February 11, 1903, Traubel to HDL, February 12, 1903.

⁴⁵*Ibid.,* HDL to Mitchell, January 23, 1903.

⁴⁶*Ibid.,* original MS, HDL to JBL, January 31, February 10, 1903; ACSCP, LII, 9221–9257; LPM, "Notes on Coal Strike Arbitration," Notebook 2 October 1902; Lloyd, *Men the Workers,* pp. 201–252.

⁴⁷LPW, Bowles to HDL, February 10, 1903, HDL to JBL, February 10, 1903; Philadelphia *Public Ledger,* February 10, 1903; *Boyce's Weekly,* March 25, 1903; *Portsmouth Herald,* March 15, 1903; *Philadelphia Press,* February 10, 1903, *New York Times,* February 10, 1903. The *New York Evening Post* and *Nation* took exception to Lloyd's statement of the moral obligation of the "scab."

⁴⁸LPW, Traubel to HDL, February 9, 12, 1903, HDL to JBL, February 11, 13, 1903.

⁴⁹ACSCP, LV, 9781–9840.

⁵⁰*Ibid.,* LV, 9841–9899, LVI, 9900–10,046; LPW, HDL to JBL, February 13, 15, 1903; *Outlook,* LXXIII (February 21, 1903), 413–414.

⁵¹LPW, T. J. Morgan to HDL, February 11, 1903, HDL to JBL, *n.d.,* MS January 1, 1903 Notebook, pp. 18–34.

⁵²LPW, HDL to JBL, February 17, 1903; *Chicago Tribune,* February 16–17, 1903; *Chicago Chronicle,* February 17, 1903; Lloyd, *Men the Workers,* pp. 253–260.

⁵³LPW, Salter to HDL, February 17, 1903, HDL to JBL, February 18, 1903; *Chicago Journal,* February 17, 1903.

⁵⁴*New York Evening Post,* February 17, 27, 1903; *The New York Times,* February 17, 1903; *Springfield Republican,* February 21, 1903.

⁵⁵LPW, HDL to JBL, February 21, 22, 26, 1903, Darrow to HDL, April 2, 1903, Notebook, p. 5.

⁵⁶LPW, Moseley to HDL, April 28, 1903, Darrow to HDL, April 2, 1903; LPM, HDL to Moseley, March 18, 1903; *United Mine Workers Journal,* XIII (March 26, 1903), 4.

[57]TR, TR to Judge Gray, March 24, 1903; CDW, address by Roosevelt, Sioux Falls, South Dakota, April 6, 1903.

[58]Anthracite Coal Strike Commission, *Report;* Eduard Losé, "Le Conflit dans le District anthracifère de Pennsylvania en 1906," extrait des *Annalles de Mines de Belgique,* tome XI (Bruxelles, 1906), pp. 3–6; Gluck, *op. cit.,* pp. 154–155; JAL, Mitchell to Labadie, August 11, 1912; Mitchell, *op. cit.,* pp. 392–396.

[59]*Boyce's Weekly,* April 8, 1903; LPW, MS two page list of "Coal Report" addresses, Moseley to HDL, April 22, 1903; LPM, HDL to J. G. Brooks, March 30, 1903, HDL to Wright, March 30, 1903; *Boston Journal,* March 22, 1903; *Outlook,* LXXIII (March 28, April 4, 1903), 696, 754–766; *Review of Reviews,* XXVII (April, 1903), 450–463; Walsh, *op. cit.,* pp. 123–126; Weyl, *op. cit.,* pp. 461–464.

[60]LPW, HDL to Mitchell, enclosed in HDL to JBL, February 27, 1903, HDL to JBL, February 26, 1903; LPM, Mitchell to HDL, February 21, March 8, 1903.

[61]LPW, HDL to Sir Ward, March 31, 1903, HDL to Reeves, April 4, 1903.

CHAPTER XXIII

[1]WG, Mead to Gladden, January 21, 1903; LPM, MS Notebook 4 April 9, 1903, p. 69; Mowry, *op. cit.,* p. 104.

[2]LPW, MS March 15 1903 Notebook, p. 99, HDL to Pinner, May 23, 1903.

[3]*Ibid.,* HDL to JBL, November 13, 1902, January 12, 17, 22, 24, M. C. Lloyd to HDL, January 16, February 24, 1903; LPM, HDL to a Miss Forbes, August 31, 1902.

[4]*Ibid.,* February 22, March 12, 1903.

[5]*Ibid.,* HDL to JBL, February 26, March 8, 12, 19, May 14, 1903; *Chicago Record-Herald,* March 9, 1903.

[6]LPW, HDL to JBL, January 3, February 18, March 6, 1903.

[7]*Ibid.,* HDL to JBL, March 2, 1903, Shibley to HDL, July 6, 1902, April 16, 1903, Herdman to HDL, August 5, September 21, 1903, circulars, leaflets; LPM, Herdman to HDL, May 2, July 29, 1902, Houghteling to HDL, March 20, 1903, HDL to Bemis, July 30, 1903, Shibley to HDL, August 5, 1903; *The Messenger* (Winnetka), November, 1903, pp. 7–8; *Chicago Daily News,* March 24, 1903.

[8]May 13, 1903; LPM, K. Durland to HDL, May 7, 1903; Earl R. Beckner, *A History of Labor Legislation in Illinois* (Chicago, 1929), pp. 160–163.

[9]LPW, MS "Introduction," HDL to Mitchell, February 27, 1902; LPM, HDL to Easley, March 31, 1903; Mason, *Brandeis,* pp. 141, 143.

[10]LPW, HDL to S. J. Forbes, August 28, 31, 1902, Simons to HDL, November 8, 1902, Simons to Darrow, November 8, 1902; *Boston Transcript,* November 6, 19, 1903: *Better Times* (New York), December 6, 1902, p. 7.

[11]LPW, HDL to Morgan, April 2, 1899.

[12]LPM, 1901 Notebook A.

[13]LIV (May 1, 1902), 1069–1072; *Chicago Tribune,* May 5, 1902.

[14]LPM, Notebook A, Italian Notebook Nos. 3, 5, 9, 11; LPW, W. H. Holt to HDL, March 4, 1902, J. Spargo to HDL, July 12, August 11, 1902; LPW, Contini to HDL, January 26, 1903; G. A. Kleene, "Bernstein vs. 'Old School' Marxism," *Annals of the American Academy of Political and Social Science,* XVIII (November, 1901), 391–419.

[15]L. T. Hobhouse, *Liberalism* (London, 1912), pp. 172–173.

[16]*Outlook,* LXXII (November 22, 1902), 670; H. D. Lloyd, "Consolidations: A Radical View," *Booklovers Magazine,* I (Philadelphia, April 1903), 391–395; LPW, for MS, F. W. S. Speirs to HDL, February 28, 1903.

[17]LPW, HDL to JBL, March 9, 1903, Fox to HDL, March 3, 1903; LPM, Morgan to HDL, February 23, 1903, HDL to Williams, March 1, 1903, Wayland to HDL, March 6, 1903.

[18]LPW, HDL to JBL, March 3–12, 1903; *Bath Times,* March 6, 1903; *Boston Herald,* March 13, 1903; Lloyd, *Lords,* pp. 224–301.

[19]LPW, HDL to JBL, March 14, 16, 17, 1903; *Boston Journal,* March 14, 22, 1903.

[20]LPW, HDL to JBL, March 10, 15, 16, 1903.

[21]LPM, HDL to JBL, March 1903, HDL to Bowles, June 12, 1903; Cf. Richard Hofstadter, *The American Political Tradition* (New York, 1948), pp. 218–220.

[22]LPM, Darrow to HDL, March 19, 1903, HDL to Fox, March 30, 1903, HDL to Darrow, March 31, 1903, HDL to Bowles, April 6, 1903, Bowles to HDL, April 8, 1903, HDL to Mailly, April 2, 1903; *Chicago Record-Herald,* March 9, 1903.

[23]LPM, Somerby to C. L. Withington, September 3, 1906; LPW, MS May 18, 1903 Notebook, p. 3; LPM, Notebook IV, March 1903, pp. 31–35; *Chicago Chronicle,* March 3, 5, 1903; Ray Ginger, *The Bending Cross: A Biography of Eugene Victor Debs* (New Brunswick, 1949), pp. 212–213.

[24]LPW, HDL to Mailly, April 20, 1903, italics added, March 15, 1903 MS Notebook; Arthur M. Schlesinger, *The Vital Center* (Boston, 1949), p. 173.

[25]*Ibid.*, HDL to Mitchell, April 17, 1903.

[26]*Ibid.*, Simons to HDL, May 14, 1903, MS (copy) "Rules for Proceedings Against Fusion or Compromise. . . . St. Louis, January 29–February 1, 1903," Mailly to HDL, May 4, 1903.

[27]LPW, HDL to JBL, February 22, 23, 27, 29, 1903; LPM, HDL to A. Lloyd, May 3, 1903; [Waldo H. Browne], *Chronicles of an American Home* ([New York], 1930), p. 98.

[28]LPW, HDL to Moseley, April 23, 25, 27, 30, 1903, Moseley to HDL, April 29, 30, May 11, 1903, John G. Palfrey to HDL, April 16, 25, 1903.

[29]*Ibid.*, MS "The Failure of Government Regulation," Brooks to HDL, June 2, 1903; *Boston Globe*, May 16, 1903; *New York Sun*, May 20, 1903; Lloyd, *Lords*, pp. 302–346.

[30]LPM, Symonds to HDL, May 1, 1903, Ely to HDL, June 5, 1903, Commons to HDL, June 5, 1903; LPW, Mitchell to HDL, May 27, 1903.

[31]*Ibid.*, HDL to Pomeroy, June 13, 1903; LPM, Pomeroy to HDL, June 22, 1903; Ginger, *op. cit.*, pp. 211–235.

[32]LPW, May 18, 1903 MS Notebook.

[33]*Ibid.*, HDL to Morgan, June 3, 30, 1903, HDL to Debs, June 8, 1903, HDL to Simons, June 8, 1903, MS "Why I Join the Socialists," HDL to Salter, June 8, 1903; Harry P. Judson, "The Municipal Situation in Chicago," *Review of Reviews*, XXVII (April, 1903), 435–439; LPM, HDL to Post, June 9, 1903.

[34]*Ibid.*, HDL to Morgan, June 21, 28, 1903, HDL to Bemis, August 2, 1903, Debs to HDL, June 12, 1903, HDL to Simons, June 21, 1903, Simons to HDL, June 24, 1903; LPW, MacDonald to HDL, June 29, 1903; LPW, Simons to HDL, June 13, 1903.

CHAPTER XXIV

[1]LPM, MS May 18, 1903 Notebook, "The Mighty Atom" in undated clipping, *Christchurch Press; The New York Times,* July 16, 1903; Lloyd, "The Abolition of Poverty," *Good House Keeping* (Springfield, Mass.), September 1903, pp. 215–230.

[2]*Chicago Chronicle,* May 25, 1903; *Pilgrim,* VII (August, 1903), 10, 30; Lloyd, "The Judicial Destruction of Law," *National Progress,* I (Chicago, August, 1903), 80–82; Lloyd, "The Public and the Coal

Question," *The Public,* III (June 2, 1900), 113–114; Lloyd, "Love and Taxes," *Boyce's Weekly,* July 8, 1903.

³*Ibid.,* March 11, 25, April 1, 15, 1903; *Warren* (Mass.) *Herald,* February 13, 1903; LPW, HDL to Tarbell, May 6, 1902.

⁴*Boyce's Weekly,* July 29, 1903.

⁵LPM, MS Notebook 11, pp. 56–57, Notebook 7 (Swiss 4), Notebook 9, p. 24, Later MS Notebooks, No. 1, p. 8, MS "The Religion of Labor," HDL to JBL, July 19, 1903; *Chicago Chronicle,* July 19, 1903; *Boyce's Weekly,* October 3, 1903. Cf. Carl J. Friedrich, *The New Belief in the Common Man* (Boston, 1942).

⁶*Boyce's Weekly,* April 22, May 27, 1902.

⁷LPM, Corrothers to HDL, March 15, September 2, 1892 to December 20, 1900, HDL to Corrothers, December 8, 1898, December 6, 1899, Corrothers to C. L. Withington, May 5, 1913, HDL to R. B. Cooper, December 3, 1898, Mead to HDL, February 17, 1892; LPW, Mather to HDL, March 18, 1903; WDH, HDL to Howells, February 5, 1895.

⁸*Ibid.,* HDL to Hadley, May 3, 1903, HDL to Du Bois, March 31, 1903; Arthur T. Hadley, *The Relations Between Freedom and Responsibility in the Evolution of Democratic Government* (New York, 1903), pp. 42–44.

⁹LPM, HDL to Hallowell, June 23, 1903, HDL to Reed, June 21, July 2, 1903, HDL to Salter, November 13, 1900, HDL to Bowles, March 18, 1903; LPW, Hallowell to HDL, April 21, June 26, 1903; W. E. Burghardt Du Bois, *Dusk of Dawn* (New York, 1932), pp. 79–97; "Reconstruction and Disfranchisement," *Atlantic Monthly,* LXXXVIII (October, 1901), 434.

¹⁰LPW, Abbot to HDL, August 20, 1903, Prichard to HDL, August 14, 1903, HDL to JBL, July 17, 19, 20, 1903; LPM, N. Kelley to C. L. Withington, *n.d.,* HDL to Wainewright, September 20, 1902.

¹¹LPW, HDL to JBL, July 20, 1903, Post to HDL, June 12, 1903, HDL to Morgan, June 3, 8, 21, 1903; LPM, Morgan to HDL, June 16, 1903.

¹²WJB, Altgeld to Bryan, September 20, 1897; WK, Kent to M. Field, June 9, 1904; LPM, Morgan to HDL, June 16, 1903, HDL to Morgan, June 21, 1903; LPW, HDL to Post, June 9, 1903, Post to HDL, June 12, 1903; *The Public,* I (December 17, 1898), 2; *Nation,* LXXII (March 28, 1901), 250; *Outlook,* LXXIII (April 18, 1903), 895–896, LXXIV (May 2, 1903), 11–12; *Social Forum,* II (April, 1900), 106–137; Taylor, *Social Frontiers,* pp. 52–53; Harrison, *Stormy Years,* pp. 140–246.

[13] H. D. Lloyd, *The Chicago Traction Question* (Chicago, 1903), pp. 3–6; George C. Sikes, *Street Railway Situation in Chicago* (Harrisburg, 1902), pp. 3–13; Harrison, *op. cit.,* pp. 218–220.

[14] *Ibid.,* pp. 218–220, 242–243; LPM, HDL to Post, June 9, 1903; Lloyd, *Traction Question,* p. 51.

[15] R. R. Bowker, "The Piracy of Public Franchises," *Atlantic Monthly,* LXXXVIII (October, 1901), 463–482; Ida M. Tarbell, "How Chicago is Finding Itself," *American Magazine,* LXIX (New York, November, 1908), 40–41.

[16] LPW, HDL to JBL, July 20, 1903, Morgan to HDL, June 23, 30, 1903, HDL to Morgan, June 29, 1903; LPM, Gompers to HDL, June 29, 1903, HDL to Post, June 9, 1903; *The Public,* VI (July 4, 18, 1903), 195–198, 225–226; C. Lloyd, *op. cit.,* II, 294–295.

[17] LPM, HDL to Bemis, July 25, 30, 1903; *Direct Legislation Record,* X (December, 1903), 66–69; *Outlook,* LXXIV (July 25, 1903), 724.

[18] LPW, Schilling to HDL, August 6, 1903; LPM, HDL to Bemis, August 2, 1903.

[19] LPW, HDL to Bemis, July 30, 1903, Sikes to HDL, July 13, 1903, HDL to JBL, July 20, 1903, Bemis to HDL, August 5, 1903, Stewart to HDL, July 13, 1903; LPM, Commons to HDL, July 27, 30, August 4, 1903.

[20] *Ibid.,* Zueblin to HDL, August 5, 1903, H. George Jr. to HDL, August 13, 1903; LPW, Abbot to HDL, August 20, 1903, HDL to Morgan, August 9, 26, 1903; *Chicago Examiner,* August 1–September 28, 1903.

[21] *Chicago Record-Herald,* September 6, 1903, *Chicago Socialist,* September 6, 1903.

[22] April 6, 1903; Louis F. Post, *The Traction Issue in the Municipal Election in Chicago* (Chicago, 1905), pp. 4–5.

[23] LPM, September 13, 1903.

[24] Addams, *Excellent,* pp. 43–46; LPW, HDL to JBL, September 9, 1903.

[25] LPW, May 18, 1903 MS Notebook.

[26] *Ibid.,* HDL to JBL, September 9, 1903, HDL to Mitchell, September 12, 1903, Mitchell to HDL, September 15, 1903; LPM to Brandeis, September 16, 1903, *n.d.,* HDL to C. L. Withington, September 12, 1903.

[27] LPW, "Traction Emergency Call, September 20, 1903," and circulars.

[28] *Ibid.,* HDL to JBL, September 20, 1903.

[29] *Chicago Record-Herald,* September 21, 1903; *Union Labor Advo-*

cate, IV (October, 1903), 11; *Chicago Socialist,* September 26, 1903; C. Lloyd, *op. cit.,* II, 302–303.

[20]*Chicago Record-Herald,* September 22, 27, 1903; *Chicago Tribune,* September 29, 1903; *The Public,* VI (September 26, 1903), 393–394.

[21]*Chicago Record-Herald,* September 22, 1903.

[22]WG, J. B. Lloyd to Gladden, November 6, 1904; LPW, Mrs. HDL to Pinner, November 2, 1903; C. Lloyd, *op. cit.,* II, 303–305; Henry D. Lloyd's estate was conservatively appraised at $282,235. Probate Court, Cook County, Illinois, *Record of Examiners and Administrators Inventories and Appraisements,* Vols. 200, pp. 10–16, 213, pp. 230–236, *Record of Wills,* LXV, 349.

[23]Lloyd, *Traction Question,* Chs. XI–XII; *Union Labor Advocate,* IV (October, 1903), 29.

[24]LPW, J. F. Willard to HDL, October 3, 1903, letters to JBL from Symonds and other Londoners; *The Public,* VI (December 5, 1903), 545–546; *Chicago Tribune,* November 30, 1903; *Chicago Commons,* VII (December, 1903), 10–13; "Workers' Compensation for Accidents Bill: Henry Demarest Lloyd," *Parliamentary Debates, Legislative Council and House of Representatives, No. 42, 20th November to 24th November* (Wellington, 1903), 991; C. Lloyd, *op. cit.,* II, 346–348.

Index